Laura McPherson
A Grammar of Seenku

Mouton Grammar Library

Edited by
Georg Bossong
Bernard Comrie
Patience L. Epps
Irina Nikolaeva

Volume 83

Laura McPherson

A Grammar of Seenku

DE GRUYTER
MOUTON

ISBN 978-3-11-077710-9
ISSN 0933-7636

Bibliographic information published by the Deutsche Nationalbibliothek
The Deutsche Nationalbibliothek lists this publication in the Deutsche Nationalbibliografie;
detailed bibliographic data are available on the Internet at http://dnb.dnb.de.

© 2021 Walter de Gruyter GmbH, Berlin/Boston
This volume is text- and page-identical with the hardback published in 2020.
Printing and binding: CPI books GmbH, Leck

www.degruyter.com

In memory of Russ Schuh

Acknowledgements

Most of this work has been financially supported by the National Science Foundation Documenting Endangered Languages program, first with grant BCS-1263150 (PI Jeffrey Heath) and later by BCS-1664335 (PI McPherson). Additional funding has come from the Dartmouth College Office of the Provost, Dickey Center for International Understanding, and Leslie Center for the Humanities. I am deeply grateful to all funding agencies for supporting this work.

Thank you to all of my patient Sambla collaborators for teaching me about your language—I hope I have accurately represented it here and accept responsibility for any remaining errors. Seenku is incredibly rich and complex, a language I could study for a lifetime and continually discover something new. I hope that the description I have provided here can serve as a jumping off point for future work, both descriptive and theoretical, on its many intricacies. My deepest thanks go to Clément Traore, Emma Traore, Fatou Traore, and Mamadou Diabate, who spent many long hours working with me and sharing their knowledge. I would also like to thank my non-Sambla support staff and friends in Burkina Faso, without whom this work would not have been possible—Zakaria Sawadogo, Valentine Dibloni, Bakari Ouattara, Minkailou Djiguiba, and Barkissa Ramdé—as well as fellow linguists who have kept me company and discussed data patterns while in field, especially Jeffrey Heath, Rasmane Congo, Lamine Sanogo, Paul Solomiac, Abbie Hantgan, Nate Severance, Kate Sherwood, and Anthony Struthers-Young.

In preparing this grammar, I have had countless helpful discussions on data patterns, typological phenomena, formatting, and presentation. I would like to specifically thank Tom Ernst, Byron Ahn, Laura Kalin, Claire Bowern, and Matthew Dryer for their insights and guidance. Finally, many thanks to all of the Dartmouth students who have helped me on various aspects of this project: Maggie Baird, Emily Grabowski, Ksenia Ryzhova, Gabriel Zuckerberg, Emma Mazzuchi, Annie Furman, Dat Vo, Katie McCabe, Jessica Zhang, Guhui Zhang, and especially Lucas James and Adeline Braverman, for helping get this manuscript and its associated archive ready for publication.

Figure 1.1: Used by permission, ©2003 SIL International, Map of the Samogho languages, further redistribution prohibited without permission.

Contents

Acknowledgements —— VII

Abbreviations —— XIX

1 Introduction —— 1
1.1 Seenku —— 1
1.1.1 Geographic location —— 1
1.1.2 Sambla villages —— 2
1.1.3 Population —— 4
1.1.4 Dialects —— 4
1.1.5 Multilingualism —— 5
1.1.6 Vitality and domains of use —— 5
1.1.7 Previous studies —— 6
1.2 Sambla history, environment, and culture —— 6
1.2.1 History —— 6
1.2.2 Environment —— 7
1.2.3 Culture —— 7
1.3 Fieldwork and methodology —— 8
1.4 Organization of the grammar —— 10

2 Sketch of the grammar —— 11
2.1 Phonology —— 11
2.1.1 Segmental phonology —— 11
2.1.2 Tonal phonology —— 12
2.2 Nominal and adjectival morphology —— 13
2.2.1 Nominal morphology —— 13
2.2.2 Adjectival morphology —— 13
2.3 Noun phrase structure —— 13
2.4 Anaphora —— 14
2.5 Verbal morphology —— 15
2.5.1 Verbal derivation —— 15
2.5.2 Verbal inflection —— 15
2.6 Main clauses and constituent order —— 16
2.6.1 Word order —— 16
2.6.2 TAMP markers —— 16
2.6.3 Negation —— 17
2.7 Relative clauses —— 17
2.8 Complement clauses —— 18
2.9 Clause chaining and event sequencing —— 18

2.10	Artistic adaptation —— 18	

3 Segmental phonology —— 20
- 3.1 Vowels —— 20
- 3.1.1 Monophthongs —— 20
- 3.1.2 Diphthongs —— 23
- 3.1.3 The status of schwa —— 25
- 3.1.4 Minimal pairs —— 27
- 3.2 Consonants —— 40
- 3.2.1 Consonant inventory —— 40
- 3.2.2 Minimal pairs —— 41
- 3.2.3 The status of [ɾ] —— 49
- 3.3 Syllable structure and phonotactics —— 50
- 3.3.1 Syllable shapes —— 51
- 3.3.2 Latent nasal codas —— 54
- 3.3.3 Phonotactic restrictions —— 61
- 3.4 Word structure —— 63
- 3.5 Phonological rules —— 64
- 3.5.1 High vowel effects —— 65
- 3.5.2 Lenition processes —— 69
- 3.5.3 Dorsal dissimilation —— 71
- 3.5.4 Hiatus resolution —— 72
- 3.5.5 Vowel centralization —— 75
- 3.6 Phonological phrasing —— 75

4 Tone —— 77
- 4.1 Tone inventory —— 77
- 4.1.1 Tonal primitives —— 77
- 4.1.2 Simple (two-tone) contour tones —— 83
- 4.1.3 Complex (three-tone) contour tones —— 86
- 4.2 Tone-bearing unit (TBU) —— 89
- 4.2.1 Tone on the initial half syllable —— 89
- 4.3 Lexical tone —— 90
- 4.3.1 General lexical melodies —— 91
- 4.3.2 Category-specific distributions —— 93
- 4.3.3 Surface tone distributions —— 96
- 4.4 Grammatical tone —— 97
- 4.4.1 Tonal affixation —— 98
- 4.4.2 Argument-head tone sandhi —— 102
- 4.4.3 Clitic elision (nascent tonal morphology) —— 110
- 4.5 Phonological tone rules —— 112
- 4.5.1 Register assimilation —— 113

4.5.2	Downstep and downdrift —— 114	
4.5.3	Tonal absorption —— 120	
4.6	Phonetic realization of tone —— 122	
4.6.1	Declination —— 122	
4.6.2	Voice quality —— 122	
4.7	Tone and intonation —— 124	
4.7.1	Falling question intonation —— 124	
4.7.2	Continuation rise —— 126	
5	**Nominal morphology** —— 128	
5.1	Noun stems —— 128	
5.1.1	Simple noun stems —— 128	
5.1.2	Reduplicated noun stems —— 130	
5.1.3	Nouns ending in -nɛ —— 131	
5.2	Nominal derivation —— 132	
5.2.1	Deadjectival derivation —— 132	
5.2.2	Deverbal derivation —— 134	
5.3	Nominal inflection —— 137	
5.3.1	Regular plural marking —— 137	
5.3.2	Irregular plural marking —— 143	
6	**Pronouns and anaphora** —— 144	
6.1	Pronouns —— 144	
6.1.1	Basic pronouns —— 144	
6.1.2	Discourse definite pronoun (anaphor) —— 146	
6.2	Emphatic marking —— 147	
6.3	Object pronouns —— 149	
6.4	Subject pronouns —— 149	
6.5	Possessive pronouns —— 151	
6.6	Oblique pronouns —— 152	
6.7	Logophoric pronouns —— 153	
6.7.1	Quotatives —— 154	
6.7.2	Adjectival predicates —— 155	
6.7.3	Reflexives —— 155	
6.7.4	Reciprocals —— 157	
7	**Compound nouns** —— 159	
7.1	Noun-noun compounds —— 159	
7.1.1	Regular compounds —— 160	
7.1.2	Possessive-type compounds —— 164	
7.1.3	Crypto-compounds —— 167	
7.2	Noun-adjective compounds —— 169	

7.3	Noun-postposition compounds —— 170	
7.3.1	Compounds with postpositions —— 170	
7.3.2	Noun-postposition compounds —— 172	
7.4	Noun-verb and verb-noun compounds —— 173	
7.4.1	Agentive compounds —— 173	
7.4.2	Instrumental compounds —— 175	
8	**Noun phrase structure —— 177**	
8.1	Linear order of NP elements —— 177	
8.2	Determiners (indefinite, definite, and demonstrative) —— 178	
8.2.1	Definite determiner *ǎ* —— 179	
8.2.2	Discourse definite determiner *kɔ́* —— 180	
8.2.3	Demonstrative expressions —— 182	
8.2.4	Indefinite determiner *tsɛ̌* —— 186	
8.3	Adjectives —— 188	
8.3.1	Adjectival vs. verbal modification —— 188	
8.3.2	Adjectival stems —— 191	
8.3.3	Adjectival modifiers —— 192	
8.3.4	Headless NPs with adjectives —— 197	
8.4	Numerals —— 197	
8.4.1	Number system —— 198	
8.4.2	Cardinal numerals —— 201	
8.4.3	Distributive numerals —— 204	
8.4.4	Ordinal numerals —— 205	
8.5	Non-numeral quantifiers —— 207	
8.5.1	All —— 207	
8.5.2	None/any —— 212	
8.5.3	Many —— 214	
8.5.4	Some/certain —— 217	
8.5.5	Few —— 218	
8.6	Possession —— 219	
8.6.1	Inalienable possession —— 219	
8.6.2	Alienable possession —— 222	
8.6.3	Free variation between alienable and inalienable —— 227	
8.6.4	Recursive possession —— 228	
9	**Ideophones and onomatopoeia —— 231**	
9.1	Phonological characteristics of ideophones and onomatopoeia —— 231	
9.1.1	Segmental characteristics —— 232	
9.1.2	Tonal characteristics —— 232	
9.2	Ideophones —— 237	
9.2.1	Intensifiers —— 238	

9.2.2	Expressive adverbials —— 241	
9.3	Onomatopoeia —— 244	
9.3.1	Animal sounds —— 244	
9.3.2	Impact sounds —— 245	
9.3.3	Other sounds —— 246	

10 Postpositions and adverbials —— 249
- 10.1 Postpositions —— 249
- 10.1.1 *k’̀n* 'on (top of)' —— 249
- 10.1.2 *gṹ* 'under' —— 251
- 10.1.3 *kəré* 'near, next to' —— 251
- 10.1.4 *kǎa* 'across from' —— 252
- 10.1.5 *nɛ́* locative —— 253
- 10.1.6 *ká* 'in hand' —— 255
- 10.1.7 *wɛ̏* 'with' —— 256
- 10.1.8 *tɛ́* genitive —— 261
- 10.1.9 *lɛ́* dative —— 267
- 10.1.10 Relational nouns as postpositions —— 271
- 10.2 Adverbials —— 274
- 10.2.1 Locative adverbs —— 274
- 10.2.2 Temporal adverbs —— 281
- 10.2.3 Manner adverbs —— 291
- 10.2.4 Quantifier adverbs —— 293

11 Coordination —— 295
- 11.1 Conjunction —— 295
- 11.1.1 NP conjunction —— 295
- 11.1.2 PP and adverb conjunction —— 298
- 11.1.3 Conjunction of adjectival modifiers —— 300
- 11.1.4 Conjunction of adjectival predicates —— 300
- 11.1.5 Clause-level conjunction —— 301
- 11.2 Disjunction —— 301
- 11.2.1 NP disjunction —— 301
- 11.2.2 Disjunction of adjectival modifiers —— 302
- 11.2.3 Disjunction of adjectival predicates —— 303
- 11.2.4 PP disjunction —— 303
- 11.2.5 Clause-level disjunction —— 304
- 11.2.6 'Whether or not' conditionals —— 306

12 Verb stems and verbal derivation —— 307
- 12.1 Verb stems —— 307
- 12.1.1 Transitive verbs —— 307

12.1.2	Intransitive verbs —— 310
12.2	Labile verbs —— 313
12.3	Antipassive —— 315
12.3.1	Morphophonological form —— 316
12.3.2	Antipassive function and semantics —— 318
12.3.3	Antipassive with an explicit object —— 319
12.3.4	Antipassive verbs in deverbal compounds —— 321
12.4	Transitive pre-verbs —— 322
12.4.1	*nɛ́-* —— 322
12.4.2	*wɛ̀-* —— 325
12.4.3	*lɛ̋-* —— 326
12.5	Compound verbs —— 327
12.5.1	Noun-verb compounds —— 327
12.5.2	Verb-verb compounds —— 330
12.6	Pluractional reduplication —— 332

13	**Verbal inflection —— 335**
13.1	Mood: irrealis and realis stems —— 336
13.2	Irrealis inflectional categories —— 340
13.2.1	Prospective —— 341
13.2.2	Habitual —— 343
13.2.3	Imperative —— 345
13.2.4	Hortative —— 349
13.2.5	Bare irrealis in insubordinate clauses —— 351
13.3	Realis inflectional categories —— 353
13.3.1	Nominalized inflections —— 353
13.3.2	Non-nominalized (verbal) inflections —— 358
13.3.3	Stative/resultative —— 362
13.4	Tense —— 365
13.4.1	Past prospective —— 366
13.4.2	Past habitual —— 366
13.4.3	Past progressive —— 367
13.4.4	Past perfective —— 367
13.4.5	Past perfect —— 368
13.4.6	Past stative/resultative —— 368
13.5	Negation —— 369

14	**Non-verbal predicates —— 371**
14.1	Copula *kɛ́* —— 371
14.1.1	Basic function —— 371
14.1.2	Past tense —— 373
14.1.3	Discourse definite copula —— 374

14.2	Existential predicates —— 375	
14.2.1	Negative existential ɲá —— 377	
14.3	Adjectival predicates —— 378	
14.4	Possessive predicates —— 380	
14.5	Volitional predicates —— 382	
14.5.1	'Want' predicates —— 382	
14.5.2	'Desire' predicates —— 383	

15 Comparatives —— 385
- 15.1 Asymmetrical comparison —— 385
- 15.1.1 fő́n 'better, more' —— 385
- 15.1.2 Comparative APs —— 388
- 15.1.3 Bare predicates —— 388
- 15.1.4 fə̀ '(sur)pass' —— 389
- 15.1.5 Superlatives —— 390
- 15.2 Symmetrical comparison —— 390
- 15.2.1 Simile comparisons —— 391
- 15.2.2 Identity comparisons with ɲagő́n —— 392
- 15.2.3 Comparisons with sɔ́ɛn 'one' —— 392

16 Interrogation —— 393
- 16.1 Polar interrogatives —— 393
- 16.1.1 Affirmative polar interrogatives —— 393
- 16.1.2 Negative polar interrogatives —— 395
- 16.2 Wh-interrogatives —— 397
- 16.2.1 Which/what —— 397
- 16.2.2 Who —— 400
- 16.2.3 Where —— 401
- 16.2.4 When —— 403
- 16.2.5 How (many) —— 404
- 16.2.6 Why —— 405

17 Relative clauses —— 407
- 17.1 Verb inflection and subject marking in the relative clause —— 409
- 17.1.1 Prospective —— 409
- 17.1.2 Habitual —— 410
- 17.1.3 Progressive —— 411
- 17.1.4 Perfective —— 412
- 17.1.5 Existential and participial predicates —— 413
- 17.2 Subject relatives —— 415
- 17.3 Object relatives —— 416
- 17.4 PP relatives —— 417

17.5	Possessor relatives —— 419
17.6	Headless relatives —— 420
17.7	Relative pronoun —— 421
17.7.1	fəlɛ́/fənɛ́/fèn nɛ́ —— 421
17.7.2	kərɛ́/kú lɛ́ —— 422
17.7.3	tərɛ́/tənɛ́/tɛ́nɛ́ —— 423
17.7.4	məlɛ́/mɛ́ɛ —— 424

18	Conditional constructions —— 426
18.1	Basic form —— 426
18.2	Hypotheticals —— 427
18.2.1	Conditionals with non-perfective verb forms —— 428
18.2.2	Hypotheticals with non-verbal predicates —— 430
18.2.3	Conditionals as temporal subordination —— 432
18.3	Counterfactual conditionals —— 434
18.4	'Even if' —— 435
18.5	'If not' —— 438
18.6	Whether or not conditionals —— 439

19	Complement and purposive clauses —— 441
19.1	Complementizers —— 441
19.2	Complement clauses with an overt complementizer —— 442
19.2.1	Quotatives —— 443
19.2.2	Complements of 'know' —— 447
19.2.3	Complements of 'think' verbs —— 449
19.3	Subjunctive complement clauses —— 453
19.3.1	Invariably subjunctive complement clauses —— 454
19.3.2	Subjunctive/subordinate complement clauses —— 461
19.4	Nominalized complements —— 465
19.4.1	'be able' with a PP complement —— 466
19.4.2	'accept' with a PP complement —— 467
19.4.3	'forbid' with a PP complement —— 468
19.4.4	'fail' with a PP complement —— 468
19.4.5	'try' with an NP complement —— 469
19.4.6	'finish' with an NP or PP complement —— 470
19.4.7	'start' with an NP complement —— 470
19.5	Purposive clauses —— 471
19.5.1	Explicit conjunction sân-kɔ́/jân-kɔ́ —— 472
19.5.2	Purposive clauses with no conjunction —— 472
19.5.3	Verbs of motion as auxiliary verbs —— 473

20	Clause coordination and event sequencing —— 476

20.1	Coordination with explicit conjunctions —— 476	
20.1.1	Because —— 476	
20.1.2	But —— 478	
20.1.3	As though —— 479	
20.2	Clause chaining —— 481	
20.3	Temporal subordination —— 484	
20.3.1	Subordination with 'before' —— 484	
20.3.2	Subordination with 'until' —— 486	
20.3.3	Subordination with verbal reduplication —— 488	
20.3.4	Conditionals as temporal subordination —— 489	
21	**Information structure and discourse —— 491**	
21.1	Focus and information structure —— 491	
21.1.1	Emphatic pronouns —— 493	
21.1.2	Focus particles —— 495	
21.1.3	Clauses introduced by the copula as a focus strategy —— 498	
21.1.4	Focused negation with discourse definite *kɔ́* —— 500	
21.2	Topicalization —— 501	
21.2.1	Phrase-final *íaa* —— 502	
21.2.2	*kɔ̀nì* 'as for' —— 502	
21.3	Discourse markers —— 504	
21.3.1	Emphatic particles —— 504	
21.3.2	Exclamative *òo* —— 505	
21.3.3	Impatience particle *sá̰* —— 506	
21.3.4	*wétanɛ̌* 'now' —— 507	
21.4	Interjections —— 508	
21.4.1	Yes and no —— 508	
21.4.2	*ì-ǎ-lɔ́* 'you know' —— 509	
21.5	Greetings and benedictions —— 510	
21.5.1	Greetings —— 510	
21.5.2	Benedictions —— 514	
21.6	Discourse structure —— 515	
21.6.1	Turn-taking —— 516	
21.6.2	Back-channeling —— 516	
22	**Artistic adaptation of language —— 518**	
22.1	Sung music —— 518	
22.1.1	Linguistic features of vocal lyrics —— 519	
22.1.2	Tone-tune association —— 520	
22.2	Surrogate speech —— 522	
22.2.1	Balafon surrogate language —— 522	
22.2.2	Horn surrogate language —— 525

22.3 Instrumental versions of vocal music —— 526

23 Texts —— 528
23.1 Explanation of traditional fonio farming, part 1 —— 528
23.2 The toad and the rabbit —— 541

Bibliography —— 565

Index —— 571

Abbreviations

ANTIP	antipassive
CLF	classifier
CMPV	comparative
COMP	complementizer
COP	copula
DAT	dative
D.DEF	discourse definite
DEF	definite
DEM	demonstrative
EMPH	emphatic
EXCL	exclamative
FOC	focus
FR	French
GEN	genitive
HAB	habitual
HUM	human
IDEO	ideophone
INDF	indefinite
INTENS	intensifier
INTERJ	interjection
IRR	irrealis
JU	Jula
LOC	locative
LOG	logophoric
NE	-ŋé (suffix associated with certain locatives)
NEG	negative
NOM	nominalized
PART	particle
PFV	perfective
PL	plural
PRES	presentative
PRF	perfect
PRO	pronoun
PROSP	prospective
PST	past
PTCP	participle
Q	question
REAL	realis
REC.PST	recent past
RECIP	reciprocal
RED	reduplicant
REL	relative
SBJV	subjunctive
SG	singular
SUBORD	subordinate
TOP	topic

XX — Abbreviations

TRANS   transitive
VOC   vocative

1 Introduction

1.1 Seenku

Seenku [ISO 639-3: sos] is a Mande language spoken by a population of around 16,000 people in southwestern Burkina Faso. It is also commonly referred to in the literature by its exonym, Sambla (variant French spelling Sembla), which is a Jula term for both the language and the ethnicity. Genetically, Seenku is said to belong to the Samogo group, which itself belongs to Northwestern (Kastenholz 1997) or Western (Vydrine 2009a; 2016) Mande. Only one other language in the group, Dzùùngoo (Solomiac 2007, 2014), has been the subject of a thorough reference grammar. The phonetics and phonology of Jowulu have been described (Djilla, Eenkhoorn, and Eenkhoorn-Pilon 2004), as has quantification in Bankagooma (Tröbs 2008), but the remaining Samogo languages Duungooma and Kpeego remain virtually unstudied. The greater Northwestern branch of Mande includes the more populous Bobo, Bozo, and Soninke language groups, with Bobo spoken in areas contiguous to Seenku territory. Non-Mande languages neighboring Seenku include the Toussian languages and Tiéfo, all early branches of Gur.

The whole southwestern region of Burkina Faso is linguistically dominated by Jula, a Mande lingua franca. Nearly everyone, including all but perhaps the oldest of Seenku speakers, are bilingual in Jula. It is used to communicate between ethnicities and is the most common vehicular language in the major urban area of Bobo-Dioulasso, where there is a large Sambla diaspora.

The name Seenku is a compound [sɛ́ɛ̃-kû], made up of *sɛ́ɛ̃*, the demonym of the people, and *kû*, meaning 'language' or '(abstract) thing'. In this grammar, I will use the term **Sambla** to refer to the people or the culture and **Seenku** to refer to the language itself. Though Sambla is an exonym, it is used by the community when referring to themselves in either French or Jula. While Coulibaly (1989) and Royer (1996) claim that the term is derogatory, I have not heard this sentiment echoed by any of my consultants. The literature typically uses the spelling *Seeku* to refer to the language, but this does not capture the phonemic nasalization of the first vowel; for this reason, I choose to write the name of the language as Seenku.

1.1.1 Geographic location

The Seenku-speaking zone is located to the west of the major city of Bobo-Dioulasso, at roughly $11\,°C$ N and $5\,°C$ W in the villages surrounding Karangasso-Sambla.[1]

---

[1] This is not to be confused with another village close to Bobo-Dioulasso, Karangasso-Vigue, where the Gur language Vigue/Viemo is spoken.

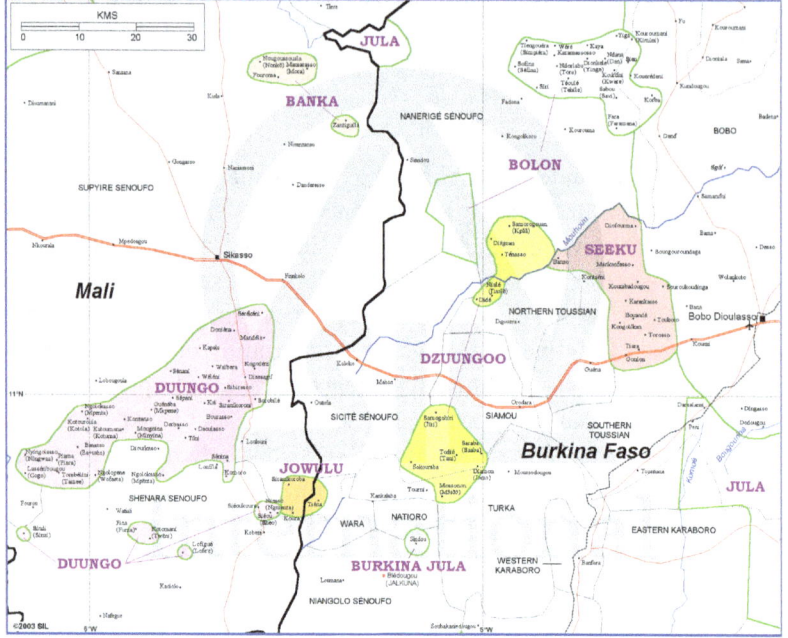

Fig. 1.1: SIL map of the distribution of Samogo languages. Used with permission.

The map in Figure 1.1 shows the Seenku-speaking zone in relation to the other languages in the area. Samogo language areas are shaded in (split across the Mali/Burkina Faso border), and other Mande languages are outlined (Jula, Bolon, Bobo, Jalkunan).

1.1.2 Sambla villages

I organized a GIS survey of Sambla country, carried out in 2018 by my assistants Minkailou Djiguiba and Sy Clement Traoré. GIS coordinates were gathered for 24 Sambla villages, along with basic information about their history, demographics, etc. The map in Figure 1.2 shows the results of this survey; the name on the top reflects the Seenku name for the village, while the corresponding Jula name is given in parentheses below.

Some of the villages, such as Sîo-gṵ̀ or Gbéncέ-məgέɛ̀wɛ̀, are ethnically mixed, mostly with Mossi, Bobo, or Fulani families. The other ethnicities do not typically learn Seenku—instead, Jula is used, even with the Fulani or the Mossi, who also maintain their own languages (Fulfulde and Moore, respectively). Other villages consist of mostly Sambla griots, whether blacksmiths, musicians, or potters.

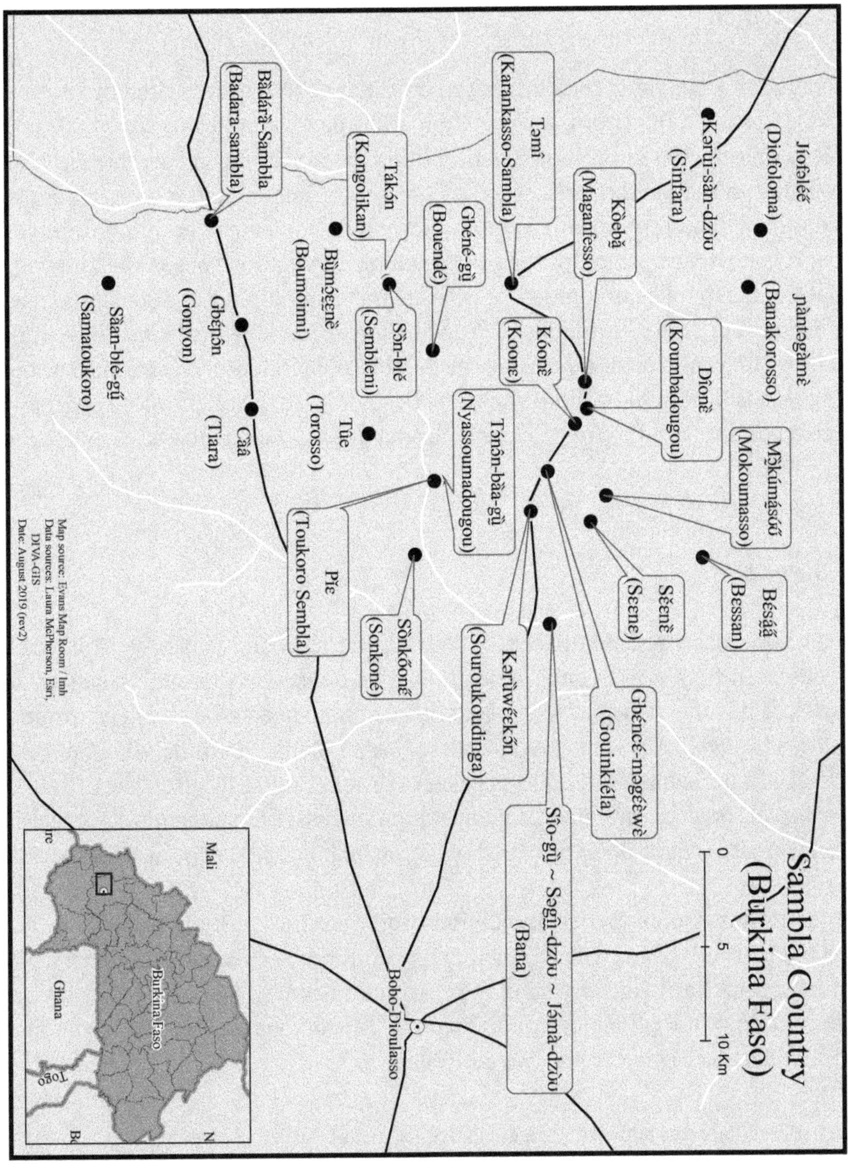

Fig. 1.2: Map of Sambla country, with village names in Seenku (and Jula)

1.1.3 Population

The population estimate of 16,000 is based on a 2009 UNSD survey cited by Lewis et al. (2016). Strand (2009) cites the population of the Sambla prefecture as 20,667 people, based on the 1996 Burkinabe census, but this number may include non-Sambla people living in the Sambla area (such as hamlets of ethnic Moore or Fula people) and it does not include ethnically Sambla people living outside of traditional Sambla country. It is unclear what proportion of the ethnic population speaks the language, especially in diaspora communities, or whether the population of speakers is increasing or decreasing. Recent unpublished sociolinguistic work by Rasmane Congo indicates severe linguistic attrition among the Sambla population in Ouagadougou, but the language is likelier to be more vital in Bobo-Dioulasso, given the close proximity to Sambla country and the frequency of movement back and forth between the two locales.

1.1.4 Dialects

There are two closely related dialects of Seenku, Northern and Southern. This grammar focuses on Southern Seenku, known also as *Gbéné-kû*, literally, 'language of Bouendé', as it is the dialect of the major village of Bouendé as well as the surrounding villages (Kongolikan, Sembleni, Toronsso, Sɛɛnɛ, Bana, Souroukoudingan, etc.), for a total of approximately 12,000 speakers (Lewis et al. 2016). Northern Seenku, known also as *Təmí-kû*, literally, 'language of Karangasso', is spoken in Karangasso and Banakorosso (*ɲàntəgàmɛ̀*) by a total of approximately 5,000 speakers (Lewis et al. 2016).

My consultants report perfect intelligibility between the two dialects, an assertion echoed by Prost (1971). My own investigations of Northern Seenku are preliminary, but what I have seen has been very similar to Southern Seenku, with just a few lexical differences and minor phonological differences. The following table gives examples of lexical differences between the two dialects:

Tab. 1.1: Lexical differences between Southern and Northern Seenku

Southern	Northern	Gloss
bɛ̀ɛ	sà-bɛ̀ɛ	'pig'
bǒontô	bǒolô	'youth'
mɔ̂ɛn-dě	ŋmêɛ-lě	'millet (grain)'

In addition, one consultant reports minor pronunciation differences in the village of Souroukoudingan (Seenku: *Kərǔwɛ́ɛkɔ̃́n*). She specifically notes cases where a long vowel in Bouendé corresponds to a VrV sequence in Souroukoudingan, e.g. gɔ̈ɔ (B) vs. gɔ̈rɔ̈ (S) 'ground'. This may shed light on the development of long vowels in Seenku.

More careful dialect comparison must await future research.

1.1.5 Multilingualism

Nearly everyone in Sambla country is bilingual in Jula, with some rare exceptions among very old women. Those with formal education, especially younger people, also speak French. There is limited Fulani presence in Sambla country, but as is typical in this area of Burkina Faso, the Fulani speak Jula; Sambla people are unlikely to speak Fulfulde. There is also a scattering of Mossi hamlets in the region, but the Sambla are unlikely to be bilingual in Moore, and the Mossi living in the area must communicate more broadly in Jula.

1.1.6 Vitality and domains of use

Seenku is currently being passed on to children in Sambla villages, where it is the language of daily life. However, families who move to Bobo-Dioulasso and especially Ouagadougou are increasingly likely to shift to Jula (even in Ouagadougou, where the majority lingua franca is Moore). I am told there has historically been social stigma attached to being Sambla (who were seen as manual laborers without much intellectual capacity), and as such, some people are hesitant to reveal their ethnic identity in Bobo-Dioulasso, adopting an urban identity instead. Other speakers, however, express great pride in being Sambla, so these value judgments could be changing.

In terms of its domains of use, Seenku is the language of the home and daily life in Sambla villages, except when interacting with non-Sambla people (locals of different ethnicities, visitors, etc.). There is no orthography for the language, and so there are no written documents, publications, or pedagogical materials; the language of education, even primary education, is French. Even in a private Facebook group for Sambla people, most posts are in French, though I have occasionally seen brief exchanges or comments in Seenku.

While French may be the threat to Seenku in written language, the more immediate threat in spoken communication comes from Jula. As noted above, every Sambla person that I know under the age of 50 speaks fluent Jula. Multilingualism is, of course, the norm in West Africa, but the equation is changing. Greater mobility, ease of communication with cell phones and mobile internet, and urban sprawl that brings the boundaries of Bobo-Dioulasso closer to Sambla country all contribute to an environment in which Jula becomes more socially and economically viable and Seenku loses ground. Even when speaking Seenku, code-switching into Jula is common, and a lot of original Seenku vocabulary has been lost to Jula loanwords, including grammatical constructions like modals (see §19.3.1.2). In addition, many traditional oral genres are being lost, including riddles, folktales, and vocal music. There are many examples in the archived corpus where a speaker begins a narration and then doesn't remember how to finish it, or where a person does not remember more than one or two songs or stories.

These are troubling signs for the long term survival of the language.

1.1.7 Previous studies

The most in-depth work on Seenku prior to the current fieldwork is Prost (1971). This 70-page work describes Northern Seenku with a short grammar sketch, lexicon, and text. More recently, Congo (2013) wrote his master's thesis on Southern Seenku, focusing mostly on an accurate phonemic analysis of the dialect of Bouendé.

To my knowledge, this exhausts the previous work done on Seenku.

1.2 Sambla history, environment, and culture

1.2.1 History

Seenku is a member of the Samogo language group; the people speaking this original Samogo language are thought to have migrated to their present-day region between Sikasso, Mali and Bobo-Dioulasso, Burkina Faso from near the border with Guinea around 1500 CE (Person 1961, Royer 1996, as cited in Strand 2009). The region was likely inhabited already by different Gur ethnicities, such as the Tiéfo or the Toussian, who remain neighbors of the Sambla to this day. The Toussian and the Sambla especially share many cultural (and even linguistic) traits from centuries of close contact. Later Senufo migrations split the Samogo group into smaller populations, and the Samogo spoken by each population evolved into the distinct languages that are spoken today.

Before French colonization, the region was invaded by warring Jula clans, the Traoré and the Ouattara. The Traoré took over Sikasso and set up the Kingdom of Kenedougou, while the Ouattara took command of Bobo-Dioulasso. The local populations between the two regions were subjugated and found themselves used as pawns in the power struggle between these two clans (Royer 1996, Strand 2009). Sambla country itself ended up divided in these struggles; residents of Karangasso volunteered as warriors for the Ouattara, whereas residents of the southern villages resisted Jula rule and later French rule. Strand (2009) notes that even to this day there remains some latent animosity between northern and southern Sambla villages.

The French took over Sambla country in July of 1898 and placed it under the rule of the tyrant Si-Boro Traoré, who was responsible for changing many Sambla family names to Traoré (Royer 1996).

1.2.2 Environment

The Sambla region is characterized by rolling hills and low forest, filling out to a lush green in the rainy season and more arid for the rest of the year. Common tree species include baobab, mango, acacia, and shea. Forests are especially dense on the rolling hills surrounding the area, which are protected by the governmental agency *Eaux et Fôrets*. The year can be divided into three main seasons: rainy season (late June through September, with a mini hot season near the end), cold season (October through February), and hot season (March through June). The climate is generally more temperate in all seasons than further north in Burkina Faso.

The Sambla are primarily agriculturalists, with staple crops of corn, millet, sorghum, and cotton. Shea butter production is also an important (and labor-intensive) activity for the women in the village. Many domestic animals are kept in the villages: chickens, ducks, pigs, guinea fowl, goats, sheep, with cows taken out to pasture by Sambla boys or by hired Fulani herders.

Karangasso is the administrative center in Sambla country, having had a governor or political chief established there by the colonial government, though Bouendé holds more traditional power (see Strand 2009). In terms of infrastructure, I arrived in the area in the summer of 2013 to find Karangasso with electricity and Bouendé in the process of having poles put up, though as of 2019, the funding has dried up and Bouendé's electricity lines still bring no current.

1.2.3 Culture

The three main religions in Sambla country are Christianity, Islam, and traditional religion. Churches, mosques, and fetishes can all be found in the villages, and my impression is that most Christians and Muslims still retain at least some degree of traditional religious practice. The production and consumption of millet beer is very common, particularly on market days. For a description of some of the Sambla's primary traditional cults, see Strand (2009).

The Sambla organize their society into roughly the same caste system as is common in Mande culture. The highest status caste are the *sáǎn* (Jula *horon*), who are landholders and farmers. Chiefs come from this caste. There is also a blacksmith caste, known as *cěe*, in addition to a griot (or 'musician-historian') caste, known as *jeli* in Jula and as *kâ* in Seenku. Among the griots, we find specific sub-castes, including leatherworkers *tsʉ̀-dəgé-kâ* and balafon-playing griots *bɑ̣a-brɛ̣́-kâ*. The craft or profession (leatherworking, balafon playing, drum playing, etc.) is hereditary in these sub-caste families. Traditionally, there is no intermarriage between the *sáǎn* and the blacksmith or griot castes. The different lower classes, however, can intermarry.

In terms of family structure, it is not uncommon for a man to have two or more wives, though polygamy is less common among the Christian population. Extended families typically live together in a "compound", consisting of several small houses, granaries, and other storage buildings around a large central courtyard. Modern houses are built rectangularly (a shape apparently imposed by the colonial government, Strand 2009:38) out of mud brick or cement, with corrugated tin rooves. Granaries are still built in a round form with pointed thatched rooves.

1.3 Fieldwork and methodology

The current volume is based on primary fieldwork on Southern Seenku carried out in Burkina Faso from January 2012 to the present with speakers from Bouendé, Torosso, and Sɛɛnɛ. My primary consultants in Burkina Faso are a male speaker, Sy Clement Traore (SCT, born 1990) and a female speaker Gni Emma Traore (GET, born 1996), both from Bouendé. I have also benefitted from the help of Sambla consultants living outside of Burkina Faso, including another female speaker Gni Fatou Traore (GFT), originally from Sɛɛnɛ and now living in New York, and the world-renowned balafonist Mamadou Diabate (MD), originally from Torosso but now living in Vienna. The text corpus represents the speech of over a dozen other Seenku speakers, mostly older, both male and female, representing the speech of Bouendé and Torosso. A couple of texts were collected with speakers of the northern dialect from Karangasso.

Most of this work has been financially supported by the National Science Foundation Documenting Endangered Languages program, first with grant BCS-1263150 (PI Jeffrey Heath) and later by BCS-1664335 (PI McPherson). Additional funding has come from the Dartmouth College Office of the Provost, Dickey Center for International Understanding, and Leslie Center for the Humanities. The overarching goal of the project is to create a multi-purpose archive of Seenku speech and verbal art and produce descriptive materials, including the current volume.

Elicitation was carried out both in Burkina Faso and abroad; the bulk of elicitation was done at a project base in Bobo-Dioulasso. The contact language was French, and elicitation was largely done based on translation of words and phrases I devised, though ethnobiological elicitation was done using both field guides and specimens, and much of the modal data was elicited using a survey designed by Margit Bowler and John Gluckman. Over the years, most of my work with speakers has shifted from elicitation to text transcription and translation, using elicitation of sentences only to clarify constructions found in natural speech.

The examples in this grammar are drawn from both elicitation and texts. Where possible, I prioritize naturally occurring examples, except where either the form or construction is unattested in the text corpus or where an elicited example illustrates the concept more clearly. All examples, whether elicited or naturally occurring, are tagged with a code that represents the recording they are drawn from, the format of which represents the date and whether the recording is elicited or textual. For instance, sos170714t1 represents the first text [t] recorded on July 14th, 2017, while sos150618e represents elicitation recordings from June 18th, 2015. A few rare cases do not have entries in the archive, as the data came from personal communication with consultants that may not have been recorded.

All cited recordings, including video of the narratives and texts, are archived at the Endangered Languages Archive (ELAR), hosted at the School of Oriental and African Studies in London. The URL for accessing these recordings is:

https://elar.soas.ac.uk/Collection/MPI1080582

Nearly all of the "bundles" (files associated with a particular recording event) are unrestricted, meaning they can be freely accessed, listened to, or downloaded by anyone registered with ELAR (registration is free). A small number of more sensitive recordings are restricted, with permission required to access them. Elicitation bundles are accompanied by scans of the original field notes (meaning that the transcriptions in these notes may not reflect the final analysis of the language). Narrative or text bundles include both audio and video, as well as ELAN annotations for all of the texts cited in this grammar. Some of the ELAN annotations are fully glossed and translated, while others are transcriptions and translations into French created by GET; the transcription system in these files, noted in the archive, is not always consistent with the transcription system that I use. This text corpus contains a variety of genres, including riddles, folk tales, procedural videos (e.g. weaving, making shea butter), vocal music, balafon music, interviews, and conversation.

Examples from narratives used in the grammar are further tagged with the annotation number, e.g. sos170714t1:28, so that the example can be easily located in the ELAN file for those interested in looking further at its context. The goal of following this system of tagging and archiving is to promote transparency in the grammar—readers can access all of the original data and can evaluate the analyses for themselves. Grammatical description is always a work in progress; there is always more data to gather, more angles to consider, more comparisons to make. By providing the original data, I hope that others will find it easier to assess the description I give here and reanalyze or reinterpret patterns if new insights come to light.

Further, it should be noted that not all speakers agree on every term or construction. Disagreements are especially common based on age, with younger (and more urban) speakers offering examples that older speakers reject. I take this as evidence for language change and note such disagreements as they arise in the text.

All elicitation sessions were recorded in WAV format on either a Zoom H4n recorder or a Marantz PMD 661 MK11. Video was recorded using a Zoom Q8, Canon

Vixia, or Canon XA30 camcorder. A range of microphones were used on both audio and video recorders; details are provided in the metadata for each bundle in the archive. Phonetic analyses reported in this grammar were done in Praat. Data was first transcribed on paper in notebooks, then digitized (scanned and typed) for storage.

1.4 Organization of the grammar

The organization and layout of this grammar reflects my background and roots as a fieldworker—the structure largely follows that of my grammar of Tommo So (2013), a Dogon language. In writing that grammar, I drew on a grammatical outline created by Jeffrey Heath for Dogon languages, reflected in his grammar of Jamsay (2008). Where appropriate, I altered the internal structure of chapters or created new chapters to accommodate Seenku's Mande grammatical structure.

There is of course a vast literature on Mande languages, replete with Mande-specific terminology. I make reference to some of that terminology (e.g. predicate markers, pre-verbs, *compacité tonale*) in this grammar for ease of comparison with other Mande languages, but I also endeavor to explain it in a way that will be accessible to a more general linguistic audience.

Otherwise, the terminology used in this grammar is meant to be relatively theory-neutral, adhering to what Haspelmath (2008) might call "Basic Linguistic Theory". My own training is in generative linguistics, especially morphophonology, and so at times I might make suggestions as to how data could be interpreted from a generative perspective, but the description I have given here should be general enough to leave theoretical analysis up to the reader and his or her own theoretical persuasions.

For an overview of the topics in the grammar, see the next chapter.

2 Sketch of the grammar

This chapter serves as a preview and roadmap for the rest of the grammar. I summarize core grammatical structures and highlight particularly interesting or unique features of Seenku, all while providing cross-references to chapters later in the volume where the patterns are discussed at length.

2.1 Phonology

Seenku has undergone a lot of phonological reduction compared to more widely spoken Mande languages like Jula, or even closely related Samogo languages. The result is a largely mono- and sesquisyllabic lexicon. To ensure that contrasts can be maintained without the presence of multiple syllables, the phoneme inventory (segmental and tonal) has increased, and diphthongs are common.

2.1.1 Segmental phonology

The consonant inventory consists of 20 core phonemes (and two more marginal ones, /p/ and /j/) across five places of articulation: bilabial, alveolar, palatal, velar, and labiovelar. Among these 20 phonemes, Seenku displays the alveolar affricates /ts/ and /dz/, rare in Mande languages. The vowel inventory appears to be in a state of flux, with speakers showing either eight or nine phonemic oral vowels and five nasal vowels. The seven vowels /i e ɛ a ɔ o u/ are attested in all people's speech, suggesting a prototypically Mande seven-vowel system, but all speakers have an additional back vowel whose F1 is intermediate between /o/ and /ɔ/ but which patterns like a high vowel and sounds heavily pharyngealized; I treat this as [-ATR] /ʊ/. Some speakers additionally have the corresponding front vowel /ɪ/. For further discussion, see §3.1.1.1. Length is contrastive for all vowels. In addition to the monophthongs, Seenku uses a wide range of diphthongs (back-to-front and/or rising sonority). Interestingly, length is also contrastive for diphthongs due to the non-moraic nature of the diphthong-initial vowel quality (§3.1.2). See §3.1 and §3.2 for further discussion of consonant and vowel phonemes, respectively.

    A unique feature of Seenku is its "sesquisyllabic" stem shape, a term coined by Matisoff (1990) and described more recently in Pittayaporn (2015). More commonly seen among Southeast Asian languages, sesquisyllabic words consist of a short half or minor syllable (Cə) before the full syllable, e.g. mənǐ 'woman', təgê 'chicken', etc. For a discussion of sesquisyllabicity and its underlying representation, see §3.3.1.2.

    The only coda consonant Seenku allows is a non-contrastive coda nasal. The behavior of the final nasal is variable, raising the question of whether it should be treated as a floating segment (as in Jowulu, Djilla et al. 2004, or Dzùùngoo, Solomiac 2014) or as a fully present coda in the underlying representation, no matter how weakly realized on the surface. See §3.3.2 for further discussion.

Some of the most prevalent segmental phonological rules include vowel hiatus resolution (§3.5.4), palatalization (§3.5.1.1), and affrication (§3.5.1.2).

2.1.2 Tonal phonology

Tone has a high functional load in Seenku, and the tone system is quite complex. There are four contrastive tonal primitives, which I call extra-low (X, ȁ), low (L, à), high (H, á), and super-high (S, a̋). The four tones are elegantly captured with a two feature system, with further evidence for tone features found in grammatical processes like plural and perfective formation; §4.1.1.1 discusses the feature system further.

These four tones can combine to create at least seven two-tone contours, some of which are attested lexically and others of which are purely morphological in nature. Three-tone contours, such as XHX, LSX, and HXS are also found.

If we could define a tone-bearing unit, we would have to say it is the syllable in Seenku, with each syllable able to host up to three tones. However, the interaction between tone and vowel length suggests a more phonetic timing-based approach (cf. Zhang 2004), where falling tones are found on short vowels, rising tones sometimes trigger lengthening of the vowel or simplification of the tone contour, and tritone contours obligatorily appear on long vowels (either underlying or lengthened on the surface); see §4.2.

Despite the complexity of the tone system, Seenku still displays downdrift and downstep, but only of S; all tones are, of course, subject to declination. Downstep and downdrift are discussed in §4.5.2 while declination is treated in §4.6.1.

A striking feature of Seenku tonology is its extensive system of argument-head tone sandhi, treated in §4.4.2. These paradigmatic tone changes take place in specific morphosyntactic configurations of a head (nominal, verbal, or postpositional) and its internal argument, and interact with other tonal processes like plural formation in interesting ways. Sandhi patterns differ from tonal changes in compound nouns. Either of these sets of tone changes may be seen as Seenku's version of Mande "tonal compactness" or *compacité tonale* (Creissels 1978, with various Mande patterns recently summarized by Green 2018 who redefines the phenomenon as replacive tone). Compound tonology is discussed in §7.1.1.2.

2.2 Nominal and adjectival morphology

2.2.1 Nominal morphology

Nouns do not carry much morphology. As is typical for Mande languages (but not Niger-Congo more broadly), Seenku lacks noun classes. The only inflectional morphology on nouns is the plural, marked by a combination of vowel fronting and tone raising (§5.3); in a few human nouns, exceptional singular and/or plural suffixes are used. There is no affixal definite marking, segmental or tonal. However, for a discussion of incipient case marking on pronouns, see §6.6. Derivational morphology is more common, particularly compounding (treated in Chapter 7). In some cases, it is unclear whether a morpheme is an affix or compounded stem. For example, the nominalizing morpheme -bé, found in forms like nérémǎn-bé 'stupidity' (cf. néremǎn 'stupid') could be a simple affix or it could be a nominalized form of the root bȅ 'do'. To my knowledge, there is no interclass derivational morphology.

2.2.2 Adjectival morphology

Adjectives differ from nouns in their plural inflection, which involves initial CV reduplication in addition to the vocalic and tonal changes; in a N+Adj sequence, plural marking can occur on both the noun and the adjective or on just the adjective. Deadjectival nouns are derived using the -bé suffix/morpheme discussed above. Comparative constructions are analytical, involving no morphological marking on the adjective. For further discussion of adjectival morphology, see §8.3.2.

2.3 Noun phrase structure

The maximal noun phrase in Seenku is made up of the following elements, roughly in order (though some variation is attested):

(1) a. (discourse) definite, indefinite determiner, or possessor
    b. noun
    c. adjective
    d. numeral
    e. demonstrative or indefinite determiner
    f. non-numeral quantifier

For example:

(2) a. móò   bì   ké-kę̃   sṳ̀ɛ
       1SG.EMPH.DAT goat.PL RED-white.PL three
       'my three white goats'

   b. ä̀ bî   dë̀n sóen lɛ́
      DEF goat CLASS one DEM
      'this one goat'

Determiners are a particularly interesting topic in Seenku, both for their distribution and their phonological effects. The discourse definite, for instance, triggers argument-head tone sandhi and must obligatorily co-occur with a demonstrative. The definite, on the other hand, can occur on its own and does not interact tonally with the noun. For further discussion, see §8.2.

Possession is also of interest in the construction of noun phrases. Seenku has two possessive patterns, alienable and inalienable. Inalienable possession involves direct juxtaposition of the possessor and the possessed noun, which undergoes complex tone sandhi alternations triggered by the tone of the possessor. Alienable possession involves an explicit genitive or dative marker between the possessor and the possessed noun, with no tonal interaction between the two. However, this dative marker can be absorbed into the preceding pronoun, as in (2a), in which case the alienable possessor behaves like an inalienable possessor in triggering argument-head tone sandhi. See §8.6.2.3 for more.

2.4 Anaphora

Pronouns and anaphora in Seenku show a typical Mande or West African range: three persons are distinguished, along with a binary distinction between singular and plural. Gender is not a grammatical category, meaning 3sg ä̀ could refer to a male or female referent; there is likewise no animacy marking, and so ä̀ could mean 'it' as well. The only divergence from a basic six-pronoun system is the presence of what appears to be an inclusive vs. exclusive distinction in the 1pl, with exclusive íwí̋ and inclusive mí̋. The noun mɔ̋ 'person' can also be used as a pronoun, meaning either a generic pronoun like 'one' or a 1pl, as we see in French with *on*. See §6.1 for description of the pronominal categories.

In addition to the basic pronouns, there is a pronoun í which I describe as logophoric. Its distribution is similar to pronouns in other Mande languages, such as Boko (Jones 2000), meaning it is found both in traditional logophoric contexts (in a complement clause co-referent with the thinker or speaker of the main clause) as well as reflexive and reciprocal contexts. It too shows limited subject agreement, with ń used for the 1sg and í found in all other contexts. See §6.7.

2.5 Verbal morphology

2.5.1 Verbal derivation

As with nouns, derivational morphology is sparse with verbs in Seenku; expressions like the causative or benefactive are expressed analytically as opposed to morphologically. Nevertheless, we find two kinds of explicit derivational marking, both of which raise interesting questions of representation and interpretation.

The first is an antipassive suffix, which sometimes surfaces as what appears to be an infix. It suppresses the patient role of a transitive verb, rendering it intransitive in canonical cases. However, many of these antipassive verbs can continue to take a patient (i.e. be used transitively), but with a modified semantics where the VP takes on a partitive meaning (e.g. bǐ sɔ̌ɔ 'sell goats' vs. bǐ síɟɛɛ 'sell (antip.) some of the goats'). Antipassives are treated in §12.3.

The other derivational data pattern is the use of so-called "pre-verbs" (Keïta 1989, Vydrine 2009b, Khachaturyan 2017, etc.), (at least) diachronically related to nouns or postpositions that group phonologically with the preceding object but syntactically form a compound with the following verb. Three postpositional pre-verbs are attested: wɛ̀- (from the associative), né- (from the locative), and lɛ̌- (from the dative), though there is little in the way of consistent semantics for the use of each one. Certain inalienable nouns like kɔ̌n 'head' or dzó 'mouth' are also found in these compound verbs. See §12.4 for further discussion.

2.5.2 Verbal inflection

Verb stems in Seenku inflect for two categories: reality status (irrealis vs. realis) and aspect. There is no participant agreement, and tense and negation are (except in irregular cases) indicated through the use of post-subject markers (see below) or particles.

Realis verb stems often involve a high vowel infix before the syllable nucleus, creating a diphthong and sometimes triggering palatalization or affrication. For example: irrealis tɔ̌ vs. realis tsǐɔ. The realis is used in the perfect, perfective, progressive, immediate past, and conditional. In contrast, the irrealis consists of the bare verb stem, though with transitive verbs, it undergoes argument-head tone sandhi with the direct object; the realis verb stem, despite following the same word order, shows no tonal interactions. The irrealis is used in the prospective, the imperative, the habitual, and in subordinate clauses like purposives. For more on realis and irrealis verb stems, see §13.1.

Some aspects are marked with only grammatical tone, such as the perfective (marked by tone lowering) and the perfect (marked with a -SX contour suffix); others, like the habitual or the progressive, are marked with verbal particles homophonous with postpositions; still others, like the prospective or the imperative, are bare. Verbal inflection is treated in great depth in Chapter 13.

2.6 Main clauses and constituent order

2.6.1 Word order

Seenku has a typical rigid Mande word order:

(3)   Subject - TAMP - Auxiliary - Object - Verb - PP/Adjunct - Negation

Only one object, the internal object, can appear before the verb; any indirect objects must appear with a postposition after the verb. The one exception to this word order is that certain adverbs, such as kɔrɔ 'yesterday', can appear clause-initially.

There are no word order changes to be found, e.g. in subordinate clauses or due to focus or topicalization.

2.6.2 TAMP markers

A typical feature of Mande languages is the presence of grammatical particles after the subject that indicate tense, mood, or other grammatical functions (see e.g. Tröbs 2003). These go by many names in the literature on Mande languages. The term "predicate marker" or "predicative marker" is common in Mandeist literature (e.g. Bearth 1995, Babaev 2011), but they are also referred to as post-subject markers (e.g. Babaev 2010), auxiliaries (e.g. Kastenholz 2003), or TAMP markers (e.g. Idiatov 2016). I will follow this last naming convention, as it is the most neutral and likely to be understood outside of the Mandeist tradition, though it should be noted that in Seenku, they do not mark aspect.

TAMP markers are not as varied in Seenku as they are in some other Mande languages (such as Jula), but a few are attested, listed below with their cross-references:
- Past tense lɛ́ (§13.4)
- Subordinate wɛ̀/lɛ̀ (Chapter 17, §19.3, §20.2)
- Subjunctive lɛ́ (§18.1, §19.3)

The subordinate marker has two forms, lɛ̀ and wɛ̀. The /l/-initial form lɛ̀ is found marking the subject of relative clauses, while either lɛ̀ or wɛ̀ can be found in certain complement clauses and in clause chaining. Similarly, the subjunctive marker is found in all conditional clauses as well as some complement clauses.

In every case, the segmental material of the TAMP markers can elide, leaving behind only their tone and a mora, which dock to the preceding subject. For instance, the past tense marker following the 1sg could be pronounced as either mó lɛ́ or móő;

/l/- and /w/-initial postpositions follow the same process of elision, but in addition undergo tone sandhi, while TAMP markers remain tonally inert. See §4.4.3 for further discussion of elision.

I treat TAMP markers as distinct from auxiliaries, such as the prospective ná, the progressive sĭ ('be'), or the immediate past sı́o. The two can co-occur, always in the order TAMP Aux.

2.6.3 Negation

Negation in Seenku is of interest in that it follows the areal pattern of clause-final marking (Dryer 2009, Idiatov 2015), with the negative particle ŋé. Even when a clause is complicated with an embedded subordinate clause, negation still is marked at the end of the whole thing, i.e. **after** the embedded clause. For instance:

(4) mó lǎ ɲá ä̀ nè̋ ä̀ nǎ nè̋ ŋé
    1SG.EMPH believe.PTCP be.NEG 3SG LOC 3SG PROSP come.IRR NEG
    'I don't think that he will come.' [sos170811e]

The clause-final negative marker ŋé belongs to the initial matrix clause, as can be discerned by the use of the irregular negative verb ɲá; in other words, this phrase does not translate as "I believe he won't come". See §13.5 for an overview of negation and §19.2.2 for more examples of negation in complex clauses.

2.7 Relative clauses

Seenku displays head-internal relative clauses; like Bambara (Bird 1968) and many other Mande languages, these clauses are typically left-peripheral and resumed by a discourse definite pronoun kʊ́ in the main clause; they can also appear after the main clause, with a relative pronoun coreferent with the head that appears in the main clause. The head of the relative clause is followed by the wh-relativizer lɛ́ (see §16.2.1 for treatment of lɛ́ as a wh-word), and the subject is followed by the subordinate TAMP marker lḛ̀; if the subject is the head of the relative clause, the two occur in the order REL SUBORDINATE (lɛ́ lḛ̀). There is no special verbal morphology associated with relative clauses.

The subordinate marker shows interesting behavior with respect to auxiliaries. Typically, other TAMP markers like the past or the subjunctive co-occur with auxiliaries and precede them. In relative clauses, the subordinate marker follows the prospective auxiliary (§17.1.1), blocks the appearance of the affirmative progressive auxiliary sĭ 'be', and is blocked by the negative progressive auxiliary ɲá (§17.1.3).

Whenever the subject of a relative clause is a noun, it is followed by a resumptive pronoun; both the noun and pronoun are followed by the subordinate predicate marker.

For further discussion of relative clauses, see Chapter 17.

2.8 Complement clauses

Seenku has three complementization strategies. The first is to use an overt complementizer, found in expressions of saying, knowing, or thinking. The most interesting aspect of these constructions is that Seenku shows limited complementizer agreement, whereby the complementizer agrees with the subject of the matrix clase. There is a two-way distinction between *né* for the 1sg and *ì* for every other person-number combination; see §19.1 for further discussion.

The other complementization strategy is to juxtapose the complement clause to the end of the matrix clause with no complementizer; the subordination of the complement clause is shown by the use of either the subjunctive or the subordinate TAMP markers. In some complement clauses, the subjunctive is used regardless of tense/aspect, while with other verbs, past and perfective aspects are correlated with the use of the subordinate rather than the subjunctive. See §19.3.

Finally, some verbs take nominalized complement clauses; these constructions are discussed in §19.4.

2.9 Clause chaining and event sequencing

In narratives, Seenku displays the phenomenon of clause chaining—sequences of foregrounded subordinate clauses introduced by a single main clause establishing the background. There may be incipient same subject marking on the subordinate TAMP marker for 3sg subjects; see §20.2.

Otherwise, Seenku displays a few temporal subordination strategies, which can involve the conditional construction, verbal reduplication, or an explicit 'before' construction; these constructions are treated further in §20.3.

2.10 Artistic adaptation

A peculiar feature of this grammar is the inclusion of a chapter on artistic adaptation. I have chosen to include this topic given the presence of a fascinating surrogate language system, particularly on the balafon, a kind of resonator xylophone: anything in Seenku can be "spoken" musically by encoding the tone and rhythm of the language on the instrument. In addition, vocal music in Seenku is tightly constrained by the language's tone system, and these melodies are fed back to instrumental music, creating two styles of musical language. See Chapter 22 for discussion.

3 Segmental phonology

This chapter focuses on the segmental phonology of Seenku; for tonal phonology, see Chapter 4. I begin with phoneme inventories, first of vowels (§3.1) and then of consonants (§3.2). The discussion then turns to syllable structure and phonotactics (§3.3) and then to a brief discussion on word structure (§3.4), which in most cases is the same as syllable structure, given the largely mono- and sesquisyllabic nature of Seenku vocabulary. Finally, I address phonological rules and processes in §3.5 before a brief discussion of phonological phrasing in §3.6.

3.1 Vowels

Between contrastive length and nasalization and a wide array of diphthongs, Seenku has a very large vowel inventory. I divide the discussion of the vowels into monophthongs (§3.1.1) and diphthongs (§3.1.2), with questions of inventory and acoustics discussed in each. Minimal pairs are addressed separately in §3.1.4, which includes both monophthongs and diphthongs.

3.1.1 Monophthongs

3.1.1.1 Oral vowels

Determining the number of phonemic vowel qualities in Seenku has proven to be a surprisingly difficult task. At first, the language appears to be a typical West African seven vowel system for the oral vowel qualities, with a two-way height or ATR contrast in the mid vowels: /e, ɛ, o, ɔ/. However, a handful of lexical items introduce a third category that falls acoustically between the regular categories in terms of F1 (height). It often has a pharyngealized quality to it, suggesting retracted tongue root, though this would benefit from articulatory study. The situation appears to be in a state of flux, with differences between speakers. For instance, while most speakers display the third category in back vowels, some speakers appear to have only the two-way contrast in front vowels.

Given this, there is no obvious way in which to transcribe the third category. If the system is basically a seven vowel system, then it makes sense to treat the more common and more stable categories as /o, ɔ/, which to my ear matches their acoustics. But if this is the case, then there is no prototypical vowel in the IPA that falls between the two in terms of height. Given the pharyngealized quality of the third category and its variable triggering of palatalization (§3.5.1.1), I hypothesize that these are [-ATR] high vowels, with extreme raising of F1 due to the retracted tongue root. As such, I will transcribe these vowels as /ɪ/ and /ʊ/.

It is unclear whether the mysterious third category is an innovation or archaic feature in Seenku. As a Western Mande language, we would expect a seven vowel system in Seenku (Vydrine 2004), but nine vowel systems are attested in Southern Mande, and Le Saout (1979) considers these to be the most archaic, with other vowel systems neutralizing these contrasts. It seems unlikely that just a single Western Mande language would retain a trace of this older archaic system, leading me to believe that these are remnants of some other contrast in Seenku, possibly diphthongs that have monophthongized or a phonologized effect of a consonant that has since been lost. An example of a four-way (near) minimal pair for the back vowel series is shown in (1):

(1) kû   'thing'
    kʊ̂   'toh (staple grain paste)'
    kô   'rock hyrax'
    (à) kɔ̂ '(his) bone'

Note that I have only ever heard short [-ATR] high vowels.

With this in mind, the inventory of oral vowels, short and long, is shown in Table 3.1, with each vowel exemplified; minimal pairs will be provided in §3.1.4.

Tab. 3.1: Seenku oral monophthong inventory

Short		Long	
i	bî 'goat'	ii	tîi 'accept'
(ɪ)	kíʼ (past tense copula)		
e	mɛ̌lɛ́ 'hot pepper'	ee	cəbɛ̌e 'shea nut'
ɛ	bɛ̂ 'do (irrealis)'	ɛɛ	bɛ̌ɛ 'pig'
a	kâ 'yam'	aa	kâa 'fight'
ɔ	(à) kɔ̂ '(his) bone'	ɔɔ	kɔ̌ɔ 'hole'
o	(à) tò '(his) testicle'	oo	(à) tǒo '(his) ear'
ʊ	jō 'water'		
u	kərù 'hyena'	uu	kərúú 'all'

Short oral vowels have an inventory of 8-9 vowels, depending on the speaker; some speakers have merged /ɪ/ and /ɛ/ (recall that /ɪ/ is acoustically intermediate between /e/ and /ɛ/ in terms of F1/F2). Long oral vowels show only the basic 7-way contrast, with the loss of [-ATR] high vowels.

Long vowels are almost exactly twice as long as short vowels on average. In a phonetic comparison of 64 short vowel tokens in a frame sentence and 54 long vowels, short vowels had an average duration of 111ms, while long vowels had an average duration of 225ms.

I assume the feature inventory in Table 3.2 to account for the vowels of Seenku. The role of this feature inventory in plural formation will be discussed in §5.3.1.2.

Tab. 3.2: Seenku vowel features

	i	e	ɛ	a	ɔ	o	ʊ	u
[front]	+	+	+	-	-	-	-	-
[back]	-	-	-	-	+	+	+	+
[high]	+	-	-	-	-	-	+	+
[low]	-	-	-	+	-	-	-	-
[ATR]	+	+	-	-	-	+	-	+

For acoustic F1*F2 plots of the vowel qualities (both oral and nasal), see §3.1.1.3.

3.1.1.2 Nasal vowels

Like many languages, Seenku has a reduced set of nasal vowel qualities; specifically, ATR distinctions in high and mid vowels are neutralized, leaving just five nasal vowel qualities. Length is contrastive for nasal vowels as well, and while in principle all five could be long, only three of the five possible long vowels are attested in the data.

Tab. 3.3: Seenku nasal monophthong inventory

Short		Long	
į	bį́ 'horns'	įį	tərį́į 'cut (antipassive)'
ɛ̨	dɛ̨̀ 'walls'	ɛ̨ɛ̨	tɛ̨̂ɛ̨ 'hunt'
a̧	bá̧ 'hit'	a̧a̧	bâ̧a̧ 'balafon'
ɔ̨	fərɔ̨̌ 'monkey'	(ɔ̨ɔ̨)	
ų	bų̂ 'grass'	(ųų)	

3.1.1.3 Vowel acoustics

To plot the acoustics of Seenku's monophthongs, I compiled a list of nine lexical items for each vowel quality, collapsing the distinction between short and long vowels (for which there are no audible quality differences). Two speakers of Seenku, one male and one female, embedded each item in a frame sentence (mó ___ sɔ́ɔ 'I bought ___' for nouns and ___ sə́sàa nɛ̀ 'do ___ now' for verbs), repeating each three times for a total of 27 tokens of each quality. Formant values were extracted from the recordings using a Praat script, with outliers rechecked and corrected by hand. The resulting acoustic information was normalized and plotted using NORM vowel normalization and plotting suite (http://lingtools.uoregon.edu/norm/index.php). The results are shown in Figure 3.1. Unfortunately the two speakers who recorded this list—both younger speakers from central Bouendé—do not have the vowel /ɪ/ as part of their inventory, and thus the chart contains only the [-ATR] high back vowel /ʊ/.

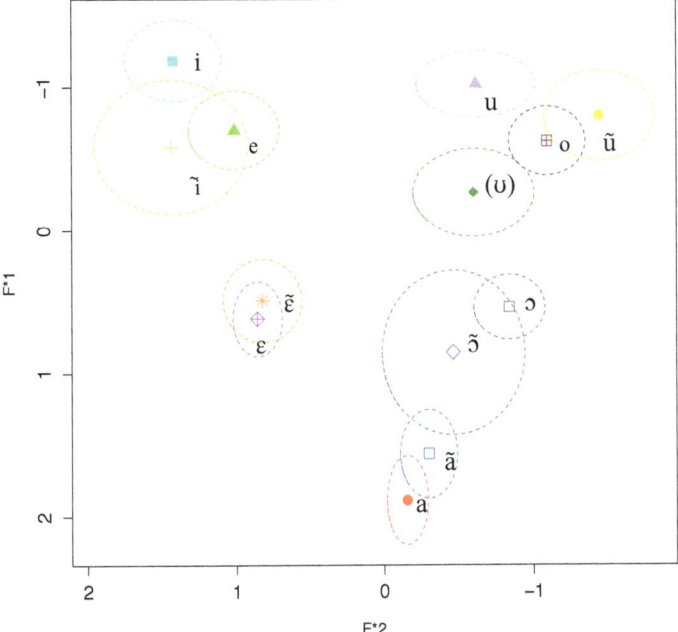

Fig. 3.1: Normalized F1*F2 plot for two speakers

This plot demonstrates the position of /ʊ/ between /o/ and /ɔ/ in terms of height, though the high series /u, ʊ/ is slightly more centralized than the mid series /o, ɔ/. The nasal vowels are interesting in that the high nasal vowels /ĩ/ and /ũ/ (using IPA conventions for nasalization here as opposed to the tilde below the vowel, as I use in most transcriptions) are acoustically quite close to /e/ and /o/; thus, while we can say that the distinction between mid vowels is neutralized in the nasal series, from an acoustic standpoint it seems possible that the height distinction between [+ATR] vowels is neutralized instead. In fact, we find alternations between /e/ and /ĩ/, such as dên 'grain' and dí̃ 'grains', where the latent nasal coda is realized as vowel nasalization in the plural. See §3.3.2 for further discussion of nasal codas and §5.3.1.3 for nasal alternations in plurals.

3.1.2 Diphthongs

Seenku also has around a dozen diphthongs, all of which are either rising sonority (moving from a higher vowel to a lower vowel) or level sonority (moving from a back vowel to a front vowel). Many diphthongs are created through morphological processes like plural formation (§5.3.1) or realis formation (§13.1), though they are also found lexically. Oral diphthongs are shown in Table 3.4, nasal diphthongs in Table 3.5.

Tab. 3.4: Seenku oral diphthong inventory

	ui		
ie	ue	oe	
iɛ	uɛ		ɔɛ
io	uo		
iɔ	uɔ		
ia	ua	(ʊa)	

Tab. 3.5: Seenku nasal diphthong inventory

	ṵḭ	
ḭɛ̰	ṵɛ̰	ɔ̰ɛ̰
ḭɔ̰	ṵɔ̰	
ḭa̰		

From a phonetic standpoint, the two elements are not on equal footing. The initial element behaves like an onglide, which I take phonologically to be a non-moraic vowel, while the second element has a duration similar to monophthongs. Because the initial vowel is non-moraic, diphthongs may also be either short or long without creating superheavy syllables.

Given that the majority of diphthongs begin with either /i/ or /u/, we may also ask whether we are dealing with diphthongs at all, or whether instead Seenku should be analyzed as having secondary palatal and labial articulation on consonants. This is the analytical route taken in Djilla et al. (2004) for related Samogo language Jowulu. The distinction between [oe] and [ue] or [ɔɛ] and [uɛ], though, point to diphthongs as the most natural explanation, since it allows the glide-like quality to retain its full set of vocalic features.

We can make a few observations about the diphthong inventory in Seenku. First, back-to-front diphthongs are attested while front-to-back (excluding /a/) are not; thus, we find no *iu, *eo, *ɛɔ, etc. Second, back-to-front diphthongs are harmonic for [ATR]. While /oe/, /ɔɛ/ are attested, *oɛ or *ɔe are not. High and low vowels are neutral and may combine freely. The diphthong /ʊa/ is in parentheses, as it is only attested in one morpheme, /sʊ́aa/ 'path, way' (in compounds like /ŋəmá-sʊ́aa/ 'blood vessel'); palatalization of /s/ to [ʃ] ([ʃʊ́aa]) points to the [-ATR] high vowel rather than /ɔ/, though this is the only case in which we find this category involved in dipththongs.

Due to the absence of [+ATR] nasal vowels, the inventory of nasal diphthongs is also smaller.

As stated above, diphthongs may also be either short or long, with the length constrast carried by the second element. Because of the onglide portion, the overall duration of diphthongs is longer than their corresponding monophthongs, 135ms for short diphthongs and 263ms for long diphthongs.

3.1.3 The status of schwa

There is some question of how to treat a surface vowel schwa [ə] in the phonology of Seenku. As will be discussed in §3.3, a large portion of the Seenku lexicon is best classified as **sesquisyllabic** (Matisoff 1990, Pittayaporn 2015), a short half syllable containing a non-contrastive vowel [ə] followed by a full syllable containing one of the vowel phonemes described above. This non-contrastive vowel does not carry its own tonal specification, instead receiving pitch either from the full syllable to the right, in the case of mono- or bitonal melodies, or by hosting the first of the three tones in a tritonal word. Examples of such sesquisyllabic words include:

(2) a. səmâ 'dance'

   b. nəgǐ 'cow'

   c. mənǐ 'woman'

The duration of this vowel is on average only 42ms, compared to 111ms for short vowels (see §3.1.1 above).

The exact quality of the vowel depends on its consonantal context and the following vowel. When it is adjacent to a palatal consonant, its realization is closer to [i] than to schwa, as in [jibé̃] 'clothing' or [ɲigâa] 'guinea fowl'; when adjacent to a velar consonant followed by a back round vowel, its realization is closer to [u], as in [dugǒɔ] 'place'. However, these qualities are not contrastive. Between a velar stop and [r], it is typically realized as a high round vowel agreeing in [ATR] specification with the following vowel:

(3) a. kərê → [kʊrê] 'man'

   b. kərǜ → [kurǜ] 'hyena'

   c. gərȅ → [gurȅ] 'voice'

No other vowel quality is found in this environment, suggesting that it is non-contrastive.

The question is: is [ə] (or its various surface allophones) in these words the realization of a schwa vowel phoneme, restricted to appearing only in these initial half syllables, or is it epenthetic or excrescent, there to break up an otherwise complex onset?

While it almost certainly has its origins in a full vowel that underwent a kind of iambic reduction, I argue that synchronically it is best treated as epenthetic. Evidence for this position is not abundant, but the following facts are suggestive. First, Seenku tolerates onset clusters in which the second consonant is a liquid, and in these environments, the schwa is optional. For example:

(4) a. [bəlĕ] ~ [blĕ] 'big'

   b. [fəlɛ́] ~ [flɛ́] 'what'

   c. [sərȁ] ~ [srȁ] 'chief'

One could argue that it is only in the position before liquids that an underlying schwa could be deleted, similar to the syncope of high vowels in languages like Bambara (see e.g. Green 2010), but it seems more likely to me that Seenku only employs this non-contrastive vowel when it is required for phonotactic reasons. Note, however, that velar-liquid clusters are not attested; a short high round vowel is always realized between the two consonants.

Second, in the balafon surrogate language (§22.2.1), the schwa is not treated as an independent vowel. Sesquisyllabic words are treated the same as long vowels, receiving a rapid grace note strike on the xylophone before the strike corresponding to the main vowel. I take this to be evidence that schwa does not have the same level of phonological representation as other vowels, suggesting that they are epenthetic rather than underlying. However, one could also posit a difference between phonologically full and reduced vowels that is represented on the balafon in this way.

Finally, in discussing orthographic possibilities, consultants had no qualms about writing sesquisyllabic words without a schwa or similar vowel, i.e. writing words like 'dance' as <smâ>. When some consultants write in Seenku, they likewise write words with initial clusters, but these spellings vary. Since the language does not have a written tradition, native speaker intuitions about orthography should be treated with caution, as they may have influences from French, Jula, or other languages in which the person may be literate, but they still offer a glimpse into their metalinguistic knowledge.

In sum, there is no uncontroversial evidence pointing to the phonemic status of schwa, but what evidence exists suggests that it is not underlying. In the transcription system used in this grammar, however, I will typically write sesquisyllabic words with a schwa, which better represents their surface pronunciation, though if C2 is a liquid and the word typically begins with a cluster, I will write it that way (i.e. *blǎ* 'fall' rather than *bəlǎ*).

3.1.4 Minimal pairs

The following subsections will run through each of the vowel phonemes, discussing allophones and providing minimal and near minimal pairs with similar phonemes. So as not to duplicate efforts, minimal pairs contrasting short and long vowels will be provided beginning in §3.1.4.8; minimals pairs contrasting nasality will be given beginning in §3.1.4.15. Diphthongal contrasts (both between diphthongs and between monophthongs and diphthongs) will be given beginning in §3.1.4.23.

3.1.4.1 /i/

The vowel /i/ is a high front unrounded vowel with just a single allophone [i]. As will be discussed in §3.5.1.1, it has a tendency to palatalize and/or spirantize the preceding consonant. The following minimal pairs show that /i/ contrasts in height with /e/ and /ɛ/ and in backness with /u/:

(5)   *Minimal pairs for /i/ vs...*

/e/	jěn	'front'	jî	'grindstone'
/ɛ/	kɛ̂	'moon'	cî	'house'
/u/	bǔ	'sand'	bǐ̋	'goats'

3.1.4.2 /e/

The vowel /e/ is a front mid unrounded [+ATR] vowel. It is the rarest vowel in Seenku, more commonly found in the diphthong /ie(e)/ than as a monophthongal vowel quality. It shows no allophonic variation. The vowel /e/ contrasts with /i/ in height, with /ɛ/ in [ATR], and with /o/ in backness:

(6)   *Minimal pairs for /e/ vs...*

/i/	jî	'grindstone'	jěn	'front'
/ɛ/	tɛ́	'who'	té̋	(genitive particle)
/o/	jǒn	'slave'	jěn	'front'

3.1.4.3 /ɛ/

The vowel /ɛ/ is a front mid unrounded [-ATR] vowel. In contrast to its [+ATR] correspondent, it is one of the most common vowels in Seenku, found in many of the function words as well as core vocabulary. Unlike the previous two vowels, the vowel /ɛ/ has two allophones: an elsewhere case [ɛ] and a centralized allophone [ɜ], found primarily after alveolar affricates. For example, the indefinite quantifier /tsɛ́/ is most commonly pronounced [tsɜ́]. Unlike the central [ə] in sesquisyllabic words, this allophone [ɜ] is more tense, with an audibly retracted tongue root quality to it. See §3.5.5 for further discussion. /ɛ/ contrasts with /i/ and /a/ in height, with /e/ in [ATR], and with /ɔ/ in backness:

(7) *Minimal pairs for /ɛ/ vs...*

/i/	cî	'house'	kê	'moon'
/a/	kâ	'griot'	kê	'moon'
/e/	tế	(genitive)	té	'who'
/ɔ/	fɔ̌	'grow'	fɛ́	'blow'

3.1.4.4 /a/

The vowel /a/ is a low central unrounded vowel in Seenku. Its pronunciation is consistent, with just the single allophone [a]. It contrasts with /ɛ/ and /ɔ/ in height and backness.

(8) *Minimal pairs for /a/ vs....*

| /ɛ/ | kê | 'moon' | kâ | 'griot' |
| /ɔ/ | sɔ́ | 'arrive' | sá | 'cry' |

3.1.4.5 /ɔ/

The vowel /ɔ/ is a back mid rounded [-ATR] vowel. It has just the single allophone [ɔ]. The following minimal pairs show that /ɔ/ contrasts with /ʊ/ and /a/ in height, with /o/ in [ATR], and with /ɛ/ in backness:

(9) *Minimal pairs for /ɔ/ vs....*

/ʊ/	kʊ̌	'rock hyrax'	à kɔ̌	'his bone'
/a/	sá	'cry'	sɔ́	'arrive'
/o/	sőn	'fun'	sɔ́n	'sky'
/ɛ/	fɛ́	'blow'	fɔ̌	'grow'

3.1.4.6 /o/

Like the [+ATR] vowel /e/, the vowel /o/ is not frequent in Seenku. It is a mid back rounded [+ATR] vowel that shows no allophony, being consistently pronounced as [o]. It contrasts with /u/ in height, with /ɔ/ in [ATR], and with /e/ in backness:

(10) Minimal pairs for /o/ vs....

/u/	tsù	'straw'	tòn	'pond'
/ɔ/	sɔ̌n	'sky'	sőn	'fun'
/e/	jěn	'front'	jön	'slave'

3.1.4.7 /u/

The vowel /u/ is a high back rounded vowel. Between a palatal onset and the high front vowel /i/ in diphthongs, it surfaces variably as the allophone [y], as in ɲűi [ɲýi] 'honey'. It contrasts with /o/ and /ɔ/ in height and with /i/ in backness, and with /ʊ/ in [ATR]:

(11) Minimal pairs for /u/ vs....

/o/	tòn	'pond'	tsù	'straw'
/ɔ/	lɔ̌	'here'	lǔ	'courtyard'
/i/	bǐ	'goats'	bǔ	'sand'
/ʊ/	jù	'year'	jô	'water'

3.1.4.8 /ii/

After labiovelars, the long vowel /ii/ is realized with a slight [ə] onglide, [əii]. It is otherwise simply a longer version of /i/. We can contrast the long vowel /ii/ with both short /i/ and with other similar long vowel phonemes, such as /ee/, /ɛɛ/, and /uu/:

(12) Minimal pairs for /ii/ vs....

/i/	à ní	'his father'	à nîi	'his tongue'
/ee/	jěe	'be day'	kpîi	'faint'
/ɛɛ/	kpɛ̌ɛ	'sew'	kpîi	'faint'
/uu/	nǘun	'hoarse'	nìi	'pregnancy'

3.1.4.9 /ee/

If /e/ is rare, its equivalent long vowel /ee/ is even rarer, attested in only a handful of words. In principle, it contrasts with /e/ in length, with /ii/ in height, with /ɛɛ/ in [ATR], and with /oo/ in backness, but minimal pairs are difficult to find. I take these to be accidental gaps, as there is nothing predictable about the distribution of /ee/. Near minimal pairs are listed below:

(13)   Near minimal pairs for /ee/ vs...

/e/	jəbĕ	'cloth'	cəbĕe	'shea nut'
/ii/	kpîi	'faint'	jĕe	'be day'
/εε/	mó cɛ̀ɛ	'my egg'	cĕe	'blacksmith'
/oo/	kôo	'be born'	jĕe	'be day'

3.1.4.10 /εε/

The long vowel /εε/ is quite common. Unlike /ε/, which has a centralized allophone, /εε/ is consistently pronounced as a front vowel; however, the environment for centralization (after alveolar affricates) is unattested for the long vowel, so it is not clear whether this process would also affect them. For more on phonotactics and combinatorial statistics, see §3.3.3. The following minimal pairs illustrate the contrast in length with /ε/, in height with /ii/ and /aa/, in [ATR] with /ee/, and in backness with /ɔɔ/.

(14)   Minimal pairs for /εε/ vs...

/ε/	nɛ̋	'come'	nɛ̋ɛ	'coil up'
/ii/	kpîi	'faint'	kpɛ̀ɛ	'sew'
/aa/	kǎa	'chase'	kɛ́ɛ	'break'
/ee/	cəbĕe	'shea'	bɛ̀ɛ	'pig'
/ɔɔ/	dɔ̋ɔ	'snatch'	dɛ̀ɛ	'accustom'

3.1.4.11 /aa/

The long vowel /aa/ has just a single allophone, [aa]. It contrasts with /a/ in length and with /εε/ and /ɔɔ/ in height.

(15)   Minimal pairs for /aa/ vs...

/a/	kâ	'griot'	kâa	'fight'
/εε/	kɛ́ɛ	'break'	káa	'chase'
/ɔɔ/	bɔ̋ɔ	'age'	bâa	'wear out'

3.1.4.12 /ɔɔ/

Like /aa/, the long vowel /ɔɔ/ shows no allophonic variation. It contrasts with /ɔ/ in length, with /aa/ in height, with /oo/ in [ATR], and with /εε/ in backness.

(16)   Minimal pairs for /ɔɔ/ vs...

/ɔ/	mó kɔ̋	'my bone'	mó kɔ̋ɔ	'my brother'
/aa/	bâa	'wear out'	bɔ̋ɔ	'age'
/oo/	sóo	'gather'	sɔ́ɔ	'sell'
/εε/	dɛ̀ɛ	'accustom'	dɔ̋ɔ	'snatch'

3.1.4.13 /oo/

The vowel /oo/ is considerably more common than its front equivalent /ee/. It contrasts with /o/ in length, with /uu/ in height, with /ɔɔ/ in [ATR], and with /ee/ in backness. However, the minimal pair with /uu/ is not a perfect illustration, as the two words differ in category (adverb vs. verb). See §3.1.4.14 below for a discussion of /uu/.

(17) Minimal pairs for /oo/ vs...

/o/	à tò	'his testicle'	ǎ tööo	'his ear'
/uu/	sǔu	'directly'	sőo	'gather'
/ɔɔ/	kɔ̌ɔ	'walk'	kôo	'be born'
/ee/	jěe	'be day'	kôo	'be born'

3.1.4.14 /uu/

There is nothing to indicate that long /uu/ should not be phonemic, given the consistent length distinctions for other vowels, yet examples of long /uu/ in core vocabulary (nouns and verbs) are lacking. The closest example is nǔun 'hoarse', a participial modifier. All other examples of /uu/ are found in either ideophones or ideophonic quantifiers, like kərúú 'all', already unusual in its tone pattern (two distinct H tones in a row, with plural kərúíì). It is unclear whether it is simply a rare vowel phoneme, yet to be gathered into the lexicon, or whether it is a gap in the core phoneme inventory. Given the lack of core vocabulary with /uu/, I will not provide the full set of minimal pairs. A near minimal pair for length, however, can be found with kərû 'thorn' vs. kərúú 'all'.

3.1.4.15 /i̤/

We now turn to the nasal vowels and their contrasts with oral vowels. The short high front vowel /i̤/ contrasts with its oral equivalent /i/ in nasality, with /ɛ̤/ in height, and with /ṳ/ in backness.

(18) Minimal pairs for /i̤/ vs...

/i/	bí	'goats'	bí̤	'horns'
/ɛ̤/	fɛ̤̋	'yet'	fí̤	'two'
/ṳ/	fərṳ̀	'bean'	fərí̤	'broom'

3.1.4.16 /ɛ̤/

The vowel /ɛ̤/ displays the same pattern of centralization as its oral equivalent, yielding two allophones: [ɜ̤] after alveolar affricates and [ɛ̤] elsewhere. Given the limited environment for [ɜ̤], it is not surprising that it is only attested in one word in most people's speech: [tsɜ̤̋] 'how'. In the speech of some people, there is variation between palatal stops and alveolar affricates, thus other examples are attested, such [à tsɜ̤] 'his foot', but most people would pronounce this as [à cɛ̰̀], with a palatal stop and the allophone [ɛ]. For discussion of the palatal/alveolar affricate variation, see §3.5.1.3.

The phoneme /ɛ/ contrasts with /ɛ̰/ in nasality, with /ḭ/ and /a̰/ in height, and with /ɔ̰/ in backness.

(19) *Minimal pairs for /ɛ/ vs...*

/ɛ/	təgɛ́	'chickens'	təgɛ̰́	'cheeks'
/ḭ/	fḭ́	'two'	fɛ̰́	'yet'
/a̰/	bã̰	'table'	kpɛ̰̂	'hunt'
/ɔ̰/	à kɔ̰̀n	'his head'	à cɛ̰̀	'his foot'

3.1.4.17 /a̰/

The low nasal vowel /a̰/ contrasts with /a/ in nasality, and with /ɛ̰/ and /ɔ̰/ in height.

(20) *Minimal pairs for /a̰/ vs...*

/a/	dán	'lie'	dá̰n	'hump (back)'
/ɛ̰/	kpɛ̰̂	'hunt'	bã̰	'table'
/ɔ̰/	tsɔ̰̂	'be submerged'	sã̰	'buy'

3.1.4.18 /ɔ̰/

The vowel /ɔ̰/ contrasts with /ɔ/ in nasality, with /ṵ/ and /a̰/ in height, and with /ɛ̰/ in backness.

(21) *Minimal pairs for /ɔ̰/ vs...*

/ɔ/	jɔ́	'brew beer'	jɔ̰́	'grill'
/ṵ/	à tsṵ̀	'his skin'	à tsɔ̰́	'his pity'
/a̰/	sã̰	'buy'	tsɔ̰̂	'be submerged'
/ɛ̰/	à cɛ̰̀	'his foot'	à kɔ̰̀n	'his head'

3.1.4.19 /ṵ/

The high back nasal vowel /ṵ/ contrasts with /u/ in nasality, with /ɔ̰/ in height, and with /ḭ/ in backness.

(22) *Minimal pairs for /ṵ/ vs...*

/u/	jù	'year'	jṵ̀	'hill'
/ɔ̰/	à tsɔ̰́	'his pity'	à tsṵ̀	'his skin'
/ḭ/	fərṵ̀	'beans'	fərḭ́	'broom'

3.1.4.20 /iḭ/

The long high front nasal vowel /iḭ/ contrasts with /ii/ in nasality, with /ḭ/ in length, and with /ɛ̰ɛ̰/ in height.

(23) *Minimal pairs for /iḭ/ vs…*

/ii/	kpîi	'faint'	kpíḭ	'spark'
/ḭ/	bḭ́	'horns'	kpḭḭ́	'spark'
/ɛ̰ɛ̰/	səgɛ̰̌ɛ̰	'grave'	səgîḭ	'market'

3.1.4.21 /ɛ̰ɛ̰/

The long mid front nasal vowel /ɛ̰ɛ̰/ contrasts with /ɛɛ/ in nasality, with /ɛ̰/ in length, and with /iḭ/ and /a̰a̰/ in height.

(24) *Minimal pairs for /ɛ̰ɛ̰/ vs…*

/ɛɛ/	kɛ́ɛ	'totem'	kɛ̰́ɛ̰	'tomorrow'
/ɛ̰/	kpɛ̰̂	'hunt'	kɛ̰́ɛ̰	'tomorrow'
/iḭ/	səgɛ̰̌ɛ̰	'grave'	səgîḭ	'market'
/a̰a̰/	bâ̰a̰	'balafon'	pɛ̰̌ɛ̰	'donkeys'

3.1.4.22 /a̰a̰/

The long low nasal vowel /a̰a̰/ is very rare. Phonemically, it appears only in the noun *bâ̰a̰* 'balafon', though it is also found on rising tones, where length contrasts are neutralized, such as *kǎ̰*. With just this one word, I will not present minimal pairs.

3.1.4.23 /ui/

We now turn to diphthongal contrasts. Diphthongs will be contrasted both with their monophthongal elements and with similar diphthongs. Where possible, I will provide minimal pairs using non-derived diphthongs, that is, diphthongs found in uninflected lexical items rather than those derived from plural formation or other morphological processes. Finally, to conserve space, I will not treat short and long diphthongs separately, but instead focus on the vocalic qualities. However, if giving an example with a long diphthong, it will be provided in a minimal pair with matching length.

First, the diphthong /ui/ is relatively rare in uninflected lexical items, but it can be found. It contrasts with both /u/ and /i/, and their long counterparts; it is also distinct from similar diphthongs /ue/ and /oe/.

(25) Minimal pairs for /ui/ vs...

/u/	bǔ	'sand'	bûi	'deaf-mute'
/i/	jəgǐ	'crush'	jəgǔi	'urinate'
/ue/	mó cǔen	'my elbow'	cûi	'turtle'
/oe/	ǐ bŏe	'their backs'	bǔi	'deaf-mutes'

3.1.4.24 /ie/

The diphthong /ie/ is attested both lexically and derivationally, though it is far more common in the latter condition through realis formation or irregular derivation (e.g. the locative cîe 'in the house' vs. cî 'house', or tsǐen 'pestle', likely from tsǐ-děn 'mortar child'). It contrasts with both /i/ and /e/, and with the diphthongs /iɛ/, /io/ and /ue/.

(26) Minimal pairs for /ie/ vs...

/i/	tsǐ	'mortar'	tsǐen	'pestle'
/e/	tě	(genitive)	tsīe	'black'
/iɛ/	fǐɛ	'blow (realis)'	fīe	'throw (realis)'
/ue/	à cùen	'his elbow'	cîe	'in the house'

3.1.4.25 /ue/

The diphthong /ue/ often co-occurs with a coda nasal. It is mainly a lexical rather than derived diphthong. It contrasts with the monophthongs /u/ and /e/, and with the diphthongs /ie/, /uɛ/, /ui/, and /uo/.

(27) Minimal pairs for /ue/ vs...

/u/	sǔ	'antelope'	sǔen	'trunkfish'
/e/	dəgěn	'remainder'	dəgǔen	'small tree (*Maranthes polyandra*)'
/ie/	tsǐen	'pestle'	cǔen	'tilapia'
/ui/	cûi	'turtle'	cǔen	'tilapia'
/uɛ/	cùɛ	'vomit'	à cùen	'his elbow'
/uo/	sǔo	'picked up'	sǔen	'trunkfish'

3.1.4.26 /oe/

The diphthong /oe/ is rare lexically. It is most commonly attested in alternations between singular /o/ and plural /oe/. As such, it contrasts with /o/ (where [oe] marks the plural), and also with /e/, /ɔɛ/, and /ue/. Even though the diphthong-initial round vowel is non-moraic and is pronounced as a glide, /ue/ and /oe/ remain distinct in that /ue/ triggers palatalization from the high vowel while /oe/ does not. Thus, the last minimal pair in the following table would be pronounced [ʃʷ̌eɲ] vs. [sǫ̌e].

(28) *Minimal pairs for /oe/ vs…*

/o/	kŏ	'rock hyrax'	kŏe	'rock hyraxes'
/e/	jĕn	'front'	jŏe	'slaves'
/ɔɛ/	à kɔ̀ɛ	'his bones'	kŏe	'rock hyraxes'
/uɛ/	sűen	'trunkfish'	sòe	'horses'

3.1.4.27 /iɛ/

This diphthong /iɛ/ is similar to its [+ATR] counterpart in terms of frequency and distribution; it is found in a handful of lexical items and is otherwise created through diphthongization processes like realis formation (§13.1). It contrasts with its component monophthongs /i/ and /ɛ/, and with the diphthongs /ie/, /iɔ/ and /uɛ/.

(29) *Minimal pairs for /iɛ/ vs…*

/i/	bǐ	'goats'	bïɛ	'grasshopper'
/ɛ/	fɛ́	'blow (irrealis)'	fíɛ	'blow (realis)'
/ie/	fie	'throw (realis)'	fíɛ	'blow (realis)'
/iɔ/	sîɔ	'feces'	sïɛ	'mean'
/uɛ/	fűɛ	'twenty'	fîɛ	'baobab'

3.1.4.28 /uɛ/

The diphthong /uɛ/ is mainly a lexical diphthong—it is not derived by realis formation, since typically the front vowel /i/ would be inserted before /ɛ/, though it is occasionally created in plural formation with singular /uɔ/ (see the fifth minimal pair below). It contrasts with its component monophthongs /u/ and /ɛ/ as well as with the diphthongs /iɛ/, /ɔɛ/, /uɔ/, and /ue/.

(30) *Minimal pairs for /uɛ/ vs…*

/u/	kû	'thing'	kûɛ	'calabash'
/ɛ/	kê	'moon'	kûɛ	'calabash'
/iɛ/	fíɛ	'baobabs'	fűɛ	'twenty'
/ɔɛ/	à kɔ̀ɛ	'his bones'	kûɛ	'calabash'
/uɔ/	gù̀ɔ	'country'	gùɛ	'countries'
/ue/	à cuè	'his elbows'	cùɛ	'vomit'

3.1.4.29 /ɔɛ/

There are no instances of lexical /ɔɛ/. It is only created via plural formation, due to fronting of /ɔ/. It contrasts with /ɔ/, as well as with /ɛ/, /uɛ/, and /oe/.

(31)   *Minimal pairs for /ɔɛ/ vs....*

/ɔ/	à kɔ̃	'his bone'	à kɔ̃ɛ	'his bones'
/ɛ/	kɛ̃́	'yams'	kɔ̃ɛ	'buttons'
/uɛ/	kűɛ	'calabashes'	kɔ̃ɛ	'buttons'
/oe/	kòe	'rock hyraxes'	à kɔ̃ɛ	'his bones'

3.1.4.30 /io/

The diphthong /io/ is rare, but there are both lexical and derived cases, with the latter the result of realis formation. It is found after coronals (which palatalize) and in one instance after /p/ (in the ideophone *pǐo* '(not) at all'). Since these are environments where /uo/ is rare, it is difficult to find minimal pairs for these two diphthongs. It contrasts with /i/ and /o/, and with /uo/, /iɔ/, and /ie/.

(32)   *Minimal pairs for /io/ vs...*

/i/	tsǐ́	'mortar'	tsǐo	'bat'
/o/	tòn	'pond'	tsǐo	'poke (realis)'
/uo/	sǔo	'picked up'	tìsǐo	'sneeze'
/iɔ/	tsǐɔ	'fart'	tsǐo	'bat'
/ie/	tsǐe	'black'	tsǐo	'bat'

3.1.4.31 /uo/

The diphthong /uo/ is very rare. It is unattested lexically, raising the possibility that the vowel quality /ʊ/ may have arisen diachronically from /uo/. However, synchronically, this analysis cannot be defended, as [uo] is derived from realis formation and is pronounced distinctly (as a diphthong) in forms such as *búo* 'killed (realis)'. It contrasts with the monophthongs /u/ and /o/, as well as with the diphthong /uɔ/.

(33)   *Minimal pairs for /uo/ vs...*

/u/	sú	'pick up'	sǔo	'picked up'
/o/	bó	'kill'	búo	'killed'
/uɔ/	bűɔ	'take out (realis)'	bűo	'kill (realis)'

3.1.4.32 /iɔ/

The diphthong /iɔ/ is found both phonemically and also derived through realis formation. Like other [i]-initial diphthongs, it triggers palatalization and spirantization of preceding consonants (see §3.5.1.1 and §3.5.1.2, respectively). It contrasts with its component monophthongs, /i/ and /ɔ/, and with similar diphthongs /io/, /iɛ/, and /ia/. It is difficult to find minimal pairs for /iɔ/ and /uɔ/, since the latter never occurs with coronal consonants (the primary environment for /iɔ/, though it is also attested after bilabials in words like *pîɔn* 'flute').

(34)   *Minimal pairs for /iɔ/ vs...*

/i/	sı̋ɔ	'excrement'	sı̋	'water jar'
/ɔ/	tsɔ̂	'bow (archery)'	tsîɔ	'fart'
/io/	tsîo	'bat (animal)'	tsîɔ	'fart'
/iɛ/	ɲíɛ	'insult (realis)'	ɲíɔ	'eat (realis)'
/ia/	ɲı̋a	'finish (realis)'	ɲíɔ	'eat (realis)'

Note that some speakers do not palatalize the /n/ in the realis of 'eat' (cf. irrealis *nɔ̋*), pronouncing the form instead as *nı́ɔ*.

3.1.4.33 /uɔ/

As stated in the last subsection, /uɔ/ appears primarily after non-coronal consonants. It is both a lexical diphthong and one derived through realis formation. It contrasts with both /u/ and /ɔ/, and with the diphthongs /uo/ and /uɛ/; due to distributional restrictions, no minimal pairs could be found with /iɔ/.

(35)   *Minimal pairs for /uɔ/ vs...*

/u/	à gù	'his neck'	gṳ̀ɔ	'country'
/ɔ/	à kɔ̀	'his bone'	kṳ̀ɔ	'grass'
/uo/	bűo	'kill (realis)'	bűɔ	'take out (realis)'
/uɛ/	kûɛ	'calabash'	kûɔ	'doum palm'

3.1.4.34 /ia/

The diphthong /ia/ is mainly a lexical diphthong, but it is sometimes created through realis formation as well. It is considerably rarer than high-mid diphthongs. It contrasts with /i/ and /a/, and with the monophthongs /iɛ/, /iɔ/, and /ua/.

(36)   *Minimal pairs for /ia/ vs...*

/i/	sı́	'tree sp. (*Terminalia* sp.)	sı́a	'Bobo-Dioulasso'
/a/	fâ	'flour'	à fìa	'his lung'
/iɛ/	fìɛ	'fourth son (birth order name)'	à fìa	'his lung'
/iɔ/	ɲíɔ	'eat (realis)'	ɲı̋a	'finish (realis)'
/ua/	kùa	'other'	kpə̰rṵ̀-kı̰̀-kīa	'snail'

3.1.4.35 /ua/

The diphthong /ua/ is only a lexical diphthong; that is, it is never derived through morphological processes like plural or realis formation. It contrasts with its component monophthongs /u/ and /a/, and with the diphthongs /uɛ/, /uɔ/, and /ia/.

(37)   Minimal pairs for /ua/ vs...

/u/	tərǘ	'gather up'	tərúa	'curve, zigzag'
/a/	kǜaa	'farm'	káa	'chase'
/uɛ/	kûɛ	'calabash'	kùa	'other'
/uɔ/	kǜɔ	'grass'	kùa	'other'
/ia/	kpərǜ-kì-kĩa	'snail'	kùa	'other'

3.1.4.36 /ʊa/

Since the diphthong /ʊa/ is only attested in one morpheme /sʊ́aa/ 'path, way', I will treat it as a marginal contrast and not provide minimal pairs here.

3.1.4.37 /u̯i/

The nasal diphthong /u̯i/ is a lexical diphthong, but can also be created in plural formation by fronting an underlying /u̯/. It contrasts with /u̯/ and /i̯/, with /ui/ in nasality, and with the similar nasal diphthong /u̯ɛ/.

(38)   Minimal pairs for /u̯i/ vs...

/u̯/	kṹ	'catch'	kû̯i	'deny'
/i̯/	fí̯	'two'	fû̯i	'bull'
/ui/	fũi	'nothing'	fû̯i	'bull'
/u̯ɛ/	ɛ̀ɛ́ fṷ̀ɛ	'his wife'	fû̯i	'bull'

3.1.4.38 /i̯ɛ/

The diphthong /i̯ɛ/ is both lexical and derived in realis formation. With its initial /i̯/, it triggers palatalization and spirantization of preceding velar, alveolar, and palatal stops and fricatives. It contrasts with non-nasal /iɛ/, its component vowels /i̯/ and /ɛ/, as well as with nasal diphthongs /i̯ɔ/, /i̯a/ and /u̯ɛ/.

(39)   Minimal pairs for /i̯ɛ/ vs...

/iɛ/	cíɛ	'baskets'	mó cí̯ɛ	'my feet'
/i̯/	mḭ̀	'drink (realis)'	mḭ̀ɛ	'understand (realis)'
/ɛ/	sɛ̰̀	'dig (irrealis)'	sḭ̀ɛ	'dig (realis)'
/i̯ɔ/	sḭ̀ɔ	'introduce (realis)'	sḭ̀ɛ	'dig (realis)'
/i̯a/	tsḭ̀a	'lean'	sḭ̀ɛ	'dig (realis)'
/u̯ɛ/	âa fṷ̀ɛ	'your wife'	tà-fḭ̀ɛ	'hot'

3.1.4.39 /u̯ɛ/

The diphthong /u̯ɛ/ is fairly rare in Seenku; where it is attested, it is lexical rather than derived. It contrasts with /ue/ in nasality, with component vowels /u/ and /ɛ/, and with similar diphthongs /i̯ɛ/, /ɔ̯ɛ/, and /u̯ɔ/.

(40)   *Minimal pairs for /u̯ɛ/ vs…*

/ue/	fúe	'twenty'	âa fṵ̀ɛ	'your wife'
/u/	fṵ̀	'wild grape'	âa fṵ̀ɛ	'your wife'
/ɛ/	à dzɛ̰̀	'his tooth'	dzṵ̀ɛ	'scold'
/i̯ɛ/	tà-fḭ̄ɛ	'warm'	âa fṵ̀ɛ	'your wife'
/ɔ̯ɛ/	bɔ̰̂ɛ	'stone throwing game'	bṵ̂ɛ	'djinn'
/u̯ɔ/	kṵ́ɔ	'bite (realis)'	kṵ̀ɛ	'corner' (French loan > *coin*)

3.1.4.40 /ɔ̯ɛ/

The diphthong /ɔ̯ɛ/ is almost always derived in Seenku, most commonly in plural formation with common roots such as *mɔ̰̂* 'person' with plural *mɔ̰̂ɛ* 'people'. However, a small number of roots with underlying /ɔ̯ɛ/ can also be found. It contrasts with /ɔe/ in nasality, with /ɔ/ and /ɛ/, and with diphthongs /u̯ɛ/ and /i̯ɛ/.

(41)   *Minimal pairs for /ɔ̯ɛ/ vs…*

/ɔe/	à kɔ́e	'his bones'	mí kɔ́ɛ	'our heads'
/ɔ/	mɔ̰̂	'person'	mɔ̰̂ɛɛ	'sorghum'
/ɛ/	dɛ̰̀	'walls'	mó dɔ̰̂ɛ	'my shoulders'
/u̯ɛ/	bṵ̂ɛ	'djinn'	bɔ̰̂ɛ	'stone throwing game'
/i̯ɛ/	mḭ̂ɛ	'snake'	mɔ̰̂ɛɛ	'sorghum'

3.1.4.41 /i̯ɔ/

The diphthong /i̯ɔ/ is most commonly derived through realis formation, but can occasionally be found underlyingly in a root as well. It contrasts with /iɔ/ in nasality, with its components /i/ and /ɔ/, and with the other nasal diphthongs /i̯ɛ/ and /i̯a/. Like their non-nasal counterparts, /i̯ɔ/ and /u̯ɔ/ are in complementary distribution.

(42)   *Minimal pairs for /i̯ɔ/ vs…*

/iɔ/	tsḭ̂ɔ	'fart'	tsḭ̂ɔ	'caterpillar'
/i/	sḭ̆	'be'	sḭ̀ɔ	'introduce (realis)'
/ɔ/	à tsɔ̰̂	'pity for him'	à tsḭ́ɔ	'its stem'
/i̯ɛ/	sḭ̀ɛ	'dig (realis)'	sḭ̀ɔ	'introduce (realis)'
/i̯a/	tsḭ̀a	'lean'	tsḭ̂ɔ	'caterpillar'

3.1.4.42 /ʋɔ̃/

The nasal diphthong /ʋɔ̃/ is found both lexically and derived from realis formation. It is in complementary distribution with /i̯ɔ̃/, found only after non-coronal consonants. It contrasts with its oral equivalent /ʋɔ/, the monophthongs /ʋ/ and /ɔ/, and the similar diphthong /ʋɛ̃/.

(43) *Minimal pairs for /ʋɔ̃/ vs...*

/ʋɔ/	kʋ́ɔ	'make apologize (realis)'	kʋ̃́ɔ̃	'bite (realis)'
/ʋ/	kʋ́	'catch (realis)'	kʋ̃́ɔ̃	'bite (realis)'
/ɔ/	mɔ̃́	'person'	mʋ̃ɔ̃	'millet'
/ʋɛ̃/	kʋ̃ɛ̃	'corner' (French loan > *coin*)	kʋ̃́ɔ̃	'bite (realis)'

3.1.4.43 /i̯a̰/

The nasal diphthong /i̯a̰/ is only attested in one root: *tsi̯a̰* 'lean'. I suspect that other forms may be possible, but they are unattested in the current data set. Given its marginal nature, I will not provide minimal pairs here.

3.2 Consonants

3.2.1 Consonant inventory

Seenku has a rich consonant inventory, with five places of articulation, including labiovelars. Stops, oral and nasal, are contrastive at each place of articulation. In addition, Seenku displays phonemic alveolar affricates /ts, dz/, which are rare in Mande but for which the voiced counterpart is attested in related Dzùùngoo (Solomiac 2014). The consonant inventory is shown in Table 3.6. For clarity in the table, phonemes are given in IPA, but where the orthographic convention used in this grammar differs from standard IPA, the grapheme is given in angled brackets after the IPA symbol:

Tab. 3.6: Seenku consonant inventory

	Labial	Alveolar	Palatal	Velar	Labiovelar
Plosive	(p) b	t d	c ɟ <j>	k g	kp gb
Nasal	m	n	ɲ	ŋ	ŋm
Affricate		ts dz			
Fricative	f	s			
Approximant		l	(j <y>)		w

Two phonemes, bilabial plosive /p/ and palatal glide /j/, are in parentheses; these are marginal phonemes in Seenku, attested in a small number of lexical items. Some of these are clearly loanwords from Jula, such as the reflexive marker *yéré*, while the origins of others are unclear (e.g. *pě̀ñ* 'donkey').

Voiced stops in Seenku are fully voiced (negative VOT), and voiceless stops are unaspirated.

Coronal and palatal phonemes are particularly prone to allophony in Seenku, producing the common surface allophones [ʃ], [tʃ], and [dʒ]. Each subsection in §3.2.2 will discuss the phoneme and any allophones, with cross-references to phonological rules later in the chapter.

3.2.2 Minimal pairs

Each consonant phoneme is discussed in detail in the following subsections, including allophonic behavior and (near) minimal pairs with similar phonemes. I will address phonemes in the following order: voiceless plosives, voiced plosives, nasal stops, affricates, fricatives, approximants.

3.2.2.1 /p/

As discussed in §3.2.1, /p/ is a marginal phoneme in Seenku. Though fairly common in ideophonic intensifiers and quantifiers (e.g. *pəré-pəré* 'intensely (white)' or *pó-pó* 'all'), it is rare in regular vocabulary. The current lexicon contains 7 instances, shown in (44):

(44) *pě̀ñ*   'donkey'
      pě̀nəgé   'sixth son (birth order name)'
      pɛ́n   'curved stick for tamping down dirt floors'
      pètè̀   'flat'
      pîɔn   'wood flute'
      plě̀n   'traditional bag'
      pɔ̀tɔ̀   'goatskin bag'

Both *pètè̀* and *pɔ̀tɔ̀* are phonotactically unusual disyllabic words with L tone whose origins are unclear. The birth order name *pě̀nəgé* is also attested among the neighboring Tusia, a Gur ethnicity with many shared cultural traits (Strand 2009); /p/ is a more common phoneme in this language, and the name may be a borrowing into Seenku. If the others are borrowings, their source is unclear.

/p/ contrasts with /b/ in the feature [voice], /m/ in the feature [nasal], /f/ in the feature [continuant], and /kp/ in the feature [dorsal]:

(45)   Minimal pairs for /p/ vs...

/b/	blĕn	'cloth for carrying load on head'	plèn	'traditional bag'
/m/	mêɛn	'bushbuck'	pɛ̀ñ	'donkey'
/f/	fên	'thing'	pɛ̀ñ	'donkey'
/t/	tɛ̋	'who (pl)'	pɛ́n	'cane for tamping floors'
/c/	cɛ̀n	'times (quantifier)'	pɛ̀ñ	'donkey'
/k/	kókô	'rooster'	pó-pó	'all'
/kp/	kpɛ̰̂	'hunt'	pɛ̀ñ	'donkey'

3.2.2.2 /t/

The voiceless stop /t/ is unaspirated. It has an allophone [ts] before high vowels, and otherwise is realized as [t]. For a discussion of the rule of affrication, see §3.5.1.1. /t/ contrasts with /d/ in voicing, /n/ in nasality, /ts/ in release, /s/ in continuancy, and /p, c, k, kp/ in place of articulation.

(46)   Minimal pairs for /t/ vs...

/d/	dəmǎ	'shrivel'	təmǎ	'praise'
/n/	nǎ	'come (realis)'	tǎ	'cook (sauce)'
/ts/	tsɛ̋	'indefinite, some'	tɛ̋	'who (pl)'
/p/	pɛ́n	'curved stick for tamping floor'	tɛ̋	'who (pl)'
/c/	cɔ̀	'village'	à tɔ̀	'like him'
/k/	kâ	'yam'	tâ	'fire'
/kp/	kpèɛ	'knives'	tèɛ	'small termites'

3.2.2.3 /c/

The phoneme /c/ is a voiceless palatal stop. After high vowels, it has the allophone [tʃ] for most speakers, though younger female speakers have a tendency to use an alveolar affricate allophone [ts] in this environment instead. This variation is discussed in greater depth in §3.5.1.3 below.

/c/ contrasts with /ɟ/ in voicing, /ɲ/ in nasality, and /p, t, k, kp/ in place of articulation. It likewise contrasts with /ts/, despite allophonic overlap.

(47)   Minimal pairs for /c/ vs...

/ɟ/	ɟɔ̀	'grill'	cɔ̰́	'scoop'
/ɲ/	à ɲèn	'her side'	à cɛ̀n	'her breast'
/p/	pɛ̀ñ	'donkey'	cɛ̀n	'peanut'
/t/	à tɔ̀	'like him'	cɔ̀	'village'
/k/	kɛ́ɛ	'break off'	cɛ́ɛ	'gather'
/kp/	kpɛ̀ɛ	'sew'	cɛ́ɛ	'gather'

3.2.2.4 /k/

The voiceless velar stop /k/ is likewise unaspirated. After the high front vowel /i/, /k/ and /c/ neutralize to [tʃ], but they are contrastive in other environments. /k/ contrasts with /g/ in voicing, /ŋ/ in nasality, and /p, t, c, kp/ in place of articulation.

(48)   *Minimal pairs for /k/ vs…*

/g/	gɔ̌ɔ	'wood'	kɔ̌ɔ	'hole'
/ŋ/	ŋanɔ̂	'oil'	kanɔ̂n	'work association'
/p/	pó-pó	'all'	kókô	'rooster'
/t/	tâ	'fire'	kâ	'yam'
/c/	cɛ́ɛ	'gather'	kɛ́ɛ	'break'
/kp/	kpənṳ̀	'stomach'	kə̀nṵ	'stone'

3.2.2.5 /kp/

The voiceless labiovelar plosive /kp/ is the most common labiovelar sound in Seenku. It has just the single allophone [kp], and contrasts with /gb/ in voicing, /ŋm/ in nasality, /w/ in the feature [approximant], and /p, t, c, k/ in place of articulation.

(49)   *Minimal pairs for /kp/ vs…*

/gb/	gbéné	'Bouendé'	kpéně	'finger'
/ŋm/	ŋmɛ̌ɛ	'chew'	kpɛ̀ɛ	'sew'
/w/	wɛ́n	'money'	kpɛ̂	'hunt'
/p/	pɛ̌ñ	'donkey'	kpɛ̂	'hunt'
/t/	těné	'soumbala'	kpéně	'finger'
/c/	cɛ́ɛ	'gather'	kpɛ̀ɛ	'sew'
/k/	kə̀nṵ	'stone'	kpənṳ̀	'stomach'

3.2.2.6 /b/

The phoneme /b/ is very common in Seenku, both initially and in C2 position of sesquisyllables. In C2 position, it has an optional allophone [β]; see §3.5.2.1. It contrasts with /p/ in voicing, /m/ in nasality, /w/ in [approximant], and /d, ɟ, g, gb/ in place of articulation.

(50)   *Minimal pairs for /b/ vs…*

/p/	plɛ̌n	'traditional bag'	blɛ̌n	'cloth for carrying load on head'
/m/	mǎn	'shea'	bǎ	'rope'
/w/	wɛ̀	(associative)	bɛ̀	'do (irrealis)'
/d/	dɔ̌ɔ	'finish'	bɔ̌ɔ	'get old'
/ɟ/	ɟɔ̌ɔ	'stroll'	bɔ̌ɔ	'get old'
/g/	gɔ̌ɔn	'hibiscus'	bɔ̌ɔn	'bag'
/gb/	gbagǎ	'servant'	bagâ	'plant sp. (*Anchomanes difformis*)'

3.2.2.7 /d/

The voiced alveolar stop /d/ is also quite common. It has two main allophones: [d] and [dz], with the latter found after high [+ATR] vowels /i, u/ and variably after /ʊ/; see §3.5.1.2 for formalization of the rule. Since the contrast between /d/ and /dz/ is neutralized before high vowels, the minimal pairs offered below will demonstrate contrasts before non-high vowels.

Additionally, /d/ may have an allophone [ɾ], found in word-medial position, but this allophone could equally belong to /l/. The status of [ɾ] will be discussed further in §3.2.3.

/d/ contrasts with /t/ in voicing, /n/ in nasality, /l/ in the features [approximant] and [lateral], /dz/ in release, and /b, ɟ, g, gb/ in place of articulation.

(51)   Minimal pairs for /d/ vs...

/t/	təmã̀	'praise'	dəmã́	'shrivel'
/n/	nân	'sauce'	dân	'mouth'
/l/	lɔ̃́	'here'	dɔ̃̀n	'today'
/dz/	à dzḛ̀	'his teeth'	dḛ̀	'walls'
/ɟ/	à jèn	'in front of it'	à dèn	'its seed'
/b/	bɔ̃̀ɔ	'get old'	dɔ̃̀ɔ	'finish'
/g/	gɔ̃̀ɔ	'ground'	dɔ̃̀ɔ	'millet beer'
/gb/	gbəgê	'approach'	dəgɛ̋	'make'

3.2.2.8 /ɟ/

The voiced palatal stop /ɟ/ has two allophones: [dʒ] before high vowels and [ɟ] elsewhere; see §3.5.1.2 for the influence of high vowels. The affricate [dʒ] is also used in C1 of sesquisyllabic words when C2 is velar, arguably a dissimilatory process; see §3.5.3. It contrasts with /c/ in voicing, /ɲ/ in nasality, and /b, d, g, gb/ in place of articulation.

(52)   Minimal pairs for /ɟ/ vs...

/c/	cɔ̰̂	'scoop'	ɟɔ̰̂	'grill'
/ɲ/	ɲǐ	'pick up'	ɟǐ	'laugh'
/b/	bɔ̃̀ɔ	'get old'	ɟɔ̃̀ɔ	'stroll'
/d/	à dèn	'its seed'	à jèn	'in front of it'
/g/	à gù	'his neck'	ɟù	'year'
/gb/	gbəgê	'approach'	ɟəgà	'descend'

3.2.2.9 /g/

The voiced stop /g/ is typically realized as [g], but in C2 position with a nasal vowel, it is occasionally realized as [ŋ] or [ɣ]. /g/ contrasts with /k/ in voicing, /ŋ/ in nasality, and /b, d, ɟ, gb/ in place of articulation, though given the rarity of /gb/ and its typical co-occurrence with C2 /g/ (an environment in which C1 /g/ is phonotactically banned), no clear near minimal pairs can be found.

(53) *Minimal pairs for /g/ vs...*

/k/	kɔ̋ɔ	'hole'	gɔ̏ɔ	'ground'
/ŋ/	ŋá̋á̋	'yawn'	gáa	'pull'
/b/	bɔ̏ɔ̂n	'bag'	gɔ̏ɔ̂n	'hibiscus'
/d/	dɔ̏ɔ	'millet beer'	gɔ̏ɔ	'ground'
/ɟ/	ɟù	'year'	à gù	'his neck'
/gb/	gbanɛ̆	'early'	gàrên	'hoe'

3.2.2.10 /gb/

As mentioned in the last subsection, the voiced labiovelar plosive /gb/ is one of Seenku's rarer phonemes, found in 8 roots in the lexicon. Of these, half are found in the sesquisyllabic configuration [gbəgV], making it very difficult to find minimal pairs with /g/ (since Seenku restricts most combinations of identical consonants in C1 and C2 position). From a phonetic standpoint, /gb/ sounds almost implosive, though instrumental evidence would be required to confirm this impression. /gb/ contrasts with /kp/ in voicing, /ŋm/ in nasality, and /b, d, ɟ, g/ in place of articulation (keeping in mind the caveat about /g/ and minimal pairs).

(54) *Minimal pairs for /gb/ vs...*

/kp/	kpénɛ̋	'finger'		gbéné	'Bouendé'
/ŋm/	ŋmáná	'lower'		gbátá̋	'shed'
/b/	bəgâ	'plant sp. (*Anchomanes difformis*)'		gbəgá̋	'servant'
/d/	dəgɛ̋	'make'		gbəgê	'approach'
/ɟ/	ɟəgà̋	'descend'		gbəgê	'approach'
/g/	gàrê(n)	'hoe'		gbanɛ̆	'early'

3.2.2.11 /m/

The bilabial nasal /m/ has just a single allophone [m]. [m] is also created when a latent nasal coda merges with a following /w/ and nasalizes it; see §3.3.2 for further discussion. The phoneme /m/ contrasts with /b/ in nasality, with /w/ in [approximant] (and nasality), and with /n, ɲ, ŋ, ŋm/ in place of articulation.

(55)   Minimal pairs for /m/ vs...

/b/	bǎ	'rope'	m̀ǎn	'shea'
/w/	wɛ́n	'money'	mɛ́ɛ	'ignited'
/n/	nɛ́ɛ	'coiled'	mɛ́ɛ	'ignited'
/ɲ/	à ɲà	'his mother'	m̀ǎn	'shea'
/ŋ/	səŋá	'lie down'	səmâ	'dance'
/ŋm/	ŋmêɛ	'chew'	mêɛ	'ignite'

3.2.2.12 /n/

The alveolar nasal /n/ has two allophones, [n] and [r̃]. The latter allophone occurs in C2 position of sesquisyllables, especially in rapid speech. In this environment, when followed by a nasal vowel, it merges with whatever we want to call the underlying form of [ɾ] (/l/ or /d/). Tapping is discussed further in §3.5.2. The allophone [n] is also derived from a latent nasal coda merging with and nasalizing /l/, as discussed in §3.3.2. Otherwise, /n/ contrasts with /d/ in nasality, with /l/ in [lateral] and nasality, and with /m, ɲ, ŋ, ŋm/ in place of articulation.

(56)   Minimal pairs for /n/ vs...

/d/	dân	'mouth'	nân	'sauce'
/l/	lɛ̆	(dative)	nɛ́	(locative)
/m/	mɛ́ɛ	'ignited'	nɛ́ɛ	'coiled'
/ɲ/	ɲà	'finish'	nà	'come (realis)'
/ŋ/	ŋâ	'ripen'	nà	'come (realis)'
/ŋm/	ŋmá	'chew'	nǎ	'lose'

3.2.2.13 /ɲ/

The palatal nasal /ɲ/ is phonemic, with just a single allophone [ɲ]. Some speakers also show it as an allophone of /n/ before [i]-initial diphthongs (but curiously not /i/ itself); this alternation can be seen most clearly in realis stem formation, discussed in §13.1. The phoneme /ɲ/ contrasts with /ɟ/ in nasality and with /m, n, ŋ, ŋm/ in place of articulation:

(57)   Minimal pairs for /ɲ/ vs...

/ɟ/	ɟí	'laugh'	ɲí	'pick up'
/m/	m̀ǎn	'shea'	à ɲà	'his mother'
/n/	nà	'come (realis)'	ɲà	'finish'
/ŋ/	à ŋamā	'his blood'	ɲamǎ	'sixth daughter (birth order name)'
/ŋm/	ŋmêɛ	'chew'	ɲɛ̀ɛ	'braid'

3.2.2.14 /ŋ/

The velar nasal /ŋ/ has a single allophone [ŋ]. It contrasts with /g/ in nasality and with the nasals /m, n, ɲ, ŋm/ in place of articulation.

(58)   Minimal pairs for /ŋ/ vs...

/g/	gáa	'pull'	ŋáǎ	'yawn'
/m/	səmâ	'dance'	səŋá	'lie down'
/n/	nằ	'come (realis)'	ŋâ	'ripen'
/ɲ/	ɲəmǎ	'sixth daughter (name)'	à ŋəmà	'his blood'
/ŋm/	ŋmá	'eat (meat)'	ŋâ	'ripen'

3.2.2.15 /ŋm/

The labiovelar nasal /ŋm/ is relatively uncommon in the language, attested in only a handful of lexical items. It has the single allophone [ŋm]. Despite its low frequency, we can still find near minimal pairs showing the contrast with /gb/ in nasality, with /w/ in [approximant] and nasality, and with the nasals /m, n, ɲ, ŋ/ in place of articulation:

(59)   Minimal pairs for /ŋm/ vs...

/gb/	gbátǎ	'shed'	ŋmáná	'lower (half)'
/w/	wěn	'money'	ŋmêɛ	'chew'
/m/	mêɛ	'ignite'	ŋmêɛ	'chew'
/n/	nằ	'come (realis)'	ŋmá	'eat (meat)'
/ɲ/	ɲèɛ	'braid'	ŋmêɛ	'chew'
/ŋ/	ŋâ	'ripen'	ŋmá	'eat (meat)'

3.2.2.16 /ts/

The voiceless alveolar affricate /ts/ is an uncommon phoneme in Mande languages. Even in Seenku, it is restricted in its environments, at least phonemically; unlike almost all other phonemes in the language, /ts/ is never found before /a/. It is also an allophone of /t/ after high vowels, neutralizing the contrast between /t/ and /ts/ in these environments. /ts/ contrasts with /dz/ in voicing, and with the plosive /t/ and the fricative /s/ in manner.

(60)   Minimal pairs for /ts/ vs...

/dz/	dzɔ̂	'amount'	tsɔ̂	'bow (archery)'
/t/	tɛ́	'who (pl)'	tsɛ́	indefinite
/s/	sɔ̂	'whistle'	tsɔ̂	'bow (archery)'

3.2.2.17 /dz/

The distribution of the voiced alveolar affricate /dz/ follows the same pattern as its voiceless equivalent. That is to say, /d/ has an affricate allophone [dz] after high vowels, and the contrast is neutralized in that environment. It contrasts with /ts/ in voicing, with /s/ in voicing and [delayed release], and with /d/ and /ɟ/ in place and manner.

(61)   *Minimal pairs for /dz/ vs...*

/ts/	tsɔ̂	'bow (archery)'	dzɔ̂	'amount'
/s/	sô	'song'	à dzò	'his mouth'
/d/	à dɔ́n	'his shoulder'	dzɔ́	'hunger'
/ɟ/	ɟô	'water'	à dzò	'his mouth'

3.2.2.18 /f/

The labiodental /f/ is one of Seenku's two fricative phonemes, both voiceless. It has only a single allophone [f], and it contrasts with /s/ in place of articulation, with /p/ in [continuant], and with /w/ in [approximant] and [voice].

(62)   *Minimal pairs for /f/ vs...*

/s/	à sa̰	'buy it'	à fa̰	'put it inside'
/p/	pḛ̆n	'donkey'	fên	'thing'
/w/	wĕ́n	'money'	fên	'thing'

3.2.2.19 /s/

The phoneme /s/ is the most common fricative in Seenku. It has two allophones, [ʃ] before high [+ATR] vowels (and variably before /ʊ/), and [s] elsewhere. It contrasts with /f/ in place of articulation, with /t/ in [continuant], with /ts/ in [delayed release], and with /ɟ/ (which has an affricate allophone [dʒ]) in voicing and place of articulation.

(63)   *Minimal pairs for /s/ vs...*

/f/	fərɛ̆	'inflate'	sarɛ̆	'look'
/t/	tǎa	'cleared space'	sǎa	'tobacco'
/ts/	tsɔ̂	'bow (archery)'	sɔ̂	'whistle'
/ɟ/	ɟḭ̀	'fetish (traditional religion)'	sḭ̀	'water jar'

3.2.2.20 /l/

Approximants in Seenku are restricted in their distribution, occurring initially only in functional elements and in a few exceptional content words. The phoneme /l/ follows this pattern, found mainly at the beginning of enclitics, but also in a few other words such as lɔ́ 'here' or lǔ 'courtyard'. In C2 position of sesquisyllabic words, it has the allophone [ɾ], which can also surface as nasalized [ɾ̃] when followed by a nasal vowel; for deeper discussion of this allophone and its underlying representation, see §3.2.3. After latent nasal codas, /l/ surfaces as [n]. The lateral approximant contrasts with /d/ in manner, /n/ in nasality, and /w/ in place of articulation.

(64)   *Minimal pairs for /l/ vs...*

/d/	dɔ̃n	'today'	lɔ́	'here'
/n/	nã́	'lost'	lã́	'certain'
/w/	wɛ̀	(associative)	lɛ̀	(subordinate)

3.2.2.21 /j/

The palatal glide /j/ is a marginal phoneme in Seenku. In initial position, it is found only in the Jula loan *jéré* 'self', which though commonly used is still a loanword. In medial position, we find it in the traditional interjection *wéějó* 'amen', which is now being replaced almost entirely by *àmínà̀* (see §21.5.2); it is also a surface allophone in the emphatic pronouns [í jó] '2pl emphatic', but the underlying form of the emphatic particle is /wó/, showing that front vowels have the tendency to front /w/. In other words, *wéějó* itself may not contain /j/ underlyingly.

Given its rarity and marginal nature, I will not provide minimal pairs here.

3.2.2.22 /w/

The labiovelar glide /w/ is very common in the language thanks to many /w/-initial grammatical particles, such as the associative postposition *wɛ̀*, the subordinate *wɛ̀* (especially in clause chaining), a focus particle *wé*, and the emphatic particle *wó*. It is otherwise found in a small number of content words, all likely loanwords. The glide has a nasal stop allophone [m] after latent nasal codas; see §3.3.2 below. /w/ contrasts with /b/ and /gb/ in manner, /m/ in nasality, and /l/ in place of articulation.

(65)   *Minimal pairs for /w/ vs...*

/b/	bɛ̀	'do (irrealis)'	wɛ̀	(associative)
/gb/	gbên	'horn'	wɛ́n	'money'
/m/	mɛ́ɛ	'ignited'	wɛ́n	'money'
/l/	lɛ̀	(subordinate)	wɛ̀	(associative)

3.2.3 The status of [ɾ]

The only phonemic liquid in Seenku is /l/. However, in C2 position of sesquisyllabic words, we find many cases of [ɾ], but never [d] and only rarely [l]. It is clear that [ɾ] should not be treated as an allophone of its own phoneme /ɾ/, but it is unclear whether to treat a word like [sərã̀] 'master' as /sədã̀/ or /səlã̀/. /d/ to [ɾ] is a common lenition pattern and is attested in related Dzùùngoo (Solomiac 2007; 2014). But on the other hand, we do find [l] after initial labials, in words such as [blã́] 'fall' or [flã̰̀] 'thrash', in complementary distribution with [ɾ] which only occurs after non-labial sounds, suggesting that both are allophones of the same phoneme /l/. Further evidence that [ɾ] is an allophone of /l/ comes from wh-words; two words for 'what' (referring to concrete and abstract things, respectively) can be produced by explicitly combining the respective word for 'thing' with the interrogative pronoun lɛ́ 'which', as in (66):

(66)   a.   fɛ́n lɛ́ [fɛ́nɛ́]
            'what' (concrete)

       b.   kú lɛ́
            'what' (abstract)

Or they can be combined into a single sesquisyllabic interrogative, in which case we see [l] after the labiodental fricative and [ɾ] after the velar plosive:

(67)   a.   fəlɛ́
            'what' (concrete)

       b.   kəɾɛ́
            'what' (abstract)

From these examples, it is clear that /l/ has an allophone [ɾ]. What is not clear is whether /d/ also does, and how we would be able to tell. In Optimality Theoretic terms (Prince and Smolensky 1993), we can ask, how would a Rich Base candidate like /sədã̀/ surface? Given the ban on [d] in C2 position, it also would likely surface with [ɾ], and given this neutralization, it is impossible to say what the underlying form would be for many surface taps. For this reason, in this grammar, I will write C2 [ɾ] as simply <r>, representing its surface pronunciation and remaining agnostic as to its underlying form. Note that these <r> do not reflect an underlying rhotic phoneme.

3.3 Syllable structure and phonotactics

This section discusses syllable structure in Seenku and any phonotactic restrictions related to it (e.g. onset and coda restrictions, etc.). Since most vocabulary is mono- or sesquisyllabic, this section can be largely read as equivalent to word structure, but this latter topic will be addressed more fully in §3.4, where polysyllabic vocabulary is also considered. In this section, I first address basic syllable types (§3.3.1), before discussing the issue of latent nasal codas (§3.3.2), and finally phonotactic restrictions in different syllable positions (§3.3.3).

3.3.1 Syllable shapes

Syllable structure in Seenku can be summarized in the following schematic:

(68) *Seenku syllable structure*
C(əC)(V)V(:)(n)

In all but a few pronouns (such as ằ '3sg' or í '2pl'), syllables in Seenku require an onset and the syllable-defining nucleus. By combining all optional syllable elements in different combinations, we arrive at the following list of 16 syllable shapes, organized by the parameters simple/sesquisyllabic and open/closed syllable in Table 3.7.

Tab. 3.7: Attested syllable shapes in Seenku

	Open	Closed
Simple	CV	CVn
	CV:	CV:n
	CVV	CVVn
	CVV:	CVV:n
Sesqui-	CəCV	CəCVn
	CəCV:	CəCV:n
	CəCVV	CəCVVn
	CəCVV:	CəCVV:n

Nasal codas and their realizations will be addressed further in §3.3.2. In the remainder of this section, I will discuss and exemplify each of the syllable shapes, first in the simple monosyllabic syllable category and then in the sesquisyllabic category.

3.3.1.1 Simple monosyllables

Simple monosyllables are defined as having a single onset consonant followed by a nucleus, which may be simplex or complex. This syllable type with a simple nucleus is widely attested, either with or without a nasal coda. Examples are shown in (69):

- (69) CV
  - kâ 'yam'
  - jü̏ 'hill'
  - sí 'tree sp.'

  CVn
  - kân 'granary'
  - à kɔ̰̂n 'head'
  - sắn 'god'

Increasing in complexity slightly, we also find simple syllables with long vowel nuclei, transcribed in this transcription system with a double vowel:

(70) CV: CV:n
      màa   'again'   màan   'rice'
      gɔ̂ɔ   'wood'   gɔ̂ɔn   'hibiscus'
      dǎa   'flatter'   dǎan   'hanging basket holder'

The nucleus can be complex, consisting of two different vowel qualities forming a diphthong. Recall from §3.1.2 that the initial vowel in these diphthongs is pronounced as a glide. Examples with complex nuclei are shown in (71):

(71) CVV   CVVn
      cùɛ   'vomit'   à cùen   'his elbow'
      pío   '(never) at all'   pîɔn   'flute'
      tsĭe 'black'   tsĭen   'pestle'

CVVn are considerably rarer than either CVV or CVn syllable types.

   Finally, diphthongs can also be long in Seenku, though more commonly these are derived diphthongs (through processes like plural formation; §5.3.1). However, I have found only a single instance of a long diphthong with a nasal coda, in *jôɛɛn*, a form irregularly derived from *jô* 'water' and part of the causative expression *bà jôɛɛn* 'make (animals) drink water':

(72) CVV: CVV:n
      gɔ̀ɛɛ   'fields'   jôɛɛn   'drink (livestock)'
      cíëe   'clear throat'
      bɔ̀ɛɛ   'remove hair'

Long diphthongs are considerably rarer than the syllable types discussed previously; the combination of a nasal coda and a long diphthong may create too heavy of a syllable, and thus we find just a single token.

3.3.1.2 Sesquisyllables

A peculiarity of Seenku is the presence of sesquisyllables, first introduced in §3.1.3 above. This term, coined by Matisoff (1990) and discussed more recently in Pittayaporn (2015), is much more commonly used in the literature on Southeast Asian languages like Burmese. It refers to a configuration where a (full) syllable is preceded by a "half" or "minor" syllables, typically with a reduced vowel like [ə] intervening. Seenku's sesquisyllables are clearly "contractive" (Matisoff 1990:551), the result of heavy iambic reduction of erstwhile disyllabic words. Iambic reduction is synchronically attested in a number of Mande languages, including Bambara, especially when V1 is a high vowel (Green et al. 2014, Green 2015). However, in Seenku, these roots have been restructured such that V1 is no longer part of the phonological representation, at least not as a full vowel, as evidenced by the fact that speakers do not reconstruct a vowel in that position even when speaking slowly.

Examples of sesquisyllabic words and their disyllabic reflexes in other Mande languages are shown in (73):

(73) a. bəlě   'big' (cf. bèlèbélé Bambara, Vydrine 2009)
      b. fərɔ̌   'monkey' (cf. fɔnɔ̀n Dzùùngoo, Traoré et al. 1998)
      c. səgǎ   'sheep' (cf. sàgá Bambara, bambara.org)

For a discussion of the status of schwa in sesquisyllabic words, see §3.1.3 above.

Sesquisyllables show the same range of nucleus types as simple syllables, and can also be either open or closed. First and most commonly, we find sesquisyllables with simple V nuclei:

(74) CəCV   CəCVn
      təgê   'chicken'   à təgàn   'his cheek'
      dərú   'suck'   dərôn   'child'
      səgɔ̀   'wrestling'   à səgɔ̀n   'his stomach'

Sesquisyllables with coda nasals are considerably rarer than those with open syllables.

The vowel in the main syllable of sesquisyllables can also be long, again, with or without a coda nasal:

(75) CəCV: CəCV:n
      jəgîi   'lay egg'   nəgḗen   'intestine'
      à nəgàa 'his enemy'   à nəgôon   'his throat'
      kəsɛ́ɛ   'watch out'   gbəgǎan   'large shed'

These examples illustrate an oddity of syllable structure distribution: all cases of CəCV:n involve /g/ as C2. As these syllables become more complex (combining sesquisyllabicity with vowel length), they become less common.

Sesquisyllables with underlying diphthongs as nuclei most commonly have the full syllable [gua]; the reason for this bias is not known, but it seems to be related to the exclusive presence of C2 /g/ in many of these complex forms. They can also be derived through plural formation, resulting in a larger number of possible diphthongs. With a nasal coda, the combination of sesquisyllabicity and a diphthong nucleus is quite rare. Examples of these word shapes are shown in (76):

(76) CəCVV   CəCVVn
      təgŭa   'blistered'   təgŭan   'slobber' (in dân-təgŭan-təgŭan)
      səgùa   'stack'   dəgŭen   'plant sp. (Maranthes polyandra)
      səgŭi   'hair'

Both open and closed versions are rare.

If short diphthong nuclei are rare in sesquisyllabic words, then long diphthongs are almost non-existent. We find just a couple of roots for both open and closed versions:

(77)   CəCVV: CəCVV:n
       dəgŭaa   'between'   təgŭaan   'tree sp. (*Carapa procera*)'
       nəgɔ́εε   'small tree sp.'
                 (*Grewia mollis*)'

Summarizing these two subsections, we find that with each added syllable structure complexity, whether to the nucleus, the coda, or the onset (assuming sesquisyllabicity to be related to onset structure), the number of attested roots drops.

3.3.2 Latent nasal codas

One of the most vexing issues in Seenku syllable structure is the question of the coda nasal. A substantial number of Seenku roots end in some sort of nasal element, though its realization is fluid and variable, dependent upon speaker, phrasing, lexical item, and sometimes just free variation. In the discussion of syllable structure above, I have given the nasal as a coda, represented by a final <n>, though it is unspecified for place and is rarely realized as a nasal stop. I will refer to the phenomenon a "latent nasal coda", representing the fact that it is often unrealized or only weakly realized, with effects more audible on following morphemes than on the root that introduces the nasal. Note that the presence or absence of the nasal coda is independent of vowel nasality; stems with oral vowels can either have the coda nasal or not (e.g. *kâ* 'yam' vs. *kân* 'granary'), and the same is true for stems with nasal vowels (e.g. *mɔ̃* 'person' vs. *kɔ̃n* 'head').

The latent nasal is Seenku's answer to Dzùùngoo and Jowulu floating nasals, but for reasons I will lay out below, I resist the term "floating" in Seenku's case. Solomiac (2007) describes for Dzùùngoo an underspecified floating nasal coda, which rarely surfaces as a consonant of its own but rather has a number of effects on following onsets. For instance, in Dzùùngoo, roots with floating nasals will nasalize a following liquid, turning it into a homorganic nasal stop (*cĩᴺ* + *rèè* → *cĩnèè* 'the corners'; pg. 49). The nasal vowel cannot be responsible for the nasalization of the liquid, since he shows contrasting examples like *χɔ̃* + *rèè* → *χɔ̃rèè* 'the noses'. When the floating nasal is realized on a following consonant, either by nasalizing it or by creating a prenasalized stop (alternatively: the coda itself is realized as a consonant), the preceding vowel of the root is nasalized. If the floating nasal is phrase-final, it is deleted.

The Jowulu facts are similar, except that in isolation, Djilla et al. (2004) note that it is realized as a "weak [i]" (e.g. [doⁱ] 'partridge', [kãⁱ] 'leg'; pg. 91) and it has a broader range of effects on following consonants. Like Dzùùngoo, the Jowulu floating nasal prenasalizes a following plosive ($ko^N + bwɔ̀ → kõmbvɔ̀$ 'man's back'; 102), with variable voicing of voiceless plosives and variable nasalization of voiced plosives (though apparently maintaining a contrast between underlying voiced stops and nasals). It also nasalizes the rhotic ($bú^N + -ru → bṹnu$ 'in the canoe'; 106). However, it differs from Dzùùngoo in triggering gemination of /l/ ($ɲã^N + lú → ɲãllú$ 'share a chicken'; 105) and voicing of voiceless fricatives ($ɲã + fɔ́ → ɲãvɔ́$ 'white chicken'; 104).

Seenku latent nasals show some similar patterns to Dzùùngoo and Jowulu, but it is not clear to me that "floating" is the best designation. The following list summarizes the behavior of the latent nasal in different environments:

(78)   Behavior of the latent nasal before a....
  - pause: Late nasalization of the vowel
  - plosive: Homorganic nasal stop (alternatively prenasalization of plosive)
  - fricative: Late nasalization of preceding vowel
  - nasal: Latent nasal deletes (absorbed into following nasal)
  - approximant: Approximant is nasalized ∼ approximant becomes a nasal stop

I will expand on and exemplify each of these environments in the subsections below.

3.3.2.1 Before a pause

In isolation, the latent nasal is barely audible, and indeed my first hypothesis was that it was deleted. However, upon closer listen, light nasalization is audible at the end of the vowel. This was confirmed by a very astute metalinguistic judgment from my consultant GET, who told me, "It's like you start by saying [a] and then end by saying [ã]." Remarkably, visual inspection of a spectrogram for the word *kân* 'granary' (in Figure 3.2) reveals that this is precisely the case.

The degree of late nasalization depends upon the speaker, with more audible nasalization for GET than for SCT, for instance. We also find that latent nasals after long vowels are pronounced with more explicit oral closure than following short vowels. The place of articulation of the closure depends on the vowel: velar after low and back vowels, palatal after front vowels. For example, we find [gɔ̀ɔ̂ŋ] 'hibiscus' but [bɛ̀ɛɲ] 'porridge'. A spectrogram of the former is shown in Figure 3.3 to illustrate the oral closure of the nasal coda:

Interestingly, the pronunciation of the latent nasal as a coda in some cases but not others predicts the behavior of stems in other morphological contexts like plural formation. Stems with a latent nasal, like *kân* 'granary', have a fully nasal vowel in the plural and no latent nasal effects on following words, while those with oral closure, like *dǎân* [dǎâŋ], lose any trace of nasality in the plural.

56 — 3 Segmental phonology

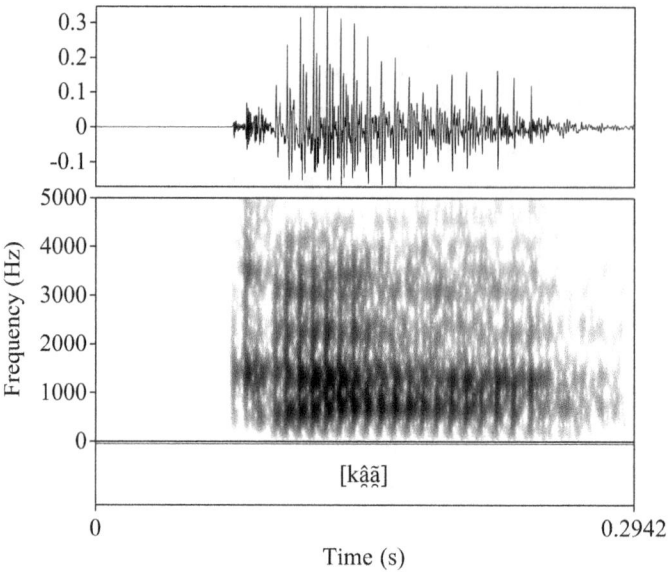

Fig. 3.2: Spectrogram for *kâ(n)* 'granary', spoken by GET

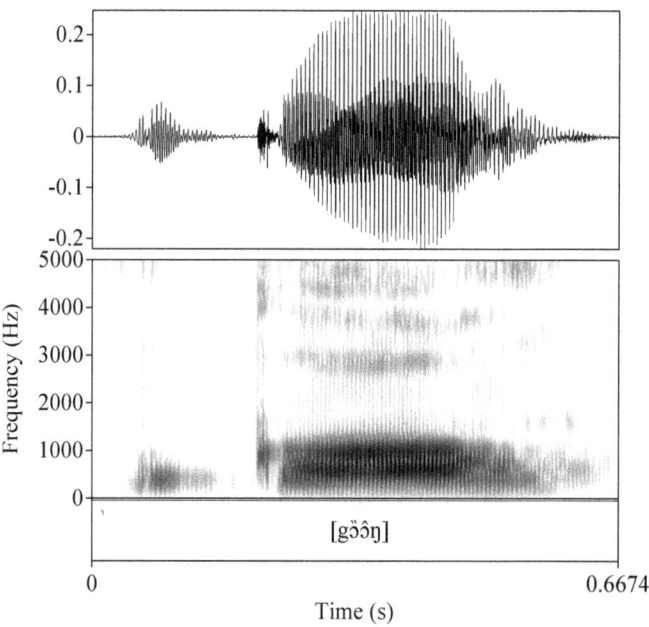

Fig. 3.3: Spectrogram for *gɔ̈ɔ̂(n)* 'hibiscus', spoken by GET

(79) a. *kân*   *bəlě* [kâm bəlě]
   granary big
   'big granary'

b. *kɛ̰̌*   *bəlě* [kɛ̰̌ bəlě]
   granary.PL big
   'big granaries'

c. *dǎân*   *bəlě* [dǎâm bəlě]
   basket.holder big
   'big basket holder'

d. *dɛ̌ɛ*   *bəlě* [dɛ̌ɛ bəlě]
   basket.holder.PL big
   'big basket holders'

This suggests either that there is a representational distinction between the two cases, beyond what can be explained phonetically by something like the increased duration of long vowels, or that both the lack of nasality in the plural and the oral closure are both related to vowel length.

It is tempting to treat these as two different classes of roots: those with floating nasals and those with pronounced nasal codas (as I did in McPherson 2017a), but the distinction is not crisp. In isolation, there is still some pronunciation of the nasal coda, as seen in 3.2, just not to the same degree as that found after a long vowel. And in context, as I will discuss below, the range of effects is the same, just with different frequencies. The fact that the nasal is pronounced at all in isolation leads me to believe that these do in fact have a slot in the syllable structure (i.e. they are not floating), but that they are weakly articulated elements.

3.3.2.2 Before plosives

Latent nasals uniformly surface as homorganic nasal stops before a following plosive. It is unclear whether this nasal should be analyzed as a coda or whether it forms part of a following prenasalized stop. Arguments in favor of the former include the fact that the nasal is introduced into the representation in coda position, so the following plosive could be seen as strengthening this realization, and the fact that prenasalized stops are otherwise unattested in Seenku. An argument in favor of the latter is that in other environments the latent nasal merges with the following onset, so treating the homorganic nasal as part of a prenasalized stop would unify the behavior of latent nasals. For clarity of transcription, I will write the homorganic nasal as a coda, but this should not be seen as support for that analytical position.

Two examples of homorganic nasals are shown in (79) above. Textual examples are given in (80) to illustrate this behavior:

(80) a. ń tɛ́ sâ[n] tsɛ́-ná ń tɛ́ kərù
 1SG dear rabbit and 1SG dear hyena
 'Mr. Rabbit and Mr. Hyena' [sos150625t2:4]

b. mɛ̀ à dô[ɲ] cɛ̀rɛ̀ mɛ̀ dô[ɲ] jəmïi
 3SG.SUBORD DEF child call.IRR but.FR child go.far.REAL.PRF
 'She called the child, but he had run far away.' [sos150626t1:145]

c. mɛ̀ bɛ́ ì à sɔ́[m] bɛ́ sǐ í tɛ̀
 3SG.SUBORD say.IRREAL COMP DEF horn DEM be LOG GEN
 'He said that he had that horn.' [sos150626t1:79]

In (80a), the latent nasal assimilates to the alveolar place of articulation of the conjunction *tsɛ́-ná*; in (80b), we see the latent nasal of *dôn* 'child' assimilating to the palatal place of articulation in two instances; finally in (80c), the latent nasal of *sɔ̂n* assimilates to the initial bilabial plosive of the demonstrative *bɛ́*.

The latent nasal is realized as a homorganic nasal regardless of vowel length or phrasal position.

3.3.2.3 Before fricatives

Before fricatives, the latent nasal is realized as nasalization on the preceding vowel, sometimes throughout the whole vowel and sometimes just at the end. In the examples in (81), I transcribe the nasal-final words as they are pronounced, with their underlying forms given after the gloss.

(81) a. íwíi kɛ́ à dɛ̃̀ɛ fəlà̰ à̰ tê
 1PL.EXCL.SBJV go.IRR DEF black.bean thrash.IRR 3SG GEN
 '[He said] that they should go thrash the black beans at his house.' (/dɛ̀n/ 'black bean') [sos150626t2:7]

b. ń tɛ́ sâ̰ sío lɛ̀ jɔ̀ɔ nɛ̀
 1SG dear rabbit REC.PST FOC stroll.REAL.NOM LOC
 'Mr. Rabbit just went out for a stroll.' (/sân/ 'rabbit') [sos130828t2:28]

c. ké jɛ́ɲ-jɛ̌ fǐ wé
 COP RED-story two FOC
 'It's two (different) stories.' (/jén-jěn/ 'story') [sos161009t1:52]

In (81a), the stem *dɛ̀n* 'black bean' is realized with late nasalization of the vowel, represented here as [dɛ̃̀ɛ]; in (81b-c), the vowel before the latent nasal of *sân* and *jén-jěn* is fully nasalized.

3.3.2.4 Before nasals

If the latent nasal is followed by a nasal stop, then the latest nasal itself is unrealized. We can understand this as the latent nasal being absorbed into the following nasal stop. Examples include:

(82) a. ké jéɲ-jéɲ   tsû sóe ŋɛ́
       COP RED-story type one NEG
       'It's not the same story.' (/sóen/ 'one') [sos161009t1:55]

    b. ì-ǎ-lɔ́   sà-bö̀-kɔ̌ɔ   kʊ́ təgì   wè ằ
       you.know.JU second.son-billygoat D.DEF stand.IRR HAB DEF
       sɔ̋-nɛ̋n-jŭ   jɛ̋ ŋɛ́
       sky-grain-water front NEG
       'You know that billygoat doesn't stand under the rain.' (/jɛ̋n/ 'front')

    c. sɔ̋ nǎ   sḭ̀ bɛ̰̂ɛ   nɛ̀
       sky PROSP be rain.ANTIP.REAL.NOM LOC
       'It must be raining.' (/sɔ̋n/ 'sky') [sos170802e]

The vowel before the nasal may get light nasalization characteristic of being followed by a nasal.

3.3.2.5 Before approximants /l, w/

Typically, sonorants /l/ and /w/ nasalize to [n] and [m] after a latent nasal, regardless of whether the nasal is after a short or long vowel (i.e. whether the latent nasal is pronounced with oral closure in isolation or not). This can be seen in (83), first with /l/ (/lɛ́/ → [nɛ́]) and then with /w/ (/wɛ̀/ → [mɛ̀]):

(83) a. ǐi   ằ jén-jɛ̋   nɛ́ təmɛ̀   wè âa
       3PL.SUBORD DEF RED-story REL tell.IRR HAB NEG.Q
       'The story they told…' [sos161009t1:181]

    b. ǐ fə̰̀   mɛ̀ cí-dɔ̀ɔ   wè í jɛ̋ mɛ̋
       3PL enter.IRR HAB house-inside with LOG front with
       'They entered into the house frontwards.' [sos161009t1:5]

In (83a), the final nasal of jén-jɛ̋ɲ 'story' causes the relative marker lɛ́ to nasalize to [nɛ́]; as this example shows, when a latent nasal nasalizes a following approximant, the nasal coda itself is lost. That is, we do not see geminate nasals arising in this case. The same behavior can be seen in (83b), with the homophonous clitics wɛ̀ 'habitual' and 'with', both of which nasalize to [mɛ] following nasal-final roots (fə̰̀n 'enter' and jɛ̀n 'front', with sandhi accounting for tone changes, §4.4.2).

Note that this nasalization pattern does not happen after nasal vowels (e.g. *mɔ̀ wɛ̀* 'with a person'), including nasal vowels derived in plural formation from stems with latent nasals (e.g. *sâ n-à kṹɔ* 'the rabbit bit him' vs. *sɛ́ l-à kṹɔ* 'the rabbits bit him', where /l/ is epenthesized to resolve hiatus between the noun and the 3sg pronoun).

While this is the general pattern we expect, it is in fact variable, even in a controlled elicitation setting. I prepared an elicitation list of 19 nasal-final stems, including both short and long vowels, and embedded them in different contexts (utterance-final, preceding an obstruent vs. a sonorant, at a phonological phrase boundary vs. within a phonological phrase, etc.). I recorded the elicitation with two speakers, GET and SCT, who repeated each context three times. Not only did the two speakers differ from one another in their patterns, they also varied their pronunciations even between repetitions of the same target. GET almost always nasalized following approximants when they fell in the same phonological phrase as the nasal-final stem (in this case, between a noun and a postposition). The only stems that showed non-application of nasalization were *kàŋáan* 'cage', where 2 out of 4 repetitions of /kàŋáan + wɛ̀/ became [kàŋáa wɛ̀] instead of expected [kàŋáa mɛ̀], and the proper noun *Cǔen*, which never nasalized /w/ (except to [w̃]), but always nasalized /l/ to [n]. In contrast, when the approximant was separated from the latent nasal by a phonological phrase boundary (like the one that falls between a subject and the verb phrase), then nasalization only variably applied in GET's speech. The context in question is shown in (84):

(84) _____ wɛ̀-gěe sĩ̀
 [target] TRANS-clean.PTCP be
 'The _____ is clean.'

Some stems, like *jö̀n* 'slave', never triggered nasalization (i.e. *jò wɛ̀-gĩi sĩ̀* 'the slave is clean' in 3/3 repetitions), while others, like *sǎn* 'god', always did (i.e. *sǎ mɛ́-gĩi sĩ̀* 'god is clean' in 3/3 repetitions). Still others showed variation between repetitions, such as *à kàn* 'its flower' (i.e. *à kà mɛ̀-gĩi sĩ̀* 'its flower is clean' in 2/3 of repetitions).

It is unsurprising that where the process applies less frequently a phrase boundary intervenes between the trigger and the target.[1] What is more surprising is that for SCT, the situation is reversed: nasalization applies almost exceptionlessly across the phrase boundary and only variably between a noun and a postposition. A larger controlled study is needed to determine whether there are any patterns in the behavior of different speakers, bolstered by looking at the corpus of texts for patterns in natural speech.

---

[1] Though, as these examples show, argument-head sandhi applies exceptionlessly across this boundary; for arguments that sandhi is not in fact a phonological process and is thus insensitive to phonological phrasing, see McPherson (2019).

What should be noted, though, is that there no indication that stems with fuller oral closure in isolation behave any differently from stems with only late nasalization, challenging any dichotomous characterization of stem types.

3.3.3 Phonotactic restrictions

Given the tight constraints on Seenku syllable structure, there are few phonotactic restrictions that arise. The most restricted location is C2 of sesquisyllabic words, which allows only a subset of Seenku's consonant inventory. In this section, I will first address onset restrictions in §3.3.3.1, before turning to C2 restrictions in sesquisyllables in §3.3.3.2, and finally discussing combinatorial restrictions between consonants and vowels in §3.3.3.3.

3.3.3.1 Onset restrictions

Every consonant in the inventory can appear in onset position of simple syllables. The approximants /l/ and /w/ are generally constrained to function words, like postpositions or TAMP markers, but both do appear sporadically in content words as well (e.g. lǔ 'courtyard', wěn 'money').

In the onset position of sesquisyllables, /l/ and /w/ never appear. In addition, both affricate phonemes are unattested in this position, as is the labiovelar nasal /ŋm/. These absences are visible in the combinatorial table in 3.4 below.

3.3.3.2 C2 restrictions in sesquisyllables

The second consonant (C2) position in sesquisyllables is the most restricted position in Seenku phonotactics. The following classes of sounds are banned:
1. Voiceless phonemes (with the exception of one /f/ in nəfòo 'animal')
2. Palatal phonemes
3. Labiovelar phonemes
4. Affricates

We find one exception for labiovelar phonemes, namely the word sə̀gbûn, a type of grass used in making mud bricks. Once these classes of sounds are removed from the phoneme inventory, we are left with the set {b, d, g, m, n, ŋ, l}, all of which are attested if we assume that some surface [ɾ] comes from /d/ and some from /l/, as discussed in §3.2.3.

	f	b	g	m	n	ŋ	l
p		x		x			
b	x			x			
t							
d							
c							
ɟ							
k			x			x	
g			x			x	
k͡p							
g͡b							
m		x		x			
n					x		
ɲ							
ŋ			x				
ŋ͡m							
t͡s					x		
d͡z					x		
f		x		x			
s							x
l							
w							

Fig. 3.4: C1/C2 combinations in sesquisyllables

Beyond the general restrictions on what can appear in C2 position, we also find restrictions on combinations of C1 and C2. The most general restriction is that combinations of homorganic consonants are banned (with the exception of /s/ + /l, d/), as the table in Figure 3.4 shows; cells where C1 and C2 are homorganic contain an <x>. Gray cells mean that the combination is attested, and white cells are unattested combinations. Every consonant phoneme is shown down the lefthand side, illustrating the gaps where they never occur in sesquisyllables (as stated in §3.3.3.1).

When C1 is /ɟ/ and C2 is /g/, /ɟ/ surfaces with its postalveolar affricate allophone [dʒ]; this dissimilatory process will be discussed further and exemplified in §3.5.3 below. Some other interesting patterns include the fact that C2 /ŋ/ never occurs after a plosive and that C1 /g/ is considerably rarer in sesquisyllabic words than the other voiced plosives, only co-occuring with C2 /l/.

3.3.3.3 Consonant-Vowel restrictions

Certain CV combinations are rare or unattested. First, labiovelars are unattested before /u/ (though /kp/ occurs in one root before /ṷ/, *kpṷ̈* 'throat'). While labiovelar sounds are rare, meaning the likelihood of accidental gaps is high, the lack of labiovelar + /u/ feels significant, since the sounds are quite similar and the combination is missing for all three labiovelar phonemes. Combinations with /e/ are likewise missing, but /e/ itself is such a rare phoneme that we find many gaps. Another unattested combination is an alveolar affricate /ts/ or /dz/ followed by the low vowel /a/.

Phonotactic restrictions can also be found between a consonant and a diphthong, even when the component vowels of the diphthong are permitted. Specifically, the diphthong /uɔ/ never appears after coronal consonants. This is a somewhat unusual restriction, in that /u/ and /ɔ/ are both attested in that environment, as is the diphthong /uɛ/, so the restriction is not strictly local. There is some evidence that this phonotactic restriction triggers alternations in realis formation, when many verb stems become diphthongs with the insertion of a high vowel infix after the onset. In this process, /i/ is typically inserted after coronal consonants and /u/ elsewhere; see §13.1 for examples. Corroborating the alternation data is the lack of roots with a combination of a coronal consonant and /uɔ/.

3.4 Word structure

The majority of Seenku vocabulary is mono- and sesquisyllabic, meaning that the discussion of syllable structure in §3.3 doubles as a discussion of word structure. However, we do find some longer words, whose structures I will briefly summarize here.

Roots can be maximally trisyllabic, though the bulk of non-monosyllabic roots are disyllabic. Most, but not all, of these can be traced to borrowings from Jula or occasionally from French. Though typically made up of simple syllables, disyllabic roots can have a sesquisyllable as one of the two syllables, in either position. The distribution of disyllabic root shapes in the current lexicon is given in Table 3.8.

Unsurprisingly, simple CV.CV are the most common, including loans from Jula like *bǎrǎ* 'work' or *jàbí̋* 'respond', and from French like *kàfé̋* 'coffee', but also purely Seenku words like *jǒŋmǎ* 'cat' (cf. Jula *jàkúmá*) or *fìsî* 'cotton'. There are also a relatively large number of CVrV words of Seenku origin, which appear to have resisted the trend towards sesquisyllabicity. Some of these, like *kǒrǒ* 'sweat' co-vary with *kǒo*, with intervocalic [ɾ] deletion creating long vowels.

Sesquisyllabicity can come in either syllabic position. Examples of initial sesquisyllables include *sərǎkǎ* 'sacrifice' and *təbàalé̋* 'table' (from French *table*, perhaps via

Tab. 3.8: Distribution of disyllabic root shapes

CV.CV	39
CV.CV:	7
CV:.CV	5
CV:.CV:	1
CV.CVN	5
CVN.CV	8
CV.CV:N	1
CəCV.CV	6
CəCV:.CV	2
CV.CəCV	7

Jula *tàbálí*). Examples of sesquisyllables in second position include *gbə̀bəgǔ* 'kitchen' (cf. Jula *gbàbúgú*) and ubiquitous adverb and discourse marker *wétənɛ̌* 'now' (§21.3.4).

There is one irregular case of a disyllabic stem with the shape CV.V, i.e. where the second syllable is onsetless: *kúɛ̂ɛ* 'sickle'. We can tell that it is disyllabic from its tone pattern and the duration of the first vowel (that is, the fact that it is actually moraic), as well as its behavior in processes like plural formation.

We can also identify a number of trisyllabic roots, whose distribution is shown in Table 3.9.

Tab. 3.9: Distribution of trisyllabic root shapes

CV.CV.CV	15
CV.CV.CVN	1
CV.CVN.CV	1
CVN.CV.CV	1

By far, simple CV.CV.CV are the most common. All trisyllabic roots are Jula loans.

Polymorphemic words can be longer still, with processes like reduplication, affixation, or compounding increasing the length of the word. One challenge is to determine whether a word is a compound with bound roots (a crypto-compound; §7.1.3) or whether it is monomorphemic. I do not dwell on this distinction here.

3.5 Phonological rules

Allophones for each phoneme were described briefly in §3.1.4 for vowels and §3.2.2 for consonants. In this section, I lay out and exemplify the phonological rules responsible for deriving these allophones.

3.5 Phonological rules — 65

Rules are grouped together by natural class, where possible (i.e. common environments or outputs). I first discuss phonological rules triggered by high vowels (§3.5.1), then turn to lenition processes triggered in sesquisyllabic words (§3.5.2) before addressing dorsal dissimilation in sesquisyllabic words (§3.5.3), vowel hiatus resolution strategies (§3.5.4), and vowel centralization (§3.5.5).

3.5.1 High vowel effects

High vowels in Seenku, especially [+ATR] high vowels, often trigger allophonic variation on the preceding consonant. There are two main processes: palatalization of velar stops and alveolar fricatives (§3.5.1.1) and affrication of alveolar stops (§3.5.1.2). However, as I will address in §3.5.1.3, certain speakers tend to swap the allophones created by these two processes, which could represent a language change in process.

3.5.1.1 Palatalization

High vowels /i, u/ trigger processes of palatalization (or perhaps more appropriately: post-alveolarization) of the preceding consonant, though the environments involved are not symmetrically distributed between /i/ and /u/. In particular, both /i/ and /u/ palatalize /s/ to [ʃ], but only /i/ will palatalize the velar stops /k/ and /g/. Palatalization also interacts with affrication, discussed in the next subsection, by turning palatal stops into post-alveolar affricates, so the palatal allophones of /k, g/ derived in this section are an abstract intermediate stop on their way to [tʃ] and [dʒ].

I begin with the more straightforward case of /s/ to [ʃ]. It is both a static generalization about Seenku vocabulary and a dynamic generalization about alternations that the alveolar fricative [s] is not found before /i/ and /u/. Instead, we find the post-alveolar fricative [ʃ]:

(85) a. sì̀   [ʃì̀]   'water jar'
     b. sú̈   [ʃú̈]   'antelope'
     c. sía   [ʃía]   'Bobo-Dioulasso'

The only exceptions to this static generalization are that the birth order name Sì 'first son' and the ideophonic adverb súu 'directly' are variably pronounced with the alveolar fricative, as is the auxiliary verb sı̌ 'be'.

We know that the allophone [ʃ] does not constitute its own phoneme since [s] and [ʃ] are in complementary distribution, with [ʃ] never appearing before non-high vowels. This is corroborated by dynamic alternations, where /s/ becomes [ʃ] in derived high vowel environments. Since /s/ is only found in onsets, the only way to derive a high vowel environment is through infixation, which is found in realis stem derivation. Examples of alternations are shown in Table 3.10.

Tab. 3.10: Palatal alternations in realis formation

	Irrealis		Realis		
a.	sɛ̋	[sɛ̋]	si̋ɛ	[ʃi̋ɛ]	'shave'
b.	sɔ́	[sɔ́]	si̋ɔ	[ʃi̋ɔ]	'bury'
c.	sə̋sɛ̋	[səsɛ̋]	sə̋siɛ̋	[ʃəʃiɛ̋]	'watch'

The case in (c) is the most interesting, where palatalization is back-copied onto what must be at some level a reduplicant, since otherwise the [ə] in sesquisyllables does not trigger palatalization; note that other speakers pronounce this pair as tsɛ̋sɛ̋ and tsɛ̋siɛ [tsɜ̋ʃíɛ], with an initial alveolar affricate that does not undergo palatalization.

The process of /s/ palatalization can be captured in the following phonological rule:

(86) */s/ palatalization*
/s/ → [ʃ] / ___ [+high, +ATR]
'The phoneme /s/ becomes the allophone [ʃ] before high [+ATR] vowels.'

Palatalization of /s/ is completely regular before [+ATR] high vowels, but only variably or lightly occurs with [-ATR] high vowel /ʊ/. For example, /sʊ̃/ 'song' is typically pronounced with [s], but /s/ can also be slightly palatalized, though typically not to the same extent as before /u/. Acoustically, the allophone of /s/ before [ʊ] has its highest amplitude frequency band around 3500 Hz for GET, similar to the palatal fricative [ʃ], but without as much low frequency energy beneath it (i.e. [ʃ] has a broader frequency distribution), perhaps reflecting a difference between laminal and apical articulation.

Alveolar stops do not palatalize but instead affricate to [ts, dz]; see §3.5.1.2 below.

Velar stops /k, g/ only palatalize before the high front vowel /i/. Before /u/, they retain their velar place of articulation (e.g. *kû* [kû] 'thing', *à gù* [à gù] 'his neck'). Before /i/, on the other hand, velars and palatals merge, and both surface as postalveolar affricates [tʃ] and [dʒ]. I analyze this as a two-part change, with velar stops first becoming palatal stops under the heading of palatalization, then the stops changing to affricates in a more general process of affrication that affects both palatals and alveolars.

Unlike the case of [s] and [ʃ], palatalization of velars represents a neutralization process, where a phonemic contrast that is clear in certain environments is lost before /i/. As such, it is not possible in the case of the static generalization to determine the underlying form as unambiguously /k/ or /c/, /g/ or /ɟ/. I will transcribe all underived stems with a palatal phoneme before the vowel /i/, more closely reflecting the surface realization, but it should be noted that an underlying sequence like /ki/ would be pronounced in the same way. For examples of non-derived palatals before high vowels, see the next subsection illustrating their affrication.

Unfortunately, we cannot see any active alternations between velars and palatals, since the process driving alternations with [s] ~ [ʃ] (that is, realis formation) inserts [u] rather than [i] after velars, which does not trigger palatalization.

Finally, palatalization fails to take place in an environment derived by the post-lexical phonological process of vowel hiatus resolution:

(87) kɛ́ í wó tɛ̀ → [kí wó tɛ̀]
      COP 2PL EMPH GEN
      'It is yours (pl.).'

See §3.5.4 for further discussion.

3.5.1.2 Affrication

A closely related process to palatalization is affrication, whereby coronal (alveolar and palatal) stops become affricates before high vowels /i, u/. The rule is given in rule notation and prose in (88):

(88) *Coronal affrication*
      [+COR, -del. rel.] → [+del. rel.] / ___[+high, +ATR]
      'Coronal stops become affricates before high [+ATR] vowels.'

I begin with palatal stops, following the discussion of palatalization in the last subsection. Palatal stops are realized as post-alveolar affricates [tʃ] and [dʒ] before high [+ATR] vowels, reflecting both static and dynamic generalizations. Non-derived roots with these post-alveolar affricates are shown in (89), though whether roots with /i/ contain a palatal or velar stop underlyingly is indeterminate due to their neutralization in this environment:

(89) a. cî   [tʃî]   'house'
      b. jí̋   [dʒí̋]   'laugh'
      c. cǜɛ   [tʃǜɛ]   'vomit'
      d. jǜ   [dʒǜ]   'year'

Affrication of /j/ is also common before /ʊ/, especially in the common root jõ̂ [dʒõ̂] 'water'.

Active alternations can be seen in realis formation, shown in Table 3.11. The high back vowel [u] is never inserted after a palatal in realis formation, so we can only see dynamic alternations with [i].

While high vowel insertion is typically only attested in realis formation, it is also found in one irregular plural form ('leg(s)'), where its insertion also triggers affrication: à cɛ̂ [à cɛ̂] 'his leg' vs. à cǐɛ [à tʃǐɛ] 'his legs'. I hypothesize that this high vowel is inserted, since otherwise the singular and plural forms would be indistinguishable. Normally, plural is marked through vowel fronting and tone raising (§5.3.1), but since

Tab. 3.11: Palatal stop/affricate alternation

	Irrealis		Realis		
a.	cɔ́	[cɔ́]	cíɔ	[tʃíɔ]	'scoop'
b.	cɛ̰̂	[cɛ̰̂]	cìɛ	[tʃîɛ]	'take off (hat)'
c.	ɟɔ́	[ɟɔ́]	jíɔ	[dʒíɔ]	'draw (water)'
d.	ɟɔ̰̀	[ɟɔ̰̀]	jìɔ̰	[dʒìɔ̰]	'grill'

/cɛ̰̂/ already has a front vowel and always surfaces as a [+raised] tone due to argument-head tone sandhi (§4.4.2), neither aspect of plural marking has an audible effect.

Alveolar stops /t, d/ likewise become affricates before high vowels. In roots, this results in the neutralization of alveolar stops and affricates. I will transcribe both with <ts, dz>, acknowledging that underlying /t, d/ in the same environment would surface the same way:

(90) a. tsí   'jump'
      b. tsû   'hippopotamus'
      c. dzḭ̀   'glue'
      d. dzûen   'roof'

There are a couple of exceptional roots where alveolar stops are retained in front of high vowels, but these are rare compared to alveolar affricates. Examples include tīi 'accept' and tûn 'pot'.

As in the case of /s/ before high [-ATR] vowels, the alveolar stops before /ʊ/ can variably surface with light affrication, as in the common expression cî-dʊ̀ʊ 'household', which surfaces variably as [tʃî-dʊ̀ʊ] and [tʃî-dzʊ̀ʊ].

The alternation between alveolar stops and affricates is found, once again, in realis formation, as shown in Table 3.12.

Tab. 3.12: Alveolar/affricate alternation in realis formation

	Irrealis		Realis		
a.	tɔ́	[tɔ́]	tsíɔ	[tsíɔ]	'leave'
b.	tɛ̰̂	[tɛ̰̂]	tsìɛ	[tsîɛ]	'show'

No examples can be found showing the alternation of /d/ and [dz], but I take this to be an accidental gap.

3.5.1.3 A change in progress?

A curious feature of GET and some other young women's speech is the tendency to swap alveolar and palatal affricates. In (91), I compare the standard pronunciations just described with GET's pronunciation:

(91)
		Standard	GET	
a.	à cìɛ	[à tʃìɛ]	[à tsìɛ]	'his feet'
b.	jõ̀	[dʒõ̀]	[dzõ̀]	'water'
c.	c̀ie	[tʃ̀ie]	[ts̀ie]	'died'

When asked about the differences in pronunciation, both SCT and GET explain that women speak "more finely", though women a generation above her from other villages (such at GFT from Sɛɛnɛ) find this affrication swap strange; it should be noted, however, that GFT has lived outside the region for several years and may be unaware of how younger women speak there today.

This could be a change in progress in the language, as it has often been seen that young women lead the charge of language change (e.g. Labov 1990).

3.5.2 Lenition processes

There are two lenition processes that specifically target C2 of sesquisyllabic words; by and large, medial consonants in disyllabic words are unaffected, suggesting that the consonant must be non-initial in the syllable rather than the word. The rules I will discuss are spirantization (§3.5.2.1) and tapping (§3.5.2.2).

3.5.2.1 Spirantization

In C2 position, stops (all of which are voiced due to phonotactic restrictions discussed in §3.3.3.2) can be lenited to voiced fricatives. The rule is given in (92) in rule notation and prose:

(92) C2 spirantization
[-cont, -nas] → [+cont] / Cə___V (optional)
'Stops optionally become fricatives in C2 position of sesquisyllables.'

Examples include:

(93) a. [dəbî] ~ [dəβî] 'mudbrick oven'

b. [səgà̰] ~ [səɣà̰] 'sheep'

The more common allophone is the stop, but especially in rapid speech, the fricative sometimes surfaces.

3.5.2.2 Tapping

Recall from §3.2.3 and §3.3.3.2 that the voiced alveolar stop [d] is not attested on the surface in C2 position. I hypothesize that /l/ and /d/ neutralize in this environment, both to the alveolar tap [ɾ]. Unfortunately there is no way to derive a sesquisyllable that would result in an alternation between /d/ and [ɾ], so this is purely a "rich base" form, to use terminology from Optimality Theory (Prince and Smolensky 1993/2001). In other words, we hypothesize that if a speaker were to pronounce an underlying form like /sədà/, it would surface as [səɾà].

In the case of /l/, we find free variation between full wh-/relative phrases like /kú lɛ́/ 'what [lit. which thing]' or /mə̀ lɛ́/ 'the person who' and their sesquisyllabic contracted forms [kəɾɛ́] and [mə̀ɾɛ́] (sometimes [mə̀lɛ́]), giving clear evidence for the [ɾ] as an allophone of /l/.

In fact, the tapping process is even more general, targeting not just /l/ and /d/ but also /n/. In C2 position, /n/ optionally becomes the nasalized tap [ɾ̃], especially in rapid speech. For example:

(94) a. ǎ [səná]   ~ [səɾ̃á]   'her husband'
      b. [wétənə̌]   ~ [wétəɾ̃ɛ̌]   'now (discourse marker)'
      c. [kə̀nû̃]   ~ [kə̀ɾ̃û̃]   'stone'

After the nasal tap, the vowel is more audibly nasalized, if it weren't already nasal to begin with (e.g. (94c)).

All three tapping processes are accounted for in the following rule:

(95)   *C2 tapping*
        [+COR, -DORS] → [+son, +approx, -lat, +tap] / Cə___V
        'Alveolar phonemes become taps in C2 position of sesquisyllables.'

In feature notation, the specification of "non-dorsal coronal" picks out alveolars from palatals, which are also coronal but in addition are specified as [+DORS]. In C2 position of sesquisyllables, all attested alveolars are voiced, consisting of the set /l, d, n/. All of these sounds become taps, but [nasal] is left unspecified on the right side of the arrow, meaning /n/ will retain its [+nasal] specification and derive [ɾ̃], while /l/ and /d/ will not.

Underlying forms become hard to ascertain in certain cases, since taps are always nasalized next to nasal vowels. This means that a form like [fəɾ̃ɔ̃] 'monkey' could be one of: /fəlɔ̃/, /fədɔ̃/, or /fənɔ̃/ underlyingly. Historically, the latter seems most likely, as the Dzùùngoo cognate is *fɔ̀nɔ̀n*, but the underlying form may have been restructured in the evolution of Seenku. In the transcription system used in this grammar, I will typically use <r> in this position, to remain neutral, unless I have heard speakers use [n] in careful speech, in which case I will use <n>.

Finally, while the rule in (95) implies that alveolars uniformly become taps in all environments, in fact /l/ surfaces with its allophone [l] in two specific environments—when C1 is labial and V is either /a/ or /e/, illustrated in the following examples:

(96) a. [blǎ] 'fall'
  b. [flâ] 'Fulani'
  c. [blě] 'big'
  d. [blěn] 'cloth put on head for carrying loads'

Additionally, the [l] allophone is found between /f/ and /ɛ/ (97a) but not between /b/ and /ɛ/ (97b):

(97) a. [fəlέ] 'what' (cf. fé né 'which thing')
  b. [brɛ̋] 'crowded'

Before all other vowels, and with all other C1 consonants, [ɾ] is used:

(98) a. [bɾí] 'mixed'
  b. [bɾɔ̰] 'be full (moon)'
  c. [fɾɔ́] 'pierce'
  d. [fɾã̌] 'thrash'

/a/ and /e/ do not form a natural class, so it is unclear why these environments should be singled out for [l]. Even if we appealed to the words with [l] containing /l/ and words with [ɾ] containing /d/, we are left with the same problem of why /l/ should only be found in this unnatural class of environments.

3.5.3 Dorsal dissimilation

There is one more phonological rule that affects sesquisyllables: dorsal dissimilation. When C1 of a sesquisyllable is palatal and C2 is velar, the palatal surfaces with its postalveolar affricate allophone [tʃ] or [dʒ], even though the schwa (whether underlying or epenthetic) is not a high vowel and thus shouldn't trigger affrication (§3.5.1.2). We can see this process apply in the following examples:

(99) a. /ɟəgḛ̀/ → [dʒəgḛ̀] 'dog'

  b. /cəgɛ̂ɛ-nɛ̰̀/ → [tʃəgɛ̂ɛnɛ̰̀] 'sandy area'

We can compare these to similar sesquisyllables where C2 is not velar, such as jəbě [ɟəbé] 'cloth' or cəběe [cəběe] 'shea nuts'; in these cases, the palatal surfaces with its palatal stop allophone.

I analyze this as a kind of dissimilation. Since palatal and velar stops are both pronounced with dorsal closure, it is difficult to articulate two such closures in quick succession. The postalveolar allophones, on the other hand, do not involve closure with the tongue body, thus easing the articulatory combination.

Dorsal dissimilation is captured in the following rule:

(100)   Dorsal dissimilation
        [+COR, +DORS] → [-DORS, +delayed release, +strident] / ___ə[+DORS]
        'Palatal consonants become postalveolar affricates before a C2 velar consonant in sesquisyllables.'

3.5.4 Hiatus resolution

Seenku does not tolerate vowel hiatus within a phonological phrase. This fact can even be seen in the language's diphthongs, where the initial vowel becomes a glide. Given the phonotactics of the language, the only vowel-initial morphemes are pronouns. When these pronouns follow another vowel, we find a range of repairs including gliding (§3.5.4.1), coalescence (§3.5.4.2), vowel deletion (§3.5.4.3), and [l] epenthesis (§3.5.4.4). In every case, the tones of both vowels are retained and surface on the resulting vowel or diphthong. For discussion of phonological phrasing, including evidence from (non-)application of hiatus resolution, see §3.6.

3.5.4.1 Gliding

If V1 in a V.V sequence is high or round, then it typically becomes a glide. As in diphthongs, this glide is simply a non-moraic version of the vowel rather than neutralizing all back vowels to [w]. For example:

(101)   a. mó   ǎ   [mǒa]   jîo
            1SG.EMPH 3SG   see.REAL.PFV
            'I saw it.' [sos170807t:1]

        b. ń   nəgí̋ sḭ̀ ǎ   [sḭ̀ã̌]   nḛ̀
            1SG mind be 3SG   LOC
            'I remember it.' [sos161009t1:24]

        c. mɔ̰̌ ǎ   [m̰ɔ̰̌a̰]   bɔ́   mɔ̰̌ ǎ   [m̰ɔ̰̌a̰] sá
            person 3SG   take.out.IRR person 3SG   carve.IRR
            'We take it out and we carve it.' [sos170711t1:32]

If V1 is nasal, then V2 is also nasalized, as in (101b-c). The resulting diphthong is longer than a single short vowel would be, but not to the extent that it should be treated as compensatory lengthening.

3.5.4.2 Vowel coalescence

If V1 is /a/ or /ɛ/ and V2 is /i/, then the two vowels can coalesce, resulting in a higher or tenser vowel. There is no compensatory lengthening in this case. First, /a/ and /i/ can optionally coalesce to produce [ɛ]:

(102) a. ä   ɲá̰   í   [ɲɛ̰́]   səgɔ̌ ŋé
     3SG be.NEG LOG   good NEG
     'It is not good.'

    b. ä   í   [ɛ̀ɛ́]   bɛ̋   ḭ̀...
       3SG LOG   say.IRR COMP
       'He said...'

When both V1 and V2 are V-only pronouns, as in (102b), coalescence is the only possible output. In the case of (102a), there is free variation between coalescence (shown here) and vowel deletion (shown in §3.5.4.3).

The combination of /ɛ/ and /i/ can variably yield [e] by coalescence, putting together the height specification of /ɛ/ and the [ATR] specification of /i/:

(103) fóo lɛ̂ɛ   sú   wɛ̀ mɔ̰̀mɛ̰̂ɛn tè lɛ̀   í
       wind REL.SUBORD get.up.IRR HAB north   GEN SUBORD LOG
       [lè]   dä̀n-kù   nɛ̀-jərä̀n-jərä̀n
                mouth-thing TRANS-RED-change.IRR
       'The north wind gave up [lit. changed his words]' [sos170807t:7]

In (103), this vowel quality coalescence can be seen in the combination of subordinate lɛ̀ and logophoric í.

3.5.4.3 Vowel deletion

In any other combination of V1 and V2, and optionally for those combinations just discussed in §3.5.4.2, V1 simply deletes/elides. Here, vowel elision is indicated by bracketing the deleted vowel. For example:

(104) a. k[é] á wóò   nìgì ŋé dö̀
     COP 2SG EMPH.DAT COW NEG EMPH
     'It's not your cow!' [sos161009t1:62]

    b. mɛ̀   təgɨ̀ m[ɛ̀]   ä bö̀-kɔ̌ɔ tsɛ́sɛ̋
       3SG.SUBORD stop 3SG.SUBORD DEF billygoat look.at.IRR
       '...he stopped and looked at the billygoat.' [sos 1 61009t1:189]

c. ằ sị̌ màa ằ t[ê] ằá tő à wè
3SG be again 3SG GEN 3SG.SBJV cross.IRR 3SG with
'He wanted to run across him again.' [sos161009t1:209]

d. fŭi kéɛ ɲ[ą́] í wó tɛ̋ ŋɛ́
nothing at.all be.NEG LOG EMPH GEN NEG
'[that] I have nothing at all.' [sos161005e]

As in other contexts, there is no compensatory lengthening, and the tones of the deleted vowel are concatenated with those of the following retained vowel and pronounced on the same syllable.

3.5.4.4 [l] epenthesis

The strategies we have seen so far have typically involved hiatus between two functional elements—TAMP markers, auxiliary verbs, pronouns, etc. If the first element in hiatus is a content word, then we tend to find a different strategy: [l] epenthesis before the V-initial pronoun. By epenthesizing this consonant, the vowel of the content word is protected from gliding, deletion, or other processes that may obscure the identity of the word. As shown in the following examples, I will gloss this epenthesized consonant simpy as L-.

(105) a. mɔ̰̋ kərúú l-í bɛ̋ wétənɛ̆
person all L-LOG do.IRR now
'Everyone says now...' [sos171009t1:105]

b. dôn kőo l-à bè wè mɔ̰ɔ́ bɔ̀ɔ
child give.birth.NOM L-3SG do.IRR HAB person.SBJV grow.old.IRR
'Having a child ages a person.' [sos170701e]

In (105a), we see l-insertion before the logophoric pronoun, and in (105b) before the 3sg.

If the preceding word ends in a latent nasal coda, an [n] can be inserted instead. It is unclear whether this is nasalization of the epenthetic [l] or whether the nasal coda simply resyllabifies as an onset; I will treat it as the former here, continuing to gloss these emergent [n] onsets as L-:

(106) sân n-í bɛ̋ ḭ̀ wétənɛ̆ í wó lɛ̰̀ í wó təgɔ̀n
rabbit L-LOG do.IRR COMP now LOG EMPH SUBORD LOG EMPH name
kʊ́ dzɛ̋ ŋɛ́
D.DEF be.good.PTCP NEG
'The rabbit said now that he doesn't have a good name...' [sos 170805t15:92]

After the nasal-final stem *sân* 'rabbit', the epenthetic L is realized as [n]; for more on the effects of latent nasal codas, see §3.3.2.

3.5.5 Vowel centralization

After alveolar affricates /ts, dz/, the vowel /ɛ/ is centralized to [ɜ]. This change can be accounted for by the following rule of centralization:

(107)   *Post-affricate centralization*
        /ɛ/ → [-front] / [+COR, -cont, +delayed release]___
        'The vowel /ɛ/ becomes the allophone [ɜ] after alveolar affricates.'

Since alveolar affricates are rare phonemes (though common allophones before high vowels), there are not many cases where we can see this realizaton. The attested examples are shown in (108):

(108)   a. *tsɛ́*   [tsɜ́]   'indefinite'
        b. *tsɛ́sɛ̀*   [tsɜ́sɜ̀]   'look at (irrealis)'
        c. *dzɛ́*   [dzɜ́]   'good, delicious'
        d. *à dzɛ̰*   [à dzɜ̰]   'his teeth'
        e. *tsɛ̰́*   [tsɜ̰́]   'how'

As these examples show, centralization applies to both oral and nasal vowels.

3.6 Phonological phrasing

Before concluding this chapter, we must first briefly address the question of phonological phrasing. As I have mentioned throughout the chapter, most of the phonological rules that apply between words only apply if both words fall in the same phonological phrase. We must therefore consider how the phonological phrase is calculated in Seenku.

Broadly speaking, phonological phrasing looks like the following, where brackets delimit phrase boundaries:

(109)   [S TAMP] [Aux Object Verb] [Adjunct Neg]

The subject will phrase together with any TAMP markers, if present. The object and verb always phrase together, and the auxiliary may also join this phrase. Finally, adjuncts such as adverbs or postpositional phrases will form their own phonological phrase, together with clause-final negation and any other clause-final discourse markers.

The strongest evidence for this phrasing comes from non-application of phonological rules that we would otherwise expect to apply. For example, consider the following utterance made up of three clauses strung together:

(110) í wóo sío nɛ́̋ ì̀ ä̀ sú í
LOG EMPH.SBJV get.up.REAL.PFV if COMP 3SG get.up.IRREAL LOG
wóo tɔgö̀ nɛ́̋ ì̀ ä̀ tɔgö̀
EMPH.SBJV sit.REAL.PFV if COMP 3SG sit.IRREAL
'[that] if I stand up, it stands up, if I sit down, it sits down.' [sos161009t1:35]

There are no pauses in this utterance, but we find that the vowel of the conditional marker *nɛ́̋* at the end of clauses 1 and 3 is retained; similarly, the vowel of *sú* 'get up' does not become a glide before the following *í*. At a minimum, then, each short clause here forms its own phonological phrase.

Looking within clauses, we find evidence of a phrase boundary between the verb and a following postpositional phrase, where once again vowel hiatus resolution fails to apply:

(111) məgɔ̆n-cəbɛ̆ɛ́ fä̀ nɛ́̋ í gü̈̀
monitor.lizard.SBJV enter.REAL.PFV if LOG under
'[he said that] when the monitor lizard ran [into the hole] underneath me...'
[sos170711t1:18]

Again, the vowel of *nɛ́̋* is retained before the initial /i/ of the logophoric pronoun.

More systematic study will be required to determine the extent to which phrasing is affected by things like speech rate, or whether short subjects of intransitive verbs would phrase with a following verb. These observations on phrasing should be seen as preliminary.

4 Tone

One of the most interesting aspects of Seenku grammar is its complex tone system. With four contrastive tone levels, multiple contour tones, and a heavy functional load for both lexical and grammatical contrasts, a firm understanding of the tone system is crucial to understanding the grammar as a whole.

This chapter provides a thorough discussion of all aspects of Seenku tone: tonal inventory (§4.1), the tone-bearing unit (§4.2), lexical tone (§4.3), grammatical tone (§4.4), phonological tone rules (§4.5), phonetics of tone (§4.6), and intonation (§4.7). Ample cross-referencing will be provided throughout, especially in the discussion of grammatical tone, which ties in with grammatical constructions treated in greater depth elsewhere in the grammar.

4.1 Tone inventory

4.1.1 Tonal primitives

Seenku has one of the richest and most complex tone systems in Burkina Faso. While its neighbors are all (to the best of our knowledge) two- or three-tone languages, as laid out in Table 4.1, Seenku boasts four distinct levels as tonal primitives.

Tab. 4.1: Neighboring languages and their tone inventories

Southern Toussian	3	Wiesmann (2001)
Northern Toussian	3	Zaugg-Coretti (2005)
Bobo	3	Boone (2016)
Jula	2	Mamadou Lamine Sanogo (p.c.)
Dzùùngoo	3 (4?)	Solomiac (2014)
Senoufo (Sicite)	3 (4?)	Garber (1988)

The Toussian languages are only beginning to be thoroughly described (ongoing work by Anthony Struthers-Young), and the tonal analyses used as references here self-identify as tentative. Dzùùngoo (Solomiac 2014) can be almost entirely described as a three-tone language, except for a fourth tone found in one verbal inflection, intermediate between L and M, which Solomiac describes as a raised L; as the most closely related language to Seenku, Dzùùngoo tone may have undergone a similar evolution to Seenku tone, or the seeds of this fourth category may have been planted before the two languages split. Nanerigé Senoufo is listed as having 2 or 4 tones, depending upon tonal analysis. Bobo has been consistently described as a three-tone language, and the vehicular Jula (a variety of Bambara, whose tone has been thoroughly analyzed) spoken in and around Bobo-Dioulasso is treated as a two-tone language.

Seenku's four tonal primitives are shown in (1), along with their abbreviations and diacritic conventions:

(1) extra-low X ä̀
    low   L à
    high   H á
    super-high S a̋

Tone will be marked just once for long vowels, on the first vowel (e.g. bɛ̀ɛ 'pig' is level X-toned), except in the case of certain contour tones where a sequence of diacritics is required; see §4.1.2 below.

Time normalized plots of these four tones for a male and female speaker are given in Figures 4.1-4.2.

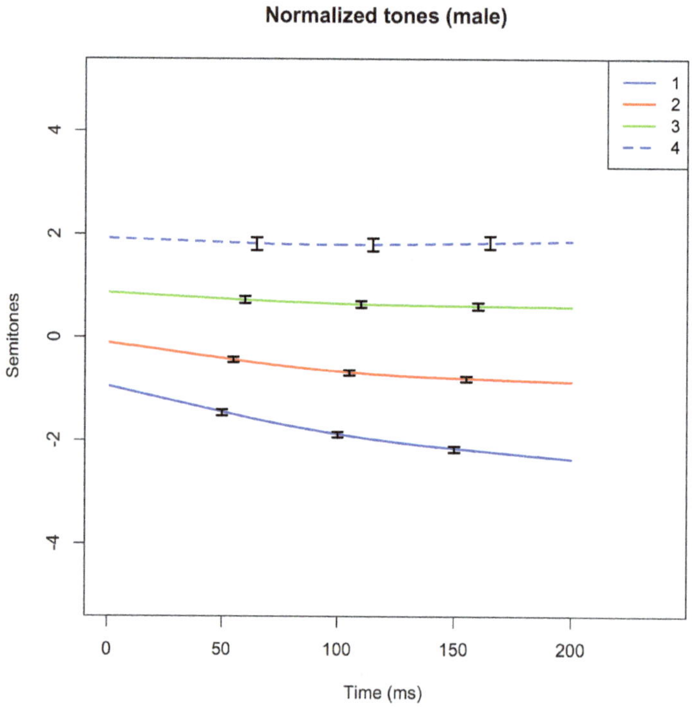

Fig. 4.1: Normalized pitch traces for Seenku's four level tones (1=X, 4=S), spoken by SCT

With two and three tone systems, there is (by and large) agreement in the naming of tones: L vs. H, or L vs. M vs. H, but once a fourth tone is introduced, a great deal of

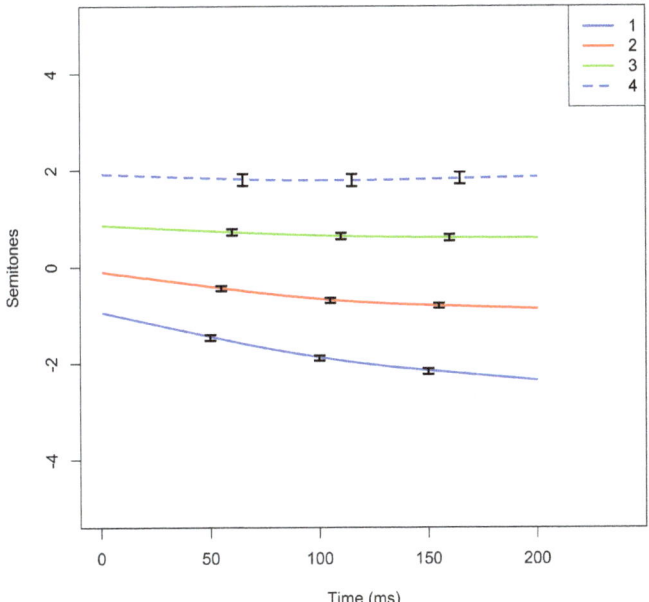

Fig. 4.2: Normalized pitch traces for Seenku's four level tones (1=X, 4=S), spoken by GET

variation is introduced in the literature. For example, Roberts-Kohno (2000) labels the four tones of Kikamba (Bantu, Kenya) as super-low (SL), low (L), high (H), and super-high (SH). Similarly, Konoshenko (2014) discusses Mande four-tone systems using the terms extra-low (eL), low (L), high (H), and extra-high (eH). Still other systems use the basic Low/Mid/High with a fourth additional tone, such as raised-L, Mid-L, Mid-H, etc. (see Odden in press). These different systems of terminology may sometimes be driven by phonological behavior, for example where there is evidence of three primary tones and one derived tone, but just as much they are driven by convention and personal preference.

Unsurprisingly, given the tonal inventories of neighboring languages, there is evidence that Seenku has evolved from a three-tone language and that one of the tones is usually derived (see §4.1.1.2 on the behavior of L). This might encourage the use of L, M, H and raised-L (as in Dzùùngoo). However, this fourth tone is not always derived, and it is far more common lexically in Seenku than in Dzùùngoo, enough so to make "raised-L" a cumbersome appellation. To remain consistent with the literature on other four-tone Mande languages, I will treat the two middle tones as L and H, but differentiate the extreme tones as "extra-low" and "super-high", which can be abbreviated to X and S, thus avoiding the need for two-letter abbreviations (either eL vs. eH or SL vs. SH); the use of diacritics remains the same.

Due to grammatical restrictions on various tones (especially the middle tones L and H), it can be a challenge to find four-way minimal sets within the same syntactic category (the surest evidence for contrast). Minimal sets, setting aside this requirement, are provided in (2):

(2) a. sí̋   'Terminalia *sp.*'
         sí   (reciprocal)
         sì   'first son (birth order name)'
         sì̏   'water jar'

     b. kő̋n   'door'
         kű   'that (discourse definite)'
         —
         kù̏   'toh'

     c. sã́n   'god'
         sá   'cry'
         sà   'second son (birth order name)'
         sằn   'stream'

     d. lé̋   (past)
         lé   (subjunctive)
         —
         lè̏   (subordinate)

As these minimal sets show, distinctions between the four levels are used for both lexical (2a-c) and grammatical (2d) contrasts. Further minimal sets will be given as contour tones are introduced in §4.1.2.

4.1.1.1 Featural representation

Throughout this grammar, I will be assuming the featural representation of the four Seenku tone levels shown in Table 4.2.

Tab. 4.2: Featural representation of Seenku tone (following Yip 1980, Pulleyblank 1986, McPherson 2017b)

	X	L	H	S
[upper]	-	-	+	+
[raised]	-	+	-	+

The two binary features [upper] and [raised] naturally account for a four-tone system. Recent work by Clements et al. (2010) and Hyman (2010) have questioned the need for, or at the very least the universality of, phonological features for tone. As I will show throughout the grammar, tone features play an active role in Seenku phonology and morphology, making them more than a simple classificatory system. For example, see tone raising in plural nouns (§4.4.1.1), tone lowering in perfective verbs (§4.4.1.2), or register agreement in contour tones (§4.1.2).

4.1.1.2 The place of L

As briefly mentioned in §4.1.1 above, three of Seenku's four tones are more heavily represented, especially at the level of the lexicon. These are the tones X, H, and S. The lower of the middle tones, L, is very uncommon in non-derived and non-inflected lexical items. It is found in only a small handful of numerals, adverbs, and proper names, except when forming part of the rising contour tone LS. On the surface, however, it is quite frequent (though still not to the same extent as the other three primitives), since it is commonly created through morphological and phonological tone processes.

If we assume that Seenku evolved from a three-tone language to a four-tone language, then we would likely posit L to be the newest tone in the system. The Seenku tones X, H, and S would correspond to the tones in a three-tone system L, M and H. While work on related Samogo languages is sparse (especially work with careful attention to the tone system), comparative evidence from Dzùùngoo (Solomiac 2014) suggests that this is on the right track, with some complications. A full lexico-comparative study of the two languages is beyond the scope of this work, but a sample of 50 cognates drawn from Solomiac (2014) yield the following correspondences:

(3) *Correspondences between Seenku tone and Dzuungoo tone*

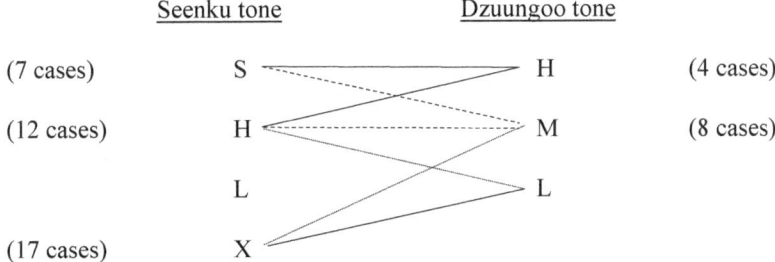

The solid lines represent the most common mappings for each of Seenku's four tones represented in the sample; the number of cases of each correspondence is given on the lefthand side. In other words, there are seven cases in which Seenku S corresponds to Dzuungoo H, twelve cases where Seenku H corresponds to Dzuungoo H, and seventeen cases where Seenku X corresponds to Dzuungoo L. It is interesting to note this neutralizing behavior, where in most cases, Seenku's two highest tones both correspond to Dzùùngoo H. The next most common correspondences are shown with dashed lines, and the number of cases is given on the righthand side, where the number of cases should be read based on the Seenku tone: in four cases, Seenku S corresponds to Dzùùngoo M and in another eight cases, Seenku H also corresponds to Dzùùngoo M. The remaining two dotted lines represent a single case each. From these correspondences, we see that the lowest tone in each system can likely be reconstructed back to a proto-Samogo stage, while it is more difficult to disentangle the two highest tones (H and S in Seenku, M and H in Dzùùngoo). Regardless, three of Seenku's four tones find correspondences in Dzùùngoo, suggesting an original three-tone system, while L remains unrepresented. A more in-depth comparative study (including both Dzùùngoo and other Samogo languages) will be required to definitively reconstruct the proto-Samogo tone system and fully understand Seenku's evolution from a three-tone to a four-tone system.

L is commonly found on the surface as the result of phonological and morphological processes. For instance, L is derived from X in nominal plurals, illustrated by the following examples:

(4) a. bɛ̋ɛ   →   bɛ̀ɛ   'pig(s)'
     b. ső   →   sòe   'horse(s)'
     c. səgä̋   →   səgɛ̀ 'sheep (pl)'

For further discussion and analysis, see §4.4.1.1 below.

It is also derived from X in argument-head tone sandhi, when an X-toned head is preceded by an X-toned argument:

(5) a. ä + kɔ̋n   →   à kɔ̀n   'his head'
     b. bɛ̋ɛ + sä̋n   →   bɛ̀ɛ sà̋n   'buy a pig'

As these examples show, both the argument and the head raise to L; this tonal process is discussed in greater depth in §4.4.2, and further examples can be found in Chapters 8 and 13 in discussions of possession and irrealis verbs, respectively.

Finally, the most common rising contour tone in Seenku is LS, not XS, presumably due to register assimilation (where L and S both share a [+raised] register feature). These rising contours can simplify to L when followed by another S, in a process of tonal absorption (formalized in §4.5.3), yielding forms like the following (L-toned words bolded):

(6) a. ä̀ **nà** mǐ bä̌
    3SG PROSP 1PL hit.IRR
    'He will hit us.' [sos150811e]

b. mó sĭ bî **sạ̀** nḛ̋
    1SG.EMPH be goat buy.REAL.NOM LOC
    'I am buying a goat.' [sos150623e]

Both bolded examples are underlyingly a LS contour tone (nǎ and sǎ̰), which simplifies, leaving a level L tone on the surface. For further discussion, see §4.5.3.

4.1.2 Simple (two-tone) contour tones

Seenku's four tonal primitives combine to create numerous contour tones, contributing to the complexity of the tone system. The following table summarizes the possible two-tone contours in the language. Cells with a check mark are attested in the dataset; if the check mark is in parentheses, the contour is theoretically possible given the language's tonal processes but I have yet to see them in the dataset. Empty cells are unattested contours that I do not expect to see.

(7)   Attested contour tones in Seenku

	S	H	L	X
S		✓		✓
H	✓		✓	✓
L	✓	(✓)		(✓)
X		✓		

As the table shows, all but three combinations are either attested or theoretically possible. The only unattested two-tone contours are either XS (possible underlyingly but surfaces as LS by register assimilation) or involve a final L tone (which is created in just one condition, with preceding H, in argument-head tone sandhi; §4.4.2).

4.1.2.1 Lexical contour tones

Not all of the contours in (7) are lexical or underlying. In fact, most are grammatical, the result of tonal morphology, tone sandhi, or elision processes. The three lexical contour tones are below, with their diacritic conventions:
- HX (â)
- LS (ǎ)
- HS (áǎ)

The distribution of these contour tones across syntactic categories is not uniform, as §4.3.2 will demonstrate. For instance, HS is far more common in verbs, while LS is more common in adjectives and nouns; HX is found in many categories, but is especially common in nouns (where it appears to be the result of a tonotactic restriction against level H; see §4.3.2 below). Thus, as before with level tones, it can be challenging to find within-category minimal sets for the contour tones. Near minimal sets, including level-toned minimal pairs where available, are given in (8):

(8) a. HS cíĕ 'clear throat'
       LS cǐe 'dead'
       HX cîe 'at home'

    b. HS ŋáă 'yawn'
       LS kăa 'next to'
       HX ŋâ 'ripen'
       X   ŋa̋a 'inside'

    c. HS kṷí̋ 'snore'
       LS kṷǐ 'grass sp.'
       HX kṷî 'deny'

    d. HS —
       LS gɔ̌ɔ 'dry'
       HX gɔ̂ɔ 'wood'
       X   gɔ̋ɔ 'field'

4.1.2.2 Grammatical contour tones

Every two-tone contour, including the lexical ones from the last subsection, can also be created grammatically. I will be transcribing the majority of these contours with a simple sequence of diacritics of the two constituent tones (since most of these contours appear only on long vowels anyway). The only new diacritic to note in this section is the use of the umlaut for SX (e.g. bä̱ 'hit (PERF)'); the use of umlaut as a "wild card" tone diacritic is common in the Mande literature.

Various grammatical processes derive these contour tones. For example, through the process of **clitic elision** (§4.4.3) alone, the contours HS, LS (from /XS/), SH, XH, SX, and HX are created (with the possibility of LH and LX as well). Examples are shown in (9):

(9) a. *Elided past tense clitic lɛ́:*
   áǎ 2SG PST
   ǎa 3SG PST (from /àá/)

b. *Elided subjunctive clitic lɛ́:*
   mɨ̌ɨ 1PL SBJV
   ǎá 3SG SBJV

c. *Elided subordinate clitic lɛ̏:*
   mɨ̏ɨ 1PL SUBORD
   âa 2SG SUBORD

In principle, LH could be created through the elision of the subjunctive clitic after a L-toned (plural) subject, and LX through the elision of a subordinate clitic in the same environment, but neither condition is attested in the current data set.

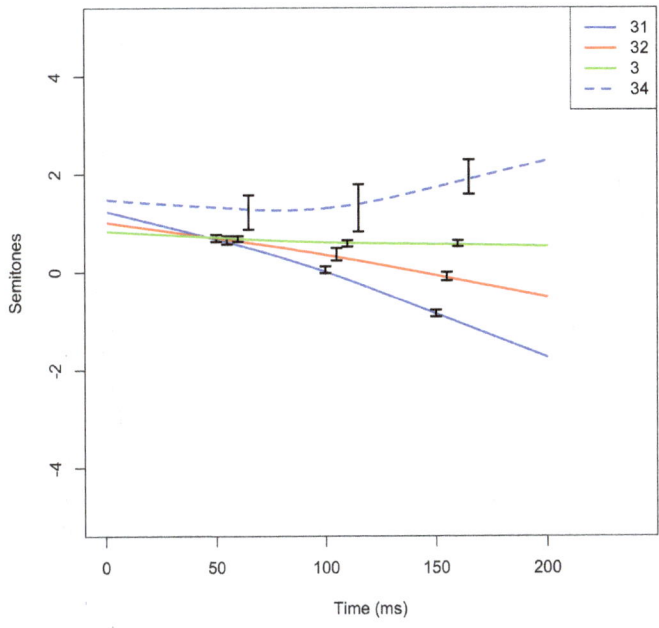

Fig. 4.3: Normalized pitch traces of HS (34), HL (32), and HX (31) contours, with level H for reference

The only attested contour tone that cannot be created by elision is HL. This contour tone is created through the same argument-head tone sandhi process that derived

L tones, discussed in §4.1.1.2 above. When a HX-toned argument precedes an X-toned head, both Xs raise to L:

(10) a. bâ̰a̰ + wɛ̏   →   bá̰a̰ wɛ̏   'with a balafon'
      b. bî + sà̰n   →   bî˺ sà̰n   'buy a goat'

In (10b), we run into a limitation of the transcription system, whereby there is no single diacritic for HL, yet it does not necessitate a long vowel; a transcription bîi̯ would imply vowel lengthening, which does not take place. I have left the L-tone diacritic floating after the vowel, showing that lengthening does not take place, but it should not be understood as a floating tone. It does link to the vowel, creating a very slight fall. Normalized pitch traces of H-intial contours (and level H) are shown in Figure 4.3.

4.1.3 Complex (three-tone) contour tones

Complex contour tones involving three level tones are also attested. In the current dataset, I have seen three such contours:
- XHX (àâ)
- LSX (ää)
- HXS (âấ)

The first "bell-shaped tone", XHX, is a lexical contour, found on nouns such as dǎân 'hanging basket holder', gɔ̀ɔ̂n 'hibiscus'. The second bell-shaped tone, LSX, is derived grammatically in the perfect through the suffixation of -SX. Examples include nàä 'come (PERFECT)' and kàä 'go (PERFECT)'; for further discussion of this grammatical tone process, see §4.4.1.3 below.

Phonetically, the lower of the two bell-shaped tones, XHX, is nearly level. A slight rise can be seen in the middle, but it is distinguished from true level tones in the fact that level tones have a tendency to fall slightly. The other bell-shaped tone LSX, in contrast, has a more visible convex shape. These two tones are plotted in Figure 4.4, from speaker SCT, with the level tones for comparison. XHX rises barely above X, which may lead the reader to question how we know there is a H involved at all; evidence comes from pluralization, where XHX becomes XS (which surfaces as LS), just like HX becomes S; see §4.4.1.1 for more details.

The last tritone contour is a typologically rare trough-shaped tone, a sequence that is often dispreferred even across multiple syllables in a word (see e.g. Yip 2002, Cahill 2007, Hyman 2010, McPherson 2016). It is created, once again, through clitic elision. For example, consider the following example with the corresponding pitch track in Figure 4.5, spoken by female speaker GET:

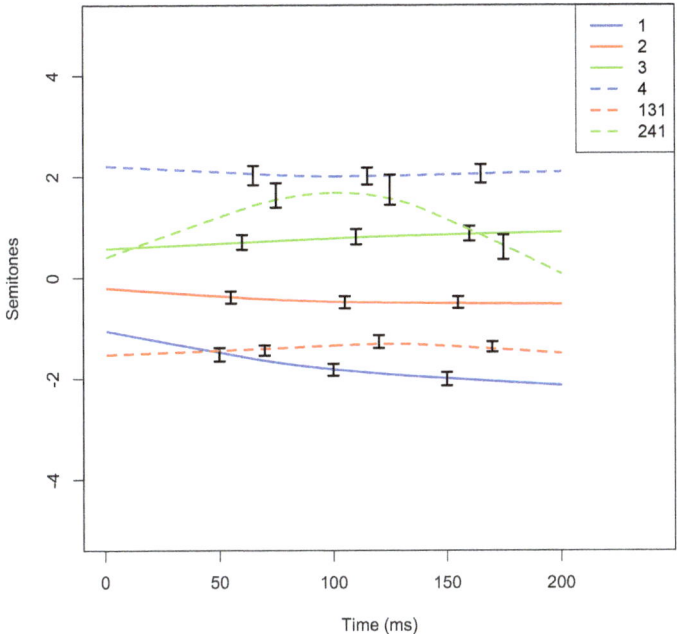

Fig. 4.4: Normalized pitch traces of three-tone contours vs. level tones.

(11) dôőn c̀ie
child.PST die.REAL.PFV
'The child died.'

The trough-shaped tone HXS is clearly visible, though the X target is unable to be fully realized between the two higher tones.

Given the typological rarity of such trough-shaped tones, it is unsurprising that some speakers simplify the contour to HS; though loss of X typically triggers downstep in Seenku (see §4.5.2), there is no evidence of downstep in the HS contour. The pitch track in Figure 4.6 illustrates the pronunciation of the same phrase by male speaker SCT.

In principle, other three-tone contours could be created through clitic elision, or even more extreme, a four-tone contour could in principle arise from the elision of a clitic after a lexical three-tone contour; though hypothetically possible, these remain unattested at the time of writing.

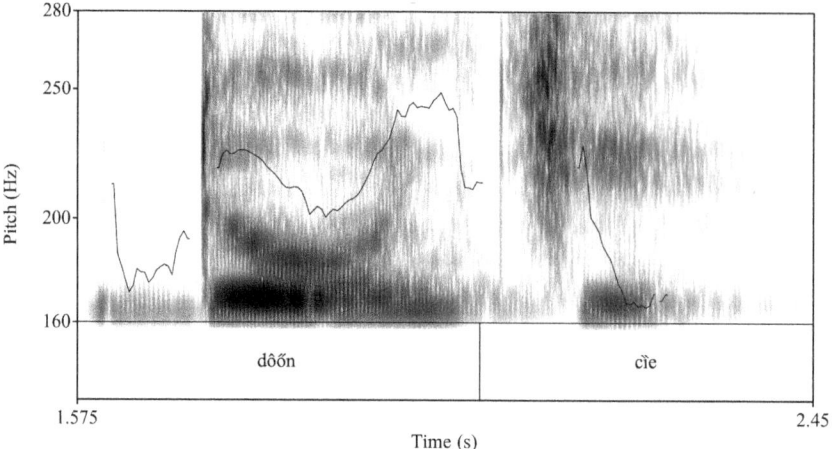

Fig. 4.5: Pitch trace of 'the child died' (GET)

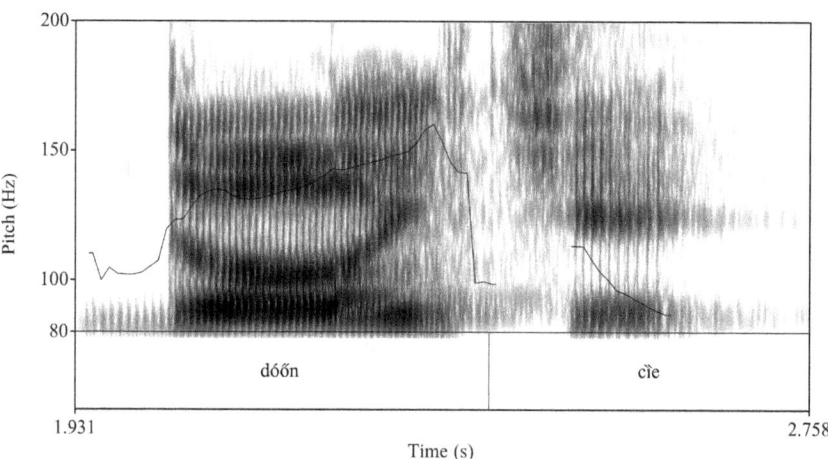

Fig. 4.6: Pitch trace of 'the child died' (SCT)

4.2 Tone-bearing unit (TBU)

The last section covered the inventory of tones in Seenku. I now turn to the question of the tone-bearing unit (TBU). If we were to identify a phonological entity as the TBU, distributional evidence would point to the **syllable**, with each syllable able to host up to three tones.

Primary evidence for this analysis comes from the fact that contour tones (or at least falling tones) are found on both short and long vowels:

(12) a. kâ 'griot'
     kâa 'fight'

b. bǎ 'hit (perfect)'
   bǎa 'balafon'

In languages where the mora is the TBU, such as Tommo So (McPherson 2013), only long vowels are able to host contour tones, since long vowels consist of two moras, and only one tone can be associated with each mora. This cannot be the case for Seenku, where short vowels can host two tones.

That being said, tone and vowel length are not entirely independent in Seenku. Specifically, length contrasts are neutralized with rising tones; all syllables are produced long when the rising tone is realized (i.e. not simplified; see §4.5.2-4.5.3 for processes that affect only underlyingly short vowels). The same situation holds for three-tone contours, except that the syllables bearing three tones are lengthened even further than those carrying rising tones.

This raises the question of whether the notion of the TBU is appropriate, or whether the distribution of tones in Seenku is more closely tied to phonetic principles of length, as proposed by Zhang (2004). Rising tones require more laryngeal effort to produce than falling tones, and consequently take more time to be fully realized. The typological ramifications of this fact are that rising tones are rarer cross-linguistically, and that when a language does have rising tones, they tend to be distributionally restricted. Seenku's answer to these restrictions is to lengthen syllables hosting rising tones.

For further discussion of phonetically driven contour tone licensing, see Zhang (2004).

4.2.1 Tone on the initial half syllable

The short half syllable in sesquisyllabic words is typically not tone bearing. In other words, sesquisyllabic words show the same lexical tone melody inventory as monosyllabic words, with the tone realized fully on the main syllable; for a discussion of lexical melodies, see §4.3. As discussed in §3.1.2, there is a question of whether half syllables are part of the underlying structure (i.e. whether the reduced vowel is underlying) or whether these words simply have a complex onset (broken up by an epenthetic vowel). The distribution of tone melodies is consistent with the epenthetic analysis, since the half syllable is non-contrastive. However, it could simply be that reduced vowels are not independently tone bearing, regardless of whether they are underlying or inserted.

On the surface, of course, the [ə] carries pitch. A controlled phonetic study will be necessary to determine whether the half syllable should be treated as phonologically specified (via spreading from the main syllable) or whether it is unspecified (receiving pitch via interpolation from surrounding tones). Either way, the tone of the initial half syllable is predictable based on the tone of the main syllable, and hence I leave it unmarked in the transcription system.

The exception is when the main syllable bears a heavy tone load—a rising tone or a three-tone contour. In this case, the first tone may be realized on the half syllable rather than on the main syllable. This allows the length contrasts on LS lexical items to be maintained. For instance, consider the two sesquisyllabic LS-toned words in (13), shown with their phonetic realization:

(13) a. dənǐ   [də̀nǐ]   'barrel drum'
      b. dəgɔ̌   [də̀gɔ̌]   'place'[1]

With three-tone contours, the initial tone is always realized on the half syllable, which is reflected in the transcription system. For instance, kə̀nû 'stone' is realized as it is transcribed; by shifting the initial X onto the half syllable, the main syllable carries only HX and can be realized as short.

4.3 Lexical tone

With a majority of Seenku stems being mono- or sesquisyllabic, the inventory of lexical tone melodies closely resembles the basic tone inventory for the language. Differences arise primarily in a) a smaller set of contour tones in lexical melodies than overall on the surface (where many are created grammatically) and b) overall frequencies (where certain tones are far more restricted lexically than they are on the surface, due again to grammatical tone processes). We also find differences in lexical tone between categories. I will first discuss the general lexical melodies of stems and words (irrespective of category) in §4.3.1 before discussing differences between categorial distributions in §4.3.2. The statistics in this section are based on a lexicon of 1654 words, with 829 distinct stems. Note that stems are defined by syntactic category, such that an adjective gɔ̌ 'dry (adj.)' is treated as a distinct stem from gɔ̌ 'dry (v.intr.)'.

4.3.1 General lexical melodies

Lexical melodies on roots (i.e. morphologically simplex words) are listed in Table 4.3, along with their frequency in the current corpus; the melodies below the line are found exclusively on polysyllabic words.

Tab. 4.3: Frequencies of lexical tone melodies in the general corpus

Melody	Count	Percentage
S	189	22.8%
H	118	14.2%
L	10	1.2%
X	188	22.7%
HX	132	16.0%
LS	84	10.1%
HS	27	3.3%
XHX	29	3.5%
LSH	1	0.1%
HLS	1	0.1%
HXS	1	0.1%
LSX	1	0.1%
SH	5	0.6%
SLS	2	0.2%
SXS	1	0.1%
XH	5	0.6%
XLS	1	0.1%
XS	33	4.0%
XSX	1	0.1%

The frequencies in the lexicon clearly demonstrate the different status of L, discussed in §4.1.1.2. There are only a handful of level L-toned stems, though the tonal primitive itself is not infrequent thanks to LS contour tones, where it is likely derived through register assimilation (§4.5.1). Of the remaining level tones, H is less frequent than either S or X (the most common lexical melodies), but this is balanced by the prevalence of HX contour tones. As §4.3.2.1 will show, a category-specific ban on final H tone triggers the epenthesis of a final X. Thus, at an underlying level, many HX stems may be /H/.

Returning to LS, it is likely that at least historically, LS and XS are the same tonal melody; XS is found on polysyllabic stems where the tones can associate to different syllables. When there is only one TBU, however, X undergoes register assimilation to [+raised], yielding a LS contour. Active register assimilation can be seen with transitive verbs in the postpositional forms; §4.5.1 provides further explanation.

There is one exceptional LSH contour, the irregular adjective *mǒén* 'small'. Its plural allomorph returns to the regular adjectival LS melody (*mənə̌*); see §7.1 for further discussion.

4.3.1.1 Issues in determining stem tone

It is not always straightforward to determine the lexical tone of a stem. This is especially true for inalienable nouns and postpositions, which obligatorily appear with an internal argument and hence always undergo argument-head tone sandhi (§4.4.2). This means that what we might call an underlyingly X-toned inalienable noun will in fact never surface as X, and thus the underlying form is abstract. Transitive verbs undergo the same sandhi, but only when irrealis, and so realis verbs offer a glimpse of underlying forms which can be extended to the nouns and pronouns. Here too, though, tonal processes obscure underlying contrasts, with H- and S-toned transitive verbs neutralizing to S. What, then, should we define as the lexical melody?

I have chosen to list sandhi-undergoers (inalienable nouns, postpositions, transitive verbs) with their abstract underlying form (X, H, or S), even though these do not always surface as such. I have left alienable nouns that surface as HX in isolation as HX, though they may be better listed as H, because it is not clear whether all HX should be treated as H, especially in other syntactic categories where grammatical tone does not provide evidence. For a discussion of the difficulties in defining underlying forms for sandhi-undergoers and a proposal to move away from the concept of a single underlying form, see McPherson (2019).

4.3.1.2 Tonal melodies on longer stems

Eighty percent of the stems in the corpus are either mono- or sesquisyllabic, and the relative proportions of each tonal melody are the same in both categories. The remaining 165 stems break down to 141 disyllabic stems (including reduplication), 22 trisyllabic stems (including two cases of retriplication), and 2 quadrisyllabic stems. This greater number of syllables introduces a broader range of tone mapping possibilities; for instance, should a HX melody be mapped as H-X, H-HX, or HX-X? It turns that there are no exceptionless principles in Seenku tone mapping. In other words, it is not the case that tones will associate left-to-right in a one-to-one fashion, as in the original autosegmental rule (Goldsmith 1976). In the HX example, there are 5 disyllabic words mapped as H-X (e.g. *jánə̏* 'evening'), 10 mapped as H-HX (e.g. *kórô* 'pigeon'), and 1 mapped as HX-X (*tôŋmòn* 'naked'). Similarly, in trisyllabic stems, XS is mapped once as X-S-S (*sìkǎrǎ* 'sugar') and once as X-X-S (*fɔ̀rɔ̀kía* 'robe').

The last noteworthy aspect of Seenku tone melodies is that, contra typological principles, trough-shaped melodies (two higher tones separated by a lower tone) are not banned. Four of the 22 trisyllabic stems show trough-shaped melodies, and these forms are listed in (14):

(14)   S-L-S   műsèlě   'sewing needle'
       S-L-S   ɲŏŋɔmě̌   'camel'
       S-S-LS   ɲămǎlɔ   'wise'
       H-X-S   músàkű   'sweet potato'

Once again, we see that there is no exceptionless tone mapping principle: SLS surfaces as both S-L-S and S-S-LS on a lexeme-specific basis.

4.3.2 Category-specific distributions

The overall distribution of tone melodies presented in the last subsection obscures the fact that tonotactics and tonal melodies often differ by syntactic category. Even different morphosyntactic classes of the same category show differences, as is the case of transitive and intransitive verbs. I provide a brief summary of these distribution patterns here, focusing on the core categories of nouns, adjectives, transitive verbs, and intransitive verbs. Cross-references are provided in each subsection to any discussion later in the grammar.

4.3.2.1 Nominal tone

The biggest characteristic of nominal tone versus general tone in the lexicon is a decrease in H melodies and a concurrent increase in HX. Statistics for the 257 nominal stems in the corpus are summarized in Table 4.4.

Tab. 4.4: Frequencies of lexical tone melodies in nouns

Melody	Count	Percentage
S	81	31.5%
H	30	11.7%
L	6	2.3%
X	79	30.7%
HX	92	35.8%
LS	42	16.3%
HS	11	4.3%
XHX	27	10.5%
SH	3	1.2%
SLS	2	0.8%
XH	5	1.9%
XS	20	7.7%

HX is the single most frequent tone melody in nouns, with H dropping to only 11.7% of the stems. Even this number is inflated, however, since it is based largely on inalienable noun stems whose abstract UR is /H/ but which never actually surface as such. In fact, the only case in which an inalienable noun surfaces with a level H melody on the surface is when an underlyingly S-toned stem is preceded by an X-toned pronoun (3sg or 3pl); see §4.4.2 for more details.

This distributional asymmetry suggests a synchronic ban on H in final position for nouns, with the preferred repair being the epenthesis of X. Diachronically, this pattern is likely tied to morphological marking that has been lost in Seenku. If we look to one of its closest relatives, Dzùùngoo (Solomiac 2007; 2014), we see that a final L tone marks the definite on nouns; this marking is inaudible on L-toned nouns, but M- and H-toned nouns surface as ML and HL contours, respectively. As argued in §4.1.1.2 above, Dzùùngoo L, M, H most likely correspond to Seenku X, H, and S. This suggests that Seenku HX contours may be a reinterpretation of erstwhile definite nouns that have been bleached of their definite meaning; for modern definite marking, see §8.2.1. Curiously, level H-toned allomorphs of nouns are still attested in Seenku in environments where definite marking would be unexpected or replaced by other determiners, such as before the relative marker lé (Chapter 17). This may provide further evidence for HX nouns being H-toned underlyingly, but there is no synchronic explanation for the final X other than a phonological restriction on H tone; it carries no other meaning.

Lest we think HX is simply a phonetic realization of H, there is evidence for its phonological reality. First, level H tones in other syntactic categories show that H is not automatically pronounced with a fall. Second, in argument-head tone sandhi, HX in argument position triggers sandhi changes associated with X, not H (§4.4.2 provides examples). And finally, words with HX contours are played with two notes in the balafon surrogate language, those corresponding to H and X; musicians, who are acutely aware of the tone system for this purpose, have explicitly told me that words like bî 'goat' have two tones. See §22.2.1 for further discussion of the balafon surrogate language.

4.3.2.2 Adjectival and participial tone

The division between adjectival stems and participial ones is not always clear-cut in Seenku, as described in Chapter 7. For this reason, I group the two together in considering their tonal melodies, for a total of 73 stems, with the frequencies laid out in Table 4.5.

Adjectives and participials diverge from most other categories in the preponderance of LS melodies, followed by S melodies. All other melodies are extremely uncommon or unattested (including the level tone L). The melodies of participal verbs are productively derived via S suffixation (§4.4.1.4 and §13.3.3), but for most adjectival stems, no active alternations can be found to point to the same process.

4.3.2.3 Transitive verb tone

Transitive verbs fall mostly into three underlying melodies: X, H, and S (Seenku's three main tones). However, as discussed in §4.3.1, these underlying representations are ab-

Tab. 4.5: Frequencies of lexical tone melodies in adjectives and participials

Melody	Count	Percentage
S	25	34.2%
H	4	5.5%
X	2	2.7%
HX	3	4.1%
LS	33	45.2%
HS	1	1.4%
XS	3	4.1%
LSH	1	1.4%
SLS	21	1.4%

stract in the sense that they do not always surface as such. When inflected in the irrealis, verb stems undergo the same argument-head tone sandhi as inalienable nouns (§4.4.2), and when inflected in the realis, H and S neutralize to S in participial forms (§4.4.1.4) and H in the perfective (§4.4.1.2). The distributions in Table 4.6, based on 166 transitive verb stems, reflect underlying tonal categories.

Tab. 4.6: Frequencies of lexical tone melodies in transitive verbs

Melody	Count	Percentage
S	49	29.5%
H	42	25.3%
X	64	38.6%
LS	3	1.8%
HS	3	1.8%
XS	4	2.4%
LSX	1	0.6%

The table clearly demonstrates that lexical melodies are more restricted in transitive verbs than they are in other categories; this falls in line with the typological generalization that verbs are often more restrictive in their prosodic categories than nouns (e.g. Smith 2001).

4.3.2.4 Intransitive verb tone

The same restrictiveness seen with transitive verbs is seen on intransitive verbs as well. The corpus contains 90 intransitive verb stems, whose tonal distributions are shown in Table 4.7.

Since intransitive verbs by definition do not take objects, they do not undergo argument-head tone sandhi, and thus their surface tones are more representative of their underlying tones. However, like transitive verbs, S and H often neutralize, but to

Tab. 4.7: Frequencies of lexical tone melodies in intransitive verbs

Melody	Count	Percentage
S	10	11.1%
H	16	17.8%
X	28	31.1%
HX	30	33.3%
LS	1	1.1%
HS	4	4.4%
XHX	1	1.1%

H; 10 exceptional verbs remain S-toned. The status of H vs. HX is less clear for intransitive verbs than it is for nouns. This distinction does not appear to be contrastive, and in fact is largely predictable based on the length of the stem vowel: most HX verbs have a long vowel and most H verbs have a short vowel. It is not clear why this distinction is in place, since short vowels have no problem hosting a HX contour, but it may be related to a general dispreference in Seenku for level H tones, a preference that gets stronger the longer the duration of the tone.

4.3.3 Surface tone distributions

The statistics provided in the last subsections represent the lexical distribution of tones, but this is not what speakers are exposed to in everyday speech. Grammatical tone and phonological tone rules result in a strikingly different tonal landscape. This section briefly reports on a pilot study of surface tone, based on forty minutes of naturalistic speech by six speakers (three male, three female). Focusing only on words with two-tone melodies, this resulted in 6374 words (tokens), or 734 types.

The token frequencies, first, are provided in Table 4.8.

There are a few things to notice about this distribution. First, the proportion of H is greatly increased compared to lexical frequencies and the proportion of HX and LS are greatly reduced. There is also a higher proportion of L, which was rare in the lexical distributions. Further, two-tone melodies that are unattested in the lexicon, such as HL, are attested on the surface, though with significantly lower frequency than the core tonal categories.

Since studies have shown that speakers may be sensitive to type frequency rather than token frequency in learning the phonotactics of their language (e.g. Bailey and Hahn 2001, Albright 2009, Richtsmeier 2011), I also provide the tonal distribution across types, where a type is defined as a lexical item with a particular tone melody. In other words, an inalienable noun in a sandhi environment that triggers S will be counted as a different type from the same lexical item in a sandhi environment that triggers X. The resulting distribution across the 734 types is given in Table 4.9.

Tab. 4.8: Token tone melody frequencies from a corpus of naturalistic speech

Melody	Count	Percentage
S	1083	17.0%
H	2091	32.8%
L	577	9.0%
X	1674	26.3%
HX	344	5.4%
LS	231	3.6%
HS	100	1.6%
SX	47	0.7%
SH	55	0.9%
HL	84	1.3%
LH	3	0.0%
LX	2	0.0%
XL	0	0.0%
SL	3	0.0%
XH	61	1.0%
XS	19	0.3%

Type frequency shows a much more even distribution across the four level tones, and crucially, a sizable proportion of L tones. Thus, even though L is quite rare in the lexicon, it is not a marginal tone in the language. The proportions of H and X are much higher in the token counts due to high-frequency pronouns and particles.

The following sections will cover the grammatical and phonological tone processes that transform the lexical melodies into their surface distributions.

4.4 Grammatical tone

Compared to its relatives, Seenku has traded in a great deal of its segmental morphology for tonal morphology. I divide Seenku grammatical tone into three overarching categories. The first is "tonal affixation" (§4.4.1), which is the most contentful kind of tonal morphology. The second is a complex sandhi process that takes place between a head and its internal argument (§4.4.2); its domain of application is grammatically defined but the tone changes do not themselves mean anything. The third and final case of grammatical tone involves the optional elision of grammatical clitics (TAMP markers and some postpositions), leaving behind only their tone and a lengthened vowel (§4.4.3); this represents a change in progress that is leaving in its wake a new range of tonal case marking.

Tab. 4.9: Type tone melody frequencies from a corpus of naturalistic speech

Melody	Count	Percentage
S	139	18.7%
H	135	18.2%
L	109	14.7%
X	137	18.5%
HX	71	9.5%
LS	48	6.5%
HS	35	4.7%
SX	17	2.3%
SH	5	0.7%
HL	21	2.8%
LH	1	0.1%
LX	1	0.1%
XL	0	0.0%
SL	3	0.4%
XH	4	0.5%
XS	16	2.1%

4.4.1 Tonal affixation

Tonal affixation encompasses cases in which tonal features or tones are exponents of morphosyntactic features. Affixation of this sort is found on both nouns and verbs.

4.4.1.1 Tone raising: Nominal plural

The only inflectional feature marked on nouns is the plural, which is marked partially through tone. The vocalic changes involved in the plural will be discussed in §5.3.1.

Plural formation involves tone raising: X becomes L and H(X) becomes S. S is the highest tone in the system and hence cannot rise any further, though in elicitation settings, speakers will sometimes pronounce singular S-toned nouns even higher in the plural, which seems to reflect a metalinguistic awareness of the tone raising process. Examples of tone raising are given in (15):

(15) a. sǒ → sòe 'horse(s)'
       nəgǐ → nəgì 'cow(s)'
       běɛ → bèɛ 'pig(s)'

    b. bî → bǐ 'goat(s)'
       təgê → təgě 'chicken(s)'
       mîɛ → mǐɛ 'snake(s)'

In McPherson (2017b), I argue that tone raising is the result of suffixing the tone feature [+raised]. Added to X, this yields L, and added to H, this yields S. Note that this presupposes that surface HX singulars like *bî* 'goat' are underlyingly H-toned, otherwise we would expect an unattested HL contour in the plural.

The fact that [+raised] is a suffix is evident from the behavior of multi-tonal words. The tone feature docks to the final tone, leaving any preceding tones unaffected:

(16) a. jŭŋmǎ → jŭŋmɛ̋ 'cat(s)'
sáǎn → séɛ̋ 'member(s) of the farming caste'

b. síên → síɛ̋ 'nail(s)'
kó-kô → kó-kőe 'rooster(s)'

c. dǎ̂ân → dɛ̌ɛ 'basket hanger(s)'
kə̀kâ → kə̀kɛ̋ 'meat(s)'

In (16a), the singular forms end in S; since this tone is unaffected by the affixation of [+raised], the plural forms retain the same tone melody as the singular. In (16b), the overall tone melody of the word is HX, but the plural gives us evidence of two adjacent H tones underlyingly. In the second example, this is unsurprising (since the form appears to be reduplicated), but in the first, this is more surprising as it looks like a diphthong. However, unlike diphthongs where the initial vowel is realized as a glide (§3.1.2), in a word like *síên*, both vowels are given equal prominence. Finally, in (16c), XHX becomes XS in the plural, unless all tones must associate to the same syllable, in which case X assimilates to S via register assimilation (§4.5.1). In every form in (16), the initial tone is not subject to tone raising.

For ordering and interaction between plural tone raising and argument-head tone sandhi, see §4.4.2. For more complete discussion of the nominal plural, see §3.1.2.

4.4.1.2 Tone lowering: Perfective

In the verbal domain, the perfective is marked in exactly the opposite way of the nominal plural: by lowering the tone of the verb. The only tone affected, though, is S, which lowers to H. This suggests the affixation of a [-raised] feature. Since X and H are both [-raised] tones to begin with, they are unaffected by the suffix. This process is exemplified in (17):

(17) bǎ → bá 'hit'
nǐɔ → níɔ 'ate'
səbɛ̌ → səbɛ́ 'wrote'

In other realis forms, both H and S verbs neutralize to S. It is not clear whether the perfective [-raised] suffix is applied to this neutralized S form (thus actively lowering both underlying /H/ and /S/) or to the underlying form; the surface form is the same either way.

Since intransitive verbs involve the neutralization of S and H to H, the perfective is marked vacuously. The current dataset lacks perfective forms of the irregular S-toned intransitive verbs, so it is not possible to test whether the [-raised] perfective affects intransitive verbs or whether it is constrained to transitive verbs.

The perfective is treated in-depth in §13.3.2.1.

4.4.1.3 -SX suffixation: Perfect

While the last two cases of tonal affixation involved tone features, the perfect involves full tones. In particular, perfect verbs are marked through the suffixation of -SX (represented with the umlaut diacritic).

First, if the verb is X-toned, a tritone LSX contour is created (with X raising to L through register assimilation). Examples of both intransitive and transitive verbs are given in (18):

(18)   a.   nä̀   →   nàä   'have come'
             kä̀   →   kàä   'have gone'

       b.   sä̀   →   sàä   'have bought'
             dɔ̈ɔ   →   dɔ̀ɔ̈   'have finished'

All other verbs surface as SX, including H- and S-toned verbs. For H-toned verbs, this could be due to a simplification of a HSX contour, or we could assume that the perfect is built off of the neutralized S form (though this neutralization to S only occurs for transitive verbs). I leave these analytical questions to future work. The examples in (19) illustrate underlyingly H-toned intransitive and transitive verbs:

(19)   a.   kpəní   →   kpəni̊   'have fallen out'
             sɔ́   →   sïɔ   'have arrived'

       b.   sɔ́ɔ   →   sɔ̈ɔ   'have sold'
             ŋmá   →   ŋmä   'have eaten (meat)'

S-toned intransitive and transitive verbs are illustrated in (20):

(20)   a.   blǎ   →   blä   'have fallen'
             sɛ̋ɛ   →   sɛ̈ɛ   'have healed'

       b.   nɪ̋ɔ   →   nïɔ   'have eaten'
             bǎ   →   bä   'have beaten'

For more on the perfect, see §13.3.2.2.

4.4.1.4 -S suffixation: Participials

Section 4.3.2.2 showed that adjectives and participial modifiers are much more likely to be either S-toned or LS-toned than any other tone melody. In the case of participial modifiers, this is due to a productive process of -S suffixation that derives participials from the verb stem. The tonal effects on the verb stem are the same as those seen with perfect -SX suffixation; X-toned stems raise to L by register assimilation in the LS contour tone, and both H- and S-toned verbs surface as S.

Examples of X-toned intransitive and transitive participials are shown in (21):

(21) a. təgò̀ → təgǒ 'seated'
gɔ̀ɔ → gɔ̌ɔ 'dry'

b. nəgè̀ → nəgě 'well pounded (outer chaff removed)'
fɔ̀ → fɔ̌ɔ 'swollen'

With sesquisyllabic verbs, the X/L can be partially realized on the initial half syllable, meaning less time is required on the full syllable to reach the S tone. When the verb stem is a monosyllable with a short vowel, the vowel lengthens to accommodate the rising tone.

Examples of H-toned intransitive and transitive participials are shown in (22):

(22) a. bɔ̂ɔ → bɔ̌ɔ 'old/aged'
ŋá → ŋǎ 'ripe'

b. bɔ́ → bǔɔ 'gone out'
né-céɛ → né-cě̌ɛ 'sorted'

The second example in (22b) carries the transitive preverb né-, treated further in §12.4.1.

Finally, examples of S-toned transitive participials are shown in (23); the current dataset does not contain any instances of the rare S-toned intransitive verbs in participial form:

(23) nǎ → nǎ 'lost'
cəmǐ → cəmǐ 'charred'

It is likely that adjectives such as səgɔ̌ 'pretty' or tsǐe 'red' may have had verbal origins, or at least that they fit into the same tonal processes that derive participials today. Since there are no alternations involving adjectives, we cannot say with any certainty.

We see the same tone patterns on verbs in the progressive, which I treat as a nominalized form (§13.3.1.1). Deeper syntactic study would be required to determine whether the participial modifier forms described here are in fact the same nominalized form. For further discussion of participial verbs, see §13.3.3.

4.4.2 Argument-head tone sandhi

The cases of grammatical tone described in the last section are all undisputably morphology—the tone changes instantiate morphosyntactic features and contribute to meaning. This is less clearly true for another prevalent set of alternations: argument-head tone sandhi.

I classify this sandhi process as grammatical due to the fact that its domains of application are defined morphosyntactically rather than phonologically: sandhi takes place between a head (nominal, verbal, or postpositional) and its preceding internal argument. Even if we were able to define phonological domains based on a syntactic distribution encompassing all three, this would be challenged again by the fact that only **irrealis** verbs undergo sandhi, despite realis verbs occurring in exactly the same position.

I will first lay out the tonal alternations involved in argument-head tone sandhi, before addressing the question of domains. For a thorough treatment of Seenku sandhi and an analysis grounded in allomorph selection, see McPherson (2019).

4.4.2.1 Sandhi alternations

In a sequence of an argument followed by its head, it is the head that undergoes sandhi. The tonal alternations depend on both the tone of the preceding argument and on the head's underlying tone. Since sandhi does not typically apply to multi-tonal forms, and since L is either rarely or never an underlying tone in the sandhi categories, the following tables summarize the tone changes involving X, H, and S only.

Sandhi alternations are slightly different depending on whether the triggering argument is a pronoun or a noun. The table in (24) lays out the tone changes with a pronominal argument. The pronoun's tone is listed down the lefthand side, and the head's underlying tone across the top. Cells in the table represent the sandhi realization of the head.

(24)   Sandhi alternations with pronominal arguments

		Head tone:		
		X	H	S
Argument tone	X	L	X	H
	H	S	X	H/X
	S	S	S	S

The only consistent tone change in the sandhi system is that heads always surface as S after S-toned arguments. Otherwise, no unifying principles like spreading, assimilation, or dissimilation can explain the sandhi patterns. In this way, Seenku tone sandhi is more similar to the paradigmatic tone sandhi of Sinitic languages (e.g. Chen 2000) than African sandhi systems.

The variability of X/H following H-toned arguments is explained in the following table, which replaces schematics with real pronouns and inalienable nouns. Two H-toned 1sg pronouns are included, the simple pronoun ń and the emphatic version mó:

(25)   *Sandhi alternations with postpositions pronominal arguments*

			Head tone:		
			kɔ̰̂n 'head'	ɲá 'mother'	nî́ 'father'
Argument tone	3SG	à̰	kɔ̰̂n	ɲà̰	ní
	1SG	ń	kɔ̰́n	ɲà̰	ní
	1SG.EMPH	mó	kɔ̰́n	ɲà̰	nḭ̀
	1PL	mî́	kɔ̰́n	ɲá̰	nî́

After the simple 1sg pronoun, S-toned nouns are realized as H, but if the emphatic pronoun is used (which is also H-toned!), S is realized as X (cf. *mó nḭ̀* 'my father', *mó bà̰* 'hit me'); the same pattern holds for the simple vs. emphatic 2sg pronouns *á* vs. *á wó*. However, if the head is instead a postposition or a verb, then S is realized as X even after simple H-toned pronouns (cf. /lɛ̌/ but *ń nɛ̀* 'to me', /bǎ̰/ but *ń bà̰* 'hit me'). These facts provide further evidence that argument-head tone sandhi is not simply a phonological process, since two pronouns with the same tone and the same basic meaning trigger different tonal alternations.

As the tables above show, a single head can have up to three surface variants, such as the case of 'father' which can surface as H, X, or S. At the very least, all heads that undergo sandhi have at least two sandhi variants. And as these charts show, X-toned and H-toned heads never actually surface as X or H, rendering the underlying form abstract. For related discussion, see §4.3.1.

Sandhi almost exclusively targets the head, with the exception of the configuration X + X. In this environment, the head surfaces as L (as shown in the tables above), but in fact, the preceding argument raises to L as well:

(26)   a. *ã̀ + wɛ̃̀*   →   *à wɛ̀*   'with her'
       b. *ḭ̀ + sã̰̀n* →   *ì sà̰n*   'buy them!'
       c. *ã̀ + kɔ̰̀n* →   *à kɔ̰̀n*   'his head'

The examples in (26) demonstrate that the same sandhi alternations apply to postpositions, inalienable nouns, and verbs, with the exception of the behavior of S-toned stems after simple H-toned pronouns, discussed above.

The sandhi patterns after non-pronominal arguments differ in two cases, namely the two cases in which S lowers to H after X-toned and certain H-toned pronouns. After nominal arguments, S lowers to X after all tones except S:

(27) *Sandhi alternations with non-pronominal arguments*

		Head tone:		
		X	H	S
Argument tone	X	L	X	X
	L	L	L	L
	H	S	X	X
	S	S	S	S

These differences are highlighted in the following examples:

(28) a. ằ + bő́n → ằ bón 'his back'
      bɛ̀ɛ + bő́n → bɛ̀ɛ bòn 'pig's back'

  b. ằ + bá̰ → ằ bá̰ 'hit him!'
      bɛ̀ɛ + bá̰ → bɛ̀ɛ bà̰ 'hit a pig!'

After the X-toned pronoun, the noun *bő́n* 'back' and the verb *bá̰* 'hit' surface as H, but if the pronoun is replaced by an X-toned noun like *bɛ̀ɛ* 'pig', they are realized as X instead.

The argument tones listed in (27) represent the final tone of the argument; for instance, if the argument is a HX-toned noun, the X will trigger sandhi alternations, as illustrated by (29):

(29) a. bî + ɲá → bî ɲà 'goat's mother'
  b. bî + kɔ̰́n → bî kɔ̰̀n 'goat's head'

Followed by a H-toned head, as in (29a), the sandhi form is straightforward: H surfaces as X. If the head is X-toned, though, it undergoes its usual rise to L, taking the X-toned portion of the HX fall with it. This leaves a HL contour tone on the surface (accounting for the HL melodies listed in §4.3.3). Falling tones do not cause vowels to lengthen, but there is no single diacritic for HL tones; thus, I transcribe these short falling tones with a L tone floating at the end of word, but this should be understand as representing a fully associated contour tone.

There are no L-toned pronouns and no underlyingly L-toned undergoers of sandhi (the handful of L-toned lexical items are numerals, adverbs, or proper nouns; §4.1.1.2 and §4.3.1). There can be L-toned non-pronominal triggers, however, if the argument is plural or a proper noun. In this case, the following head obligatorily surfaces as L regardless of its lexical tone:

(30) a. bὲɛ sạ̀n   'buy pigs!'   (cf. sạ̀n)
     b. bὲɛ sɔ̀ɔ   'sell pigs!'   (cf. sɔ́ɔ)
     c. bὲɛ bạ̀   'hit pigs!'   (cf. bǻ)

Ambiguity arises in cases like (30a), since X+X would also surface as L L. Context disambiguates the singular from the plural. As discussed in §4.4.2.4, plural tone raising applies to the output of argument-tone sandhi, meaning L is never the undergoer of sandhi.

Multi-tonal morphemes are impervious to sandhi. Consider, for instance, the postposition *kǎa* 'next to' with X-toned, H-toned, and S-toned pronominal arguments:

(31) a. ạ̀ kǎa   'next to him'
     b. mó kǎa   'next to me'
     c. mǐ kǎa   'next to us'

In every cases, the LS rise is maintained.

We must draw the distinction between multi-tonal morphemes and multi-tonal heads more broadly construed. If the head is a compound, each morpheme with its own tone, it will undergo tone sandhi from left to right; see §4.4.2.3 for further discussion and examples.

4.4.2.2 Sandhi domains

With the tonal alternations described, I now turn to the domains of argument-head tone sandhi. As the name suggests, sandhi occurs between a head and its internal argument. Seenku is mostly a head-final language, typical of Mande languages, and thus the internal argument precedes the head and triggers sandhi.

The three most common domains for argument-head tone sandhi are listed below:
1. Possessor + Inalienable Noun
2. Object + Verb (irrealis mood)
3. Noun + Postposition

These three configurations are united by the fact that the argument is a noun phrase/DP, which more often than not consists of just a single noun or pronoun, but which may be more complex (see Chapter 8 for noun phrase structure). From a syntactic point of view, they are all complements to the head, regardless of the head's syntactic category. Examples of tone sandhi occurring with more complex arguments in each of the three domains are given in (32):

(32) a. mənǐ   bɔ́ɔ̀ kɔ̀̌n   (cf. /kɔ̀̌n/)
        woman old head
        'old woman's head' [sos150703e]

b. bɛ̏ɛ-kərê sóen sǽ   (cf. /sɑ̏/)
   pig-man one buy.IRR
   'buy a male pig!' [sos141124e]

c. ằ mằan bɛ́ wɛ̋   (cf. /wɛ̏/)
   3SG rice DEM with
   'with that rice' [sos170807e]

In (32a), the possessor consists of a N Adj sequence; it ends in X, which triggers the following X-toned inalienable noun to raise to L (taking the end of the HX contour with it). In (32b), the object consists of a compound noun followed by a H-toned numeral, which triggers the X-toned verb to raise to S. Finally, in (32c), the complement to the postposition consists of a Det N Dem sequence; this final H-toned demonstrative likewise triggers raising of the X-toned postposition to S.

The fact that sandhi occurs only when the verb is irrealis can be seen in the following pair of examples:

(33) a. mí̋ nǎ bí̋ sɔ́ɔ
       1PL PROSP goat.PL sell.IRR
       'We will sell goats.' [sos130905e]

   b. mí̋ lɛ̋ bí̋ sɔ́ɔ
       1PL PST goat.PL sell.REAL.PFV
       'We sold goats.' [sos150201e]

Even though the word order is exactly the same, the irrealis verb in (33a) undergoes sandhi and the realis verb in (33b) does not.

Extensive examples of sandhi in each configuration will be provided in their respective sections: §8.6 for possession, §10.1 for postpositions, and §13.2 for irrealis verbs.

Argument-head sandhi occurs in two other domains that appear to be at least diachronically linked to the core domains listed above. These are:
1. Object + "Preverb" (incorporated noun or postposition)
2. Verb + Inflectional particle

First, many Mande languages display compound verbs, where the verb stem is preceded by what is referred to in the literature as a "preverb" (e.g. Vydrine 2009). In Seenku, these preverbs can be either nominal or postpositional. Syntactically, they belong to the verb (contributing to its semantics), but phonologically, they group with the preceding object, behaving exactly like a possessed noun or a postposition.

To begin with nominal preverbs, Seenku displays N+V compounds such as kɔ̰̋n-tsí̧ 'slaughter' (lit. head-cut) or dán-cɛ̧́ 'unbury, disinter' (lit. mouth-take.off.hat). These noun-verb combinations carry the specific semantics indicated by their glosses, and the nouns are never inflected independently, all of which suggests that the two stems form a compound. However, tone sandhi occurs between the object and the nominal preverb as if the object were acting as a possessor. This sandhi occurs between the object and preverb even if the verb is inflected for realis, rendering the verb stem impervious to sandhi:

(34) a. ä̀ sío mɔ̰̀-fṵ̀ dä̀n-cɛ̰̋ nɛ̋
3SG REC.PST person-corpse mouth-remove.hat.REAL.NOM LOC
'He just unburied a cadaver.' [sos150618e]

b. ä̀ sío mɔ̰̀-fṵ̋ḭ dä̋n-cɛ̰̋ nɛ̋
3SG REC.PST person-corpse.PL mouth-remove.hat.REAL.NOM LOC
'He just unburied cadavers.' [sos150618e]

In (34a), the nominal preverb *dán* surfaces as X after the HX-final object; when the object is inflected for plural, as in (34b), the preverb surfaces as S. Notice that this sandhi occurs even though the verb stem *cɛ̰́* itself has neutralized to S in the realis and does not undergo sandhi. When the verb stem is inflected in the irrealis, a recursive sandhi domain is formed; the resulting tonal forms of these recursive domains will be addressed in §4.4.2.3.

The same behavior holds of transitive preverbs (diachronically postpositions), as we can see in the following examples.

(35) a. mó sḭ̏ jəbɛ̋ nɛ̋-jṵ̋ɛ nɛ̋
1SG.EMPH be cloth TRANS-tear.REAL.NOM LOC
'I am tearing the cloth' [sos150630e]

b. jəbɛ̋ sḭ̏ í nɛ̏-jṵ̋ɛ nɛ̋
cloth be LOG TRANS-tear.REAL.NOM LOC
'The cloth is tearing.' [sos150630e]

After the S-toned object in (35a), *né-* surfaces as S, while after the logophoric/reflexive pronoun in (35b), it surfaces as X; the verb stem, in realis form, is unaffected. For more discussion of preverbs, see §12.4.

The second domain derived from postpositions are verbal inflectional particles. These particles are likely derived from the locative *né* and the associative *wɛ̀* at a time when many Mande verbal constructions involved deverbal nouns (Babaev 2011, Nikitina 2011), and in fact, constructions with *né* (§13.3.1) can be synchronically analyzed as nominal. However, there is no evidence that the habitual, which uses the particle *wɛ̀*, is a nominalized construction, and yet sandhi occurs much as it would with a postposition. In the interest of space, see §13.2.2 for discussion and examples.

One final domain of sandhi is somewhat surprising. I noted above that sandhi occurs between a possessor and an inalienable noun, which falls in line with the other core domains of sandhi if we consider a possessor to be an internal argument of a relational or inalienable noun. Alienable possession, on the other hand, typically involves an explicit genitive marker between the possessor and the possessed noun (either the genitive postposition *tě* or the dative postposition *lě*). When the genitive marker is present, the possessed noun does not undergo sandhi (though the postposition does):

(36) a. mí tě bî   'our goat'
     b. ằ tê bî   'his goat'

The genitive postposition *tě* has an irregular HX variant after X-toned pronouns, as shown in (36b).

However, as will be discussed in §4.4.3 below, the dative postposition can be elided, leaving its tone and length on the preceding noun or pronoun. In this case, the dative-marked possessor becomes a sandhi trigger:

(37) a. mǖ bǐ   'our goat'
     b. ɛ̌ɛ́ bǐ   'his goat'

This domain of sandhi application challenges an account based purely on syntactic configuration, since alienable possessors should not be an internal argument, regardless of whether the genitive marking is an overt postposition or marking on the possessor. For further discussion of clitic elision, see §4.4.3. For more examples of elided dative possession, see §8.6.2.3.

Note, finally, that Noun + Modifier is **not** a sandhi domain; argument-head tone sandhi is not the equivalent of *compacité tonale* (Dwyer 1973, deZeeuw 1979, etc.), which typically occurs in compound nouns and between nouns and modifiers. Tone changes in Seenku compound nouns will be treated in Chapter 7. Similarly, sandhi does not take place between subjects and following TAMP markers, despite these being enclitics and segmentally identical to postpositions. The tonology of TAMP markers will be discussed in §4.4.3.

4.4.2.3 Recursive sandhi domains

Argument-head sandhi can occur in more complex configurations, with either a complex argument, a complex head, or both. Interestingly, sandhi always applies left to right regardless of the direction of branching.

Most commonly, it is the argument that is complex. This occurs, for instance, if the argument is itself a possessor + inalienable noun sandhi domain. Consider first a case of recursive possession, with the bracketing [[Poss N] N]:

(38) a. ằ   +   ɲá   +   bőn   → ằ ɲằ bǒn
        3SG   mother   back
        'his mother's back'

b. mó   +   ɲá   +   kɔ̰n   → mó ɲà kɔ̰̀n
   1SG.EMPH   mother   head
   'my mother's head'

In (38a), X + H first becomes X X, then S of 'back' lowers to X after the non-pronominal X-tone preceding it. If calculated from right to left in this case, the outcome would be the same, but in the case of (38b), the left-to-right directionality is clear. First, H + H becomes H X, then the combination of the derived X sandhi tone and the X of the head (incidentally, 'head') causes **both the underlying and derived** X to raise to L. If the phrase had been calculated from right to left, then ɲá 'mother' plus kɔ̰n would become ɲá kɔ̰n, and the addition of H-toned mó would either lower only ɲá to X or the whole domain to X.

In these cases, the application of sandhi is consistent with the direction of branching: first the innermost domain is computed, then the larger domain. When the head is complex, however, we see that sandhi always applies left-to-right, even though this is inconsistent with syntactic structure. Consider an inalienable compound noun, tsín-ŋmä 'hip' with an X-toned and H-toned possessive pronoun:

(39) a. ä̀ tsín-ŋmǎ   'his hip'
      b. mó tsìn-ŋmà   'my hip'

Both of these tonal outputs are consistent with left-to-right application. In the case of (39a), ä̀ + tsín becomes ä̀ tsín, and this derived H tone triggers the underlying X of ŋmä̀ to raise to S. In (39b), the H tone of mó causes tsín to lower to X; when this derived X comes into contact with ŋmä̀, both the derived and underlying X raise to L. There is no right-to-left (or inner-to-outer) application of sandhi that will derive these surface forms.

4.4.2.4 The interaction of argument-head sandhi with other tonal processes

Argument-head tone sandhi must occur before other grammatical tone processes, since it is the sandhi form that acts as an input to the other tone processes. The clearest case of ordering occurs between sandhi and plural formation. The forms in (40) show the singular and plural possessed forms of dɔ̰n 'shoulder' with a H-toned possessor:

(40) a. mó dɔ̰̀n   'my shoulder'
      b. mó dɔ̰̀ɛ   'my shoulders'

Plural tone raising clearly applies to the sandhi form and not to the underlying form; here, the sandhi form X raises to L. If the plural applied to the underlying form, then both singular and plural of 'shoulder' would be S-toned, and both would lower to X during sandhi (yielding ungrammatical *mó dɔ̰̀ɛ). This same effect can be seen with an X-toned possessor:

(41) a. ǎ dɔ́n   'her shoulder'
     b. ǎ dʒ̋ɛ   'her shoulders'

Argument-head tone sandhi lowers the S to H after an X-toned possessor; H then serves as the input to plural formation, and the noun raises back to its original S.

The verbal cases of tonal affixation (§4.4.1.2-4.4.1.4) use the realis verb stem and hence do not undergo sandhi.

Finally, argument-head tone sandhi must apply before clitic elision, since it is the sandhi tones that are left on the surface. This will be discussed in depth in the next subsection.

4.4.3 Clitic elision (nascent tonal morphology)

The last case of grammatical tone to be discussed involves a process of segmental elision which appears to be a change in progress. In short, the segmental material of certain functional elements (including TAMP markers, some postpositions, and some verbal particles) can be elided; their tone is realized on the preceding vowel with concurrent compensatory lengthening. This elision is optional, and speakers vary in their rates of application, but consultant commentary suggests that it is becoming more common in younger generations. Different rates of elision in different grammatical contexts would make a fascinating topic of further study. With only tone (and length) left on the surface, clitic elision represents a case of nascent morphological tone marking tense, case and aspect. A similar trajectory has been followed in other Mande languages, such as Dan-Gwèètaa (Vydrine 2011, 2016).

All of the functional elements that elide are sonorant-initial (/l/ or /w/), which §3.3.3.1 showed to be rare word-initially in all but function words. Clitic elision may be related to this phonotactic restriction, going so far as to all but eliminate sonorants from the phoneme inventory.

The functional elements that undergo elision are listed below:

1. TAMP markers:
   (a) Past tense lɛ̋
   (b) Subjunctive lɛ́
   (c) Subordinate lɛ̏ or wɛ̏
2. Postpositions:
   (a) Associative wɛ̏
   (b) Dative lɛ̋
3. Habitual wɛ̏

The TAMP markers, all post-subject, do not undergo tone sandhi, and hence the resulting tone of the elided form is always whatever tone the marker carries; thus, the segmental minimal triplet of lɛ̋ PAST, lɛ́ SUBJUNCTIVE, and lɛ̏ SUBORDINATE is carried over to the elided forms. Let us first consider the past tense marker lɛ̋. The pairs of forms in (42) represent non-elided and elided variants:

(42) a. mî̋ lɛ̋ /mî̋ı̋   bî   bá̰
       1PL PST /1PL.PST goat hit.REAL.PFV
       'We hit a goat.' [sos150201e]

   b. mó   lɛ̋ /móő   blâ   ŋɛ́
      1SG.EMPH PST /1SG.PST fall.REAL.PFV NEG
      'I did not fall.' [sos130821e]

   c. mó   nȉ   lɛ̋ /nȉı̋   cȉe   jȉee
      1SG.EMPH father PST /father.PST die.REAL.PFV last.year
      'My father died last year.' [sos130821e]

The examples in (42) show the tonal effects of elision on preceding S, H, and X tones, and give examples of both pronominal (42a-b) and non-pronominal (42c) subjects. In every case, when lɛ̋ elides, it leaves behind its S tone and lengthens the preceding vowel. In doing so, it leaves tense to be fully realized on the subject.

The same behavior is seen with the H-toned subjunctive marker lɛ́, found after the subject in conditionals (Chapter 18) or complement clauses (Chapter 19). Examples of variation are shown in (43):

(43) a. í   ȁwǎ mî́ lɛ́ /mî́ı́   bî   sà̰
       2PL HORT 1PL SBJV /1PL.SBJV goat buy.IRR
       'Let's buy a goat!' [sos170803e]

   b. á   lɛ́ /áa   bî   sɔ́ɔ   nɛ́ á ȁ jú   ń   nɛ̏
      2SG SBJV /2SG.SBJV goat sell.REAL.PFV if 2SG 3SG say.IRR 2SG DAT
      'If you sell a goat, tell me. [sos170803e]

   c. ȁ   lɛ̋ /ȁa   sı̰̈ ȁ tê ȁ lɛ́ /ȁá   cɛ̏rɛ̏
      3SG PST /3SG.PST be 3SG GEN 3SG SBJV /3SG.SBJV sleep.IRR
      'He wanted to sleep.' [sos170728e]

When the subjunctive marker is elided, the only difference between these subjects and past tense subjects is tone. The same pattern holds for subordinate markers, but in the interest of space, I refer readers to §17.1, §19.3, and §20.2 for examples.

The elision of postpositions is more interesting in that argument-head tone sandhi takes place before the elision of the segmental material. This means that the resulting forms for any particular postposition are not uniform (i.e. they do not always contribute a S or a H, as the TAMP markers do). Table 4.10 compares the surface form of pronouns when the associative and dative are elided.

Tab. 4.10: Pronominal paradigms for elided postpositions

	Associative (wɛ̀)	Dative (lɛ́)
1SG	móő/móȅ	môo/môe
2SG	áǎ/á wéě	âa/á wêe
3SG	àa	ǎá/ɛ̀ɛ́
1PL	míî	míî
2PL	íǐ	îi
3PL	ìi	ǐi

The associative forms of pronouns incorporate the result of argument-head tone sandhi with the X-toned postposition wɛ̀, while the dative pronouns incorporate the result of sandhi with the S-toned postposition lɛ́. For summaries of sandhi alternations, see §4.4.2 above. In other words, the 1sg associative pronoun ends in S and the dative pronoun in X, despite the fact that underlyingly the tones of these two postpositions are reversed, because these are the sandhi variants of each postposition after H. Because sandhi forms depend on the preceding tone, pronouns resulting from elided postpositions do not end uniformly on the same tone, unlike pronouns resulting from elided TAMP markers. The table in (43) also shows segmental variants of some pronouns, where the elided postposition has left both its tone and a vocalic effect. Such vocalic effects are never seen with elided TAMP markers.

The pronouns resulting from elision show what looks to be the beginning of tonal case marking. If speakers ever cease to use the full form of the postposition, opting instead for purely tonal marking, it will leave an unusual pattern indeed, resistant to an account of tonal affixation. See §6.6 for further discussion of these oblique pronouns.

Dative pronouns, when used in possessive constructions, trigger argument-head tone sandhi, even though the head is an alienable noun. See §4.4.2.2 above and §8.6.2.3.

More examples of postposition elision can be found in §10.1.

4.5 Phonological tone rules

Given the high functional load of both lexical and grammatical tone in Seenku, there are very few phonological processes that affect the realization of these tones. The three processes discussed in this section are register assimilation (§4.5.1), downstep and downdrift (§4.5.2), and tonal absorption (§4.5.3). Downstep and tonal absorption form a conspiracy that simplifies rising tones in different environments.

4.5.1 Register assimilation

Table 4.2 above showed that Seenku's four tone levels are naturally categorized by two tone features, [upper] and [raised]. All lexical contour tones share at least one feature, and usually that feature is the register feature [raised]. LS is a [+raised] contour, while HX is a [-raised] contour. (HS, the remaining lexical contour, shares the feature [+upper].) For underlyingly LS vocabulary, we are unable to determine whether the more common X is underlying, which raises to L by assimilating to S's register feature, but a few derived cases show that register assimilation of this sort is an active process in Seenku. An autosegmental rule of register assimilation is given in (44):

(44)   Register assimilation

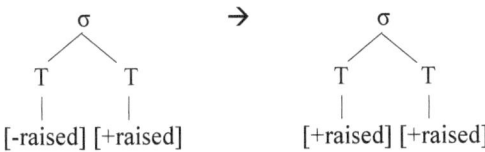

In other words, a [-raised] tone becomes [+raised] when followed by a [+raised] tone on the same syllable. It is indeterminate whether register assimilation happens as shown above, by simply changing the specification of the underlyingly [-raised] tone's register feature, or whether the [+raised] feature spreads backward. As this rule formulation shows, register assimilation is quite specific, only raising X to L **before** S in a regressive assimilation process. The falling contour SX, derived in perfect formation (§4.4.1.3), does not progressively become SL, nor does [-raised] of X trigger regressive assimilation of S to H. The fact that this process targets a rising tone may relate to the greater effort required to realize rising tones; see §4.1.2 for discussion. Finally, it should be noted that register assimilation does not automatically apply to HS contours, creating level S-toned syllables. There are cases where such a process seems to occur (with perfect formation and participial formation in §4.4.1.3 and §4.4.1.4), but HS contours also remain on the surface. It may be that regressive register assimilation is a general process, but lexical contours are exempted (a derived environment effect).

Alternations from register assimilation can be seen in four processes that result in S following an underlying X: nominal plural, perfect aspect, participial formation, and progressive aspect of transitive verbs.

Looking first at the nominal plural, when underlying /XH/ nouns (which surface as XHX in the singular due to final H avoidance, §4.3.2.1) are suffixed with [+raised], H raises to S. This leaves an XS contour tone, with X raising to L by register assimilation. The result is a LS contour tone in the plural. These steps are shown in (45) (though see Chapter 5 for a discussion of the segmental changes in the plural):

(45)   /dǎán [+raised]/ → dɛ̀ɛ̌ → [dɛ̌ɛ] 'basket hanger'

We know the [+raised] of the plural suffix is not directly responsible for the raising of X to L, since it is a suffix and only affects the final tone; see §4.4.1.1 for discussion.

In the perfect, verb stems are suffixed with -SX. When the verb stem is X, the resulting form is LSX, rather than XSX, due to register assimilation. The examples in (46) show X-toned verb stems and their perfect forms:

(46) kä̀   kàä   'go'
     nä̀   nàä   'come'
     dɔ̈̀ɔ dɔ̀ɔ̈   'finish'
     sä̀   sà̀ä   'buy'

For further discussion of the tonal affixation involved in perfect formation, see §4.4.1.3 above. For treatment of perfect as an aspectual category, see §13.3.2.2.

Participial formation is like perfect formation, except only -S is suffixed. X-toned stems raise to L with the suffixation of S; see §4.4.1.4 above for examples.

Progressive verbs are the most complex case, in that they show tonal absorption (§4.5.3) in addition to register assimilation. In fact, transitive and intransitive verbs differ in their tonal behavior in the progressive, and it is only the transitive verbs that demonstrate this register assimilation and will be discussed here. Their formation looks like that of participial verbs, suffixed with S, but since intransitive verbs take X instead (while participials are formed the same way regardless of transitivity), it is unclear whether we should treat them synchronically as the same process.

As in participial formation, the addition of S causes X-toned stems to raise to L, creating a LS contour tone. Since progressives (a nominalized verb form) are followed by the locative *né*, which undergoes the same tone sandhi as the postposition, the LS contour ends up immediately before an S-toned morpheme—the environment for tonal absorption. For formalization and examples, see §4.5.3 below.

4.5.2 Downstep and downdrift

Like many African languages, Seenku displays both downstep and downdrift. The tone literature is often inconsistent in the usage of these terms, so I define them explicitly below in a general way (i.e. not specific to Seenku):

(47) a. **Downstep:** The lowering of a high tone following another high tone, triggered by either a floating low or as a dissimilatory response.
e.g. HH → H!H, or H(L)H → H!H

b. **Downdrift:** The lowering of the second of two high tones with an intervening low tone.
e.g. HLH → HL!H

Since downstep and downdrift are at some level the same process, Stewart (1965) referred to them as non-automatic and automatic downstep, respectively. The term "downdrift" appears to have originated with Hombert (1974) and has been adopted by many researchers (including Snider and van der Hulst 1993, Hyman 2001), though it has also been used to describe the phonetic process of declination (see §4.6.1). I will be using all three terms in the description of Seenku. Downstep and downdrift, defined above, are both phonological processes, while declination is an automatic phonetic process.

In Seenku, only the highest tone S undergoes downstep and downdrift, but both of the lower two tones (X and L) are triggers. Additionally, the tone preceding the trigger can be either S or H. If viewed as a featural process, then, the environment for downstep and downdrift can be characterized as a sequence of [+upper][-upper][+upper, +raised]. However, unlike in some analyses of downstep (or upstep) in which the features themselves are responsible for the surface realization of the tones, through spreading or assimilation (such as Snider 1991), Seenku downstep and downdrift cannot be analyzed as feature changes. I will demonstrate this first for downdrift and then for downstep.

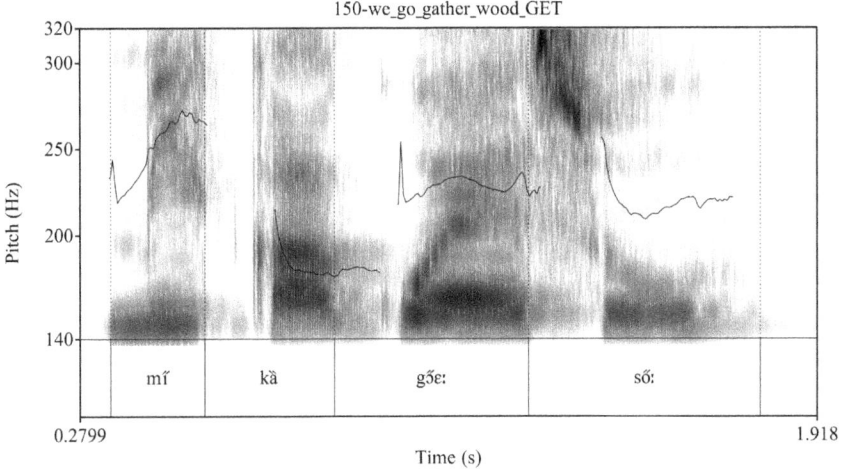

Fig. 4.7: Pitch track of 'We are off to gather wood'

4.5.2.1 Downdrift

In downdrift environments, the triggering [-upper] tone is present on the surface. Consider the following examples:

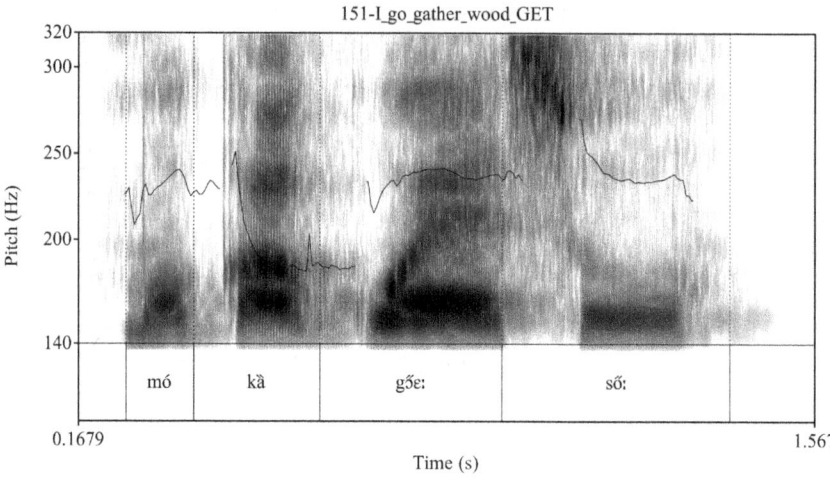

Fig. 4.8: Pitch track of 'I am off to gather wood'

(48) a. mǐ kà̰ !gɔ̋ɛɛ sőo
 1PL go.REAL.PFV wood.PL gather.IRR
 'We are off to gather wood.' [sos170825e]

b. mó kà̰ !gɔ̋ɛɛ sőo
 1SG.EMPH go.REAL.PFV wood.PL gather.IRR
 'I am off to gather wood.' [sos170825e]

In (48a), there is an average of 56Hz difference between the two S tones; this difference is enough to bring S down to the same level as the preceding H in (48b). Pitch tracks of the two utterances are given in Figures 4.7 and 4.8, respectively.

If we took downdrift to be a featural process, assimilation of S to H would involve a change from [+raised] to [-raised]. While we could view this as the result of X spreading its [-raised] feature to S, there are a couple of issues with this account. First, it predicts that S does in fact become H (by virtue of being [+upper, -raised]) and so a following H would be pronounced at the same level. As we will see shortly, this is not the case. Second, [-raised] could only spread from a tone specified as [-raised], i.e. X or H. Instead, both X and L are triggers of downdrift in Seenku, which form a natural class for [-upper] rather than [-raised]. The examples in (49) show that both X and L trigger downstep:

(49) a. mǐ sǐo bɛ̏ɛ !sɔ̋ɔ nɛ̋
 1PL REC.PST pig sell.REAL.NOM LOC
 'We just sold a pig.' [sos150201e]

b. mǐ sı́o bɛ̀ɛ !sɔ́ɔ nɛ̃̋
 1PL REC.PST pig.PL sell.REAL.NOM LOC
 'We just sold pigs.' [sos150201e]

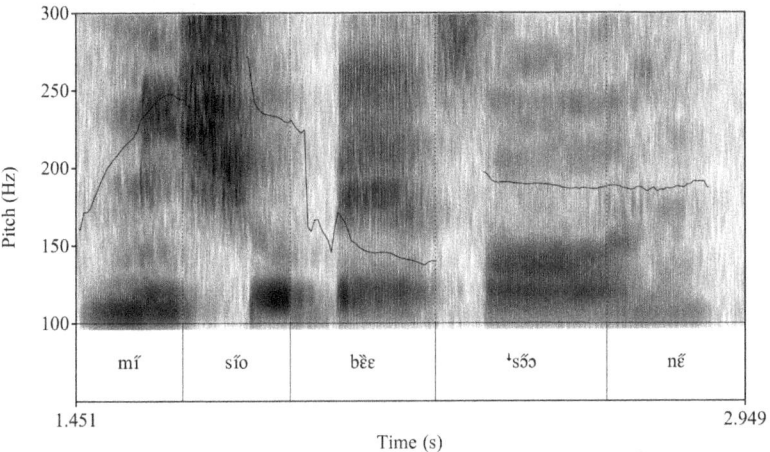

Fig. 4.9: Pitch track of 'We just sold a pig'

Curiously, the amount of downstep is greater following L (49b) than following X (49a): 56Hz (as above, despite being a different female speaker) vs. 44HZ, but even more curiously, X and L are realized the same; it is precisely the difference between the amount of downstep on the second S that encodes the plurality distinction; the interval between bɛ̀ɛ !sɔ́ɔ in (49a) is larger (about a major fourth in a Western musical scale) than the interval between bɛ̀ɛ !sɔ́ɔ in (49b). Pitch tracks of these two examples are given in Figures 4.9 and 4.10.

There are not enough repetitions of these examples to determine whether this is a consistent pattern in the realization of downdrift in Seenku. Regardless, the fact that both L and X trigger downdrift means that the lowering of S cannot be due to the spread of [-raised].

If we wished to defend the analysis that downstepped S is the featural equivalent of H, a very unnatural rule would be required: [+upper] → [-raised] / [-upper]___, or "A [+upper] tone becomes [-raised] after a [-upper] tone." The trigger [-upper] and the change [-raised] have virtually nothing to do with one other, except for both being related to lower pitch.

However, it is clear that downstepped S is **not** the equivalent of H, since a following H is pronounced lower (the same as any S-H sequence). The easiest way to illustrate this is to place the H-toned negative particle ŋɛ́ after a downdrift environment;

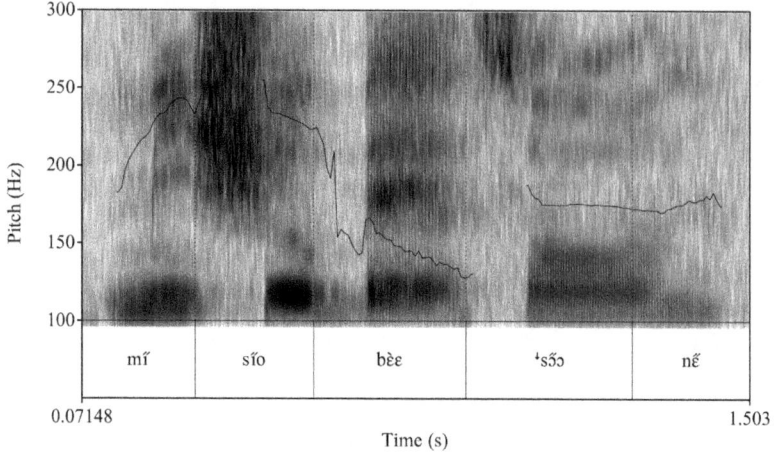

Fig. 4.10: Pitch track of 'We just sold pigs'

it is realized as lower. This can be seen in the following example, given in (50) along with its pitch track in Figure 4.11:

(50) à ɲá tâ !mɛ̰́ɛ̰ nḛ́ ŋé
 3SG be.NEG fire ignite.REAL.NOM LOC NEG
 'She is not lighting the fire.' [sos150807e]

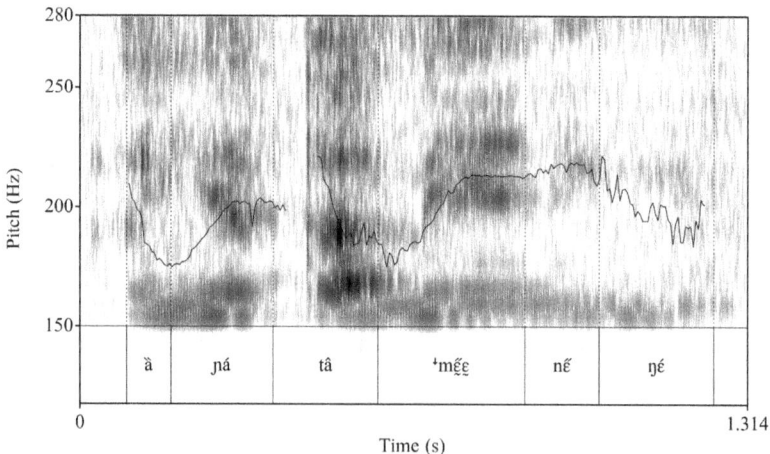

Fig. 4.11: Pitch track for 'she is not lighting the fire'

In summary, downdrift involves the lowering of S after the sequence of another [+upper] tone (H or S) followed by a [-upper] tone (X or L). While the amount of lowering brings it down to roughly the same level as a H tone, it is not a H tone representationally; as in most cases of downdrift and downstep, the S ceiling is simply lowered, pushing all other tones down with it.

4.5.2.2 Downstep

Downstep is the equivalent of downdrift, only the triggering [-upper] tone is not realized on the surface. The only configuration that yields floating [-upper] tones in Seenku is the simplification of LS rising tones.

In §4.1.2, I discussed the fact that rising tones have been shown to require greater effort, which leads them to be typologically dispreferred (Zhang 2004). While Seenku has a good deal of LS rising tones, both underlying and created by grammatical tone, they often simplify on the surface to either L through tonal absorption (see §4.5.3) or to !S, by delinking the L and leaving it floating. This latter simplification strategy is used when the LS rising tone is preceded by a [+upper] tone (except when followed by S, in which case tonal absorption occurs). Note that this is precisely the same configuration that triggers downdrift. The autosegmental rule of L delinking is given in (51):

(51) *L delinking in Seenku*

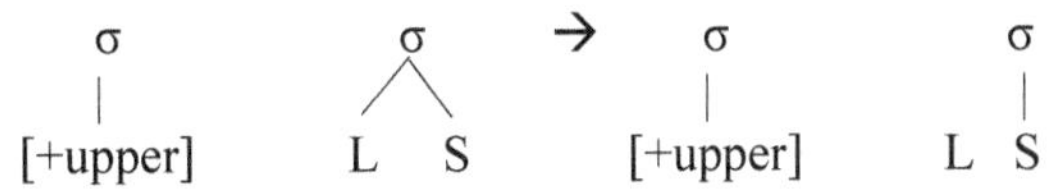

When LS is preceded by a [+upper] tone, L delinks and is left floating. This L causes the following S to downstep.

Downstep of this sort is especially common with the auxiliary verbs *sɪ̰̌* 'be' and the prospective *nǎ*. For instance:

(52) a. *ń !sɪ̰̋ jʊ̂ cɪ̰̋ɔ̰ nɛ̋*
1SG be water scoop.REAL.NOM LOC
'I am scooping up water.' [sos150812e]

b. *mɪ̋ !nǎ̋ fîɛ-kʊ̏ blȁ*
1PL PROSP baobab-plant fell.IRR
'We will fell a baobab tree.' [sos150706e]

In (52a), *sɪ̰̌* 'be' is preceded and followed by a H tone; L delinks, leaving the auxiliary realized as a downstepped S, which is still slightly higher than the preceding H tone. In (52b), the prospective *nǎ* is preceded by S and followed by H; once again, the rising tone simplifies, and the downstepped S is pronounced lower than the preceding S (but higher than the following H).

Interestingly, the application of L delinking and subsequent downstep is sensitive to vowel length, as predicted by Zhang (2004). Rising tones on long vowels are less likely to undergo simplification resulting in downstep, as shown in the following:

(53) sû sǐ í gɔ̌ɔ gùɔ-dəgèɛ
get.up.NOM be LOG difficult day-morning.LOC
'Getting up is hard in the morning.' [sos150317e]

Despite the fact that *gɔ̌ɔ* appears in a configuration that matches the environment for L delinking, the rising tone does not simplify since the vowel is long and there is ample time to realize the rise.

4.5.3 Tonal absorption

A related process to L delinking and downstep is tonal absorption. One of the original "universals of tone rules" from Hyman and Schuh (1974), tonal absorption refers to the process by which a contour tone followed by a tone identical to the endpoint of the contour simplifies to a level tone; it is as if the endpoint of the contour tone becomes absorbed into the following tone. In Seenku, tonal absorption only occurs with LS rising tones when they are followed by S. The rule is formalized in (54):

(54) Tonal absorption in Seenku
LS → L / ___ S

In other words, a LS rising tone simplifies to L when followed by another S tone.

In the last subsection, we saw how the auxiliary verbs *sǐ* 'be' and *nǎ* PROSPECTIVE simplify to downstepped S by delinking the L in many environments. When these auxiliary verbs are followed by S, then tonal absorption takes place rather than L delinking and downstep. Examples of each auxiliary verb undergoing tonal absorption are provided in (55):

(55) a. mó sì jəbě kpɔ̌ɔ ně
1SG.EMPH be clothes sew.REAL.NOM LOC
'I am sewing clothes.' [sos170717e]

b. ằ nà mí bǎ
3SG PROSP 1PL hit.IRR
'He will hit us.' [sos150811e]

In (55a), the S of *sǐ* is absorbed by the S-toned object *jəbě* 'clothes', while the same happens to the S of *nǎ* in (55b), triggered by the following S-toned pronoun *mí*. Further, in (55a), the rising tone on the nominalized progressive *kpɔ̌ɔ* is absorbed into the locative postposition, realized here as ně due to sandhi; further examples of this opaque interaction are given below.

Tonal absorption applies to all rising tones in this configuration, regardless of whether they are function or content words, and regardless of vowel length. The sentence in (56a) shows tonal absorption applying to the quantifier bagǔ 'numerous' before the S-toned past tense marker lě (and another example of sǐ, this time undergoing tonal absorption before the adverb lɔ́ 'here'). In (56b), the adjective gɔ̌ɔ 'dry' undergoes tonal absorption, but in this case the environment for tonal absorption was created by tone sandhi with the following associative postposition wɛ̀ (§4.4.2).

(56) a. kərê ɲámálɔ́ɛ bəgù   lě   sḭ̀   lɔ́
          man wise.PL numerous PST be here
          'Wise men were numerous here.' [sos170728e]

      b. jəbě   bě   !sḭ̌ í   gɔ̀ɔ wě
          clothes DEM.PL be LOG dry with
          'These clothes are dry.' [sos150630e]

The example in (56b) shows that argument-head tone sandhi must occur before tonal absorption, which is to be expected if the former is a grammatical process and the latter a postlexical phonological one.

This same combination of tone sandhi and tonal absorption is responsible for X-toned transitive verbs raising to L in the progressive. In forming the progressive, S is suffixed to transitive verb stems and X to intransitive ones. The suffixation of the S triggers register assimilation in X-toned verbs, as discussed in §4.5.1. The verbal particle né, derived from the locative postposition, follows the verb stem in the progressive and undergoes tone sandhi with either the final S or X. In the case of transitive verbs, this means né raises to S-toned ně. This creates the environment for tonal absorption: a LS-toned verb stem is followed by a S-toned postposition, and in response, the rising tone on the verb simplifies to L:

(57) /sǎ̰ -S né/   Underlying form
      sǎ̰ né   Register assimilation (§4.5.1)
      sǎ̰ ně   Argument-head-tone sandhi (§4.4.2)
      sà̰ ně   Tonal absorption (current section)

This surface form is opaque in the sense that the trigger for tone sandhi that leaves né as S-toned is no longer present on the surface.

Note, finally, that neither tonal absorption nor L delinking and downstep occur in the balafon surrogate language. That is, grammatical tone processes are encoded in musical adaptation but purely phonological ones are not, pointing once again to a concrete distinction between the two in speakers' metalinguistic awareness. For further discussion of musical adaptation of Seenku, see Chapter 22.

4.6 Phonetic realization of tone

This section addresses some phonetic aspects of tonal realization. I first address whether we can discern any specific declination effects in Seenku, before discussing a preliminary study of voice quality (phonation) and its relation to tone.

4.6.1 Declination

Declination is a phonetic rather than phonological effect and refers to "a gradual modification (over the course of a phrase or utterance) of the phonetic backdrop against which the phonologically specified F0 targets are scaled" (Connell and Ladd 1990: 2). It is thought to be due to physiological reasons and is not specific to tone languages; in fact, much of the discussion of declination has dealt with European intonation languages (Connell 2001).

It is difficult to differentiate declination from downdrift in Seenku, since most Seenku phrases contain jumps from [-upper] to [+upper] tones and back again. However, S is the only tone to undergo extreme f0 lowering after a [-upper] tone, suggesting that the lesser reductions on other tones may be the result of declination.

Consider the following example, consisting of only H and X tones:

(58) mó   ɲǎ̀   mó   dȍn təgɔ̏n bǎ̀
      1SG.EMPH mother 1SG.EMPH child name give.REAL.PFV
      'My mother named my child.' [sos150618e]

The initial H-X-H sequence could be viewed as a downdrift environment, but the difference between the two H tones is only 10Hz–considerably smaller than the 56Hz drop seen between S tones. Across the utterance, even the X tones descend, which points to declination rather than downdrift. The pitch track in Figure 4.12, augmented with tone labeling and declination parameters, illustrates both the overall lowering and the overall narrowing of the phonetic backdrop characteristic of declination.

The true test of declination will be phrases uttered entirely on the same tone. If these show gradual lowering, then we can be sure that declination is at play. Future data collection will need to target these phrases.

4.6.2 Voice quality

In a language with so many tone contrasts, it is natural to ask whether the differences between categories are enhanced with measures other than pitch (fundamental frequency, f0). A common parameter associated with tone cross-linguistically is **voice quality**, or phonation. Voice quality refers to the state of the vocal folds (the glottis) when vibrating, producing voiced sounds. When the vocal folds are in their natural

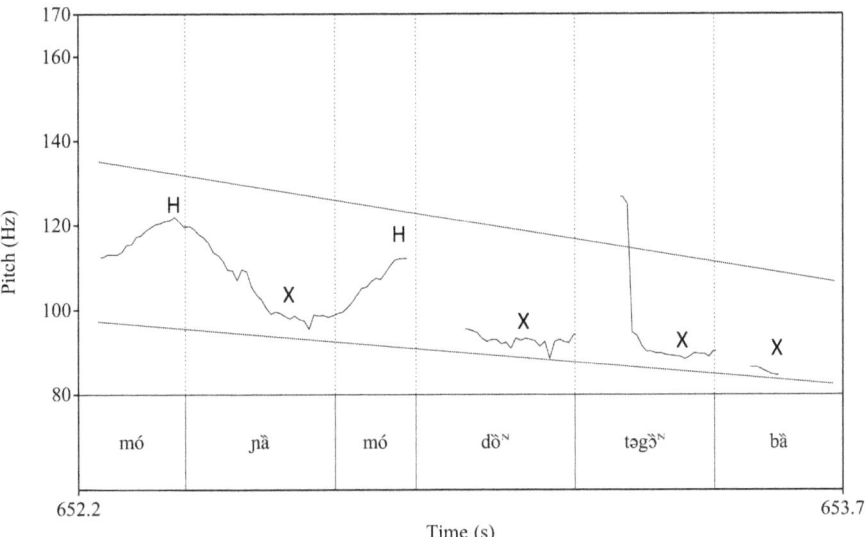

Fig. 4.12: Declination in Seenku

state for maximum vibration (that is, neither too tense nor too slack), this is referred to as **modal voice**, and it is the usual unmarked voice quality in most languages. If the vocal folds are pressed together more tightly during phonation, **creaky voice** results. If the vocal folds are held further apart, allowing more air to pass through them, then **breathy voice** results.

Voice quality itself can be a phonemic contrast on vowels, in both non-tonal languages (e.g. Burmese) and tonal languages (e.g. Zapotec). That is, it can be a parameter independent of f0 that can be used to distinguish meaning. This is not the case for Seenku; Seenku has no phonemic voice quality.

However, preliminary study of voice quality in Seenku shows that certain tones correlate with non-modal phonation. Two speakers (MD, male, and GFT, female) read through an elicitation list with 7 words from each level tone (X, L, H, S), plus 5 cases of HX and 2 cases of XHX. The list was repeated three times, embedding each word in the frame sentence ǎa _____ sạ̀ 'he bought _____'. The resulting acoustic data were processed with VoiceSauce (Shue 2010, Shue et al. 2011), a voice analysis program measuring a number of parameters associated with voice quality in different languages.

The acoustic measure that showed the most difference is H1-H2, calculated by measuring the difference in the peaks of the first (H1) and second (H2) harmonics. This paints a picture of **spectral tilt**, or how rapidly the energy decays across the harmonics. Breathy voice has been associated with steep spectral tilt (high H1-H2), creaky voice with low spectral tilt (low H1-H2); modal voice is in the middle.

For both speakers, X was significantly different from the other tones, but curiously, the male and female speakers differed in their voice quality. For the male speaker MD, X was associated with the lowest H1-H2 value, indicative of creaky phonation. This is unsurprising, considering creaky voice is often found on lower pitches (and at the ends of phrases), even in languages like English. XHX showed even lower H1-H2. Recall from §4.1.2 that XHX contours have a relatively flat pitch track, never reaching their H target, so it may be that voice quality helps distinguish them from either X or L. For the female speaker GFT, X was also significantly different from the other tones, but with the highest H1-H2 value. This suggests that for the female speaker, X is breathy rather than creaky. XHX does not differ significantly from the other tones.

These results are preliminary, but they are suggestive that contrasts, particularly among the lower tones where f0 contrasts are muddied by the flat nature of XHX contrasts, may be enhanced by voice quality. Then again, creakiness or breathiness may be automatic on these lower pitches and not significant enough for speakers to use it as a categorial cue, and as the normalized tone traces showed earlier in this chapter, f0 is significantly different for each of the tone categories. Future work should include more participants to test whether the gender differences seen here are systematic or idiosyncrasies of these two particular speakers.

4.7 Tone and intonation

The final topic to be addressed in this chapter is the relationship between Seenku's complex tone system and intonation. Given the high functional load of tone, intonation has a drastically reduced role in the language compared to European languages (e.g. it plays no role in focus), but we still find intonation involved in polar questions (§4.7.1) and in marking non-final clauses (continuation rise, §4.7.2).

4.7.1 Falling question intonation

Rialland (2009) has shown that many African languages use falling question intonation rather than the typologically more common rising question intonation. Seenku is no exception. Only found in polar (yes-no) interrogatives, falling question intonation affects the final syllable of the phrase, causing it to lengthen and fall. This will be indicated in transcriptions as ↘, glossed with Q.

If the final syllable ends in a tone other than X, the fall is particularly audible.

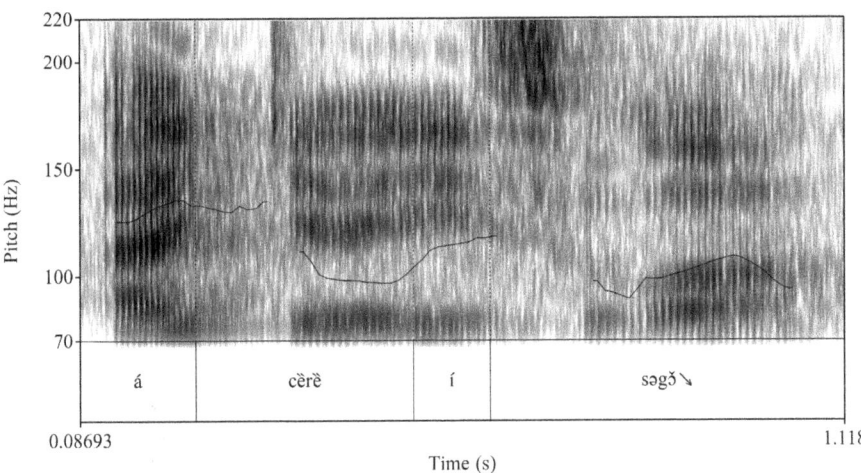

Fig. 4.13: Pitch track of 'Did you sleep well?'

(59) a. Fàatű á wó sḭ̀ à̰ tê á fä́ mó wɛ̋↘
Fatou 2SG EMPH be 3SG GEN 2SG fight 1SG.EMPH with.Q
'Fatou, you want to fight me?' [sos161008t1:100]

b. í sïo ɲəgâan-cɛ̀n gərṵ́a̰ nɛ̋↘
2PL REC.PST guinea.fowl-egg fry.REAL.NOM LOC.Q
'Have you cooked guinea fowl eggs?' [sos161008t1:227]

c. á cɛ̈rɛ̈ í səgɔ́↘
2SG sleep.REAL.PFV LOG good.Q
'Did you sleep well?' [sos150622e]

Each of these examples is realized on the surface as a fall from S down to X. A pitch track of (59c) is shown in Figure 4.13 for illustration.

When the final tone is already X, lengthening becomes the primary indication of the question, which allows more time for the X-tone to sag. An example of this lengthening effect is illustrated in (60), first glossed, then presented as a pitch track in Figure 4.14:

(60) á sḭ̀ cɛ̈rɛ̈ nɛ̏↘
2SG be sleep.REAL.NOM LOC.Q
'Are you sleeping?' [sos150622e]

Both Figures 4.13 and 4.14 end in a short vowel, but the lengthening in the latter is considerably greater. The final vowel of *səgɔ́*↘ lengthens to just shy of 300ms, while *nɛ̏* lengthens to 385ms—despite the fact that the former carries a complex contour tone!

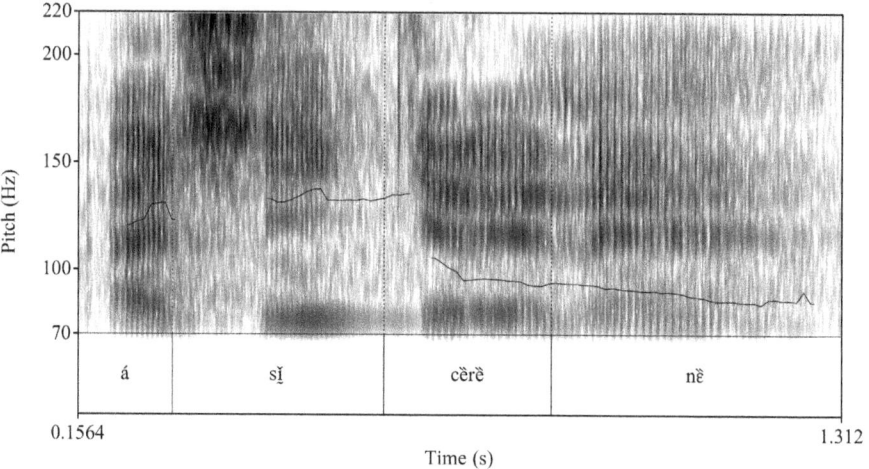

Fig. 4.14: Pitch track of 'Are you sleeping?'

For further discussion of falling question intonation, including negative yes-no questions, see §16.1.

4.7.2 Continuation rise

As in many intonation-only languages, Seenku marks the end of non-final clauses and phrases with a rising intonation to indicate that the speaker has not finished. In tonal terms, this continuation rise is realized as the tonal target of the syllable rising towards S.

A clear example is illustrated in (61), a snippet of two sentences from a text where the same clause is repeated twice in a row. In the first sentence, it is utterance-final. In the second, it is non-final, followed by another clause, and the end is marked with the continuation rise (transcribed here with ↗). I first give the glossed example in (61), with the corresponding pitch track in Figure 4.15.

(61) ...í ǎ kərá nȅ-jəràn-jəràn.   í ǎ kərá nȅ-jəràn-jəràn↗
 2PL 3SG tail TRANS-RED-change.IRR 2PL 3SG tail TRANS-RED-change.IRR
 '...you swing it around by the tail. You swing it around by the tail...' [sos170714t3: 7-8]

The final X of the reduplicated verb is clear in utterance-final position, but when it is marked as continuing, it rises sharply to S.

This intonation contour will not be explicitly marked in examples or transcribed texts, but it is clearly audible when listening to Seenku speech.

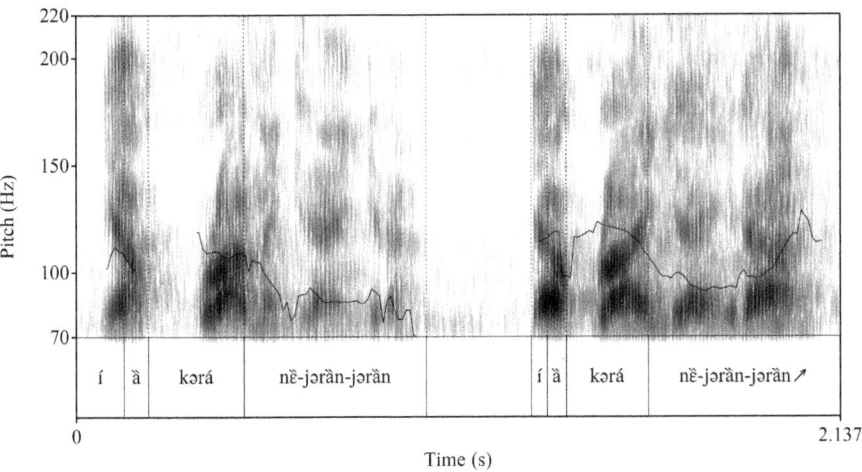

Fig. 4.15: Pitch track of continuation rise

5 Nominal morphology

In this chapter, I address the shape and construction of nouns in Seenku. The following morphosyntactic criteria separate nouns from other syntactic categories like pronouns or adjectives:
1. The ability to take a possessor (alienable or inalienable; §8.6)
2. The ability to take determiners (definite, indefinite, demonstrative; §8.2)

Their number inflection (§5.3.1) is shared by other categories, like quantifiers, and their ability to stand alone to fill an argument position is shared by pronouns (§6.1). For criteria differentiating nouns from adjectives, see §8.3 and McPherson (2017a).

In this chapter, I begin with a discussion of nominal roots and stems (§5.1), then turn to morphologically complex nouns, including nominal derivation (§5.2) and inflection (§5.3). Due to their complexity, I treat compound nouns separately in the next chapter. For treatment of pronouns, see Chapter 6, which focuses specifically on pronouns and anaphora.

Note that this chapter only addresses nouns in isolation; noun phrase structure, including modifiers, quantifiers, and possession, will be treated in-depth in Chapter 8.

By and large, Seenku does not display much nominal morphology, especially inflectional morphology. There is no morphological case marking[1] and no true diminutives or augmentatives besides compounding with 'child'. However, we find productive number marking for inflection, and derivational processes (both tonal and segmental) deriving nouns from other syntactic categories.

5.1 Noun stems

Before turning to morphologically complex nouns, let us first discuss nominal stems. I use the term "noun stems" in this section to designate both nominal roots (§5.1.1) and cases of borderline morphological complexity, which include reduplicated noun stems (§5.1.2) and an irregular class of nouns ending in -nɛ, which carries no meaning but acts like a suffix (§5.1.3).

5.1.1 Simple noun stems

Simple noun stems, by which I mean morphologically simplex nominal roots, can be any of the word shapes described in §3.4. Like most of the Seenku lexicon, the majority

---

[1] For possible incipient case marking on pronouns, see §4.4.3 and §6.6.

of nominal roots are mono- and sesquisyllabic, with Jula and French loans making up the bulk of longer roots.

While there is nothing unusual about nouns in terms of their syllable structure or segmental make-up, we do find noun-specific tonology. As mentioned in §4.3.2.1, (singular) nouns see a tonotactic restriction against H in final position. The result of this restriction is a gap in level H-toned nouns, filled instead with a large number of HX contour-toned nouns, as shown in Table 5.1.

Tab. 5.1: Most common nominal tone melodies

X		H(X)		S	
bɛ̀ɛ	'pig'	bî	'goat'	bű	'sand'
sə̀gà̂	'sheep'	tagê	'chicken'	manī́	'woman'
mà̂an	'rice'	kân	'granary'	wɛ́n	'money'

As this table shows, tone patterns cross-cut syllable shapes, with X-, HX-, and S-toned nouns found with both open and closed, mono- and sesquisyllabic roots. Notice here in (0) that where we expect to see *bí or *tagé, we find instead falling contours. I will provide evidence in §5.3 that these are in fact /H/ underlyingly.

There is also a lack of L-toned open class noun roots, presumably due to the evolutionary path of the tone system by which L was last to be added; see §4.1.1.2. However, this is the most common tone pattern for Seenku's closed class of birth order names.

5.1.1.1 Birth order names

Birth order names are a core part of naming in Sambla culture, and also neighboring ethnicities including the Toussian (whose birth order names share commonalities suggestive of borrowing; Strand 2009).[2] The first part of a traditional Sambla name is a proper noun indicating both the sex of the person and their birth order with respect to sex (first girl, first boy, second girl, etc.); though monogamy is becoming more common, Sambla men could have multiple wives, so birth order names are tied to the woman's children, not the man's. The Sambla birth order names are given in Table 5.2.

The most distinctive morphophonological feature of these names is the prevalence of L, otherwise virtually non-existent in regular nouns. In fact, all birth order nouns are either L- and LS-toned, and it is the presence of the latter that hints at the origins of the former. As discussed in §4.5.1, L can be derived from X by register assimilation in rising tones, even in the synchronic grammar (see e.g. the transitive progressive, §4.5.3). If all of these birth order names were historically rising tones, the present

---

[2] Birth order onomastics is attested more broadly in Africa, including among the Kamuə of Nigeria (Jauro et al. 2013).

Tab. 5.2: Sambla birth order names

	Male	Female
1st	Sî	Jɛ̀
2nd	Sà	Gà
3rd	Gùɔ	ɲì
4th	Fìɛ	Fɛ̰̀
5th	Tagɔ̃	Sərè
6th	Pĕnagɛ̀	ɲəmă
7th	Cŭen	Pà

day L tone can be explained if many of them underwent contour tone simplification. In fact, I have heard these names played in the balafon surrogate language (§22.2.1) with rising tones, despite the fact that they are never pronounced that way, not even in isolation, suggesting artistic crystallization of what are very commonly played Seenku words, offering a glimpse into their past.

5.1.2 Reduplicated noun stems

We find a small class of noun stems created by reduplication. I do not discuss this as a derivational or inflectional process, since it is unproductive and there are no clear semantic underpinnings of the reduplication. Reduplication is almost universally full reduplication in Seenku, with the exception of initial CV reduplication in plural adjectives (§8.3.3.2). Reduplicated nouns are exceptionlessly fully reduplicated.

Unsurprisingly, the proportion of reduplicated nouns goes up substantially in flora-fauna names, especially insects. In many languages, these semantic classes have a tendency to show non-canonical morphophonological form, with more reduplication, sound symbolism, or other phonological patterns reminiscent of ideophones (Berlin 1992, Haynie et al. 2014, etc.). Examples of Seenku reduplicated flora-fauna names are shown in (1):

(1)   a. *fɔ̃-fɔ̃*   'Commelina sp. (small plant)'
       b. *kúɔ-kûɔ*   'small termite-eating ant'
       c. *dəmí-dəmǐ*   'stingless bee sp.'
       d. *fṵ́ɔ-fṵ́ɔ*   'small biting bee'
       e. *pərŭn-pərŭn*   'hedgehog'
       f. *dzɛ̰́-dzɛ̰́*   'tawny-flanked prinia (bird)'

All of these reduplicated nouns follow the same tone patterns that are licensed in compounding; see Chapter 7. Reduplicated noun stems may themselves form part of larger compounds, as in:

(2) a. sǎnɛ̀-kərɛ̀-kərɛ̋   'whirlygig beetle' (cf. sǎnɛ̀ 'river')
    b. gɔ́ɔ-nɛ̀-bṵ̀ɔ-bṵ̀ɔ   'powderpost beetle' (cf. gɔ́ɔ nɛ̀ 'in wood')
    c. sà-dərée-ɲənǎ-ɲənǎ 'gecko' (cf. sà dərée 'I desire Sa!'; exclamation)

Reduplicated nouns are not confined to flora-fauna vocabulary. We find reduplicated noun stems among both regular alienable nouns and even inalienable/relational nouns. Examples of the former include:

(3) a. jén-jěn   'story'
    b. jé-jě̋   'shed'
    c. ɲîɛ-ɲîɛ   'metal rattles worn on hands by balafonists'
    d. kó-kô   'rooster'
    e. ŋənɛ́-ŋənɛ̋   'whirlwind'

Like the flora-fauna examples, tone patterns of reduplicated words adhere to compounding tone patterns. Notice also that every syllable shape can be reduplicated, regardless of complexity.

The attested reduplicated inalienable nouns are listed in (4):

(4) a. ǎ kú-kú   'his body'
    b. ǎ cì-cì   'its chaff (millet)'
    c. ǎ dö̀-dó   'its thigh'

The tone sandhi behavior of these reduplicated nouns varies, from acting like a regular monomorphemic noun (4a-b) to being invariant (4c). For more discussion of tone sandhi, see §4.4.2.

5.1.3 Nouns ending in -nɛ

There are a number of disyllabic noun stems that end in -nɛ. Already, disyllabic nouns are rare, raising the question of whether these nouns should be considered morphologically complex. But further, their behavior in plural formation also suggests that -nɛ is not part of the root.

The nouns in question are shown in (5) in both the singular (left) and the plural (right):

(5) a. kǎnɛ̀   kènɛ̀   'bird(s)'
    b. jǎnɛ̋   jɛ̌nɛ̋   'corn(s)'
    c. jánɛ̀   —   'evening'
    d. sənǎanɛ̋   sənɛ́ɛnɛ̋ 'star(s)'
    e. sánɛ̀   sɛ̋nɛ̋   'well(s)'

In each case, the vowel of the initial syllable is targeted by plural vowel fronting (§5.3.1.2), or perhaps both the vowel of the root and the vowel of -nɛ are but vacuously so. However, as I will show in §5.3 below, there are some other disyllabic noun roots that do not end in -nɛ but likewise show vowel raising on both vowels.

Clearer evidence that -nɛ may be a crystalized suffix comes from related words that appear to use the noun root rather than the form with -nɛ. For instance, *kæ̀nɛ̈* refers to a bird, while *kæ̀n-kù* refers to a swarm of birds. Similarly, *jæ̌nɛ̋* refers to corn in a general sense, while *jæ̌n-dɛ̋n* refers specifically to corn kernels or grains.

Nevertheless, it is unclear what -nɛ means, if anything, and it is not productive. Hence, I include it in transcriptions as part of the noun stem.

5.2 Nominal derivation

In this section, I consider processes that derive nouns through morphological processes other than compounding (here, affixation and tone changes). This is sometimes a difficult line to draw—when is a morpheme an affix versus its own root in a compound? When in doubt, I consider the process to be affixation.

Nominal derivation in Seenku takes adjectives and verbs and derives nouns. While in principle it is possible to derive nouns from other nouns (denominal derivation), this is achieved exclusively through compounding in the language and will be addressed in Chapter 7.

5.2.1 Deadjectival derivation

Abstract nouns denoting the property of an adjective can be derived by suffixing -*bé* to the adjectival stem. Tonally, we find two different patterns, depending on how the derived noun will be used. If the derived noun will stand on its own denoting an abstract concept, then the adjectival stem takes H tone and the suffix takes HX tone; in other words, the whole abstract noun has a HX tone pattern characteristic of nominal tonology (§4.3.2.1):

(6) a. *bɔ̌ɛɛ* 'crazy' *bɔ́ɛɛ-bê* 'craziness'
    b. *sǐɛ* 'mean' *sɛ́-bê* 'meanness'

These nouns are found in examples like the following, from both elicitation and texts:

(7) a. *bɔ́ɛɛ-bê sɔ̋ ŋɛ́*
    crazy-NOM be.good.IRR NEG
    'Craziness isn't good.' [sos190803e]

b. sé-bê cəbáà-dərò wè ằ ɲá̰ í səgɔ̌ ŋɛ́
mean-NOM orphan-child with 3SG be.NEG LOG good NEG
'Meanness towards an orphan is not good.' [sos130828t1:5]

In both cases, the speaker is making a value judgment about a general quality, unrelated to any person or thing who may have that quality.

In most cases, though, the deadjectival noun refers to a property of someone. In this case, it is inalienably possessed (§8.6.1), and the tonology changes. The suffix is level H-toned, and the tone on the stem depends on the adjective: X tone for LS-toned adjectives and H tone for S-toned adjectives. Examples of possessed deadjectival nouns are shown in (8):

(8) a. bəlě   'big'   bəlȅ-bɛ́   'largeness, fatness'
    b. bɔ̌ɔ   'tall'   bɔ̏ɔ-bɛ́   'height'
    c. jǔ   'long'   jȕ-bɛ́   'length'
    d. sǐɛ   'bitter'   sɛ̏-bɛ́   'bitterness'
    e. tsǐe   'black'   tsȉi-bɛ́   'blackness'

In (8d-e), we also see segmental changes in the root, where the adjectival stem on its own carries a diphthong which is monophthongized in the derived noun; these changes are reminiscent of realis/irrealis verb stems, discussed further in §13.1. Recall that vowel length distinctions are neutralized with LS rising tones, but the difference between 'bitter' and 'black' appears to reemerge in the derived noun. Finally, the same stem sǐɛ means both 'mean' and 'bitter'; when nominalizing the concept 'mean', it becomes a stand-alone abstract noun with HX tone; as the bitter property of something here, it is a possessed deadjectival noun, with X-H tone.

The following examples illustrate how property nouns are possessed:

(9) a. ì   ằ   bɔ̏ɔ-bɛ́, ì   ké   bȍ-kɔ̌ɔ
       COMP 3SG tall-NOM COMP COP billygoat
       'From his height, [it looked like] it was a billygoat.' [sos161009t1:204]

   b. fərṵ̂ mó   bəlȅ-bɛ́ nɔ̀ wè
      bean 1SG.EMPH   big-NOM eat.IRR HAB
      'Beans make me fat.' [sos170719e]

The person or thing whose quality the deadjectival noun encapsulates is encoded as a possessor. The 'eat' construction is illustrated in (9b), where the idiomatic expression 'eat (somebody's) adjective-ness' means to essentially become the quality of that adjective.

This deadjectival derivation pattern appears to be totally productive; consultants easily produced deadjectival nouns from every adjective I offered, regardless of any tonal or other morphosyntactic irregularities of the adjectival stem (e.g. pètè 'flat' → pȅté-bɛ́ 'flatness', mɔ̌ɛ̰n 'small' → mɔ̰̏ɛ-bɛ́ 'smallness').

5.2.2 Deverbal derivation

We find three kinds of deverbal derivation. The first looks just like deadjectival derivation, raising the possibility that the roots used in deadjectival derivation are in fact verbal. The second deverbal derivation pattern is purely tonal, involving no affixation or other segmental changes.

5.2.2.1 Abstract deverbal nouns derived with -bɛ́

In a few sporadic cases, we find the same suffix -bɛ́ on verbs that we saw on adjectives, though this does not appear to be a productive pattern. For example:

(10) mó   nǎ   à   nɔ́   bűrű tɛ̋ ŋé, mó   sɔ́ɔ̀
      1SG.EMPH PROSP 3SG eat.IRR bread GEN NEG 1SG.EMPH be.able
      móo   à   dɔ̀nəgɛ̀ dɔ́nəgé-bé lɛ̀
      1SG.EMPH.SUBORD 3SG taste.IRR taste-NOM DAT
      'I won't eat it with bread, I'll taste it for tasting's sake.' [sos161009t1:230]

In this example, the verb dɔ̀nəgɛ̀ 'taste' (variant pronunciation dzɛ̀nəgɛ̀) is used first as a verb, followed by a deverbal noun in a postpositional phrase lending the idiomatic sense of tasting for the sake of tasting. The tone of the verb in this case has been raised to H in the deverbal noun.

We also see -bɛ́ suffixation in one noun-verb compound: jì-kɛ́ɛ-bê 'fetish worshiping', where jì is the noun stem for 'fetish' (in the sense of traditional religion) and kɛ́ɛ is a verb stem meaning 'worship' or 'follow'. For more on noun-verb compounds, see §7.4.

5.2.2.2 Manner deverbal nouns derived with -cíɛ

Manner nominals ('how to do', 'how to sing') can be derived from verbs in Seenku using the suffix -cíɛ. There is some variation in the segmental make-up of this suffix, ranging from -cíɛ to -cé or even to -tsɛ̋. This latter variant is reminiscent of the manner adverb tsɛ̋ 'how', which could suggest a common origin, but synchronically 'how' is never pronounced with the oral vowel always found in manner nominals.

This derivational process appears to be productive; consultants were able to produce manner nominals from whatever verb I offered.

In most examples in the corpus, the suffix -cíɛ (and its variants) takes the irrealis form of a verb as its base; this verb can see its stem vowel lengthened in a manner suggestive of the antipassive (§12.3) (11a-c), or it can have a short vowel.

(11) a. bậa̰   nɛ̀ɛ-cíɛ   sɛ́ɛ-ŋɛ̀   tè
          balafon come.ANTIP-manner Sambla-HUM.PL GEN
          'How the balafon came to the Sambla.' [sos170711t1:3]

b. gbɛ̋nɛ̋ mɔ̰̀ɔ̰ kű lɛ̋ bɛ̋ wɛ̋ tsɛ̋-ké dɔ̀ⁿ ì
   before person.PST thing REL.PL do.IRR HAB and today 3PL
   bɛ̀ɛ-cíɛ
   do.ANTIP-manner
   'What people did before and how they are done now.' [sos170702t1:43]

c. Bon, bǎrǎ bɛ̀ɛ-cíɛ   pó-pó nɛ̀-jərán-jərǎn   sḭ̀
   well.FR work do.ANTIP-manner RED-all TRANS-RED-change.PTCP be
   'Well, the way we do work, it has all completely changed.' [sos170702t1:50]

d. kʊ́ ȁ dəgéɛ-cíɛ   gɔ́ɔ lé wɛ̋
   D.DEF 3SG make.ANTIP-manner wood REL with
   'How it is made, with which wood.' [sos170711t1:50-51]

e. mó   nəgȉ bűɔ   sḭ̀ ȁ təméɛ-cíɛ   lɛ̏ quoi
   1SG.EMPH mind go.out.PTCP be 3SG tell.IRR-manner DAT what.FR
   'I've forgotten how to tell it.' [sos161009t1:145]

In one example, the realis form is used instead:

(12) bâ̰ɑ̰   lɛ̏   nằ-cé   tsɔ́ lé nɛ̀
     balafon SUBORD come.REAL-manner type REL LOC
     'The way the balafon arrived.' [sos171009t1:25]

However, attempts to elicit manner nouns with other realis verb forms were unsuccessful. For instance, in asking how to say 'the way he ate' with a perfective verb, a headless relative clause with the wh-word *tsɛ̋* 'how' was offered instead (see §17.6). The suffix *-cíɛ* appears to only be productively used with irrealis verbs.

Looking at the previous examples, we can see that the suffix *-cíɛ*, while attaching to a verb stem, nominalizes a whole clause; other arguments may be present, such as the subject *bâ̰ɑ̰* 'balafon' in (12), marked with the subordinate TAMP marker *lɛ̏*, or the object *bǎrǎ* in (11c) above. The clauses are clearly nominalized, though, since they can act as the complement to a postposition, as in (11e) above with the dative postposition.

5.2.2.3 Actional nominals derived tonally

Verbs can be nominalized without any affixation. Typically, the resulting noun is an action nominal, a pure nominalization of the action described by the noun. There can be tonal changes that occur in nominalization, typically to make the resulting noun fit nominal tonotactics.

Transitive verbs retain their objects when nominalized. The verb stem takes the same form that it does in the progressive, namely it is the realis stem ending in S-tone (LS rise in the case of X-toned verbs and neutralization of H and S to S; see also §4.4.1.4). There is no argument-head tone sandhi:

(13) a. cî   ɲɛ́   gɔ̌ɔ
house build.REAL.NOM be.difficult
'Building a house is difficult.' [sos150317e]

b. jǎnɛ́ kɔ̌gɔ́ ŋmǎ   dzɛ́   môe
corn sturdy eat.REAL.NOM be.delicious 1SG.EMPH.DAT
'I like eating sturdy corn.' [sos170728e]

c. kʊ̌ ɲɪ́ɔ   ɲìä   lɔ́
toh eat.REAL.NOM finish.REAL.PRF here
'Eating toh is finished here.' [sos170728e]

d. jǎn-dɛ́n sərě   ɲìä   lɔ́
corn-grain pound.REAL.NOM finish.REAL.PRF here
'Pounding corn is finished here.' [sos170728e]

Intransitive verbs likewise surface in their progressive forms. For most intransitive verbs, this means ending in X, though irregular S- or HS-toned intransitive verbs retain this tone pattern:

(14) a. sû   sɪ̰̌ í gɔ̌ɔ   ń mɛ́ gùɔ-dəgèɛ
get.up.NOM be LOG difficult 1SG with morning.ADV
'It is difficult for me to get up in the morning.' [sos150317e]

b. kùaa   dzɛ́   ń nɛ̀
farm.ANTIP.REAL.NOM be.good 1SG DAT
'I like farming.' [sos150317e]

c. səmâ   ɲìäa   lɔ́
dance.REAL.NOM finish.REAL.PRF here
'Dancing is finished here.' [sos170728e]

d. ŋáɛ́   dzɛ́   ń nɛ̀ ŋɛ́
yawn.REAL.NOM be.good 1SG DAT NEG
'I don't like yawning.' [sos190803e]

e. sɛ́   dzɛ́   kɛ̀nɛ̀ lɛ̀
fly.REAL.NOM be.good bird.PL DAT
'Birds like flying.' [sos190803e]

Examples (14a-c) show regular HX- and X-toned intransitive verb stems, while (14d-e) show irregular HS- and S-toned stems. In every case, the tonal form seen in these deverbal nouns is the same as what is used in the progressive.

In one unusual case, a tonally derived noun is an agentive rather than an action nominal. The case in question is the compound verb *dân-bǔɔ* 'lie (realis)', with irrealis equivalent *dân-bù*. The deverbal noun *dán-bû* means 'liar' rather than 'lying'. Note that, unlike the action nominals above, the irrealis stem is used and the tone pattern is consistent with those found in compound nouns, meaning this is likely a deverbal compound noun rather than a nominalized verb stem per se. See §7.4 for further examples and discussion.

Tonal derivation of action nominals is a productive pattern in Seenku.

5.3 Nominal inflection

Nouns carry little inflectional morphology in Seenku. To give an example of its morphological paucity, while many Mande languages like Bambara (e.g. Courtenay 1974), Zialo (Babaev 2010), Jalkunan (Heath 2017), or related Dzùùngoo (Solomiac 2007) show suffixed definite markers (whether segmental or tonal), these are entirely absent in Seenku, with definiteness marked instead with an independent preceding determiner (§8.2.1). The only inflectional morphology we find is plural marking, which has both a regular pattern and some irregular marking strategies.

5.3.1 Regular plural marking

The majority of plural forms in Seenku are marked by one or more of the following changes on the surface:

1. Tone raising
2. Vowel fronting
3. Diphthongization
4. Nasalization

In (15), I show a selection of nouns whose plurals are marked only through tone raising:

(15)
Sg	Pl	Gloss
bȅɛ	bèɛ	'pig(s)'
təgê	təgě	'chicken(s)'
bî	bǐ	'goat(s)'

Nouns with only vowel fronting are shown in (16):

(16)	Sg	Pl	Gloss
jŏŋmǎ	jŏŋmɛ̋	'cat(s)'
gbátǎ	gbétɛ̋	'shed(s)'

Nouns with both vowel fronting and tone raising are shown in (17):

(17)	Sg	Pl	Gloss
səgà	səgɛ̀	'sheep'
kâ	kɛ̂	'yam'
flâ	flɛ̂	'Fulani'

Nouns with diphthong formation, a special case of vowel fronting, are shown in (18):

(18)	Sg	Pl	Gloss
sǔ	sǔi	'antelope'
bŏo	bŏee	'mat(s)'
màafɔ̃	màafɔ̃ɛ	'gun(s)'

Nouns that combine diphthong formation and tone raising are shown in (19):

(19)	Sg	Pl	Gloss
gɔ̀ɔ	gɔ̀ɛɛ	'field(s)'
kû	kûi	'thing(s)'
dò-dó	dò-dóe	'thigh(s)'

Finally, we find nouns that display vowel nasalization as part of plural formation, typically in conjunction with one or more of the other changes:

(20)	Sg	Pl	Gloss
kân	kɛ̰̂	'hut(s)'
sân	sɛ̰̂	'rabbit(s)'
dôn	d(u)ḭ̂	'child(ren)'

These effects are diverse, but the patterns are systematic. First, we find that tone raising always occurs except on S tones: S in the singular remains S in the plural, being the highest possible tone already. In terms of vowel changes, front vowel stems show no overt changes while /a/ becomes [ɛ] and back vowels become a diphthong with a following front vowel with the same height and ATR value. Finally, nasalization occurs only on those stems followed by a latent nasal coda in the singular, which is subsequently lost in the plural.

In McPherson (2017b), I argue that these changes derive from the affixation of two floating features that make up the plural morpheme, a vocalic feature [+front] and a tonal feature [+raised]. In the subsections below, I cover each in turn.

5.3.1.1 Tone changes

Recall from Chapter 4 that the Seenku tone system can be decomposed into the following feature specifications in Table 5.3.

Tab. 5.3: Seenku tonal features

	X	L	H	S
Upper	-	-	+	+
Raised	-	+	-	+

When the feature [+raised] is affixed to an X [-upper,-raised] tone, it creates L [-upper,+raised]; when it is affixed to a H [+upper,-raised], it creates a S tone [+upper,+raised]. Because S is already designated as [+raised], the addition of the [+raised] featural affix causes no change:[3]

(21) a. bɛ̏ɛ → bɛ̀ɛ 'pig(s)'
      b. bȋ → bǐ   'goat(s)'
      c. sű → sűi 'antelope'

As discussed in §4.3.2.1, part of the motivation for treating HX contours as underlying H is the fact that surface HX nouns raise to S in the plural, the expected result of adding [+raised] to a H tone. The epenthesis of X to satisfy a tonotactic constraint against final H must take place after any morphological processes like plural formation, since only the H tone is involved in the plural; that is, we do not see the affixation of [+raised] to final X, which would create an unattested HL plural allomorph of HX singular nouns (e.g. *gɔ́ɛ̀ɛ 'woods').

The tonal feature [+raised] is a suffix that combines with only the final tone of the word. For example:

(22) a. Tone change on final syllable only

      gɔ̏ɲâ   → gɔ̏ɲɛ̋   'basket(s)'
      kpɛ́nɛ̏(n) → kpɛ́nì 'finger(s)'

   b. Tone change absorbed by final S

      jŏŋmǎ → jŏŋmɛ̋ 'cat(s)'
      gbátǎ → gbétɛ̋ 'shed(s)'

---

[3] Interestingly, however, speakers appear to have metalinguistic knowledge that plurals involve a raised tone, and when producing S-toned singulars back to back with S-toned plurals, they will sometimes raise the tone of plural S even higher.

In (22a), we see final H- and X-toned syllables raising to S and L, respectively; in both cases, the preceding syllable is unaffected, retaining either X or H tone. In (22b), we see no overt tone changes, because the final syllable is already S. Like the examples in (22a), though, the initial syllable is unaffected by the suffixation of [+raised].

The fact that the tone feature is a suffix provides evidence for whether a word has one or two tonal nodes associated with it underlying. For example, the minor syllable in sesquisyllabic words like jəgè 'dog' or kərê 'man' may phonetically realize part of the tonal melody (here X or HX), but they do not carry an independent tone; if they did, we would see this tone remain unchanged in plural formation, but instead, the whole melody raises (to L in jəgè 'dogs' or to S in kərě̋ 'men'). This is even true for some disyllabic words that seem to have escaped iambic reduction, such as kórô 'pigeon', with its corresponding plural kőrě̋ 'pigeons'. However, we find a small number of seemingly mono- or sesquisyllabic words with underlyingly complex tone:

(23)   a. síên   →   síě̋   'spike(s)'
       b. kərúú →   kərúíi 'all'

In these cases, we might expect underlying /HX/ or /H/, but this would result in plural forms that are entirely S. Instead, it appears that we are dealing with underlying /H-HX/ or /H-H/ sequences, of which only the final tone is affected by [+raised] suffixation.

5.3.1.2 Vocalic changes

Let us now turn to the vocalic changes, which I argue to be the result of a featural suffix [+front]. The feature system for the vowel inventory is repeated in Table 5.4 from §3.1.1.1.

Tab. 5.4: Seenku vowel features

	i	e	ɛ	a	ɔ	o	ʊ	u
[front]	+	+	+	-	-	-	-	-
[back]	-	-	-	-	+	+	+	+
[high]	+	-	-	-	-	-	+	+
[low]	-	-	-	+	-	-	-	-
[ATR]	+	+	-	-	-	+	-	+

When [+front] is suffixed to an underlyingly [+front] vowel, no change occurs (24a). Added to a [+low] vowel, the [+low] feature is changed to [-low] due to the fact that [+low,+front] is not a permissible vowel in Seenku (24b); the result is the vowel [ɛ]. Finally, the most interesting change occurs with back vowels, where the [+back] feature is retained by diphthongization (24c). In (24), a concrete example is given on top, followed by a schematic of the featural affixation process for that class of nouns (front vowels, low vowels, back vowels).

(24) a. bɛ̈ɛ → bɛ̈ɛ   'pig(s)'

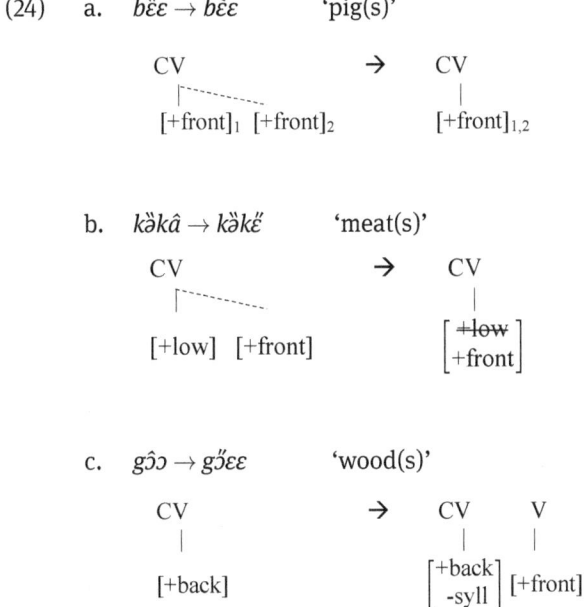

b. kə̀kâ → kə̀kɛ̈́   'meat(s)'

c. gɔ̂ɔ → gɔ̈́ɛɛ   'wood(s)'

As discussed in §3.1.2, the diphthongs formed with back vowel stems retain all of the root vowel's original features, i.e. height, ATR specification, etc. In other words, it is not the case that every back vowel becomes the glide [w] in the plural.

Finally, there is one exceptional context in which the expected diphthong is not created, and that is with mid back vowels after [r]. Rather than create the diphthongs [roe] or [rɔɛ], we find that the back vowel simply fronts, creating [re] or [rɛ] instead:

(25) a. kórô   →   kőrɛ̈́   'pigeon(s)'
     b. sörö̀   →   sòrè   'Nile monitor(s)'
     c. sö̀rɔ̈́   →   sö̀rɛ̈́   'hartebeest(s)'

These examples are also unusual in retaining disyllabic rather than sesquisyllabic form. Curiously, the very similar configuration fənɔ̈̀ [fərɔ̀] 'monkey' does surface with a diphthong in the plural, i.e. fənɔ̀ɛ 'monkeys'. It is difficult to untangle whether it is the sesquisyllabic vs. disyllabic distinction that motivates the presence vs. absence of the diphthong, or whether it has to do with underlying /n/ vs. /l/ (or /d/; §3.2.3).

5.3.1.3 Nasalization changes

The last plural alternation to discuss is nasalization. As we saw above, singular nouns with latent nasal codas typically alternate with plural forms with a nasal vowel (but no nasal coda). The underlying root vowel can be either oral or nasal. The forms in (26) expands upon the examples given in ??:

(26)
Sg	Pl	Gloss
kân	kę̋	'hut(s)'
sân	sę̋	'rabbit(s)'
-sân	-sę̋	'thing(s)' (compound final)
dǎ̀n	dę̀	'wall(s)'
cên	cę̋	'breast(s)'
dɔ̋n	dɔ̋ɛ	'shoulder(s)'
dên	dį̋	'grain(s)'
dôn	d(u)į̋	'child(ren)'
kɔ̀̋n	kɔ̀ɛ	'head(s)'
nṵ̂n	nṵ̋i	'wound(s)'

We can understand these examples as the nasal feature of the coda in the singular instead being realized on the nucleus of the syllable itself in the plural. For an analytical account in which the nasal coda is a floating feature [+nasal], see McPherson (2017b). Note that in some cases with a [+ATR] mid vowel in the singular, the vowel raises to [+high] in the plural, e.g. dên → dį̋ 'grain(s)'. This is arguably due to the fact that there are no vowels ẹ or ọ in Seenku, so to retain the [+ATR] feature, the vowel must raise to high.

What makes Seenku plural formation complicated is the fact that nasal codas do not always trigger nasalization. For some nouns, the nasal coda is simply deleted in the plural. For the most part, nasal codas are deleted after long vowels, but we also find cases of short [+ATR] mid vowels that delete the coda in the plural rather than nasalize and raise the vowel:

(27)
Sg	Pl	Gloss
dǎ̀ân	dĕɛ	'basket hanger(s)'
kǎŋăan	kɛ̀ŋɛ̋ɛ	'cage(s)'
kpǎan	kpɛ̌ɛ	'head herder(s)'
kpôon	kpȅe	'seat(s)'
bɔ̀ɔ̂n	bɔɛɛ	'bag(s)'
(ń) cűen	(ń) cűe	'(my) elbow(s)'
(ǎ) bón	(ì) bőe	'(his/their) back(s)'

For further discussion of latent nasal codas and their behavior, see §3.3.2.

5.3.2 Irregular plural marking

5.3.2.1 Human plural suffix -ŋɛ

We find a few irregular subpatterns in plural formation. The first pattern is found on some human nouns. Here, plurals are formed by the suffixation of -ŋɛ, sometimes accompanied by changes in the noun stem itself:

(28) a. kùɔnɔ̃-mɔ̂ → kùɔné-ŋɛ̋ 'youth(s)'
 b. sɛ́ɛ-məgɔ̂ → sɛ́ɛ-ŋɛ̀ 'Sambla person(s)'
 c. dərôn → dəró-ŋɛ̋ 'child(ren)'

In (28a), the root for 'youth' carries what appears to be a singular suffix -mɔ̂, likely related to the term for person məgɔ̂ or mɔ̃̀. In (28b), the actual term məgɔ̂ is used in the singular. In both cases, these singular affixes or roots are replaced by -ŋɛ (with a [+raised] tone) in the plural. When the plural suffix is added, the root does not take the regular plural fronting and raising morphology discussed in the last section.

This same -ŋɛ suffix is found in some common expressions used in greetings to refer to members of the family. In these cases, -ŋɛ is added to various locative expressions:

(29) a. cí-dɔ̀ɔ-ŋɛ̀ 'people of the house'
 b. lǔ-ŋǎa-ŋɛ̋ 'people of the courtyard/family'
 c. lɔ̌-ŋɛ̋ 'people here'
 d. ń jɛ̌-ŋɛ̋ 'people in front of me'

I have not seen an equivalent singular form of any of these.

5.3.2.2 Reduplicated plurals

One noun, 'infant' or 'baby', has its plural form created by reduplication:

(30) dò-nɛ́ɛ → dò-né-nɛ́ɛ 'infant(s)'

This is the only noun I have seen behaving in this way.

6 Pronouns and anaphora

This chapter describes the range of pronouns and anaphoric expressions in Seenku. A range of intersecting issues make pronominal expression somewhat complicated. This includes emphatic marking, the merger of pronouns with TAMP markers and postpositions, coreferential pronouns, and marginal distinctions between first person inclusive and exclusive.

The layout of this chapter is as follows: I first provide an overview of the person, number, and discourse statuses that are represented by pronouns in §6.1. Next, I briefly address emphatic marking, both form and function, in §6.2; more discussion can be found later in §21.1.1. The following sections (§6.3-§6.6) cover pronouns in different structural positions, including the variable merger with grammatical markers that yields what looks like an incipient case system. Finally, coreferential pronouns are addressed in §6.7 on logophoric pronouns, which are also used in reflexive (§6.7.3) and reciprocal (§6.7.4) constructions.

6.1 Pronouns

6.1.1 Basic pronouns

Seenku makes use of the three basic persons: 1st, which references the speaker; 2nd, which references the interlocutor; and 3rd, which references those people who are neither the speaker nor the interlocutor. Number is a simple singular vs. plural distinction. The only complication that arises is a possible 1pl inclusive vs. exclusive distinction.

Table 6.1 summarizes the basic pronouns.

Tab. 6.1: Basic pronominal paradigm for Seenku

	SG	PL
1	ń	mǐ (incl)
		íwǐ (excl)
2	á	í
3	ä̀	ì̌

As this table shows, 2nd and 3rd person pronouns are distinguished tonally, with the former carrying H tone and the latter X. In addition to the basic 3pl pronoun ì̌, the form kǔɛ (literally 'others', though possibly a pluralization of the discourse definite pronoun kʊ́; see §6.1.2) is often used. For instance:

(1) kűɛ   kɔ́kɔ́ fő́n   à   wò   wὲ, kűɛ   sĭ̧ kɔ̂ɔn
     other.PL short more 3SG EMPH with other.PL be eggplant
     bű́ɔ   nɛ̋ dőrő́n mɛ̋
     take.out.REAL.NOM LOC pole   with
     'They were shorter than him, they were picking eggplants with a long pole.'
     [sos161009t1:155]

This form *kűɛ* can also be added to single nouns or names (X) to mean 'X and others' or 'X and family':

(2) ä̀ wɛ̏   í   tə̀bɛ̏   wétənɛ̆ lɔ̋ ä̀ kərù̀ kűɛ   tɛ̋
     3SG SUBORD LOG stand.next.to.IRR now   here DEF hyena other.PL GEN
     dân tɛ̏
     wall GEN
     'He huddled next to the wall of hyena's family's house.' [sos150626t4:4]

Turning to the first plural, examples suggesting the inclusive vs. exclusive distinction are given in (3):

(3) a. ä̀ à jərà   ì̀   íwí̋   ké kɔ̀sí̋
         3SG 3SG think.IRR COMP 1PL.EXCL COP friend.PL
         'He thinks we [exclusive] are friends.' [sos170724e]

     b. ä̀ à jərà   ì̀   mí̋ ké kɔ̀sí̋
         3SG 3SG think.IRR COMP 1PL COP friend.PL
         'He thinks we [inclusive] are friends.' [sos180717e]

     c. ä̀ kərê, ä̀ səná   wɛ̏   í   bɛ̋   ì̀   íwí̋   nǎ
         DEF man 3SG husband SUBORD LOG do.IRR COMP 1PL.EXCL PROSP
         kɛ̋   í   sí tê, ì̀i   kɛ̋   ä̀ gő́ɛɛ   sőo
         go.IRR LOG RECP GEN 3PL.SUBORD go.IRR DEF wood.PL gather.IRR
         'The man, her husband said, let's go together, [and] they went to gather wood.' [sos150626t5:51]

     d. ä̀ səná   wɛ̏   í   bɛ̋   ì̀   mí̋ nǎ   kɛ̋   í   sí
         3SG husband SUBORD LOG do.IRR COMP 1PL PROSP go.IRR LOG RECP
         tê
         GEN
         'Her husband said that we [you and I] should go together.' [sos180717e]

In other words, the use of *mí̋* implies that the listener is included, while *íwí̋* does not. This definition is consistent with the fact that it is typically *íwí̋* that is found in quoted speech in narratives (as in (3c)), since the listener of a narrative would clearly not be involved in the action being quoted.

In addition to these person/number distinctions, there are two additional pronouns that are common in discourse. The first is a pronoun *mɔ̰̌*, synonymous with the word for 'person', that functions as a "generic" pronoun like French *on*. Like French, it can be used for unspecified people, where English may use a passive, or it can be used in place of *mǐ* for the 1pl. Examples of the former usage are given in (4a-b) and the latter in (4c-d).

(4) a. *mɔ̰̌ ǎ   jú   sɛ́ɛ-kû   nɛ̰̀ kɛ̰̀*
person 3SG say.IRR Sambla-thing LOC EMPH
'It is said in Seenku too!' [sos161009t1:113]

b. puisque *mɔ̰̂ɛ́ɛ   nɛ́̋ kʊ́   nɛ̰̀ mɔ̰̌   mɔ̰̂ɛ̀ɛ tsṵ̀*
since.FR millet.SBJV if D.DEF LOC person millet cut.IRR.HAB
ɲì-nà   kpéɛ̀ wɛ̀
there-towards knife with
'If it was millet, people used to harvest millet with a knife.' [sos170702t1:44]

c. *ɛ̰̀ɛ́   kɛ̰̀, ké mɔ̰̌   nǎ í   sí nəgì nɛ̀-təgò   âa*
3SG.LOG EMPH COP person PROSP LOG RECP mind TRANS-sit.IRR NEG.Q
'Okay, we'll remind each other, right.' [sos170702t1:30]

d. *ké mɔ̰̌   nǎ   tɛ̰̀ɛ   á lɛ̰̀*
COP person PROSP touch.IRR 2SG DAT
'We will catch up with you.' [sos161009t1:65]

This pronoun is also commonly found in hortatives, discussed in §13.2.4.

6.1.2 Discourse definite pronoun (anaphor)

In addition to the basic pronouns discussed above, Seenku commonly uses a pronoun *kʊ́* that explicitly refers back to a singular discourse entity, whether human or non-human, animate or inanimate. I refer to *kʊ́*, which can also be used as a determiner (§8.2.2), as a **discourse definite**. It could also be referred to as a discourse anaphor, since the crucial condition for its use is that its referent has been explicitly introduced in the discourse (i.e. it cannot be deictic, unlike the regular 3rd person pronouns above, which can be either deictic or discourse anaphoric). However, I avoid the term "anaphor", which has varied usage in the literature (all pronouns, only bound pronouns like reflexives and reciprocals, etc.).

While 3rd person pronouns can also be discourse anaphoric, the discourse definite pronoun exclusively has this use and it emphasizes the fact that the referent has been previously brought up in the discourse. The following examples illustrate a human referent (5a) and an inanimate referent (5b) for discourse definite *kʊ́*:

(5) a. Jὲ mὲ̀   kű̄ɔ   kʊ́   kɛ́ ɛ̀ɛ́   fṵ̀ɛ mὲ̀   kɛ̋
       Jɛ 3SG.SUBORD go.IRR D.DEF COP 3SG.DAT wife 3SG.SUBORD go.IRR
       tằasó   ầ   bò̰-kɔ́ɔ   lɛ̂
       be.surprised DEF billygoat PRES
       'Jɛ got up and went, she was his wife, she went and to her surprise, there was a billygoat.' [sos150626t4:13]

   b. kɛ́ mə̰̀   kʊ́ cɛ̀rɛ̀ɛ   ầ   sɛ́ɛ-məgɔ́-bɛ̂
       COP person D.DEF call.IRR.HAB DEF Sambla-person-NOM
       'That's what we call being Sambla.' [sos170714t1:3]

In (5a), the discourse definite refers to Jɛ, the wife of hyena; its first reference is present in the beginning of the clause. The use of *kʊ́* in this context makes it clear to the listener that the speaker is referring explicitly to the referent who was just introduced. In (5b), *kʊ́* refers to the video of traditional fonio farming that the two speakers are watching; in the first line of the text, the speaker does not use the discourse definite, but uses a presentative construction (§8.2.3.2) to say that what they are watching is Sambla-hood (*sɛ́ɛ-məgɔ́-bɛ̂*). He repeats this sentiment again as (5b), this time with the discourse definite, since he has already set up the reference by implication in his first utterance.

Discourse definite pronouns are common as a resumptive pronoun with relative clauses, since the relative clause will have just introduced the referent for *kʊ́*; for more information, see Chapter 17.

Both *ầ* and *kʊ́* are also used as definite determiners, the former as a general definite (cf. English 'the') and the latter emphasizing the reference back to a discourse entity (cf. English 'that (very/aforementioned)'); see §8.2 for further discussion. For the use of *kʊ́* as a negative focus marker, see §21.1.4.

The discourse definite pronoun is distinct from a logophoric pronoun *í*, also found in reflexive contexts; while *í* must be bound by an antecedent (overt or implied by a quotative complementizer), *kʊ́* is never bound. The logophoric pronoun will be discussed in-depth in §6.7 below.

6.2 Emphatic marking

The personal pronouns (but not the discourse definite or the generic *mə̰̀*) commonly occur with emphatic marking in the form of an enclitic *wo* whose tone is identical to that of the preceding pronoun. All human pronouns except the 1pl have emphatic forms though some are more commonly attested than others: the 1sg is the most common, followed by the second person, followed by the third person. For further discussion and corpus statistics, see §21.1.1. The emphatic pronouns are laid out in Table 6.2.

In the 1sg, the nasal pronoun *ń* merges with the emphatic particle, yielding *mó*. The 2sg pronoun can be pronounced either *á wó* or as an elided version *óo*; the same

Tab. 6.2: Emphatic pronominal paradigm for Seenku

	SG	PL
1	mó	—
2	á wó/óo	í wó
3	ǎ wǒ/ǒo	ǐ wǒ

variation is found in the segmentally identical but tonally distict 3sg. In the 2pl and 3pl, where the vowel is instead a high front vowel, no elision is found, though the /w/ will often front to a palatal glide, yielding [i yo].

The logophoric pronoun, which commonly takes the place of the 1st person in narratives, is likewise common in its emphatic form *í wó*. For instance, consider the following:

(6) a. kűɛ   dǒon jərǎ   kűɛ   sǐ ǎ   bűɔ   nɛ́ á
       other.PL pole use.IRR other.PL be 3SG take.out.REAL.NOM LOC 2SG
       wó   ǎ   səmí   ì̌   í   wó   ké   mɔ̋   kɔ́kɔ́ quoi
       EMPH 3SG think.IRR COMP LOG EMPH COP person short what.FR
       'They used the long pole to pick them, and you thought you were short.'
       [sos161009t1:159]

   b. ì̌   í   wóo   sío   nɛ́ ì̌   ǎ   sú   ì̌
       COMP LOG EMPH.SBJV get.up.REAL.PFV if COMP 3SG get.up.IRR COMP
       í   wóo   təgò   nɛ́ ì̌   ǎ   təgò   ì̌   ìi
       LOG EMPH.SBJV sit.REAL.PFV if COMP 3SG sit.IRR COMP LOG.SBJV
       səŋá   nɛ́ ì̌   ǎ   səŋá
       lie.down.REAL.PFV if COMP 3SG lie.down.REAL
       'If I get up, he gets up, if I sit down, he sits down.' [sos161009t1:34]

In (6a), the subject of the matrix verb is the 2sg, which takes its emphatic form *á wó*; in the subordinate clause, the coreferential subject is the logophoric, also in its emphatic form. In (6b), the logophoric pronoun is used throughout (as it is in the environment of a riddle, with the whole thing embedded as a quotation under the complementizer ì̌, §19.1); the first two references are in the emphatic, but by the third repetition, the bare form of the pronoun is used.

I choose here to use the neutral term "emphatic" rather than "focus", since it does not appear that the emphatic argument is always focused. For instance, they are often found in subject position in wh-questions, where the default assumption is not that the subject would be focused. For further discussion, see §21.1.1.

6.3 Object pronouns

The simplest argument position to address is object position. Here, there is no possibility for pronouns to merge with grammatical markers like TAMP markers or postpositions, and hence the only variation in form is whether the pronoun is emphatic or non-emphatic.

Examples of object pronouns are given in (7), illustrating a variety of different pronouns:

(7) a. ằ nǎ mǐ́ bǎ̰
3SG PROSP 1PL hit.IRR
'He will hit us.' [sos150811e]

b. ḭ̀ ằ jú kʊ́ tő ŋɛ́
3PL 3SG say.IRR D.DEF like NEG
'It's not said like that. [Lit. They don't say it like that]' [sos161009t1:39]

c. gɔ̌ɔ, ằ gɔ̌ɔ səgɔ̌ yɛ̀rɛ̀ ɲá ŋɛ́, mǐ́ kʊ́ tsɪ̀ mɛ̀ ŋɛ́
dry 3SG dry good self.JU be.NEG NEG 1PL D.DEF cut.IRR HAB NEG
'Dry, what's not properly dry, we don't cut it.' [sos170711t1:56]

(7a) illustrates a 1pl inclusive pronoun mǐ́, (7b) shows a 3sg pronoun in object position, and finally (7c) illustrates the discourse definite in object position.

6.4 Subject pronouns

In principle, subject pronouns are exactly the same as object pronouns (or any pronouns in Seenku), but there is rampant clitic elision (§4.4.3) of TAMP markers after the subject that yields portmanteau subject pronouns. There are three TAMP markers that undergo these mergers:
- lɛ̌: past tense
- lé: subjunctive (conditionals, embedded clauses)
- lɛ̏: subordinator (relative clauses, clause chaining)

In each case, when the TAMP marker merges with the pronoun, it lengthens the vowel and leaves its tone, yielding tonally differentiated subject pronouns. These are summarized in Table 6.3 (where I use the emphatic 1sg, which is more common than its plain form ń).

As this table demonstrates, pronouns in each TAMP condition all end in the same tone (S for past, H for subjunctive, and X for subordinate); the vowel quality and initial tone are taken from the base pronoun. In each cell above, the elided pronoun can be replaced with simply the plain pronoun followed by the TAMP marker (e.g. for 1sg mó lɛ̌,

Tab. 6.3: Subject pronouns in Seenku

	Plain	Past	Subjunctive	Subordinate
1sg	mó	móő	móo	môo
2sg	á	áǎ	áa	âa
3sg	ằ	ǎa	ằá	ằa
1pl	mḯ	mḯǐ	mḯí	mïï
2pl	í	íǐ	íi	îi
3pl	ỳ	y̌i	y̌í	y̏i
Generic	mɔ̰̋	mɔ̰̋ɔ̰	mɔ̰̋ɔ̰́	mɔ̰̂ɔ̰

mó lé, mó lɛ̀) with no change in meaning. Different speakers have different preferences when speaking, but if offered the other choice, they accept it without any hesitation. Generally speaking, the elided forms seem to be preferred to the non-elided forms.

Examples of each 1sg subject pronoun are given in (8):

(8) a. mó   kằ   tsɛ̋ gṳɔ nɛ̀
       1SG.EMPH go.REAL.PFV INDF country LOC
       'I went to a country.' [sos161009t1:20]

   b. móő   sɪ̰̀ ằ mḯrḯ   nɛ̋ né   kɛ́ mó
      1SG.EMPH.PST be 3SG think.REAL.NOM LOC 1SG.COMP COP 1SG.EMPH
      nǎ   né
      PROSP come.IRR
      'I thought that I would come.' [sos170720e]

   c. móo   sɪ̰̀ nɛ̋ bậa̰   brɛ̰̋   nɛ̋ á wó
      1SG.EMPH.SBJV be if balafon play.REAL.NOM LOC 2SG EMPH
      sɔ́   wè á wóo   nɛ̀ mḯ tɔ̋   bậa̰
      be.able.IRR HAB 2SG EMPH.SBJV come.IRR 1PL leave.IRR balafon
      brɛ̰̋   nɛ̋ âa   nɛ̀ dŏondǎan ŋé
      play.REAL.NOM LOC 2SG.SUBORD come.IRR step.over NEG
      'If I am playing the balafon, you can't come leave us playing the balafon and step over [it].' [sos170711t1:288]

   d. mó   nǎ   sɪ̀   nɛ̋-kɔ̰̋   môo   ɲəgâan
      1SG.EMPH PROSP water.jar TRANS-break.IRR 1SG.SUBORD scorpion
      jĩo   tré   gṳ̀
      see.REAL.PFV REL.PRO under
      'I will break the water jar that I saw the scorpion under.' [sos170718e]

Each of these TAMP markers, and their mergers with subject pronouns, are treated elsewhere in the grammar. For past tense, see §13.4; for subjunctive, see §18.1 and §19.3;

6.5 Possessive pronouns

Inalienable (relational) nouns take basic pronouns as their possessors; the pronoun triggers argument-head tone sandhi on the possessed noun, as described in §4.4.2 and §8.6.1.2. In all cases, the pronoun's form is left unaltered, with the exception of X-toned pronouns before X-toned nouns, in which case both raise to L. Examples of inalienable possession are shown in (9):

(9) a. mó   nï̀
       1SG.EMPH father
       'my father'

   b. ä̀   ɲä̀
       3SG mother
       'her mother'

   c. à   kɔ̰n
       3SG head
       'her head'

With alienable nouns, there are two postpositions that can intervene between the pronoun and the possessed noun: the genitive pronoun tě and a lengthened form of the dative pronoun lěe, addressed in §10.1.8 and §10.1.9.3, respectively. Unlike TAMP markers, which have invariable tone, postpositions undergo tone sandhi with the preceding noun or pronoun. Like other l-initial clitics, the dative postposition can elide to create a series of possessive pronouns. When it elides, it leave behind the tone of its sandhi variant, meaning that possessive pronouns do not uniformly end in the same tone. The paradigm of basic possessive pronouns is given in Table 6.4.

Tab. 6.4: Possessive pronominal paradigm for Seenku

	SG	PL
1	nɛ́n/môo	mî́î (incl)
2	âa/á wôo	îi/í wôo
3	ä̀á/ɛ̀ɛ́	ï̀ï

Tonally, H-toned pronouns result in a HX contour; X-toned pronouns result in an XH contour; and S-toned pronouns remain S (with the vowel lengthened). The 1sg, 2sg, and 2pl show the plain and emphatic form of possessive pronouns; note that the 1sg plain form is irregular *nɛ́n*. The 3sg also shows two forms, a regular *ǎá* and a fronted version *ɛ̌ɛ́*. By and large, *ɛ̌ɛ́* appears to be possible anywhere we find *ǎá*, but the reverse is not true. Specifically, some speakers appear to have analyzed *ɛ̌ɛ́* as a plural form of *ǎá*, by analogy with regular plural vowel fronting (§5.3.1). First, the examples in (10) show that *ɛ̌ɛ́* can be used in either the singular or the plural:

(10)   a.   ɛ̌ɛ́   kǎn
             3SG.DAT granary
             'his granary' [sos150810e]

      b.   ɛ̌ɛ́   kę̌
             3SG.DAT granary
             'his granaries' [sos150810e]

In the same elicitation session, the speaker produced the following data:

(11)   a.   ǎá   jəgɛ̋
             3SG.DAT dog
             'his dog' [sos150810e]

      b.   ɛ̌ɛ́   jəgɛ̋
             3SG.DAT dog.PL
             'his dogs' [sos150810e]

It is tempting to see this as a way to disambiguate the number of an otherwise neutralized plural distinction (since argument-head tone sandhi raises *jəgɛ̀* to *jəgɛ́*, where plural tone raising is inaudible). However, there is some variation or inconsistency with this construction, since in a similar configuration with *bɛ̌ɛ* 'pig' instead of *jəgɛ̀* 'dog', the speaker rejects the possessive form **ǎá bɛ́ɛ* 'his pig' in favor of the overt genitive marker *ǎ tê bɛ̌ɛ*; nevertheless, *ɛ̌ɛ́ bɛ́ɛ* 'his pigs' is accepted in the plural.

For further discussion of this possessive strategy, see §8.6.2.2.

6.6 Oblique pronouns

I use the term "oblique pronoun" here for any pronoun that occurs in post-verbal position, either explicitly as the complement of a postposition or through merger with a postposition. Like the possessive pronoun series discussed in §6.5, oblique pronouns may end in different tones due to tone sandhi on the postposition (which then elides). The postpositions that elide are the following:

- Associative *wɛ̀*
- Dative *lɛ̋*

Given that the tone differs between the two postpositions, the resulting series of pronouns remain mostly distinguishable (with the exception of S-toned pronouns, which are invariably S-toned). By and large, oblique pronouns are only created from emphatic pronouns, with the exception of the 1pl (which has no emphatic form) and marginally the 3sg.

The pronoun series is summarized in Table 6.5.

Tab. 6.5: Oblique pronouns in Seenku

	Plain/Emphatic	Associative	Dative
1sg	mó	móő	môo/môe
2sg	á wó	á wóő	á wêe
3sg	à̰	àa	—
1pl	mǐ	mǐi	mǐi
2pl	ǐ wó	ǐ wóő	ǐ wêe
3pl	ḭ̀ wö̀	—	ḭ̀ wèe

Any attempts to create dative 3sg oblique pronouns were rejected, as were associative 3pl pronouns based on ḭ̀ or ḭ̀ wö̀. Plain oblique pronouns like *áő or *âa for the 2sg were likewise rejected.

The formation of these oblique pronouns is reminiscent of what Vydrine (2006) describes for South Mande languages, like Guro.

In the text corpus, we also see cases of dative-marked discourse definite pronouns (kṹɛ), associative-marked generic 3sg (mɔ̀ɛ), and both dative- and associative-marked 3pl variants with the form 'others' (kǔɛɛ in both cases).

For examples of usage, see §10.1.7 for the comitative and §10.1.9 for the dative.

6.7 Logophoric pronouns

The pronoun í in Seenku is a co-referential pronoun found in a large variety of environments. I call the pronoun "logophoric", though its distribution does not fit the canonical distribution of logophoricity (namely, as referring to the person whose "speech, thoughts, or feelings are reported or reflected in a given linguistic context", Clements 1975: 141). The distribution in Seenku is very similar to that described for Boko (Jones 2000), where the author likewise uses the term "logophoric" while challenging its standard definition. Similar pronouns are described as "reflexive" in other Mande languages (e.g. Guro, Vydrine 2006, or Mano, Khachaturyan 2015), but this is also not an unproblematic description, as the dominance relationships between logophoric pronouns and their antecedents do not always meet the criteria for reflexivity. Following Jones (2000), I will refer to í and its variants as logophoric.

The same logophoric pronoun *í* can be co-referential with all persons and numbers with the exception of the 1sg, which repeats the simple 1sg pronoun *ń* instead.

In the following subsections, I lay out common environments for the logophoric pronoun.

6.7.1 Quotatives

Cross-linguistically, logophoric pronouns are canonically found embedded in quotative contexts; the use of the logophoric pronoun reflects co-referentiality of the speaker (or thinker or feeler) with the pronoun in the embedded clause. Seenku is no exception, with this being one of the most common uses of the logophoric pronoun:

(12) a. ì̀ ǎ̀ tré wé ì̀ ǎ̀ wò̀ nǎ̀ fènɛ́
  3PL 3SG ask.REAL.PFV FOC COMP 3SG EMPH come.REAL.PFV what
  sòo lő, mè̀ í bɛ̋ wé ǎ́! ì̀ ké í
  search.IRR here 3SG.SUBORD LOG say.IRR FOC EXCL COMP COP LOG
  wó sǐ jù̀-jő̀ɔ nɛ̋
  EMPH be mountain-stroll.REAL.NOM LOC
  'They asked him what he came to look for here, he said, "Ah! I was hunting."' [sos170711t1:16]

 b. ǎ̀ sǎ̀n mè̀ í bɛ̋ wétənɛ̀ ì̀ í nǎ̌ ǎ̀ dənɨ̋
  DEF spring SUBORD LOG do.IRR now COMP LOG PROSP DEF child.PL
  bɛ̋ ǎ̀ mənɨ̋ kǎ́
  put.IRR DEF woman in.hand
  'The spring said now it would give the woman children.' [sos170805t9:13]

 c. ǎ̀ ǎ̀ sɨ̋ɔ̀ môe mó lɛ́ íi nígí
  3SG 3SG explain.REAL.PFV 1SG.EMPH.DAT 1SG.EMPH SBJV LOG.DAT COW
  búo
  kill.REAL.PFV
  'He explained to me that I killed his cow.' [sos170816e]

In (12a-b), we see a quotative construction, where the logophoric pronoun is used as the subject of the complementizer clause, co-referential with the one speaking. Note that the logophoric pronoun is also a fixed part of the quotative clause itself, filling the object position of the verb *bɛ̋* 'put/do/say'. In (12c), the main clause contains the verb *sɨ̋ɔ̀* 'explain'; its 3sg subject is co-referential with the possessive logophoric pronoun in the complement clause. In each case, if the logophoric pronoun were replaced with a 3sg, it would obligatorily indicate another person other than the speaker.

For more on quotative constructions, see §19.2.1.

6.7.2 Adjectival predicates

Adjectival predicates involve the logophoric pronoun before the adjective:

(13) a. à̰ sı̌ í sĭɛ
3SG be LOG bitter
'It is bitter.' [sos170724e]

b. mó sı̌ ń bəlĕ
1SG.EMPH be 1SG fat
'I am fat.' [sos130821e]

The example in (13b) illustrates the use of the 1sg in place of the logophoric pronoun with a 1sg subject.

For further discussion, see §14.3.

6.7.3 Reflexives

As a co-referential pronoun, the logophoric pronoun can also be used to indicate the reflexive in Seenku. Simple examples from elicitation illustrate this point in (14):

(14) a. à̰ lɛ̃́ í tsı̣́
3SG PST LOG cut.REAL.PFV
'He cut himself.' [sos150623e]

b. á lɛ̃́ í tsı̣́↘
2SG PST LOG cut.REAL.PFV.Q
'Did you cut yourself?' [sos150623e]

c. mó nă ń bą́
1SG.EMPH PROSP 1SG hit.IRR
'I will hit myself.' [sos150623e]

Examples (14a-b) are both included to show that the same logophoric pronoun *í* is used with both second and third persons; the 1sg takes *ń* instead, as shown in (14c).

The reflexive meaning can be emphasized by using the Jula loanword *yéré* 'self' after the logophoric pronoun:

(15) a. mı̋ nă í yéré jɔ̰̋
1PL PROSP LOG self.JU burn.IRR
'We will burn ourselves.' [sos150623e]

b. à lɛ̋ í yéré tsí̧
3SG PST LOG self.JU cut.REAL.PFV
'He cut himself.' [sos150623e]

The example in (15a) illustrates the use of the logophoric pronoun with the 1pl (showing that it is indeed only the 1sg that behaves differently in taking ń), while the example in (15b) is the equivalent of (14a) above but with a greater emphasis placed on the reflexive.

Interestingly, the co-referent must be explicit for the logophoric pronoun to be used as a reflexive. For instance, 2sg imperatives where the subject pronoun is omitted use the 2sg pronoun rather than the logophoric pronoun to indicate the reflexive:

(16) a. á yéré jĭ̧ ŋé
2SG self.JU burn.IRR NEG
'Don't burn yourself!' [sos150623e]

b. á məgö̀
2SG hide.IRR
'Hide yourself!' [sos150710e]

As the glosses indicate, this differs from the distribution of reflexive pronouns in English.

Many verbs in Seenku are inherently reflexive, taking the logophoric (or 1sg) pronoun as their direct object. (17) illustrates a few such verbs:

(17) a. mó sĭ ń wɛ̋-jəgă nɛ̋
1SG.EMPH be 1SG TRANS-lower.REAL.NOM LOC
'I am bending over.' [sos150622e]

b. nìgì nǎ í bĕmbɔ̀
COW.PL PROSP LOG refuse
'The cows will refuse.' [sos150808e]

c. kûɛ lɛ̋ í nɛ̀-ŋɔ́
calabash PST LOG TRANS-collapse.REAL.PFV
'The calabash is broken.' [sos150707e]

As the examples in (17a) and (17c) show, derived transitive verbs are especially likely to be reflexive verbs. For more on transitive verb formation, see §12.4.

The subject is able to control a reflexive not only in direct object position but also indirect object position. For example:

(18) à̰ nä̀ bî̧ wè í kä̀
3SG come.REAL.PFV goat with LOG in.hand
'He brought a goat [Lit. he came with a goat in his own hands].' [sos190803e]

Here, the subject is co-indexed with the logophoric pronoun in the PP í kằ 'in hand'.

This example also highlights the use of the logophoric in obviation, i.e. to co-index two third person arguments in possessive contexts. Consider the following:

(19) a. Sà Jɛ̀ jîo í tê cîe
second.son first.daughter see.REAL.PFV LOG GEN house.LOC
'Sa$_i$ saw Jɛ$_j$ in his$_i$ house.' [sos190803e]

b. Sà Jɛ̀ jîo ằ tê cîe
second.son first.daughter see.REAL.PFV 3SG GEN house.LOC
'Sa$_i$ saw Jɛ$_j$ in her$_j$$_/$$_k$ house.' [sos190803e]

c. mó Jɛ̀ jîo í tê cîe
1SG.EMPH first.daughter see.REAL.PFV LOG GEN house.LOC
'I saw Jɛ$_i$ in her$_i$ house.' [sos190803e]

In (19a-b), there are two third person participants—the subject and the direct object. The locative PP refers to the house of one of the participants. If the logophoric pronoun is used, as in (19a), the most natural interpretation is that the house belongs to Sa, i.e. the subject; my consultant's first inclination when using the 3sg pronoun, as in (19b), is that the house belongs to Jɛ, though it could also belong to another person (i.e. neither Sa nor Jɛ). However, as we see from (19c), it is not the case that the direct object cannot control the logophoric pronoun of the possessor; the only possible reading in (19c) is that the house belongs to Jɛ. After some discussion, my consultant decided that in fact (19a) could be ambiguous, with the house belonging to either Sa or Jɛ, and that explicit repetition of the name would be needed to disambiguate.

Patterns of co-reference in cases like this would benefit from a corpus study.

6.7.4 Reciprocals

The logophoric pronoun is also involved in marking the reciprocal. In this construction, the logophoric pronoun is followed by the reciprocal morpheme sí, as in the following:

(20) a. ɛ̀ɛ́ kɛ̀ kɛ́ mɔ̰̀ nǎ í sí nəgì̀ nɛ̀-təgò
3SG.LOG EMPH COP person PROSP LOG RECP mind TRANS-sit.IRR
âa
NEG.Q
'Okay, we'll remind each other, right.' [sos170702t1:30]

b. íi   só   nɛ́̃ íi   expliquer dəgɔ̌ɛɛ lɛ́ lɛ̰̀   í
   2PL.SBJV be.able if 2PL.SBJV explain.FR place.PL REL SUBORD LOG
   bɔ́   i   sí   nɛ̰̀
   go.out.IRR LOG RECP LOC
   'If you could explain the places where they differ from each other.'
   [sos170702t1:36]

c. ḭ̀ à trùu   tɔ̋-tɔ̋ i síí̋   kǎa sóen tɛ̰̀
   3PL 3SG sweep.IRR.HAB RED-like LOG RECP.with side one GEN
   'They sweep it up together like that to one side.' [sos170714t3:146]

d. mí̋ sɪ̌ i sí jǐo   nɛ̋
   1PL be LOG RECP see.REAL.NOM LOC
   'We are seeing each other.' [sos170728e]

In these examples, we see the reciprocal acting as a possessive pronoun in (20a) and as the complement to a postposition in (20b-c). In (20c), we see the emergence of an oblique reciprocal pronoun *síí̋*, where the associative postposition in the sequence *sí wɛ̋* elides and leaves its tone and lengthening; see §6.6 above for further discussion of oblique pronouns. Finally, the elicited example in (20d) shows the reciprocal as the direct object of the verb.

7 Compound nouns

Compounding is one of the most common morphological processes in Seenku, a language with very little affixal morphology. Compounds are most commonly nouns, regardless of the syntactic categories of their constituents; for compound verbs, see §12.5.

The majority of compounds nouns involve tonal modification of one or more of their constituent stems, though the exact tonal changes depend on the internal syntactic make-up (e.g. noun-noun, noun-verb, etc.) as well as on lexical class. For quick overviews, see the introductions to each section below.

This chapter is organized around the internal make-up of the compound noun. First, I address noun-noun compounds, compounds whose constituent stems are nominal to begin with (§7.1). Next, I turn to noun-adjective compounds, lexicalized N Adj sequences that I argue have been reanalyzed as compound nouns (§7.2). Lastly, I address deverbal compounds, defined as compound nouns in which at least one stem is verbal (§7.4).

7.1 Noun-noun compounds

First we discuss noun-noun compounds. From a tonal perspective, noun-noun compounds tend to fall into two main categories. The first, which I call "regular compounds", follow a set of tonal rules seen only in compound nouns in the language. These tonal rules are Seenku's reflex of *compacité tonale* found in other Mande languages (see, for example, Dwyer 1973, deZeeuw 1979, Green 2018). However, unlike most Mande languages, where the tone of the initial element (the non-head) overwrites or alters the tone of the head, tone changes can be bidirectional in Seenku, i.e. the non-head may also change its tone. The overall result is the reduction of surface tone patterns from nine logical possibilities to five. Regular compounds will be discussed in §7.1.1.

The second tonal category of compound are what I call "possessive-type compounds". These are so named because they follow the same tonal changes found in inalienable possession and a small set of other argument-head constructions. These tonal changes are almost entirely head-neutralizing, while leaving non-head elements with their original tones. Possessive-type compounds are treated in §7.1.2.

In addition to transparent noun-noun compounds, there are also a number of words in the lexicon that have the phonological structure of a compound but with one or more bound roots. I refer to these as "crypto-compounds" and discuss them separately in §7.1.3.

7.1.1 Regular compounds

Regular compounds are the clearest case of true noun-noun compounds in the language, by which I mean two or more noun stems coming together to create a single prosodic word corresponding to a single terminal N node as opposed to a lexicalized phrase. Evidence for this is found in the fact that the overarching tone melodies of regular compounds tend to be the same as those found on simple (non-compound) words.

I will first address headedness of regular compounds in §7.1.1.1, before turning to their morphophonological form in §7.1.1.2.

7.1.1.1 Headedness

The majority of regular noun-noun compounds are right-headed. In the examples below, the head is underlined:

(1) a. sɛ́ɛ-gûa
Sambla-country
'Sambla country'

b. cë̀n-fâ
peanut-powder
'peanut flour'

c. ɲəná-bű
mouse-sand
'mouse burrow'

In (1a), 'Sambla country' is right-headed, since it is a sort of country; in (1b), similarly, 'peanut flour' is a kind of powder. Finally, (1c), though less transparent, can still be considered right-headed, since a mouse's burrow can be recognized by the pile of sand it has kicked up from digging the burrow—thus, it refers to a kind of sand.

Exceptional left-headed compounds mostly involve 'male' and 'female', which appear on the right but are best interpreted as modifiers of the head on the left.

(2) a. fíɛ-kərê
baobab-man
'non-fruiting (male) baobab'

b. bí-mənǐ
goat-woman
'nanny goat'

The example in (2a) refers to a kind of baobab tree, not a kind of man; the same can be said for (2b), which refers to a kind of goat.

Ambiguous cases are those compounds with 'child', such as *bíe-lôn* 'kid, baby goat' or *təgé-lôn* 'chick, baby chicken'. Should these be considered a kind of baby or a kind of goat/chicken? Such structurally ambiguous compounds with 'baby' or 'child' are not uncommon cross-linguistically; for instance, very similar constructions are found in the Dogon language Tommo So (McPherson 2013).

The morphophonological form of noun-noun compounds does not appear to differ depending upon whether they are left- or right-headed.

7.1.1.2 Morphophonological form

Segmentally, regular noun-noun compounds do not show any systematic changes to the segmental form of their stems. There is no linker morpheme, no voicing alternations, etc. A few compounds show irregular morphophonological changes. Examples include compounds for baby animals, such as *bíe-lôn* 'kid, baby goat' (cf. *bí* 'goat' and *dôn* 'child'), or compounds for territory names like *sɛ́ɛ-gûa* 'Sambla country' (cf. *sɛ́ɛ* 'Sambla' and *gùɔ* 'country').

While segmentally unaltered, regular noun-noun compounds undergo complex tonal changes that can affect either the non-head or the head (though typically not both). The resulting tonal melodies all comply with stem-level tonotactics, but this cannot be the only driving factor to the tone changes, as we see alternations in stems whose simple combination would already satisfy these constraints.

If we consider only stems with one of the three underlying lexical tones (X, H, S) and their combinations, there are nine logical possibilities; however, on the surface, only five are attested, as shown in Table 7.1.

Tab. 7.1: Tone combinations and their surface outputs in regular noun-noun compounds

Stem1	Stem2	Output
X	X	X-S; X-HX; H-HX
X	H	X-HX
X	S	X-S
H	X	H-HX
H	H	H-HX
H	S	H-S; S-S
S	X	S-S
S	H	S-S; H-HX
S	S	(S-S?)

S+S with the output S-S is placed in parentheses with a question mark, as I have found no unequivocal cases of this combination; based on tonal behavior elsewhere in the system, I suspect S-S would be the surface form. Every case where multiple variants are listed is type variation; in other words, certain compounds behave categorically in one way, and other compounds behave categorically in the other.

A few generalizations can be drawn from these patterns:
1. Stem2 S always remains S
2. Stem2 H always remains H(X)
3. Stem2 X never remains X; it assimilates to a preceding non-X tone
4. Stem1 X remains X, except for irregular cases where X-X raises to H-HX
5. If Stem1 surfaces as S, Stem2 will always be S
6. Stem1 H optionally raises to S before S

Most combinations show a single categorical output form, with the exception of X+X, H+S, S+H, which display variation. We can also notice that the restriction on final H tones is only applicable to the whole word, not to the individual stems. Thus, stems like *bí* 'goat' that would surface as [bî] in isolation are able to appear in their underlying form in Stem1 position, as in *bí-mənǐ* 'nannygoat'.

X+H and X+S show no tonal alternations in regular noun-noun compounds:

(3) a. cə̀n   + fá   →   cə̀n-fâ
        peanut + powder
        'peanut flour'

    b. nəgɨ̀ + mənǐ   →   nəgɨ̀-mənǐ
        cow + woman
        'heifer'

Both Stem1 and Stem2 retain the same tone in the compound as they do in isolation.

X+X combinations, however, show a high degree of lexical variation. Uniting the output forms, however, is the generalization that final X cannot remain; it must raise to either H or S. If it raises to H, Stem1 X sometimes raises as well. Examples in (4) illustrate the outputs X-S, X-HX, and H-HX, respectively:

(4) a. kpɛ̀ɛ + kɔ̌ɔ   →   kpɛ̀ɛ-kɔ́ɔ (X-S)
        knife + handle
        'knife handle'

    b. bəgɔ̀ + gǔɔ   →   bəgɔ̀-gûɔ (X-HX)
        Bobo + country
        'Bobo country'

    c. cəbɛ̀ɛ + kərǔ   →   cəbée-kərû (H-HX)
        shea.nut + coop
        'shea nut storage'

The case in (4c) is the only instance I am aware of of X+X raising to H-HX. Turning to the other two patterns, we see that all instances of X-HX involve the same Stem2 *gûɔ*, which suggests that this HX allomorph may be an irregular form used in compounds; the unusual cases where *gûɔ* surfaces as [gûa] support the hypothesis that these compounds are irregular and shouldn't define the general rules of compounding. Thus, X-S may be seen as the normal output of X+X in regular noun-noun compounds. While a polar change from X to S may seem unusual, it is also attested in argument-head tonal alternations, wherein X becomes S after a H-toned argument (see §4.4.2).

Both H+X and H+H neutralize to H-HX in regular noun-noun compounds. This is illustrated by the following examples:

(5) a. təgé + kərù̀ → təgé-kərû
    chicken + coop
    'chicken coop'

   b. né + fá → né-fâ
    néré + powder
    'néré powder'

In (5a), we see the same HX allomorph of underlying X-toned *kərù̀* 'coop' that we saw in (4c) above. It is possible that paradigm uniformity effects are responsible for the irregular realization of this X+X compound.

With the input H+S, we see variation between H-S and S-S in the output:

(6) a. bí + mənǐ → bí-mənǐ
    goat + woman
    'nanny goat'

   b. ɲəná + bű → ɲənǎ-bű
    mouth + sand
    'mouse burrow'

Neither combination is common, making it difficult to assess which pattern should be regarded as the default.

With S+H, the behavior is even more difficult to discern. S+H compounds that surface as H-HX are unquestionably regular noun-noun compounds, but we see many cases of S-S as well. Here, it is difficult to determine whether this is a tonal possibility for regular noun-noun compounds or whether these are possessive-type compounds, where S-S is the expected output. First, examples of S+H becoming H-HX are shown in (7):

(7) a. mənǐ + tí → mə̀nì-tî
woman + bachelor
'unmarried woman'

b. ɲəgə̋ + fá → ɲəgé-fâ
salt + powder
'powdered salt'

We see clear cases of lowering in these compounds, a tonal outcome that is not attested in argument-head tonal alternations where initial S exceptionlessly spreads to the following head, regardless of its underlying tone.

But many noun-noun compounds are attested whose underlying stems are S+H and whose surface form is S-S, and is not always clear whether these should be treated as regular noun-noun compounds or as possessive-type compounds. Consider the following examples:

(8) a. sǒn + tá → sǒn-tǎ
sky + fire
'sun'

b. ɲǚį + cí → ɲǚį-cǐ
honey + house
'bee hive'

In both examples, the head noun is an alienable noun, thus not a noun that would regularly undergo argument-head tonal alternations. On the other hand, this is true for most possessive-type compounds: the head is not obligatorily an inalienable noun, yet they form compounds using the same mechanism. I leave the question open as to whether the forms in (8) are a tonal option for regular noun-noun compounds or whether they are possessive-type compounds. For a discussion of the latter, see §7.1.2.

7.1.2 Possessive-type compounds

Possessive-type compounds are also noun-noun compounds, but they are phonologically identical to inalienable possessive constructions (see §8.6.1). The initial (non-head) acts as the possessor and the head noun as the possessed, meaning tonally, it is the initial stem that determines the overall tonal form of the compound. For example, we can compare a productively formed inalienable possessive construction in (9a) with a possessive-type compound in (9b):

(9) a. kərê dön
 man child
 'the man's child'

 b. kərê-dərön
 man-child
 'boy'

With the inalienable noun *dôn* 'child', the possessive construction in (9a) refers to the child of the man. Using the variant stem *dərôn* in (9b), the compound means 'boy'; in other words, *kərê* 'man' is a modifier referring to the gender of the child rather than the child's parent. In both cases, though, the phonological form is the same. The ban on final H applies to the initial stem, yielding a HX contour (/kəré/ → [kərê]), and the final tone of the possessor/initial stem spreads onto the second element, neutralizing its tone. For further discussion of these tonal rules, see §4.3.2.1 and §4.4.2.

The interesting thing about possessive-type compounds is that they follow the behavior of inalienable possession, despite the fact that the head nouns in this type of compound are not obligatorily inalienable. For example, consider an older vocabulary item referring to a mouse burrow (cf. (6b) above):

(10) ɲəná + tɔ́ɔn → ɲənâ-tɔ̀ɔn
 mouse + beer.jar
 'mouse burrow'

The head noun, *tɔ̂ɔn* 'beer jar', is not an inalienable noun. To refer to the beer jar of someone, the alienable possessive strategy with the genitive particle *tě* is used (e.g. *à tê tɔ̂ɔn* 'her beer jar'). But in this compound, the tighter syntactic connection between an inalienable noun and its possessor is co-opted to create compound nouns.

As noted in §7.1.1.2 above, it is sometimes difficult, if not impossible, to tell whether a compound is being treated as a regular noun-noun compound or as a possessive-type compound without simply saying that any compound that could conceivably be following argument-head tonal alternations must therefore be a possessive-type compound. For instance, *sə̆məŋǎ-sǔ* 'religion', consists of the modifier *sə̆məŋǎ* 'god' and the head noun *sô* 'path'. The S of the modifier raises the H of the head, which is the pattern in argument-head tonal relations, but it is also consistent with the drive of regular noun-noun compounds to have a lexical tone melody.

The following subsections illustrate some common heads in possessive-type compounds.

7.1.2.1 Compounds with *sân* 'thing'

Many compounds (including some regular compounds) are found with the head *sân*, which I take to mean roughly 'thing'. It is a bound root, never occurring on its own. Examples of possessive-type compounds with *sân* are shown in (11):

(11) a. dân-sǎn
mouth-thing
'crop'

b. gùɔ-sərà-sàn
country-chief-thing
'thing for the chief'

c. ŋàa-sàn
inside-thing
'guts'

All compounds with *sân* refer to objects, whose definition is elaborated upon by the initial stem(s). There does not appear to be very fixed semantics for *sân* except that it is a concrete object, unlike *kû*, which can be applied to things like languages and situations. As we can see in these examples, *sân* compounds follow argument-head tone sandhi rules, and thus X+X raises to L L, which we do not see in regular compounding.

7.1.2.2 Compounds with *dên* 'seed'

Among the most common possessive-type compounds are those in which the head is *dên* 'grain'. Related to *dôn* 'child', this stem can refer to literal grains, or it can be used more figuratively to refer to small seed-like objects.

First, in (12), examples are given illustrating literal 'grain' uses of *dên*:

(12) a. mǎan-dẽn
rice-grain
'grain of rice'

b. jǎnɛ́-dẽ́n
corn-grain
'kernel of corn'

c. tɑ̰́ɑ̰́-dẽ́n
palm-nut
'palm nut'

In each case, *dên* takes on the final tone of the preceding non-head noun.
More figurative uses of *dên* are shown below:

(13) a. kɔ́-dẽ̀n
bone-grain
'button'

b. kpṹn-dὲn
   throat-grain
   'esophagus'

c. səgɔ̂ɛ-nὲn
   stomach-grain
   'navel'

In (13a), traditional buttons (made of bone) are referred to as little grains of bone– not literally a seed or grain, but similar in shape and size. In (13b), the head noun *dên* refers to one of the smaller elements (tubes) that make up the throat. In other words, *dên* here does not refer to a small seed-like object, but a smaller component of a whole. In (13c), there is some irregular segmental phonology: 'stomach' surfaces as *səgɔ̂ɛ* rather than regular *səgɔ̀* and *dên* mutates to *nên*. Here, 'grain' refers to the navel or bellybutton, another small component element of the whole.

7.1.3 Crypto-compounds

Crypto-compounds (cf. Heath 2008, Matisoff 2008, McPherson 2013) are nouns that show all of the phonological hallmarks of being a compound, but in which one or both of the roots are bound. In the case where only one root is bound, these compounds are analogous to English "cranberry" compounds (where *cran-* means nothing outside of the compound, while *berry* is, of course, a free and transparent stem).

I begin with these simpler cases. Compounds of this type tend to be regular noun-noun compounds rather than possessive-type compounds, perhaps reflecting stronger lexicalization/less productively formed compounds. The examples in (14) lists some cases of cranberry-type crypto-compounds, with only one bound root:

(14) gɔ̀ɔ-frɔ̂   ground-??   'ground'
     kṹ-jəgɔ̂   toh-??   'leftover toh (the next day)'
     kpénén-mɔ̃̀ɲɔ̃̌ finger-??   'pinky finger'
     kprṳ̀-kíkíaa   stomach-??   'snail'
     mənĭ-frṹ   woman-??   'wedding'
     mɔ̀̃-tî   person-??   'person'
     sɔ̃̀n-sân   ??-thing   'animal pen'
     sɔ̃́n-kərĭ   sky-??   'sunset'

As these examples show, it is more common for the final stem to be bound than the initial stem (though interestingly, in two of the cases, this initial stem could conceivably be the head: 'leftover toh' and 'pinky').

It is sometimes possible to see that these crypto-compounds were historically transparent, but one of the stems has evolved over time in its independent form while retaining a different form in the compound. For instance, it is tempting to tie the *mɔ̰́ɲɔ̰́* in *kpénén-mɔ̰́ɲɔ̰́* 'pinky' to the adjective *mɔ̌ɛ́n* 'small', itself an irregular-sounding adjective. Similarly, in the compound *bíaa-cî* 'mudbrick house', *cî* is the regular noun for 'house', while *bíaa* is most likely related to the noun *bîɛɛ* 'mud'. In other cases, like *gɔ̀ɔ-frɔ̂* 'ground, dirt', there are no likely synchronic candidates to shed light on the bound stem *frɔ̂*.

A sample of fully opaque crypto-compounds in which neither stem can be identified (thus obscuring whether or not we should even be calling these forms compounds) are shown in (15):

(15) *bé-dɛ̋-kɔ̋*   'high dry spot'
       bö-kɔ̌ɔ   'billygoat'
       dɛ̀n-fɔ̂   'fermented grain (for beer)'
       dɔ̰̋-ŋmɔ̰̀n   'jaw'
       gɛ̀n-fəlɛ́n   'soap'
       kú-tằa   'forehead'
       kṵ̀-gbằn   'fritters'
       tô-ŋmön   'naked'

The final morpheme *kɔ̋* in *bé-dɛ̋-kɔ̋* 'high dry spot' could be the postposition 'on', but it would still leave *bé-dɛ̋* opaque. It is tempting to see *dɛ̀n* in *dɛ̀n-fɔ̂* 'fermented grain' as 'grain', but it differs both vocalically and tonally, making such a connection tenuous at best. In the case of *kú-tằa* 'forehead', a parallel could be drawn to *cé-tằa* 'palm', where *cé* 'hand' is transparent; in both, *tằa* could refer to a large flat expanse.

A corner of the lexicon with many crypto-compounds is vocabulary for times of the day, most of which contain the bound root *gùɔ-* combined with another bound root. This vocabulary is illustrated in (16):

(16) *gùɔ-cɛ̋rɛ̋*   'dawn'
       gùɔ-dəgɛ̀   'morning'
       gùɔ-fḭ́ɛ   'night'
       gùɔ-təgằ   'middle of the night'

It is not clear whether there is any relation between *gùɔ* in these compounds and *gùɔ* meaning 'land, country, village'. The most transparent case is *gùɔ-cɛ̋rɛ̋* 'dawn', where *cɛ̋rɛ̋* is likely related to *cɛ̀rɛ̀* meaning 'day' or 'sleep'. There is some variation between speakers in whether this compound-initial is pronounced as *gùɔ* or *gö*; the latter I have also heard in the reduplicative adverb *gö-őo-gö* 'everyday'.

7.2 Noun-adjective compounds

Noun-adjective compounds are compounds in which one stem is an adjective. This is typically the final stem (following the noun, i.e. the normal position for an adjective), but tone patterns or semantics point to these combinations being lexicalized compounds as opposed to productively formed phrases. Nevertheless, there is a bit of a spectrum in this regard, with certain combinations more ambiguous than others.

(17) sú-bɔ̂ɔ   path-old   'animism'
     cəbâa-pètè   shoe-flat   'sandal'
     bṹ-kǎ   sand-white   'ash'
     gɔ̃̀ɔ-kǎ   ground-white   'white clay'
     gɔ̃̀ɔ-tsĭe   ground-black   'black clay'
     kəré-bɔ̂ɔ   man-old   'old man'
     məní-bɔ̂ɔ   woman-old   'old woman'
     mɔ̃̌-bɔ̂ɔ   person-old   'old person'
     nəgɛ́́ɛn-bəlě   intestine-large   'large intestine'
     nəgɛ́́ɛn-məŋě   intestine-small   'small intestine'
     ɲá-bəlě   mother-big   'grandmother'
     ɲá-bəlè̈   mother-big   'mother-in-law'

Certain compounds are clearly compounds because they follow compound tonology; for instance kəré-bɔ̂ɔ 'old man', where kəré retains its underlying final H rather than forming the characteristic HX compound of a noun in final position (cf. kərê bɔ̌ɔ 'tall man'). Others, such as gɔ̃̀ɔ-kǎ are more ambiguous. Speakers report that this is the term for a kind of white clay, but if the only white ground in the area is made of this clay, then this term does not necessarily reflect lexicalization and compounding. An interesting case in the table above is the tonal difference between 'grandmother' and 'mother-in-law', both of which involve the stems ɲá 'mother' and bəlě 'big'; analogous terms exist for 'grandfather' (nǐ-bəlě) and 'father-in-law' (nǐ-bəlè̈). Argument-head tone sandhi typically does not extend to adjectives, nor does it apply to multitonal stems; by either account, then, it is unsurprising that bəlě is unaffected by sandhi in 'grandmother' and 'grandfather'. For the in-law terms, though, bəlè̈ does undergo sandhi, emphasizing the fact that it is a compound and not a N+Adj sequence. (18a-b) contrast 'my grandfather' vs. 'my father-in-law', while (18c-d) contrast 'his grandfather' vs. 'his father-in-law'.

(18) a. mó nì̃-bəlě
        'my grandfather'

     b. mó nì-bəlè
        'my father-in-law'

c. ǎ ní-bələ̆
   'his grandfather'

d. ǎ ní-bələ̋
   'his father-in-law'

Seenku also shows a small number of noun-adjective bahuvrihi compounds, in other words, compounds that refer to a person or thing by some characteristic belonging to it. The two attested bahuvrihi compounds both refer to ethnicities: *dzṳ̈-tsı̆e* 'Dafin, Marka' (lit. mouth-black) and *tsṳ̀-kǎ* 'European' (lit. skin-white). Note that Dafin also means 'black mouth' in Jula.

While all of the noun-adjective compounds given above follow the usual noun-adjective order, one compound is attested in which this order is reversed: *bəlè-kənɔ̂* 'large work party (sometimes involving the whole village)', which appears to be made up of the adjectival stem *bəlĕ* (here [bəlè]) followed by the noun *kənɔ̂*, meaning 'work association'.

7.3 Noun-postposition compounds

There is a small class of compound nouns in Seenku that contain a postposition. Most commonly, this postposition is found between two nouns, but in a few cases, it can be the head. The two configurations are treated separately in the subsections below.

7.3.1 Compounds with postpositions

Noun-postposition-noun compounds tend to be possessive-type compounds tonally. This may be due to the fact that the most commonly attested postposition is the dative, which can be used in possessive constructions (see §8.6.2.2). For example:

(19) a. *cê-lè̈-körö̈*
       hand-DAT-jewelry
       'bracelet'

   b. *nâ-nè̈-sàn*
       sauce-DAT-thing
       'condiments'

   c. *nɔ́-nè̋-sǎn*
       eat-DAT-thing
       'food'

The example in (19a) is an example of a template for jewelry in Seenku; "jewelry for the hand" is a bracelet, "jewelry for the finger" is a ring, etc. The examples in (19b-c) both are headed by *sân* 'thing' (see §7.1.2.1 above), but in both cases, dative *lɛ̋* is nasalized to [nɛ̋] by the preceding nasal-final stems (*nân* 'sauce' and *nɔ́n* 'eat'), making it ambiguous as to whether the postposition should be analyzed as the dative or the locative.

Some compounds do explicitly use the locative, including:

(20) a. *pɛ̏n̂-bö̏-nɛ̏-sǎ̀n*
          donkey-back-LOC-thing
          'donkey's back padding'

      b. *pɛ̏n̂-gǜ-nɛ̏-sǎ̀n*
          donkey-neck-LOC-thing
          'yoke for donkey'

In (20a), it is a bit ambiguous between the locative and the dative, since *bőn* 'back' ends in a latent nasal, but *gù* 'neck' does not; the nasal must then be a part of the postposition's underlying representation, identifying it as the locative.

Also attested are compounds with the postposition *gṵ̀* 'under', such as:

(21) a. *tőo-gṹ-sǎn*
          eat-under-thing
          'wattle (chicken)'

      b. *tǎ̀n-gṹ-sḭ̏ɛ*
          wing-under-??
          'inner wing of a grasshopper'

In (21b), it is unclear what the head *sḭ̏ɛ* means independently.

Finally, we find cases where the associative postposition *wɛ̏* is used. Unlike with the dative compounds, regular compound tonology rather than possessive tonology is used:

(22) *dǎ̀-mé-təbê*
      wall-with-be.up.against.NOM
      'side pillar of a house'

At a deeper level, this compound consists of a nominal stem *dǎ̀n* 'wall', a postposition *wɛ̏* 'with', and a verb stem *təbé* 'be up against'. As part of the compound, the verb stem is nominalized.

There is an expression in Seenku meaning 'up above', namely *sǎ mɛ̋*, where the nasal on the associative *mɛ̋* is indicative of an underlying nasal coda on *sǎn*. This suggests that it is related, at least historically, to words like *sɔ́n* 'sky' or *sǎn* 'god', both indicative of something up high. The expression can be used on its own as an adjunct PP (23a) but it is also found in a couple of compound nouns:

(23) a. (səgɔ́) tsí sǎ mě mȅ kě təgì
(partridge) jump.REAL.PFV above with 3SG.SUBORD go.IRR stop.IRR
sǎ mě
above with
'[The partridge] jumped up high and stopped up high.' [sos170805t15:220]

b. sǎ-mě-dzȩ̏
above-with-teeth
'upper teeth'

c. sǎ-mě-tǎn
above-with-wing
'front wing (grasshopper)'

Both of these compounds are inalienable and undergo compound argument-head tone sandhi with the possessor. Interestingly, though, sǎ-mě is treated as one morpheme for the purposes of sandhi, creating the output ȁ sá-mé-dzȩ̋, where sǎ-mě lowers to H after X, and then that H triggers X to raise to S. See §4.4.2 for further discussion of argument-head tone sandhi.

7.3.2 Noun-postposition compounds

We find a small number of compounds that end in a postposition, rather than sandwiching it between two noun stems. These are listed in the table in (24), organized by final postposition:

(24) bòee-dàn-dəgŭaa   bricks-mouth-between   'space between mudbricks'
      jṳ̀i-dəgŭaa   mountain-between   'valley'
      cî-gṳ̀   house-under   'inside of the house'
      cüen-gṳ̀   arm-under   'armpit'
      jṳ̀-kɔ̌n   mountain-on   'summit, mountaintop'
      cəgêɛ-nȅ   sand-LOC   'place with sandy soil'
      ɲəmȁ-cě-nȅ   (cryptocompound)   'dry season'
      tsǚ-ně   (cryptocompound)   'forest'

The compounds in this table vary in their semantic transparency. Compounds with dəgŭaa 'between' are completely transparent, as is the one instance with kɔ̌n 'on'. Of the two compounds with gṳ̀ 'under', 'armpit' is transparent (cf. English 'underarm'), while cî-gṳ̀ looks like it should mean 'under the house' but instead refers to its interior. The final compounds in the table all appear to contain the locative postposition; each refers to a time or a place, in other words an expression that would likely be used with the locative, but more often than not the elements in the compound itself are not used on their own, hence making the whole form a cryptocompound.

7.4 Noun-verb and verb-noun compounds

In the last chapter, §5.2.2 addressed deverbal derivation through affixation and tone changes. However, the primary means of deriving nouns from verbs in Seenku is compounding, though oftentimes the line between the two processes is blurred as compounding itself can involve the same kind of tone changes.

In this section, I divide deverbal compounds up by their semantics. I first address different kinds of agentive compounds (§7.4.1), then turn to instrumental compounds (§7.4.2). Action nominals are typically created through tone changes on the verb root but without explicit compounding of the object and verb; see §5.2.2.3 for examples.

As this section will demonstrate, the majority of noun-verb and verb-noun compounds use the antipassive form of the verb root. It is unclear whether this is related to the semantics of antipassives in particular, or whether there is a confound whereby Seenku has a nominalizing strategy that happens to be homophonous with the antipassive. See §12.3 for further discussion of antipassive formation.

7.4.1 Agentive compounds

We find three different kinds of compounds denoting the agent of the verb stem. The most common and productive appears to be compounds with the head noun *sərà* 'master' following the verb stem (§7.4.1.1), but we also find verb-final compounds that simply employ tone changes to mark the change of category (§7.4.1.2) and compounds that use the human singular and plural suffixes discussed in §5.3.2 after the verb stem (§7.4.1.3). I discuss each type of agentive compound in turn below.

7.4.1.1 Compounds with *sərà* 'master'

One of the most common forms of agentive compounds in Seenku uses the noun stem *sərà* 'master' after the verb. A restriction on this kind of agentive is that it only takes intransitive verbs; the verb cannot have its own internal argument. For underlying intransitive verbs, this is no issue, but for transitive verbs, the verb stem must be made antipassive first, suppressing the internal argument. Agentive compounds with underlying intransitive verb stems are shown in (25):

(25) səmâ-sərà   'dancer'
      sérê-sərà   'Muslim (one who prays)'

More often than not, the verb in the agentive compound is rendered intransitive by the antipassive (§12.3). These examples are shown in (26), along with the underlying transitive verb stem:

(26) dəgêɛ-sərȁ   'cook'   cf. dəgɇ̋
      kəsîɛɛ-sərȁ   'careful person'   cf. kəsɇ́ɛ
      kùaa-sərȁ   'farmer'   cf. kùa
      kŏee-sərȁ   'singer'   cf. kŏo
      kpèɛ-sərà   'tailor'   cf. kpɔ̋ɔ
      sɇ̋ɛ-sərɇ̋   'buyer'   cf. sə̏
      səmêɛ-sərȁ   'beggar'   cf. səmɇ̋ɛ

The tone patterns of the derived compounds are not entirely consistent, ranging from all X-toned, to raised L-toned, to a LS contour tone on the antipassive noun that spreads to the head sərȁ.

The stem sərȁ is not just found in verb-noun compounds, but also with noun-noun compounds, indicating a person who possesses a certain thing or quality expressed in the non-head. For instance:

(27) dá̰-sərȁ   hump-master   'hunchback'
      fəŋá̰ḛ̀-sərà   power-master   'strong person'
      kŏkɔ̋ɔ-sərɇ̋   laziness-master   'lazy person'
      kṵ̀kő-sərà   quandary-master   'person with a problem'
      sɇ̋ɛkú-sərɇ̋   cleverness-master   'clever person'

However, most commonly, sərȁ literally means owner or master, found in the common compound gùɔ-sərȁ 'chief (lit. 'village-master')'.

7.4.1.2 Compounds with verb stem and tone changes

The agentive form of transitive verbs tends to be a compound consisting of the object and the verb, with the same kind of nominalizing tone changes discussed in §5.2.2.3. Examples from the current dataset are shown in (28):

(28) sắn-cérê   god-call   'muezzin'
                                         cf. céré 'call'
      jì-kɇ̰̂ɛ   fetish-worship   'customary chief'
                                         cf. kɇ̋ɛ 'worship'
      jì-ɲî   fetish-carry   'talisman'
                                         cf. ɲí 'carry'
      kú-səgɔ́-bâ   thing-good-do   'do-gooder'
                                         cf. bȁ 'do'
      sṵ̀gṵ̀nḭ̀-cên   navel-swallow   'mantis sp.'
                                         cf. cén 'swallow'

tsį̂ɔ-ŋmâ	caterpillar-eat	'Bobo (caterpillar eater)' cf. *ŋmá* 'eat'
cə̀n-fá-nɔ́	peanut-flour-eat	'Sambla (ground peanut eater)' cf. *nɔ́* 'eat'

Both realis and irrealis verb stems are used in these compounds. For instance, *bà* is the realis form of 'do', but *nɔ́* is the irrealis form of 'eat'; for most verbs, the two are segmentally identical and thus we cannot tell. As these examples show, the resulting tone pattern of these agentive compounds fits the general rules for compound tonology laid out in §7.1.1.2.

7.4.1.3 Compounds suffixed with human singular/plural

In two cases, we find an agentive compound that employs an antipassive verb stem, like in *serà* compounds above, but with the internal object as part of the compound as well. These constructions are additionally identifiable by their human singular and plural marking with the suffixes discussed in §5.3.2. The attested examples are as follows:

(29) a. *sə́məŋá̌-tsíɛɛ-jú-rí-mɔ̌*
   god-word.PL-say-ANTIP-HUM.SG
   'preacher' (lit. 'one who says the words of God')

   b. *sə́məŋá̌-tsíɛɛ-mɛ́ɛ̌-ŋɛ̌*
   god-word.PL-listen.ANTIP-HUM.PL
   'church congregation' (lit. 'those who hear the words of God')

It is unclear whether this is a productive construction.

7.4.2 Instrumental compounds

Instrumental compounds, expressing a noun used as an instrument in the action of a verb, use roughly the same construction as the agentive compounds discussed in §7.4.1.3. In particular, we can schematize them as follows:

(30) Object-Verb.ANTIP-Instrument

Examples are shown in (31):

(31) kṳ̀-bréɛ-tɔ́ɔn   toh-take.out-jar   'clay dish for toh'
                                                              cf. bɔ́ 'take out'
     dɔ̋ɔ-mərį́-kų̋   beer-drink-calabash   'beer calabash'
                                                              cf. mų̀ 'drink'
     sắn-cέrέέ̋-jŏ   god-call-water   'ablutions water'
                                                              cf. cέrέ 'call'
     dân-sằn-dəgέέ̋-wăatí́   mouth-thing-make-time   'harvest time'
                                                              cf. dəgέ 'make'

The initial object retains its own tone, rather than being incorporated into a compound tone pattern. This blurs the line between compounds like these vs. verb stems nominalized with tone, discussed in §5.2.2.3.

We find similar instrumental compounds where the antipassive actually suppresses the internal argument of the verb, if one was present originally. These include:

(32) tsį́-bréɛ-kəré   cut-take.out-man   'fiancé'
                                                              cf. tsį́-bɔ̋ 'get engaged'
     dəgêɛ-cì̀   cook-house   'kitchen'
                                                              cf. dəgέ 'cook'
     səŋέ̋ɛ-sắn   lie.down-thing   'bed'
                                                              cf. səŋá 'lie down'
     ŋmέɛ-dzę̋   chew-teeth   'molars'
                                                              cf. ŋmá 'eat (meat)'
     kṳaa-gə̀rêen   farm-hoe   'hoe (daba) for farming'
                                                              cf. kṳ̀a 'farm'
     fəgę̌ɛ-jṳ̀ê   plant-hoe   'hoe for planting'
                                                              cf. fəgę̏ 'plant'
     səgěɛ-jṳ̀ê   plow-hoe   'hoe for hand plowing'
                                                              cf. səgèɛ 'plow by hand'

The first example in the table shows that even idiomatic compound verbs like *tsį́-bɔ̋* 'get engaged' can be involved in compounds. In this case, a fiancé isn't an instrument of getting engaged per se, but still a necessary ingredient in the process. Similarly, the second example shows that the same construction can create a locative noun instead of an instrument, reminiscent of the range of participants possible in applicative constructions (Peterson 2007). The other examples are uncontroversial instrumental nouns. The compound *səŋέ̋ɛ-sắn* 'bed' is interesting in that *səŋá/səŋǎ* is an ambivalent verb that can mean either 'lie down' (with H tone in the intransitive) or 'lay somebody down' (with S tone in the transitive); despite having an intransitive counterpart already, the antipassive is still used in this construction, suggesting once again a connection between the antipassive and nominalization. For more on the antipassive, see §12.3.

8 Noun phrase structure

The preceding chapters have focused on nominal morphology, including root and stem shapes, affixation, and compounding; in every case, nouns were treated in isolation. In this chapter, we turn to how nouns combine with other elements to create noun phrases (NPs). This includes modification (adjectives), quantification (numerals and other quantifiers), determiners, possession, and combinations thereof. Relative clauses, another form of nominal modification, will be discussed separately in Chapter 17. Note that the use of NP to describe noun phrases is meant purely descriptively. The facts could easily fit into a theory of syntax involving the DP (Determiner Phrase).

In the course of this chapter, I will address morphological characteristics of nominal modifiers, including adjectives and quantifiers, so as to avoid repetition that would result from treating them in their own chapters.

8.1 Linear order of NP elements

Before turning to individual NP elements as they combine with the head noun, I first lay out the maximal NP structure in Seenku. The linear order of a complex noun phrase can be summarized as follows:

1. Possessor or (In)definite determiner
2. **Noun**
3. Adjective*
4. Numeral
5. Demonstrative/Indefinite determiner
6. Quantifier

The head noun is shown in bold. Preceding the head noun, we find a slot that can contain either a possessor or a determiner, either indefinite or definite. Definite determiners, which can be either a general definite or discourse definite, often though not obligatorily combine with a demonstrative determiner following the noun, in a position that can also host the indefinite determiner (though it will only appear in one slot for any given NP). All other noun phrase elements follow the head noun: adjectives (where the asterix indicates one or more), numerals, demonstrative determiners, and quantifiers.

The following examples illustrate these orders:

(1) a. mó sɔ̀n bəlě (Poss N Adj)
1SG.EMPH heart big
'my big heart'

b. ǎ   bí-dḭ̀   fín ně̋   (Det N Num Dem)
    DEF goat-CLF.PL two DEM.PL
    'these two goats'

c. bî   tsĭe lê   (N Adj Dem)
    goat black DEM
    'this black goat'

d. môo   bḭ̀   tsí-tsĭe   fí́   (Poss N Adj Num)
    1SG.GEN goat RED-black.PL two
    'my two black goats'

e. mó   tòee   fí́ lě̋   (Poss N Num Dem)
    1SG.EMPH ear.PL two DEM
    'my two ears/these two ears of mine'

f. môo   bḭ̀   tsí-tsĭe   kərúi̋   (Poss N Adj Quant)
    1SG.EMPH.GEN   goat RED-black   all.PL
    'all of my black goats'

The example in (1a) illustrates the order <1, 2, 3>. In (1b) we see <1, 2, 4, 5>. (1c) combines adjectives and demonstratives, illustrating both the order <2, 3, 5> as well as the fact that the demonstrative pronoun is optional. (1d) shows the order <1, 2, 3, 4>, combining an adjective and a numeral. In (1e), we see evidence for numeral before demonstrative with the order <1, 2, 4, 5>, while (1f) combines the first and last elements of the NP, a possessor and a quantifier, in the order <1, 2, 3, 6>.

All of the slots in the NP can be filled simultaneously, resulting in quite complex NPs, if we place possessors and pre-nominal determiners in the same slot; evidence for this move comes from the fact that there are no examples in the data corpus combining a possessor and a pre-nominal determiner. This is reminiscent of English, where a noun can be preceded by either a possessor (John's cat) or a determiner (the cat) but not both (*John's the cat).

The sections below treat each of the NP elements. The order of presentation deviates from the linear order of the NP in order to make the discussion more coherent, e.g. discussing determiners and demonstratives in adjacent sections, since they often obligatorily co-occur. I also defer the discussion of possession until the end of the chapter (§8.6), after non-possessive modifiers have been addressed.

8.2 Determiners (indefinite, definite, and demonstrative)

Unlike many Mande languages, including closely related Dzùùngoo (Solomiac 2007), Seenku has no suffixal definite marking. Whether anything can be truly construed as definite marking at all is a matter of debate. In elicitation settings, consultants do not distinguish between definite and indefinite nouns. In narratives, however, we find many instances in which a noun is preceded by what looks like a pronoun, either the 3sg or the discourse definite, and these may carry a definite meaning (or at least a discourse definite meaning). The former is discussed in §8.2.1 and the latter in §8.2.2. Demonstrative determiners are unequivocally attested, and these follow the noun (see §8.2.3), though they are often combined with a pre-nominal determiner. There is also what I treat as an indefinite determiner *tsɛ́*, which can appear either pre- or post-nominally, though this may be best analyzed as a quantifier ('a certain, one'). Since it cannot combine with other determiners or quantifiers, it is not possible to distinguish between the two analyses on combinatorial grounds; I discuss NPs with *tsɛ́* below in §8.2.4. Most NPs in the data corpus carry no determiners, with context to differentiate between definite and indefinite NPs.

8.2.1 Definite determiner *à*

Though uncommon in elicited forms, NPs in narratives are often preceded by what appears to be the 3sg pronoun *à*. NPs carrying *à* are seldom the first mention of a referent in the narrative, suggesting a definite or discourse definite reading to this pronoun.

In terms of form, this construction is reminiscent of inalienable possession, as it involves the direct juxtaposition of a pronoun and a noun. Unlike possession, however, argument-head tone sandhi (§4.4.2) does not take place; there is no tonal interaction between the determiner and the noun. Further, all of the attested examples of this form involve alienable nouns, which in possessive constructions would require either a genitive particle or lengthening of the pronoun. As laid out in §8.1, the definite *à* may be blocked with inalienable nouns, which obligatorily appear as possessed in Seenku.

It is unclear whether speakers think of the definite *à* as the same as the 3sg; to distinguish the two in glossing, I gloss the definite usage as DEF in what follows. Examples of this form include:

(2) a. ì à cî ɲɛ̀ kó tő mɛ̀ kɛ́
  3PL DEF house build.REAL.PFV D.DEF like 3SG.SUBORD go.IRR
  ɲà
  be.finished.IRR
  'They built the house like that until it was done.' [sos130828t2:8]

 b. ǎ sà-bö-kɔ̌ɔ sǐ ǎ kə̀ká` kɔ̀ɛ dəgǔaa
  DEF second.son-billygoat be DEF meat head.PL between
  'The billygoat was between the animal heads.' [sos150626t3:61]

c. mɔ̀ɔ́   fà   ä̀ jén-jén sí́   té̋
    person.SBJV enter.IRR DEF RED-tale female.PL GEN
    'Let's get into folk tales.' [sos150626t2:1]

d. ä̀   kɛ̀nɛ̀ tà-fíɛ̰   lé màa
    DEF bird.PL fire-heat.REAL.PTCP FOC again
    'The birds also warmed up.' [sos150626t3:30]

As these examples show, the form of the definite is invariant, always ä̀ regardless of whether the noun that follows is singular (as in (2a-b)) or plural (as in (2c-d)).

To show how the definite pronoun appears on subsequent mentions of a reference, consider in (3a-b) two consecutive sentences of a narrative.

(3) a. ä̀   kǎa-kà   wé́ tsé̋ fên sɲ̀ì, məgɔ̌n-cəbḛ̌e íaa, á
       3SG RED-go.REAL.PRF FOC INDF thing be.there monitor   TOP 2SG
       məgɔ̌n-cəbḛ̌e tő̋   kɛ̀
       monitor   know.IRR EMPH
       'When he went out, there was something there, a monitor lizard, you know monitor lizards.' [sos170711t1:9]

b. mɛ̀̋   ké̋ wé́ ä̀ məgɔ̌n-cəbḛ̌e kǎa
    3SG.SUBORD go.IRR FOC DEF monitor   chase.IRR
    'And he went to chase the monitor lizard.' [sos170711t1:10]

In the first sentence, the referent 'monitor' is introduced with no definite marking; in fact, this first introduction of the monitor is preceded by an explicit indefinite noun 'something', and then the speaker confirms with the listener that he knows what this animal is. In the second sentence in (3b), 'monitor lizard' is now accompanied by the definite pronoun, leading to a literal translation like "He went to chase the [aforementioned] monitor lizard."

Many other examples of pre-nominal ä̀ occur in conjunction with demonstratives; for these examples, see §8.2.3 below.

8.2.2 Discourse definite determiner *kó̰*

A very similar construction is found with the discourse definite pronoun *kó̰*, discussed in §6.1.2, in place of the regular definite *ä̀*. This also commonly stands alone, for instance as a resumptive pronoun in relative clauses. However, as a determiner, the discourse definite must occur in conjunction with a following demonstrative *bḛ́*, discussed on its own in §8.2.3. Here, I will specifically address the *kó̰ X bḛ́* construction.

This construction is resolutely discourse definite (anaphoric), inappropriate in deictic contexts. It is used to make reference to some aforementioned discourse entity. Unlike the regular definite determiner *à* (even when used in conjunction with the demonstrative *bɛ́*), the discourse definite *kʊ́* triggers tone sandhi on the following noun, following the same pattern as inalienable possessors: X-toned nouns become S, H- and S-toned nouns become X. The following examples illustrate these constructions, which are bolded for ease of reading:

(4) a. ké **kʊ́ jěn-jěn** bɛ́ yɛ̌rɛ̌ ŋɛ́
COP D.DEF RED-story DEM self.JU NEG
'It's not that riddle [that we were just talking about].' [sos161009t1:87]

b. ì ǎ wótərő gǎa à wɛ̀ mɔ̌ nǎ lɛ̌ à
3PL DEF donkey.cart pull.IRR 3SG with person PROSP REL.SBJV 3SG
bɛ̀ mǐ í sí wɛ̋, wótərő lɛ̋ né wétənɛ̌ ǎ
put.IRR where LOG RECP with donkey.cart PST come.IRR now 3SG
jəgà **kʊ́ dəgɔ̌ɛɛ** bɛ́ nɛ̌
put.down.IRR D.DEF place DEM LOC
'They would pull a donkey cart with it, and where it was put down together, the donkey cart would come and put it down in that place.' [sos170702t1:45]

c. áǎ **kʊ́ sʊ̀** bɛ́ kòo wɛ́ têɛ
2SG.PST D.DEF song DEM sing.REAL.PFV FOC who.DAT.Q
'Who did you sing that song for?' [sos170805t3:140]

The example in (4a) is drawn from a narrative where the participants were telling various riddles and discussing their answers. The speaker, MD, was just referring to a different riddle when he made the statement in (4a), stating that it was not that discourse-defined riddle. The context for the discourse definite is explicitly provided in (4b); the clause before the discourse definite expression refers to a place where the farmers and their donkey carts would put down the grain that they had harvested, and in the next clause, the discourse definite is used to refer back to that place. Note that *dəgɔ̌ɛɛ* 'place' escapes tone sandhi due to the fact that it is multitonal (§4.4.2). In (4c), the women were describing the meaning of a song that they had just sung, and the interviewer GET then poses this question; the discourse entity is quite salient in this case.

One more example is provided in (5), where the first mention of the noun 'mud-brick house' is set up in (5a), followed up with a discourse definite expression in (5b).

(5) a. Bon,   kərɔ̀   ǎ-né   dɔ̌n ǐ   ɲá̰   sóen ŋɛ́ kú lɛ́
       well.FR yesterday and.then today 3PL be.NEG one NEG thing which
       tɔ́, ǎ-lɔ́   kərɔ̀   mḯi   kóò   mí' wɛ̀   i
       like you.know.JU yesterday 1PL.PST be.born.IRR.HAB 1PL SUBORD LOG
       jó   bi̋aa-cî̋   gṵ̀
       see.IRR mudbrick-house under
       'Well, the way in which yesterday and today are not the same, you know that before we used to be born in mud brick houses.' [sos170702t1:46]

   b. mais kǔ   bi̋aa-cí   bé kɛ́   sáŋgá̰nső
      but.FR D.DEF mudbrick-house DEM COP.PST two.level.house
      'But those traditional houses had two levels.' [sos170702t1:47]

In the first sentence, the speaker introduces the topic of mudbrick houses; here, it carries no determiners. In the following utterance, the speaker refers to the mudbrick houses again, this time with the discourse definite and the demonstrative. Interestingly, the tone of *bi̋aa-cî* is largely unaffected; *cí* is allowed to maintain a final H tone before the demonstrative, but there is no sandhi, possibly because *bi̋aa-cí* is being interpreted as a single morpheme, hence making it a multitonal morpheme impervious to sandhi.

There is at least one expression involving the discourse definite determiner that does not take the demonstrative, and that is the postpositional expression *kǔ dəgɔ̀ nɛ̏* 'at that moment' (variant *kǔ dəgṵ̀ɛɛ nɛ̏*). The variation between *dəgɔ̀* and *dəgṵ̀ɛɛ* is reminiscent of the noun *dəgɔ̌ɔ* ~ *dəgɔ̌ɛɛ* 'place', but a) the length isn't consistent and b) generally LS-toned morphemes should be resistent to sandhi. I assume a diachronic relation between the two. An example of this expression include:

(6) Emma drée, non, kǔ   dəgɔ̀   nɛ̏   fáná áǎlí mó
    Emma want no.FR D.DEF moment LOC also even 1sg.emph
    dzïa   kɛ̰̀
    be.tired.REAL.PRF EMPH
    'Emma is for me, no, in that moment, even if I'm tired!' [sos170714t3:136]

This is likely a fixed expression, which would explain its deviant structures.

8.2.3 Demonstrative expressions

Unlike the discourse definite determiners we just saw, demonstrative determiners follow the noun in Seenku. There are two main constructions used to express a demonstrative meaning: what I call a "true" demonstrative *bé*, and a presentative expression with *lɛ́* followed by a resumptive pronoun that fills the same role; when asked, consultants say the two constructions are interchangeable. Like French *ce*, these are general demonstrative expressions which can be used deictically or to specify a discourse entity. Any deictic information, like proximal or distal, must come from context.

Typically, both *bé* and *lé* co-occur with a preceding definite determiner, either the discourse definite *kʊ́* as we have just seen or the regular definite *à*. However, the demonstrative *bé* is occasionally attested on its own without a definite.

In the subsections below, I first cover *bé*, then turn to *lé*.

8.2.3.1 *bé* demonstratives

Most commonly, the noun marked by *bé* is preceded by another definite determiner. We saw many examples of the discourse definite *kʊ́ X bé* construction in §8.2.2; here, I provide examples with the regular definite determiner *à*. Unlike the discourse definite, this construction does not trigger any tone changes. The only notable tonal fact with *bé*, as with *lé*, is that /H/ nouns can remain H-toned before the demonstrative; the process of H → HX that we see with nouns in isolation does not apply before the demonstrative. This is almost certainly due to the fact that the final X used to be a definite suffix which would not be used before an overt demonstrative determiner, though synchronically it must be learned as simply a tonal irregularity; for more on final X epenthesis, see §4.3.2.1.

A selection of textual and elicited examples of the *à X bé* demonstrative construction are shown in (7):

(7) a. ǎa   sú   wè à   bá̰a̰-dón   bé   sṵ̀
       3SG.SUBORD get.up.IRR HAB DEF balafon-child DEM pick.up.IRR
       'He would get up and pick up the little balafon...' [sos170711t1:40]

   b. mais à   tǎa   bé
      but.FR DEF proverb DEM
      'But that proverb...' [sos161009t1:159]

   c. à   dəgɔ̌ɔ bé təgɔ̀n cèrè   wè Tûe
      DEF place DEM name call.IRR HAB Toronsso
      'That place is called Toronsso.' [sos171009t1:13]

   d. mó   nǎ   à   bí bé sǎ̰
      1SG.EMPH PROSP DEF goat DEM buy.IRR
      'I will buy this goat.' [sos150805e]

The demonstrative is also occasionally attested without a preceding determiner. Examples include the following:

(8) a. jəbɛ́̋ bɛ́ kpɔ́ɔ sį̀
       clothes DEM sew.PTCP be
       'Those clothes are sewn.' [sos150806e]

   b. səgɔ̀ bɛ́ fɛ̋ fɔ̋
      wrestling DEM heat.up.IRR more
      'The wrestling heats up.' [sos170714t3:71]

   c. kú bɛ́ kàä Kanazoe kɔ̋n nɛ̋
      thing DEM go.REAL.PRF Kanazoe head LOC
      'Kanazoe is taking this seriously! [Lit. 'this thing has gone into Kanazoe's head!]' [sos161009t1:163]

These constructions are considerably rarer than those with the initial determiner, and there is always the risk that textual examples are simply accidental omissions of short grammatical elements.

The plural form of the demonstrative is *bɛ̋*, created by regular plural tone raising of H to S (§5.3.1). This can be seen both when the noun is preceded by a determiner (9a) and when it is not (9b):

(9) a. kó bà̰à̰-dḭ̀ bɛ̋ sį̀ í mú-mənɛ̋
       D.DEF balafon-grain.PL DEM.PL be LOG RED-small
       'Those keys there are small.' [sos170711t1:104]

   b. kó sɛ́ɛ̋ bɛ̋ kó wɛ̏ ḭ̀ ɲá màa kó
      D.DEF farming.caste.PL DEM.PL D.DEF SUBORD 3PL refuse again D.DEF
      nɛ̏
      LOC
      'Those farmers also refused and rejected him.' [sos171009t1:88]

   c. à̰ tsɛ́ɛɛ bɛ̋ sį̀ í gɔ̀ɔ
      DEF word.PL DEM.PL be LOG dry
      'These questions are hard.' [sos171009t1:120]

   d. ḭ̀ á wôo kà̰ bų̀ɛ̀-dḭ̀ bɛ̋ jő
      COMP 2SG EMPH.SUBORD go.REAL.PFV djinn-child.PL DEM.PL find.IRR
      dán né nɛ̏
      place REL LOC
      '[He asked,] "Where did you go to find those djinns?"' [sos130828t2:29]

In all of these examples, the noun is also plural-marked.

8.2.3.2 The presentative *lê* as a demonstrative

As mentioned at the beginning of this section, the presentative *lê* can be used like a demonstrative. This term is likely a contraction of *lé lḛ̀*, possibly related to the relative marker and the subordinate TAMP marker, since the plural of this presentative is *lë*, i.e. the X remains after plural raising. Since I am not certain of this synchronic connection, I will simply gloss these as PRES and PRES.PL for the singular and plural presentative, respectively. These expressions differ from those with *bé* in that they are obligatorily followed by a resumptive pronoun. Vowel hiatus resolution (§3.5.4) means that these typically surface as *lâ* in the singular and *lï* in the plural, though as always my transcriptions represent the level before regular phonological processes.

The presentative-marked NP is typically not fronted or otherwise extracted from its base position, but as (13) shows, it is possible to front them.

Like *bé* demonstratives, the presentative *lê* more commonly co-occurs with a preceding definite marker. The following examples are drawn from both text and elicitation, and represent a mix of singular and plural uses:

(10) a. mó   yɛ̀rɛ̰̀   nəgì   lɛ́   büɔ   ằ   kú   lê   ằ   lɛ́
1SG.EMPH self.JU mind PST go.out.REAL.PRF DEF thing DEM 3SG DAT
'Myself, I had forgotten that thing.' [sos161009t1:110]

b. ì̀   á   wó   káká̰   ì̀   á   ằ   bá̰ɑ̰   lê   kɔ́
COMP 2SG EMPH should COMP 2SG DEF balafon PRES D.DEF
brɛ̰̀
play.ANTIP.IRR
'That you should play that balafon.' [sos170711t1:269]

c. ì̀   sḭ̀   ằ   mɔ̰̀ɛ   lë   kṵ̋ɛ   cɛ́rɛ̋   nɛ̋   ȉi
3PL be DEF person.PL PRES.PL others call.REAL.NOM LOC 3PL.SBJV
né
come.IRR
'They are calling those people [to tell them] to come.' [sos170711t1:393]

d. mó   nă   ằ   bí   lë   ȉ   bá̰
1SG.EMPH PROSP DEF goat PRES.PL 3PL hit.IRR
'I will hit these goats.' [sos150811e]

In (10a), the presentative-marked NP is in adjunct position after the verb; it is followed by a resumptive pronoun *ằ*, which carries the postposition. In (10b), it is in object position before the verb, and it is resumed by the discourse definite pronoun *kɔ́*. In (10c), it is likewise in object position, where the presentative carries the plural and is resumed by the pronoun *kṵ̋ɛ*. Finally, in (10d), it is also in object position and plural marked, but here, curiously, the noun itself is singular. The presentative-marked NP is resumed by the pronoun *ȉ*.

In one case, the 3pl pronoun ì is used in place of the regular definite à; in this example, the presentative-marked NP is in subject position:

(11) ì   dənį̃   lë̈   ì   lɛ̋   à   jío   tsɛ̋́ ì   ké   kʊ́   tɔ̋
     3PL child.PL PRES.PL 3PL PST 3SG say.REAL.PFV how COMP COP D.DEF like
     'Like those kids said, it's like that.' [sos150626t3:15]

As with the demonstrative bɛ̋, the presentative can also follow a noun without a preceding determiner, though this configuration is less common:

(12) a. brún nɛ̂ɛ   təgɔ̋n í   bɛ̋   ì   gɔ̋ŋgɔ̀rɔ̀ŋgɔ̋
        cane DEM.DAT name LOG do.IRR QUOT curved.staff
        'That cane is called gɔ̋ŋgɔ̀rɔ̀ŋgɔ̋.' [sos170714t3:83]

    b. Vraiment, vraiment, fɔ̋   mɔ̀̈   tsɔ́ɛ̀ wɛ̀   kűi   lë̈   ì   lɛ́
       really.FR really.FR must person ask.IRR HAB thing.PL DEM 3PL DAT
       tsɛ̋́ sɔ̋n   nɛ̋́
       INDF moment LOC
       'Really, really, we need to ask about these things sometime.' [sos161009t1:160]

    c. mənı̋   lê   à   sị̈ í   bəlɛ̆
       woman PRES 3SG be LOG big
       'That woman is fat.' [sos150808e]

In one case, I have seen fronting of the NP marked with this demonstrative strategy, with the resumptive pronoun kʊ́ taking its place in situ:

(13) bî   tsǐe lê   mó   kà   kʊ́   sɑ̋́n
     goat black PRES 1SG.EMPH go.REAL.PFV D.DEF buy.IRR
     'That black goat, I am going to buy that one.' [sos150703e]

The NP 'the black goat' is pre-posed; it functions as the object of the main clause, where the discourse definite kʊ́ stands in its place.

8.2.4 Indefinite determiner tsɛ̋́

Indefinite nouns can be explicitly introduced in discourse using the determiner tsɛ̋́, which can appear either before or after the noun. The post-nominal position appears to be the more general position, with the pre-nominal position more common for semantically light nouns like 'thing' or 'person'. As mentioned in the introduction to this section, it may also be possible to analyze tsɛ̋́ as a quantifier like "one" or "a certain", but it is not clear how to disambiguate these two analyses.

The indefinite determiner is found most commonly in discourse to introduce a referent who will go on to be a recurring character, giving it a translation closer to English colloquial "this one" ("there was this one woman...") rather than an unmarked indefinite "a".

Cases of post-nominal indefinite determiners are shown in (14):

(14) a. ké jén-jén tsɛ́, mó nă ằ təmé
COP RED-story INDF 1SG.EMPH PROSP 3SG tell.IRR
'It's a story, I will tell it.' [sos130828t1:3]

b. donc, cəbâa-dərɔ̀ tsɛ́, ằ ní cìë ằ ɲằ
so.FR orphan-child INDF 3SG father die.REAL.PRF 3SG mother
mɛ̈ cì̀
3SG.SUBORD die.REAL.PFV
'So, there was an orphan, her father had died, her mother was also dead.' [sos130828t1:10]

c. dónô fɔ́ɔ mǒén tsɛ́ kʊ́ í bɛ́ ì̀ ằ tɛ̀ɛ ɲì
child skinny small INDF D.DEF LOG do.IRR COMP 3SG leave.IRR there
'A small skinny child said, "Leave him there".' [sos170711t1:26]

d. sɔ́n bəlĕ băa tsɛ́ bi̱ɛ̱
sky big IDEO INDF rain.REAL.PFV
'A huge rain fell.' [sos150626t3:1]

In each case, the indefinite serves to introduce a new referent in the discourse. After this initial introduction, the NP will either be unmarked or marked with the definite or demonstrative determiners introduced in §8.2.1–§8.2.3.

The indefinite determiner is also attested in the pre-nominal position. This is most common with light nouns, such as 'thing', 'person', 'man', or 'woman', but it can be attested with less common nouns like 'story' or 'country' as well. For instance:

(15) a. mɛ̈ kɛ́ mɛ̈ í bɛ́ ɛ́! ì̀
3SG.SUBORD go.IRR 3SG.SUBORD LOG say.REAL.PFV INTERJ COMP
bùbă̆ tsɛ́ fên si̱ nɔ̋-ŋɛ́ ằ dáǹ gù̱
dad.VOC INDF thing be here-NEG DEF wall under
'He went and shouted, "Eh! Dad, there is something over there next to the wall!"' [sos150626t3:6]

b. tsɛ́ mənɩ́ búɔ, kɛ́ cɔ́ɔ-bâ-mənì̀, ằ
INDF woman go.out.REAL.PFV, COP magic-do.NOM-woman 3SG
sɛ́ gərû
be.mean too.much
'A woman went out who was a sorcerer, she was very mean.' [sos130828t1:8]

c. í wó kà tsɛ́̋ gǜɔ nɛ̏
LOG EMPH go.REAL.PFV INDF country LOC
'I went to a country.' [sos161009t1:2]

d. ń nǎ wɛ́ màa tsɛ̋́ jén-jɛ̋́n jű í lɛ̏
1SG PROSP FOC again INDF RED-story say.IRR 2PL DAT
'I am going to tell you another riddle.' [sos161009t1:1]

The example in (15d) can be compared to that in (14a), showing the interchangeability of pre-nominal and post-nominal position for the indefinite determiner. However, this interchangeability may be limited to simple nouns; I have seen no instances where a noun modified by an adjective has a preceding indefinite determiner.

As all of these examples show, the indefinite remains tonally independent of the noun regardless of whether it precedes or follows it.

8.3 Adjectives

This section addresses adjectival modifiers, including the morphology of adjectival stems and structural aspects of adjectival modification. For adjectival predicates, see §14.3. For ideophonic adjectival intensifiers, see §9.2.1.2.

I begin in §8.3.1 with a discussion of "adjective" as a syntactic category in Seenku. In §8.3.2, I address adjectival stem shape, before turning to adjectives as modifiers in §8.3.3. Finally, I address the question of headless NPs with adjectives in §8.3.4.

See also McPherson (2017a) for further discussion of the morphosyntax of adjectives in Seenku.

8.3.1 Adjectival vs. verbal modification

As in many other African languages (Welmers and Welmers 1969, Ameka 2001, Segerer 2008, etc.), nouns may be modified in two ways in Seenku: 1) using a small set of true adjectives, or 2) using verbs in participial form. The two overlap in both form and function to a great extent, blurring the line between the two supposed categories, but they can be distinguished in two ways. Let us take the example of 'black', an adjective, and 'dry', a participial modifier. As modifiers, the two look indistinguishable:

(16) a. jəbɛ̋́ tsǐe
clothes black
'black clothes'

b. *jəbě gɔ̌ɔ*
   clothes dry
   'dry clothes'

However, the two differ in that 'black' and other true adjectives have no corresponding verb stem, while participial modifiers like 'dry' do:

(17) a. *mənǐ sɪ̰ jəbě bǎ ně ǎá təgö̀ í tsǐe*
      woman be clothes make.REAL.NOM LOC 3SG.SBJV sit.IRR LOG black
      'The woman is blackening the clothes (lit. the woman is making the clothes become black).' [sos150630e]

   b. *mó   sɪ̰ gɔ̂ɔ gɔ̌ɔ   ně*
      1SG.EMPH be wood dry.REAL.NOM LOC
      'I am drying the wood.' [sos150630e]

The adjective in (17a) requires a causative construction with a subordinate clause (§19.3.2.4), while (17b) simply uses the transitive form of the verb from which the participial is derived.

Second, in predicate constructions, participials can precede the copular verb while true adjectives cannot:

(18) a. *jəgè̤ sɪ̰ í tsǐe*
      dog be LOG black
      'The dog is black.' [sos120108e]

   b. **jəgè̤ tsǐe sɪ̰*
      dog black be
      'The dog is black.'

   c. *gɔ̂ɔ sɪ̰ í gɔ̌ɔ*
      wood be LOG dry
      'The wood is dry.' [sos150630e]

   d. *gɔ̂ɔ gɔ̌ɔ sɪ̰*
      wood dry be
      'The wood is dry.' [sos150630e]

Consultants laughed when offered the order in (18b) while both orders with the participial modifier are regularly attested and judged equally good.

These differences suggest a distinction between true adjectives on the one hand and deverbal modifiers on the other. Nevertheless, it is not quite so simple, in that stems that by these two tests appear to be adjectival can display verb-like qualities in other constructions. An example of this is the adjective *bəlě* 'big, fat'. This stem cannot be used as a transitive verb meaning 'fatten', so a construction with a deadjectival noun is used instead (19a); similarly, it can only be used as an adjectival predicate after the noun and not before it (19b-c):

(19) a. frṷ̀ mó bəlȅ-bɛ́ nɔ̀ wɛ̀
bean 1SG.EMPH big-NOM eat.IRR HAB
'Beans make me fat.' [sos170719e]

b. jȕŋmǎ sɪ̌ í bəlĕ
cat be LOG big
'The cat is big.' [sos160825e]

c. *jȕŋmǎ bəlĕ sɪ̌
cat big be
'The cat is big.' [sos160825e]

The expression in (19c) is ungrammatical with the meaning 'the cat is big', i.e. as an adjectival predicate. Instead, it means 'there is a big cat', where *jȕŋmǎ bəlĕ* is an NP consisting of a noun and an adjectival modifier.

While these facts line up with the adjective vs. verb distinction laid out above, we also find that *bəlĕ* 'big' can be used as a predicate without the auxiliary verb *sɪ̌* 'be', suggesting that it is at some level verbal:

(20) a. ȁ brɔ̰̀ bəlȅ
3SG liver be.big
'He gets mad easily [lit. his liver is big]' [sos170701e]

b. mɔ̰̀ ȁ tȍ ȉ sɛ́ɛ-gûa bəlȅ
person 3SG know.IRR COMP Sambla-country be.big
'We know that Sambla country is big.' [sos170711t1:438]

These X-toned stems look like the verbal base of a participial form *bəlĕ*.

Thus, it is not totally clear that Seenku has a binary distinction between verbs and adjectives, but rather different classes of stems can have differing levels of verb-like or adjective-like properties. In the sections below, I will take a wide view of adjectives, treating anything as an adjectival stem that is used primarily as a modifier, even if a verbal counterpart exists. In other words, I will exclude explicitly participial forms like *kpɔ̌ɔ* 'sewn' from *kpɔ̰̌ɔ* 'sew', since this is more commonly used as a verb, but include forms like *bəlĕ* 'big' or even *gɔ̌ɔ* 'dry' whose modifier form is more common than corresponding verbs.

8.3.2 Adjectival stems

Like noun stems, adjectival stems tend to be mono- or sesquisyllabic in length, but the distribution of tone patterns differ. In the data thus far, the most common tonal melody for adjectives is a LS rising tone. As we saw in §4.3.2.1, this rising tone pattern is comparatively rare on nouns. The attested LS adjectival stems in the dataset are listed in Tables 8.1 and 8.2, for mono- and sesquisyllabic stems, respectively.

Tab. 8.1: Monosyllabic adjectives

CV	jǔ	'long'
	kǎ̰	'white'
CV:	fɔ̌	'skinny'
	gɔ̌ɔ	'dry'
CVV	tsǐe	'black'
	sǐɛ̰	'red'
	sǐɛ	'mean'
	mǔi	'in shape'
CVC	gǔn	'curved'

Tab. 8.2: Sesquisyllabic adjectives

CəCV	balě	'big'
	sagɔ̌	'good, pretty'

This tonal melody likely has morphological underpinnings, as it is the same melody we frequently see on participial forms derived from verbs; see §4.3.2.2 for further discussion.

While rising tones are the most common, other tone patterns are also attested, summarized in Table 8.3. The stems in this table are used in various predicate constructions, from the typical sɪ̰̌ í X construction (e.g. à̰ sɪ̰̌ í bɔ̌ɔ 'he is tall') to X sɪ̰̌ constructions (e.g. à̰ pètè sɪ̰̌ 'he is flat') to more unusual constructions like sɪ̰̌ í X wɛ̀ (e.g. à̰ sɪ̰̌ í kɔ̌gɔ̌ wɛ́ 'he is sturdy'). For further discussion, see §14.3 on adjectival predication.

Plural morphology on adjectives will be discussed in conjunction with their role as modifiers in §8.3.3.2 below.

Tab. 8.3: Adjectives with other tone patterns

X	sagěe	'new'
	kùa	'other'
L	pètè	'flat'
H	kɔ́-kɔ́	'short'
	ɲúɛ	'bad'
S	bɔ̌ɔ	'tall'
	dzíɛ	'good, delicious'
	cərǎ	'fresh'
	kɔ̌gɔ̌	'sturdy'
LSH	mŏén	'small'
HS	nɔ́gɔ̌	'skinny'

8.3.3 Adjectival modifiers

Both adjectives and deverbal qualificative participials fill the same slot in the NP directly following the noun, with no tonal interaction. I will first address NPs with a single adjective then turn to multiple adjective ordering.

8.3.3.1 Singular NPs
Modifiers follow the modified noun (N Adj/N Ptcp). They do not carry any special morphological marking and do not display any special phonological interaction with the noun. Examples of both adjectives (Adj) and participles (Ptcp) are shown in (21):

(21) a. bṷ̀ cərǎ
grass fresh
'fresh grass'

b. jŭŋmǎ tsĭe
cat black
'black cat'

c. gɔ̂ɔ gɔ̌ɔ
wood dry
'dry wood' [sos170711t1: 55]

Textual examples of NPs with an adjective include:

(22) a. ké mʝ̀ bɔ̂ɔ âa
COP person old NEG.Q
'He's an old person, you know?' [sos170714t2:71]

b. kótê   bəlĕ tsɛ́́ sɪ̰̂
    calabash big INDF be
    'There is a big calabash.' [sos170711t1:286]

c. dónô fɔ́ɔ   mŏén tsɛ́́ kʊ́ í bɛ́́ ɪ̰̀ à   tɛ̀ɛ   ɲì,
    child skinny small INDF D.DEF LOG do.IRR COMP 3SG leave.IRR there
    dôn mŏén quoi
    child small what.FR
    'A small skinny child said, "Leave him," a small child.' [sos170711t1:26]

In (22a), we see a simple NP consisting of a noun and an adjective. In (22b), this N Adj sequence is followed by an indefinite determiner *tsɛ́́*. In (22c), there are two NPs with adjectives; the first is a complex NP consisting of a noun, two adjectives (see §8.3.3.3 below), and an indefinite determiner, while this is repeated at the end of the utterance as a simple N Adj sequence. As these examples show, there is no tonal interaction between the noun and the adjective; a N Adj sequence is prosodically distinct from a compound noun (§7.1.1.2).

8.3.3.2 Plural NPs

When plural nouns are modified, plurality is obligatorily marked on the modifier and only optionally marked on the noun. Plural modifiers follow the same pattern as pluralized nouns, i.e. they undergo suffixation of a [+front] vocalic feature and a [+raised] tonal feature, but in addition, they also undergo initial CV reduplication. The template for a reduplicated modifier is shown in (23):

(23) *Pluralization of modifiers*
      $C_1 í$-$C_1 V_2$... -[+front], -[+raised]

In this schematization, [i] stands in as a default high vowel in the reduplicant, but the realization of this vowel can be either [i] or [u] depending on segmental properties of the stem. Some speakers even pronounce the reduplicant with a schwa.

(24) provides examples of correspondences between singular and plural adjectives:

(24) | Singular | Plural | Gloss |
|---|---|---|
| bəlĕ | bú-bəlĕ | 'big' |
| tsĭe | tsí-tsĭe | 'black' |
| kǎ̰ | kí-kḛ̌ | 'white' |
| jṵ̆ | jú-jṵ̌i | 'long' |

The examples in (25) show plural NPs with an adjective; in examples (25a-b), only the adjective is inflected for plural, while in (25c-d), the same forms are shown with both the noun and the adjective inflected:

(25) a. səgà̰   bú-bələ̆
          sheep RED-big.PL
          'big sheep'

     b. kó-kô   tsí-tsĭe
         RED-rooster RED-black.PL
         'black roosters'

     c. səgὲ   bú-bələ̆
         sheep.PL RED-big.PL
         'big sheep'

     d. kó-kőe   tsí-tsĭe
         RED-rooster.PL RED-black.PL
         'black roosters'

Examples of NPs with plural adjectives in the text corpus are shown in (26):

(26) a. mɔ̰̀ɛ   lέ   í   jío   ḭ̀   ɲìä   kʊ̌
          person.PL SBJV LOG say.REAL.PFV 3PL refuse.REAL.PRF toh
          sɔ́-səgɔ̌ɛ   nέ   ḭ̀   fáakέɛ   lë̀   ḭ̀   té   nǎ   kʊ́
          RED-good-.PL LOC 3PL chaff.PL PRES.PL COMP who PROSP D.DEF
          tò̰   à   wò̰   kà̰
          take.IRR 3SG EMPH in.hand
          'When the people said they had refused the good kinds of toh, that chaff there, they asked who would take it from her?' [sos170805t9:46]

     b. mí̋ ní̋   bú-blĕ   kű́ɛ   lὲ̰   à   jú   tsɛ̋   mí̋ì
         1PL father.PL RED-big.PL others SUBORD 3SG say.IRR how 1PL.DAT
         tsɛ̋-ké mí̋ ní̋   lὲ̰   à   jú   tsɛ̋
         and 1PL father.PL SUBORD 3SG say.IRR how
         'How our grandfathers told us, and how our fathers told it...' [sos170711t1:6]

     c. sò̰   ké-kɛ̆   kɔ́ɔ   í   sí   tə̰nḭ̀   brú-brú-brú
         horse RED-white.PL walk.IRR.HAB LOG RECP behind IDEO
         'White horses were walking one after another.' [sos170805t9:20]

In (26a), the speaker uses a copy of the stem vowel [ɔ] in the reduplicant instead of a high vowel.

We will see more examples of plural adjectives in §14.3 in the discussion of adjectival predicates.

There is one adjective with an irregular stem form in the singular vs. the plural: 'small'. In the singular, we find *mŏén* with an aberrant LSH tone pattern, while the corresponding plural is *mú-məŋĕ*, in line with other adjectival stems. In adjectival predicates, discussed in §14.3, we see the reduplicated plural, but in one exceptional case of 'small' as an adjectival modifier, we see it with its plural stem form but lacking the initial reduplicant:

(27) áa à jío né̋ kótê məŋĕ lɛ̏ kä̤a̤
2SG.SBJV 3SG see.REAL.PFV if calabash small.PL REL.SBJV go
ɲì-nà
there-towards
'If you see there, there are little calabashes.' [sos170711t1:103]

It is unclear whether this is a speech error or a possible variant, or even whether the speaker intended this a singular adjective and used the plural stem. I judge this latter possibility to be the most likely, since the same speaker uses the expression *kótê məŋĕ* 'small calabash' seemingly in the singular in one other place in the text (phrase 106).

Some adjectives do not follow the reduplicative plural pattern; instead, they form their plurals through regular featural suffixation, like nouns. These include the following:

(28) Singular Plural Gloss
      bɔ́ɔ   bɔ̋ɛɛ   'old'
      kɔ́-kɔ́   kɔ́-kɔ̋ɛ 'short'

With these adjectives as well, the preceding noun can either be marked for plural or left in the singular; the latter option appears to be more common:

(29) a. mó sị̌ ä̀ tê fʝ̋ ä̀ mɔ̰̀ kɔ́-kɔ̋ɛ lɛ̏ kɛ̂
1SG.EMPH be 3SG GEN until 3SG person RED-short.PL PRES.PL COP
fəné-ŋä̀
what-Q
'I want to know those short people there, what are they?' [sos161009t1:153]

b. mɔ̰̀ bɔ̋ɛɛ sị̌ ä̀ fôn-cìcì gä́a né̋
person old.PL be DEF fonio-chaff pull.REAL.NOM LOC
'The old people are pulling the fonio chaff.' [sos170714t3:42]

c. mɔ̰̀ɛ bɔ̋ɛɛ sị̌ ɲì ì ä̀ fô-nèn trù
person.PL old.PL be there 3PL DEF fonio-grain gather.up.IRR
'The old people are there gathering up the fonio grain.' [sos170714t3:145]

In (29a), we see one of three repetitions of the phrase 'short people' in the plural in the text, all of which leave 'person' in the singular. In (29b), we have two utterances referring to old people from the same text spoken by the same speaker; in the first instance, he uses the singular 'person' and in the second he uses the plural, with no apparent change in meaning. The example in (29a) also shows that the presentative demonstrative (§8.2.3) follows the plural adjective.

8.3.3.3 Multiple adjectives

Instances of multiple adjectives are rare in the current data set. In elicitation data, the attested cases involve a size adjective (e.g. 'big') and a color adjective (e.g. 'white' or 'black'). Surprisingly given cross-linguistic tendencies towards a hierarchy of adjective ordering (see e.g. Sproat and Shih 1991), these adjectives can appear in either order in Seenku. An example with a singular noun is given in (30):

(30) a. jəgê kă̰ bəlě
       dog white big
       'big white dog' [sos120107e]

   b. jəgê bəlě kă̰
       dog big white
       'big white dog' [sos120107e]

The consultant expressed no preference. In a separate elicitation asking about a big red cat, 'big' was placed inside of 'cat' (e.g. jŏŋmǎ bəlě sḭ̀ɛ); the elicitation does not ask for the opposite order.

When pluralized, both adjectives show reduplicative plural marking; again, they can appear in either order:

(31) a. jəgê bú-bəlě tsí-tsĭe
       dog RED-big RED-black
       'big black dogs' [sos190803e]

   b. jəgê tsí-tsĭe bú-bəlě
       dog RED-black RED-big
       'big black dogs' [sos190803e]

In these examples, the noun is left unmarked for plural, but consultants report that plural marking is also possible (i.e. jəgè bú-bəlě tsí-tsĭe).

There are only two cases of multiple adjectives in the text corpus:

(32) a. dónô fɔ́ɔ mŏén tsẽ́ kʊ́ í bẽ́ ḭ̀ à tɛ̀ɛ ɲì
       child skinny small INDF D.DEF LOG do.IRR COP 3SG leave.IRR there
       'A small skinny child said, "Leave him there".' [sos170711t1:26]

   b. à̰ gɔ̃ɔ səgɔ̃ yɛ̀rɛ̀ ɲá ŋé, mɪ́ kʊ́ tsḭ̀ mɛ̀ ŋé
       3SG dry good self.JU be.NEG NEG 1PL D.DEF cut.IRR HAB NEG
       'What's not good and dry, we don't cut it.' [sos170711t1:56]

In (32a), both adjectives refer to physical size and dimensions. When I asked a consultant whether the opposite order 'small and skinny' would be possible, she agreed, though personally said she would not use those two adjectives together as they are redundant. The example in (32b) is more equivocal, either representing a headless NP (§8.3.4), in which case it is truly a case with two modifiers, or it is a participial predicate (§13.3.3). Regardless, the evaluative adjective 'good' comes outside of the physical property adjective 'dry'. In this case, the order of the adjectives could not be reversed.

This may be a property of value adjectives. For instance, in asking about a phrase like 'a good little lamb', only the order in (33) was accepted:

(33) səgà-nòn   mŏén səgɔ̌
      sheep-child little good
      'a good little lamb' [sos190803e]

The consultant reported that if the order of the adjectives were reversed, mŏén 'small' would be read as an afterthought, i.e. 'a good lamb, and so small!'.

8.3.4 Headless NPs with adjectives

There are no true headless NPs in Seenku. In other words, the N slot cannot be left empty to express an idea like 'the big [one]' or 'a red [one]'. Where in English we use the placeholder 'one', in Seenku the 3sg pronoun ằ is used to support the adjective. We saw one putative example of the 3sg replacing the modified noun in (33b). Clearer cases are shown in (34), from both elicitation and narrative data:

(34) a. ằ   mə́-mənĕ   təgɔ̈́ɛɛ   sı̌
          3SG RED-small.PL certain.PL be
          'There are some small ones.' [sos170711t1:369]

      b. mí sı̌ ằ tsı̌e sặ   nɛ̋
          1PL be 3SG black buy.REAL.NOM LOC
          'We are buying a black one.' [GFT, p.c.]

We can see in these examples that the default 3sg is used regardless of the number of the adjective; this is reminiscent of the behavior of the definite marker ằ, discussed in §8.2.1.

8.4 Numerals

In this section, I lay out the numeral system for Seenku, including cardinal (§8.4.2), distributive (§8.4.3), and ordinal (§8.4.4) numerals as modifiers of nouns. Non-numeral quantifiers will be discussed in §8.5. Throughout the subsections, I will provide examples showing how numerals combine with other elements in the NP.

8.4.1 Number system

Before turning to the deployment of numerals in the NP, I first lay out the number system. As we will see, Seenku is a mixed-base system, with base ten up to 40, and base twenty beyond.

8.4.1.1 1-10
The numerals 1-10 are listed in (35):

(35) 1   sɔ́ɛn
      2   fĩ́n
      3   sṹɛ
      4   nằa
      5   nɔ̀
      6   tsï̀i
      7   ɲɛ̂ɛ
      8   kằa
      9   kṹomɛ̂̃
      10 tő

There is some variation in the pronunciation of 'one', from [sɔ́ɛn] to [sɔ́̃ɛ̃n] to [sóen]. I will transcribe it in examples as pronounced by the speaker. The numeral 'five' is one of the few lexically L-toned words in Seenku.

8.4.1.2 Decimals 20-210
The formation of decimal numerals (20, 30, 40, etc.) is a somewhat mixed system. There is a special lexeme for '20', fṹɛ, which is also used in the formation of '30':

(36) fṹɛ né tő
      '30' (literally 'ten on twenty')

The system from 40 upwards is a base-20 system, but rather than using fṹɛ, the stem təgê is used. The use of this term probably harks back to an earlier system of commerce whereby a chicken (təgê) was worth twenty monetary units. The decimal numerals 40-210 are listed in (37):

(37) 40   təgê fĩ́n   (2x20)
     50   təgê fĩ́n né tő   (2x20+10)
     60   təgê sṳ̀ɛ   (3x20)
     70   təgê sṳ̀ɛ né tő   (3x20+10)
     80   təgê nằa   (4x20)
     90   təgê nằa né tő   (4x20+10)
     100 təgê nɔ̀   (5x20)
     110 təgê nɔ̀ né tő   (5x20+10)
     120 təgê tsʾ̀ì   (6x20)
     130 təgê tsʾ̀ì né tő   (6x20+10)
     140 təgê ɲɛ̀ɛ   (7x20)
     150 təgê ɲɛ̀ɛ né tő   (7x20+10)
     160 təgê kằa   (8x20)
     170 təgê kằa né tő   (8x20+10)
     180 təgê kṳ̀omɛ̃̀   (9x20)
     190 təgê kṳ̀omɛ̃̀ né tő (9x20+10)
     200 təgê tő   (10x20)
     210 təgê tő né tő   (10x20+10)

As we can see, multiples of twenty are counted up by adding the multiplicant after *təgê* (whose final X tone element is sometimes left unpronounced, inducing downstep in the case of H and S tones and to no effect before S tones, e.g. [təgɛ́ !fĩ́n] '40'). Intermediate 10s between multiples of twenty are created by adding *né tő* 'on ten'. The tone of the postposition *né* seems to surface with its underlying tone, perhaps because it cannot undergo tone sandhi with a preceding numeral in this construction. It is also likely related to a *né* found in conjunctions like *à-né* or *tsɛ́-né*; see §11.1.1.

8.4.1.3 Hundreds, thousands, and above

The system of decimal numerals up to 290 is roughly the same as what we have seen so far, but with slightly different means of adding the numerals beyond 200. In 220, we see the use of both '20' lexemes, *təgê* and *fűɛ*:

(38) təgê tő fűɛ wɛ́
     '220' (literally 10x20 with twenty)

Here, *fűɛ* is added not with the postposition *né* after the base but with what looks like the postposition *wɛ̃̀* 'with' after the additive itself, lending the meaning 'X with 20'.

The numeral 230 is formed much as expected, by adding *né tő*, but in addition, a form *báǎ* is added at the end in place of the postposition *wɛ̃̀*. This may be a contraction of *bá wɛ́*, but it is unclear what *bá* would mean in this case. One consultant reports that this particle can also be used after lower decimal numerals like 90, but it gives the sense of being a response to a question. With 230, however, it is obligatory:

(39) təgê tő fűɛ né tő báǎ
'230' (literally 10x20 10 on 20)

More data are required to test this metalinguistic knowledge.
The numerals 240-290 are listed in (40):

(40) 240   təgê tő təgê fĭn mééɛ́   (10x20 with 2x20)
      250   təgê tő təgê fĭn né tő báǎ   (10x20 with 2x20+10)
      260   təgê tő təgê sùɛ wěɛ́   (10x20 with 3x20)
      270   təgê tő təgê sùɛ né tő báǎ   (10x20 with 3x20+10)
      280   təgê tő təgê nằa wěɛ́   (10x20 with 4x20)
      290   təgê tő təgê nằa né tő báǎ   (10x20 with 4x20+10)

The postposition wɛ̀ has highly unusual tone patterns in these numeral constructions. Note that the vowel isn't actually pronounced particularly longer; I have simply transcribed them this way to accommodate the diacritics. The examples in (40) show that wɛ̀ (with its tonal variants) is used after multiples of 20 while báǎ is used in its place after odd multiples of ten.

At 300, the numerals switch over to a monetary counting system, where every numeral is divided by 5 (the smallest coin denomination). Thus, 300 takes the same form as 60, 400 the same form as 80, 500 the same as 100, etc.

While 1000 is the same as 200 (təgê tő), the base lexeme for counting thousands is bí. Just as the counting numeral təgê could mean 20 or 'chicken', so too does bí mean both 1000 and 'goat'; note that as a numeral, it does not take the HX contour tone seen when it is used as a noun, even though təgê does. The numerals 2000-9000, all of which are compositional (n x 1000) are listed in (41):

(41) 2000   bí fĭn
      3000   bí sùɛ
      4000   bí nằa
      5000   bí nɔ́
      6000   bí tsìi
      7000   bí ɲěɛ
      8000   bí kǎa
      9000   bí kùomɛ̀

We encounter a new counting lexeme at 10,000, dán, and multiples of 10,000 are formed compositionally just as we see with multiples of 1000. For example:

(42) a. dán sóen
          '10,000'

b. *dán sùɛ*
'30,000'

c. *dán tő*
'100,000'

As (42a) shows, *dán* is typically not used alone to mean 10,000; it is instead followed by *sóen* 'one'.

8.4.1.4 11, 34, 57 etc.

When combining a digit 1-10 with a decimal numeral or above, the digit comes at the end followed by the postposition *wɛ̀* 'with', again with unusual tone patterns. Some examples given in (43):

(43) a. *tő fĩ́n méɛ̋*
'12'

b. *tő kǎa wéɛ̋*
'18'

c. *təgê fĩ́n né tő sóen méɛ̋*
'51'

d. *təgê tő təgê nằa né tő tsɨ̀i wéɛ̋*
'296'

The example in (43a) amounts to "10+2"; (43b) is "10+8"; (43c) equals "2x20+10+1"; finally, (43d) equals "20x10+20x4+10+6".

8.4.2 Cardinal numerals

Cardinal numerals are used to count the number of nouns in question. Here, we can distinguish between the canonical use of cardinal numerals (e.g. "three pigs") vs. a partitive expression, counting a subset or fraction of nouns (e.g. "three of the pigs"). I consider these two expressions under the same heading of "cardinal numeral", since the morphological form of the numeral remains the same.

Cardinal numerals can be used in two constructions: direct juxtaposition, in which the numeral is placed immediately following the noun (and adjective), and a classifier construction.

8.4.2.1 Direct juxtaposition (Noun Numeral)

Generally speaking, cardinal numerals simply follow the noun:

(44) a. jəgĕ́ sɔ́ɛn
    dog one
    'one dog'

b. bɛ̀ɛ sùɛ
    pig.PL three
    'three pigs'

c. bǐ tő nằa wéɛ́
    goat.PL ten four with
    'fourteen goats'

As these examples show, nouns are marked as plural with numerals two and above. Example (44c) shows that composite numerals like 'fourteen' (lit. "10+4") follow the noun in the same way as a simple digit.

Examples of N Num constructions in the text corpus include the following:

(45) a. ì ǎ né jù̀ tő nɔ̌ wéɛ́ mi̤-nǎ ǎ jərá sŏn
    COMP 3SG come.IRR year ten five with where-toward 3SG become fun
    'If he reaches the age of fifteen, we're having fun.' [sos170711t1:154]

b. mɔ̰̌ nɛ̀ ǎ dzi̤ tá` kɔ̀n jù̀ sùɛ jù̀ nằa jù̀ nɔ̌
    person come.IRR 3SG put.IRR fire on year three year four year five
    'We come and put it on the fire for three years, four years, five years.' [sos170711t1:58]

c. ǐi ǎ tsi̤ tɔ̌-tərɔ̌ dəgɔ̌ɛɛ fi̤n nɛ́
    3PL.PST 3SG cut.REAL.PFV RED-like place.PL two LOC
    'They cut it like that into two pieces.' [sos170714t2:15]

d. ǎá jərá nɛ́ sɔ́sáa nɛ̀ mɔ̰̀ɛ tsì̤i ɲəgɔ̀ɛ
    3SG.SBJV become.REAL.PFV if right.now LOC person.PL six same.PL
    'If it were six people like that...' [sos170714t3:19]

e. dằn nɛ̀-tá̤ mɛ̀ cǐ kàa blà
    wall TRANS-chop 3SG.SUBORD house.PL eight fell.IRR
    'Cut the wall and it makes eight houses.' [sos150626t1:20]

The first two examples have the noun jù̀ 'year' modified by the numerals. As we can see, it is not pluralized; this may be a peculiarity of the noun. In (45c), the noun dəgɔ̌ɛɛ 'place' is pluralized, but in the dialect of the speaker, 'place' is always used in the plural. The clearer examples of a plural noun are seen in (45d), where mɔ̀ɛ 'people' is the head noun, and (45e), where cí 'houses' is inflected for plural.

8.4.2.2 The use of classifier dị̈

Sometimes in elicitation, consultants will decide that numerals need to be preceded by a classifier derived from the word 'grain': singular dén and plural dị̈, which form a compound with the preceding noun and hence often differ tonally on the surface. For example:

(46) a. bî-děn   sɔ́ɛn
          goat-CLF one
          'one goat' [sos150805e]

      b. bǐ-dị̈   nɔ̀ ~ bî-dị̀   nɔ̀
          goat.PL-CLF.PL five goat-CLF.PL five
          'five goats' [sos150804e]

      c. bɛ̀ɛ-dị̀   fűɛ   fín̰   méɛ́ɛ̰́
          pig.PL-CLF.PL twenty two with
          'twenty-two pigs' [sos150805e]

The example in (46b) shows that plural marking on the noun root itself is optional in the presence of the classifier, which is obligatorily plural-marked.

Interestingly, I have never seen this classifier construction in texts. It is unclear why it would be reported in elicitation, especially since French has no classifier of the sort to calque from, if it is not naturally attested in speech.

8.4.2.3 Partitive constructions

All of the N Num sequences we have seen thus far in this section have been pure cardinal numerals, referring to a set of entities commensurate with the value of the numeral. But N Num expressions can also be partitive, or in other words, the numeral can denote that amount of a larger set denoted by the noun. In Seenku, there is no morphosyntactic distinction; the difference must be made by context. Consider the following example from elicitation:

(47) móò   bì   tsí-tsi̋e   fín̰ cȉe
      1SG.EMPH.DAT goat.PL RED-black.PL two die.REAL.PFV
      'My two black goats died' or 'Two of my black goats died.' [sos150703e]

In the first interpretation, the number of goats possessed by the speaker is coextensive with the number of goats that died: two. In the second interpretation, the speaker may own more goats, but two of them died.

There is only one textual example in the corpus that looks like a partitive construction:

(48) kʊ́   mənì-dəròn   bɛ́   sɔ́ɛn ằ   kú-bê   dəbê   wétənɛ̌
      D.DEF woman-child DEM   one DEF thing-NOM be.good.REAL.PFV   now
      kʋ̃ɛ
      D.DEF.DAT
      'One of the girls fell in love with him.' [sos171009t1:56]

We might expect 'girl' to be in the plural somewhere in this NP; there is no segmental evidence, though the compound *mənì-dəròn* is unusually L-toned here where we would expect X, reminiscent of plural tone raising.

More examples are needed to fully elucidate the partitive construction.

8.4.3 Distributive numerals

Distributive numerals indicate that the noun modified by that numeral is distributed across other events or participants in the sentence. Distributive numerals are formed by reduplication in Seenku. Like other numerals, they follow the noun and do not interact tonally. For example:

(49) mó   gbɛ̰̀   fɪ́n-fɪ́n   bằ   dənɪ̰̋   bɛ̋   kǎ
      1SG.EMPH zaban RED-two   give.REAL.PFV child.PL DEM in.hand
      'I gave the children two zabans each.' [sos 1 50702e]

Here, the quantity 'two zabans' (an indigenous sour fruit that grows on a vine) is distributive across each child in the discourse. Interestingly, despite the fact that two zabans indicates plurality, the noun is left in the singular.

One textual example is in (50):

(50) mɪ̋ fáná ằ   sɔ́n-sɔ́ɛn   jɵ̋   âa
      1PL also 3SG RED-one   find.IRR   NEG.Q
      '[so that] we also find one [cow] each.' [sos161009t1:31]

This example shows that distributive reduplication is not full reduplication, but rather CV(N) reduplication; the first half of the diphthong is copied, as is the final nasal, but not the second half of the diphthong.

Distributive numerals can also be used as adverbs, as in the following examples:

(51) dóró-ŋɛ̋   nǎ   səmâ   sɔ́n-sɔ́ɛn
      child-HUM.PL PROSP   dance.IRR   RED-one
      'The children will dance one by one.' [sos150702e]

For more on adverbs, see §10.2.

8.4.4 Ordinal numerals

The cardinal numerals we have seen designate the absolute number of the modified noun. For instance, *bǐ˝sùɛ* means 'three goats'. Ordinal numerals, on the other hand, refer to the "order number" of the modified noun, i.e. 1st, 2nd, 3rd, etc.

In Seenku, as in many other languages, 'first' does not follow the regular pattern. There seem to be a few options for how 'first' is expressed, depending upon context and speaker preference. The first is *gbènɛ̋*, which can also mean 'early' or 'before'. In the limited available data, this form precedes the modified noun and triggers argument-head tone sandhi, suggesting that it itself is a noun and is acting as a possessor (or at the very least it forms a compound with the head noun):

(52) gbènɛ̋ bɛ̋ɛ
    first   pig
    'first pig'

Another strategy seen in texts to express 'first' is the expression *tsį́-kų́nį̋*, derived from the verb *tsį́-kų̀* 'begin' with what appears to be antipassive derivation (§12.3). For example:

(53) í   wôo   tsı̋ɛɛ tsį́-kų́nį̋
    2PL EMPH.DAT   word cut-grab.ANTIP
    'Your first question...' [sos170711t1:1]

Even though this expression looks to have verbal origins, it is used as a regular modifier.

Finally, I have heard speakers simply use French *premier*, even if they themselves do not speak French. For example:

(54) kʊ́   jərâ   ằ   sô   kòee-sắn   prɔ́mîɛ prɔ́mîɛ ằ
    D.DEF   become   DEF song sing.ANTIP-thing   first.FR first.FR DEF
    sɛ́ɛ̀-ŋɛ̀   tè
    Sambla-HUM.PL   DAT
    'That became the very first thing the Sambla used to play songs.' [sos170711t1:336]

The ordinal here follows the noun—the Seenku but not the French word order—and it is repeated twice for emphasis.

All other ordinals are formed with the suffix *-bé*. I am unsure of whether this suffix should be viewed as at some level the same suffix as nominalizer *-bé* (§5.2.2.1), or whether this is accidental homophony. I will gloss it as ORD here.

The ordinal suffix triggers tone changes on the numeral, but they are irregular and variable. The only consistency is that the tone of the preceding numeral stem is typically lowered. For instance, '2nd' surfaces variably in my notes as *fį̀-bé* and *fį̄-bé* (cf. *fí̵* 'two'). A similar ambivalence between X- and H-toned realizations is found with other lexically S-toned numerals:

(55)   a.   *tó-bé*
              '10th' (cf. *tő*)

       b.   *fùɛ-bé*
              '20th' (cf. *fűɛ*)

Interestingly, when 'ten' or 'twenty' is part of a compound numeral, there is no tonal effect of the suffix:

(56)   təgê   fí̵n   né   tő-bé
        twenty two on ten-ORD
        'fiftieth'

The affix can even be added to a large composite number ending in a postposition, suggesting that the affix may be a "phrasal affix" like the English genitive, or possibly a clitic:

(57)   təgê   fí̵n   né   tő   sóen   méɛ̋ɛ-bé
        twenty two on ten one with-ORD
        '51st'

X- and L-toned numerals remain unchanged.
     Ordinal numerals 3rd through 6th are shown in (58):

(58)   3rd   *sùɛ-bé*
        4th   *nằa-bé*
        5th   *nɔ̀-bé*
        6th   *tsìi-bé*

In the case of 'five', the numeral is already lexically L-toned.
     The only instance of a true ordinal in the text corpus is shown in (59):

(59)   kɛ́   móò   nìgì   nằa-bé   lɛ̋
        COP 1SG.EMPH.DAT cow four-ORD EMPH
        'It's my fourth cow.' [sos161009t1:126]

As this example shows, ordinal numerals follow the noun they modify and do not induce tonal changes (the raising of *ǹ̩gì* to *nìgì* in this example is due to the preceding possessor; §8.6.2.2).
     One other example of an ordinal in form but only tangentially in function is shown in (60):

(60) gṳ̀ɔ-fíɛ̰ fã̌   fṳ̀ɛ-bɛ́   nɛ̰̀
      night pass.REAL.PTCP twenty-ORD LOC
      'The night passed at 20:00.' [sos170714t3:55]

Here, the ordinal *fṳ̀ɛ-bɛ́* 'twentieth' stands in as a headless NP, where the noun 'hour' is understood. This expression was used by the speaker to replace French code switching to *vingt heures* just two utterances prior.

8.5 Non-numeral quantifiers

Non-numeral quantifiers likewise follow the noun and remain tonally independent from it. They are distinct from adjectives in their plural morphology (they do not undergo reduplication; §8.3.3.2), and in the sole case in which a non-numeral quantifier acts like a predicate (*mɔ̰̌mã̌* 'a lot, many'; §8.5.3), it does not behave like an adjectival predicate (§14.3).

In this section, I will first address quantifiers of totality ('all', 'nothing', 'each') before moving to amount quantifiers ('many', 'few', 'certain'). For adverbial quantifiers, see §10.2.4.

8.5.1 All

There are three main expressions denoting 'all' in Seenku, which may be combined with one another for emphasis. I will address each in turn in the subsections below. For distributive nouns ("each X", "every X"), see §10.2.2.4.

8.5.1.1 *kərúú*

By far the most common form of 'all' in Seenku is the form *kərúú* (or sometimes [kúrúú]). The unusual double-marking of H on the long vowel represents the fact that the plural raises only one half of the syllable, to *kərúíi*, suggesting two distinct H tones. The final vowel is often held for quite some time, longer than a regular long vowel, making this quantifier more ideophonic in nature (cf. *kǔrǔυυ* 'for a long time'; see Chapter 9 for more on ideophones).

In elicitation of universal quantifiers, this is the first form offered. Elicited examples include:

(61) a. jəgè   kərúíi
          dog.PL all.PL
          'all of the dogs' [sos120107e]

b. *móò   bì   tsí-tsĭe   kərúíĭ c̀ìe*
   1SG.EMPH.DAT goat.PL RED-black all.PL die.REAL.PFV
   'All of my black goats died.' [sos150703e]

c. *kʊ́   kùi   bɛ̋   kúrúíĭ nɔ̰́n   tɛ̋,   Yàkű kájǹ   ằá*
   D.DEF thing.PL DEM.PL all.PL that.for GEN   Yakou should 3SG.SUBJ
   kɛ̋   kʊ́   sɔ̀n bé   tằ   nɛ̀
   go.IRR D.DEF play DEM attend LOC
   'For all of those reasons, Yacou should go to that concert.' [sos170809e]

We can see in all three of these examples that both the noun and the quantifier carry plural marking. The examples in (61b-c) show how various NP elements are arranged in more complex NPs: in (61b), we see the order Poss N Adj 'all', while in (61c) we see Det N Dem 'all'.

Singular 'all' in elicitation settings is rare, but it surfaces not infrequently in texts.

(62) a. *ì̀ wɛ̀   ằ   ɲì̀   ì̀   wɛ̀-   ằ   məní-sân   kərúú*
       3PL SUBORD 3SG carry.IRR 3PL SUBORD DEF woman-thing all
       'They took it, they– all the plates.' [sos 170805t9:51]

b. *bâ̰a̰-dɛ̀n   kərúú gűrɛ̋ sḭ̌ ằ   nɛ̀*
   balafon-grain all   voice be 3SG LOC
   'All of the notes of the balafon are there.' [sos170711t1:344]

c. *ì̀   kərúú lɛ̀   ằ   bɑ̋rɑ̋ lé   bɛ̋ɛ   bâ̰a̰   kɔ̀n*
   3PL all   SUBORD DEF work REL do.IRR.HAB balafon on
   'The work that all of them do on the balafon...' [sos170711t1:194]

d. *mɔ̰̀   kərúú l-í   bɛ̋   wétənɛ̌*
   person all   L-LOG do.IRREAL now
   'Everyone says now...' [sos171009t1:105]

As example (62c) showed, pronouns can also take 'all'. Further examples are shown in (63):

(63) a. *mɔ̰̀-bɔ́ɔ-bé   nă   mí̋ kərúíĭ kṵ̋*
       person-old-NOM PROSP 1PL all.PL catch.IRR
       'Age will catch all of us.' [sos170719e]

b. ì̀ kə́rúú sɔ́ɔ̀ íì à bâ̰a̰ dàn-kù
   3PL all   be.able.HAB 3PL.SBJV DEF balafon mouth-thing
   mɛ̰̀   ŋɛ́
   understand.IRR NEG
   'Not all of them can understand the balafon speech.' [sos170711t1:219]

c. kűɛ kə́rúíi̯ɲì̀   í   mæ̀
   others all.PL run.REAL.PFV LOG all
   'They all ran away.' [sos170711t1:142]

d. á wó sɔ́ɔ̀   óo   kʊ́ jǜ   dɔ̀ɔ̀nì í
   2SG EMPH be.able.IRR.HAB 2SG.EMPH.SBJV D.DEF say.IRR a.little 2PL
   fin̰ kə́rúíi̯ quoi
   two all.PL what.FR
   'Can you talk about that a little bit, I mean both of you.' [sos170711t1:157]

e. mɔ̰̀ sɔ́ɔ̀   mɔ̰̀ɔ̰́   à kə́rúú jǜ bâ̰a̰ nɛ̰̀
   person be.able.IRR.HAB person.SBJV 3SG all   say.IRR balafon LOC
   'Can it all be said on the balafon?' [sos170711t1:218]

Even with plural pronouns, 'all' can be either in the singular or the plural. The example in (63d) shows how, when following the numeral 'two', the universal quantifier takes on the meaning of 'both'. The singular pronoun à in (63e) surfaces, as expected, with singular 'all'.

Further study is required to determine what influences the use of singular vs. plural 'all'.

8.5.1.2 pó-pó

We find another ideophonic form for 'all', pó-pó. It is less common overall, but in certain contexts such as greetings, it is the form that is typically used. In nearly all of the textual examples (except for the example in (64a)), pó-pó (plural variant pó-pőe) is used with a pronoun:

(64) a. bon, bǎrǎ́ bèɛ̀-cíɛ   pó-pó nɛ̰̀-jə́rán-jə́rǎn   sḭ̆
     well.FR work do.NOM-manner RED-all TRANS-RED-change.PTCP be
     'Well, how we work has changed completely.' [sos170702t1:43]

   b. à pó-pó sḭ̆ bâ̰a̰   nɛ̰̀
     3SG RED-all be balafon LOC
     'It is all there on the balafon.' [sos170711t1:227]

c. ì̀ pó-pŏe sį̈ kɔ̋ɔ ně̋
   3PL RED-all.PL be walk.REAL.NOM LOC
   'They were all walking.' [sos161009t1:3]

d. ŋ́gàa mó nă wé à jú í lě̈ né í
   but 1SG.EMPH PROSP FOC 3SG say.IRR 2PL DAT 1SG.COMP 2PL
   pó-pŏe kúnàwê
   RED-all.PL good.morning
   'But I will say to all of you, "good morning".' [sos171009t1:7]

In these examples, the use of the singular or the plural quantifier correlates with the number of the pronoun, but that is not always the case. In one example, the speaker retriplicates the quantifier rather than the usual reduplication, and in this case, there is no plural marking:

(65) ì̀ pó-pó-pó mɔ̰̈ kʋ́ jù bâ̰ɑ̰ nè̈ í mà̀
     3PL RED-RED-all person D.DEF say.IRR balafon LOC LOG all
     'We can say all of it on the balafon.' [sos170711t1:222]

The lack of plural marking may be due to the fact that the quantifier is being used unequivocally as an ideophone rather than a nominal modifier.

Unlike kərúú, which only ever appears in NPs, pó-pó can also appear clause-finally in conjunction with another 'all' expression, í mà̀(məlĕ), which always appears after the verb. I have seen two instances of this construction, once in a text and once in elicitation:

(66) a. ǐi nă kű́ɛ tɔ̋ ɲì ŋé ǐi kű́ɛ bő̋ í
        3PL.SBJV PROSP others leave.IRR there NEG 3PL others kill.IRR LOG
        màməlĕ pó-pó
        all   RED-all
        'To not leave them, to kill them all.' [sos150626t5:23]

b. mó nɔ́nɛ́sắn à̀ nìɔ í màməlĕ pó-pó
   1SG.EMPH food   3SG eat.REAL.PRF LOG all   RED-all
   'I ate all of the meal.' [sos150807e]

The other 'all' expression will be addressed in the next subsection.

8.5.1.3 í mà̀(məlĕ)

The examples in (66) show pó-pó combining with another way of marking totality in Seenku, the form í mà̀(məlĕ). This form is reminiscent of the adjectival plural, but with the vowel /a/ in the initial syllable rather than /u/ (cf. mú-mənĕ 'small (pl)') and X tone rather than H. However, unlike adjectival plurals, it is the məlĕ that is optional, not the mà̀; that is, we find examples of both í màməlĕ and simply í mà̀. Since it is not clear what *mǝlě* would mean on its own, I do not parse it out as its own morpheme, and will simply gloss both *mà* and *mǎmǝlě* as 'all'.

The most common use of *mà(mǝlě)* is after the verb, combined with the logophoric pronoun. I begin with examples of simply *í mà* in (67):

(67)   a. kű́ɛ   kərúíĭ   ɲì̀   í   mà
           others all.PL.PST   run.REAL.PFV   LOG   all
           'They all ran away.' [sos170711t1:142]

   b. ĭĭ   ɲì̀   í   mà
       3PL.PST   run.REAL.PFV   LOG   all
       'They all ran away.' [sos 170711t1:143]

   c. kʊ́   kərúú lɛ́́   sɪ̆   í   mà
       D.DEF all   PST   be   LOG all
       'There was all of that.' [sos170714t3:72]

   d. kű́ɛ   fəná kɛ̀ɛ   sɪ̆   í   mà ká̰ ì̀   kəré   bɛ́   bâ̰a̰
       others also taboo be LOG all go 3PL.SUBORD what do.IRR balafon
       kʊ̀rɛ̀   ŋɛ́
       next.to NEG
       'Do they all also have a taboo, something they can't do next to the balafon?' [sos170711t1:280]

These examples show that *í mà* is often, though not obligatorily, combined with another 'all' expression earlier in the clause. Examples (67a-b) are spoken nearly on top of one another by two different speakers, the first of whom uses *kərúíĭ* and the second of whom does not.

We also find *í mǎmǝlě* in this environment:

(68)   a. í   ké̋   dằn   tɛ̀   í   mǎmǝlě
           2PL go.IRR wall GEN   LOG all
           'Go by the wall, all of you!' [sos150626t5:30]

   b. kʊ́   kʊ́   tő   í   mǎmǝlě
       D.DEF D.DEF like LOG all
       'It's like all of that.' [sos170711t1:200]

   c. fő̰   í   kʊ́   temps   bɛ́   sù̀   í   mǎmǝlě
       must 2PL D.DEF time.FR DEM   take.IRR LOG all
       'You have to take all of this time.' [sos170711t1:202]

In each of these examples, the clause-final *í mǎmǝlě* refers back to an NP earlier in the clause.

Despite the prevalence of clause-final *í mà̰(məlě)*, *mámələ̌* can also be used as a modifier in the NP, in which case the logophoric pronoun is absent and the initial syllable is H rather than X:

(69) a. mais ằ káká̰ kɛ́ kú mámələ̌ mɔ̰̂ɔ́ ằ káná
but.FR 3SG should COP thing all person.SBJV 3SG learn.JU
'But then we should learn all of it.' [sos170711t1:163]

b. sɔ̋n-tǎ-kɔ̰̋n mámələ̌ lɛ̋ kɛ̋ búɔ
sky-fire-head all PST go.IRR go.out.REAL
'The sun rose completely.' [sos130828t2:57]

c. mɔ̰̂ mámələ̌ l-ằ tó
person all L-3SG know
'Everyone knows.' [sos170702t1:122]

d. mɔ̰̂-tî jĩ́o dəgɔ̂ɔ mámələ̌ nɛ̏
person find.PPL place all LOC
'People are found everywhere.' [sos170702t1:182]

In (69a), *mámələ̌* is combined with the generic noun *kú* 'thing', yielding an expression like 'everything', while in (69b), it follows a compound noun meaning 'sunrise'; combined with this noun, the quantifier 'all' gives the sense that the sunrise has happened in its entirety. In (69c), 'all' once again follows a light noun 'person', once again in the singular. Like (69a), this gives the reading of 'everyone' rather than 'everything'. The same holds for (69d), which with the noun *dəgɔ̂ɔ* 'place' yields the expression 'everywhere'.

I have never seen simply *mà̰* used in the NP as a modifier.

8.5.2 None/any

We now turn to negative expressions of totality, namely the expressions 'nothing/no' or 'anything/any'. These forms are negative polarity items (NPIs) in Seenku, requiring negation in the sentence to license them. The main NPI used in this capacity is *füi*, which can be used on its own meaning 'nothing' or as a nominal modifier to mean 'no'. Some consultants don't like the use of this term, since they identify it as Jula, though whether it is a borrowing or simply a close cognate is unclear.

It is not necessary to include the NPI *füi* to modify a noun; the meaning of 'any' can be inferred simply from a negative sentence, like the following:

(70) ằ kə̰̂kâ jĩo ŋɛ́
3SG meat see.REAL.PFV NEG
'He did not find any meat.' [sos161009t1:185]

Two sentences later, *kəkâ* 'meat' is replaced with the NPI *füi* 'nothing'; see (73b) below.

Nevertheless, we do find examples of the quantifier used as a modifier, as in (71), which gives an example from both the text corpus (71a) and elicitation (71b):

(71) a. kɔ̀ɔ füi nǎ təgò ɲì ŋé
hole nothing PROSP remain.IRR there NEG
'Not (even) one hole will remain there.' [sos130828t2:75]

b. mó bî füi bä̀ dôn kä̀ ŋé
1SG.EMPH goat nothing give.REAL.PFV child in.hand NEG
'I gave no goat to the child.' [sos150702e]

Similarly, in elicitation I have seen *füi* combined with *mɔ̀* 'person' to indicate 'no one', as in (72a), but by and large simple negation in conjunction with an indefinite noun creates this reading without an explicit NPI, (72b-c):

(72) a. mɔ̀ füi lɛ́ nä̀ ŋé
person nothing PST come.REAL.PFV NEG
'No one came.' [sos150630e]

b. tsɛ́ mɔ̀ lɛ́ nä̀ ŋé
INDF person PST come.REAL.PFV NEG
'No one came.' [sos150630e]

c. tsɛ́ mɔ̀ bậạ dzǔ-tsị́ fɛ́ í wó tè
INDF person balafon mouth-cut.REAL.PFV yet LOG EMPH GEN
fɔ́ɛ́-fɔ́ɛ́ ŋé
RED-at.all NEG
'No one has given to the balafon at all.' [sos161005e]

The examples in (72a-b) were offered more or less back-to-back as meaning the same thing. The example in (72c) has the same form as (72b), with the indefinite expression *tsɛ́ mɔ̀* 'someone' taking on the negative meaning 'no one' under the scope of negation. The ideophone *fɔ́ɛ́-fɔ́ɛ́* may be related to *füi* 'nothing'.

Most typically, however, *füi* is used alone as an NPI, a rare case of a headless NP:

(73) a. ń nǎ füi bɔ̀ ŋé
1SG PROSP nothing take.off.IRR NEG
'I'm not removing anything.' [sos150626t5:5]

b. à kɔ́ ɲá füi jîo nɛ́ ŋé
3SG D.DEF be.NEG nothing see.REAL LOC NEG
'He hadn't found anything.' [sos161009t1:187]

c. mó   füi   bà̠   ŋɛ́
   1SG.EMPH nothing do.REAL.PFV NEG
   'I didn't do anything.' [sos150629e]

In every case, *füi* alone takes the place of the NP.

There are variants of *füi* attested in the text corpus, including the following:

(74) a. föe   ä̠   sǝbɛ̈   ŋɛ́
        nothing 3SG succeed.REAL.PFV NEG
        'Nothing succeeded.' [sos170714t3:47]

   b. gbɛ̈nɛ̈ wótǝrŏ   ɲá   ŋɛ́ fú-fú   ɲá   ŋɛ́
      before donkey.cart be.NEG NEG RED-nothing be.NEG NEG
      'Before, there were no donkey carts, there was nothing.' [sos170714t3:156]

In (74a), the diphthong is [oe] instead of [ui], while in (74b), we see a loss of the diphthong but reduplication. Tonally, the use of H tone here also suggests a singular-plural connection between *fú-fú* and *füi*. In one more example, we find unreduplicated *fû*, but this example is unusual in that consultants translated it with a double negative:

(75) mǝnǐ-bǎrǎ   kɛ́ fû   ŋɛ́
     woman-work COP nothing NEG
     'Women's work isn't nothing.' [sos170714t3:55]

The speaker goes on to describe different kinds of work that women did. It is unclear whether the use of *fû* here rather than *füi* allows for this double negative interpretation (implying that women's work is, in fact, something).

8.5.3 Many

The quantifier *mɔ̀mǎ* 'many' is very common in Seenku, especially used with nouns that would not otherwise have a plural form (either through lexical blocking or accidental homophony of the singular and plural). Examples from elicitation are provided in (76) to illustrate the basic behavior of the quantifier:

(76) a. í   bɛ̀ɛ   mɔ̀mǎ sǎ
        2PL pig.PL many buy.IRR
        'Buy a lot of pigs!'

   b. tsïe   mɔ̀mǎ
      pestle many
      'a lot of pestles'

c. jòn   mɔ̀mɛ̰́
    slave many.PL
    'many slaves'

d. kûɛ   mɔ̀mǎ̰
    calabash many
    'many calabashes'

Like other modifiers, the quantifier 'many' follows the noun. As with the universal quantifiers (§8.5.1), the quantifier 'many' can be marked for plural. There is variation in plural marking, however, both on the noun and on the quantifier. In (76a), the noun is overtly marked as plural and the quantifier is not. In (76b), the quantifier is not marked as plural and the noun is ambiguous—the singular form is also *tsíe*, so the quantifier is necessary to disambiguate the number of the noun. In (76c), the noun is singular and the quantifier is plural; the avoidance of plural marking 'slave' appears to come from two sources, the first being homophony avoidance with *jòe* 'things being said', and the second being to avoid the issue of needing to dock a nasal feature to a [+ATR] vowel in the plural (see §5.3.1.3). (76d) likewise leaves the noun in the singular (to avoid homophony with the 3pl variant *kűɛ* 'others') but also leaves the quantifier unmarked. It would be interesting to track plural marking patterns with the quantifier in a large corpus of texts to determine whether there are any rules or at least statistical patterns.

From texts, we find the following examples of *mɔ̀mǎ̰* (or its plural form) as a modifier.

(77) a. tsîɛɛ   mɔ̀mǎ̰ nŏo   ɲì   tənḭ̂
         word   a.lot come.IRR.NE   there after
         'A lot of questions will follow.' [sos171009t1:116]

    b. mɔ̀   mɔ̀mǎ̰ tîi   dəró-mɔ̰̀   cìamǎ̰ tîi   kằ   nɛ̀
        person a.lot accept child-HUM.SG a.lot.JU accept go.REAL.NOM LOC
        fón-bɛ̰́ɛ̰́   ŋɛ́
        fonio-beat.ANTIP.NOM NEG
        'A lot of people, a lot of young men didn't accept to go to the fonio beating.'
        [sos170714t3:64]

    c. donc, mó   nǎ   wé   nìgì   mɔ̀mɛ̰́ tő   dɔ̀n   í   wó
        SO.FR 1SG.EMPH PROSP FOC   COW.PL a.lot.PL take.IRR today 2SG   EMPH
        kằ
        in.hand
        'So, it's me who will get a lot of cows with you all today.' [sos161009t1:13]

In (77a-b), both the noun and the quantifier are in the singular; in (77c), both are in the plural. We find no textual cases of mismatch. Note in (77b) that the speaker also uses a borrowed quantifier *cìamą́* from Jula *càmán*.

In one case, the quantifier is repeated multiple times for emphasis using the "bouncing ball intonation" pattern, discussed in §9.1.2.2:

(78) kúɔné-ŋɛ̋ mɔ̰̀mɑ̰́ mɔ̰̀mɑ̰́ mɔ̰̀mɑ̰́ fa̰a̰̋
 youth-HUM.PL a.lot a.lot a.lot pass.REAL.PRF
 'Many many many generations have passed.' [sos171009t1:78]

An interesting fact about the quantifier *mɔ̰̀mɑ̰́* is that it does not have to appear in the NP. It can appear at the end of the clause, even when it is understood to be modifying the noun:

(79) a. ǎ ɲǐa-ɲǐa ì ɲűi bà ǎ kà mɔ̰̀mɑ̰́
  3SG RED-finish.REAL.PFV 3PL honey give.REAL 3SG in.hand a.lot
  'When he finished, they gave him a lot of honey.' [sos130828t2:10]

 b. jén-jěn sḭ̀ mó tɛ̀ mɔ̰̀mɑ̰́ mɛ̰̀ fa̰̋
  RED-story be 1SG.EMPH GEN a.lot 3SG.SUBORD pass.REAL
  'I [used to] have so many stories.' [sos150626t2:27]

 c. mənı̋ nɛ̰̀ lɛ̋ màa mɔ̰̀mɑ̰́
  woman come.IRR PST again a.lot
  'A lot of women come.' [sos170714t2:87]

 d. dərı̋-sɛ̋ sḭ̀ ǎ tê mɔ̰̀mɑ̰́
  raise-thing.PL be 3SG GEN a.lot
  'He has a lot of animals.' [sos150804e]

In (79a), the sentence implies that a lot of honey was given to the rabbit, but 'a lot' comes at the end rather than after 'honey'. The same can be said for (79b-c), where the speaker is indicating a lot of stories and a lot of women, respectively, but without 'a lot' being part of the NP. In the elicited example in (79d), we might expect 'many' to modify 'animals' (as in the French sentence offered for translation, *il a beaucoup d'animaux*), but it comes instead at the end of the phrase, acting more like an adverb modifying the possession of said animals. In fact, this Seenku order can be calqued into French by my consultants, with sentences like *elle a payé du riz beaucoup* 'she bought a lot of rice' a common occurrence. Note that for (79d), the opposite order is also attested in elicitation, with seemingly no difference in meaning:

(80) nìgì mɔ̰̀mɛ̰̋ sḭ̀ mó nı̀ tɛ̀
 cow.PL many.PL be 1SG.EMPH father GEN
 'My father has a lot of cows.' [sos150702e]

The use of *mɔ̃mǽ* at the end of the clause is consistent with its use as an adverb, as in:

(81) kərɔ́   mó   cḛ̀rḛ̀   mɔ̰̀mǽ dɛ̋
    yesterday 1SG.EMPH sleep.REAL.PFV a.lot EMPH
    'I slept a lot yesterday!' [sos150806e]

For more on adverbial *mɔ̰̀mǽ*, see §10.2.4.1.

8.5.4 Some/certain

To designate 'some' or 'certain', the quantifier *təgɔ̋ɛ* is used. The singular equivalent appears to be the indefinite *tsɛ̋*. While the form of the modifier itself indicates a plural (an S-toned *ɔ̋ɛ* diphthong), the noun that precedes it may be either in the singular or the plural; the reading of the whole NP is always plural.

(82) a. ằ   má-məɲɛ̆   təgɔ̋ɛ sǐ
      3SG RED-small.PL certain be
      'There are some small ones.' [sos170711t1:369]

   b. est-ce que   mɔ̰̀   sɔ́ɔ̀   mɔ̰̀ɔ̰́ tsîɛɛ   təgɔ̋ɛ
      Q.FR   person be.able.IRR.HAB person.SBJV word certain say.IRR
      jű   bâa nɛ̀   mais mɔ̰̀   sɔ́ɔ̀   mɔ̰̀ɔ̰́ ì
      balafon LOC but.FR   person be.able.IRR.HAB person.SBJV 3PL say.IRR
      jű   í   dzʊ̏   âa
      LOG mouth NEG.Q
      'Are there things that one can say on the balafon that one can't say with one's mouth?' [sos170711t1:229]

   c. mɔ̰̀ bɔ̋ɛɛ   təgɔ̋ɛ fəná sǐ
      person old.PL certain also be
      'There are also some old people.' [sos170714t3:151]

   d. búɛ̀-dḭ̀   təgɔ̋ɛ sǐ wétənɛ̆ ï̀   ɲűi-cí   ɲɛ̋
      fetish-child.PL certain be now 3PL.SBJV honey-house build.IRR
      wɛ̋
      HAB
      'There were some djinns who were building an apiary.' [sos130828t2:1]

In (82a), there is no head noun, but rather a plural adjective is propped up by the 3sg pronoun *ằ*, and this is in turn modified by *təgɔ̋ɛ*. In (82b), the noun *tsîɛɛ* 'word' is left in the singular, with plurality indicated by the quantifier. In (82c), the noun is singular, the adjective plural, and the quantifier also plural. In (82d), the noun and the quantifier are plural.

The distribution of this quantifier is similar to the indefinite *tsɛ́* seen in §8.2.4; it often introduces referents, though in this case plural referents, as we can see in (82d), which is the first line of a folk tale.

The text corpus contains one instance of a reduplicated form:

(83) ǎ   sɔ̃́n bəlě dzɔ̃́-gbǎa lɛ̃́ kɛ̀nɛ̀ təgʒ́ɛ-təgʒ́ɛ   bíɛ̣   ì
     DEF sky big IDEO-IDEO PST bird.PL certain-certain rain.REAL.PFV 3PL
     blǎ-blǎ
     fall-fall
     'A huge rain beat down on certain birds, they fell and fell.' [sos150626t3:27]

The quantifier *təgʒ́ɛ*, like 'nothing', can be used as its own stand-alone NP; if anything, this usage is more common than its use as a modifier:

(84) a. təgʒ́ɛ wɛ̀   í   bɛ̃́   ì   à   tɛ̀ɛ   ɲì-nà
        certain SUBORD LOG do.IRR COMP 3SG leave.IRR there-towards
        'Some of them said to leave him there.' [sos170711t1:26]

     b. ì   kərúú sɔ́ɔ́   ǐi   ǎ   bá̰ą̰ dàn-kù
        3PL all   be.able.IRR.HAB 3PL.SBJV DEF balafon mouth-thing
        mɛ̰̀   ŋɛ́, mais təgʒ́ɛ l-à   mɛ̰̀   wɛ̀
        understand.IRR NEG but.FR certain L-3SG understand.IRR HAB
        'Not everyone understands the speech of the balafon, but some of them understand it.' [sos170711t1:219]

     c. souvent təgʒ́ɛ sḭ̌ í   bú-bəlě təgʒ́ɛ sḭ̌ í   mú-məɲě
        often.FR certain be LOG RED-big certain be LOG RED-small
        'Often some of them are big, some of them are small.' [sos170711t1:86]

In (84b), the universal quantifier *kərúú* (§8.5.1) in the first clause is contrasted with the more constrained quantifier *təgʒ́ɛ* in the second.

8.5.5 Few

The quantifier 'few' or 'a little' is borrowed from Jula: *dɔ́ɔní*. This form is much more commonly used as an adverb, a usage discussed in §10.2.4.3. In fact, this is the only attested usage in texts. In elicitation, however, I have seen it used as a nominal modifier:

(85) a. nìgì dɔ́ɔní sḭ̌ mó   nǐ̃   tɛ̰̀
        cow.PL a.little be 1SG.EMPH father GEN
        'My father has few cows.' [sos150702e]

b. mó bǐ́ dɔ́ɔní sɔ́ɔ
   1SG.EMPH goat.PL a.little sell.REAL.PFV
   'I sold a few goats.' [sos150702e]

In (85a), *dɔ́ɔní* modifies the plural noun *nìgì* 'cows' to mean 'a few cows'. In (85b), the same usage is seen with *bǐ́* 'goats'.

8.6 Possession

Seenku is a typical Mande or West African language in drawing a distinction between alienable and inalienable nouns. Inalienable nouns include kinship terms and body parts (including parts of plants), while all other nouns are treated as alienable. In this section, I address inalienable and alienable possessive NPs (Possessor + Possessed), including complex NPs in which either the possessor or the possessed noun is modified by other NP elements. For possessive predicates, see §14.4. I will first discuss inalienable possession, then turn to alienable possession.

8.6.1 Inalienable possession

In inalienable possession, there is a tight semantic relationship between the possessor and possessed noun, and this tight semantics is mirrored in a tighter morphosyntactic relation. While alienable possession involves a possessive particle (see §8.6.2 below), inalienable possession involves a direct juxtaposition of the possessed noun and its possessor. For both nonpronominal and pronominal possession, the possessor precedes the possessed noun:

(86) Schematic of inalienable possession
     Possessor$_{NP}$ Possessed$_N$

The possessor NP triggers argument-head tone sandhi with the possessed noun, summarized in §4.4.2. Because inalienable nouns must be uttered with a possessor (typically 3sg in the elicitation context), it is quite difficult to determine the lexical tone of inalienable nouns. However, since the same tonal changes occur between an object and a verb and verbal tone is more easily determined, the underlying tone of inalienable nouns can be deduced. Note simply that where the underlying form of an inalienable noun is provided in the following, that form is abstract and never seen on the surface.

8.6.1.1 Nonpronominal possession

When the possessor is nonpronominal (nominal), the final tone of the possessor spreads onto the possessed noun, neutralizing lexical contrasts. The exception is X-final nouns with an X-toned possessed noun; in this case, the would-be X-toned stretch surfaces as L instead.

The examples in (87) show a H-toned noun *bərṹ* 'nose' with different nonpronominal possessors:

(87) a. sŏ̀ bərṹ̀
horse nose
'a horse's nose'

b. jŭŋmǎ bərṵ̃́
cat nose
'a cat's nose'

The neutralizing nature of inalienable possessive tone is clear if we compare the examples in (87) with those in (88), with a lexically S-toned word like *bŏn* 'back':

(88) a. sŏ̀ bŏn
horse back
'a horse's back'

b. jŭŋmǎ bőn
cat back
'a cat's neck'

If the possessor is plural, the effects of plural tone are spread onto the possessed noun; this is visible in (89), with the underlyingly H-toned noun *ɲá* 'mother':

(89) a. bὲɛ ɲà
pig.PL mother
'pigs' mother'

b. bḯ ɲǎ
goat.PL mother
'goats' mother'

In (89a), the L created by affixing [+raised] to the X-toned noun triggers the possessed noun to also raise to L; in (89b), the S created from a H-toned noun likewise spreads.

Plural marking on the possessed noun happens after argument-head tone sandhi has taken place. Its tonal effects are inaudible on nouns that have become S-toned, but when a noun has become X-toned, that X will raise to L; if the preceding possessor is also X-toned, it too will raise. Both the possessed noun and the possessor whose tone had spread raise to L:

(90) a. bî tsɛ̋
    goat foot
    'a goat's foot' [sos150620e]

b. bî̂ tsı̏ɛ
    goat foot.PL
    'a goat's feet' [sos150620e]

In the examples in (90), the X that has spread is part of a HX contour on the possessor. When this X tone is raised to L in plural formation, the X of HX raises, creating a HL contour.

If the NP possessor is complex, the final tone of the NP (not the noun) is the trigger of sandhi. For instance:

(91) a. jʊ̏ŋmá̋ tsı̆e cı̋ɛ
    cat   black foot.PL
    'a black cat's feet' [sos190803e]

b. bî tsı̆e cı̋ɛ
    goat black foot.PL
    'a black goat's feet' [GFT, p.c. 8/5/19]

The final S of the adjective is the trigger of sandhi. Note that there is interspeaker variation in the pronunciation of 'foot' (initial alveolar affricate vs. initial palatal).

8.6.1.2 Pronominal

Pronominal inalienable possession looks a lot like non-pronominal inalienable possession: no possessive marker is required, so the possessed noun is simply preceded by an independent pronoun (either emphatic or non-emphatic). As described in §4.4.2, argument-head tone sandhi results in even more complicated tonal changes when the possessor is a pronoun. Table 8.4 shows the resulting tonal forms with different pronouns, arranged by person and number. In the table, non-emphatic pronouns are given first for each person-number specification, followed by emphatic pronouns, if applicable. For tables of argument-head tone sandhi arranged by tonal form of the pronoun, see §4.4.2.1.

Just as we saw with non-pronominal possession, plural formation on the possessed noun affects the pronoun as well in the case of derived X-X sequences. This is illustrated in (92) with the underlyingly H-toned noun cé 'hand' (pronounced by GET in this example as tsé; see §3.5.1.3 on this variation):

Tab. 8.4: Examples of tonal changes involved in pronominal inalienable possession

		/kɔ̰̂n/ 'head'	/ɲá/ 'mother'	/ní/ 'father'
1sg	ń	kɔ̰́n	ɲȁ	ní
	mó	kɔ̰́n	ɲȁ	nȉ
2sg	á	kɔ̰́n	ɲȁ	ní
	á wó	kɔ̰́n	ɲȁ	nȉ
3sg	ȁ	kɔ̰̀n	ɲȁ	ní
1pl	mǐ	kɔ̰́n	ɲa̋	nǐ
2pl	í	kɔ̰́n	ɲȁ	ní
	í wó kűɛ	kɔ̰́n	ɲa̋	nǐ
3pl	ȉ	kɔ̰̀n	ɲȁ	ní
	kűɛ	kɔ̰́n	ɲa̋	nǐ

(92)   a.   ȁ   tsɛ̏
              3SG hand
              'his hand' [sos150804e]

       b.   ȁ   tsìɛ
              3SG hand.PL
              'his hands' [sos150804e]

When 'hand' is pluralized in (92b), the raising of X to L extends leftward into the pronoun.

8.6.2 Alienable possession

Alienable possession is more complicated than inalienable possession in that there is more than one construction used. In all cases, the word order is the same as in inalienable possession (possessor precedes the possessed noun), but the two are linked with intervening material. In the most canonical case, this is the genitive postposition *tě*, but it can also be a lengthened dative postposition *lěɛ*, or this postposition can be subsumed into the preceding possessor via clitic elision (§4.4.3). The latter two constructions trigger argument-head tone sandhi, while the former does not.

I divide this section by construction-type, with both non-pronominal and pronominal possession discussed together for each.

8.6.2.1 Alienable possession with genitive *tě*

Genitive-marked alienable possession can be schematized as follows:

(93)   *Schematic of alienable possession with* tě
        Possessor$_{NP}$ *tě* |Possessed$_N$|

With this construction, no tone changes are attested on the possessed noun, represented in the schematic in (93) by the vertical bars surrounding the possessed noun. The genitive, being a postposition, does undergo argument-head tone sandhi with the preceding possessor. Examples of possession with *tě* are shown in (94), with the NPs taken from texts:

(94) a. óo tè̤ kənâ
    2SG.EMPH GEN elder
    'your older brother' [sos170714t1:44]

  b. mǐ tě sɛ́ɛ-gûa
    1PL GEN Sambla-country
    'our Sambla country' [sos171009t1:29]

  c. ä̀ kərù kűɛ tě dằn
    DEF hyena others GEN wall
    'the wall of the hyena's family'

  d. kərù tè̤ cîe
    hyena GEN house.LOC
    'in hyena's house'

In these examples, we can see the genitive particle *tě* undergoing argument-head tone sandhi with the preceding noun or pronoun, creating the surface variants [tè̤] and [té] here (cf. HX after an X-toned pronoun, [à tê]). The possessed noun, on the other hand, retains its base tones. In (94d), the possessed noun 'house' has locative marking, rendering the whole phrase postpositional in nature.

For more on the postposition *tě* and its uses beyond possession, see §10.1.8.

8.6.2.2 Alienable possession with dative *lɛ́́ɛ*

Though rare, we find a few instances from elicitation where the consultant uses a lengthened version of the dative postposition *lɛ́́ɛ* after the possessor. Not only does *lɛ́́ɛ* undergo argument-head tone sandhi, but the resulting tonal form also triggers sandhi on the possessed noun. The schematic in (95) captures this construction, with the lack of vertical bars around the possessed noun indicating that argument-head tone sandhi pervades the whole construction:

(95) *Schematic of alienable possession with* lɛ́́ɛ
    Possessor$_{NP}$ *lɛ́́ɛ* Possessed$_N$

I have never seen this construction in texts, which raises questions about how common it is, whether all speakers employ it, etc. For completeness' sake, I present data from elicitation here and leave this construction as a topic for future research:

(96) a. mó lèɛ jəgè
1SG.EMPH DAT dog
'my dog' (cf. *jəgè*) [sos170705e]

b. mó l̋ɛ̈ɛ bï̀
1SG.EMPH DAT goat
'my goat' (cf. *bî*) [sos170705e]

c. mï̋ l̋ɛ̈ɛ bï̋
1PL DAT goat
'our goat(s)' (cf. *bî* (sg) or *bï̋* (pl)) [sos170705e]

d. sân nɛ̈ɛ cï̀
rabbit GEN house
'rabbit's house' [sos180716e]

The data from sos170705e were provided by SCT, while those in sos180716e were provided a slightly older speaker, GFT, who is also from a different village in the southern dialect. She generally disprefers this construction. In (96c), where the possessed noun raises to S, it is ambiguous as to whether 'goat' is in the singular or the plural, since the stem has a front vowel so no vocalic changes are audible.

8.6.2.3 Alienable possession with an elided dative *l̋ɛ̈ɛ*

Far more common than the construction with an overt dative postposition is the same construction with the dative elided. With the process of clitic elision (§4.4.3), the postposition loses its segmental form but adds its tone and a mora to the preceding possessor. This morphologically complex possessor continues to trigger argument-head tone sandhi, just as the dative postposition did when in its independent form. The construction is schematized in (97):

(97) *Schematic of alienable possession with elided dative*
Possessor.Dative$_{NP}$ Possessed$_{N}$

The period separating "Possessor" and "Dative" in (97) shows that the two have merged and it is not possible to parse off part of the possessor as the dative postposition (at least at the segmental level). With pronouns, we find two irregular changes when the dative postposition is elided. These are shown in (98):

(98) a. à̋ + l̋ɛ̈ɛ → ɛ̈́ɛ́ ~ à̋á (3sg)

b. ń + l̋ɛ̈ɛ → nɛ́n (1sg)

There is variation with the 3sg between a form with vowel fronting and a form without (98a). This is irregular since the same vowel changes are not found with the 2sg, which only differs tonally from the 3sg (i.e. á + lɛ́ɛ → âa). In (98b), we see that when a non-emphatic 1sg combines with the dative, an irregular form nén is created; the emphatic form is totally regular (mó + lɛ́ɛ → môo). For a summary of these possessive pronouns, see §6.5.

This construction is found both in elicitation and in texts. I first provide elicited examples that are counterparts of those in (96):

(99) a. móò jəgè
       1SG.EMPH.DAT dog
       'my dog(s)' [sos170705e]

   b. môo bỉ̀
       1SG.EMPH.DAT goat
       'my goat' [sos170705e]

   c. mḯi bḯ
       1PL.DAT goat
       'my goat(s)' [sos170705e]

   d. sâan cỉ̀
       rabbit.DAT house
       'rabbit's house' [sos180716e]

In every case, speakers felt more comfortable with the elided version than with the non-elided version.

Before turning to textual examples, I would like to point out an interesting tonal phenomenon in elicitation settings. A form like (99a) is also ambiguous for whether the possessed noun is marked as plural or not, since the L tone formed by argument-head tone sandhi is already [+raised] and the front vowel of the stem means that no vocalic changes are audible. When vocalic changes are audible, as in (100) with the X-toned noun jụ̀ 'hill', the singular and plural nouns are given with the same pitch for L tone:

(100) a. móò jụ̀
         1SG.EMPH.DAT hill
         'my hill' [sos150810e]

    b. móò jụ̀ị
         1SG.EMPH.DAT hill.PL
         'my hills' [sos150810e]

When the possessed noun has a front vowel, as in bɛ̀ɛ 'pig', and consultants are asked to provide the singular and plural back-to-back, they will sometimes stumble and attempt to differentiate the two, often by slightly raising or lengthening the plural, reflecting their metalinguistic knowledge that plural forms are typically higher. This is audible in the following pair of examples from elicitation, where the up arrow indicates a slightly raised L tone:

(101) a. móò bɛ̀ɛ
1SG.EMPH.DAT pig
'my pig' [sos150810e]

b. móò ↑bɛ̀ɛ
1SG.EMPH.DAT pig.PL
'my pigs' [sos150810e]

I suspect that these differences would not be maintained in fluent speech. Context would be necessary to disambiguate.

Examples of elided dative possession from texts are shown in (102):

(102) a. ɛ̀é fṳ̀ɛ
3SG.DAT wife
'his wife' [sos150626t3:13]

b. ằá fṳ̀ɛ
3SG.DAT wife
'his wife' [sos150626t4:63]

c. móò nìgì
1SG.EMPH.DAT cow.PL
'my cows' [sos161009t1:124]

d. ɛ̀é cɪ̀ɛ
3SG.DAT hand
'his hand' [sos161009t1:156]

e. kəré béè fṳ̀ɛ
man DEM.GEN wife
'that man's wife' [sos130828t1:14]

The examples in (102a-b) show the variation between ɛ̀é and ằá for the 3sg (with the very same noun). In (102e), the noun 'wife' is seen again, this time with a complex NP as the possessor consisting of a noun and a demonstrative; the dative postposition is elided into the demonstrative, just as it would be into a noun.

One final note is required on pronominal possession with the dative elided: even with all of the tonal changes seen above, we find that multitonal possessed nouns are not affected. This fact is illustrated in (103) with a couple of multitonal nouns:

(103) a. ɛ̌ɛ́   dǎân
           3SG.DAT basket.hanger
           'his basket hanger'

       b. mǔi   dǎân
           1PL.GEN basket.hanger
           'our basket hanger'

       c. môo   jö̀ŋmǎ
           1SG.EMPH.DAT cat
           'my cat' [sos180716e]

This behavior is consistent with argument-head tone sandhi more generally (§4.4.2).

8.6.3 Free variation between alienable and inalienable

I have found one example so far of a noun that can be treated either as alienable or inalienable, and that is the word dò̈-nɛ́ɛ 'baby, infant'. I show this word as morphologically complex, since it appears to contain the word dôn 'child', but the meaning of nɛ́ɛ (possibly lɛ́ɛ with nasalization from the latent nasal on 'child') is unknown. Examples (104a) and (104b) show true free variation, since both involve a 1sg possessor. Examples (104c) and (104d) show further examples of inalienable possession and alienable possession, respectively:

(104) a. mó   dò̈-nɛ́ɛ
           1SG.EMPH baby
           'my baby' [sos130904e]

       b. mó   tè̈ dò̈-nɛ́ɛ
           1SG.EMPH GEN baby
           'my baby' [sos130904e]

       c. ä̀   dò̈-nɛ́ɛ
           3SG baby
           'his/her baby' [sos130904e]

       d. mǐ tě dò̈-nɛ́ɛ
           1PL GEN baby
           'our baby' [sos130904e]

Note that the root *dôn* 'child' on its own is always treated as inalienable (though unlike most inalienable nouns, it can be used on its own without a possessor).

8.6.4 Recursive possession

Recursive possession simply combines the elements we saw above with few surprises. I break this section into each combination of alienable and inalienable.

8.6.4.1 Inalienable-inalienable

In the construction [[Possessor Noun$_1$] Noun$_2$], in which the head noun (Noun$_2$) is itself possessed by an embedded possessive phrase, the embedded possessive phrase has its regular tonology as described in §8.6.1. The head noun, possessed by this complex possessor, follows the same pattern of argument-head tone sandhi, with the resulting sandhi form of Noun$_1$ triggering the alternation on Noun$_2$.

Recursive possession is rare in texts, so I provide examples from elicitation here, first with a consistent head noun *bő́n* 'back' :

(105) a. *ǟ ní bòn*
3SG father back
'his father's back' [sos150618e]

b. *á wó nì̀ bòn*
2SG EMPH father back
'your father's back' [sos150618e]

c. *mó tsí̀ɔ bő́n*
1SG.EMPH co.wife back
'my co-wife's back' [sos150620e]

In (105a-b), both Noun$_1$ and Noun$_2$ are held constant, varying just the embedded possessor. The X-toned pronoun in (105a) causes *ní̋* 'father' to lower to H, and this H tone causes the S of *bő́n* to flip to X. In (105b), the pronoun is H-toned, which causes S to lower to X, and the newly created non-pronominal X on *nì̀* has the same effect on S-toned *bő́n*. In (105c), underlying X-toned *tsí̀ɔ* 'co-wife' raises to S after a H-toned pronoun, and this S spreads onto *bő́n* (vacuously, since the noun was S-toned to begin with).

With an X-toned head noun *kǒ̰n* 'head', we find the following selection of results:

(106) a. *ǟ ní kǒ̰n*
3SG father head
'his father's head' [sos150618e]

b. mó   nì   kɔ̰̀n
    1SG.EMPH father head
    'my father's head' [sos150618e]

c. mǐ́   nǐ́   kɔ̰̋n
    1PL   father head
    'our father's head'

All three examples in (106) hold the two nouns constant and vary just the initial embedded possessor. In (106a), X-toned ǎ causes S-toned nǐ́ to lower to H. By argument-head tone sandhi, H causes X of kɔ̰̀n to flip to S. In (106b), H-toned mó lowers nǐ́ to X-toned nḭ̀. The combination of this derived X and the underlying X of kɔ̰̀n causes both nouns to raise to L. In (106c), the 1pl mǐ́ starts the process of S spreading, causing nǐ́ to remain S-toned; this S tone then spreads onto kɔ̰̀n.

A couple of examples from texts are shown in (107):

(107) a. í   dòn   kɔ̰̀n
          LOG   child head
          'her own child's head' [sos130828t1:22]

      b. mənǐ́   dőn   kɔ̰̋n
          woman child head
          'the woman's child's head'

8.6.4.2 Inalienable-alienable

If the complex possessor involves inalienable possession and the head possessed noun is alienable, we find the schematized form [[Possessor Noun$_1$] tɛ̋ Noun$_2$]; in other words, as is expected for alienable possession, the possessor is separated from the possessed noun with the genitive postposition tɛ̋, and no tonal alternations occur on the alienable noun. Examples from elicitation include:

(108) a. mó   ɲǎ̰   tɛ̏   cî
          1SG.EMPH mother GEN   house
          'my mother's house' [sos120109e]

      b. á   ɲǎ̰   tɛ̏   tàafíɛ
          2SG   mother GEN   wrapskirt
          'your mother's wrap skirt' [sos150707e]

The embedded inalienable possessive phrase has its regular tonal alternations, but the alienable noun is not affected. I have not seen any instances of dative alienable possession in these recursive NPs, either elided or otherwise.

8.6.4.3 Alienable-alienable

If both parts of recursive possession are alienable, the genitive particle is found twice: [[Possessor *tɛ́* Noun₁] *tɛ́* Noun₂]. Examples of this kind are sparse in the current data set, in both elicitation and textual data, but the attested cases are shown in (109):

(109)   a.   mó   tɛ̏   jə̀gɛ̏ tɛ̀   cî
                 1SG.EMPH GEN dog GEN house
                 'my dog's house' [sos150619e]

        b.   ä̀   kä̀nkù   tɛ̏   fṳ̀ɛ   tɛ̀   tə̀nɔ̋
                 DEF big.bird GEN wife GEN hearth
                 'the big bird's wife's hearth' [sos150626t6:30]

Alternatively, one or the other alienable construction can use the dative strategy instead. The example in (110) is very similar to that in (109b), but a dative-marked pronoun is used for the embedded possession rather than the genitive:

(110)   ȉì   fṳ̀ɛ   tɛ̀   tə̀nɔ̋
        LOG.DAT wife GEN hearth
        'his wife's hearth' [sos150626t5:29]

Noun₁ undergoes argument-head tone sandhi, due to the use of the dative possessor, and this L tone then causes the following genitive marker to be L. Noun₂, though, preceded by the genitive marker, has its base tone.

8.6.4.4 Alienable-inalienable

Finally, if the embedded possessive construction is alienable but the head possessed noun is inalienable ([[Possessor *tɛ́* Noun₁] Noun₂]), then the final tone of the embedded possessive phrase triggers tone sandhi on the head noun.
     Examples include:

(111)   a.   ń   tê   jə̀gè cɛ̰̀
                 1SG GEN dog foot
                 'my dog's foot'

        b.   ń   tê   mɔ̰̀-têɛ kɔ̄-dɛ̏n
                 1SG GEN shirt bone-grain
                 'my shirt's buttons' [sos170717e]

In both examples, the embedded possessor is a 1sg with a genitive marker. In (111a), the X of *jə̀gɛ̏* 'dog' combines with the X of *cɛ̰̀* 'foot', and both raise to L. In (111b), the final X of *mɔ̰̀-têɛ* causes H-toned *kɔ́* to lower to X, and this X causes the H of the latter half of the compound to likewise lower.

9 Ideophones and onomatopoeia

This chapter addresses a class of sound symbolic or iconic words in Seenku known as "ideophones". Dingemanse (2012) characterizes ideophones as "marked words depictive of sensory imagery". If we unpack this definition, ideophones can be seen as "marked" due to their often divergent phonology and to the fact that they often seem to defy syntactic category membership. The broad definition—"depictive of sensory imagery"—means that ideophones can invoke any of the senses. This includes sound, where onomatopoeia form a specific subclass of ideophones, but also visual characteristics like color, tactile sensations like stickiness or texture, kinds of movement, smells, or tastes.

Though found in languages all around the world, ideophones are a common characteristic of African languages (Samarin 1965, Blench 2010, etc.), including Mande languages. Seenku makes extensive use of different kinds of ideophones. For ease of presentation, I will make a distinction between ideophones and onomatopoeia, where the latter is meant to capture a sound, while the former captures other sensory imagery, but this is likely not a meaningful distinction in terms of anything like word class. As such, in §9.1, I address phonological characteristics of this broad class of words together, including segmental, tonal, morphological, and intonational characteristics. Then, in §9.2, I turn to different kinds of ideophones, which we can put into two categories: intensifiers and expressive adverbials. Finally, in §9.3, I discuss onomatopoeias, under the headings of animal noises, impact sounds, and other sounds.

Generalizations in this chapter are drawn from a set of 72 distinct ideophones and onomatopoeias attested in the corpus of texts and elicitation data. There are sure to be many more ideophones in the language that have simply not come up.

9.1 Phonological characteristics of ideophones and onomatopoeia

Ideophones often have unusual phonological characteristics that set them apart from "regular" vocabulary. This could be through the use of non-phonemic sounds, but as Dingemanse (2012) points out, most commonly it is by combining the regular inventory of the language in atypical ways. For instance, the Dogon language Tommo So has strict vowel harmony in regular roots, but these rules are flauted in ideophones (McPherson 2013).

In Seenku, ideophones are typically identifiable by repetition (reduplication or more), lengthening, or unusual prosody, but segmental and tonal characteristics can also be identified. I will discuss each in turn below.

9.1.1 Segmental characteristics

Ideophones do not contain any segments that are unattested in the phoneme inventory. Instead, the phonemes can be deployed in different ways, disobeying regular phonotactics. The most noticeable exceptional quality of ideophones is the presence of initial /l/, otherwise only attested in function words (and a small number of other exceptions; §3.3.3.1). Examples of /l/-initial ideophones are shown in (1):

(1)   lébáalée   'high in the air'
        ləgɔ̃-ləgɔ̃-ləgɔ̃   'movements of a toad's throat'
        lɛ́-lɛ́-lɛ́   'staunchly (refuse)'
        lɛ̋-lɛ̋-lɛ̋-lɛ̋   'very far away'

The last two examples in the table show that ideophones can differ from one another tonally; see §9.1.2 for more on the tonal structure of ideophones.

In addition to phonotactic differences, ideophones also have a higher instance rate of marginal phonemes such as /p/:

(2)   pà-pà-pà   'very hot'
        pằntừn-pằntừn   'sound of shea butter slapping in a bowl'
        pín   'sound of dropping a grinding pin'
        pǐo   '(not) at all'
        pó-pó-pó-pó   'all'
        préee   'middle of nowhere'
        pü-pü-pü-pü   'sound of a billygoat'

The example *pó-pó-pó-pó* takes the universal quantifier *pó-pó* 'all' (already an ideophone, even in this basic reduplicated form) as its base and adds further repetitions to it, together with "bouncing ball" intonation discussed in §9.1.2.2.

The closest we get to a unique segment in ideophones is the diphthong [ou] found in the ideophone *gbŏûn* 'swollen' (sometimes pronounced [gŏûn]).

Finally, it should be noted that many ideophones, particularly non-reduplicated ones, are held for considerably longer than a regular long vowel. This has the effect of making the ideophone "pop out" of speech. I will transcribe these with three identical vowels (e.g. *bəgɛ̀ɛɛ* 'contaminated') rather than the regular two of long vowels.

9.1.2 Tonal characteristics

While ideophones can be any of the tonal melodies found in non-ideophonic vocabulary, we find the middle tones L and H most frequently. First, L-toned ideophones are shown in (3):

(3) bəgɛ̀ɛɛ 'contaminated'
   bəŋɛ̀-bəŋɛ̀ 'very dirty (house, dishes)'
   bò-bò-bò 'sound of beating fonio'
   brɔ̀-brɔ̀-brɔ̀-brɔ̀ 'very dirty (clothing)'
   bùrù-bùrù-bùm 'sound of lots of wings flapping'
   nəŋà̰-nəŋà̰ 'very dirty (shea nuts)'
   ŋɔ̀mì-ŋɔ̀mì-ŋɔ̀mì 'stealthily (like a hunter)'
   pà-pà-pà-pà 'very hot'
   pètè 'flat'
   yèee 'dirty'

Considering how few L-toned stems there are in the rest of the vocabulary (only a small handful, §4.1.1.2), the use of L tones in ideophones is one way to set them apart from the regular vocabulary.

We find even more H-toned ideophones than L-toned ones. In the interest of space, I do not list all of them here, but provide a representative selection:

(4) bóen 'intensely red'
   gó-gó-gó 'very hot and dusty'
   préee 'middle of nowhere'
   kɔ́rɔ́ɔɔ 'for a long time'
   súi-súi 'separated, in pieces (shea butter)'
   bríii 'lot of smoke'
   cɛ́ɛɛ '(not) at all'
   céi 'sound of dropping a broom or a branch'

There are far more monosyllabic lengthened ideophones with H tone than with L tone, where reduplication is the usual strategy. The long extended H tone likewise sets ideophones apart, since nouns resist having a final H tone (§4.3.2.1) and H-final verbs at the end of the clause (i.e. without a following particle) are also rare, confined to just the perfective.

Note that it is often very hard to tell L- and H-toned ideophones apart, since they are generally phrase final and thus are not followed by any other reference point. Indeed, there appears to be variation. For instance, I have heard the ideophone fəgáaa 'light, feeling good' both with a H tone and as L-toned fəgàaa. Looking at the balafon surrogate language (§22.2.1), which can often shed light on tonal identity due to the discrete nature of the notes, we find cases where the same ideophone appears to be played as either H or L. For instance, the intensifier for 'white' pəɾɛ́-pəɾɛ́ is played on the same note as preceding H tones by SAD (sos170711m:12), but on the same note as preceding L tones by MD (sos161005e). It may be the case that H and L are non-contrastive in ideophones.

Table 9.1 lays out the other attested tone melodies along with an example of each. However, there does appear to be some tonal variation, as another speaker produced the X-toned ideophone bùgù-bùgù-bùgù with L tone.

Tab. 9.1: Other ideophonic tone melodies

X	bùgù-bùgù-bùgù	'rolling boil'
HX	céɲâ-céɲâ-céɲâ	'hopping (partridge)'
HS	fɔ́ɛ̋-fɔ́ɛ̋	'nothing at all'
LS	mṳ̋	'sound of thrashing'
S	kɐ̋gɐ	'very far away'
SX	pü̋-pü̋-pü̋-pü̋	'sound of a billygoat'
X-S	krɛ̏n-krɛ̋n	'fast footsteps (rabbit)'
XHX	dṳ̂ɡu	'distended (belly)'

9.1.2.1 Reduplication and repetition

Reduplication and extended repetition are common features of ideophones in Seenku. I define reduplication here as a single repetition of the stem (resulting in two copies), with extended repetition being three or more repetitions. There does not appear to be an upper bound on repetitions, with the number reflecting the amount of emphasis a speaker wishes to put on the meaning or on aesthetic principles of story telling.

First, the following ideophones have only been heard with simple reduplication:

(5) bəɲè-bəɲè   'very dirty (house, dishes)'
     krɛ̏n-krɛ̋n   'fast steps (rabbit)'
     kùrù-kùrù   'squat down wide'
     fɔ́ɛ̋-fɔ́ɛ̋   'nothing at all'
     nəŋɑ̂-nəŋɑ̂   'very dirty (shea nuts)'
     pərí-pərí   'very black'
     sɔ́yá-sɔ́yá   'very first'
     súi-súi   'separated, in pieces (shea butter)'

Since this table reflects only attested examples, it is not clear whether any of these could be repeated further. One thing we notice about these forms is that the stems are complex, either sesquisyllabic, with a diphthong, or even disyllabic in the case of sɔ́yá-sɔ́yá 'very first' and kùrù-kùrù 'squat down wide'. None of them are simple CV syllables, unlike the extended repetition cases, where simple CV is widely attested. The intensifier pərí-pərí 'very black' here is only attested with reduplication; the equivalent for 'white', pəré-pəré, is likewise only reduplicated in **spoken** data, but in the balafon surrogate language, we find it undergoing extended repetition. More data are required to say whether extended repetition is possible when speaking.

A sample of ideophones with extended repetition are shown in (6). Note that most of these have some sort of iconic intonation (§9.1.2.2), whether descending pitch or the bouncing ball pattern of duration.

(6) brű-brű-brű 'one after another'
    brɔ̀-brɔ̀-brɔ̀-brɔ̀-brɔ̀ 'very dirty (clothing)'
    gó-gó-gó 'very hot and dusty'
    kǔa-kǔa-kǔa-kǔa 'sound of birds crying'
    lέ-lέ-lέ 'staunchly refuse'
    lɛ̌-lɛ̌-lɛ̌-lɛ̌ 'very far away'
    mɔ́-mɔ́-mɔ́-mɔ́-mɔ́ 'up very high'
    ŋɔ̀mì-ŋɔ̀mì-ŋɔ̀mì 'stealthily (like a hunter)'
    pó-pó-pó-pó-pó 'all'

Comparing these to the reduplicated forms, we can see the greater portion of CV stems. The number of repetitions in this table reflects the actual number of repetitions used by the speaker in the corpus. As we can see, this varies between three and five, though I have seen up to ten repetitions in the case of cɔ̌, an onomatopoeia for the cry of a partridge; a spectrogram of this example is found in Figure 9.1 below.

9.1.2.2 Iconic intonation

One of the most interesting aspects of Seenku ideophones is the presence of what I call "iconic intonation", or in other words, fixed prosodic templates into which ideophonic stems can be slotted. There are three such prosodic templates, which I term as follows:
1. Lengthened monosyllable
2. Stepwise descending
3. Bouncing ball

The lengthened monosyllables were first noted in §9.1.1. These are usually H-toned, but the odd S-toned lengthened monosyllable can also be found. I treat this lengthening as a fixed prosodic template, since it is not a length found phonemically in Seenku and many different ideophonic stems can be put into this frame. The lengthening is extreme, up to 1285ms (i.e. over a second long!) at the end of a phrase, but more typically around 600ms in non-final position. Examples of lengthened monosyllables will be seen in the subsections below, identifiable from their sequences of three vowels.

The second pattern I call "stepwise descending". In this prosodic template, the stem undergoes extended repetition, with each repetition of equal duration but steadily decreasing pitch. A spectrogram and pitch trace of one such ideophone is shown in Figure 9.1.

In the last iteration (the 10th) at the end, another speaker begins to talk as the primary speaker finishes her ideophone. We can see that the pitch falls between each iteration, steeply at first then more shallowly as the speaker reaches the bottom of her

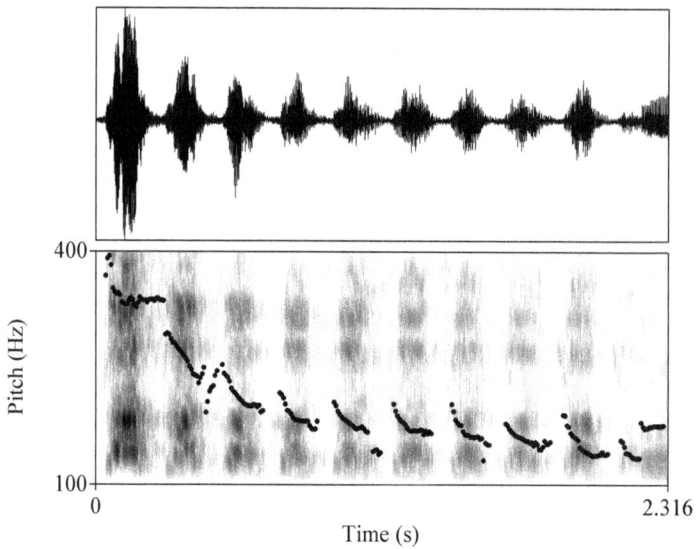

Fig. 9.1: Spectrogram and pitch trace of stepwise descending *cɔ́-!cɔ́-!cɔ́...*

range; with the exception of the first iteration, which is slightly longer, each repetition is roughly the same duration. I represent stepwise descending ideophones of this sort with exclamation marks between each repetition, as in downstep, though it should be noted that the descent is steep, taking an initial S-tone down to an X-tone by the end.

The last and most interesting iconic intonation pattern is what I call "bouncing ball" prosody. Imagine if you drop a ball and listen to its bouncing pattern: the first bounces are spaced further apart (as the ball bounces higher), gradually increasing in speed (as they decrease in height) before coming to a stop. This is shown in Figure 9.2.

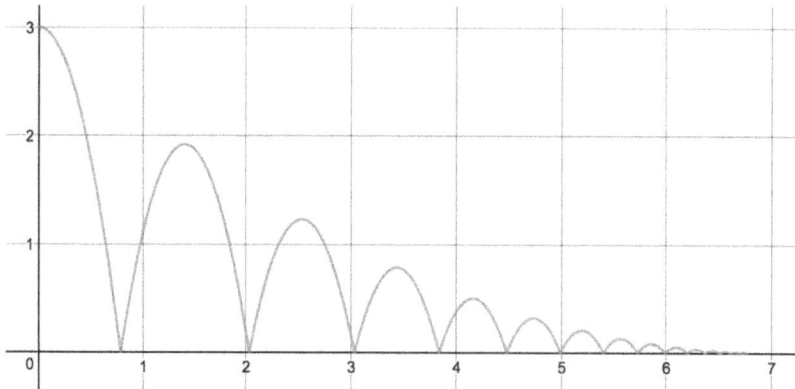

Fig. 9.2: Graph of a bouncing ball

The extended repetitions of some Seenku ideophones follow a frequency pattern like this, where the initial repetitions are longer and more spaced out, growing gradually more rapid. A pitch trace of one instance, using the ideophone *pó-pó-pó-pó* 'all', is shown in Figure 9.3. An interesting feature of bouncing ball prosody is visible here: the pitch remains constant. Thus, in the stepwise descending pattern, pitch drops continously while duration remains constant, and the opposite is true in the bouncing ball pattern. The speeding up in spoken language is typically most audible between the first three repetitions, as we can see here, with later ones matching approximately the same duration.

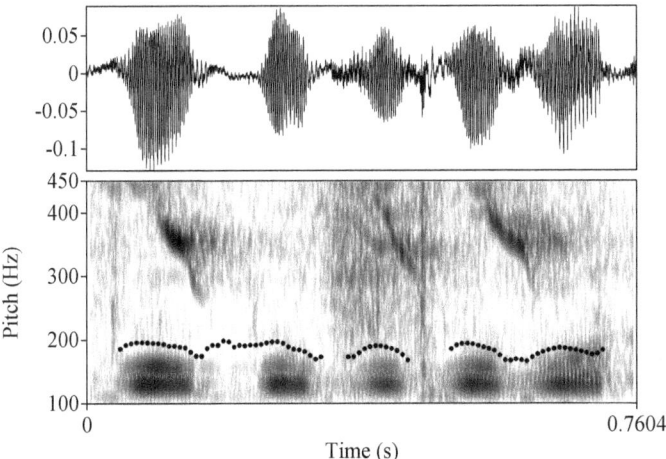

Fig. 9.3: Bouncing ball prosody on *pó-pó-pó-pó* [sos170805t15]

However, this "bouncing ball" target can be heard more clearly when Seenku is played instrumentally, as is shown in the spectrogram in Figure 9.4 from the balafon playing the ideophone *pəré-pəré...* 'intensely white'.

The textgrid shows the gradually decreasing durations between each iteration.

Bouncing ball prosody of this sort can be heard consistently in Seenku musical surrogates, which could be seen as more faithfully encoding a target that spoken language can only approximate (due, perhaps, to limitations of the vocal apparatus).

9.2 Ideophones

This section addresses the two main kinds of non-onomatopoetic ideophones in the language: intensifiers and expressive adverbials. Onomatopoeia will be discussed in §9.3.

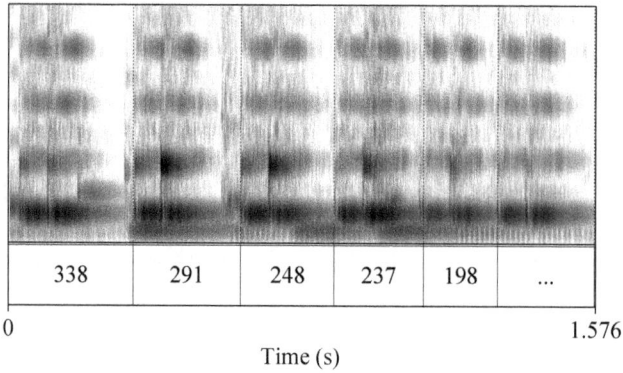

Fig. 9.4: Spectrogram of bouncing ball prosody on the balafon [sos170711m8]

9.2.1 Intensifiers

Ideophonic intensifiers behave like adverbs. They can follow a modifier (adjective, qualificational verb, numeral) or they can follow a non-qualificative predicate, adding an intensification to the action or to some other aspect of the clause.

9.2.1.1 Modificational intensifiers

Modificational intensifiers are most commonly associated with adjectives, and indeed, we find that adjectives in Seenku tend to be associated with one or more ideophonic intensifiers. Attested combinations are listed in Table 9.2.

Tab. 9.2: Adjectives and their intensifiers

Adjective	Intensifier	Gloss
bəlě	bǎa	'very big'
jǔ	dzı̰̀n-dzı̰́n	'very long'
kǎ	pɛ́-pɛ́	'very white'
sḭ̄ɛ	bóen	'very red'
tsǐe	prí-prí	'very black'

Textual examples showing the use of these intensifiers are provided in (7):

(7) a. sɔ̌n bəlě bǎa tsɛ̋ bḭ́ɛ
sky big INTENS INDF rain.REAL.PFV
'A really big rain fell.' [sos150626t3:1]

b. ì   á   wóo   né   bậạ   dzǔ-tsì̧   í   wó   tè̀
   COMP 2SG EMPH.SBJV come.IRR balafon mouth-cut.IRR LOG EMPH GEN
   wě́n   bí   nɔ̀   kǎ   prè-prè
   money hundred five white RED-INTENS
   '[I said] you should be the first to come and give to the balafon with a fresh new [lit. bright white] 500 CFA note.' [sos161005e]

c. ì   á   ằ   tɔ́   sɔ̋n-tǎ-kɔ̋ń   lò̤   né̋ bɔ́,   ằ
   COMP 2SG 3SG leave.IRR sky-fire-head.SBJV come if go.out.IRR 3SG
   bǔɔ   í   si̧̋ɛ   bóen
   go.out.PTCP LOG red INTENS
   '[He said] wait til the sun comes up, til it rises bright red.' [sos130828t2:31]

The intensifiers simply follow the adjectival stem, whether that adjective is used as a modifier (7a-b) or in a predicate (7c).

Qualificational verbs can also take intensifiers. Examples from the corpus include the following:

(8) a. ăa   fi̧ɛ   pà-pà-pà-pà
       3SG.PST heat.REAL.PFV RED-INTENS
       'It is very hot.' [sos161003e]

   b. á   kəmě   si̧   gó-gó-gó
      2SG dry.PTCP be RED-INTENS
      'You're so dusty!' [sos170724e]

   c. ằá   mù̧ɔ   né̋ sɔ̋ń   tè̀   ằ   kǎa nǎ   kəmè̀   lɔ̋
      3SG.SBJV cook.REAL if time.REL GEN 3SG side PROSP bleach.IRR here
      tóee
      INTENS
      'When it has cooked, one side will get very bleached.' [sos170822t4:141]

The intensifiers come at the end of the clause, since they are in fact adverbial intensifiers (see the subsection below), but they intensify the meaning of the qualificational verb. Thus, they straddle the boundary between modificational intensifiers and adverbial intensifiers.

In the case of one numeral, sóen 'one', we also find an intensifier: dén-dén (possibly related to the word dên for a grain or a small piece). Its usage is illustrated in (9):

(9) təné   brȩ̂   tɔ̋-tɔ̋   ì   mɔ̧̀   sóen dén-dén
    REL.PRO beat.ANTIP.IRR RED-like COMP person one RED-INTENS
    'What we play one at a time.' [sos170711t1:324]

This example emphasizes that just a single player is playing at a time, even though the norm (for balafons, in this case) is to play with three people at once.

9.2.1.2 Adverbial intensifiers
Adverbial intensifiers are used after the predicate to intensify some non-qualificational aspect of the preceding clause. This can be another adjunct, such as a location, as in (10):

(10) a. ì̃ wɛ̈ kɛ́̃ wétənɛ̌ sɔ́ jɥ̀ brɔ̂-nɛ̈ préee nɛ̈
3PL SUBORD go.IRR now arrive.IRR bush center-LOC INTENS LOC
'They arrived now in the absolute middle of the bush.' [sos150626t4:57]

b. mɛ̈ kɛ́̃ à bè gɔ̂ɔ-kù nɛ̈ bǘɔɔ tsɛ́̃ nɛ́̃
3SG.SUBORD go.IRR 3SG put.IRR wood-plant LOC INTENS INDF LOC
'and went and put her in a tree, in a very tall one.' [sos130828t1:31]

In (10a), the ideophone *préee* intensifies the meaning of the *jɥ̀ brɔ̂-nɛ̈* 'middle of the bush', indicating that the location is absolutely the middle of nowhere. The construction in (10b) is interesting, in that *bǘɔɔ* adds an intensified meaning of 'tall' that refers back to the tree, even though there is no explicit adjective meaning 'tall' before it. It also seems to form a resumptive NP with the indefinite determiner *tsɛ́̃*, but I classify *bǘɔɔ* as an intensifier rather than an adjective (cf. *bɔ́ɔ* 'tall'), since adjectives cannot head an NP and require a 3sg pronoun *ằ* to prop them up (§8.3.4).

In most cases of adverbial intensifiers, though, it is either the intention of the action, its intensity, or its duration that is intensified by the ideophone. This is illustrated in the following examples:

(11) a. ɛ̋! mó bɔ̀n dzïa lɛ̋, ń bón dzïa
INTERJ 1SG.EMPH back tire.REAL.PRF EMPH 1SG back tire.REAL.PRF
lɔ̋ tsɛ̰́ɛɛ nɛ̈
here INTENS LOC
'Eh! My back is tired! My back is really really tired now.' [sos170822t2:444]

b. mɛ̈ təgɔ̀ wɛ́ ằ kɔ́ɔ lɛ̀ kúrúʊʊ
3SG.SUBORD sit.IRR FOC DEF hole DAT INTENS
'…and he sat in that hole for a looong time.' [sos170711t1:27]

c. mɛ̈ néɛ̀ mɛ̈ kú təgǐ fúrúuu
3SG.SUBORD come.IRR.HAB 3SG.SUBORD D.DEF climb.IRR INTENS
'…and she kept coming and climbing it over and over.' [sos150626t4:132]

In (11a), the intensifier *tsɛ̰́ɛɛ* intensifies the meaning of the predicate 'tired'; it is, however, a general intensifier that is found in other contexts, meaning something like 'really' or 'truly'; see, for instance, (15b) below. The two ideophones in (11b-c) are similar in being temporal: kúrúʊʊ (sometimes kɔ́rɔ́ɔ or kpɔ́rɔ́ɔ) indicates a long duration, while fúrúuu appears to indicate multiple iterations. However, it is unclear whether there is a clear division between durative and iterative intensifiers, considering the following example:

(12) kpɔ́rɔ́ɔ mɛ̀ kɛ́ɛ́ né kʊ́ sǎn bé tsʉ́ʉ́
INTENS 3SG.SUBORD go.IRR come.IRR D.DEF river DEM cross.IRR
'Time after time, she would cross that river...' [sos150626t5:153]

Here, whenever the child being pursued by the sorcerer would smash an egg, it would turn into a river that the sorcerer had to cross. This happened multiple times, indicated by kpɔ́rɔ́ɔ. More data are required to tell whether fúrúuu and kpɔ́rɔ́ɔ are interchangeable.

Finally, we find adverbial intensifiers that express extreme locations, as in the following:

(13) a. ì wò kɛ́ɛ́ lɛ́ɛ́-ǃlɛ́ɛ́-ǃlɛ́ɛ́-ǃlɛ́ɛ́ ìì fʉ̰ɛ wè
3PL EMPH go.IRR INTENS LOG.DAT wife with
'They had gone far far far away with his wife.' [sos150626t4:60]

b. á wó sɪ̰ à bǎrǎ bǎ nɛ́ɛ́ á dərǒn kɡ̰ɑ nɛ́ɛ́
2SG EMPH be DEF work do.REAL.NOM LOC 2SG child INTENS LOC
'You're working, and your child is faaaar away.' [sos170822t3:203]

c. səgɔ̂ lɛ́ɛ́ íi ɲ̀ia nɛ́ɛ́ àa sɛ́ɛ́ sǎn
partridge PST LOG.SBJV finish.REAL.PFV if 3SG.SUBORD fly.IRR up
mɛ́ɛ́ mɔ́-mɔ́-mɔ́
with INTENS
'When the partridge was done, he flew high high up.' [sos170805t15:164]

d. səgɔ̂ tsɪ̰́ sǎn mɛ́ɛ́ léebáaléee
partridge jump.REAL.PFV up with INTENS
'The partridge jumped way up high.' [sos170805t15:220]

All of these intensifiers give a sense of distance, either on the horizontal (13a-b) or vertical (13c-d) axis.

9.2.2 Expressive adverbials

Expressive adverbials have the same morphosyntactic distribution as intensifiers, but they differ semantically. Instead of intensifying the meaning of another element in the clause, expressive adverbials add highly specific meanings (typically) evoking some physical movement or characteristic. This class of words expands the descriptive and expressive capability of the language, balancing the relative lack of adjectives. The following table lays out some of the expressive adverbials that describe characteristics:

(14) bəgèɛɛ 'dirty, contaminated'
bəŋè-bəŋè 'dirty (house, dishes)'
brɔ̀-brɔ̀* 'very dirty (people, clothing)'
déɛ-déɛ* 'just a little remaining (of a tree being chopped)'
dɔ́ɛɛ 'fine, back to normal'
dṳ̀ṳ̂ṳ 'distended'
fəgáaa 'light, in good health'
fúiii 'sprouted, spoiled'
gbɔ̰̀ɔ̰̂ɔ̰ 'distended'
kṵ̋ɔ-ɲénéɲ́ɛ́ 'very fresh'
nəŋà̰-nəŋà̰ 'very dirty (shea nuts)'
ŋḭ́ɔ-ŋḭ́ɔ* 'pointy'
pètè 'flat'
sá̰a̰a̰ 'blood red'
súi-súi 'separated, not smooth (shea butter)'
wéee 'bright, clean'
yèee 'oily, dirty'

Forms with asterisks are represented in the corpus with extended repetition, not shown here in the interest of space. It is possible that other reduplicated forms could also be repeated multiple times, but we would need more data to be sure. We can see in this table that there are several different expressive adverbials for dirtiness, each with a specific kind of dirtiness evoked. For instance, *yèee* represents an oily or sticky dirtiness, while *bəŋè-bəŋè* could refer to clutter in a house or old food stuck to plates. Some examples of dirtiness expressive adverbials in context are provided in (15):

(15) a. ḭ̀ á cìe sḭ̌ bəgèɛɛ
COMP 2SG hand.PL be dirty
'[They say] your hands are dirty [from the shea nuts].' [sos170822t1:83]

b. à̰ nəŋà̰-nəŋà̰ lɔ́ tséɛɛ nɛ̋
3SG RED-dirty here INTENS LOC
'They are so dirty [shea nuts sitting in the mud].' [sos170822t1:71]

c. mḭ́ bé wé brɔ̀-brɔ̀-brɔ̀-brɔ̀-brɔ̀
1PL DEM FOC RED-dirty
'Look at how dirty we are [doing shea butter work].' [sos170822t2:456]

Though all of these expressive adverbials arose in the process of creating shea butter, they refer to different kinds of dirtiness, from the sort of sticky dirtiness of contaminated hands, to somewhat rotten mud-covered nuts, to general dirtiness of the clothing and person when doing manual labor of this sort. In (15b), the expressive adverbial is combined with the intensifier *tsɛ́ɛɛ* seen in (11a) the last subsection.

Other expressive adverbials refer to highly specific physical states, such as *súi-súi* for mixing shea butter that is not smooth but is rather breaking up in chunks (see sos170822t2:235), or *déɛ-déɛ*, which indicates the state right before a tree will fall when just a little bit of wood remains uncut.

The other use of expressive adverbials is to describe specifics of movement. For instance:

(16) a. ŏo   lɛ̀   bɔ́   wétənĕ í   sɔ̀,   ŋɔ̀mì-ŋɔ̀mì-ŋɔ̀mì
         3SG.EMPH SUBORD go.out.IRR now   LOG alone IDEO
         mɛ̀   kɛ̋   mɛ̀   kɛ̋   tàasò̀   à   bö̀-kɔ̃   lê
         3SG.SUBORD go.IRR 3SG.SUBORD go.IRR surprised DEF billygoat PRES
         'He went out himself this time, stealthily, like a hunter, he went, he went and to his surprise there was a billygoat.' [sos150626t3:18]

   b. í   nǎ   kùrù̀-kùrù̀ í   blǎ bö̀-kɔ̃   kɔ́n
      LOG PROSP IDEO   LOG fall billygoat on
      '[and] he would squat down wide to block his passage, and set about pouncing on the billygoat.' [sos150626t3:52]

   c. blö̀kɔ̋   fúɛn-jɔ̂ fúɛn-jɔ̂ fúɛn-jɔ̂
      Blokɔ IDEO   IDEO   IDEO
      'Blokɔ [the name of a dog's head] limped along.' [sos170805t15:56]

   d. mɛ̀   ɲá   mɛ̀   í   tsí̧   nɛ̀-bù̀ɔ
      3SG.SUBORD refuse 3SG.SUBORD LOG backside TRANS-go.out.REAL
      cɛ̀ɲä̀ cɛ̀ɲä̀ cɛ̀ɲä̀
      IDEO IDEO IDEO
      '[The partridge] refused and hopped away.' [sos170805t15:217]

All of the expressive adverbials are evocative of a specific stance or kind of movement, from careful, stealthy stalking to the hopping of a bird. While English expresses these with simile or semantically narrow verbs like 'squat', Seenku shifts the burden onto ideophones. Note that in (16b), the expressive adverbial immediately follows the prospective auxiliary, taking the place of a main verb. In (16c-d), I have written spaces between repetitions of the ideophone, since there are short pauses, suggesting that the whole ideophone is being repeated as separate prosodic words rather than a kind of reduplication.

9.3 Onomatopoeia

This last section addresses the subclass of ideophones that are meant to mimic sounds, better known as "onomatopoeia". I divide this section into three subsections based on natural classes of sounds: animal sounds, impact sounds, and finally any other onomatopoetic ideophones that do not fit into the other two classes.

9.3.1 Animal sounds

Onomatopoeias for animal sounds are language-specific. While English speakers may find it natural that pigs make the sound *oink-oink*, French speakers would feel the same about *groin-groin*. The current dataset does not include many instances of animal sounds, but we do see a few. The following lists the animal sounds seen thus far:

(17) cow   *múu*
     dog   *wɔ́w*
     cat   *ɲǎaŋ*
     goat   *pü-pü-pü*
     sheep   *bȅɛ̀ɛ̏, mȅɛ̀ɛ̏*
     duck   *cṳ́ɛŋ-cṳ́ɛŋ*
     rooster *ké-ké̱ɛlí-kê̱ɛ* or *kó-kőolí-kôo*
     partridge *cő-cő-cő*

These animal sounds arise most commonly in the folktale genre, where we find some other specific animal sounds not necessarily associated with a species or associated with a context-specific sound made by an animal. For instance, the rooster's call in (17) is crowing, the equivalent of English "cockadoodledoo", but in (18c), the onomatopoeia refers to the sound of roosters scattering.

(18) a. *ì   ɛ̏ɛ́   bɛ̋   ì   pü-pü-pü-pü*
        COMP 3SG.LOG do.IRR COMP IDEO
        'He said, "Ba-a-a-ah!"' [sos161009t1:219]

   b. *kó-kô   lɛ́   bǎ   lɛ̋   ì   ké-ké̱ɛlí-kê̱ɛ*
      rooster SBJV say PART COMP IDEO
      'When the rooster crowed, "cockadoodledoo!"' [sos170805t3:114]

   c. *kó-kô   sá   ì   kő-!kő-!kő-!kő*
      rooster cry.REAL.PFV COMP IDEO
      'The roosters went "ko-ko-ko-ko" (while scattering).' [sos130828t2:49]

d. ằ kànè dàn-cèɛ   gűrɛ̋ kǔa-!kǔa-!kǔa-!kǔa
   DEF bird.PL mouth-break.PFV voice IDEO
   'The birds were crying out kwa kwa kwa kwa!' [sos150626t4:53]

e. mɛ̀   í   bɛ̋   ì   cɔ́-!cɔ́-!cɔ́-!cɔ́
   3SG.SUBORD LOG do.IRR COP IDEO
   '[The partridge] said, "cɔ-cɔ-cɔ-cɔ!"' [sos170805t15:223]

The billygoat's cry in (18a) is pronounced with bouncing ball prosody, while the three bird sounds in (18c-e) are pronounced with stepwise descending intonation. This fact does not appear to be significant—the partridge's call is pronounced with bouncing ball prosody elsewhere in the text.

More targeted elicitation is required to fill in more animal sounds and test how consistent they are across speakers.

9.3.2 Impact sounds

Another class of onomatopoeia found in texts are different impact sounds. In English, too, this is a common source of onomatopoeia (e.g. "thud!", "bam!", "thwack!", etc.). Since impacts tend to involve a single (loud) sound, it comes as no surprise that most impact onomatopoeia in Seenku are monosyllabic.

The following three examples show onomatopoeia for different objects falling and making impact:

(19) a. səgɔ̂ lɛ̋ sɛ̋ sǎn mɛ̋ ằ   né   blǎ í bón kɔ̌n ì̀   gbɛ̰̈
        partridge PST fly up with 3SG come.IRR fall LOG back on COMP IDEO
        'The partridge flew up high and came falling back down onto his back, gbɛ!' [sos170805t15:157]

   b. mɛ̀   jé-lén-tɔ̂   blằ   pín
      3SG.SUBORD grindstone-child-pin drop.IRR IDEO
      'He would drop a stone grinding pin, pin!' [sos150626t5:130]

   c. mɛ̀   ằ   fənɨ̋ bɛ̋   céi
      3SG.SUBORD 3SG broom put.IRR IDEO
      'He would drop the broom, cei!' [sos150626t5:156]

One can imagine the sound symbolism in these onomatopoeia: the high front vowel and nasality in *pín* capturing the high pitched resonance of a stone rolling pin being dropped, the noisier palatal in *céi* capturing the rustle of a broom. Since these examples are drawn from texts, there is always the possibility that the speaker invented them on the spot, that is, that they are not general lexicalized ideophones in the language, but still we get a glimpse into the kinds of onomatopoetic ideophones that are used.

Other impact sounds involve the impact from swinging an object and having it hit something else (either vertically or laterally). Three cases are illustrated in (20):

(20) a. ántȅ sân nɛ́ kpɔ̃́ ȅɛ́   kɔ̃́n-sɛ̋ ä̀ gɔ́ɔ̀ wɛ̀
       dear rabbit PST IDEO 3SG.LOG head-look DEF wood with
       'When Mr. Rabbit gave it another thwack, he looked up at the tree.'
       [sos150626t5:77]

   b. ń tȅ sân né ä̀ gɔ́ɔ tsi̠   nɛ̋ kpṵ̂
      1SG dear rabbit SBJV DEF wood cut.REAL.PFV if IDEO
      'If Mr. Rabbit cuts the tree, thud!' [sos150626t5:96]

   c. dȅn-ká̈ flá̈ dȅn kóò wɛ̀ fő mṳ̆
      bean-flower thrash bean grow.IRR HAB better IDEO
      'Thrash the bean flower, the bean grows better, mu!' [sos150626t2:9]

The examples in (20a-b) both represent the sound of chopping wood, and the two ideophones appear to be variants of one another: both with a voiceless labiovelar stop and a back nasal vowel. In (20c), the impact is the sound of thrashing black beans; however, it should be noted that this example is produced in a sort of half-singing fashion, raising the question of whether *mŭ* is ever used in regular spoken language or whether it is a playful aesthetic choice here. From elicitation by a different speaker, referring this time to fonio rather than a kind of bean species, we find the ideophone *bí*:

(21) ä̀ si̠ fɔ̂   nȅ ä̀ nȅ bí
     3SG be thrash.REAL.NOM LOC 3SG LOC IDEO
     'He is thrashing it, *bí*!' [sos170801e]

More data are required to see whether thrashing onomatopoeias (or any onomatopoeias, for that matter) are standard across speakers or not.

9.3.3 Other sounds

Onomatopoeia representing sounds not in these two categories do, of course, pop up. As with the impact sounds in (21), it's hard to say whether these are innovations by the individual speakers or not. Some I have checked with other speakers, others I have not. Where the ideophone has been independently confirmed by another speaker, I will point it out.

First, speaker GRT makes extensive use of ideophones in telling stories. The following two are onomatopoeia from his story about the billygoat and the hyena [sos150626t4]:

(22) a. plěn-gṳ̀ dǎn-cě̀n í ɲá nḛ̀ kɛ̀nɛ̀ sɛ́ brùbrùbrùm ä̀
bag-under mouth-open LOG side LOC bird.PL fly.IRR IDEO DEF
cîe
house.LOC
'He opened up the bag on his side and the birds flew out into the house with a WHOOSH!' [sos150626t4:54]

b. ...ḭ̀ nəgḭ̀ bṳ́ɔ lɛ́ ḭ̀ nɔ́nɛ̰́sán dəgë í lö̀
3PL mind go.out.PTCP FOC 3PL food prepare.REAL.PRF LOG come
ä̀ nɔ́ wïrrrraaaa
3SG eat.IRR IDEO
'...they had forgotten that they had made food, they were going to eat it, wrrrraaa [sound of the billygoat emerging from between the hanging animal heads].' [sos150626t4:65]

Both of these examples are difficult to transcribe; in (22a), the <r> is heavily trilled and breathily voiced, representing the movement of air created by lots of wings. In (22b), the pitch excursion is extreme across the whole ideophone, and both the trill and the vowel have long durations.

These examples represent the sound of a rapid, chaotic sort of movement. Other onomatopoeias are far more repetitive and discrete, such as the two in (23):

(23) a. mó brɔ̰̀ lɛ́ sḭ̀ tě̀n tě̀n tě̀n
1SG.EMPH heart PST be IDEO IDEO IDEO
'My heart was beating hard, ten ten ten.' [sos170805t3:83]

b. pǎntùn pǎntùn pǎntùn pǎntùn
IDEO IDEO IDEO IDEO
'(Mimicking the sound of GMT mixing shea butter)' [sos170822t2:154]

Both of these involve slower, more spaced out repetitions matching approximately the rate of the sound in real life.

Finally, one ideophone blurs the line between an onomatopoeia and an expressive adverbial:

(24) dɔ́ɔní tûn mḛ̀ í bɛ́ ḭ̀ bǔgù-bǔgù-bǔgù
a.little pot SUBORD LOG do.IRR COMP IDEO
'After a little while, the pot started going bugu-bugu-bugu.' [sos170805t3:125]

This ideophone represents a rolling boil, but we can tell it is intended as an onomatopoeia here since it is introduced with a quotative complementizer ɲ̀ (§19.1).

Many more examples will be required to build a thorough picture of how segmental, tonal, and prosodic information combine in a system of sound symbolism in Seenku.

10 Postpositions and adverbials

This chapter discusses postpositional phrases and adverbials in Seenku, both of which are found post-verbally in the X position of the Mande word order S Aux O V X.

For ease of presentation, I divide this chapter into sections on postpositions (§10.1) and adverbials (§10.2), respectively, where each construction will be discussed in turn. However, running through many of these subsections, we find a general directional morpheme *nǎ* that modifies the meaning of both postpositions and adverbs, giving a sense of 'towards'. I do not dedicate a subsection to this morpheme, since it does not appear to be its own postposition: It never appears on its own, and other postpositions do not stack in this way. For examples with *nǎ*, see (24), (31a), and especially §10.2.1.2 on the adverb 'there', with which it commonly combines. It is also discussed in §16.2.3 for the wh-expression 'towards where'.

10.1 Postpositions

Seenku has a fairly large inventory of specific postpositions compared to some other West African languages, where many spatial relationships are expressed with a general locative and a relational noun (often a body part). Seenku has a few of these expressions (discussed in §10.1.10), but they are relatively rare compared to simple postpositions.

The following subsections cover the main uses of each postposition, which may be varied. The postpositions are: *kɔ̃n* 'on (top of)' (§10.1.1), *gú* 'under' (§10.1.2), *kəré* 'next to' (§10.1.3), *kǎa* 'across' (§10.1.4), *né* 'at, to, in' (a general locative, §10.1.5), *ká* (§10.1.6), *wɛ̀* 'with' (comitative or associative, §10.1.7), *tɛ̋* (genitive, §10.1.8), and *lɛ̋* (dative, §10.1.9).

10.1.1 *kɔ̃n* 'on (top of)'

The postposition *kɔ̃n* has slightly more restricted semantics than English 'on' or French *sur*, used primarily for vertical relations rather than horizontal ones (e.g. something hanging **on** a wall in English). In this way, it has more of a sense of 'on top of' than the more varied uses of English 'on'. Historically, it appears to be derived from the relational noun *kɔ̃n* 'head', though the two differ in modern Seenku in the nasality of the vowel.

The postposition carries X tone underlyingly and undergoes tone sandhi with the preceding noun; see §4.4.2 for discussion of argument-head tone sandhi.

Elicited examples include:

(1) a. mó   sį̌ təgò̌   nɛ̈ kpóòn dzʋ̀ kɔ̀n
       1SG.EMPH be sit.REAL.NOM LOC seat edge on
       'I am sitting on the edge of the chair.' [sos150622e]

   b. kằnɛ̈ təgŏ sį̌ gɔ́ɔ̀ cìen kɔ̀n
       bird sit.PTCP be wood branch on
       'The bird is perched on the branch.' [sos150622e]

   c. mó   nǎ   təgò̌ ń   cəmį̀-kɔ̰̀n kɔ̀n
       1SG.EMPH PROSP sit.IRR 1SG knee-head on
       'I will kneel (Lit. sit on my knees).' [sos150622e]

From texts, we find examples like the following:

(2) a. ằ   wò   tərų̃́   jɛ̋n   ɲì-nà   ằ   wɛ̈   í   jó   í
       3SG EMPH hearth front there-towards 3SG SUBORD LOG see.IRR LOG
       nǎ   kʋ̀rʋ̀-kʋ̀rʋ̀ í blǎ bò̤-kɔ̌ɔ kɔ́n
       PROSP RED-IDEO LOG fall.IRR billygoat on
       'There in front of his hearth, he set his sights on him, squatted down wide to block his passage, and set about pouncing on the billygoat.' [sos150626t4:52]

   b. fà-kʋ́ɔ   sîɔ   jəgì̈   wɛ̈   máàn   kɔ̀n cɛ̀n sóen ŋɛ́
       sandfox feces excrete.IRR HAB termite.mound on time one NEG
       'The sandfox doesn't defecate just once on the termite mound.' [sos150710e]

   c. mɔ̰̌   nɛ̈   ằ   dzį́   tá̀ kɔ̀n jʋ̀ sʋ̀ɛ
       person come.IRR 3SG put.IRR fire on year three
       'We come and put it on the fire for three years.' [sos170711t1:58]

   d. mɔ̰̌ɔ́   bʋ́ dzį́̌   kʋ́   kɔ̋n mɔ̰̌ɔ́   fằ
       person.SBJV dirt put.IRR D.DEF on person.SBJV pass.IRR
       'Let's stop that and move on.' [sos150626t2:24]

From these examples, we can see the consistency of the vertical orientation of *kɔ̀n*: The hyena is pouncing onto the billygoat from above in (2a); the sandfox is defecating on top of the termite mound in (2b); in (2c), the wood of the balafon is being placed on the fire; finally, in (2d), the idiomatic expression 'put dirt on something', meaning to stop it or let it go, implies piling dirt onto something.

10.1.2 gṹ 'under'

The postposition gṹ expresses the notion of 'under' or 'underneath'. It requires that the complement of the postposition be physically above the subject. However, this does not have to be as strictly a vertical relationship as kɔ̀n; for instance, as we will see in (4a), 'under' can be used if the subject is at the base of a wall that extends up above it without physically being over its head.

The following elicited phrases show simple examples of the postposition:

(3) a. bɛ̀ɛ sənǎ sɪ̰̌ gɔ̂ɔ gṳ̀
pig lie.PTCP be wood under
'The pig is lying under the tree.' [sos150623e]

b. mó təgŏ sɪ̰̌ gbátǎ gṹ
1SG.EMPH sit.PTCP be shed under
'I am seated under the shed.' [sos150703e]

Examples from the text corpus show more varied uses of the postposition:

(4) a. mɛ̏ kɛ̋ mɛ̏ í bɛ̋ ɛ̋! ɪ̀ bǜbǎ
3SG.SUBORD go.IRR 3SG.SUBORD LOG do.IRR INTERJ COMP dad.VOC
tsɛ̋ fên sɪ̰̌ nɔ̋-ŋɛ̋ ằ dân gṳ̀
INDF thing be here-NEG DEF wall under
'He went out and shouted "Eh! Dad, there is something over there next to the wall!"' [sos150626t4:6]

b. kótê blĕ sɔ́ɔ̀ ằá fằ kʊ́ gṳ̀ ŋέ
calabash big be.able.IRR.HAB 3SG.SBJV enter.IRR D.DEF under NEG
'A big calabash can't fit under there.' [sos170711t1:105]

c. á ằ jó ɪ̀ fôn tsɪ̰̀ ɪ̀ ằ bɔ́ kɑ̰̋ tɔ̋-trɔ̋
2SG 3SG see.IRR 3PL fonio cut.IRR 3PL 3SG take.out.IRR go RED-like
í sí gṳ̀
LOG RECP under
'You see they are cutting fonio underneath each other.' [sos170714t2:24]

10.1.3 kəré 'near, next to'

The postposition kəré implies close proximity, which can be translated either as 'near' or 'next to'. As is usually for sesquisyllabic words with a velar stop in C1 and [r] in C2, the schwa of the sesquisyllabic sounds more like a round vowel, here [u] or [o], but there is no evidence this is contrastive. See §3.1.3 for further discussion.

First, elicited examples lay out the basic use of the postposition:

(5) a. bɛ̋ɛ sənɑ̆ sḭ̄ gɔ̂ɔ kərɛ̏
pig lie.PTCP be wood next.to
'The pig is lying next to the tree.' [sos150623e]

b. á wó gbəgɛ̋ sḭ̄ mó kərɛ̏
2SG EMPH approach.PTCP be 1SG.EMPH next.to
'You are close to me.' [sos150623e]

In texts, we find the following examples:

(6) a. ʽìi mlé təgö̏ bɑ̰́ɑ̰ bé kərɛ̏ kű́ɛ fəná kɛ̏ɛ sḭ̄
3PL.SUBORD REL.PRO sit.IRR balafon DEM next.to 3PL also taboo be
í mɑ̀ kɑ̰́ ʽìi kəré bɛ̋ bɑ̰̀ɑ̰ kərɛ̏ ŋɛ̋
LOG all go 3PL.SUBORD what do.IRR balafon next.to NEG
'Do those who sit next to the balafon have a taboo, something they can't do next to the balafon?' [sos170711t1:280]

b. kɛ́ í wó kərɛ̏, təgŏee-mɔ̰̆ dərɔ̰́
COP 2PL EMPH next.to seated-person only
'The ones sitting next to you only...' [sos170711t1:252]

c. ʽì wɛ̏ təgö̀ à frɔ̰̀ɛ kərè
3PL SUBORD sit.IRR DEF monkey.PL next.to
'They sat down next to the monkeys.' [sos150626t6:34]

In each case, the postposition *kəré* is most naturally translated as 'next to'.

10.1.4 *kǎa* 'across from'

The postposition *kǎa* is similar to *kəré* in indicating proximity, and it is offered in translation to both 'across from' (French: *en face de*) and 'next to' (French: *à côté de*). When asked specifically about the difference between *kəré* and *kǎa*, I am told that *kǎa* means 'across from', but it appears that there is overlap in their semantics. This fluidity is illustrated first with examples from elicitation, where (7a) shows *kǎa* with the meaning 'across from' (provided in explicit contrast to *á jərá kərɛ̏* 'next to your house'), while (7b) shows a reading of 'next to':

(7) a. mó sḭ̄ á jərá kǎa
1SG.EMPH be 2SG home across
'I am across from your house.' [sos170707e]

b. *móő   à tò   né   à ɲá   mí̋ kǎa   ŋɛ́*
   1SG.EMPH.PST 3SG know.IRR 1SG.COMP 3SG be.NEG 1PL across NEG
   'I didn't know that he was next to us.' [sos181206e]

This same variation is seen in natural examples from the text corpus, where (8a) gives the reading of 'across from' but (8b-c) are better translated as 'next to':

(8) a. *kʊ́ kʊ́ tɛ̀ wé méɛ̋   lɛ̏   tə̀gò̰ mɔ̰̏   kǎa,*
   D.DEF D.DEF GEN FOC REL.PRO.PL SUBORD sit.IRR person across
   məré   lɛ̏   à dɔ̰̀nɪ̋ brɛ̋   mɔ̰̏ kǎa tsɛ̋-né à
   REL.PRO SUBORD DEF drum play.IRR person across and DEF
   də̀nṵ̀-brɛ̋
   talk.drum-play.NOM
   'That's why we have those sitting next to us, those that play the drum and the talking drum players.' [sos170711t1:240]

b. *méɛ   lɛ̏   kà̰   bâ̰a̰ gɔ̰̏   sô dzʊ̀ kǎa*
   REL.PRO SUBORD go.REAL.PFV balafon learn.IRR road mouth across
   tsɛ̋-ké mí̋ nɔ̰̋n   ké sɔ́ɛn ŋɛ́
   and 1PL that.for COP one NEG
   'Someone who has gone and learned balafon on the side of the road and what we do, it's not the same.' [sos170711t1:75]

c. *à̰ wɔ̀ kʊ́ sṳ̀   lɛ̋   à̰ kʊ́ bɛ̋   ḭ̂ kǎa*
   3SG EMPH D.DEF take.IRR EMPH 3SG D.DEF put.IRR LOG across
   'She takes it and puts it down next to her.' [sos170714t2:101]

More in-depth spatial study could reveal differences between configurations that allow *kǎa* and *kəré*.

10.1.5 *né* locative

The most general locative postposition in the language is *né*, which can carry a variety of meanings, from 'in', to 'to', to 'at'. As such, I will gloss it LOC. Its semantic center, however, appears to carry the meaning of 'inside', which no other postposition indicates.

The locative expression with *né* has evolved into verbal expressions, particularly the progressive (to be **in** the state of doing) or the recent past (via an expression meaning to arrive **in** the action); for more on these periphrastic expressions, see §13.3.1.

Examples of *né* from elicitation include:

(9) a. ä̀ sĭ fâ̰   nȅ jô nȅ
       3SG be enter.REAL.NOM LOC water LOC
       'She is entering the water.' [sos150630e]

   b. mí' bɛ̀ɛ bá̰   gɔ̀ɛɛ nɛ̀
      1PL pig.PL hit.REAL.PFV field.PL LOC
      'We hit the pigs in the fields.' [sos150317e]

   c. óo kà̀   gùe tsɛ̋ nɛ̋
      2SG.EMPH go.REAL.PFV country.PL how LOC
      How many countries have you been to? [sos150317e]

Like most postpositions seen thus far (barring the tonally complex kǎa), the locative undergoes argument-head tone sandhi. In (9a), both a periphrastic verbal usage and a postpositional usage are attested. In its postpositional usage, the meaning of 'in' or 'inside' is clear, as entering water implies being in the water. Likewise, in (9b), the hitting of the pigs took place in the fields. The postposition in example (9c) is translated into English as 'to', but nevertheless, having been to a country means having been in a country, so the 'inside' semantics are still applicable.

The following examples are selected from texts illustrating the physical locative uses of *né*:

(10) a. ì̀ fəgǎ   sĭ plɛ̀ngṳ̀   nɛ̏ bò̰-kǒo tɛ̋
        3PL be.full.PTCP be traditional.bag LOC billygoat GEN
        'They were full in the billygoat's bag of tricks.' [sos150626t4:28]

    b. ń́ tɛ̋ bò̰-kɔ̃̀ ä̀ síɔ   ì̀ wò̰ lɛ̏ kʊ́ dəgɔ̀ɛɛ
       1SG dear billygoat 3SG be.able.REAL.PFV 3PL EMPH DAT D.DEF place
       bɛ́ nɛ̏ íaa
       DEM LOC TOP
       'Mr. Billygoat showed them up in that place, didn't he.' [sos150626t4:69]

    c. ä̀ pó-pó sĭ bâ̰ɑ̰   nɛ̏
       3SG RED-all be balafon LOC
       'It's all on the balafon.' [sos170711t1:227]

    d. ké lɔ̋ ké ì̀ kà̀ä   ä̀ gɔ̀ɔ nɛ̏
       COP here COP 3PL go.REAL.PRF DEF field LOC
       'It's here, they've gone to the field.' [sos170714t1:4]

While some of these clearly exemplify the notion of 'inside' ((10a) or (10b)), examples (10c) and (10d) show the more general locative nature of *né*, though still referring to a concrete location.

The postposition *né* can also be used figuratively, for things like languages or memories, as illustrated in (11):

(11)   a.   mɔ̈   ä̀   jú   sɛ́ɛ-kû   nɛ̈   kɛ̈
           person 3SG say.IRR Sambla-thing LOC EMPH
           'They say it in Seenku too!' [sos161009t1:113]

       b.   Vraiment, ń   nəgí sɪ̈ ä̀ nɛ̈
           really.FR 1SG mind be 3SG LOC
           'Really, I remember it...' [sos161009t1:22]

In (11a), the locative *né* encodes that something is **in** a language (here, Seenku); in (11b), the use is still figurative, stating that something is **in** the speaker's mind (i.e. she remembers it).

10.1.6 *ká* 'in hand'

We find a postposition *ká* that is best defined as 'holding', having something in one's hands. Most commonly this postposition follows the goal or benefactor in 'give' constructions, which suggests a benefactive reading. However, when used in other situations, it implies being in the hands of the complement of the postposition.

The following examples show the use of *ká* in 'give' constructions, which may translate literally to something like 'put something in someone's hands':

(12)   a.   ä̀ bî bä̀   mó   kä̀
           3SG goat put.REAL.PFV 1SG.EMPH in.hand
           'He gave me a goat.' [sos150703e]

       b.   ä̀ pîɔn bä̀   bö̀-kɔ̌ɔ ká
           3SG flute put.REAL.PFV billygoat in.hand
           'He gave the flute to the billygoat.' [sos150626t4:44]

       c.   ì wɛ̈ à bɛ̌ɛ   ɲì ä̀ wɔ̀ kä̀
           3PL SUBORD 3SG put.IRR.NE there 3SG EMPH in.hand
           'They gave her to him.' [sos171009t2:15]

The postposition has an underlying H tone that undergoes argument-head tone sandhi with its complement, resulting in X- and S-toned allomorphs.

The reason not to treat *ká* as a benefactive can be seen in the following non-'give' examples, all of which display a meaning of proximity or holding in the hands of the complement. First, the following examples were elicited to better understand the semantics of the postposition:

(13) a. ằ   nǎ   səmâ   mó   kằ
3SG PROSP dance 1SG.EMPH in.hand
'He will dance in my hands (e.g. holding a baby).' [sos150703e]

b. ằ   nǎ   bîˆ   sə̀   mó   kằ
3SG PROSP goat buy.IRR 1SG.EMPH in.hand
'He will buy the goat that I have with me.' [sos150703e]

c. kûɛ   lɛ́ˉ   í   nɛ̀-kúɔ   mó   kằ
calabash PST LOG TRANS-break.REAL.PFV 1SG.EMPH in.hand
'The calabash was broken by me.' [sos150707e]

The sentence in (13a) implies that the dancing is happening in the speaker's hands, making it appropriate for something like a baby dancing in its mothers hands while she holds it up. Example (13b) makes it clear that *ká* is not a benefactive: it does not mean 'he will buy the goat for me', but rather that the goat that he will buy is the one held by the speaker. Finally, in a reflexive construction like (13c), the agent who broke the calabash can be added by using *ká*, indicating that the breaking was done with the speaker's hands.

Textual examples show the same:

(14) a. ì̀   wɛ̀˜   í   bɛ́ˉ   ɛ́ˉ!   ì̀   ằ   mɔ̰̀   lê   ì̀   ằ
3PL SUBORD LOG do.IRR INTERJ COMP DEF person PRES COMP 3SG
sïɛ   dɔ̀n   tsɛ́ˉ   fɛ́ǹ   mè   í   kằ
return.REAL.PRF today INDF thing with LOG in.hand
'They said, eh! that person has returned with something.' [sos170711t1:33]

b. kɛ́   nïgì̀   tsïi   sï̌   mó   kằ   lɛ́ˉ
COP cow six be 1SG.EMPH in.hand EMPH
'It's six cows for me!' [sos161009t1:76]

10.1.7 *wɛ̀˜* 'with'

The postposition *wɛ̀˜* covers both instrumental and comitative uses, like English 'with' or French *avec*, though it extends beyond that as well. For instance, it is used as a comparative in Seenku, whereas English uses 'than' in this context. Each subsection below will address one of these uses.

10.1.7.1 Instrumental

The standard way of expressing an instrument in Seenku is to mark it with the postposition *wɛ̀˜*. Elicited examples include:

(15) a. mó   nǎ   kân   dzʊ̌-kpa̰   tsù   wὲ
1SG.EMPH PROSP granary mouth-close.IRR thatch with
'I will cover the granary with thatch.' [sos150622e]

b. ä̀   fəgâ̰   bä̀   í   yɛ̌rɛ̈ kä̀   dɔ̀ɔ   wὲ
3SG strength put.REAL.PFV LOG self in.hand beer with
'He gave himself courage with beer.' [sos150630e]

Example (15b) also illustrates the 'give' usage of the postposition ká; see §10.1.6 above. Instrumental uses are further illustrated by textual examples:

(16) a. kűɛ kɔ́-kɔ́   főn   à   wò   wὲ,   kűɛ sḭ̌   kɔ̂ɔn
3PL RED-short more 3SG EMPH with 3PL be eggplant
bűɔ   nɛ̋   dőrőn mɛ̋
take.out.REAL.NOM LOC pole with
'They were shorter than him, they were picking eggplants with a long pole.' [sos161009t1:155]

b. á   wó   ä̀   jú   kű   tő   á   cè   wὲ
2SG EMPH 3SG say.IRR D.DEF like 2SG hand.PL with
'You say it like that with your hands.' [sos170711t1:251]

c. ì   tê   kɔ̰̌nä̀   kúrúú lê   kűʊ   nǎa-nä̀   sɔ́,
3PL GEN eldest all   PRES D.DEF.SBJV RED-come.REAL.PRF arrive.IRR
kű   fà̰   í   bòn   mὲ
D.DEF pass.REAL.PFV LOG back with
'When the oldest among them arrived, he entered backwards (lit. with his back).' [161009t1:4]

The first example, (16a), contains a clear instrumental usage of wὲ. In fact, it contains two instances of the postposition—the first a comparative (see §10.1.7.2) and the second the instrumental usage, where once again the /w/ is nasalized to [m] by the latent nasal coda of dőrőn 'long pole for harvesting'. The example in (16b) likewise has a clear instrumental reading, where the speaker is talking about the balafon surrogate language (§22.2.1) and is referring to hands being the means or instrument of speaking on the instrument. In (16c), the instrumental meaning is less clear cut; the postposition might be better translated as 'by' rather than 'with', but it still indicates the means by which the action of entering takes place, and thus I group it with the instrumental.

10.1.7.2 Comitative

Another common usage of wὲ is the comitative, doing something **with** or **accompanied by** something or someone else. Canonical examples from elicitation include the following:

(17) a. à̀ nằ mó wɛ́̋
3SG come.REAL.PFV 1SG.EMPH with
'He came with me/he brought me.' [sos150619e]

b. mó nǎ səmâ à wè ŋɛ́
1SG.EMPH PROSP dance.IRR 3SG with NEG
'I will not dance with him.' [sos150703e]

c. móő kằ bǐ wɛ́̋
1SG.EMPH.PST go.REAL.PFV goat.PL with
'I took goats (lit. went with goats).' [sos150618e]

While the postposition *wɛ̀* is commonly used in examples like (17a), the genitive *tê* can also be used, presumably to distinguish 'come with' from 'bring', which is periphrastically expressed as the former; see §10.1.8.3 below.

The comitative usage is particularly common in texts. For example:

(18) a. mɛ̏ kɛ́̋ sú à bá̰à̰ wè à jəmɨ̰̏
3SG.SUBORD go.IRR get.up.IRR DEF balafon with DEF bush
mɛ̏ nɛ̏ à wè
3SG.SUBORD come.IRR 3SG with
'He came back from the bush with the balafon.' [sos170711t1:32]

b. ì̀ wɛ̏, í kʊ́ bɔ̌, mɔ̰̂-mâa bɔ̌ kərù
3PL SUBORD LOG D.DEF take.out.IRR association take.out.IRR hyena
wè
with
'They would, they would make this association, make the association with the hyena.' [sos150626t2:3]

c. í wó səgɔ̌ kʊ́ wɛ́̋
2PL EMPH wrestle.IRR D.DEF with
'You would wrestle with him.' [sos170714t3:68]

d. ì̀ á kɛ́̋ ằ wɛ̏, ì̀ ắá kằ nɛ́̋ sɔ́
COMP 2SG go.IRR 3SG with COMP 3SG.SBJV go.REAL.PFV if arrive.IRR
ì̀ á fà̰ à wè cîe
COMP 2SG enter.IRR 3SG with house.LOC
'[They said] you should go home with that, and when you get home, go inside with it.' [130828t2:72]

In at least one context, however, a different construction based on coordination can also be used. Consultants report no difference in meaning between (19a) and (19b):

(19) a. mó   sḭ̀ lű-ŋǎa   tsɛ́-ké jʊ̃ŋmǎ kǎ
       1SG.EMPH be courtyard-inside and   cat   white
       'I am in the courtyard with a white cat.' [sos130821e]

   b. mó   sḭ̀ lű-ŋǎa   jʊ̃ŋmǎ kǎ   wɛ̋
      1SG.EMPH be courtyard-inside cat   white with
      (=(19a)) [sos 170705e]

As this is the only attested example of this construction, it is difficult to determine how productive it is or whether there are any subtle differences between the two.

10.1.7.3 Comparative

In comparative constructions, the standard of comparison (the noun to which the subject is being compared, also known as the comparandum) is also marked with the postposition wɛ̀. These constructions will be discussed in-depth in Chapter 15, but I provide a small selection of examples here to illustrate the usage of the postposition:

(20) a. ń tɛ̋ sân kú-tío   főn   ń tɛ̋ kərù wè âa
       1SG dear rabbit thing-know better 1SG dear hyena with NEG.Q
       'Mr. Rabbit was cleverer than Mr. Hyena, wasn't he.' [sos150626t2:22]

   b. ń təgǒ gɔ̀ɔ   bɔ́ɔ főn ń tàgï̈   ń tsìɛ̰̀ mè
      1SG sit.PTCP ground.ADV tall more 1SG stand.PTCP 1SG foot.PL with
      wè
      with
      'If I am sitting on the ground, I am taller than when I stand on my feet.' [sos161009t1:59]

(20b) displays two instances of wɛ̀, with the postpositional phrases nested in such a way as to put both postpositions next to each other: The comparative postposition follows a clause, which itself ends in a PP headed by wɛ̀.

10.1.7.4 Other uses of wɛ̀

Finally, the postposition wɛ̀ is found in a variety of environments adjacent to these other meanings but not neatly contained within them. For instance, it is found in contexts of putting something on or taking something off:

(21) a. mó   nǎ   mɔ̰̋-têɛ   dzḭ̀   mó   wɛ̋
       1SG.EMPH PROSP imported.clothes put.IRR 1SG.EMPH with
       'I will put on imported clothes.' [sos150702e]

b. *mó   sị̌ bî tsụ̀ bűɔ   nɛ́ à wè*
   1SG.EMPH be goat skin take.off.REAL.LOC in 3SG with
   'I am skinning the goat.' [sos150805e]

This can be imagined as an extension of the earlier uses if we think of the skin or the clothing as being with the person or animal on which they are found.

Similarly, it can be used to mark a theme of the verb 'fill':

(22) *mó   dằn   fəgă   sị̌ nɔ́nɛ́sắn mɛ̋*
      1SG.EMPH mouth fill.PTCP be food   with
      'My mouth is filled with food.' [sos150620e]

Here, the nasal coda of *nɔ́nɛ́sắn* nasalizes the initial /w/ to [m].

Other more divergent uses include:

(23) a. *ằ   nă   dɛ̀ɛ   cɔ̀   wè*
         3SG PROSP accustom.IRR village with
         'He will get used to the village.' [sos150629e]

      b. *sû   gɔ̋ɔ   à wè gừɔ-dəgɛ̀ɛ*
         get.up.NOM be.difficult 3SG with morning.LOC
         'It is difficult for him to get up in the morning.' [sos150317e]

      c. *bɛ̀ɛ səŋă   nɛ́-bɔ̋   sị̌ gɔ́ɔ̀ wè*
         pig lie.down.PTCP TRANS-go.far.PTCP be wood with
         'The pig is lying down far from the tree.' [sos150623e]

All of these examples appear to use the postposition *wɛ̀* to express a relation between its complement and the predicate that is neither locative nor benefactive. It is, in this sense, the general relational postposition, while *nɛ́* (§10.1.5) is the general locative postposition.

However, when combined with the directional morpheme *nằ*, *wɛ̀* can take on a locative meaning:

(24) *mó   tɛ̋ gɔ̋ɔ sị̌ Wằgàdűgű   wɛ́-nằ*
      1SG.EMPH GEN field be Ouagadougou with-towards
      'My field is towards Ouagadougou.' [sos170705e]

This example indicates that the field in question is in the direction of or on the way to Ouagadougou. For other examples of *nằ* with other postpositions and adverbs, see especially (31a) and §10.2.1.2,.

10.1.8 *tɛ́* genitive

The postposition *tɛ́* is most commonly used as a genitive particle in alienable possessive constructions (§8.6.2), but it is also found in other contexts, including ones with more of comitative or locative reading. I will first discuss the canonical genitive uses before turning to other uses.

Note that *tɛ́* undergoes the same argument-head tone sandhi processes as other postpositions, except that where other postpositions would surface as H (after X-toned pronouns), *tɛ́* surfaces as HX [tê].

10.1.8.1 Genitive

In alienable possessive constructions, the possessor is often followed by the postposition *tɛ́*, which is in turn followed by the possessed noun. In (25a-b), I present simple examples from elicitation, with a longer phrase from a narrative in (25c):

(25) a. ằ   tê   bő̋o
         3SG GEN mat
         'his mat'

     b. sân tɛ̏ cî
         rabbit GEN house
         'rabbit's house'

     c. ɛ́ɛ! ì   fên   fǎ̰   kərȕ   tɛ̏ cîe
         INTERJ COMP thing pass.PTCP hyena GEN house.LOC
         'Eh! Something entered hyena's house.' [sos150626t4:16]

The postposition is also used in possessive predicates, which translate literally to something like 'Possessed exists for the possessor'. For example:

(26) a. jəbɛ̋   ɲá   mó   tɛ̏   ɲɛ́
         clothes be.NEG 1SG.EMPH GEN NEG
         'I don't have clothes.' [sos150702e]

     b. cî   səgɛ̏e sḭ̀ ń   tê
         house new be 1SG GEN
         'I have a new house.' [sos150617e]

In narratives, we find examples like the following:

(27) a. mənı̋-dərő̋n   kő̋nǎ ɲá   ì   tê   ɲɛ́
         woman-child elder be.NEG 3PL GEN NEG
         'They don't have an elder daughter.' [sos170714t3:113]

b. *jén-jẽn   sĩ mó   tẽ   mɔ̃mɑ̃ mɛ̀   fɑ̌*
   RED-story be 1SG.EMPH GEN a.lot 3SG.SUBORD pass
   'I [used to] have so many stories.' [sos150626t2:27]

This construction is quite similar to the expression of volition, described in 10.1.8.4 below. For more on possessive predicates, see §14.4.

We find similar expressions of possession, such as:

(28) a. *kǘʋ   nəgì̀ tsɛ̌   mó   tẽ*
       D.DEF.COP cow how 1SG.EMPH GEN
       'How many cows it that for me?' [sos161009t1:24]

   b. *ɛ́!   ì̀   ké à   cí   ké á   wó tẽ âa*
      INTERJ COMP COP DEF house COP 2SG EMPH GEN NEG.Q
      'Eh! That's your house, isn't it?' [sos150626t4:22]

   c. *ì̀ fəgǎ   sĩ plɛ̌ngṳ̀   nɛ̀ bò̌-kǒo   tɛ́*
      3PL be.full.PTCP be traditional.bag LOC billygoat GEN
      'They were full in the billygoat's bag of tricks.' [sos150626t4:28]

The example in (28a) is clearly possessive, asking about the number of figurative cows for the speaker (counting how many riddles she has won); the same can be said for (28b). In (28c), a clearly genitive usage would have put the PP *bò̌-kɔ̌ɔ tɛ́* 'billygoat's' before the bag; this order is reported to be possible by consultants, but the attested order gives *tɛ́* more of a locative flavor ('in the bag the billygoat had on him'). If *ká* were used instead, then the bag would be held in the billygoat's hand, whereas the current reading suggests that the bag is slung over his shoulder. Other clear locative uses of *tɛ́* will be discussed in the next subsection.

As will be described below in §10.1.9, the postposition *lɛ́* is also used in genitive constructions. For more on possession, see §8.6.

10.1.8.2 Locative

Locative uses of *tɛ́* can sometimes be understood under the umbrella of genitive constructions, as referring to someone's house (cf. French *chez*). For instance:

(29) a. *ì̀ dɛ̀n sĩ í   kőo   wɛ́ ä̀ kərṳ̀   tê*
       COMP bean be LOG grow.IRR with DEF hyena GEN
       'There was this bean that grew at the hyena's place.' [sos150626t2:6]

b. *féé-ŋé,   mè̀   sú   mè̀   kɛ̋ ń   tɛ̋ sân*
   thing-NEG 3SG.SUBORD get.up.IRR 3SG.SUBORD go.IRR 1SG dear rabbit
   tè̀.
   GEN
   'Um, he got up and went to Mr. Rabbit's.' [sos130828t2:58]

Here we can imagine a possessive flavor to *tɛ̋*, implying the house or courtyard of the possessor.

Other locative expressions are less convincingly genitive in nature. It may be that certain verbs select PPs with *tɛ̋* rather than other postpositions. The following textual examples show a range of other locative uses:

(30) a. *mɔ̀̌ɔ́   fà̀   à̀   jén-jén   sí̋   tɛ̋*
       person.SBJV enter.IRR DEF RED-story female.PL GEN
       'Let's get into folktales.' [sos150626t2:1]

   b. *à̀   wè̀   í   tə̀bè̀   wétə̀nĕ lɔ̋   à̀   kə̀rù̀ kűɛ*
      3SG SUBORD LOG huddle.against.IRR now   here DEF hyena other.PL
      tɛ̋   dân tè̀
      GEN wall GEN
      'He huddled next to the wall of hyena's family's house.' [sos150626t4:4]

   c. *sì-bɔ́rɔ́ wáatí̋ nɛ̋ kʊ́ fə̀gà̀   nà̀   kʊ́   wɛ̋ bə̀̂ə*
      Sy-Boro time   LOC D.DEF power come.REAL.PFV D.DEF with balafon
      tè̀
      GEN
      'At the time of Sy-Boro, power brought it to the balafon.' [sos170711t1:329-331]

In (30a), *tɛ̋* marks the figurative location into which the narrator suggests entering: folktales. This is typically not the postposition used for 'enter'; instead, the locative *né* is often used (see above §10.1.5), or most commonly, 'enter' is used with the adverbial *cîe* 'in the house'. In this context, though, consultants only accept *tɛ̋*. In (30b), there are two instances of *tɛ̋*. The first is canonically genitive ('hyena's family's wall'), whereas the second one marks this wall as the location against which the billygoat is huddling. Here, it is reported that *wè̀* can also be used without any difference in meaning. Finally, in (30c), it is not clear whether *tɛ̋* is functioning more like a locative or more like a comitative, that is, whether power was brought to the balafon or with the balafon.

The postposition *tɛ̋* is one of the elements with which the directional morpheme *nà̀* can be compounded. This morpheme encodes the meaning of 'towards'. The examples in (31) contrast a sentence with and without *nà̀*:

(31) a. mó   sɪ̌ kằ   nɛ̏ cɔ̀ tè-nà
        1SG.EMPH be go.REAL.NOM LOC village GEN-towards
        'I am going towards the village.' [sos170705e]

   b. mó   sɪ̌ kằ   nɛ̏ cɔ̀ tề
        1SG.EMPH be go.REAL.NOM LOC village GEN
        'I am going to the village.' [sos170705e]

As these examples show, *nà* participates in argument-head tone sandhi, and when it is added to the X-toned PP *cɔ̀ tề*, it causes the whole phrase to raise to L; see §4.4.2 for more examples of X to L raising.

10.1.8.3 Comitative *tê*

While most comitative expressions employ *wɛ̀*, we find some examples where *tê* is used instead. The most consistent usage of comitative *tê* is found in the reciprocal expression *í sí tề* (variant *í sí tê*), meaning 'together', where *í sí* is the general reciprocal pronoun (see §6.7.4). Examples, both elicited and natural, include:

(32) a. mǐi   nằ   í sí tê
        1PL.PST come.REAL.PFV LOG RECP GEN
        'We came together.' [sos150619e]

   b. ằwǎ mɔ̰̌ɔ̰́   səmâ   í sí tê
        HORT person.SBJV dance.IRR LOG RECP GEN
        'Let's dance together.' [sos150317e]

   c. mó   tsɛ̋-kɛ́ Fàatű sɪ̰̌ í sí tề
        1SG.EMPH and   Fatou be LOG RECP GEN
        'Me and Fatou are together.' [161009t1:63]

It may be this same construction extended to pronouns other than the reciprocal in sentences like the following:

(33) a. móő   nằ   ằ   tê
        1SG.EMPH.PST come.REAL.PFV 3SG GEN
        'I came with him/I came to his place.' [sos150619e]

   b. mó   sɔ́ɔ̀   móo   tsiɛ   í wó tề
        1SG.EMPH be.able.IRR.HAB 1SG.EMPH.SBJV speak.IRR 2PL EMPH GEN
        bá̰a̰-kű   kɔ̋n
        balafon-thing on
        'I can speak to you about the balafon.' [sos171009t1:23]

The curious thing about (33a) is that it was produced immediately after sentences like (17a), using the comitative postposition wè. As discussed above, it appears that wè is sometimes avoided with the verb 'come', since it gives the meaning of 'bring', but the first interpretation of tế (if read back to another consultant) is the *chez* 'home of' interpretation. In (33b), the genitive tế is used to mean 'speak with' or 'speak to'; with the verb 'say', the dative lế is often used instead (§10.1.9).

An 'accompaniment'-like usage of tế is found in texts when referring to eating different foods together. For example:

(34) a. mó   ná à nɔ́ bűrű tế ŋɛ́
        1SG.EMPH PROSP 3SG eat.IRR bread GEN NEG
        'I'm not going to eat it with bread.' [161009t1:223]

     b. à̰ wò sɔ́-nɛ́-jɔ̌   gű kɛ́ à ná à nɔ́
        3SG EMPH rain-grain-water under COP 3SG PROSP 3SG eat.IRR
        bɔ̀-kɔ́ɔ   kə̀ká tḛ̀
        billygoat meat GEN
        'In the rain, he was going to eat [it] along with the meat of the billygoat.'
        [sos150626t4:34]

The first example makes reference to an omelette that has just been made, which the speaker said she would not eat with bread, whereas the second, from a folk tale, refers to birds the clever billygoat had released from his bag as a distraction to the hyena, who wished to eat him. In (34a), tế could plausibly be a locative, with omelettes often being placed in or on bread, whereas in the second, such an explanation is less readily available.

10.1.8.4 Desire

The postposition tế is exceptionlessly found in the volitional construction. At first glance, it closely resembles possession, but the distribution of arguments in the construction is not the same. Both have the same general form N1 be N2 tế, but in possession, N2 is the possessor (and the subject of the sentence in English) whereas in wanting, N1 is the experiencer and subject of the sentence in English. Compare the following:

(35) a. à̰ sɪ̰ mó   tḛ̀
        3SG be 1SG.EMPH GEN
        'I have it.'

     b. mó   sɪ̰ à̰ tê
        1SG.EMPH be 3SG GEN
        'I want it.'

Of course, given the right context, (35a) could also mean 'he wants me' (and less likely (35b) could mean 'he has me').

If the desired thing is a noun, then it is the complement of the genitive postposition:

(36) a. ń sɪ̆ bǎ pètétè
1SG be table flat GEN
'I want a flat table.' [sos160825e]

b. Mm-mm, mó ɲá bűrű tê ŋé
EXCL 1SG.EMPH be.NEG bread GEN NEG
'Uh-uh, I don't want bread.' [sos161009t1:225]

If the desired thing is an action, then the complement of the genitive postposition is a dummy 3sg pronoun ǎ, followed by the subordinated clause:

(37) a. ǎ sɪ̆ ǎ tê ǎá ǎ ŋmǎ
3SG be 3SG GEN 3SG.SBJV 3SG eat.IRR
'He wanted to eat him.' [sos161009t1:211]

b. Fàatű á wó sɪ̆ ǎ tê áa fǎ mó wɛ́↘
Fatou 2SG EMPH be 3SG GEN 2SG.SBJV fight 1SG.EMPH with.Q
'Fatou, you want to fight me, don't you?' [sos161009t1:96]

For more on volitional predicates, see §14.5.

10.1.8.5 Other uses of *tĕ*

Other scattered examples are attested that don't fall into any of the categories laid out above. These are given below.

(38) a. kʊ́ kʊ́ tɛ̀ wé mɛ́ɛ́ lɛ̀ təgʊ̀ mɔ̰̀ kǎa,
D.DEF D.DEF GEN FOC REL.PRO.PL SUBORD sit.IRR person across
məré lɛ̀ ǎ dɛ̀ɲǐ bɽɛ̆ mɔ̰̀ kǎa tsɛ́-né ǎ
REL.PRO SUBORD DEF drum play.IRR person across and DEF
dənʊ̰̀-bɽɛ̆
talk.drum-play.NOM
'That's why we have those sitting next to us, those that play the drum and the talking drum players.' [sos170711t1:240]

b. ǎ gùrè kǎa ɲá bʊ̀-kɔ́ɔ gűrɛ̆ tɛ̆ ŋé
3SG voice resemble.PTCP be.NEG billygoat voice GEN NEG
'His voice didn't resemble the voice of a billygoat.' [sos161009t1:205]

c. móő   bậa   brɛ̋   gúɔ   ń   ní   tɛ̏
   1SG.EMPH.PST balafon play.REAL.NOM learn.REAL.PFV 1SG father GEN
   'I learned how to play the balafon from my father.' [sos150703e]

In (38a), the genitive postposition is used in a purposive construction (also found in the wh-word 'why', see §16.2.6); in (38b), it marks the PP complement of 'resemble'. (38c) may be a figurative case of the locative/genitive *chez* construction, learning the balafon 'at the place of' or 'with' my father.

10.1.9 *lɛ̋* dative

The postposition *lɛ̋* most closely resembles a dative or lative postposition, with the major exception that it is not used in 'give' constructions (where the specific postposition *ká* is used instead; §10.1.6). In addition to meanings of action towards something or someone (quintessentially dative or lative), it is also found in possessive constructions and other locative constructions.

Phonologically, it appears to sometimes undergo clitic elision, though the resulting form does not appear to be determinable based on phonology alone. For instance, when used in the dative, a contracted form of the 1sg *môe* is found, with a diphthong; in the possessive, however, the pronoun *môo* is found instead. It may be that these possessive pronouns are not derived from *lɛ̋*, instead derived from genitive *tɛ̋*, but more likely these pronouns were diachronically derived from productive rules of elision but now exist as independent forms in a pronominal paradigm. I will set aside these forms here and refer the reader to §8.6.2.2 on dative possession and §§6.5-6.6 on possessive and oblique pronouns, respectively. For discussion of clitic elision, see §4.4.3.

The following subsections will address each usage of *lɛ̋* in turn.

10.1.9.1 Dative/lative

I describe *lɛ̋* as both dative and lative, since it can mark both recipients and benefactives (dative) as well as physical locations and movement towards them (lative). For consistency, however, I will gloss the postposition as DAT for 'dative'.

This dative usage is especially common with verbs like 'say', 'show', 'introduce' or other ditransitives. For example:

(39) a. mó   sɪ̰̌ ń sḭ̀ɔ   nɛ̋ á wó lɛ̏
         1SG.EMPH be 1SG introduce.REAL.NOM LOC 2SG EMPH DAT
         'I am introducing myself to you.' [sos150805e]

b. á tě̋ mó lɛ̀
   2SG show.IRR 1SG.EMPH DAT
   'Show yourself to me!' [sos150617e]

c. ằ jú ằ lɛ́
   3SG say.IRR 3SG DAT
   'Say something to him!' [sos150617e]

In each of these examples, the listener or experiencer is marked with *lɛ̋*.
Examples in texts include:

(40) a. ń nǎ wɛ́ màa tsɛ̋ jén-jěn jǔ í lɛ̀
       1SG PROSP FOC again INDF RED-story say.IRR 2PL DAT
       'I am going to tell you another riddle.' [sos161009t1:1]

b. ǎa dəgɔ̀ màa ằ lɛ́
   3SG.PST greet.REAL.PFV again 3SG DAT
   'He greeted him again...' [sos161009t1:208]

c. ké mó sɪ̌ dəgɔ̀ nɛ̀ í kərúı̋ lɛ̋
   COP 1SG.EMPH be great.REAL.NOM LOC 2PL all.PL DAT
   'I greet you all.' [sos171009t1:4]

The dative is also the most common marker of benefactives in Seenku, as shown by the following examples:

(41) a. kʋ́ lɛ̀ jɔ́ɔ-jɔ́ɔ wɛ́ kʋ́ bı̰̂ɛ à
       D.DEF SUBORD RED-stroll.REAL.PFV FOC D.DEF play.REAL.PFV DEF
       mɔ̰̀ɛ lɛ̀
       person.PL DAT
       'When he would go around playing for the people...' [sos171009t1:36]

b. mɛ̀ ı̀ tərɛ̀ ı̀ mɔ̰̀ sɔ́ɔ̀ mɔ̰̀ɔ́
   3SG.SUBORD 3PL ask.IRR COMP person be.able.IRR.HAB person.SBJV
   kúnî í wêe
   help.IRR 2PL EMPH.DAT
   'And he asked, "Could we be of help to you?"' [sos130828t2:3]

c. ńjʋ́wɛ́ ní cé-tǎa nɛ̋-bǎ̰a̰ ı̀ lɛ́
   Njʋwɛ L-LOG hand-palm TRANS-beat.IRR.HAB 3PL DAT
   'Njʋwɛ claps her hands for them.' [sos170714t1:49]

Not every verb appears able to take a benefactive argument, however. For instance, attempts to use *lɛ̋* as a benefactive with 'dance' were not successful, being interpreted instead as the presentative lé, at times homophonous depending upon the results of argument-head tone sandhi.

Lative uses of lě encode physical movement towards the complement. For instance:

(42) a. ké à nìgì nŏo ɲǜ í wó lɛ̋
COP DEF COW.PL come.NEG there 2PL EMPH DAT
'There are the cows coming towards you!' [sos161009t1:46]

b. ằ lö̀ lě gbəgɛ̀ ằ lé mɛ̀ ằ fərḭ́ bɛ̋ céi!
3SG come if approach 3SG DAT 3SG.SUBORD DEF broom put.IRR IDEO
'When she got close to him [the child], he dropped the broom, kei!' [sos150626t5:156]

In other instances with the verb gbəgɛ̀ in (42b), we see the use of the postposition kəré (§10.1.3) rather than the dative.

10.1.9.2 Locative uses

Other locative uses of lě are attested that don't seem to encode lative movement. This movement can be either physical (spatial) or metaphorical, as the following examples indicate:

(43) a. ằ wɔ̀ təgŏ-təgɔ̀ kʋ́ tɔ́ ằ tâ lɛ̋, ằ bö̀-kɔ́ɔ
3SG EMPH RED-sit.REAL.PFV D.DEF like 3SG fire DAT DEF billygoat
tá-fḭ̀ɛ âa
fire-heat.REAL.PFV NEG.Q
'When he had sat down like that, next to the fire, the billygoat warmed up.' [sos150626t4:29]

b. mó yɛ̀rɛ̀ nəgì lě büɔ ằ kú lɛ̋ ằ lé
1SG.EMPH self.JU mind PST go.out.REAL.PRF DEF thing DAT 3SG DAT
'I myself had forgotten that thing!' [sos161009t1:107]

c. í dòn-mənì-dənòn sɔ́ wɛ̀ ằá təgɔ̀ ằ
LOG child-woman-child be.able.IRR HAB 3SG.SBJV sit.IRR DEF
bá̰a-brɛ̰̂ lɛ̋ ằ lé ŋɛ́
balafon-play.NOM DAT 3SG DAT NEG
'[They said that] their daughter could not get married to that balafon player.' [sos171009t1:42]

In (43a), the meaning of lě is something like 'next to' or 'near' rather than 'towards'. Example (43b) is figurative, an expression for 'forget' that translates literally to something like '(one's) mind go out (from something)'. In that sense, lě encodes more of a direction away from whatever has been forgotten, rather than towards. Finally, in (43c), we see the expression for '(woman) marry (a man)', which involves the verb 'sit' followed by a PP with *lé̤*. In both (43b-c), when the dative is used after a noun, the postpositional phrase is repeated, this time with a pronoun. It is not clear whether this resumptive pronoun is obligatory or not.

10.1.9.3 Possessive uses

What appears to be a lengthened version of the dative, *lɛ́ɛ* can also be used for alienable possession in place of the genitive postposition. Consultants report no difference in meaning between the two constructions, though I would not be surprised to find one with systematic corpus investigation.

Unlike possessive constructions with the genitive postposition *tě*, where there is no tonal interaction between the possessor and the possessed noun, the postposition *lɛ́ɛ* triggers argument-head tone sandhi with the possessed noun. For instance, we can contrast the dative and the genitive in the following supposedly synonymous expressions:

(44) a. mó   lɛ̀ɛ   jəgè
       1SG.EMPH DAT dog
       'my dog' [sos170705e]

   b. mó   tȅ   jəgȅ
       1SG.EMPH GEN dog
       '=(44a)' [sos150810e]

Typically, however, it undergoes clitic elision (§4.4.3), particularly with pronouns. This creates a series of possessive pronouns, though it is not clear whether these possessive pronouns are the result of the dative or the genitive eliding. Since the dative and the genitive are both S-toned postpositions, the sandhi alternations they trigger are the same. But then again, when the dative elides in its use as a dative, it typically leaves a front vowel element (e.g. *mó lȅ* = *môe*), whereas possessive pronouns lack these front vowels (e.g. *môo* 'my'). For more discussion of possessive pronouns, see §6.5.

The dative postposition can be found in the possessive-like predicate used for hunger, though here, the locative postposition §10.1.5 can also be used. For example:

(45) kərȕ dzi̋a-dzía   sőń   nȅ, dző   sǐ ȁ lé, ȁ kő
     hyena RED-tired.REAL.PRF moment.REL LOC hunger be 3SG DAT 3SG D.DEF
     ɲá   fűi   jïo   nȅ ŋé
     be.NEG nothing see.REAL.NOM LOC NEG
     'When hyena got tired out, he was hungry, he wasn't finding anything [to eat].'
     [sos161009t1:186]

For examples with locative *né*, see §10.1.5.

10.1.10 Relational nouns as postpositions

We find a small subset of relational nouns (body parts and others) that can be used like postpositions. The attested nouns in the data corpus are *jẽ́n* 'front', *jǚnį̌* 'eyes', and *tənį̌* 'behind'. These forms are distinguished from postpositions in that they can be used in compound nouns (in the case of 'front' and 'back') or to refer to physical body parts (in the case of 'eyes'); this is not the case for true postpositions.

10.1.10.1 *jẽ̀n* 'front'
The relational noun *jẽ̀n* 'front' can be used nominally in expressions like the following:

(46) a. ằ jén-ts̬ɩ̌ɛ
    3SG front-leg.PL
    'its front legs' [sos150623e]

  b. í jẽ́n-kpɛ́ɛ kɔ̃́n
    LOG front-paw.LOG on
    'on its (own) front paws' [sos150804e]

  c. ń jẽ́n-ŋɛ̋ wɛ́ òo
    1SG front-HUM.PL FOC EXCL
    'How about the people in front of me? (greeting)' [sos150624e]

  d. ì fạ̀n mɛ̀ cí-dɔ̀ɔ wè í jẽ́n mɛ̋
    3PL enter.IRR HAB house-inside with LOG front with
    'They entered into the house frontwards.' [sos161009t1:20]

In (46a) and (46b), *jẽ̀n* is clearly nominal, not only in the fact that it can form compounds with other nouns but also in the fact that in (46b), the compound is separately marked by the postposition *kɔ̃́n* 'on'. In (46c), the *jẽ̀n* acts as the nominal root, inflected with the irregular human plural suffix *-ŋɛ̋*, to create a noun meaning 'those people in front'. Finally, in (46d), the relational noun refers to the front of the body, and again it is marked with an independent postposition *wɛ̀*.

It can also be used as a postposition, however, in which case it means simply 'in front':

(47) a. bɛ̀ɛ sənǎ sɩ̌ mó jẽ́n
    pig lie.PTCP be 1SG.EMPH front
    'The pig lying in front of me.' [sos150623e]

b. *sənɛ́ sị̌ í   ɲ̀-jǎa   nɛ́ ń jɛ́n*
   fly be LOG RED-buzz.REAL.NOM LOC 1SG front
   'The fly is buzzing around in front of me.' [sos150703e]

c. *ǎ wɔ̀ tənɔ̰̌ jɛ́n ɲì-nà   ǎ wɔ̀ í jío*
   DEF EMPH hearth front there-towards 3SG EMPH LOG say.REAL.PFV
   ì̀ í nǎ kùrù-kùrù   í blǎ bɔ̀-kɔ̃ɔ kɔ́n
   COMP LOG PROSP RED-crouch.IDEO LOG fall billygoat on
   'There in front of that hearth, he set his sights on him, squatted down wide to block his passage, and set about pouncing on the billygoat.' [sos150626t4:52]

In these examples, the post-verbal adjunct requires no further postpositional marking, suggesting that the relational noun is being used postpositionally.

10.1.10.2 *jűnị̌* 'eyes/front'

The inalienable noun *jűnị̌* literally means 'eyes', as shown in examples like the following:

(48) a. *mó   sị̌ ń jűnị̌ nɛ́-tì-tǎ   nɛ́*
      1SG.EMPH be 1SG eye.PL TRANS-RED-rub.REAL.NOM LOC
      'I am rubbing my eyes.' [sos150622e]

   b. *ǎ jűnị̌ dzŏ-kpá̰*
      3SG eye.PL mouth-close.REAL.PFV
      'He closed his eyes.' [sos150622e]

In both examples, *jűnị̌* refers literally to the eyes.

Examples of it used postpositionally are rare in the text corpus but are attested. The clearest case is shown in (49):

(49) *ǎa   ǎ təmɛ̀   ń jűnị̌ ŋɛ́, ń nəgí ɲá bɔ̀   ǎ*
     3SG.PST 3SG tell.REAL.PFV 1SG eye.PL NEG 1SG mind be.NEG anymore 3SG
     nɛ̀̀ ŋɛ́
     in NEG
     'She didn't tell it in front of me, I don't remember it anymore.' [sos150626t6:26]

Here, all that is needed to indicate 'in front of' the speaker is the relational noun *jűnị̌*.

10.1.10.3 *tənị̌* 'behind'

The relational noun *tənị̌* corresponds to the noun *jèn*; while the former is for front, this latter is for rear or hind. As a noun, it is found, for example, in the following compound:

(50) ă   təgĭ   sį́ í   tənį̋-kpɛ́ɛ   kɔ̋n
      3SG stand.PTCP be LOG hind-paw.PL on
      'It is standing on his hind legs.' [sos150804e]

This same relational noun can also be used postpositionally to indicate 'behind', but only if the complement is in motion. Examples from elicitation and texts illustrate this condition:

(51) a. bíe-nô   sį̀ ɲǜ   nɛ̏ í   ɲǎ   tənį̏
         goat-child be run.REAL.PFV LOC LOG mother behind
         'The baby goat is running behind its mother.' [sos170707e]

    b. mɛ̏   ä̀ gɔ̋ɛɛ   blǎ   ɲì   súu   mɛ̏   í
        3SG.SUBORD DEF wood.PL drop.IRR there directly 3SG.SUBORD LOG
        bɛ̋   ä̀ cəbâa-dərǒn tənį̏
        put.IRR DEF orphan-child behind
        'She dropped the wood straight away and set about chasing after the orphan.' [sos130828t1:29]

In (51a), the sentence implies that the mother goat is moving and the baby goat is following behind. In (51b), the orphan is running away and the sorcerer is following behind him.

If the complement (whether animate or not) is stationary, 'behind' is expressed with the postposition tɛ̋ following the relational noun bő́n 'back':

(52) a. bɛ̏ɛ səŋǎ   sį̀ gɔ̂ɔ   bȍn tɛ̏
         pig lie.PTCP be wood back GEN
         'The pig is lying behind the tree.' [sos150623e]

    b. bíe-nô   sį̀ sâ   nɛ̏ sánɛ̏ bȍn tɛ̏
        goat-child be cry.REAL.NOM LOC well back GEN
        'The baby goat is crying behind the well.' [sos170707e]

In each of these cases, the tree and the well are stationary, but consultants report that the same expression can be used even if a person or animal is stationary. Similarly, 'behind the car' would be expressed as móbílí̋ tənį̋ if the car is in motion but móbílí̋ bő́n tɛ̋ if the car is stationary, showing that it is the state the complement is in rather than the identity of the complement itself that determines which expression is used.

For the use of tənį̂ as an adverb, see §10.2.2.10.

10.2 Adverbials

Adverbial expressions are also found in post-verbal position. They carry no special adverbial marking in Seenku (i.e. no prefixes, suffixes, or postpositions), nor is there a prototypical adverbial tone melody. This section will cover locative, temporal, and manner adverbs; expressive adverbials and ideophones are discussed separately in §9.2.2.

10.2.1 Locative adverbs

10.2.1.1 lɔ́ 'here'
The adverb lɔ́, with the variant nɔ́ (found after nasal vowels and latent nasal codas), is used to indicate 'here'. This adverb is unusual in beginning with a liquid, typically a segment reserved for functional elements, but since adverbs are closer to being functional elements than true open class vocabulary (nouns and verbs), it is less surprising.

Simple elicited examples include:

(53) a. à   bὲ   lɔ́
          3SG put.IRR here
          'Put it here!' [sos150617e]

    b. ăa   bị̀ɛ   dɔ́ɔní lɔ́
          3SG.PST rain.REAL.PFV a.little here
          'It rained a little here.' [sos150702e]

    c. ằ   nǎ   sɔ́   kę́ɛ̨   lɔ́
          3SG PROSP arrive.IRR tomorrow here
          'He will arrive here tomorrow.' [sos150617e]

In terms of linear order when more than one adverb or adjunct follows the verb, 'here' and other locative adverbs typically follow other adverbs (i.e. they are more peripheral). This can be seen with a quantity adverb in (53b) and with a temporal adverb in (53c). This same ordering principle will be seen in naturalistic examples from texts as well.

From texts, we find:

(54) a. kɛ́ ȉ   l-ằ   kŭa   tsị́-kų́   wétanɛ̆ lɔ́
          COP 3PL L-3SG farm.REAL.NOM cut-grab.REAL.PFV now   here
          'They have started farming here now.' [sos170714t1:12]

b. kṹ gǘrḗ sį̀ nɔ́ í blĕ
   D.DEF voice be here LOG big
   'Its voice is big here.' [sos170711t1:94]

c. mó nă à dà̰ wétənĕ lɔ́
   1SG.EMPH PROSP 3SG stop.IRR now here
   'I'll stop here now.' [sos150626t1:25]

d. Mǎadù, vraiment, fɔ̰́ mɔ̰̌ɔ nă wé jén-jẽ́n təmḗ
   Madou really.FR must person.PST PROSP FOC RED-story tell.IRREAL
   dɔ̀n nɔ́, sinon, ăa nă bɛ̀n ŋέ
   today here if.not.FR 3SG.PST PROSP be.good NEG
   'Madou, really, we had to tell riddles here today otherwise it wouldn't be good.' [sos161009t1:12]

In (54a) and (54c), the spatial adverb lɔ́ follows the discourse adverb wétənĕ (§21.3.4). In (54b), it precedes the adjectival predicate. Finally, in (54d), the temporal adverb dɔ̀n precedes 'here', and its latent nasal coda nasalizes the /l/ of lɔ́ to [n].

'Here' can also be used in a compound adverb with the negative marker to mean 'there', or literally, 'not here': lɔ́ɔ-ŋḗ, with the vowel of lɔ́ typically lengthened. We know this must be a compound adverb and not simply a negated phrase based on three pieces of evidence: first, the negative marker is S-toned rather than its regular H tone. Second, it is not clause-final but always adjacent to the adverb. And third, if the predicate is 'be', the affirmative form sį̀ rather than negative form ɲá is used.

Examples of this compound adverb are shown in (55):

(55) a. à̰ sį̀ kú lé bă nḗ lɔ́ɔ-ŋḗ
     3SG be thing which do.REAL.NOM LOC here-NEG
     'What is he doing over there?' [sos170707e]

b. mɛ̀ kḗ mɛ̀ í bɛ̀ ɛ́! ḭ̀ bùbǎ
   3SG.SUBORD go.IRR 3SG.SUBORD LOG do.IRR INTERJ COMP dad.VOC
   tsḗ fên sį̀ nɔ́ɔ-ŋḗ à̰ dân gṵ̀
   INDF thing be here-NEG DEF wall under
   'He went out and shouted "Eh! Dad, there is something over there next to the wall!"' [sos150626t4:6]

This compound adverb emphasizes the spatial difference between the speaker and the action being referenced; the action is clearly 'over there', not in the same location as the speaker. As consultants report, perhaps the two interlocutors were once in the same place, and one has moved elsewhere or come back from somewhere else, which allows them to assert that the place in question is not or no longer where they are. In contrast, *ɲì-nà*, to be discussed in §10.2.1.2, represents a more general 'there' or 'over there' without any necessary reference to the location of the speaker.

In fact, the general 'there' adverb *ɲì-nà* can be combined with *lɔ́* to give a sense of 'around here'; *lɔ́ ɲì-nà* . It appears to encode a wider circle than simply *lɔ́* 'here', perhaps something akin to 'hereabouts'. For instance:

(56) a. á nɛ̏-dəgɛ̏   á nɛ̏   lɔ́ ɲì-nà
 2SG TRANS-hurry.IRR 2SG come.IRR here there-towards
 'Come here quick!' [sos150704e]

b. ì sɔ́n bəlě dzɔ̋-gbǎa lê   kʊ́ bɪ́ɛ̣   ŋáa-bɛ́   lɔ́
 COMP rain big IDEO   PRES D.DEF rain.REAL.PFV mean-NOM here
 ɲì-nà
 there-towards
 'There's a huge rain out there, raining like meanness.' [sos150626t4:20]

In (56a), the use of *lɔ́ ɲì-nà* rather than *lɔ́* gives the meaning of 'come this way', rather than specifically where the speaker is. In (56b), it implies that the rain was not just specifically 'here' (as rains are seldom so narrowly concentrated) but here and in the vicinity.

10.2.1.2 *ɲì(-nà)* '(over) there'

As discussed above, *ɲì* or *ɲì-nà* is a general and very common adverb meaning 'there'; with the directional morpheme *nà*, it takes on the meaning of 'over there' or 'towards there', similar to *wɛ̀-nà* (24) or *tɛ́-nǎ* (31a). Unlike the more specific compound adverb *lɔ́ɔ-ŋɛ́* (55), it does not appear to set up any opposition between the location of the speaker and the location under discussion. It means a simple general 'there'.

Elicited examples include:

(57) a. á wóő   kàä   ɲì-nà   cɛ̏n tsɛ̋
 2SG EMPH.PST go.REAL.PRF there-towards time how
 'How many times have you been there?' [sos150619e]

b. à jərà   ɲì-nà
 3SG dump.IRR there-towards
 'Dump it out over there!' [sos150623e]

c. à fì   ɲì
 3SG throw.IRR there
 'Throw it over there!' [sos170701e]

In texts, we find examples like:

(58) a. təgɔ́ɛ wɛ̀ í bɛ̋ ì̀ à tɛ̀ɛ ɲì-nà
certain.PL SUBORD LOG do.IRR COMP 3SG leave.IRR there-towards
'Some of them said to leave him there.' [sos170711t1:26]

b. kɛ̋ mǐ ká̰ ằ fôn-tsḭ́ gɔ̋ ɲì-nà
COP 1PL go DEF fonio-cut.REAL.NOM learn.IRR there-towards
'We went there to learn fonio cutting.' [sos170714t2:67]

Without the directional morpheme, the adverb *ɲì* often combines with the preceding verb with seemingly very little in added meaning. Further, it often correlates with a lengthening and S-tone addition on what precedes it (usually the verb, but occasionally an adverb). There is some indication that this comes from a particle or suffix *ŋɛ̋*, whose meaning is unclear, which normally elides; it is glossed in the following examples as NE. For example:

(59) a. ì̀ ằ nǎ kɛ̋ təgŏ ɲì (Expected: [təgò])
COMP 3SG PROSP go.IRR sit.NE there
'[They said] that she should go get married there.' [sos171009t1:67]

b. ằ nìgì nŏo ɲì, óo kʊ́ jǜ (Expected: [nò])
DEF COW.PL come.NE there 2SG.EMPH D.DEF say.IRR
'The cows are coming, you have to say [the answer].' [sos161009t1:9]

c. ằ dôn mɛ̀ bɔ́ mɛ̀ kɛ̋ ằ cɛ̋n-kɛ̋
DEF child SUBORD go.out.IRR 3SG.SUBORD go.IRR DEF peanut-shell.PL
sɛ̋ɛ ɲì (Expected: [sɛ̋])
throw.NE there
'The child went outside to throw out some peanut shells.' [sos150626t4:5]

d. ằ kórô lɛ̀ kɛ̋ ằ dzö̀-tò màǎ ɲì
DEF pigeon SUBORD go.IRR 3SG mouth-reply.IRR again.NE there
'The pigeon replied to him again there.' [sos150626t6:17]

In (59a-c), it is the verb that is lengthened with a S-tone addition. In (59d), it is the adverb *màa* 'again'. There is not a strong locative sense in any of these examples, suggesting *ɲì* itself has relatively weak semantics.

The following examples show the suffix *-ŋɛ̋* that this lengthening may be derived from:

(60) a. á nǎ ằ fì-ŋɛ̋ ɲì-nà ŋɛ́
2SG PROSP 3SG throw-NE there-towards NEG
'Don't throw it there!' [sos170707e]

b. mɛ̏ kʊ́ bìaa-cí   bé kɛ̋ sáŋgə̣́sőʼ
   but.FR D.DEF mud.brick-house DEM COP.PST multi.story.house
   mɔ̣̏ɔ   təgı̀   mɔ̣̏ɔ́   səŋá-ŋɛ̋   ɲì
   person.PST climb.IRR person.SBJV lie.down-NE there
   'Those mudbrick houses, they were two-story houses, we used to go upstairs to sleep.' [sos170702t1:54]

For example (60a), my consultant reports that the verb can also be pronounced *fıi*, with the lengthening and S-tone seen in the examples in (59).

10.2.1.3 *sərɛ̋* 'outside'

The adverb *sərɛ̋* means 'outside', as illustrated in the following examples from both elicitation and texts:

(61) a. ń   sı̣̀   sɛ̋   nɛ̋   sərɛ̋
       1SG be fly.REAL.NOM LOC outside
       'I am going outside.' [sos150812e]

b. ə̀á   jîaa   nɛ̋ ì   bɔ́   kʊ́   sɔ̀ɔ̀   nɛ̏
   3SG.SBJV return.REAL.PFV if 3PL go.out.IRR D.DEF moment LOC
   sərɛ̋
   outside
   'If he left, they would go outside then.' [sos170702t1:165]

c. ı̋ı   í   bə̏   nɛ̋ sə̋sə̀a   nɛ̏   í   bɔ́   bə́ą̀
   3PL.SBJV LOG do.REAL.PFV if right.now LOC 2PL go.out.IRR balafon
   wɛ̀   sərɛ̋
   with outside
   'If they told you right now that you should go outside with your balafon...' [sos170711t1:422]

10.2.1.4 *cîe* 'at home'

The noun *cî* 'house' has a related locative form *cîe*, meaning 'at home'. This is likely derived from a contraction of 'house' with one of the postpositions, but it is no longer recoverable which postposition it would have been, since consultants know this expression only as *cîe*. Examples include:

(62) a. m̰ɛ̀ kúrúíi sḭ̀ kɔ́ɔ ně ǐi fɑ̰̀n mè í
person.PL all.PL be walk.REAL.NOM LOC 3PL.SBJV enter.IRR HAB LOG
jěn mɛ́ cîe
front with house.LOC
'All of the people were walking and entering a house frontwards.'
[sos161009t1:3]

b. kɔ̀ɔ fůi nǎ bɔ́ cîe ɲɛ́
hole nothing PROSP go.out.IRR house.LOC NEG
'Not even one hole will remain in the house.' [sos130828t2:75]

Its nominal origins, however, are betrayed by the fact that it is commonly preceded by the determiner ǎ or even by a possessor, indicating whose home is in question:

(63) a. ǎ bö̀-kɔ́ɔ wɛ̀ təgǒ ɲì ǎ cîe
DEF billygoat SUBORD remain.IRR.NE there DEF house.LOC
'The billygoat remained in the house.' [sos150626t4:57]

b. ɛ̋! ì̀ fên fɑ̰̌ kərǔ tɛ̀ cîe
INTERJ COMP thing pass.PTCP hyena GEN house.LOC
'Eh! Something entered hyena's house...' [sos150626t4:16]

These examples suggest that, syntactically, it is best treated as a locative noun, but since it behaves adverbially, I have included it here.

10.2.1.5 *lű-ŋǎa* 'in the courtyard'

A similar locative compound is found with *lű-ŋǎa*, combining *lű* 'courtyard' with *ŋǎa* 'interior' (cf. *à ŋàa-sɛ̰̀* 'his guts'). To date, there are no textual examples, but elicited examples show the following:

(64) a. mí̋ bɛ̀ɛ bɑ̰́ lű-ŋǎa
1PL pig.PL hit.REAL.PFV courtyard-interior
'We hit the pigs in the courtyard.' [sos150317e]

b. mó sḭ̀ lű-ŋǎa tsɛ̋-ké jö̰ŋmǎ kɑ̰̌ wɛ̋
1SG.EMPH be courtyard-inside and cat white with
'I am in the courtyard with a white cat.' [sos170705e]

Consultants report that these forms are ungrammatical with the postposition *né*.

Like the relational noun *jěn*, which can be used like a postposition or as a noun, *lű-ŋǎa* can also be turned into a noun *lű-ŋǎa-ŋɛ̋* 'people of the courtyard' with the human suffix *-ŋɛ̋*; this noun is commonly found in greetings ('how are the people of this courtyard?'). For more on the human plural suffix, see §5.3.2.

10.2.1.6 jəmɨ̀ 'in the bush'

Another locative noun adverb is *jəmɨ̀*, meaning 'in the bush' or 'in the wild' (in other words, not in the village). The following examples are selected from folktales, where it is a common theme:

(65) a. mɛ̀   kɛ́   jɨ̀-jɔ̋ɔ   jəmɨ̀
          3SG.SUBORD go.IRR hill-stroll.IRR bush
          'He went out to hunt in the bush.' [sos170711t1:8]

   b. kʊ́ nɛ̀ mɨ́ ǎ tsɨ́   kǎ jəmɨ̀
       D.DEF LOC 1PL 3SG cut.IRR go bush
       'For that, we go cut it in the bush.' [sos170711t1:54]

   c. ǎá   kǎ   nɛ́ ǎá   kôo   nɛ́ ǎ jəmɨ̀
       3SG.SBJV go.REAL.PFV if 3SG.SBJV give.birth.REAL.PFV if DEF bush
       ǎ   sò-bǔn   tərɨ́ɨ́   ǎ   sà-nɛ̀ kʊ́ dòn bé tò
       DEF horse-grass cut.ANTIP.NOM DEF spring D.DEF child DEM take.IRR
       'If she went out and if she gave birth in the fields [where] she cut horse grass, the spring would take that child.' [sos170805t9:2]

As (65c) shows, *jəmɨ̀*, like *cîe*, can also take a determiner, indicating that it is syntactically a locative noun.

10.2.1.7 gɔ̀ɔ 'on the ground'

As a noun, 'ground' or 'field' is X-toned: *gɔ̋ɔ*. As an adverbial locative noun, however, it is L-toned, most likely due to the elision of another X-toned postposition in its development. Unlike the other locative nouns in the preceding subsections, *gɔ̀ɔ* is never preceded by a determiner *ǎ*, presumably due to the fact that it gives the general sense of 'on the ground'; there is no need to differentiate one ground from another. Examples include:

(66) a. ǎ sɨ́ təgɔ́ ǎ sɨ́o   mənɛ̀-sɑ́n dzɨ́ɨ́   nɛ́ gɔ̀ɔ
          3SG be like 3SG REC.PST iron-thing put.REAL.NOM LOC ground.LOC
          'It's like a piece of iron was just dropped on the ground.' [sos170711t1:69]

   b. ń   təgǒ   gɔ̀ɔ   bɔ́ɔ fɔ́n ń   təgǐ   ń   tsɨ̀ɛ̀   mɛ̀
       1SG sit.PTCP ground.LOC tall more 1SG stand.PTCP 1SG foot.PL with
       wɛ̀
       with
       'If I am sitting on the ground, I am taller than when I stand on my feet.' [sos161009t1:58]

As we can see in these examples, *gɔɔ* has a locative meaning without an explicit locative postposition. I have glossed it as LOC due to its semantics, even though the postposition *né* does not productively elide, and if it did, it would not raise X to L since it is not an X-toned pronoun.

10.2.1.8 *cɔ̌* 'in the village'

The noun *cɔ̌* 'village' can be used unaltered as an adverbial locative noun. It is not commonly attested in texts, where action is typically directed back towards houses (thus implying the village), but it can be found. Examples from both elicitation and texts illustrate this form:

(67) a. mó   sɔ́ɔ̀   móo   ké̃   cɔ̌   ŋé
         1SG.EMPH be.able.IRR.HAB 1SG.SBJV go.IRR village NEG
         'I am not able to go to the village.' [sos150618e]

   b. móo   kà̃   né̃ cɔ̌   mó   nă   tséɛ
       1SG.EMPH.SBJV go.REAL.PFV if village 1SG.EMPH PROSP ask.IRR
       'If I go to the village I will ask.' [sos161009t1:162]

   c. puisque mɔ̂ɛɛ né̃ kʊ́   nè̃   mɔ̌   mɔ̂ɛɛ tsɪ̀   ɲì-nà
       since.FR millet if D.DEF LOC person millet cut.IRR there-towards
       kpèɛ wè,   ǐi   à̃   ɲù̃   tásía   nè̃ ì̃ nè̃   à
       knife with 3PL.SBJV 3SG pick.up.IRR container LOC 3PL come.IRR 3SG
       bè   wótərŏ   né̃ kʊ́   nè̃   kʊ́   sɔ̌   nè̃ à   wè
       put.IRR donkey.cart LOC D.DEF come.IRR D.DEF moment LOC 3SG with
       cɔ̌
       village
       'If it's millet now, we use knives to cut it, they brought them in containers, they came and piled it in donkey carts and used that to bring it to the village.' [sos170702t1:51]

10.2.2 Temporal adverbs

Temporal adverbs typically come close to the verb in Seenku, before any locative adverbs, if they appear post-verbally. However, they also can appear pre-clausally, a position not available to locative adverbs.

10.2.2.1 *dɔ̌n* 'today'

The following examples illustrate the use of *dɔ̌n* 'today' in texts:

(68) a. təgɔ́́ɛ   sı̰̆ səsɛ̋   dzɛ̋   sı̰̆, bă   sı̰̆, təgɔ́́ɛ   sı̰̆
certain.PL be spider glue.PTCP be put.PTCP be certain.PL be
mànà-sàfɛ̋ bă   sı̰̆ dɔ̏n
plastic-bag put.PTCP be today
'Some of them have spider egg sacs glued on, put on, some of them have plastic bags put on today.' [sos170711t1:121]

b. Donc, mó   nă   wé nìgì   mɔ̏mɛ̋   tő   dɔ̏n   í   wó
SO.FR 1SG.EMPH PROSP FOC COW.PL a.lot.PL take.IRR today 2PL EMPH
kə̏̀
in.hand
'So, it's me who will get a lot of cows with you all today.' [sos161009t1:11]

c. Mǎadṵ̀, vraiment, fɔ̰̋   mɔ̰̀ɔ̰   nă   wé jén-jɛ̋n   təmɛ̋
Madou really.FR must person.PST PROSP FOC RED-story tell.IRR
dɔ̏n nɔ̋, sinon, ăa   nă   bɛ̏n   ŋé
today here if.not.FR 3SG.PST PROSP be.good NEG
'Madou, really, we had to tell riddles here today otherwise it wouldn't be good.' [sos161009t1:12]

These examples show that dɔ̏n 'today' typically appears post-verbally, though not necessarily clause-finally (PPs or locative adverbs may follow). This is in contrast to kərɔ̀ 'yesterday', discussed in the next subsection.

As in English, the adverb 'today' can be used as a noun, as shown in examples like the following:

(69) a. est-ce que bon   gbènɛ̋-kűi   tsɛ̋kɛ́ dɔ̀n-kùi
Q.FR   well.FR past-thing.PL and today-thing.PL
sɛ́ɛ̰-kû   nɛ̰̏ est-ce que í   wó   kűɛ   tɛ̋   ì-yèrè-màní
Sambla-language LOC Q.FR   2PL EMPH other.PL GEN change.JU
sı̰̆ ou   bien   təgɔ́ ì-yèrè-màní ɲá   ŋé
be or.FR well.FR or change.JU be.NEG NEG
'Well, between things in the past and things today, in your opinion, have they changed or not?' [sos170702t1:21]

b. bon, kərɔ̀   ǎ-né dɔ̏n   ḭ̀   ɲá   sóen ŋé   kú   lɛ́ tɔ̋
well.FR yesterday and today 3PL be.NEG one NEG thing-which like
'Well, yesterday and today, why they aren't the same.' [sos170702t1:53]

In (69a), 'today' forms a compound with kû 'thing' ('things of today'), while in (69b), it is conjoined with 'yesterday', and this coordinated NP forms a topic resumed by the 3pl pronoun ḭ̀.

10.2.2.2 kərɔ̀ 'yesterday'

The adverb *kərɔ̀* 'yesterday' often appears in pre-clausal position in elicitation, though as (69d) shows, this position is also attested in texts (suggesting that it is not only a calque from French):

(70) a. *kərɔ̀ bὲɛ lɛ́̋ tsį́*
yesterday pig.PL PST jump.REAL.PFV
'Yesterday the pigs jumped.' [sos150317e]

b. *kərɔ̀ móő mɔ̰́ɛn-kȭ sà̰*
yesterday 1SG.EMPH.PST millet-toh buy.REAL.PFV
'Yesterday I bought millet toh.' [sos150805e]

c. *kərɔ̀ mó cȅrȅ dɛ̋*
yesterday 1SG.EMPH sleep.REAL.PFV EMPH
'Yesterday, I slept a lot!' [sos150806e]

d. *ì-ǎ-lɔ́ kərɔ̀ míí kóo mí̋ íwí̋*
you.know.JU yesterday 1PL.PST be.born.IRR 1PL 1PL.EXCL
jîo bìaa-cî gṳ̀
see.REAL.PFV banko-house under
'You know that yesterday [in the past] we were born in traditional mud-brick houses.' [sos170702t1:53]

It may be that the clause-initial order in this example is a focus strategy, with contrastive focus on 'yesterday' (**yesterday** we were born in mudbrick houses, as opposed to today when we are not).

The post-verbal position is also possible, however, seen in both elicitation and texts. For instance:

(71) a. *nɛ̋ səmâ kərɔ̀*
1SG.PST dance.REAL.PFV yesterday
'I danced yesterday.' [sos120107e]

b. *ń ǎ mṵ̈ kərɔ̀*
1SG 3SG drink.REAL.PFV yesterday
'I drank it yesterday.' [sos170822t3:211]

While (71a) could be seen as a calque from French in the elicitation process, (71b) is from a naturalistic text, showing that it is not simply a product of translation.

10.2.2.3 *kɛ́ɛ̋* 'tomorrow'

The adverb *kɛ́ɛ̋* 'tomorrow' can appear either clause-initially or post-verbally. It is rare in texts, found (adverbially) only in the example shown in (72c):

(72) a. *kɛ́ɛ̋   mó   nǎ   ǎ   dzį́   ǎ   nɛ̏*
   tomorrow 1SG.EMPH PROSP 3SG flee.IRR 3SG LOC
   'Tomorrow, I will run away from him.' [sos150811e]

b. *ǎ   nǎ   sɔ́   kɛ́ɛ̋   lɔ̋*
   3SG PROSP arrive.IRR tomorrow here
   'He will arrive here tomorrow.' [sos150617e]

c. *ɩ̏   fəŋǎmá nǎ   sɪ̌ ɩ̀   kɛ́ɛ̋   íwíí   ǎ*
   COMP chief   come.PTCP be COMP tomorrow 1PL.EXCL.SBJV 3SG
   dəgɛ̏   tɔ́-tərɔ̋
   make.IRR RED-like
   '[They would say] that the chief has come, that tomorrow we should do it like this.' [sos170823t8:357]

More data are required to determine which word order is more common.

10.2.2.4 *X-óo-X* 'every X'

To express 'every day' or 'every evening', a reduplicated structure is used, with a linker *-óo-* separating the reduplicants. Like other temporal adverbs, this can be placed either clause-initially or post-verbally, as shown in the following examples:

(73) a. *(cɛ̏rɛ̏-óo-cɛ̏rɛ̏) ǎ   bɛ́ɛ̂   wè   (cɛ̏rɛ̏-óo-cɛ̏rɛ̏)*
   day-LINK-day 3SG beat.ANTIP.IRR HAB day-LINK-day
   'It rains every day.' [sos150702e]

b. *mó   à   tò   kəré lêɛ   nɔ́nɛ́sán nɔ̋ɔ   lɔ̋*
   1SG.EMPH 3SG know.IRR man REL.SUBORD food   eat.IRR.HAB here
   gù̏ɔ-óo-gù̏ɔ
   day-LINK-day
   'I know the man who eats here every day.' [sos180717e]

In most cases, the reduplicated element is a temporal noun like *cɛ̏rɛ̏* 'day' or *jánɛ̏* 'evening', but (73b) shows a form unique to this construction with the element *gù̏ɔ*; though this is often found in time expressions like *gù̏ɔ-dəgɛ̏* 'morning' or *gù̏ɔ-fɪ́ɛ̣* 'night', *gù̏ɔ* cannot be used on its own.

10.2.2.5 kúcı̋ı̋ 'the other day'

An adverbial expression *kúcı̋ı̋* indicates a timeframe of a few days ago. Though its phonological form is suggestive of a compound, it is not transparently decomposable. Given the loose timeframe associated with it, its translation is flexible, anything from 'the other day' to 'last week'.

For example:

(74) a. môo   bî   tsǐe lɛ́ jı̀o   kúcı̋ı̋   mó
       1SG.EMPH.SUBORD goat black REL see.REAL.PFV other.day 1SG.EMPH
       ká̋   dɔ̀n   à   sà̰
       go.REAL.PFV today 3SG buy.IRR
       'The black goat I saw the other day, I'll go buy it today.' [sos150703e]

   b. sɛ̋́   cı̀e   kúcı̋ı̋   ŋɛ́
      rabbit.PL die.REAL.PFV other.day NEG
      'The rabbits did not die last week.' [sos150709e]

This form has yet to appear in the text corpus.

10.2.2.6 jǐee 'last year'

The adverb *jǐee* refers specifically to 'last year'; it is not related in any obvious way to the word *jṵ̀* 'year', though they may share a common diachronic origin. It is currently attested in:

(75) mó   nı̋ı̋   cı̀e   jǐee
     1SG.EMPH father.PST die.REAL.PFV last.year
     'My father died last year.' [sos130821e]

Consultants report that there is no difference in meaning if the adverb is placed clause-initially.

10.2.2.7 jánɛ̋ 'in the evening'

Like *dɔ̀n* 'today', the form *jánɛ̋* can be either a noun 'evening' or an adverb 'in the evening'. Once again, it can appear clause-initially or post-verbally.

(76) a. jánɛ̋   ȁ   nǎ   cèrȅ
        evening 3SG PROSP sleep.IRR
        'She will sleep this evening.' [sos170713e]

b. ǎá   bî   kɔ̰̂-tsḭ́   òo   ǎá   səgà
    3SG.SBJV goat head-cut.REAL.PFV whether 3SG.SBJV sheep
    kɔ̰̂-tsḭ́   òo   mɔ̰̀   nă   nɔ́nɛ́sǎn nɔ́   í   səgɔ́
    head-cut.REAL.PFV whether person PROSP food   eat.IRR LOG good
    dɔ̂n   jánɛ̀
    today evening
    'Whether he slaughters a goat or a sheep, we are going to eat well tonight.'
    [sos150702e]

In (76b), it is not clear whether dɔ̂n jánɛ̀ is a sequence of two adverbs ('today in the evening') or a single compound adverb ('today-evening').

10.2.2.8 gùɔ-dəgɛ̀ɛ 'in the morning'
The noun gùɔ-dəgɛ̀ 'morning' has an adverbial form gùɔ-dəgɛ̀ɛ 'in the morning', with a lengthened final vowel. As with gɔ̀ɔ 'on the ground' above, this is most likely the result of coalescence between the noun and a postposition, though this origin is now lost; speakers do not accept any of the postpositions in place of lengthening.

(77) a. sû   gɔ̀ɔ   à   wè   gùɔ-dəgɛ̀ɛ
        get.up.NOM be.difficult 3SG with morning.ADV
        'It is difficult for him to get up in the morning.' [sos170315e]

    b. ḭ̀   tàa   kṹ   nɛ̋ ŋɛ́ í   wó   lɛ̀   kəná   tsɛ̋
        QUOT otherwise D.DEF if NEG LOG EMPH SUBORD wake.REAL.PFV how
        gùɔ-dəgɛ̀ɛ   tsɛ̋   mɔ̰̀   bâ̰a̰   dzṵ̀-tsḭ́   fɛ̋ í
        morning.ADV INDF person balafon mouth-cut.REAL.PFV yet LOG
        wó   tɛ̀   fɔ́ɛ̋-fɔ́ɛ̋   ŋɛ́
        EMPH GEN RED-nothing NEG
        'If not, since I woke up this morning, no one has opened the balafon [given me anything] at all.' [sos161005e]

As noted above, many time expressions contain the compound initial gùɔ, found in the expression gùɔ-óo-gùɔ 'every day' (§10.2.2.4), but since this is not ever used on its own and consultants can offer no translation for it, I do not gloss it separately.

10.2.2.9 gbɛ̆nɛ̋ 'early'
The form gbɛ̆nɛ̋ can be used as a noun to mean '(the) past' (found also in irregularly inflected nouns like gbɛ̆nɛ̋-ŋɛ̋ 'ancestors') or as an adverb meaning 'early' or 'before'. For instance:

(78) a. ń nă kənâ gbɛ̀nɛ́
     1SG PROSP wake.up.IRR early
     'I will wake up early.' [sos150618e]

   b. á nằ gbɛ̀nɛ́
     2SG come.REAL.PFV early
     'You came early.' [sos150622e]

It can also be found clause-initially when the speaker is emphasizing the timeframe, such as:

(79) gbɛ̀nɛ́ mɔ̀ɔ̀ kú lé bɛ́ wɛ́ tsɛ́-ké dɔ̀n ìi
     before person.SUBORD thing REL do.IRR HAB and today 3PL.SUBORD
     béɛ-cé
     do.NOM-manner
     'The things that people did before and how they are done now.' [sos170702t1:41]

10.2.2.10 tənî̀ 'late(r)'

Related to the postposition tənî̀ 'behind', we find the adverb tənî̀, meaning either 'late' or 'later'.

(80) a. móő səŋâ tənî̀
     1SG.EMPH.PST lie.down.REAL.PFV late
     'I went to bed late.' [sos150623e]

   b. mɔ̀ nă jó tənî̀
     person PROSP see.IRR late
     'See you later.' [sos171009t1:128]

In every case I have seen, this adverb is clause-final.

10.2.2.11 sə́sằa (nɛ̀) 'just now'

The adverb sə́sằa nɛ̀ (sometimes [sísằa nɛ̀]) is likely a loan from Jula sísá̰, meaning '(right) now'. It can appear either clause-initially or post-verbally. In terms of TAM, it is compatible with present (81a), perfect (81b), and immediate past (81c).

(81) a. ì-á-lɔ́ sísằa nɛ̀ kʊ́ kʊ́ ɲá bò ŋɛ́
     you.know.JU right.now LOC D.DEF D.DEF be.NEG anymore NEG
     'As you know, that doesn't exist anymore now.' [sos170702t1:69]

b. ằ   bǚɔ   sə́sằa   nȅ
    3SG go.out.REAL.PERF right.now LOC
    'She has gone out just now.' [sos150617e]

c. ằ   sǐo   tsı̂   nȅ sə́sằa   nȅ
    3SG REC.PST jump.REAL.NOM LOC right.now LOC
    'He just [now] jumped.' [sos150317e]

In (81a), *sə́sằa nȅ* is clause-initial, while in (81b-c), we see it clause-finally.

10.2.2.12 *fɛ̋* 'yet'

The adverb *fɛ̋* 'yet' indicates an action that has yet to happen. It is not solely a negative polarity item (NPI), since it is able to occur in both the affirmative and the negative. Examples of the negative include:

(82) a. mó   cȉe   fɛ̋ ŋé
         1SG.EMPH die.REAL.PFV yet NEG
         'I haven't died yet.' [sos130821e]

b. óo   nǚgì sóen jȉo,   Kanazoe á   wó   ằ   nǚgì
    2SG.EMPH cow one see.REAL.PRF Kanazoe 2SG EMPH DEF cow
    jȉo   fɛ̋ ŋé
    see.REAL.PFV yet NEG
    'You got one cow, Kanazoe, you haven't gotten a cow yet.' [sos161009t1:73]

c. mó   kʊ́   ɲȉa   fɛ̋ ằ   nȅ ŋé
    1SG.EMPH D.DEF finish.REAL.PFV yet 3SG LOC NEG
    'I haven't finished with it yet.' [171009t1:115]

In these examples, the adverb is always accompanied by the negative marker *ŋé*.

In the affirmative, it carries a range of meanings from, 'first' to 'already' to 'before'. For example:

(83) a. mó   yȅrȅ   nǚgì sóen jȉo   ké ń   nȍ   fɛ̋ fı́n
         1SG.EMPH self.JU cow one see.REAL.PRF COP 1SG come yet two
         jő
         see.IRR
         'I got one cow, I'll get two yet.' [sos161009t1:64]

b. mó   nɔ̀ɛ   ké fı́ fɛ̋ ké mɔ̀   ká̋ fɛ̋ âa
    1SG.EMPH that.for.PL COP two yet COP person go yet NEG.Q
    'For me it's two already, are we not leaving yet?' [sos161009t1:77]

c. donc mɔ̰̌ nǎ à tsíɛ bɛ́ tɔ̀ fɛ̰́ lɔ̋
    SO.FR person PROSP DEF word DEM leave.IRR yet here
    'So we'll leave these questions here for now.' [sos171009t1:126]

Note that in (83b), there are two instances of *fɛ̰́*, the first affirmative and the second negative (licensed by the negative question marker *âa*; §16.1.2). More research is needed to determine the semantic range of *fɛ̰́* in the affirmative.

10.2.2.13 *bö̀* 'anymore'

The adverb 'anymore' is expressed as *bö̀* in Seenku. It can appear in one of two positions: either after the auxiliary or after the verb (where it may be preceded by other adjuncts). From elicitation, we find:

(84) a. ń nǎ cȅrȅ bö̀ ŋɛ́
    1SG PROSP sleep.IRR anymore NEG
    'I will no longer sleep.' [sos130821e]

b. mó ɲá bö̀ səkɛ́ɛtí̋ mḭ̌ nɛ̰́ ŋɛ́
    1SG.EMPH be.NEG anymore cigarette drink.REAL.NOM LOC NEG
    'I don't smoke cigarettes anymore.' [sos181204e]

Textual examples include:

(85) a. à̰ nǎ ɲì̀ ǎa fɑ̰̀ í tê cîe kərṵ̀
    3SG PROSP run 3SG.SUBORD enter.IRR LOG GEN house.LOC hyena
    nǎ bö̀ à̰ jó ŋɛ́
    PROSP anymore 3SG see.IRR NEG
    'He would run and enter his house and the hyena would not be able to see him anymore.' [sos161009t1:212]

b. kɛ́ Sɛ́ɛ̰-kû yèrè-yèrè ɲá bö̀ ŋɛ́
    COP Sambla-language RED-self.JU be.NEG anymore NEG
    'True Seenku doesn't exist anymore.' [sos170702t1:148]

c. ì̀ wɛ̰̏ í bɛ̰́ ì̀ kɛ́ íwí̋ dő̰n bö̀ ŋɛ́
    3PL SUBORD LOG do.IRR COMP COP 1PL.EXCL child anymore NEG
    'They said that she is not their child anymore.' [sos171009t1:64]

Unlike *fɛ̰́* 'yet' in the last subsection, *bö̀* is purely an NPI and requires negation to be realized.

10.2.2.14 kà-bǎ́ 'already'

The adverbial expression *kà-bǎ́* 'already' is borrowed from Jula (meaning 'it's done', a combination of the TAMP marker *kà* and the verb *ban* 'finish'). It is found post-verbally, often combined with perfect verbal aspect (§13.3.2.2) as shown in the following examples from both elicitation and texts:

(86) a. mó cërë kà-bǎ́
 1SG.EMPH sleep.REAL.PRF already
 'I have already slept.' [sos150806e]

 b. ǎá nɔ́nɛ̌sǎn nïɔ nɛ̌ kà-bǎ́ ń nǎ bɔ̀
 3SG.SBJV food eat.REAL.PRF if already 1SG PROSP anymore
 dəgéɛ   ŋé
 cook.ANTIP.IRR NEG
 'If you have already eaten, I won't cook anymore.' [sos170811e]

 c. á wó kűɛ tsï kà-bǎ́
 2SG EMPH other.PL cut.REAL.PRF already
 'You have already cut them.' [sos170714t2:34]

10.2.2.15 màa 'again'

The adverb *màa* 'again' is very common in texts. Its most typical position is post-verbal, as shown in the following examples from texts:

(87) a. ì á jáa màa fɛ̌ á kɛ̌ sənǎ
 COMP 2SG return.IRR again yet 2SG go.IRR lie.down.IRR
 '[He said that] you should just go home again and go back to bed.' [sos130828t2:43]

 b. ì jïa màa
 3PL return.REAL.PRF again
 'They have turned around again.' [sos170714t2:40]

 c. ì fôn cɛ̀n ì ǎ kəké màa
 3PL fonio take.out.IRR 3PL 3SG spread.out again
 'They take the fonio and pour it out again.' [sos170714t3:147]

The adverb *màa* can also be used with other meanings, such as 'also' (88a-b), or even in cases where the exact meaning contributed by *màa* is unclear, such as (88c-d):

(88) a. bö-kɔ̌ɔ   fáná   kằ   lɛ̋ màa, dằnɛ̀-bɛ́ nɛ̀
       billygoat also.JU go.REAL.PFV PST again hunt-NOM LOC
       'Billygoat had also gone out hunting.' [sos161009t1:183]

   b. kɛ́ gɔ̂ɔ sɔ́ɛn dərɔ̌ màa
      COP wood one only again
      'It's also just one type of wood.' [sos170711t1:70]

   c. móo   ɲìa   nɛ̋ màa kʊ́ nɛ̀ mó   nǎ
      1SG.EMPH.SBJV finish.REAL.PFV if again D.DEF LOC 1SG.EMPH PROSP
      ń   kőo   jű   lɛ̋-jű   í   wêe
      1SG be.born year TRANS-say.IRR 2PL EMPH.DAT
      'Now that I've finished that, I'll tell you the year I was born.' [sos171009t1:14]

   d. kʊ́   cɛ́ɛ-cé   sị̌ né màa í   sɔ̌   kɛ̀
      D.DEF gather.NOM-manner be FOC again LOG alone EMPH
      'That way of gathering [fonio] is sure different!' [sos170714t2:99]

If a clause-initial discourse marker or conjunction is used, often borrowed from French, *màa* can occur after this:

(89) Et   puis   màa fáná á   wó təgő-bɛ̀ɛ   tsɛ̋
     and.FR then.FR again also.JU 2SG EMPH sit.NOM-be.NOM how
     móo   sị̌ nɛ̋ bậa brɛ̋   nɛ̋
     1SG.EMPH.SBJV be if balafon play.REAL.NOM LOC
     'And then also how you're seated, if I'm playing the balafon...' [sos170711t1:288]

I have never seen it at the very beginning of a clause, suggesting that prosodically, it must follow another element.

10.2.3 Manner adverbs

Manner adverbs appear exclusively post-verbally; I have never seen them in the post-auxiliary position available to some of the other temporal or locative adverbs.

Many manner adverbs are ideophonic, and as such are addressed in Chapter 9. Here, I focus specifically on two manner adverbials, *í səgɔ̌* 'well' and *fə-fìɔ* 'quickly'.

10.2.3.1 *í səgɔ̌* 'well'

The adverbial expression 'well' in Seenku takes the form *í səgɔ̌*, consisting of a logophoric pronoun *í* and the adjective *səgɔ̌* 'good'. This is precisely the construction used after the copular auxiliary *sị̌* in adjectival predicates (§14.3). The following examples are drawn exclusively from texts:

(90) a. mó   năá   təgò̰   mó   nəgì   nè-təgò   í   səgɔ̌
       1SG.EMPH PROSP.FOC sit.IRR 1SG.EMPH mind TRANS-sit.IRR LOG good
       'I will sit down to remember well.' [sos171009t1:47-48]

   b. mó   ká-kán   móo   ằ   jú   í   səgɔ̌
      1SG.EMPH AFF-good.JU 1SG.EMPH.SBJV 3SG say.IRR LOG good
      'I have to say it well.' [sos171009t1:121]

   c. ằ   ằ   grṹa   í   səgɔ̌
      3SG 3SG fry.IRR LOG good
      'She fries it well.' [sos170714t3:74]

There is, to my knowledge, no antonym 'poorly' or 'badly'. Instead, the clause with í səgɔ̌ would simply be negated.

10.2.3.2 (fə-)fìɔ 'quickly'

The adverb 'quickly' can either be expressed with simple fìɔ or reduplicated fə-fìɔ. Younger speakers seem to offer the reduplicated version more frequently, whether in elicitation (91a-b) or in texts (91c), whereas the unreduplicated version has been offered by an older speaker in a text setting (91d):

(91) a. ằ   nèɛ   lɔ̌   fə-fìɔ
       3SG come.IRR.HAB RED-fast
       'He comes here quickly.' [sos170713e]

   b. ń   nǎ   təgḭ̀   sò   kɔ̀n təré   lɛ̈̀   ɲì   wè
      1SG PROSP stand.IRR horse on REL.PRO SUBORD run.IRR HAB
      fə-fìɔ
      RED-fast
      'I will ride the horse that runs quickly.' [sos150620e]

   c. í   kɛ̈́   à   bèɛ   fə-fìɔ   fə-fìɔ   í   jîaa   í
      2PL go.IRR 3SG do.IRR.HAB RED-fast RED-fast 2PL return.c irr 2PL
      nɛ̈̀   cèrḛ̀ fĩ́n   ằ   bṵ́-kǎ́   nǎ   né
      come.IRREAL day two DEF grass-empty PROSP come.IRR
      'You go do it quickly quickly, you return, and in two days time, weeds are coming up.' [sos170714t3:128]

   d. máná nɛ̈́ kɔ́   í   nè-frɔ́   wè fìɔ ŋɛ́
      bag   if D.DEF LOG TRANS-pierce.IRR HAB fast NEG
      'If the bags are plastic, they don't pierce [as] quickly.' [sos170711t1:137]

In (91c), we see repetition or reduplication of the already reduplicated adverb.

10.2.4 Quantifier adverbs

The last kind of adverb to be addressed in this chapter are quantifier adverbs. For quantification in the NP, see §8.5.

10.2.4.1 'a lot'

The same quantifier *mɔ̰̀má̰* used as a nominal modifier (§8.5.3) can also be found as a quantifier adverb. This is clearly shown in the following elicited examples with intransitive verbs, where the adverb cannot be interpreted as a nominal modifier:

(92) a. kərɔ̀   mó   cěrɛ̀   mɔ̰̀má̰ dɛ̋
    yesterday 1SG.EMPH sleep.REAL.PFV a.lot EMPH
    'Yesterday I slept a lot!' [sos150806e]

   b. ä̀ bı̤ɛ̰   mɔ̰̀má̰
    3SG rain.REAL.PFV a.lot
    'It rained a lot.' [sos150702e]

In both cases, the adverb *mɔ̰̀má̰* must modify the verb; there is no object nominal for it to modify, and it is not semantically tied to the subject.

This construction is not common in texts, suggesting that it may be a French calque. Instead, the ideophonic adverb *tsɛ́ɛ* (§9.2.1.2) is often seen, or even the universal quantifier *pó-pó* 'all' (§8.5.1.2). These two constructions are shown in the following exchange:

(93) a. ń̀ kòee   lɔ̋ pó-pó
    1SG sing.ANTIP.IRR.HAB   here RED-all
    'I sing a lot!' [sos170822t12:402]

   b. áä̋ kɔ̀nɛ̀   kòee   tsɛ́ɛ nɛ̰̀
    2SG.PST TOP.JU sing.ANTIP.IRR.HAB IDEO LOC
    'In any case you used to sing a lot.' [sos170822t12:403]

In (93a), the quantifier *pó-pó* does not literally mean 'all', but rather simply 'a lot'. In the next line, which follows immediately in the text, another speaker uses the ideophonic intensifier *tsɛ́ɛ* instead.

10.2.4.2 'too much'

The adverb *gərû* gives the reading of 'too much'. Like *mɔ̰̀má̰* above, it is attested in elicitation with intransitive verbs, as in:

(94) a. ằ sáà gərû
3SG cry.IRR.HAB too.much
'He cries too much.' [sos170713e]

b. ằ bíɛ gərû
3SG rain.REAL.PFV too.much
'It rained too much.' [sos150702e]

In fact, (94a) was offered in translation to the French prompt *il pleure beaucoup*, or 'he cries a lot', suggesting that *gərû* may not necessarily encode the notion of excess.

This adverb is also attested in the text corpus. For instance:

(95) a. dɔ̀ɔnì ằá dəbɛ̈ nɛ́ gərû dərɔ́ ɛ̈ɛ́
a.little 3SG.SBJV be.good.REAL.PFV if too.much only 3SG.LOG
nɛ̀-frɔ̃
TRANS-pierce.IRR
'If it's too good, it pierces.' [sos170711t1:136]

b. á wó jɔ́ɔ̀ wɛ̀ gərû
2SG EMPH stroll.IRR HAB too.much
'You walk around too much.' [sos170822t4:135]

As these examples suggest, *gərû* is only ever found post-verbally.

10.2.4.3 'a little'

The adverb 'a little' is borrowed from Jula: *dɔ̀ɔnì* (sometimes *dɔ́ɔní*). Though typically found in post-verbal position, the example in (95a) shows that it can also be used in a discourse role at the beginning of the clause.

In its role as a quantifier adverb, we find examples like the following:

(96) a. í í gərɛ́ bɔ̌ dɔ̀ɔnì quoi
2PL LOG voice take.out.IRR a.little what.FR
'Speak a little louder if you will.' [sos170822t1:5]

b. áa ằ kòo nɛ́ á sɔ́ɔ̀ ằ tsḭ́-mɛ́-kű
2SG.SBJV 3SG sing.REAL.PFV if 2SG be.able.IRR.HAB DEF meaning
jű dɔ́ɔní mɔ̰̀ɛɛ quoi
say.IRR a.little person.DAT what.FR
'Once you have sung it, would you be able to tell us a little about its meaning.' [sos170822t12:101]

In both cases, the adverb follows the verb.

11 Coordination

This chapter covers coordination strategies, both conjunction (§11.1) and disjunction (§11.2), at the levels of the NP, PP, and AP; clause-level disjunction will also be covered, but since clause-level conjunction is typically achieved through other means, these constructions will be discussed separately in Chapter 20.

11.1 Conjunction

This section first covers NP conjunction (§11.1.1), then turns to PP conjunction (§11.1.2), the conjunction of adjectival modifiers (§11.1.3), and finally the conjunction of adjectival predicates (§11.1.4). A brief section discusses clause-level conjunction (§11.1.5), but mainly provides cross-references to discussion later in the grammar.

11.1.1 NP conjunction

There are several conjunctions in Seenku, listed in (1) from most common to least commonly attested:

(1) a. tsɛ̃́-kɛ́

b. tsɛ̃́-nɛ́

c. ã̀-nɛ́

In (1a-b), the initial element is homophonous with the indefinite (§8.2.4); in (1a), this is followed by an element homophonous with the copula ké, while in (1b-c) the final elements are more like the locative. The initial element in (1c) looks like the definite (§8.2.1) rather than the indefinite. The form in (1a) is by far the most common, offered consistently in elicitation; the other forms appear more commonly in texts and may be a property of older speakers. While the conjunctions have internal structure, I will gloss them simply as 'and', since it is not clear whether meanings like indefinite or the copula are recoverable synchronically in these constructions.

In NP coordination, the conjunction appears between the two conjuncts; it does not interact phonologically with either. Examples of coordinated NPs in isolation or in simple copular phrases are provided in (2):

(2) a. dɔ̋ɔ tsɛ́-kɛ́ jṵ̂
     beer and water
     'beer and water' [sos170714e]

  b. kɛ́ cɔ́ɔ-bâ-mənı̋ tsɛ́-kɛ́ cəbâa-dərõ̀n
     COP magic-do.NOM-woman and orphan-child
     'It's [the story of] the sorcerer woman and the orphan.' [sos130828t1:4]

  c. ń tɛ̋ sân tsɛ̋-nɛ́ ń tɛ̋ kərṵ̀
     1SG dear rabbit and 1SG dear hyena
     'Mr. Rabbit and Mr. Hyena.' [sos150626t2:4]

The elicited example in (2a) contain the conjunction *tsɛ̋-kɛ́*, also attested at the beginning of a folktale with the same younger speaker in (2b). The example in (2c) likewise comes from the introduction to a folktale told by an older speaker, where *tsɛ̋-nɛ́* is used instead. When asked about the order of conjuncts, consultants report that it does not matter; in both instances, the order could be reversed.

The following examples, two back-to-back utterances from different speakers in a text, show the equivalency of *tsɛ̋-kɛ́* and *tsɛ̋-nɛ́*:

(3) a. est-ce que bon gbɛ̀nɛ́-kűi tsɛ́-kɛ́ dɔ̀n-kùi
     Q.FR well.FR before-thing.PL and today-thing.PL
     sɛ́ɛ̰-kû nɛ̀ est-ce que í wó kű́ɛ tɛ̋ ì-yɛ̀rɛ̀-mànı́
     Sambla-language LOC Q.FR 2PL EMPH other.PL GEN change.JU
     sḭ̀ ou bien təgɔ́ ì-yɛ̀rɛ̀-mànı́ ɲ́á ŋɛ́
     be or.FR or change.JU be.NEG NEG
     'Between things from the past and things today, are there any changes or not?' [sos170702t1:21]

  b. ı̀ kərɔ́ tsɛ̋-nɛ́ dɔ̀n
     COMP yesterday and today
     'Between yesterday and today?' [sos170702t1:22]

The younger speaker in (3a) uses *tsɛ̋-kɛ́* while the older speaker in (3b) repeats the question using *tsɛ̋-nɛ́*.

Note that the conjuncts must be NPs and not simply nouns. For instance, if wishing to say 'a big cat and dog' (meaning both the cat and the dog are big), the adjective must be repeated in each conjunct:

(4) jṳ̀ŋmɑ̋ bəlɛ̌ tsɛ́-kɛ́ jəgɛ̀ bəlɛ̌
     cat big and dog big
     'a big cat and a big dog' [sos130818e]

When offered a form jǒŋmǎ tsɛ́-ké jəgɛ̀ bəlɛ̌, consultants interpreted this as 'a cat and a big dog'; the adjective does not scope over both conjuncts.

Placed into context, we find that conjoined NPs may appear in their regular syntactic positions, first as a subject (5a-b), then as an object (5c) (conjoined object NPs could not be found in the text corpus); for complements of postpositions and postpositions themselves, see §11.1.2. However, there is a preference for a resumptive pronoun when the conjoined NPs are sentence initial, even if this is the regular subject position:

(5) a. á   wó   à   tò   kərǔ tsɛ́-né bɔ̌-kɔ̌ɔ   ǐ   bèn   mè
       2SG EMPH 3SG know.IRR hyena and   billygoat 3PL get.along.IRR HAB
       ŋɛ́
       NEG
       'You know the hyena and the billygoat do not get along.' [sos161009t1:182]

    b. Bon,   kərɔ̀   ǎ-né dɔ̌n ǐ   ɲá   sóen ŋɛ́ kú   lɛ́   tɔ̌...
       well.FR yesterday and today 3PL be.NEG one NEG thing which like
       'Well, as for why yesterday and today are not the same...' [sos170702t1:53]

    c. mǐ   nǎ   bɛ̀ɛ tsɛ́-ké bî   sà̰
       1PL PROSP pig and   goat buy.IRR
       'We will buy a pig and a goat.' [sos150617e]

These examples show a variety of conjunctions: tsɛ́-ké in (5c), tsɛ́-né in (5a), and finally the less common ǎ-né in (5b). In subject position in (5a-b), the conjoined NPs of the subject are followed by the 3pl pronoun ǐ; though consultants do not outright reject forms without the pronoun, one can sense that the presence of the resumptive pronoun is far more natural. In object position, interestingly, no such pronoun is required. In fact, such a resumptive pronoun is unnatural in object position if the conjoined NPs remain in situ. A resumptive pronoun is only accepted if the conjoined NPs are preposed, e.g. bɛ̀ɛ tsɛ́-ké bî, mǐ nǎ ì sà̰ 'a pig and a goat, we will buy them'.

NPs themselves can be quite long, for example, nominalized clauses. In these cases still, the conjunction tsɛ́-ké can be used:

(6) a. gbɛ̌nɛ́ mɔ̀ɔ   kú   lɛ́ bɛ̌   wɛ̌ tsɛ́-ké dɔ̌n ǐi
       before person.SUBORD thing REL do.IRR HAB and   today 3PL.SUBORD
       bɛ̀ɛ-cé
       do.ANTIP-manner
       'The things people did before and how they are done now.' [sos170702t1:41]

b. *bâa   nà   tsɛ̋́ sɛ́ɛ-ŋɛ̀   tè íaa, mí̋ nǐ́ì*
balafon come.REAL.PFV how Sambla-HUM.PL GEN TOP 1PL father.PST
bú-blĕ   kűɛ   lɛ̌   ǎ   jú   tsɛ̋́ mǐ́ì   tsɛ̋́-ké mí̋ nǐ́
RED-big.PL other.PL SUBORD 3SG say.IRR how 1PL.DAT and 1PL father
lɛ̌   ǎ   jú   tsɛ̋́...
SUBORD 3SG say.IRR how
'Well, as for how the balafon came to Sambla country, as our grandfathers told us and how our fathers told us...' [sos170711t1:5-6]

In (6b), the first conjunct is the long nominalized clause 'the way our grandfathers told us', conjoined with 'the way our fathers told us' with the conjunction *tsɛ̋́-ké*.

These conjunctions can also be translated to 'and then' (cf. French *et puis*). For example:

(7) a. *ǎ   wɔ̀   kǜ,   ǎ-né ǎ   jəgɛ̀, ǎ-né ǎ   bɔ̀-kɔ̌ɔ*
3SG EMPH take.REAL.PFV and DEF dog and DEF billygoat
'They started with him (the hyena), and then the dog, and then the billygoat.' [sos150626t4:74]

b. *dìnǐ́ lɛ̂ɛ lɔ̋ ké dìnǐ́ tsɛ̋́ sǜɛ sǐ nɔ̋ ì̀ kà̀   tsɛ̋́-ké dìnǐ́*
drum PRES here COP drum INDF three be here 3PL in.hand and drum
sǐ   tsɛ̋́-ké sèn-sèn tsɛ̋́-ké kɔ̰-kɔ̰ ǎ-né ǎ   dənǜ
female and   sen-sen and   kɔ-kɔ and DEF talking.drum
'The drums that are here, there are three kinds of drums here that they have, the female drum, the *sen-sen*, and the *kɔ-kɔ*, and then [also] the talking drum.' [sos170714t1:9]

In (7a), the speaker is talking about how the animals made an association, starting first by taking the hyena, and then the dog, and then the billygoat. The use of *ǎ-né* in particular gives a sense of 'and then' rather than simply 'and'. In (7b), we see two conjunctions used; first *tsɛ̋́-ké* is used, interestingly, not just between the conjuncts for the three drum types, but before the first one too. After the three types of *dìnǐ́* are listed, the speaker then uses *ǎ-né* to note that additionally the talking drum (*dənǜ*) is also found. It is unclear why the conjunction *tsɛ̋́-ké* appears at the beginning of the list.

11.1.2 PP and adverb conjunction

Conjunction involving PPs depends partially on whether the same postposition is shared by both nouns or not. If different postpositions are involved, then conjunction obligatorily involves the conjunction of the PP, with each conjunct containing its own postposition. For instance:

(8) mó   ɲəgâan jîo   mó   tḛ̀ cəbâa nḛ̀ tsɛ́-ké sḭ̀
    1SG.EMPH scorpion see.REAL.PFV 1SG.EMPH GEN shoe LOC and water.jar
    gṵ̀
    under
    'I found a scorpion in my shoe and under the water jar.' [sos170717e]

Since each PP involves both a different noun and a different postposition, it is logical that the whole PP must be repeated. However, consultants also accept forms with conjunction of full PPs even when the postposition is the same:

(9) mó   ɲəgâan jîo   mó   tḛ̀ cəbâa gṵ̀   tsɛ́-ké
    1SG.EMPH scorpion see.REAL.PFV 1SG.EMPH GEN shoe under and
    sḭ̀   gṵ̀
    water.jar under
    'I found a scorpion under my shoe and the water jar.' [sos170717e]

The postposition gṵ̀ is repeated after each noun.

In other cases, we see what appears to be conjunction of the NP complements of the postpositions with just a single postposition attested:

(10) a. à̰   nà̰   à   dò̰n tsɛ́-ké à   kɔ̀sí́ wɛ́
        3SG come.REAL.PFV 3SG child and 3SG friend with
        'She came with her child and her friend.' [sos170717e]

     b. sân   nḛ̀   jáa   mḛ̀   kɛ̋   à̰   jú   à
        rabbit SUBORD return.IRR 3SG.SUBORD go.IRR 3SG say.IRR 3SG
        dḭ̀   tsɛ́-ké è́é   fṵ̀ɛɛ   lè
        child.PL and   3SG.LOG wife.PL DAT
        'When the rabbit came back, he went to tell his children and his wives.'
        [sos170805t15:183]

When asked about (10a), a consultant reports that the postposition could be repeated but that this is not necessary.

The difference appears to lie in whether both NPs are involved in a single event or not. In the case of (10a), the woman's arrival occurred once with both the child and the friend in tow; in (10b), Rabbit will tell both his children and his wives ostensibly at the same time. Both of these examples stand in contrast to (9), where different scorpions were found, one under a shoe and another under a water jar, requiring two separate acts of finding.

Thus, it appears that these coordination strategies depend in large part on semantics; even though it is syntactically permissible to conjoin NP complements of a postposition, it is only felicitous when the two are linked together in a single event or action.

11.1.3 Conjunction of adjectival modifiers

The conjunction of adjectival modifiers depends on whether a single noun is characterized by both adjectives or whether multiple nouns are involved. Of course, in most instances, multiple adjectives can simply be stacked, as in English (e.g. *dənôn fɔ̌ɔ mŏén* 'a small skinny child'), but if two are mutually incompatible, such as colors, they can be coordinated. For example, one can speak of a 'black and white cat'; the whole cat cannot be characterized as either black or white, but both colors exist in patches. In this case, a simple conjunction *né* is used between the two adjectives:

(11) mó ná jö̀ŋmǎ kǎ né tsĭe sǎ́
1SG.EMPH PROSP cat white and black buy.IRR
'I will buy a white and black cat.' [sos150703e]

If, on the other hand, the colors refer to different instances of the same noun, the noun must be repeated. This is unlike in English, where we can say 'a black and a white pig', to refer to one pig of each color. In Seenku, this must be expressed by coordinating full NPs:

(12) mó ná bɛ̀ɛ tsĭe tsɛ̋-kɛ́ bɛ̀ɛ kǎ sǎ́
1SG.EMPH PROSP pig black and pig white buy.IRR
'I will buy a black pig and a white pig.' [sos150703e]

Since NPs are being coordinated, the regular NP conjunction *tsɛ̋-kɛ́* is used.

11.1.4 Conjunction of adjectival predicates

The formation of adjectival predicates is discussed in §14.3. As discussed there, the verb 'be' is followed by a dummy logophoric pronoun that props up the adjective, since headless NPs are not allowed. This pronoun+adjective behaves like an NP, and thus when it comes to the conjunction of adjectival predicates, regular NP conjunctions are used. For example:

(13) a. jö̀ŋmǎ sɪ̆ í kǎ tsɛ̋-kɛ́ í tsĭe
cat be LOG white and LOG black
'The cat is white and black.' [sos130821e]

b. kərê sɪ̆ í bɔ̋ɔ ǎ-né í bəlĕ
man be LOG tall and LOG big
'The man is tall and fat.' [sos170717e]

At least one consultant prefers the use of the conjunction *ǎ-né* with adjectival predicates; she states that *tsɛ̋-kɛ́* would also be possible here, but that *ǎ-né* sounds a little more natural. This is likely related to the adjectival modifier conjunction *né* seen in §11.1.3.

11.1.5 Clause-level conjunction

Conjunction at the clause level is not achieved through the use of conjunctions. Rather, clauses are often conjoined either by simple juxtaposition or, in narratives, through the use of the subordinator *mɛ̈*; see Chapter 20 for further discussion of clause chaining.

11.2 Disjunction

Disjunction in Seenku is now most commonly expressed using French loans like *ou*, *ou bien*, or *sinon* rather than a native Seenku strategy. These loans can be used to coordinate either NPs or clauses. The native Seenku disjunction *təgɔ́*, only rarely attested, is found more commonly with clause-level disjunction than NP disjunction.

11.2.1 NP disjunction

Seenku does not appear to allow disjoined NPs to appear in their regular argument positions. For example, when disjoining an object NP, the first disjunct appears in situ in the object position (pre-verbal), while the disjunction and the second disjunct appear after the verb. In the current data set, only French loans are attested in these constructions:

(14) a. mó nă bî sɔ́ɛn sǎ́ ûu bɛ̈ɛ sɔ́ɛn
1SG.EMPH PROSP goat one buy.IRR or.FR pig one
'I will buy one goat or one pig.' [sos150622e]

b. mó nă bî sɔ́ɛn sǎ́ sínɔ́ bɛ̈ɛ sɔ́ɛn
1SG.EMPH PROSP goat one buy.IRR if.not.FR pig one
'I will buy one goat or one pig.' [sos150622e]

c. á wó nɛ̈ bâ̰a̰ dzü̈-tsḭ̀ mó tɛ̈ bí
2SG EMPH come.IRR balafon mouth-cut.IRR 1SG.EMPH GEN thousand
nɔ́ ou bien dán sóen âa
five or.FR well.FR ten.thousand one NEG.Q
'That you should come open up the balafon for me with 5000 or 10,000 CFA.' [sos170711t1:237]

The example in (14a) uses French *ou*; (14b) uses French *sinon*, while finally in (14c) the longer French conjunction *ou bien* is used.

In subject position, a different strategy is used, repeating the disjunction *ûu* before each disjunct:

(15) ûu   mó   ûu   á   wó   nǎ   kɛ́   Sía
      or.FR 1SG.EMPH   or.FR 2SG EMPH PROSP go.IRR Bobo
      'Either you or I will go to Bobo-Dioulasso.' [sos150622e]

The disjuncts are limited to pronouns, and this complex coordinated phrase is left in situ in subject position.

11.2.2 Disjunction of adjectival modifiers

As before, which disjunction is used depends on whether the utterance is a statement or a question; if the former, then the French loan *ou bien* is used; if the latter, then *təgɔ́* can be used.

In either case, disjunction of adjectival modifiers is much more clearly the disjunction of NPs than the conjunction of said modifiers. While in §11.1.3 above, we saw that modifying adjectives can be conjoined simply with *né*, in disjunction, the second adjective must be supported by a 3sg pronoun; it cannot occur alone. This is true of both statements and questions:

(16) a. ä̀   nǎ   təgê   tsǐe   ou   bien   ä̀   kǎ   bő
          3SG PROSP chicken black or.FR well.FR 3SG white kill.IRR
          'He will sacrifice either a black or white chicken.' [sos170717e]

      b. ä̀   nǎ   təgê   tsǐe↘   təgɔ́ ä̀   kǎ   bő
          3SG PROSP chicken black.Q   or   3SG white kill.IRR
          'Will he sacrifice a black or white chicken?' [sos170717e]

      c. á   cî   bəlɛ̌ ou   bien   ä̀   mɔ̌én ɲɛ̋↘
          2SG house big or.FR well.FR 3SG small build.IRR.Q
          'Did you build a big or small house?' [sos170717e]

An interesting phenomenon is seen with falling question intonation in (16b), where rather than being applied clause-finally as we normally see (§16.1.1), it occurs instead on the first disjunct, followed by the native Seenku disjunction *təgɔ́*. We do not see this distribution of question intonation in (16c) with the French disjunction *ou bien*. As I suggest below, it may be that questions like (16b) involve clause-level disjunction with ellipsis, and thus the question intonation is still clause-final.

11.2.3 Disjunction of adjectival predicates

With adjectival predicates, disjunction looks much like conjunction; the disjunction is placed after the first adjective, and the second adjectival predicate follows, preceded by its usual logophoric pronoun:

(17) a. ǎ sǝná   sị̈ í bǝlě↘ tǝgɔ́ í mŏén
         3SG husband be LOG big or LOG small
         'Is her husband fat or skinny?' [sos170717e]

   b. ǎ tê jǝgȅ sị̈ í tsǐe ou bien í kǎ
      3SG GEN dog be LOG black or.FR well.FR LOG white
      'His dog is either black or white.' [sos170717e]

As we have seen, in questions with *tǝgɔ́* as the disjunction, the falling question intonation is found before this disjunction, with no question intonation in the disjunct that follows.

The disjunction of adjectival predicates can also involve full clauses. We see this optionally in (18a) and obligatorily with the embedded construction in (18b):

(18) a. ɛ̀ɛ́   jǝgȅ sị̈ í tsǐe tǝgɔ́ (ǎ sị̈) í kǎ
         3SG.DAT dog be LOG black or   3SG be LOG white
         'Is his dog black or white?' [sos170717e]

   b. mó   nǝgı̏ ɲá   ǎ nȅ̀ cî   nǝgɔ̌ ɲá   nɛ̋ ɲɛ́ ou
      1SG.EMPH mind be.NEG 3SG LOC house dirty be.NEG if NEG or.FR
      bien ǎ gṵ̀ gı̆i   sị̈ nɛ̋
      well.FR 3SG under clean be if
      'I don't remember if the house is dirty or clean.' [sos170717e]

Rather than simply marking the adjectives or participles themselves as disjuncts, each disjunct contains a full clause.

11.2.4 PP disjunction

PPs are disjoined in the same way as NPs: typically with a French loan disjunction (19a). If, however, the utterance is a question, then the native Seenku *tǝgɔ́* may appear, as in (19b):

(19) a. ăa   kà   Kɔ́dìvɔ̂ar ou   bien   Kǎmɛ̌rűn mɛ̏
      3SG.PST go.REAL.PFV Ivory.Coast or.FR well.FR Cameroon but.FR
      mó   à   tò   ké   tə́né   ŋɛ́
      1SG.EMPH 3SG know.IRR COP which.one NEG
      'He went to either Cote d'Ivoire or Cameroon, but I don't know which.'
      [sos170714e]

   b. ăa   bǎrǎ   bà   Sía↘ təgɔ́ Wàgàdǔgǔ
      3SG.PST work do.REAL.PFV Bobo.Q or   Ouagadougou
      'Did he work in Bobo or in Ouaga?' [sos170714e]

It is likely, however, that these are also clause-level disjunctions with ellipsis. The reasoning behind this is that in (19b), a question, the location before the disjunct is marked with falling question intonation, indicating the end of a clause. The same can be seen with PPs with overt postpositions:

(20) mó   ɲà   nă   móò   jəbè   bɛ̀   ă   gɔ̂ɔ-kù
     1SG.EMPH mother PROSP 1SG.EMPH.DAT clothes put.IRR DEF wood-plant
     gṵ̀↘   təgɔ́ cî   bön tɛ̏
     under.Q or   house back GEN
     'Will my mother put my clothes under the tree or behind the house?' [sos170717e]

As a statement, *ou bien* is used:

(21) mó   ɲà   móò   jəbè   bà   gɔ̂ɔ-kù   gṵ̀
     1SG.EMPH mother 1SG.EMPH.DAT clothes put.REAL.PFV wood-plant under
     ou bien   cî   bön tɛ̏
     or.FR well.FR house back GEN
     'My mother put my clothes under the tree or behind the house.' [sos170717e]

11.2.5 Clause-level disjunction

The preference for disjunction in Seenku is clearly clause level. For instance, if a verbal disjunction is offered in elicitation, it is translated with clause-level disjunction in Seenku:

(22) a. á   nɔ́nɛ̋sǎn nɔ̋   ű   á   sú
        2SG food   eat.IRR or.FR 2SG get.up.IRR
        'Either eat or get up!' [sos150622e]

   b. mə̰̂   nă   kȍee   ûu   mə̰̂ɔ́   səmâ
      person PROSP sing.ANTIP.IRR or.FR person.SBJV dance.IRR
      'We will either sing or dance.' [sos150622e]

These are statements rather than questions. When the utterance is a question, the Seenku disjunction *təgɔ́* appears, either in conjunction with its French equivalent (23a) or on its own:

(23) a. est-ce que bon   *gbə̏nə̋-kűi   tsə̋ké dɔ̀-kùi*
    Q.FR   well.FR past-thing.PL and   today-thing.PL
    sɛ́ɛ-kû   nɛ̀ est-ce que *í   wó   kűɛ   tə̋   ì-yɛ̀rɛ̀-mànî*
    Sambla-language LOC Q.FR   2PL EMPH other.PL GEN change.JU
    sǐ ou   bien   *təgɔ́ ì-yɛ̀rɛ̀-mànî ɲá   ŋɛ́*
    be or.FR well.FR or   change.JU be.NEG NEG
    'Well, between things in the past and things today, in your opinion, have they changed or not?' [sos170702t1:21]

  b. *á   kǎ   mó   tɛ̏↘ təgɔ́ á   nǎ   təgǒ   ɲì*
     2SG go.REAL.PFV 1SG.EMPH GEN.Q or   2SG PROSP sit.IRR.NE there
     'Are you going with me or are you staying?' [sos170714e]

The example in (24) shows the same preference for clause-level disjunction, even where English or French would use NP disjunction for the object NPs:

(24) a. *ȁ   sǐ dɔ̌ɔ mǐ   nə̋↘ təgɔ́ ȁ   sǐ jõ̂*
    3SG be beer drink.REAL.NOM LOC.Q or   3SG be water
    mǐ   nə̋
    drink.REAL.NOM LOC
    'Is he drinking beer or water?' [sos170714e]

  b. Parce   que *mó   à   tò   ȁá   jərá*
     because.FR   1SG.EMPH 3SG know.IRR 3SG.SBJV become.REAL.PFV
     nə̋ ì̏   í   bə̋   wə̋ ì̏   Fátárá ou   bien *ì̏   í   bə̋*
     if 3PL LOG do.IRR HAB COMP Fatara or.FR well.FR 3PL LOG do.IRR
     ì̏   Pátárá...
     COMP Patara
     'Because I know if they say Fatara or Patara...' [sos161009t1:51]

The example in (24a) is a question, and hence *təgɔ́* is used; as seen in (19b), the first clause before the disjunction carries falling question intonation; the second clause, introduced by *təgɔ́*, does not. In (24b), on the other hand, the disjunction is not a question. Rather, it is embedded under the verb *tò* 'know'; here, the French *ou bien* is used instead.

11.2.6 'Whether or not' conditionals

'Whether or not' conditionals involve disjunction of two hypothetical possibilities, making them at once conditionals (discussed at length in Chapter 18) and disjunction, addressed in this section. I defer treatment of this construction to §18.6.

12 Verb stems and verbal derivation

The aim of this chapter is to cover the morphological form and function of verb stems, encompassing both simple (non-derived) stems as well as morphologically complex ones that result from verbal derivation.

As previous chapters have laid out, Seenku is not a morphologically rich language, even as far as Mande languages go. Many derivational concepts that other languages mark via affixes, such as causative or passive, are expressed periphrastically in Seenku. Nevertheless, four cases of verbal derivational morphology can be identified. The first of these, the antipassive (§12.3), is suffixing, while transitive pre-verbs (§12.4) and (of course) compound verbs (§12.5) are cases of compounding. Finally, full reduplication of the verb stem can also be used to mark pluractionality (§12.6).

Before turning to these derivational processes, I will first cover the basic morphological properties of non-derived verb stems. Though most of these properties carry over to derived verb stems, some interesting differences can be identified. Section 12.1 discusses the basic properties of verb stems, both transitive and intransitive. In §12.2, I turn to labile verbs, those stems that can be used either transitively or intransitively.

12.1 Verb stems

Verbs in Seenku can be distinguished from other syntactic categories in a number of ways. Functionally, they can serve as the predicate of the sentence without the need for a copular verb (necessary to form a nominal or adjectival predicate). They are also morphologically distinct: They inflect for mood and aspect (Chapter 13) rather than number, and their derivational morphology (discussed below) involves affixes that are unattested on other syntactic categories.

Transitive and intransitive verbs are no different in terms of stem length or segmental make-up, but the two differ tonally. Specifically, a three-way underlying tone contrast (X, H, S) is neutralized to a two-way contrast in many inflectional categories, with intransitive verbs neutralizing H and S to H and transitive verbs neutralizing the two to S. I will address transitive verbs first, then turn to intransitive verbs.

12.1.1 Transitive verbs

Transitive verbs have the same segmental make-up as any roots in Seenku: they are generally mono- or sesquisyllabic, and the vowel can be short or long. The tonal behavior of both transitive and intransitive verb roots is convoluted, with the underlying tone obscured by inflectional properties or sandhi with the direct object, if applicable.

Nevertheless, we can determine that the majority of Seenku transitive verb roots fall into one of the three main tonal classes of the language: X, H, or S.

In the irrealis, the underlying tone of the verb never surfaces, since irrealis verbs undergo argument-head tone sandhi with the preceding object, but the underlying three-way contrast is sometimes maintained in the different outcomes of this tonal process; see §4.4.2 for further discussion. In realis forms, the contrast between H and S is neutralized—to H in the perfective (§13.3.2.1) and to S in nominalized forms like the progressive (§13.3.1).

What this means is that there is no single verb form in which the underlying tone of the verb is pronounced; rather the tonal classes of verbs have to be learned based on the distribution of tonal forms across multiple inflectional categories. Tables 12.1-12.3 below divide transitive verbs into their underlying tone patterns, X, H, and S; an abstract irrealis form is provided showing this tone, alongside the same verb with a 3sg object pronoun, then two realis forms: the lowered perfective stem and the nominalized progressive stem. As the table shows, the realis often has segmental changes associated with it as well. For further discussion of inflection, see the next chapter.

Tab. 12.1: X-toned transitive verb stems

	UR	Irrealis w/3sg	Perfective	Progressive	Gloss
Monosyllabic:	sǎ	à sǎ	sǎ	sǎ	'buy'
	sɛ̀	à sɛ̀	sǐɛ	sǐɛ	'dig'
	kŏo	à kòo	kŏo	kŏo	'count'
	kpɔ̌ɔ	à kpɔ̀ɔ	kpɔ̌ɔ	kpɔ̌ɔ	'sew'
Sesquisyllabic:	sarè̌	à sarè	sarè̌	sarě	'pound'
	təgì̌	à təgì	təgì̌	təgǐ	'erect'
	dəbǎa	à dəbàa	dəbǎa	dəbǎa	'poison'

Tab. 12.2: H-toned transitive verb roots

	UR	Irrealis w/3sg	Perfective	Progressive	Gloss
Monosyllabic	bɔ́	à bɔ̀	búɔ	bűɔ	'take out'
	cɔ́	à cɔ̀	cíɔ	cĩ́ɔ	'scoop'
	gáa	à gàa	gáa	gǎa	'pull'
	sɔ́ɔ	à sɔ̀ɔ	sɔ́ɔ	sɔ̃́ɔ	'sell'
Sesquisyllabic	fəgá	à fəgà	fəgá	fəgǎ	'fill'
	təgá	à təgà	təgá	təgǎ	'divide'
	tərɛ́	à tərɛ̀	tərɛ́	tərɛ̌	'ask'

In these tables, we can see how determining the tonal form of a transitive verb is not straightforward. An underlyingly X-toned verb surfaces as X-toned in the perfec-

Tab. 12.3: S-toned transitive verb roots

	UR	Irrealis w/3sg	Perfective	Progressive	Gloss
Monosyllabic	bǎ	à bá	bá	bǎ	'hit'
	dzǐn	à dzín	dzí	dzǐ	'put'
	měɛ	à méɛ	méɛ	měɛ	'ignite'
	sěɛ	à séɛ	séɛ	sěɛ	'spit out'
Sesquisyllabic:	səbě	à səbɛ́	səbɛ́	səbě	'write'
	səgě	à səgɛ́	səgɛ́	səgě	'filter'
	səměɛ	à səméɛ	səméɛ	səměɛ	'beg'

tive, but otherwise undergoes tonal changes; it raises to L with an X-toned pronoun in argument-head tone sandhi and becomes LS in the progressive. H-toned verbs also show their base tonal form in the perfective, but lower to X with an X-toned pronoun in the irrealis and raise to S in the progressive. S-toned verbs show identical behavior to H-toned verbs in realis forms (H in the perfective, S in the progressive), but diverge in their behavior after an X-toned pronoun in the irrealis.

Tables 12.1-12.3 account for the majority of transitive verb stems in Seenku, but we find other patterns in the lexicon that differ in terms of tone, segmental and syllabic form, or both.

Cases of tonally divergent mono- and sesquisyllabic stems are rare. In the current dataset, only one unequivocal case is attested: *dǎa* 'praise, flatter', which retains an invariably LS tone regardless of whether it is used in the irrealis or the realis, and regardless of inflectional category.

We also find verbs whose stems may be underlyingly mono- or sesquisyllabic, but which are lexicalized as reduplicated. In the progressive, these verbs all tend to surface as H-S (see also §12.5 on the tonal patterns of verb compounds), though the tone patterns can diverge in the irrealis. The attested reduplicated verbs are summarized in Table 12.4; note that the perfective form of these verbs is unattested in the current dataset and thus is omitted.

Tab. 12.4: Reduplicated transitive verb stems

	UR	Irrealis w/3sg	Perfective	Progressive	Gloss
X-S	jěn-jěn	à jèn-jɛ́n	jɛ̌n-jèn	jěn-jěn	'sift'
H-S	krú-krǔ	à krù-krǔ	krú-krû	krú-krǔ	'encircle'
	(nɛ́-)jarán-jarǎn	à nɛ̀-jaràn-jarǎn	nɛ̀-jarán-jarân	nɛ́-jarán-jarǎn	'change'
S-S	gbɛ̌n-gbɛ̌n	à gbɛ́n-gbɛ́n	gbɛ́n-gbên	gbɛ́n-gbɛ̌n	'affix, stick'
	brǐ-brǐ	à brí-brí	brí-brî	brí-brǐ	'go around'

In the progressive, the verbs are largely indistinguishable, with the exception that X-S surfaces with its X tone. Otherwise, both H-S and S-S neutralize to H-S. The underlying tone patterns can be distinguished in the irrealis, where H-S becomes X-X after an X-toned pronoun, and S-S becomes H-H; this is a rare case in which sandhi affects multiple morphemes but does not appear to apply cyclically from left-to-right (in which case we might expect [H-X] for underlying S-S, where the derived non-pronominal H tone causes S to drop to X). See §4.4.2 for more on argument-head tone sandhi.

Finally, we find around a dozen bi- or trisyllabic verb stems, most commonly loanwords from Jula. More often than not, these carry multitonal melodies that behave irregularly in inflection. The attested stems are listed below:

(1) H-H   jábí   'reply'
     H-S   (né-)dóonǎn   'step over'
              sánkǎ   'compete'
              (né-)blěntǎ   '(donkey) roll on the ground'
     H-H-S   ɲáŋgóyǎ   'be jealous'
     X-S   wè̂-kǔkǎ   'scrub (hard object)'
              pǒmpě   'pump'
              màkrǐ   'praise'
              ɲ̀ǐjǎa   'buzz around'
     LS-X   běmbɔ̀   'refuse'
     S-S   bɔ̋mǎa   'hustle'
              ɲəŋǎmɛ̋   'mix'

Most of these stems are missing a complete paradigm in the corpus, and hence I present just a single form, the realis from the progressive here.

12.1.2 Intransitive verbs

Intransitive verb stems do not show any special marking or stem shapes that differentiate them from transitive verbs. Their underlying tonal contrasts are also likely the same (X, H, S), but H and S neutralize to H(X) in both realis and irrealis forms; by virtue of being intransitive verbs, they never carry a direct object that could reveal contrasts via sandhi patterns. As a result, in most cases, it is impossible to say what the underlying tone of a surface H-toned intransitive would be. In a few cases where the same verb stem can be used transitively (labile verbs; §12.2), the underlying form can be identified, but for most verbs, it is not possible.

There are two curious tonal aspects of intransitive verbs that I will discuss below. The first is that, while S generally lowers to H, this cannot be a completely productive process, since we do find a small number of S-toned intransitive verbs. The second is determining why some intransitive verbs carry level H and others carry HX.

X-toned verbs are straightforward, surfacing as expected with X unless they raise to L with a following X-toned aspectual particle (e.g. the habitual, §13.2.2). Examples are listed in (2), with monosyllabic forms in (2a) and sesquisyllabic forms in (2b):

(2)   a.   Monosyllabic:

kà̰	'go' (irrealis: kḛ́ or kṵ́ɔ)
nà̰	'come' (irrealis: nḛ́ or nɛ̰̀)
ɲḭ̀	'run'
cǜɛ	'vomit'
cḭ̀	'die'
dɛ̰̀ɛ	'become accustomed'

b.   Sesquisyllabic:

cèrḛ̀	'sleep'
səbɛ̰̀	'succeed'
səgɔ̰̀	'wrestle'
təgḭ̀	'stand'

With the exception of high frequency verbs 'go' and 'come', these X-toned intransitive verbs would surface the same regardless of whether they are in a realis or irrealis form. Thus, while transitive progressive verbs take a LS surface form, intransitive progressive verbs remain X; see §13.3.1 for further discussion and exemplification.

Surface H(X)-toned verbs, on the other hand, present more of a challenge. On the whole, we find both level H- and HX-toned verbs, but there is no indication that this distinction is contrastive; that is, there are no minimal pairs contrasting H- and HX-toned verbs. But at the same time, it is not free variation, nor is it an entirely predictable distinction based on phonological factors alone. Some factors do favor H over HX, such as vowel length: stems with short vowels tend to carry H, leaving HX generally constrained to long vowels. However, long vowels themselves may carry either HX or H, such as the distinction between kɔ́ɔ 'walk, travel' (also pronounced kɔ̌ɔ with exceptional S tone) and jɔ́ɔ 'stroll'. Further complicating matters are verbs that are H in the irrealis but HX in the realis (or in one case vice versa).

Tables 12.5-12.7 list H- and HX-toned intransitive verbs in their irrealis form (taken from the prospective or imperative) and their realis form (taken from the perfective). The most common H-toned verb stems are simple CV: sú/sío 'get up', tsí 'jump', etc. With more complex syllable structure comes the possibility of HX; we see this with sesquisyllabic stems in Table 12.6, even though their main vowel is still short. We also find CVV stems in this category, like sôo 'dream', which is HX-toned regardless of inflection. This contrasts with a verb like kóo/kôo 'give birth', which is H-toned in the irrealis and HX in the realis. While it is tempting to see the lack of HX on CV verbs as a statement about their tone bearing ability, sâ 'cry (perfective)' in Table 12.7 shows that it is possible for these short stems to host a HX contour; this fact is corroborated elsewhere in the language (e.g. nouns), where HX is in fact the norm regardless of syllable weight (§4.2). We must take these tone patterns to be a lexical peculiarity of intransitive verbs.

Tab. 12.5: H-toned intransitive verb stems

	Irrealis	Perfective	Gloss
Monosyllabic:	só	síɔ	'arrive'
	tsḭ́	tsḭ́	'jump'
	sú	sío	'get up'
	ŋá	ŋá	'ripen (change colors)'
Sesquisyllabic:	kəŋǵ	—	'wake up'

Tab. 12.6: HX-toned intransitive verb stems

	Irrealis	Perfective	Gloss
Monosyllabic:	kɔ́ɔ	kɔ̂ɔ	'walk'
	sôo	sôo	'dream'
Sesquisyllabic:	səmâ	səmâ	'dance'
	jərâ	jərâ	'become'
	gbəgê	gbəgê	'approach'

Tab. 12.7: Mix of H and HX-toned intransitive verb stems

	Irrealis	Perfective	Gloss
Monosyllabic:	sá	sâ	'cry'
	jáa	jîaa	'return'
	fôo	fóo	'detach'
	jɔ́ɔ	jɔ̂ɔ	'stroll'
	kóo	kôo	'give birth'
Sesquisyllabic:	səŋá	səŋâ	'lie down'

We can also ask whether the difference between H and HX verbs can be attributed to an underlying H vs. S. It would appear not. Both 'lie down' and 'get up' are labile verbs (§12.2), able to be used both transitively and intransitively without any overt morphological change. When these stems undergo argument-head tone sandhi with an object, the resulting form shows that they are both underlyingly S-toned (ằ sú 'pick it up', ằ səŋá 'lay it down'), and yet as intransitive verbs, sú is uniformly H-toned while səŋá varies between H and HX. The HX-toned verb stem kɔ́ɔ 'walk' likewise appears to be underlyingly S-toned, since some speakers in fact pronounce the progressive this way (kɔ́ɔ nɛ̋ ~ kɔ́ɔ nɛ̏ 'walking').

Though X- and H(X)-toned verb stems constitute the vast majority of intransitive verbs, there are a few that remain invariably S-toned, except in the perfective, where they lower to H (due to a featural affix marking the perfective; see §13.3.2.1). These stems are listed in (3):

(3)   a.   Monosyllabic:
           jǐ̋   'laugh'
           sɛ̋   'fly'
           sɛ̋ɛ   'heal'

     b.   Sesquisyllabic:
           dəmɑ̋   'shrivel'
           tərɔ̋   'slip'

These stems show that the process lowering S to H in the intransitive is not exceptionless or totally productive.

HS-toned intransitive verbs are rarer still (as underived verbs), but a handful are attested, such as ŋɑ́ɑ̏ 'yawn', ŋúɑ̏ 'breathe', or səgí-səgí nɛ̋ 'have the hiccups', where H-S is mapped onto a reduplicated verb. For HS contour tones on antipassive verbs, see §12.3.1 below.

12.2 Labile verbs

Labile verb stems can be used either transitively or intransitively. This could be viewed as a case of (almost) zero derivation (though it is not possible to identify which form is the base and which the derived); I designate it as "almost" zero derivation, since the verb stem will conform to the tone patterns of either intransitive or transitive verbs (specifically with regards to H/S neutralizations), which can result in tonal alternations. Additionally, some intransitive verbs display vowel lengthening reminiscent of the antipassive (§12.3) but without the other vocalic changes (raising and/or fronting).

X-toned verbs remain more or less unchanged regardless of transitivity, as can be seen in the following examples with the stem təgi̋ 'climb, stand, stop (intr.)' or 'stop, erect (tr.)'.

(4) a. ì-ǎ-lɔ́   sà-bò-kɔ̌ɔ   kʊ́   təgì   wè   ằ
       you.know.JU 2nd.son-billygoat D.DEF stand.IRR HAB 3SG
       sɔ̌-nɛ́n-jʊ̌   jĕn ŋɛ́
       rain-grain-water front NEG
       'You know, billygoat, he won't stand under the rain.' [sos150626t3:2]

   b. ằ   sɪ̰̌ kókó   təgĭ   nɛ̋
       3SG be enclosure erect.REAL.NOM LOC
       'He is building an enclosure.' [sos170721e]

The form in (4b) shows the final S tone characteristic of nominalization in the transitive. Otherwise, the same verb stem is used both intransitively (4a) and transitively (4b) with no change in form.

With H- and S-toned stems, we see alternations between intransitive and transitive uses. (5) shows the corresponding progressive forms of the same S-toned stem used intransitively (5a) and transitively (5b):

(5) a. mó   sɪ̰̌ sənâ   nɛ̏
       1SG.EMPH be lie.down.REAL.NOM LOC
       'I am lying down.' [sos150623e]

   b. mó   sɪ̰̌ dôn sənǎ   nɛ̋
       1SG.EMPH be child lay.down.REAL.NOM LOC
       'I am laying the child down.' [sos150623e]

The intransitive takes the tonal melody HX while the transitive becomes S. The neutralizing nature of these tone changes is shown by comparing (5) with a case of underlyingly H-toned stems in (6):

(6) a. fôo sɪ̰̌ fîɛ   nɛ̏
       wind be blow.REAL.NOM LOC
       'The wind is blowing.' [sos150617e]

   b. mó   sɪ̰̌ pîɔn fíɛ   nɛ̋
       1SG.EMPH be flute blow.REAL.NOM LOC
       'I am playing the flute.' [sos150710e]

The progressive forms are the same here, HX in the intransitive and S in the transitive, despite the fact that the irrealis shows that this verb stem is underlyingly H (ằ fɛ̋ 'blow it' vs. ằ sənǎ 'lay it down').

Table 12.8 lists the attested labile verb stems; transitive verbs are presented in their underlying forms and intransitive verbs are given in their irrealis form. In the case of one verb, there is vowel lengthening in the intransitive, similar to what is seen in the antipassive. The stem in question is transitive kùa 'farm', with intransitive kùaa; if the intransitive were formed through the suffixation of the antipassive, however, we would expect fronting of the vowel to kǔɛɛ. I treat this as an irregular labile stem.

Tab. 12.8: Labile verbs in Seenku

Intransitive		Transitive	
báa	'get worn out'	bǎa	'wear out'
blǎ	'fall'	blǎ	'fell'
bɔ́	'go out'	bɔ́	'take out'
fə̰̀	'enter'	fə̰̀	'put in'
fɛ́	'(wind) blow'	fɛ́	'blow (horn)'
fóo	'come undone'	fóo	'undo'
gɔ̀ɔ	'dry out (intr.)'	gɔ̀ɔ	'dry out (tr.)'
jəgà̰	'go down'	jəgà̰	'take down'
jərâ	'spill (intr.)'	jərá	'pour out'
mɛ́ɛ	'(fire) ignite'	mɛ́ɛ	'light (fire)'
sə̰ná	'lie down'	sə̰ňá	'lay down'
təgḭ̀	'stand, stop'	təgḭ̀	'stop, erect'
tsɔ̰́	'be submerged'	tsɔ̰́	'submerge'

12.3 Antipassive

The single unequivocal case of non-tonal affixation in verbal morphology (both derivational and inflectional) is the antipassive. Though its function and semantics will be discussed in greater depth in §12.3.2 below, antipassive formation in brief is a valency-changing operation that suppresses the verb's internal argument. In other words, it is detransitivizing. It is possible that this morphological process is better characterized as "deobjective", but cognate processes in other Mande languages are referred to in the literature as antipassive, and so I will use that terminology here for consistency.

The antipassive appears to be of limited productivity. Not every verb offered to consultants can be put into the antipassive, and allomorph selection (between its two allomorphs, -i and -ri) is lexically-specific (though trends can be identified). What is more, the verb root in certain antipassive/transitive pairs appears to have undergone different evolutionary paths, such as gərɔ̰̀ 'butcher (transitive)' vs. gɔ̀ɛɛ 'butcher (antipassive)', where the bare root shows the compression of presumed disyllabic *gərɔ to sesquisyllabicity, while the antipassive shows loss of intervocalic [r] resulting in a long vowel. This lack of productivity is unsurprising given the general lack of affixation in the language.

In the subsections below, I will first address the morphophonological form of the antipassive before turning to its meaning. Next, unusual cases in which the internal argument of the verb co-occurs with the antipassive are discussed in §12.3.3. Finally,

I briefly touch on the use of antipassive verbs in deverbal compound nouns, though readers are referred to §7.4 for further exemplification.

12.3.1 Morphophonological form

The Seenku antipassive has two allomorphs that are lexically-specific; that is, each antipassive verb selects for one or the other suffix. While some phonological conditioning can be identified, it is still in many cases an unpredictable choice.

The two allomorphs are *-i* and *-ri*. Given the diachronically unstable nature of intervocalic [r], it is tempting to see these as having a single antipassive ancestor. But in fact, other distantly related Mande languages show reflexes of two antipassive suffixes as well (Creissels 2012). Soninke, for instance, has two suffixes *-i* and *-ndi*, while other languages show only one or the other (e.g. Bozo has *-i* while Mandinka has *-ri*). Creissels analyzes these two suffixes as being the result of different diachronic paths (the former from the reflexive and the latter from a 'do' verb). The same may be true of Seenku, or there may only have been *-ri* with the intermittent loss of intervocalic [r]. I return to this question in §12.3.2 below.

Tab. 12.9: Antipassive verbs with the /-i/ allomorph

bǎ	'hit'	bɛ̌	'rain'
dəgɛ́	'cook, make (tr.)'	dəgêɛ	'cook (intr.)'
jagǐ	'lay, excrete (tr.)'	jagîi	'lay, excrete (intr.)'
jagɔ̌	'eat (stodgy food)'	jagɔ̌ɛ	'eat (stodgy food, intr.)'
kǒo	'sing (tr.)'	kǒee	'sing (intr.)'
kpǐ	'extinguish'	kpîi	'go out, faint'
kpɔ̌	'sew (tr.)'	kpɛ̀ɛ	'sew (intr.)'
ɲɛ̀	'braid (tr.)'	ɲɛ̀ɛ	'braid (intr.)'
ŋmá	'eat (meat)'	ŋmêɛ	'chew'
sǎ	'buy (tr.)'	sɛ̀ɛ	'do some buying'
səbɛ̌	'write (tr.)'	səbêɛ	'write (intr.)'
sɔ́ɔ	'sell'	sîɔɛɛ	'do some selling'

12.3.1.1 Vocalic suffix *-i*

I have suggested an underlying form *-i* for the vocalic antipassive suffix, but on the surface, it always coalesces with the final vowel of the verb root. It is similar to the nominal plural (§5.3.1) in that it raises /a/ to [ɛ] and creates back-front diphthongs from back vowels. But unlike the plural, which was analyzed as a featural suffix [+front], the antipassive often causes the final vowel to lengthen, suggesting that the suffix is itself a full vowel. The exact nature of the vowel itself is unclear, given that it blends with the final vowel of the root. However, it must be front and it must be non-low, given the raising effect on /a/, so for simplicity's sake, I will analyze it as /-i/.

Verb roots that take the /-i/ allomorph of the antipassive are shown in Table 12.9, in their abstract underlying forms and antipassive suffixed forms. Tone patterns will be discussed shortly. This table includes only those verbs that are used predicatively (i.e. as verbs). In §12.3.4 below, other verb roots with the /-i/ suffix are identified in deverbal compounds.

The allomorph /-i/ occurs more commonly after non-high vowels; in the table above, only two out of twelve verb roots have a high vowel. As we will see below for the allomorph /-ri/, the reverse is true. This table also shows that, with the exception of 'hit'/'rain' (which shows evidence of semantic drift and lexicalization), all antipassive verbs show lengthening of the final vowel. Finally, the antipassive form of 'sell' shows unusual palatalization of /s/, presumably from an [i]-initial diphthong.

Tonally, antipassive verbs fit into the broader template in Seenku for intransitive verbs, with S- and H-toned verbs neutralizing to H (realized as HX on long vowels); X remains X. However, unusual HS tone patterns are also attested. I hypothesize that these are the tone patterns imposed on productively formed antipassive verbs, while verbs that have been lexicalized as intransitive verbs fit the regular tonal scheme for such verbs. These tonal realizations are not always stable. For instance, the antipassive of 'buy' is attested in the data corpus as both X-toned and HS-toned:

(7) a. mó sǐ sɛ̀ɛ̀ nɛ̀
       1SG.EMPH be buy.ANTIP.REAL.NOM LOC
       'I am doing some buying.' [sos150623e]

   b. mó sǐ sɛ́ɛ́ nɛ́
       1SG.EMPH be buy.ANTIP.REAL.NOM LOC
       'I am doing some buying.' [sos170802e]

These were spoken by two different speakers, so there may be interspeaker variation in either tone patterns or degrees of lexicalization; however, in the case of (7b), this verb was elicited after another antipassive verb with a HS tone pattern, so it may have primed the antipassive category for an otherwise lexicalized verb. This topic would benefit from further investigation.

12.3.1.2 CV suffix -ri

The antipassive allomorph -ri is found more commonly after roots with a high vowel, as demonstrated by Table 12.10.

Though less common than the vocalic allomorph, the -ri allomorph appears disproportionately with high-vowel roots. In the case of 'put' and 'cut', the antipassive offers a glimpse at the underlying identity of the initial consonant: an alveolar plosive in both cases, which become affricates [dz] and [ts] before high vowels. In the case of

Tab. 12.10: Antipassive verbs with the /-ri/ allomorph

jǔ	'say (tr.)'	júrǐ	'say (intr.)'
dzḭ̌	'put (tr.)'	dərḭ̌	'put (intr.)'
mɪ̰̀	'drink (tr.)'	mərɪ̰̀	'drink (intr.)'
tsí	'cut (tr.)'	tərḭ̌	'cut (intr.)'
səsɛ̌	'look at'	sərɛ́	'look, watch'
bɔ́	'take out'	bərɛ́ɛ̌	'remove (intr.)'

'look', the non-antipassive root has undergone reduplication, absent in the antipassive.

The suffix *-ri* undergoes vowel harmony with the root; for instance, rather than *sɛ́-ri* 'look, watch', the antipassive surfaces as *-rɛ*; the same holds true for the antipassive in *bərɛ́ɛ̌* 'remove (intr.)', from the root *bɔ́* 'take out'. But as we can see, in every case except *jǔ* 'say', the addition of the antipassive suffix co-occurs with sesquisyllabic reduction; in other words, the vowel of the root itself is lost. It is unclear why 'say' is an exception to this process.

Alternatively, we could see this antipassive pattern as synchronically being the combination of an infix /-r-/, after the initial consonant, with the suffix /-i/; this would make this antipassive pattern a case of multiple exponence (Harris 2017). This would still leave unexplained why *jǔ* does not have the antipassive form **jərǔi̯*, though avoidance of back-front diphthongs after [r] is seen elsewhere (§5.3.1.2).

I remain agnostic as to the best analysis of the /-ri/ antipassives and how to tease apart synchrony and diachrony. Given the limited productivity of the pattern, I suspect a diachronic explanation, but future work (including experimental work) may shed light on how current speakers of Seenku treat these alternations.

From a tonal standpoint, the melody HS is more common with *-ri* antipassives. Where the verb has become sesquisyllabic, the vowel of the suffix must lengthen to accommodate the rising tone; in other words, the source of the long final vowels with *-ri* antipassives is not the same as for *-i* antipassives, where it is the result of adding a moraic suffix to another vowel. In *júrǐ* 'say', where the vowel of the root is retained, H-S is distributed across the two syllables. As before, there are verbs whose tone simply falls in line with regular intransitive verbs. This can be seen in *sərɛ́* 'look' (from *(sə)sɛ̌* 'look at') and *mərɪ̰̀* 'drink (intr.)' (from *mɪ̰̀* 'drink (tr.)') above.

12.3.2 Antipassive function and semantics

The antipassive is an intransitivizing operation that takes a transitive verb and suppresses the patient; the agent (subject) remains unchanged. Thus, the prototypical use of the antipassive is as an intransitive verb, though exceptional cases where the antipassive co-occurs with a patient argument are discussed below in §12.3.3. Examples of an underived root and its antipassive counterpart are shown below, with 'sing' in (8a-b) and with 'drink' in (8c-d):

(8) a. m̀ kűɛ bɔ́ wɛ́ kʊ́ tɔ́, m̀ kűɛ kőo
person other.PL take.out.IRR HAB D.DEF like person other.PL sing.IRR
'We created them like that, to sing them.' [sos170822t12:422]

b. m̀ kòee lɛ̋
person sing.ANTIP.IRR.HAB EMPH
'We used to sing!' [sos170822t12:401]

c. ń sḭ̌ dɔ̀ɔ mḭ̌ nɛ̋
1SG be beer drink.REAL.NOM LOC
'I am drinking beer.' [sos150620e]

d. mó sḭ̌ mərḭ̀ nɛ̏
1SG.EMPH be drink.ANTIP.REAL.NOM LOC
'I am drinking.' [sos150620e]

In (8a), the transitive verb 'sing' takes the 3pl emphatic pronoun kűɛ as its object, which is then absent in (8b); similarly, in (8c), the verb 'drink' takes dɔ̀ɔ 'beer' as its object, but no object is present with the antipassive verb in (8d).

12.3.3 Antipassive with an explicit object

Though the very role of the antipassive is to suppress the verb's internal argument, the patient, it is not uncommon to find cases in Seenku in which an antipassive verb is used transitively. All of these cases share a similar semantics of non-totality: the action is performed on the object, but only on a subset. For ease of presentation, I will first provide simple examples from elicitation, then draw on naturally occurring cases in the text corpus.

We can contrast, for example, the transitive verb dzḭ́ and its antipassive form dərḭ̋ used transitively in (9):

(9) a. mó nǎ cɛ̀n-nḭ̀ dzḭ̀ bɔ̀ɔ̃n nɛ̏
1SG.EMPH PROSP peanut-grain.PL put.IRR bag LOC
'I will put peanuts in the bag.' [sos170803e]

b. mó nǎ cɛ̀n-nḭ̀ dərḭ̋ bɔ̀ɔ̃n nɛ̏
1SG.EMPH PROSP peanut-grain.PL put.ANTIP.IRR bag LOC
'I will put some/a few peanuts in the bag.' [sos170803e]

In (9a), the use of the transitive verb creates a general statement about putting peanuts in a bag. Depending upon the context, it could mean all of the peanuts, a handful of peanuts, etc. In (9b), however, with the antipassive verb, the statement obligatorily means just some of the available peanuts (e.g. a handful from a pile). There is also a greater morphophonological division between the object and verb in (9b), with the verb resisting argument-head tone sandhi with the object, though this may be due to the fact that the verb carries a complex tone melody; see §4.4.2 for discussion of tone sandhi and the immutability of complex tone.

Another example is provided in (10) with the same partitive meaning:

(10) a. mó lɛ̌ bǐ sɔ́ɔ
 1SG.EMPH PST goat.PL sell.REAL.PFV
 'I sold (the) goats.' [sos150623e]

 b. mó lɛ̌ bǐ sìɔ̃ɛɛ
 1SG.EMPH PST goat.PL sell.ANTIP.PRF
 'I have sold some of the goats.' [sos150623e]

Using the transitive verb in (10a) is neutral: it could be all of the goats one intended to sell or some goats. In (10b), the use of the antipassive suggests that only a part of the goats were sold; others remain in the possession of the seller.

Curiously, in some cases, the HS tone pattern appears when the antipassive verb is used transitively and not when it is used intransitively:

(11) a. mó sĭ sɛ̰̀ɛ nɛ̀
 1SG.EMPH be dig.ANTIP.REAL.NOM LOC
 'I am digging.' [sos150623e]

 b. mó sĭ tònkű sɛ́ɛ́ nɛ̋
 1SG.EMPH be hole dig.ANTIP.REAL.NOM LOC
 'I am digging some holes.' [sos150623e]

It may be that the intransitive verb patterns variably override the antipassive HS when the verb is used intransitively, but when an object is present, this force is reduced. Another interesting difference to note between the antipassive verb and its underived root is that the antipassive version tends not to show realis stem modifications (§13.1); the regular transitive verb 'dig' in the realis is sɪ̀ɛ.

Textual examples of antipassive verbs used transitively are shown in (12):

(12) a. ǎá   kằ   nɛ́ ǎá   kôo   nɛ́ ằ   jəmɯ̀
       3SG.SBJV go.REAL.PFV if 3SG.SBJV give.birth.REAL.PFV if DEF bush
       ằa   sò̰-bṵ̂n   tə̰rɯ̰́
       3SG.SUBORD horse-grass cut.ANTIP.IRR
       'If she goes and gives birth in the bush, where she cuts horse grass.'
       [sos170805t9:2]

   b. á kɛ̋   ằ nɔ́   á cèn-nḭ̀   də̰rɯ̰́   á tḛ̀
       2SG go.IRR 3SG eat.IRR 2SG peanut-grain put.ANTIP.IRR 2SG GEN
       jŏ̰fá̰   nɛ̋
       pocket LOC
       'You go and eat it, you put some peanuts in your pockets.' [sos170714t3:94]

In (12a), the use of the antipassive verb tə̰rɯ̰́ 'cut' implies cutting a portion of horse grass from a larger field. In (12b), the natural example that inspired (9), the use of the antipassive implies that just a few peanuts are put into the pocket.

12.3.4 Antipassive verbs in deverbal compounds

While antipassive verbs are found as verbal predicates, one of the most common places they are found in Seenku is in deverbal compound nouns. This is reminiscent of the patterns seen in Mandinka (Creissels 2012), where the *-ri* antipassive is commonly found in agent and instrumental nominalizations. Some Seenku examples are listed in (13):

(13) dəgêɛ-sə̰rằ   'cook, chef'   < dəgêɛ 'cook (intr.)'
     dɔ̀ɔ-mə̰rɯ̰́-kɯ̰̋   'calabash for beer'   < mə̰rɯ̰̀ 'drink (intr.)'
     kʊ̀-bə̰rɛ́ɛ-tŏ̰ɔn   'dish for toh'   < bə̰rɛ́ɛ̋ 'take out (intr.)'
     sṵ̆mə̰ŋắ-tsḭ̆ɛɛ-jṵ́rḭ́-ŋɛ̋ 'preachers'   < jṵ́rḭ́ 'say (intr.)'
                             (lit. sayers of god's words)

The first example in the table, 'chef', understandably contains an antipassive verb, as no object is present. The others, however, explicitly contain the patient role in the instrumental or agentive compound: a calabash for drinking beer, a dish for toh, one who says God's words. Nevertheless, the antipassive verb is used.

For further discussion, see §7.4.

There appears to be a link between the antipassive and nominalization, even beyond compound nouns. Consider the following examples:

(14) a. ằ sḭ̆ɔ̰ɛɛ   ɲá bò̰   ŋɛ́
        3SG sell.ANTIP.NOM be.NEG anymore NEG
        'There's no question of selling anymore.' [sos170803e]

b. à kéɛ́ ɲá bɔ̈ ŋɛ́
   3SG go.ANTIP.NOM be.NEG anymore NEG
   'She can't go anywhere anymore (There's no question of going anymore).'
   [sos170714t3:115]

In (14a), the transitive stem sɔ́ɔ takes its antipassive form síɔ́ɛɛ and acts as a noun with the negative existential verb ɲá; more surprising is the example in (14b), where an antipassive is built off of an intransitive verb kà/kɛ̃́ 'go', which has no patient role to suppress in the first place. Constructions like these raise the question of whether the antipassive is accidentally homophonous with a nominalization strategy rather than being the nominalization strategy itself. I leave this question to future theoretical work, and will continue to gloss forms like this as the antipassive throughout the grammar.

12.4 Transitive pre-verbs

In addition to the valency-decreasing antipassive, Seenku also shows a valency-increasing operation: transitive "pre-verbs". Attested across Mande languages, these prefixal pre-verbs are typically derived from postpositions, and the Seenku data are no exception. The two most common pre-verbs in Seenku are né- and wè-, derived from the locative (§10.1.5) and the associative (§10.1.7), respectively. Sporadic cases of a pre-verb lɛ̃́-, presumably related to the dative (§10.1.9), are also attested. For treatment of pre-verbs in other Mande languages, see Keïta (1989), Vydrin (2009), and Shluinsky (2014), among others.

The pre-verbs have been treated as verbal prefixes, in e.g. Shluinsky (2014), but they depend phonologically on the preceding object, just as their related postpositions do. In this regard, they act more like enclitics, phonologically grouped with the preceding word and undergoing argument-head tone sandhi, though morphologically they appear to be part of the following verb. In order to make explicit this latter grouping, however, I will transcribe them as prefixes, attached to the verb with a hyphen.

Each preverb will be treated in its own subsection below. The semantics of these transitive pre-verbs are highly varied; no clear patterns of use can be identified, and deeper study of their meanings could be a volume unto itself. Here, I aim to simply document attested cases of transitive pre-verbs and suggest semantic patterns where possible.

12.4.1 né-

The transitive preverb né- has its origins in the locative postposition. Like the locative, the preverb né- is underlyingly H-toned, which can be deduced from its sandhi patterns with the preceding object. It is the most common of the preverbs and the most consistent in that the resulting verb is always transitive (hence the term "transitive pre-verbs"). However, there is no such consistency in the semantics. It is not the case that it acts as a causative, adding a new agent role, given that many verbs with and without the preverb have very similar semantics.

For example, the underived verb *bǎ* 'beat, hit' is already transitive, involving an agent and a patient; this verb may take the transitive prefix *né-*, which alters the meaning slightly. Depending upon context, *né-bǎ* can mean either 'hurt (sb), beat (sb) up' or 'mash seeds with a stone to extract oil'. Similarly, the labile verb *fà̰* can mean either 'enter' as an intransitive verb or 'put in' as a transitive verb. With the prefix *né-*, it can be used in the context of sucking in one's stomach: *â səgö̃n ně-fà̰* 'suck in your stomach!'. In both of these cases, it is not clear exactly what it is that the transitive prefix adds.

The semantic murkiness of the transitive preverb *né-* can be felt in full looking at the attested verbs listed in Table 12.11.

Tab. 12.11: Verbs with transitive preverb *né-* and their underived counterparts

né-bǎ	'mash seeds (for oil)'	bǎ	'hit, beat'
né-bǎ	'beat up, hurt'	bǎ	'hit, beat'
né-bɔ́	'sift grains'	bɔ́	'remove'
né-bɔ́	'move far away'	bɔ́	'go out'
né-fà̰	'suck in (stomach)'	fà̰	'put inside'
né-fɛ́	'winnow grain'	fɛ́	'blow on'
né-frɔ́	'puncture'	frɔ́	'puncture'
né-kɛ́ɛ	'break up'	kɛ́ɛ	'break'
né-nɛ́ɛ	'coil up'	nɛ́ɛ	'coil up'
né-təgǎ	'divide'	təgǎ	'share'
né-təgò	'remind'	təgò	'seat (sb)'
né-tɛ̀	'lean back (in chair)'	tɛ̀	'show'
né-tsḭ́	'cut across (road, field)'	tsḭ́	'cut'
né-tsḭ́-tsḭ́	'cut into pieces'	tsḭ́	'cut'
né-tsɔ́	'crush'	tsɔ́	'submerge'

The uses range from an intensifying one ('crush' vs. 'submerge'), to one that renders the verb more figurative ('cut across (road, field)' vs. 'cut'), to no difference in meaning whatsoever ('puncture' or 'coil up'). Note that *né-təgò* 'remind' must be used with the object *nəgí* 'mind' (e.g. *mó nəgì nè-təgò* 'remind me!').

In other cases, it becomes impossible to untangle the meaning of the prefix, since the derived verb has no attested underived counterpart:

(15) né-bléntǎ '(donkey) roll on ground'
né-brɔ̌ 'press out oil'
né-dəgɛ̀ 'do quickly'
né-dóonǎn 'step over'
né-jərán-jərǎn 'change'
né-jǜɛ 'tear'
né-ką̀ 'verify'
né-kę́ 'uncrumple'
né-kŏo 'scrape'
né-kɔ́ 'break open'
né-cənɨ̌ 'barter'
né-nəgɔ̌ 'knead'
né-səgá 'pound fruits'
né-sɔ̌ɔ 'push, come close'
né-tą́ 'crush (bone to get marrow)'

The transitive prefix always undergoes argument-head tone sandhi with the preceding object; whether or not the verb stem itself participates depends, as usual, on whether the verb is realis or irrealis.

For instance, consider the following two examples:

(16) a. ì nǎ wétənɛ̌ ằ nɛ̏-fɛ̀
3PL PROSP now 3SG TRANS-blow.IRR
'They are going to winnow it now.' [sos170714t3:153]

b. mó nǎ ń nəgì nɛ̀-təgò í səgɔ̌
1SG.EMPH PROSP 1SG mind TRANS-sit.IRR LOG good
'I'm going to remember well.' [sos161009t1:124]

In (16a), both the transitive prefix and the verb stem are H. With the X-toned object pronoun, ằ + né becomes ằ nɛ̏-, and this X-toned prefix then causes fɛ́ to likewise drop to X. In (16b), the transitive prefix is H but the verb stem is X. When the final H of ń nəgí 'my mind' (itself a sandhi domain) comes into contact with the transitive prefix, it causes it to drop to X, as in (16a). But when this X tone is combined with the verb stem's X, the whole stretch of X tones raises to L.

The following elicited example shows how the verb root is impervious to sandhi when in the realis, even though sandhi still occurs between the object and the transitive prefix:

(17) mənǐ sɪ̌ ằ nɛ̏-fíɛ nɛ́
woman be 3SG TRANS-blow.REAL.NOM LOC
'The woman is winnowing it.' [sos150704e]

The root *fíɛ* remains S-toned, despite the preceding X-toned prefix. The same sandhi rules apply to all of the transitive prefixes, with exact alternations dependent upon the suffix's underlying tone as per regular argument-head sandhi patterns (§4.4.2).

12.4.2 wɛ̀-

The preverb *wɛ̀-* has its origins in the associative postposition *wɛ̀* ('with'). There are fewer verbs that take this preverb as compared to *né-*, which makes identifying any semantic patterns even more difficult.

I begin by giving derived verbs whose roots are not bound, i.e. those cases where the underived verb is also present in the lexicon, in Table 12.12.

Tab. 12.12: Verbs with transitive preverb *wɛ̀-* and their underived counterparts

wɛ̀-fəgɔ̀	'clean, wash'	fəgɔ̀	'bathe (tr. or intr.)'
wɛ̀-fì	'toss wet mudbrick onto wall'	fì	'throw'
wɛ̀-gɔ̀ɔ	'warm oneself up by fire'	gɔ̀ɔ	'dry'
wɛ̀-jəgà	'bend over, tilt'	jəgà	'go down'

The verb stem *fəgɔ̀* can be used transitively or intransitively, with the meaning of 'bathe (a person)'; with the transitive prefix, the verb stem can now be used to indicate the cleaning of other things, like dishes, houses, or even pounded millet. The addition of the transitive prefix to the verb 'throw' narrows it semantically, to mean throwing wet mudbrick onto a wall when plastering a house. In the case of 'dry', adding the transitive broadens the meaning slightly, to general warming up rather than drying out specifically. The case of 'go down' is similar, where adding the transitive prefix refers to a tilt rather than an actual larger displacement downwards.

There are more cases of transitive verbs with *wɛ̀-* with no underived counterpart. These are shown in (18):

(18) wɛ̀-dəgɛ̀   'go into hiding'
      wɛ̀-gĩi   'clean (used as a participle)'
      wɛ̀-jəgá   'rinse'
      wɛ̀-kö̀ká   'scrub (hard surface)'
      wɛ̀-nəgɔ̀   'replaster mudbrick roof'
      wɛ̀-ŋüɔ   'scratch'

Note that *wɛ̀-jəgá* 'rinse' forms a tonal minimal pair with *wɛ̀-jəgà* 'tilt'.

12.4.3 lɛ̋-

Most of the preverbs originated in the locative and the associative, as described in the last subsections. A very small number, however, can be tied back to the dative lɛ̋ (see §10.1.9). The three clearest cases are illustrated in (19):

(19) a. á lɛ̏-jȕ kɛ̏
2SG TRANS-say.IRR EMPH
'Introduce yourself!' [sos150626t5:14]

b. mɛ́ɛ lɛ̏ à lɛ́-kpá̰ nɛ̋
REL.PRO REL.SBJV 3SG TRANS-close.REAL.NOM LOC
'The one who is playing the accompaniment...' [sos170711t1:197]

c. mó nǎ à lɛ́-dɔ̋ɔ
1SG.EMPH PROSP 3SG TRANS-fray.IRR
'I will fray it.' [sos170811e]

In (19a-b), the root is also attested in underived environments, but in (19c), it is not clear whether the root dɔ̋ɔ is related to homophonous verbs 'finish' or 'snatch'; the semantic connection seems tenuous. The verb in (19b) is constrained to the specific case of the middle player of a balafon "closing" the space between the two more advanced players seated across from him playing the treble and bass. The transitive-marked lɛ̋-jǔ likewise has narrower semantics than general jǔ 'say'; it is used to mean both 'introduce', as in (19a), and 'explain'.

We find two Jula loanwords that appear to be derived in a similar fashion, though using lá- rather than lɛ̋-. These are illustrated in (20):

(20) a. ì təgö wétənɛ̋ ì kʊ́ lá-mɛ̰́
3PL sit now 3PL D.DEF listen.JU.IRR
'They sat now to listen to it.' [sos150626t6:36]

b. mó ɲà̰ blɛ̆ lɛ̋ mó lá-mɔ̀
1SG.EMPH mother big PST 1SG.EMPH raise.JU.REAL.PFV
'My grandmother raised me.' [sos150617e]

As loanwords, they are also resistent to argument-head tone sandhi; neither the level H sequence after kʊ́ in (20a) nor the S-X pattern after mó in (20b) are typically found on native Seenku verbs.

12.5 Compound verbs

In addition to verbs derived through affixation (or the incorporation of erstwhile postpositions), Seenku also displays a small number of compound verbs. These can be split into two broad groups: noun-verb compounds and verb-verb compounds. I will treat each group separately below.

12.5.1 Noun-verb compounds

Noun-verb compounds are more common than verb-verb compounds. They have almost exclusively relational body part terminology as their initial nominal element, most commonly *dzú* 'mouth (outer)' and *dán* 'mouth (inner)', but are also attested with *kɔ̌n* 'head', *brɔ̂* 'liver', and *gú* 'neck'. Given the fact that postpositions in many Mande languages evolved from relational nouns, such noun-verb compounds have been considered under the heading of preverbs in other Mande languages, such as Kla-Dan (Makeeva 2009). In Seenku, however, nouns and postpositions are more tenuously related (with the exception of *kɔ̌n* 'head' and the postposition *kɔ̀n* 'on'); thus, I consider them here as a separate processes, though one could argue that they are part and parcel of the same phenomenon.

While it is clear that these noun-verb combinations form a semantic unit in Seenku, as similar combinations do in many other Mande languages, it is not always clear what the best morphosyntactic analysis of the constructions are. As Khachaturyan (2017) summarizes in a treatment of Mano noun-verb compounds, these constructions have fallen under various headings, from compounds, to idioms, to noun incorporation. In this treatment, I will privilege the term "compound" as a simple way to express the tight relationship between the two stems and the unpredictable semantics of the resulting form.

As with the transitive preverbs, the noun of noun-verb compound phrases phonologically with the object. It is these two, rather than the compound noun-verb itself, that obligatorily undergo argument-head tone sandhi, with the object ostensibly acting as a possessor of the relational noun; of course, when the verb is inflected for irrealis, the verb stem too is incorporated into this sandhi domain. From a phrasing standpoint, then, a noun-verb compound is indistinguishable from a complex NP object and a simplex verb, as the following example shows:

(21) a. *mó   sı̆ ń dzṳ̈ kpǎ   nɛ̋*
         1SG.EMPH be 1SG mouth close.REAL.NOM LOC
         'I am closing my mouth.'

b. à   sḭ̀ mó   dzʊ̀-tsío   nɛ̰́
    3SG be 1SG.EMPH mouth-meet.REAL.NOM LOC
    'He is replying to me.' [sos150617e]

In (21a), the noun *dzʊ́* 'mouth' is possessed by the 1sg, which triggers sandhi creating *ń dzʊ̀*; this complex noun phrase is the object of the verb *kpā̰* 'close'. In (21b), the verb is a compound *dzʊ́-tsío* 'reply', or literally 'mouth-meet'. Though from a semantic standpoint, *dzʊ́-tsío* is the compound form, the initial noun still phrases phonologically with the object *mó*; it acts as a possessor, triggering *dzʊ́* to lower its tone to X.

It is difficult to say with certainty whether these noun-verb combinations in Seenku are compounds or simply idiomatic phrasal verbs. One of the most common criteria for distinguishing compound nouns from phrases is separability: can the noun and verb (in this case) be separated with intervening material? Unfortunately, Seenku offers few means of testing the hypothesis due to its rigid constraints on word order. Only one object can precede the verb (meaning the noun could not be separated by another object), and even adverbs must be post-verbal. The only morphosyntactic means we are left with to test whether the noun forms part of the compound is to inflect the noun or embed it in more complex noun phrases.

Since the nouns are inalienable/relational nouns, they must obligatorily have a possessor (the direct object plays this role with noun-verb compounds), and the presence of a possessor reduces the probability that the noun will carry an additional determiner like the demonstrative *bɛ̰́* (see §8.2.3). Thus, the fact that we never see an intervening determiner between the noun and the verb is not surprising.

A small bit of evidence that noun-verb combinations are not phrasal can be found in the fact that the noun cannot be modified by an adjective, nor is it inflected for plural, which the same noun would be when used outside of the compound. For instance, the noun *dzʊ́* 'mouth' in the noun-verb compound *dzʊ́-tsío* 'respond, talk back' does not inflect for plural, even when the object (its possessor) is plural:

(22) à   sḭ̀ mí́ dzʊ́-tsío   nɛ̰́
      3SG be 1PL mouth-meet.REAL.NOM LOC
      'He is responding to us.' [sos150617e]

Despite the fact that the possessor is plural, and thus by definition multiple mouths would be involved, the plural *dzʊ̆ɛ* is ungrammatical. This can be contrasted with a simplex verb for which 'mouth' is the object; in this case, a plural possessor is most naturally accompanied by a plural noun. The following example employs the word for the inner mouth *dán* rather than the outer mouth:

(23) mí́ sḭ̀ í dḛ̀   fəgā̰   nɛ̰́
      1PL be LOG mouth.PL fill.REAL.NOM LOC
      'We are filling our mouths.' [sos150620e]

I say "most naturally" since consultants will often accept forms in which the possessor is plural but the possessed noun is singular, but usually with a caveat that "it sounds like they speak Seenku in Bobo-Dioulasso" or some other indication that it is not "good" Seenku. Nevertheless, consulants have offered singular nouns with plural possessors in other contexts in the corpus when number was not the focus of discussion, such as the following:

(24) ǎ sį̌ kű́ɛ dǎn fəgǎ nɛ̋
 3SG be others mouth fill.REAL.NOM LOC
 'He is filling their mouths.' [sos150620e]

Thus, number marking on the object noun or noun in a compound may not be the best indicator of compound status.

These verbs may also form a spectrum, from true compounds like dzṹ-tsı́o 'respond' that resist inflection of the noun and are not semantically transparent to combinations like kɔ̂n-tsı̨́ 'slaughter', which is more semantically transparent (literally 'head-cut') and the noun inflects for plural:

(25) ǎ nǎ mı̋ kɔ̂ɛ-tsı̨́
 3SG PROSP 1PL head.PL-cut.IRR
 'He will slaughter us.' [sos171006e]

I suspect that there may be cases of interspeaker variation, with some speakers analyzing a combination as a phrase and others treating the combination as a compound, but a large corpus study would be needed to test this hypothesis.

The attested noun-verb compounds are given in Table 12.13, organized by the identity of the noun.

Tab. 12.13: Noun-verb compounds in Seenku

	Compound	Literal gloss	Gloss
a.	dzṹ-bǎ	mouth-do	'light (fire)'
	dzṹ-blǎ́	mouth-fall	'knock it off/let it go'
	dzṹ-kpǎ́	mouth-close	'cover'
	dzṹ-tsı́o	mouth-take.back	'reply'
	dzṹ-tsı̨́	mouth-cut	'give first (to the balafon)'
b.	dán-cɛ̋	mouth-open	'open'
c.	kɔ̂n-bűɔ	head-remove	'winnow'
	kɔ̂n-kű	head-catch	'meet'
	kɔ̂n-sɛ̋	head-look	'look up'
	kɔ̂n-tsı̨́	head-cut	'slaughter'
d.	brɔ̂-fı̀ɛ	liver-heat	'make someone angry'
e.	gű-ɲı́	neck-lift	'pick up, straighten up'

Some combinations, like 'give first (to the balafon)' are clearly semantically opaque, while others like 'open' or 'close' are quite transparent. I have grouped them together with noun-verb compounds, but they are likely towards the phrasal end of the spectrum.

12.5.2 Verb-verb compounds

Verb-verb compounds are less common than noun-verb compounds, but they are more clearly compounds, since there is no longer an option of treating them as possessed nouns or otherwise forming a complex object. The two clearest cases both involve the verb *tsį̋* 'cut' as the compound-initial stem. These are given in (26):

(26) *tsį̋-bɔ̋*   cut-take.out   'explain, retell, get engaged'
      tsį̋-kų́   cut-catch   'start'

However, there is the possibility that rather than the verb 'cut', these involve the bound root *tsį̋n* found in compound nouns like *tsį̋n-gų́* 'lower half' or *tsį̋n-ŋmǎ* 'upper half'. I will treat them as verbs here.

The tonal behavior of these verb-verb compounds is the same as noun-verb compounds: the initial verb stem always undergoes sandhi with the preceding object, regardless of whether the verb is inflected for realis or irrealis, while the second stem will also join the sandhi domain if it is irrealis. The following two examples show the same verb in the progressive, first with an X-toned pronominal object and then with an S-toned object noun:

(27) a. mó   sį̋   ǎ   tsį̋-bű̋ɔ   ně̋   ǎ   lɛ́
         1SG.EMPH be 3SG cut-take.out.REAL.NOM LOC 3SG DAT
         'I am retelling it to him.' [sos170728e]

     b. mó   sį̋   mənı̋ tsį̋-bű̋ɔ   ně̋
         1SG.EMPH be woman cut-take.out.REAL.NOM LOC
         'I am getting engaged to the woman.' [sos170728e]

In (27a), *ǎ* causes *tsį̋* to lower to H. In (27b), the S on *mənı̋* 'woman' vacuously triggers S on *tsį̋*. Note that in both cases, *bű̋ɔ* retains the S tone characteristic of the progressive.

In the irrealis, the sandhi tone of the first verb stem triggers sandhi on the second:

(28) ń   kě̋   ǎ   tsį̋-bɔ̋
      1SG go.IRR 3SG cut-take.out.IRR
      'I will go retell it.' [sos150805e]

Other compound verbs are less clear. For instance, *tá-fɛ̰̋* 'heat' looks at first glance to be a compound verb, consisting of a tonally different version of *tà* 'cook (sauce, toh)' and *fɛ̰̋* for 'hot' or 'heat', as in the following examples:

(29) a. mó sḭ̌ jô tà-fḭɛ nɛ̋
    1SG.EMPH be water cook-heat.REAL.NOM LOC
    'I am heating the water.' [sos150630e]

   b. mó tà-fɛ̰̀
    1SG.EMPH cook-heat.IRR
    'Heat me!' [sos150630e]

The tone pattern in (29b) shows that *tá* cannot have the same X tone as *tà* 'cook', otherwise the H-toned pronoun would raise it to S, creating a surface form *mó tă-fɛ̰̋*.

However, other forms suggest that *tá* may in fact be a noun (possibly related to *tâ* 'fire'), separable from the verb:

(30) jô tà sḭ̌ fɛ̰̋ nɛ̋
    water fire? be heat.IRR LOC
    'The water is heating up.' [sos150630e]

Here in the intransitive, *tà* remains with the experiencer, which is now the subject; it is separated from the main verb by the auxiliary *sḭ̌*. We also see a curious tone change on the verb stem, from X in the transitive to S in the intransitive. More data are needed to unravel this case, since in other instances, the intransitive verb remains X-toned:

(31) à̰ bŏ-kɔ̌ɔ tă-fḭɛ âa
    DEF billygoat cook-heat.REAL.PFV NEG.Q
    'The billygoat warmed up, didn't he.' [sos150626t4:29]

A final class of possible verbal compounds is synchronically opaque. These are compounds that end in the stem *sò̰* or *só*. We find two such verbs, listed in the following table:

(32) kằn-sò̰   'wait for'
    tằa-só   'surprise'

First, 'wait for' is fairly regular in its behavior, shown in the following examples:

(33) a. mó kắn-ső
    1SG.EMPH wait.for.IRR
    'Wait for me!' [sos150620e]

   b. à kàn-sò
    3SG wait.for.IRR
    'Wait for him!' [sos150620e]

The second verb, *tằa-só*, is irregular. It is common in this form in texts, as the following examples indicate:

(34) a. ȋȋ   kɛ́   tằa-só   mɔ̰̀ɛ   kúrúȋȋ kʊ́   nɛ̰̀   cèrè
       LOG.SUBORD go.IRR surprise person.PL all.PL D.DEF LOC sleep.IRR
       wè
       HAB
       'To my surprise, everyone was sleeping.' [sos161009t1:42]

   b. ɛ̰̌ɛ́   fṵ̀ɛ mɛ̰̀   kɛ́   tằa-só   ằ   bö̀-kɔ̃ɔ   lê
       LOG.DAT wife SUBORD go.IRR surprise DEF billygoat PRES
       'His wife went, and to her surprise, it was a billygoat.' [sos150626t4:13]

   c. mɛ̰̀   jəgǎ-jəgằ   wétənɛ̌ ɲì-nà   mɛ̰̀   ằ
       COMP RED-go.down.REAL.PFV now   there-towards 3SG.SUBORD 3SG
       tằa-só   ằ   bɛ́   wé mɔ̰̀ɛ   dəgɔ̌aa
       surprise 3SG do.IRR FOC person.PL between
       'When he had gone down there now, to his surprise, he was surrounded by people.' [sos170711t1:6]

The form is consistently in the irrealis in texts, typically following the 3sg subordinate marker *mɛ̰̀* or the irrealis form of 'go' *kɛ́*. In elicitation, I tried to get 'surprise' in different inflections, with interesting results:

(35) a. á   mó   tằa-wö̀
       2SG 1SG.EMPH surprise.REAL.PFV
       'You surprised me.' [sos150623e]

   b. á   nǎ   tằa   mó   nɛ̰̀ ŋé
       2SG PROSP surprise 1SG.EMPH LOC NEG
       'Don't surprise me!' [sos150623e]

In the perfective, *-só* is replaced with *-wö̀*. In the imperative, an irrealis form that we might expect to have the same form as that found in texts, we find instead an unsuffixed form *tằa*. However, both of these are transitive uses of 'surprise' as opposed to the intransitive form found in texts. Regardless, the verb is irregular and will require more data to clarify.

12.6 Pluractional reduplication

The final type of verbal derivation to discuss is derivational reduplication. Here, we must distinguish between two kinds: unproductive lexical reduplication and productive pluractional reduplication. In §12.1 above, we saw that some verb stems are lexically reduplicated: that is, an unreduplicated form is unattested, and there is no clear semantic contribution of the reduplication (though some stems, like 'have the hiccups', is consistent with a pluractional reading).

In contrast to the lexically reduplicated verbs, Seenku also has a productive pluractional reduplication process. Pluractionality in Seenku is event-related rather than participant-related. That is to say, a reduplicated pluractional verb expresses that the event takes place multiple times in a row rather than happening once with multiple participants. Further, the typical reading of pluractional reduplication in Seenku is what has been characterized as "event-internal" or repetitive (Wood 2007) rather than "event-external" or iterative, where the multiple events are spaced out over time.

We can see this reading clearly in the following example, contrasting the unreduplicated and reduplicated versions of the verb *tsí̧* 'cut':

(36) a. mí̋ nǎ gɔ̂ɔ tsì̧
 1PL PROSP wood cut.IRR
 'We will cut wood.' [sos150706e]

 b. mí̋ nǎ gɔ̂ɔ nɛ̏-tsì̧-tsì̧
 1PL PROSP wood TRANS-RED-cut.IRR
 'We will cut the wood into pieces.' [sos150706e]

The unreduplicated verb in (36a) has a rather neutral semantics. The degree and manner of cutting is not specified and can be read from the context. In (36b), on the other hand, the reduplication of the verb encodes multiple cutting strokes as part of the same event, with the result that the wood ends up being cut into multiple pieces. A very similar case is found with *nɛ-təgǎ* 'divide up' and *nɛ-təgǎ-təgǎ* 'divide into multiple small quantities'; the pluractionality is event-internal.

Transparent pluractional semantics can be found with intransitive verbs as well, such as the following:

(37) a. frɔ̏ sı̧̆ tsı̧́ nɛ̏
 monkey be jump.REAL.NOM LOC
 'The monkey is jumping.' [sos150811e]

 b. frɔ̏ sı̧̆ tsı̧́-tsı̧́ nɛ̏
 monkey be RED-jump.REAL.NOM LOC
 'The monkey is jumping up and down.' [sos150811e]

Once more, the reduplicated verb in (37b), compared with the simple verb in (37a), indicates that the monkey is jumping over and over again.

From texts, we find examples like the following:

(38) ké á wó nă à nè-bà̰-bà̰ á sɔ́ɔ̀ á
 COP 2SG EMPH PROSP 3SG TRANS-RED-hit.IRR 2SG be.able.IRR.HAB 2SG
 wóo à fəgà̰ bɔ̀ âa
 EMPH.SBJV 3SG oil take.out.IRR NEG.Q
 'Are you going to beat it and beat it until its oil comes out?' [sos170822t2:159]

The use of *né-bá̰-bá̰* implies beating or mixing the ground shea nuts again and again until the oil comes out; the pluractional reduplication is indicating an action repeated in close succession.

13 Verbal inflection

Having introduced verb stem formation in the last chapter, I turn now to verbal inflection—how those stems are inflected for tense, aspect, mood, and negation. The main inflectional features realized on the verb itself are mood and aspect; tense is typically encoded through auxiliary verbs or TAMP markers, and negation is always marked with a clause-final negative particle *né*, though one auxiliary has an irregular negative form.

Verb inflection in Seenku is best understood hierarchically, illustrated in Figure 13.1 with the main inflectional categories:

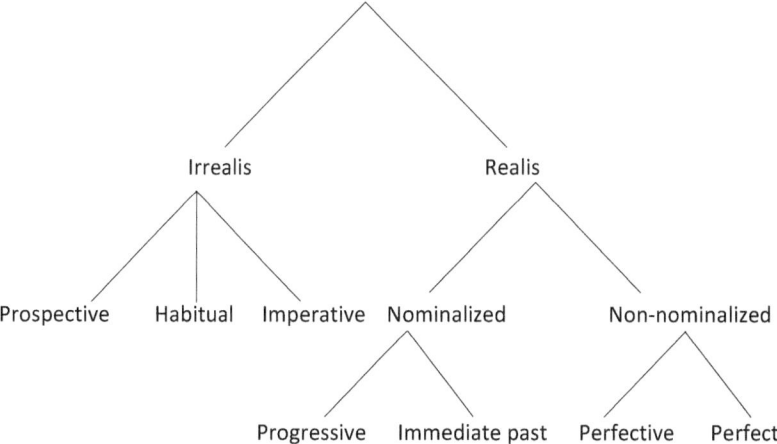

Fig. 13.1: Inflectional hierarchy of Seenku verbs

The first split divides verbs into two basic stem forms based on mood, corresponding to irrealis and realis. The two stem forms are distinguished by tonal behavior and in many cases also by the presence or absence of a high-initial diphthong triggering palatalization on many consonants; formal differences between the two are discussed in §13.1, before turning to the aspects that fall under the irrealis and realis headings themselves in §13.2 and §13.3, respectively. Realis forms are further split into two broad classes: those that use a nominalized stem (in conjunction with a postposition) and those that do not. The former are addressed in §13.3.1 and the latter in §13.3.2 below. In addition, the stative/resultative construction uses a participle derived from the realis stem; this construction is discussed in §13.3.3. At the end of the chapter, I turn briefly to tense (§13.4) and negation (§13.5).

13.1 Mood: irrealis and realis stems

As the split above indicated, verb stems in Seenku have two forms: a realis form and an irrealis form. For arguments that it is indeed reality status underlying the stem split, I refer the reader to McPherson (2017c). I will also briefly touch on the motivations in §13.2 and §13.3 below.

There are two main ways in which irrealis and realis stems can differ from one another: 1. tone sandhi behavior and 2. vowel nucleus changes. Neither difference is obligatory (for instance, intransitive verbs have no object to trigger sandhi), meaning that for some verbs, there is no audible difference between the irrealis and the realis. However, given the number of verbs for which two different forms do exist, I treat this as a fundamental split in Seenku verbal morphology.

First, recall from §4.4.2 that transitive verbs undergo argument-head tone sandhi in irrealis inflections but not in realis ones (whether nominalized/post-positional or not), despite sharing the same O V word order. This is illustrated with the pair of examples in (1) with the underlying H-toned verb *káa* 'buy':

(1) a. ń ná bɛ̀ɛ kàa
       1SG PROSP pig chase.IRR
       'I will chase a pig.' [sos130823e]

   b. móő bɛ̀ɛ káa
       1SG.EMPH.PST pig chase.REAL.PFV
       'I chased a pig.' [sos130823e]

The example in (1a) employs the prospective, an irrealis inflection, and the verb undergoes argument-head tone sandhi with the preceding object; (1b) shows the exact same word order but uses the perfective, a realis inflection, and here the X-toned object *bɛ̀ɛ* 'pig' has no tonal effect on the verb.

Intransitive verbs, on the other hand, do not have an object that could trigger sandhi. In many cases, then, the two stem forms are indistinguishable, as in (2):

(2) a. mi nǎ səmâ
       1PL PROSP dance.IRR
       'We will dance.' [sos120107e]

   b. nɛ̋ səmâ
       1SG.PST dance.REAL.PFV
       'I danced.' [sos120107e]

In both the irrealis and the realis, the verb stem remains HX-toned *səmâ* 'dance'. In other cases, the irrealis has a level H tone and the perfective has HX:

(3) a. mó ná jáa
1SG.EMPH PROSP return.IRR
'I will return.' [sos130911e]

b. móő jîaa
1SG.EMPH.PST return.REAL.PFV
'I returned.' [sos130911e]

This is a tonal difference, but not one tied to argument-head tone sandhi. See also §12.1.2 for more on these tonal differences in intransitive verbs.

The most noticeable difference between irrealis and realis verb stems is an ablaut process affecting the stem nucleus. The most common manifestation of ablaut is the appearance of a high vowel ([i] or [u]) before the stem vowel, which creates a diphthong and may trigger palatalization or spirantization of the onset, as described in §3.5.1. This could be analyzed as infixation, but since other verbs display changes to the root vowel itself (as I will describe below), I will remain neutral and treat all changes under the heading of ablaut.

First, we find a substantial class of verbs whose realis stem has an [i]-initial diphthong. In Table 13.1, the perfective will be used to represent the realis stem, which neutralizes the contrast between H and S in transitive verbs; this is contrasted with the irrealis stem, here represented by the abstract underlying form of the stem (i.e. the segmental material of the irrealis but without any sandhi changes).

Tab. 13.1: Verbs with [i]-initial diphthongs in the realis

Irrealis	Realis	Gloss
cɛ̌	cíɛ	'open, take off hat'
cɔ̌	cíɔ	'scoop water'
fɛ̀	fi̯ɛ	'heat'
fɛ́	fíɛ	'blow'
jɔ̂	ji̯ɔ	'grill'
jő	jîo	'see'
mɛ̀	mi̯ɛ	'hear, understand'
nɛ́	níɛ	'insult'
ɲà	ɲi̯a	'finish'
nɔ̌	nɪ́ɔ	'eat'
sǎsɛ́	sísíɛ	'look at'
sɛ̀	si̯ɛ	'dig'
sɔ́	síɔ	'bury'
sɔ̌	si̯ɔ	'introduce'
tɛ̀	tsi̯ɛ	'show'
tő	tsíɔ	'leave'

The initial consonants of stems in this class are drawn from every place of articulation except velar, and the stem vowels are drawn from the class of [-ATR] sounds /ɛ, ɔ, a/. The palatal and alveolar stops affricate before the high front vowel (resulting in neutralization of /t/ and /ts/ for alveolar stops) and /s/ palatalizes to [ʃ]. For some speakers, /n/ also palatalizes to [ɲ] (another neutralizing alternation), though I have heard from other speakers that this may be a marker of urban Seenku. Note finally that the perfective of 'see' jĩo has an irregular HX tone pattern.

Verb stems with initial velar stops either do not undergo ablaut, or in the case of stems with the vowel /ɔ/ or /o/, they form [u]-initial diphthongs. Three bilabial-initial stems also fall into this category, as shown in Table 13.2.

Tab. 13.2: Verbs with [u]-initial diphthongs in the realis

Irrealis	Realis	Gloss
bɔ́	búɔ	'take out'
bő	búo	'kill'
nɛ́-fɔ́	nɛ́-fúɔ	'detonate, make pop'
gɔ̋	gúɔ	'learn'
kɔ̋	kúɔ	'make sb apologize'
nɛ́-kɔ́	nɛ́-kúɔ	'crack open'
kɔ̰́	kṵ́ɔ	'bite'
kɔ̰̀	kṵ̀ɔ	'cool'

We find a pattern here with the bilabial stems: if the stem vowel is back, then the diphthong is [u]-initial; if it is front, as in fɛ́ 'blow' and fɛ̰̀ 'heat' above, it is [i]-initial. It is tempting, looking at the stems in (3), to say that all stems with back vowels will have an [u]-initial diphthong as a sort of vowel harmony, but stems with non-velar or bilabial initial consonants in Table 13.1 show that this cannot be the case.

In the forms shown so far, the realis stem with the diphthong is used as expected in all realis inflections. We find two cases of intransitive verbs where the diphthong is limited to the perfective and perfect, i.e. the non-nominalized realis forms. The first of these is the verb sɔ́ 'arrive'; the examples in (4) illustrate this verb in the prospective (an irrealis form), the progressive (a nominalized realis form), and the perfect (a non-nominalized realis form):

(4) a. à nǎ sɔ́ kɛ̰́ɛ
    3SG PROSP arrive.IRR tomorrow
    'He will arrive tomorrow.' [sos150617e]

b. à̰ sı̆ sɔ̂   nɛ̏
   3SG be arrive.REAL.NOM LOC
   'He is arriving.' [sos150617e]

c. à̰ si͡ɔ
   3SG arrive.REAL.PRF
   'He has arrived.' [sos150617e]

Both the prospective and the progressive show a monophthongal /ɔ/ in the stem, despite the progressive being a realis form, while the diphthong [iɔ] appears only in the perfect. The verb bɛ́/bı̣́ɛ 'rain' likewise shows this distribution of the diphthong. It is unclear why these verbs deviate from the regular pattern in the language.

We find a small number of irregular irrealis/realis pairs, all with high stem vowels. Three of these verbs whose irrealis form has [u] form a subclass, with an alternation between irrealis /u/ and realis [io] (rather than the expected [iu]). These verbs are shown in Table 13.3.

Tab. 13.3: Alternations between irrealis /u/ and realis [io]

Irrealis	Realis	Gloss
sŭ	sío	'pick up'
jŭ	jío	'say'
tsŭ	tsi͡o	'poke'

This lowering of the stem vowel could be due to the fact that *iu is an unattested diphthong in Seenku.

A high front vowel /i/ in the stem also can yield irregular results; in this case, we find an alternation between irrealis /i/ and realis [ie], as shown in Table 13.4.

Tab. 13.4: Alternations between irrealis /i/ and realis [ie]

Irrealis	Realis	Gloss
cì	cìe*	'die'
fì	fìe	'throw'

I have listed 'die' here, since it does follow the /i/ vs. [ie] pattern, but like 'arrive', the diphthong is only found in the perfect and perfective. This alternation is not widespread; most verbs with stem /i/ (e.g. ɲì 'run', jĭ 'laugh', ɲĭ 'pick up', etc.) maintain the monophthong /i/ in both stem forms. Given the rarity of /e/ in verb stems, it may be that these verbs represent historical *ce or *fe, whose mid vowel is now only retained in the diphthong.

Finally, two very common verbs, 'come' and 'go', have irregular irrealis/realis forms. In the realis, both are X-toned with the vowel /a/, but both show tone raising and vowel changes in the irrealis; in the case of 'go', there are two interchangeable realis forms, shown in Table 13.5.

Tab. 13.5: Irregular irrealis/realis pairs for 'come' and 'go'

Irrealis	Realis	Gloss
nɛ́	nã̀	'come'
kɛ̌/kǔɔ	kã̌	'go'

It is unsurprising that such common verbs would be irregular.

To summarize, many verb stems in Seenku alternate in the realis, forming a high vowel-initial diphthong. Though typically this diphthong consists of an initial [i] followed by the stem's original underlying vowel, we find deviations due to phonotactic pressures and lexical exceptions; we also find that some verbs only alternate in the perfect and perfective.

13.2 Irrealis inflectional categories

In this section, I cover inflectional categories that use the irrealis verb stem, namely the prospective (Seenku's future equivalent), the habitual, and the imperative. We also find a bare use of irrealis verbs in narratives, where tense/aspect is clear from the narrative context. With the exception of the bare form, the explicit inflectional categories that use the irrealis stem are all consistent with Mithun's (1999:173) characterization of irrealis as "portray[ing] situations as purely within the realm of thought, knowable only through imagination", as opposed to the concrete, actualized events encoded by the realis. Actions that will occur in the future, for instance, belong to the realm of thought, as do imperatives, since there can be no guarantee that the listener will follow through on the orders. The habitual refers to a pattern of events, some of which may have been actualized, but many of which are assumed to take place or continue taking place. See McPherson (2017c) for further discussion.

I begin this section with the prospective (§13.2.1), then discuss the imperative (§13.2.3), the habitual (§13.2.2), and finally the use of bare irrealis verbs in narratives (§13.2.5).

13.2.1 Prospective

Future events are encoded in Seenku using the prospective aspect. Evidence that this is aspect rather than tense comes from the fact that the prospective auxiliary verb *nǎ* is compatible with past tense marking; for further discussion, see §13.4. I characterize *nǎ* as an auxiliary verb, since it can be preceded by a TAMP marker. This auxiliary has cognates in many Mande languages, and is most likely derived from the verb *nà* (realis) 'come'.

We can schematize the prospective construction as follows:

(5) *Schematization of the prospective*
Subject (TAMP) *nǎ* (Object) Verb$_{irrealis}$

The verb is inflected for irrealis; if an object is present, then it will trigger argument-head tone sandhi on the verb.

Examples from texts are shown in (6):

(6) a. kʊ́   nǎ   fɑ̰̀   í   bòn   mè
       D.DEF PROSP enter.IRR LOG back with
       'It will enter backwards.' [sos161009t1:29]

   b. mó   nǎ   sɔ́   ŋɛ́
       1SG.EMPH PROSP arrive.IRR NEG
       'I wouldn't be able to.' [sos171009t1:81]

   c. kɛ́   mɔ̰̀   nǎ   í   sí   nəgì   nè-təgò   âa
       COP person PROSP LOG RECP mind TRANS-sit NEG.Q
       'We'll remind each other, right.' [sos170702t1:30]

   d. kűɛ   nǎ   í   nè-sɔ̀ɔ   ɑ̰̀   bɑ̰̰̀ɑ̰̀   wè
       others PROSP LOG TRANS-push.IRR DEF balafon with
       'They will approach the balafon.' [sos170714t3:52]

Intransitive verbs are shown in (6a-b), where there is not much to show explicitly that the verb is irrealis. In (6c-d), the verb is transitive (in both cases, marked with a transitive pre-verb, §12.4); the verbs undergo sandhi with the object (cf. /né-təgò/ 'remind' and /né-sɔ̀ɔ/ 'approach'). The example in (6b) also shows negation, which is marked solely by a clause-final particle *ŋɛ́*; nothing about the auxiliary or the verb stem itself is affected.

The prospective auxiliary can also be followed by a focus particle *wé*, shown in (7):

(7) mó   ná   wé   nìgì   mɔ̀mɛ́ tő   dɔ̀n í   wó   kà̈
    1SG.EMPH PROSP FOC COW.PL a.lot take.IRR today 2PL EMPH in.hand
    'I'm going to get a lot of cows from you today.' [sos161009t1:13]

This *wé* appears to be a broad focus marker, and is most often found in conjunction with an emphatic 1sg subject, as in (7). For more discussion of *wé*, see §21.1.2.1.

The prospective has no apparent restrictions in terms of what timeframes it refers to; it could be an event that is about to occur, as in (7), or it could be a statement about the distant future. That is, we find no difference between immediate future and distant future constructions, a distinction we will see for completed events in §13.3 below.

The prospective auxiliary *ná* is also used to mark present inference, similar to an epistemic modal. This "future-as-present-inference" pattern is found in many languages (Aikhenvald 2004, Winans 2016), including English, in statements such as "John will be at home" to mean that John is at home right now. Examples of this usage are attested in a structured elicitation focusing on modal constructions.[1]

(8) a. *Gilles là   jərà   wè   jəgě ná   jó   cîe   ŋɛ́ à̈*
       Gilles 3SG think.IRR HAB dog PROSP find.IRR house.ADV NEG 3SG
       ná   jó   sərɛ̋
       PROSP find.IRR outside
       'Gilles thinks that the dog might not be in the house, he might be outside.' [sos170802e]

    b. *Robert ná   sɪ̰ dɔ̀ɔ-cîe*
       Robert PROSP be beer-house.LOC
       'Robert must be at the bar.' [sos170802e]

    c. *sɔ̋n ná   sɪ̰ bệ   nɛ̈ sɑ́sàa   nɛ̈ Gbéné-gʉ̈*
       sky PROSP be rain.REAL.NOM LOC right.now LOC Bouendé-under
       'It will be raining now in Bouendé.' [sos170807e]

In all three of the examples in (8), the prospective is used but the statement implies something about the present: the dog is outside, Robert is at the bar, it is raining. The use of the prospective indicates that the speaker is inferring that fact from what they know about the world around them and the patterns of the individuals involved. For instance, if Robert spends every afternoon at the bar, and it is currently the afternoon, the speaker knows by all accounts Robert should be there. Even in English in this context, we can say, "Robert will be at the bar." The example in (8c) is particularly interesting, showing a combination of the prospective with the progressive. Here, the prospective auxiliary scopes over the progressive auxiliary 'be'.

---

1 Modal elicitation list adapted from Bowler and Gluckman.

13.2.2 Habitual

The habitual in Seenku uses the irrealis verb form, but instead of using an auxiliary verb like the prospective, it uses a habitual particle after the verb. This particle is wḛ̀, homophonous with and likely derived from the postposition 'with' (§10.1.7). It cliticizes to the verb stem, which triggers argument-head tone sandhi, but with one modification I will address below.

The habitual construction is schematized in (9):

(9)   *Schematization of the habitual*
      Subject (TAMP) (Object) Verb$_{irrealis}$ wḛ̀

As we can see, there is no auxiliary verb between the TAMP marker and the VP. If an object is present, it triggers sandhi on the irrealis verb, which itself triggers sandhi on the habitual particle. By and large, sandhi applies to the particle as expected (wḛ̀ raises to L after X and to S after S), but H-toned verbs, whether underlying or themselves derived through sandhi with the object, always behave as though they are HX-toned in the habitual; this means that the habitual particle surfaces as L rather than the expected S triggered by H tone.

To take an example, consider the following two irrealis expressions, the first in the imperative and the second in the habitual:

(10) a. ằ   bá̰
          3SG hit.IRR
          'Hit him!' [sos130905e]

      b. dôn   n-ằ   bá̰`   wḛ̀   cȅrḛ̏-óo-cȅrḛ̏
          child L-3SG hit.IRR HAB day-LINK-day
          'The child hits him everyday.' [sos150709e]

The S-toned verb bá̰ becomes H in the irrealis after an X-toned pronominal object, as seen in (10a). However, instead of creating the expression ằ bá̰ wḛ́ in the habitual, instead we see the addition of an X tone to the end of the irrealis verb, which then triggers wḛ̀ to raise to L. This is a peculariatity of the habitual and is not attested with postpositions or other undergoers of sandhi.

Like the homophonous postposition 'with', the habitual particle commonly undergoes clitic elision (§4.4.3), with its length and tone concatenated onto the preceding verb. Note that the tone that is left behind is the sandhi tone, not the underlying

X tone. For example, we can contrast a form with the overt particle in (11a) and the elided particle in (11b):

(11) a. ǎ sɔ́` wè
3SG arrive.IRR HAB
'He is able.' [sos171009t1:6]

b. ǎ sɔ́ɔ̀
3SG arrive.IRR.HAB
'He is able.' [sos170714t3:56]

These examples also illustrate the addition of X to the H-final verb sɔ́ 'arrive, be able to'. As we can see in (11b), it is the sandhi tone L that is left behind when the particle elides.

The habitual denotes repeated, ongoing actions, either in the present (in which case there is no TAMP marker) or the past (in which case the past TAMP marker lɛ̋ is used). It has an imperfective reading, but does not cover cases of action in the process of taking place, which are encoded specifically by the progressive (§13.3.1.1). By virtue of using the irrealis stem, some repetitions of the actions must be understood as unrealized but expected.

Examples from texts using the overt particle are shown in (12); the underlying form of the verb is given in parentheses for the purposes of understanding the argument-head tone sandhi:

(12) a. ì ǎ dəgɔ́ɔ bɛ́ təgɔ̀n cèrè wè Tûe
3PL DEF place DEM name call.IRR HAB Toronsso
'They call the name of that place "Toronsso."' (/cɛ́rɛ́/) [sos171009t1:13]

b. kɛ́ kʊ́ à gərè dəbè wè
COP D.DEF 3SG voice make.good.IRR HAB
'It makes its voice good.' (/dəbɛ̋/) [sos170711t1:123]

c. ì í bɛ̋ wɛ̋ ì tsɛ̋?
3PL LOG do.IRR HAB COMP how
'How is it said?' (/bɛ̀/) [sos161009t1:40]

Since both X- and H-toned verbs both trigger L on the habitual particle, this is the tone we most commonly see associated with it. The example in (12c) shows that it can also surface as S-toned wɛ̋.

Elided habitual particles are illustrated in (13), once again with the underlying form of the verb in parentheses:

(13) a. *Pátárá mɔ̀̃   sóen dərɔ́̃ cèrèe   ŋɛ́*
        Patara person one only sleep.IRR.HAB NEG
        'Patara was the one person not sleeping.' (/cèrè̀/) [sos161009t1:43]

   b. *kɛ́ mɔ̀̃   kʊ́   cèrɛ̀ɛ   ằ   gərên-blă*
        COP person D.DEF call.IRR.HAB DEF hoe-drop.NOM
        'That's called "dropping the hoe".' (/cɛ́rɛ́/) [sos170714t1:18]

   c. *ằ   bɔ́ɔ̀   bò̀   ŋɛ́*
        3SG go.out.IRR.HAB anymore NEG
        'It doesn't go out anymore.' (/bɔ́/) [sos170711t1:358]

   d. *ì̀ à dəgɛ̀ɛ   gɔ́ɔ   lɛ́   wɛ̋?*
        3PL 3SG make.IRR.HAB wood which with
        'Which wood do they make it with?' (/dəgɛ́/) [sos170711t1:51]

The examples in (13) are a combination of intransitive and transitive verbs. The example in (13b) is the same verb we saw with the overt particle in (12a), showing that elision is truly a case of free variation and not lexically or phonologically determined. Examples (13a) and (13c) also show negative habituals, which, as expected, are formed simply by adding the negative particle *ŋɛ́* to the end of the clause; see §13.5 for further discussion.

Past habituals will be discussed and illustrated in §13.4.

13.2.3 Imperative

The imperative is quite simple in Seenku: it is simply the irrealis form of the verb without any auxiliaries or affixes. The only complexity that arises is in the presence or absence of subject pronouns, whose basic behavior is summarized in Table 13.6.

Tab. 13.6: Behavior of subject pronouns in imperative forms

	2sg	2pl
Affirmative	(á)	í
Negative	á	í

In other words, 2sg affirmative imperatives typically do not employ the subject pronoun, while the 2pl does (the pronoun being the only indication of number). In the negative, both the singular and plural obligatorily employ pronouns.

Let us begin with affirmative imperatives. The form of 2sg and 2pl affirmative imperatives is schematized in (14):

(14) a. *Schematization of 2sg affirmative imperative*
(á) (Object) Verb$_{irrealis}$

b. *Schematization of 2pl affirmative imperative*
í (Object) Verb$_{irrealis}$

For affirmative singular imperatives, the subject pronoun is optional but typically absent. For intransitive verbs, then, the imperative clause consists of only the verb stem:

(15) a. *cĕrȅ*
sleep.IRR
'Sleep!' [sos130821e]

b. *səmâ*
dance.IRR
'Dance!' [sos120107e]

We find cases in texts where the 2sg pronoun is used:

(16) a. *Fatou, á jïjä̀ lɛ̋*
Fatou 2SG try.hard.JU EMPH
'Fatou, try hard (Jula)!' [sos161009t1:49]

b. *á bɔ́ ń kɔ̋n*
2SG go.out.IRR 1SG on
'Leave me alone!' [sos150626t5:23]

In (16a), the verb *jïjä̀* is a borrowing from Jula, and during translation of the text, it was corrected by a speaker with the phrase *á ŋɛ́ɛn* 'try hard!' (French *faut grouiller!*).

With transitive verbs, we most commonly find just an object and the verb stem, which form a sandhi domain:

(17) a. *bɛ̏ɛ sɔ̋ɔ*
pig sell.IRR
'Sell a pig!' [sos130905e]

b. *bǐ sɔ̋ɔ*
goat.PL sell.IRR
'Sell goats!' [sos130905e]

c. *ä̀ fɛ̀*
3SG blow.IRR
'Blow on it!' [sos150807e]

The examples in (17a-b) show the same verb sɔ́ɔ 'sell' with two different objects to illustrate the effects of sandhi in the imperative construction. In (17c), the verb fέ 'blow (on)' takes a 3sg object pronoun, causing it to lower its tone to X.

Here too the subject pronoun á can be used (with or without the emphatic particle wó):

(18) a. óo   kʊ́   jǜ
          2SG.EMPH D.DEF say.IRR
          'Say it!' [sos161009t1:11]

    b. á   wó   ằ   dzǜ-tò̀   kḯ
          2SG EMPH 3SG mouth-take.IRR EMPH
          'Respond to her!' [sos150626t6:14]

    c. á   kû   jǜ   lḯ   sạ̈́
          2SG thing say.IRR EMPH IMP
          'Please say something!' [sos150626t6:85]

These subject pronouns are not to be confused with 2sg possessive pronouns; typically, if the 2sg subject were present then the logophoric pronoun í would be used to indicate possession, but since in the imperative it can be omitted, the 2sg pronoun can be used:

(19) a. á   tòo bɛ̀   í   səgɔ̃   lḯ
          3SG ear put.IRR   LOG good   EMPH
          'Listen up well!' [sos150626t1:2]

    b. á   nṳ̀   təmɛ̃̀
          2SG that.for tell.IRR
          'Tell yours!' [sos150626t5:37]

When the subject of the imperative is plural, the 2pl pronoun í must be present, since this is the only way to mark number. Examples of intransitive (20a-b) and transitive (20c-d) verbs are given below:

(20) a. í   cì̀
          2PL die.IRR
          'Die (all of you)!' [sos130821e]

    b. í   kʉ́ɔ   gbéné-gṳ̀
          2PL go.IRR Bouende-under
          'Go to Bouende (all of you)!' [sos130910e]

c. í bèɛ sā̰
 2PL pig buy.IRR
 'Buy a pig (all of you)!' [sos150317e]

d. í wó kʊ́ jṵ̀ kɛ̀
 2PL EMPH D.DEF say.IRR EMPH
 'Say it (all of you)!' [sos161009t1:46]

The example in (20b) is the plural equivalent of (18a) above from the same speaker in the same text.

The exception to needing the 2pl subject pronoun is when a 2pl possessor is present, since the number can be inferred from this possessor:

(21) a. í kɔ̋ɛ wɛ̋-jəgǎ
 2PL head.PL TRANS-lower.IRR
 'Lower your (pl.) heads!' [sos150709e]

b. í gərɛ̋ bɔ̋ dɔ́ɔní
 2PL voice take.out.IRR a.little.JU
 'Speak up a little (you both)!' [sos170822t1:5]

By virtue of using the 2pl possessive pronoun, it is clear that the speaker is addressing multiple people.

Turning now to negative imperatives (prohibitives), we find that the subject pronoun is always obligatory, regardless of whether the subject is singular or plural. The basic negative imperative construction can be schematized as in (22):

(22) *Schematization of negative imperative (prohibitive)*
 á/í (Object) Verb$_{irreal}$ ŋɛ́

As before, the irrealis verb will undergo sandhi triggered by the object, if present.
Singular subjects are shown first in (23):

(23) a. á ɲəgɛ̋ dzɨ̋ ŋɛ́
 2SG salt put.IRR NEG
 'Don't put salt!' [sos150807e]

b. á ń dǎa ŋɛ́
 2SG 1SG flatter.IRR NEG
 'Don't flatter me!' [sos170728e]

c. á à̰ kɛ̀n ŋɛ́
 2SG 3SG swallow.IRR NEG
 'Don't swallow it!' [sos170728e]

An example of the negative plural imperative is shown in (24):

(24) í jăn-dě́n sərě́   ŋɛ́
      2PL corn-grain pound.IRR NEG
      'Don't pound corn!' [sos150317e]

Oftentimes, the prospective construction is used for the negative imperative, schematized in (25):

(25) *Schematization of prospective negative imperative*
      á/í nă (Object) Verb$_{irreal}$ ŋɛ́

It is completely indistinguishable in form from the regular prospective construction. Examples include:

(26) a. ì̀ á nă dâmbù̀ ŋɛ́
         COMP 2SG PROSP lie.IRR NEG
         'He said, don't lie!' [sos150626t3:8]

     b. á wó nă ằ sò̀o   ằ jô sù̀   ŋɛ́
         2SG EMPH PROSP 3SG search.IRR DEF water pick.up.IRR NEG
         'Don't just try to get the water!' [sos170822t1:113]

     c. í nă mɔ́ɛ̀ɛ-dèn sərè ŋɛ́
         2PL PROSP millet-grain pound.IRR NEG
         'Don't pound millet (all of you)!' [sos150317e]

In (26c), the consultant offered this negative imperative both with and without the prospective auxiliary. It is not clear how different the regular prohibitive construction is from the prospective construction in terms of illocutionary force. I suspect that the prospective construction is a firmer demand, but more data will be necessary to test this hypothesis.

13.2.4 Hortative

Hortatives are similar to imperatives in suggesting an action, but now the speaker is included in the command. Either the 3sg generic pronoun *mɔ̀* (like French *on*, see §6.1) or the regular 1pl inclusive pronoun *mí́* can be used, followed by a subjunctive marker *lɛ́*. There is also an optional clause-initial expression *ằwắ*, which I gloss as simply HORT. This construction is schematized in (27):

(27) *Schematization of the hortative*
      (ằwắ) mɔ̀/mí́ lɛ́ (Object) Verb$_{irrealis}$

While the schematization shows an overt segmental TAMP marker *lé*, this typically undergoes clitic elision (§4.4.3), leaving only its H tone and lengthening on the preceding subject pronoun.

Examples of the 3sg generic pronoun *mɔ̃́* are shown first in (28), drawing where possible from the text corpus:

(28) a. *Fatou, ằwắ mɔ̃́ɔ́   à   fəlé kʊ́   ŋmằ*
      Fatou HORT person.SBJV DEF what D.DEF eat.IRR
      'Fatou, let's eat the thing.' [sos161009t1:218]

   b. *né   mɔ̃́ɔ́   ằ   ŋmằ   kɛ̈*
      come.IRR person.SBJV 3SG eat.IRR EMPH
      'Come, let's eat!' [sos161009t1:224]

   c. *mɔ̃́ɔ́   fằ   à   jén-jén   sí   tɛ̈*
      person.SBJV enter.IRREAL DEF RED-story female.PL GEN
      'Let's get into folktales.' [sos150626t2:1]

We can see examples both with the hortative expression *ằwắ* and without. In elicitation, one consultant differentiates between singular ('me and you') and plural ('me and you all') hortatives in the following way:

(29) a. *ằwắ mɔ̃́ɔ́   mɔ̂ɛɛ-dèn   sərɛ̈*
      HORT person.SBJV millet-grain pound.IRR
      'Let's pound millet (me and you)!' [sos150317e]

   b. *í   ằwắ mɔ̃́ɔ́   mɔ̂ɛɛ-dèn   sərɛ̈*
      2PL HORT person.SBJV millet-grain pound
      'Let's pound millet (me and you all)!' [sos150317e]

The 2pl pronoun *í* at the beginning marks that the speaker is talking to multiple people, in the same way that this pronoun does in plural imperatives (§13.2.3).

The 3sg generic *mɔ̃́* is far more common in natural speech than the 1pl *mí̋*, which is found in elicitation:

(30) *í   ằwắ mí̋   bî̀ sà̰*
     2PL HORT 1PL.SBJV goat buy.IRR
     'Let's buy a goat (me and you all)!' [sos170803e]

Finally, we see instances in texts where the translation suggests a hortative but the prospective form is used; this is likely the same parallel we find with the imperative and the prospective. Examples are shown in (31):

(31) a. mɔ̌   nǎ   ä̀   tsiɛ   bé   tɔ̀   lɔ́
         person PROSP DEF word DEM leave.IRR here
         'Let's leave the discussion off here.' [sos171009t1:126]

   b. íwí̋   nǎ   ä̀   sɛ́ɛ́-kû   gɔ̀
       1PL.EXCL PROSP DEF Sambla-language learn.IRR
       'Let's [exclusive] learn Seenku.' [sos170702t1:31]

   c. ä̀   səná   wɛ̀   í   bɛ̋   ì̀   íwí̋   nǎ   kɛ̋   í
       3SG husband SUBORD LOG do.IRR COMP 1PL.EXCL PROSP go.IRR LOG
       sí   tɛ̀
       RECP GEN
       'Her husband said, "Let's go together".' [sos150626t5:50]

In the negative, ŋé is added at the end; the hortative itself can take any of the forms seen thus far, including subjunctive hortatives (32a) and prospective hortatives (32b):

(32) a. mɔ̰̌ɔ́   bɛ̀ɛ sɑ̰̀   ŋé
         person.SBJV pig buy.IRR NEG
         'Let's not buy a pig.' [sos150317e]

   b. mɔ̌   nǎ   jǎn-dɛ́n   sərɛ̋   ŋé
       person PROSP corn-grain pound.IRR NEG
       'Let's not pound corn.' [sos150317e]

13.2.5 Bare irrealis in insubordinate clauses

In narratives and folktales, we find a construction where stand-alone clauses have a bare (uninflected) irrealis verb as the main verb and the subject is usually (though not obligatorily) followed by the subordinate TAMP marker; in other words, these clauses look morphosyntactically like subordinate clauses, but there is no subordinating main clause. In translating these tales, the past tense is often offered in French (which I then translate into English), despite no past or perfective marking in the actual clause.

I take these clauses to be examples of what Evans (2007) calls **insubordinate clauses**: "the conventionalized independent use of a formally subordinate clause" (Evans 2007:377). Like some quotative clauses discussed in §19.2.1, bare irrealis insubordinate clauses are likely evidential in nature, making it little surprise that we would find them in folktales.

I schematize the bare irrealis insubordinate clause in (33):

(33)   *Schematization of bare irrealis insubordinate clause*
       Subject (wɛ̀) (Object) Verb$_{irrealis}$

This clause construction, with a subordinate marker and a bare irrealis verb, is also found in clause chaining; see §20.2. Occasionally instead of *wɛ̈*, the allomorph *lɛ̈* is used, with no apparent difference in meaning.

Some examples are shown in (34):

(34) a. Donc, kərù   kɛ́   jɔ́ɔ   mɛ̈   kɛ́   dzîaa,   à
       SO.FR hyena go.IRR stroll.IRR 3SG.SUBORD go.IRR get.tired.IRR 3SG
       kə̀kâ jîo   ŋé
       meat see.REAL.PFV NEG
       'So, hyena went out for a stroll but tired himself out without finding any meat.' [sos161009t1:184]

   b. ì̈   wɛ̈   ä̀   bậa   dəgɛ̈   wé   ì̈   wɛ̈   à   bè   à
      3PL SUBORD DEF balafon make.IRR FOC 3PL SUBORD 3SG put.IRR 3SG
      kä̀
      in.hand
      'They made a balafon and gave it to him.' [sos170711t1:31]

   c. ä̀   dôn   mɛ̈   bɔ́   mɛ̈   kɛ́   ä̀   cɛ̈n-kɛ́
      DEF child SUBORD go.out.IRR 3SG.SUBORD go.IRR DEF peanut-shell.PL
      sɛ́ɛ   ɲì
      throw.IRR there
      'The child went outside to toss out some peanut shells.' [sos150626t4:5]

   d. ö̀o   lɛ̈   bɔ́   wétənɛ̈   í   sɔ̀   ŋɔ̀mì-ŋɔ̀mì-ŋɔ̀mì
      3SG.EMPH SUBORD go.out.IRR now   LOG alone IDEO
      mɛ̈   kɛ́   mɛ̈   kɛ́   tä̀asö̀   ä̀   bö̀-kɔ́ɔ
      3SG.SUBORD go.IRR 3SG.SUBORD go.IRR be.surprised DEF billygoat
      lɛ̈
      PRES
      'He went out himself this time, carefully, like a hunter, he went, he went and to his surprise there was a billygoat.' [sos150626t4:18]

In (34a), the first clause shows a case where the bare irrealis is used without a subordinate TAMP marker; the first clause is chained with another irrealis clause using *mɛ̈*. The last clause here uses the perfective. In (34b), two clauses both contain a 3pl subject followed by the TAMP marker *wɛ̈*. Note that the particle after the verb *dəgɛ̈* is a focus particle, not the habitual, as evidenced by its tone. In (34c), the subordinate marker nasalizes due to the latent nasal on *dôn* (§3.3.2); the second clause is chained using the 3sg form of the subordinate, also the nasalized *mɛ̈*. Finally, (34d) illustrates the TAMP marker *lɛ̈* used in place of *wɛ̈*, even though the context is exactly the same as (34c), which was uttered just a few lines earlier in the folktale.

For more on clause chaining of the sort seen in (34), see §20.2.

13.3 Realis inflectional categories

In contrast to irrealis categories (§13.2), the use of the realis stem implies that a situation has been actualized or realized. In Seenku, this can mean that it is currently ongoing (in the case of the progressive, §13.3.1.1), or that it has been completed (in the case of the immediate past, §13.3.1.2, the perfective, §13.3.2.1, and the perfect, §13.3.2.2).

As we saw in the hierarchy at the beginning of the chapter, realis forms split into two constructions: 1. A nominalized construction where an auxiliary verb is obligatory and the nominalized verb is followed by a postposition, and 2. A non-nominalized construction where the verb stem acts as the main verb. I cover the former in §13.3.1 and the latter in §13.3.2.

13.3.1 Nominalized inflections

Given the general lack of overt derivational morphology in Seenku, it can be difficult to tell if a stem has changed categories. This is the case for the "postpositional" or "nominalized" verb constructions. On the one hand, they run exactly parallel to locative expressions, as illustrated in (35) where (35a) is a locative construction and (35b) a progressive:

(35) a. bɛ̏ɛ sǐ gɔ̂ɔ nɛ̏
         pig be tree LOC
         'The pig is in the tree.' [sos150623e]

     b. kʊ̏ sǐ gɔ̏ɔ   nɛ̏
         toh be dry.REAL.NOM LOC
         'The toh is drying out.' [sos150812e]

It is clear that the progressive has, if nothing else, a diachronic connection to nominal constructions, which has been argued for progressives in other Mande languages (see e.g. Nikitina 2011). The question is: should the realis verb stems in these forms be seen as nominalized in the synchronic grammar?

The answer appears to be "yes". We find the same form of the stem (and the same lack of tonal interaction between the object and the verb) in explicitly nominalized constructions as we do in the progressive. For instance:

(36) a. kʊ̏ ɲíɔ   ɲǜä   ɪ̋
         toh eat.REAL.NOM finish.REAL.PRF here
         'Eating toh is finished here.' [sos170728e]

b. mó   sḭ̆ kʊ̀ ɲɪ́ɔ   nɛ̋
1SG.EMPH be toh eat.REAL.NOM LOC
'I am eating toh.' [sos120109e]

More telling still, X-toned transitive verbs take a LS contour in both the explicitly nominalized form and in the periphrastic realis verb constructions:

(37) a. jăn-dɛ́n   sərě   ɲìä   lő
corn-grain pound.REAL.NOM finish.REAL.PRF here
'Pounding corn is finished here.' [sos170728e]

b. ḭ̀   sḭ̆ jăn-dɛ́n   sərě   nɛ̋
3PL be corn-grain pound.REAL.NOM LOC
'They are pounding corn.' [sos170713e]

Thus, I will treat these realis constructions as nominalized synchronically. The nominal marking is purely tonal: transitive verbs are either S-toned (for underlying H- and S-toned verbs) or LS-toned (for underlying X-toned verbs). Table 13.7 compares the abstract underlying form of transitive verb stems to their nominalized realis form. The horizontal line divides the two nominalized surface forms (LS and S), with underlying H and S neutralizing.

Tab. 13.7: Nominalized realis stems of transitive verbs

UR	Nominalized	Gloss
sà̰	să̰	'buy'
kpɔ̀ɔ	kpɔ̆ɔ	'sew'
sɔ́ɔ	sɔ̋ɔ	'sell'
sɔ́	sɪ̋ɔ	'bury'
bá̰	ba̰̋	'hit'
nɔ̋	nɪ́ɔ/ɲɪ́ɔ	'eat'

As discussed in §12.1.2, it is difficult to tell what the underlying form of an intransitive verb would be. On the surface, though, the nominalized realis forms do not differ greatly from other forms (irrealis, non-nominalized realis forms); X-toned verbs surface as X, and H/HX-toned verbs err towards HX when nominalized. For instance, while sá 'cry' is a level H in the irrealis, it varies between H and HX when nominalized. All long vowels, whether H- or HX-toned in the irrealis, are HX when nominalized. The rare surface S-toned intransitive verbs remain S-toned when nominalized.

These nominalized forms are used in two constructions that differ by auxiliary verb: the progressive (§13.3.1.1), with its auxiliary verb sḭ̆ 'be', and the immediate past (§13.3.1.2), with its auxiliary verb sɪ́o (likely derived from 'get up').

13.3.1.1 Progressive

The progressive in Seenku uses the auxiliary verb sǐ 'be', which is the one verb with an irregular negative form ɲá. I begin with affirmative progressives, whose form is schematized in (38):

(38) Schematization of the affirmative progressive
Subject (TAMP) sǐ (Object) Verb$_{Realis.Nom}$ né

The verb is nominalized, and by virtue of being a realis form, it does not interact tonally with the preceding object. Like the prospective auxiliary nǎ, I treat sǐ as an auxiliary since it can co-occur with a preceding TAMP marker, such as the past tense lɛ̌. The final particle né is the locative postposition. As a postposition, it undergoes argument-head tone sandhi with the preceding nominalized verb. All transitive verbs end in S, so it is uniformly S-toned in transitive constructions, while the majority of intransitive verbs end in X, making it usually X-toned in the intransitive (except for the rare cases of S-toned intransitives). Underlyingly X-toned transitive verbs become LS when nominalized; when the postposition becomes S-toned via sandhi, it creates the LS-S environment for tonal absorption (§4.5.3), which leaves these verbs L-toned on the surface:

(39) sǎ   + né → sǎ nɛ̋ → sà̰ nɛ̋
buy.REAL.NOM   LOC
'buying'

I will continue to transcribe the tonal forms below with their morphophonemic tone, i.e. their tone before postlexical processes like downstep or tonal absorption have occurred, but note that this process is exceptionless in these nominalized verb constructions.

The progressive indicates that an action is taking place at the reference time, whether that is the present/time of speaking or a past reference point. For example:

(40) a. ä   sǐ ä̀   máantón   sɪ̰̌ɛ   nɛ̋
3SG be DEF termite.mound dig.REAL.NOM LOC
'He is digging up the termite mound.' [sos170711t1:5]

b. kűɛ sǐ kɔ̂ɔn   bṵ̋ɔ   nɛ̋ dőrőn mɛ̋
others be eggplant take.out.REAL.NOM LOC pole with
'They are picking epplants with a long pole.' [sos161009t1:155]

c. á ɲəmà-kőrő́n jîo   âa,   kʊ́   sɪ̌   ằ   fôn
    2SG Nyumakoro see.REAL.PFV NEG.Q D.DEF be DEF fonio
    cɛ́́ɛ   nɛ́̋
    gather.REAL.NOM LOC
    'You see Nyumakoro, right? She's gathering fonio.' [sos170714t2:96]

d. ằ   sɪ̌   kằ   nɛ̋̀   jəmɪ̋̀
    3SG be go.REAL.NOM LOC bush
    'He is going to the bush.' [sos161009t1:182]

e. ɪ̀   pó-pőe   sɪ̌   kő́ɔ   nɛ́̋
    3PL RED-all.PL be walk.REAL.NOM LOC
    'They are all walking.' [sos161009t1:4]

Transitive examples are shown in (40a-c); we can see that in every case, the object has no tonal effect on the nominalized verb. Intransitive examples are given in (40d-e), one with X tone and one with irregular S tone.

The negative progressive involves suppletive allomorphy of the auxiliary verb, with *sɪ̌* replaced by *ɲá*. This is schematized in (41):

(41)   *Schematization of the negative progressive*
        Subject (TAMP) *ɲá* (Object) Verb$_{Realis.Nom}$ *nɛ́̋ ŋɛ́*

This negative auxiliary obligatorily co-occurs with the clause-final negative particle *ŋɛ́*.

The negative progressive is far less common in texts, but we find the following examples:

(42)   a. ɪ̀   á   ɲá   pîɔn fɪ́́ɛ   nɛ́̋   í   səgɔ̌   ŋɛ́
            COMP 2SG be.NEG flute blow.REAL.NOM LOC LOG good NEG
            '[He said] you're not playing the flute well.' [sos150626t4:50]

        b. ɪ̀   mɔ̌̀ɛ   yèrè ɲá   ằ   kʊ̀-səgɔ̌   səgɔ̌ mɪ̌
            COMP person.PL self be.NEG DEF toh-mix.PTCP good drink.REAL.NOM
            nɛ́̋ ŋɛ́
            LOC NEG
            '[They say that] the people themselves are not drinking good mixed toh porridge.' [sos170809t5:38]

For more on negation, see §13.5.

13.3.1.2 Immediate past

The second nominalized realis construction is an immediate or recent past construction. Instead of the auxiliary verb *sɪ̌* 'be', an auxiliary *sío* ([ʃő]) is used. This is likely derived from the realis form *sío* 'get up' (generally H-toned *sío* in the perfective for the intransitive verb), which is also used as an expression meaning 'come from' (cf. *á sío lɛ̀ dəgɔ́ɔ lɛ́ nɛ̀* 'where do you come from?'). I gloss it as REC.PST for 'recent past'. Otherwise, the construction is identical to the progressive:

(43) *Schematization of the immediate past*
Subject (TAMP) *sío* (Object) Verb$_{Realis.Nom}$ *nɛ́*

Usually, this is the construction offered in translation of the French expression *venir de faire* (which I translate as 'have just done'). From elicitation, we find the following:

(44) a. ằ ní sío mí̋ bǎ̰ nɛ̋
3SG father REC.PST 1PL hit.REAL.NOM LOC
'His father just hit us.' [sos150811e]

b. dón nêɛ səgû ŋmá ằ sío
child REL.SUBORD caterpillar eat.REAL.PFV 3SG REC.PST
cǜɛ nɛ̀̋
vomit.REAL.NOM LOC
'The child who ate caterpillars, he just threw up.' [sos170729e]

c. ằ sío kṵ́ḭ̋ nɛ̋
3SG REC.PST snore.REAL.NOM LOC
'He just snored.' [sos150622e]

d. mí̋ sío bî sɔ́ɔ nɛ̋
1PL REC.PST goat sell.REAL.NOM LOC
'We just sold a goat.' [sos150201e]

We know that this construction must refer to an immediately completed action (within the last hour), since even the addition of 'yesterday' is ungrammatical. Contrast (45a), with the adverb *sə́sǎa nɛ̀̋* 'just now', and ungrammatical (45b), with the adverb *kərɔ̀* 'yesterday":

(45) a. ằ sío tsḭ̂ nɛ̀̋ sə́sǎa nɛ̀̋
3SG REC.PST jump.REAL.NOM LOC just.now LOC
'He jumped just now.' [sos150317e]

b. *kərɔ̀ ằ sío tsḭ̂ nɛ̀̋
yesterday 3SG REC.PST jump.REAL.NOM LOC
'?He just jumped yesterday.' [sos150317e]

Even in English, the translation in (45b) is marginal.
Textual examples of the immediate past aren't very common, but we find a few:

(46) a. í sío ɲəgâan cɛ̀ɛ gurɑ̌ nɛ́↘
2PL REC.PST guinea.fowl egg fry.REAL.NOM LOC.Q
'Have you all cooked guinea fowl eggs just now?' [sos161009t1:220]

b. á sío məŋɛ̀-sǎn dzį̌ nɛ́ gɔ̀ɔ
2SG REC.PST iron-thing put.REAL.NOM LOC ground.ADV
'You just dropped a piece of iron on the ground.' [sos170711t1:69]

c. kɛ́ ằ mɔ̰̀ bɛ́ sío bậa gǔɔ nɛ́
COP DEF person DEM REC.PST balafon learn.REAL.NOM LOC
sô-dzʊ̆ kǎa
road-mouth next.to
'[You'll know that] that person just learned the balafon on the side of the road.' [sos170711t1:183]

In the first context, an interlocutor suggested that the group go and eat since cooking in the kitchen just wrapped up. Thus, the question posed in (46a) refers to an event (frying) that just completed. In (46b), the example comes at the end of a longer clause, translating to 'If you took out one [wooden] key and dropped it on the ground, you realize that it's like you just dropped iron on the ground.' Thus, the realization comes immediately after having dropped the wood (which has become hard like iron thanks to a long period of smoking and drying). In (46c), the sentence refers to an unskilled balafon player, who may have just learned the music haphazardly.

The rarity of the immediate past in the text corpus is likely due to the fact that most of the corpus consists of tales and narratives, rather than conversation, where events in the immediate surroundings are likely to be discussed.

For a similar meaning, see the perfect construction in §13.3.2.2.

13.3.2 Non-nominalized (verbal) inflections

We cannot say that the realis form is inherently nominalized, or in other words, that realis marking is nominal marking, since we find two common verbal constructions that use realis verb stems without an auxiliary or anything else that could be taken as the main verb. These are the perfective (§13.3.2.1) and the perfect (§13.3.2.2), which are segmentally identical but tonally divergent. Both of these are clearly aspects, since they can occur either in the present tense or the past tense with the TAMP marker lɛ̌.

13.3.2.1 Perfective

The perfective is formed with the realis stem and a featural suffix [-raised], which triggers lowering of the verb's tone; since X and H are both [-raised] already, these verbs are unaffected, but S lowers to H. For more on tone features, see §4.1.1.1. The one exception to this tonal pattern is the verb *jó* (irrealis) 'see', whose perfective form has a HX tone pattern *jîo*.

The regular perfective construction is schematized in (47):

(47)   *Schematization of the perfective*
Subject (TAMP) (Object) Verb$_{realis}$-[-raised]

Tables of underlying forms and perfective equivalents can be found in §12.1.1 and §12.1.2 and will not be repeated here.

The perfective encodes a completed action, but not necessarily one with continued present relevance (unlike the perfect, to be addressed in §13.3.2.2 below).

(48)   a.   í   wó   kà   tsɛ́   gùɔ   nɛ̀
LOG EMPH go.REAL.PFV INDF country LOC
'[They say] I went to a country.' [sos161009t1:2]

b.   sɔ̃́n   bəlɛ̌   bǎa   tsɛ́   bįɛ
rain big IDEO INDF rain.REAL.PFV
'A huge rain fell.' [sos150626t4:1]

c.   mó   ằ   bâa   gùɔ   mó   lɛ̀   sɔ̃́ń
1SG.EMPH DEF balafon learn.REAL.PFV 1SG.EMPH SUBORD time.REL
tɛ̀   jù   nɔ̀
GEN year five
'I learned the balafon when I was five.' [sos171009t1:21]

d.   ké   ì   ằ   sío   píɔn gùrè tè
COP 3PL 3SG pick.up.REAL.PFV flute voice GEN
'They got it [the notes] from the tuning of the flute.' [sos170711t1:342]

In each of the cases, the reported action has been completed, sometimes many years ago in (48c-d), sometimes without any implicit timeframe, as in (48a-b) from the set up of a riddle and a folktale, respectively.

This is the form offered most readily in translation of the French *passé composé*, often with the past TAMP marker (here elided into the subject):

(49)   a.   mű   bî   sằ
1PL.PST goat buy.REAL.PFV
'We bought a goat.' [sos150201e]

b.   mű   bî   bą́
1PL.PST goat hit.REAL.PFV
'We hit a goat.' [sos150201e]

c. *móő   nằ   ằ   tê*
1SG.EMPH.PST come.REAL.PFV 3SG GEN
'I came to his house.' [sos170705e]

The examples in (49a-b) show explicitly that the verb does not undergo sandhi with the preceding object (otherwise we would expect *sạ̀* and *bạ̀*, respectively). (49b) also shows the lowering of underlying S on *bą́* 'hit' to H as a result of the featural suffix.

For textual examples of past perfectives, see §13.4.4.

13.3.2.2 Perfect

The perfect has the same segmental form as the perfective, but the tone pattern differs. While the perfective suffixes a tonal feature [-raised], the perfect suffixes a full tone sequence -SX (a super-high to extra-low falling tone). On X-toned verbs, this creates the tone pattern LSX, as the verb's tone assimilates to [+raised] (see §4.5.1). H- and S-toned verbs are neutralized to S. These tone changes (X to L and H to S) are reminiscent of the nominalized realis form found in the progressive and the immediate past, but since the perfect lacks an auxiliary verb (i.e. the verb stem itself acts as the verbal predicate), I hesitate to say that these tonal overlaps are anything but coincidence, or the same result from pressure to assimilate to a following S tone.

The form of the perfect is schematized in (50):

(50) *Schematization of the perfect*
Subject (TAMP) (Object) Verb$_{realis}$-SX

In Table 13.8, I illustrate the tonal behavior of the perfect by comparing perfect forms to underlying and perfective forms of verbs.

Tab. 13.8: Tonal effects of the perfect

UR	Perfective	Perfect	Gloss
sạ̀	sạ̀	sạ̈ä	'buy'
kà	kà	kàä	'go'
tsí̧	tsí̧	tsï̧	'cut'
bɔ́	búɔ	büɔ	'go out'
səmâ	səmâ	səmä	'dance'
nɔ́	nínɔ	nïɔ	'eat'
bą́	bą́	bą̈	'hit'

As this table shows, H- and S-toned verbs neutralize in both the perfective and the perfect: to H in the perfective and to SX in the perfect. The table includes a mix of both intransitive and transitive verbs, whose tonal outcomes are the same in this inflection.

The perfect is used to encode a completed action that still has relevance to the time of reference. Often, for present perfects, this means that an action has just been completed, similar to the immediate past discussed in §13.3.1.2. Further data are required to fully tease apart the two constructions.

Like many other inflectional categories, the perfect can be inflected for either the present or the past. Present perfects are illustrated here; for past perfects, see §13.4.5.

The following examples are drawn from the text corpus:

(51) a. mó nìgì fín jïo
     1SG.EMPH cow.PL two find.REAL.PRF
     'I've gotten two cows.' [sos161009t1:74]

b. á wó kűɛ tsï̱ kà̱-bá̱
   2SG EMPH other.PL cut.REAL.PRF already
   'You and the others have already cut them.' [sos170714t2:33]

c. ì dɔ̈ɔ̈
   3PL finish.REAL.PRF
   'They're finished.' [sos170714t2:37]

d. kúɔné-ŋɛ́ mɔ̰̀má̰ mɔ̰̀má̰ mɔ̰̀má̰ fà̱á̱
   youth-HUM.PL a.lot a.lot a.lot pass.REAL.PRF
   'Many many many generations have passed.' [sos171009t1:78]

All of these examples encode an action that has been completed recently, but whose implications can be felt in the present. In (51a), the group telling riddles is comparing how many "cows" they have gotten for getting riddles right or stumping their opponents. In (51b), the speaker is talking about duping an opponent during farming competitions by making him try to cut fonio that has already been cut, resulting in him cutting his own fingers. In (51c), the speakers are watching a video of farming and are commenting on the farmers having just completed a row of farming and they await their next move. Finally, in (51d), the speaker is talking about how the balafon players have arrived where they are today from their origins; by virtue of discussing the present state, he uses the perfect to refer to the generations that have passed to bring them to this moment.

Interestingly, the perfect cannot be put into the negative; instead, the perfective form is used. It is as though if an action has not been completed, there is no way it can have present relevance.

For the use of a reduplicated perfect form in event sequencing, see §20.3.3.

13.3.3 Stative/resultative

The last realis form to discuss is a participial form used in conjunction with the auxiliary sɪ̧ 'be' to express a stative/resultative meaning. Participial formation is closely related to nominalization seen in §13.3.1 except that all verbs, whether transitive or intransitive, become either S or LS; in other words, all verbs behave like transitive verbs. These tonal rules are laid out in (52):

(52) *Tonal rules of participial formation*
/H, S/ → S
/X/ → LS

In other words, H- and S-toned verbs become level S-toned as participles, whereas X-toned verbs become LS. This common LS tone pattern on adjectives likely has its roots in participial formation, though synchronically, adjectives and participles have diverged in their (especially predicate) behavior; for adjectival predicates, see §14.3.

Like the nominalized forms found in progressives, participles take the realis form of the verb as their base. Table 13.9 exemplifies participial formation with a few illustrative verbs.

Tab. 13.9: Examples of participial formation

UR	Participle	Gloss
jɔ̀	jǐɔ	'grilled'
tàgì̧	tàgǐ̧	'standing'
nɛ́-frɔ́	nɛ́-frɔ̌	'punctured'
bɔ́	bǔɔ	'gone out'
mɛ̃́ɛ	mɛ̃́ɛ	'ignited'
brǐ̧	brǐ̧	'mixed'

The use of the realis verb stem is particularly clear with 'grill' and 'go out', where the realis shows diphthong formation; see §13.1 for further details. This table also illustrates how transitive and intransitive words behave the same in participial formation. For instance, the participial form of intransitive tàgì̧ 'stand' is LS-toned tàgǐ̧ rather than the X-toned nominalized form tàgì̧ we would be find in, e.g., progressives (§13.3.1.1).

This participial form combines with the auxiliary sɪ̧ to create a stative/resultative predicate, as schematized in (53):

(53) *Schematization of stative/resultative predicates*
Subject Participial sɪ̧

The construction expresses that the subject is in a state of being, which may be the result of a dynamic verb like 'grill'; for instance, if one grills meat, then this action results in the meat being grilled. Since the object of the dynamic clause becomes the subject of the stative/resultative clause, this form is reminiscent of passives. Consider the following, which shows first a dynamic transitive clause, and then a corresponding stative/resultative:

(54) a. ń sǐ kə̀kâ cəmí̋ ně̋
         1SG be meat grill.REAL.NOM LOC
         'I am charring meat.' [sos150805e]

     b. kə̀kâ cəmí̋   sǐ
         meat grill.PTCP be
         'The meat is charred.' [sos150805e]

The subject in the participial predicate is the argument that has undergone the action; in other words, the apparent subject of participial predicates (though see §13.4 to complicate this idea) is the internal argument of the verb (object of transitives and subject of intransitives). Unlike a passive, though, no agent is implied; the participial simply refers to the subject's present state.

This same dynamic/stative alternation can be seen for intransitive verbs; in this case, the subject is the same in both constructions. Examples from the text corpus include:

(55) a. ä̀ nḛ̀-jərán-jərã́n   sǐ
         3SG TRANS-RED-change.PTCP be
         'It has changed.' [sos170702t1:21]

     b. óo   té̋-məní̋   təgǐ   sǐ
         2SG.EMPH dear-woman stand.PTCP be
         'Your girlfriend is standing [there].' [sos170714t3:134]

     c. mó   nəgì bű͗ɔ   sǐ ä̀ lɛ́ dɔ̀ɔnì
         1SG.EMPH mind go.out.PTCP be 3SG DAT a.little
         'I have forgotten it a little.' [sos171009t1:104]

In each case, the participial predicate refers to a state of being or the result of an action undergone by the subject—changes have occurred, a person has stood up and is still standing, "the mind has left" (the metaphor for forgetting) and is still gone, etc.

Given that stative/resultative predicates describe a state of being, it is unsurprising that much qualification in Seenku is expressed through participial forms of verbs rather than adjectives. Examples of qualificational predicates, from both the text corpus and elicitation, are given in (56):

(56) a. mó   fəgɛ̌   sĭ
       1SG.EMPH fill.PTCP be
       'I'm full.' [sos161009t1:228]

   b. sàʃɛ̃́ dəmǎ   sĭ
      bag shrivel.PTCP be
      'Bags are tough.' [sos170711t1:128]

   c. jõ̀   kŭɔ   sĭ
      water cool.PTCP be
      'The water is cold.' [sos150806e]

   d. mó   dzía   sĭ
      1SG.EMPH be.tired.PTCP be
      'I'm tired.' [sos150811e]

These forms differ morphosyntactically from adjectival predicates (§14.3) by the fact that the auxiliary *sĭ* follows the participle, whereas it precedes the adjective, with an intervening logophoric pronoun (§6.7). There are a small number of forms, however, that can be treated as either an adjective or a participial, such as *gɔ̌ɔ* 'dry':

(57) a. gɔ̂ɔ gɔ̌ɔ   sĭ
       wood dry.PTCP be
       'The wood is dry.' [sos150630e]

   b. gɔ̂ɔ sĭ í   gɔ̌ɔ
      wood be LOG dry
      'The wood is dry.' [sos150630e]

There is no apparent difference in meaning between these two constructions. When asking consultants if a participle could follow *sĭ*, I have generally been offered the following:

(58) a. jõ̀ sĭ í   tǎ-fĭɛ   wɛ̃́
       water be LOG cook-heat.PTCP with
       'The water is heated.' [sos150630e]

   b. jəbɛ̃́ sĭ í   sənɛ̃́   wɛ̃́
      cloth be LOG wet.PTCP with
      'The clothing is wet.' [sos150630e]

These look like adjectival constructions, except that the participle is followed by *wɛ̀̃* (which I take here to be the associative postposition and not the habitual particle, but there is no way of distinguishing the two). The default construction for the forms in (58) would put the participle before sĭ (i.e. *jõ tằ-fį̄ɛ sĭ* and *jəbɛ̋ sənɛ̋ sĭ*).

Negative participial predicates follow the same pattern as other predicates with sĭ, using the suppletive verb *ɲá* and clause-final *ŋɛ́*:

(59) ằ   nɛ̋-jərán-jərǎn   ɲá   ŋɛ́
      3SG TRANS-RED-change.PTCP   be.NEG NEG
      'It has not changed.' [sos170711t1:110]

For more on negation, see §13.5.

13.4 Tense

Tense is a distinct inflectional dimension from aspect in Seenku. There is a binary distinction, present vs. past. Present tense is unmarked, but past tense is encoded not on the verb itself but by a TAMP marker *lɛ̋* after the subject. This is schematized in (60):

(60) *Schematization of past tense*
      Subject *lɛ̋* (Object) Verb

In this schematization, I have used simply a neutral designation of "verb", since both realis and irrealis forms can be put into past tense. The one exception to this schematization is the stative/resultative predicate, where the past tense marker follows the participle; this will be discussed further below. While (60) shows an overt segmental TAMP marker, this commonly undergoes clitic elision (§4.4.3), leaving behind only its tone and lengthening on the preceding subject. Its tone is uniformly S, since TAMP markers (unlike post-verbal particles or postpositions) do not undergo argument-head tone sandhi. For example:

(61) a. mó   lɛ̋   ~ móő
          1SG.EMPH   PST   1SG.EMPH.PST
      b. dôn   nɛ̋   ~ dôőn
          child PST   child.PST

In (61b), the /l/ of the past TAMP marker nasalizes due to the latent nasal on *dôn* 'child'. As we can see, this clitic elision process can create some lexically-unattested contour tones, such as this trough-shaped tone HXS.

Past tense formation is very straightforward, since it does not interact with the inflected form of the verb. For illustration's sake, I briefly provide examples of each aspect that can combine with past tense in the subsections below; note that imperatives (§13.2.3) and the immediate past (§13.3.1.2) do not combine with the past TAMP marker.

13.4.1 Past prospective

The main evidence that *ná* marks prospective aspect and not future tense comes from the fact that it can combine with the past tense.

(62) a. mó lɛ́ ná bî sà̰
       1SG.EMPH PST PROSP goat buy.IRR
       'I was going to buy a goat.' [sos150317e]

   b. mó ń bà̰ né móő ná kɛ́
       1SG.EMPH 1SG do.REAL.PFV 1SG.COMP 1SG.EMPH.PST PROSP go.IRR
       'I said that I was going to go.' [sos170822t1:2]

A different auxiliary verb *lò* 'come' instead of *ná* can also be used:

(63) nɛ́ lò ń dəgá bà̰
     1SG.PST come 1SG younger.brother hit.IRR
     'I was going to hit my younger brother.' [sos150808e]

The past prospective is also used in counterfactual constructions, meaning 'would have':

(64) a. mʒ̀ɔ ná à̰ nɔ́ í səgɔ̃́
       person.PST PROSP 3SG eat.IRR LOG good
       'We would have eaten well.' [sos170803e]

   b. nɛ́ ná wɛ́ ḭ̀ dzį̀ à̰ dəbî nɛ̰̀
       1SG.PST PROSP FOC 3PL put.IRR DEF oven LOC
       'I would have put them in the oven.' [sos170822t1:47]

For more on counterfactuals, see §18.3.

13.4.2 Past habitual

The habitual can be put into the past tense to create a past imperfective or past habitual reading, similar to English 'used to'. For example:

(65) a. mɔ̃ɔ̰   à   təmɛ̀   wɛ̀
       person.PST 3SG tell.IRR HAB
       'We used to tell it.' [sos161009t1:111]

   b. mɔ̃ɔ̰   nəfòo nəgɛ̀   wɛ̀
       person.PST animal herd.IRR HAB
       'We used to herd animals.' [sos170702t1:87]

   c. kɛ́ ĩ   à   sərè   wɛ̀ tsí̋   nɛ̋
       COP 3PL.PST 3SG pound.IRR HAB mortar LOC
       'They used to pound it in mortars.' [sos170702t1:75]

This construction is common in narratives discussing past practices.

13.4.3 Past progressive

To form a past progressive, the past TAMP marker *lɛ̋* simply precedes the progressive auxiliary *sĭ* 'be'. (Incidentally, this is the same construction for the past tense of *sĭ* 'be' used in copular or existential constructions; §14.2.)

(66) a. móő   sĭ kɔ̀sɛ́́ɛ   nɛ̋
       1SG.EMPH be be.careful.REAL.NOM LOC
       'I was being careful.' [sos150629e]

   b. móő   sĭ ɲǜnɛ̀   nɛ̀̈
       1SG.EMPH.PST be be.sick.REAL.NOM LOC
       'I was sick.' [sos130821e]

I have not seen any cases of the past progressive in the text corpus.

13.4.4 Past perfective

The past perfective is quite common compared to the other past aspects, since of course it is most likely that actions that occurred in the past would be completed with respect to the time of reference (usually the time of speaking). As we already saw in §13.3.2.1, the past perfective is most common form offered in elicitation when translating the French *passé composé*.

The following is a selection of examples from the text corpus:

(67) a. Parce que mó lɛ́ á wó céré
because.FR 1SG.EMPH PST 2SG.EMPH call.REAL.PFV
'Because I called you.' [sos170711t1:216]

b. kərù lɛ́ ɲḭ̀
hyena PST run.REAL.PFV
'Hyena ran.' [sos161009t1:207]

c. ǐi fä̰ kʊ́ wɛ́
3PL.PST pass.REAL.PFV D.DEF with
'They passed her.' [sos170805t9:26]

13.4.5 Past perfect

Finally, the perfect aspect can be in the present, as we saw in §13.3.2.2, or the past tense. We do not find many examples of past perfects in the text corpus; the following examples are a mix of naturally occurring and elicited:

(68) a. mó yɛ̀rɛ̰̀ nəgḭ̀ lɛ́ büɔ ä̰ kú lê ä̰ lɛ́
1SG.EMPH self.JU mind PST go.out.REAL.PRF DEF thing PRES 3SG DAT
'I myself had forgotten that thing.' [sos161009t1:107]

b. kɛ́ cǘen-sǎn nɛ́ ä̰ kṵ̈ ɲì-nà jəmɯ̰̈
COP monster-thing PST 3SG catch.REAL.PRF there-towards bush
'[They thought] a monster had caught him in the bush.' [sos170711t1:28]

c. móő̰ səmä
1SG.EMPH.PST dance.REAL.PRF
'I had (already) danced.' [sos150317e]

13.4.6 Past stative/resultative

In all of the past constructions just described, the past TAMP marker lɛ́ follows the subject. In the case of participial predicates, however, it follows the participial:

(69) a. bíe-lôn təgǐ lɛ́ sɪ̰̌ kpénéǹ kɔ̀n
goat-child stand.PTCP PST be mound on
'The baby goat was standing on the mound.' [sos170728e]

b. ằ təgǒ lɛ̋ sɪ̌
   3SG sit.PTCP PST be
   'He was seated.' [sos150709e]

If the location of the past TAMP marker is an indication of constituency and the boundaries of the subject, then we would have to say that participles are in fact a nominalized form, and this nominalized clause is the subject of an existential predicate with sɪ̌ 'be'. For instance, (69a) would translate literally to 'the baby goat's standing was on the mound'. It is certainly possible that this is the correct syntactic interpretation, but more data are required to fully tease out the syntactic structure.

13.5 Negation

As we have seen throughout this chapter, negation is remarkably simple in Seenku: in all but one case (constructions with the auxiliary sɪ̌), the only indication of negation is a particle ɲé at the end of the clause. This clause-final negation is an areal feature, attested in other local Mande languages like Jalkunan (Heath 2017) but also in unrelated Gur and Kru languages (Dryer 2009, Idiatov 2010); it is not a feature of Mande languages more broadly.

Only inflectional constructions that use the auxiliary sɪ̌ (the progressive, §13.3.1.1, and stative/resultative predicates, §13.3.3) have distinct negative morphology, where the affirmative auxiliary verb sɪ̌ 'be' has a suppletive negative form ɲá.

We also see the collapse of different affirmative inflections in the negative, specifically when it comes to completed actions; while there are distinct perfect, perfective, and immediate past forms in the affirmative, these are neutralized to the negative perfective. As a consultant has told me, if something hasn't occurred, why does it matter how recently it didn't take place?

The examples in (70) illustrate the negative for the prospective (70a), habitual (70b), imperative (70c), hortative (70d), progressive (70e), and perfective (70f).

(70) a. mó   nǎ   ằ   nɔ́   bűrű tɛ̋ ɲé
        1SG.EMPH PROSP 3SG eat.IRR bread GEN NEG
        'I'm not going to eat it with bread.' [sos161009t1:223]

   b. mí̋ kó̰   tsɪ̰̀n   mɛ̀ ɲé
      1PL D.DEF cut.IRR HAB NEG
      'We don't cut that.' [sos170711t1:56]

   c. á   tɛ̈ɛ   ằ   kɔ̀rő lɛ̋ ɲé
      2SG touch.IRR 3SG steam DAT NEG
      'Don't touch the steam!' [sos150807e]

d. mɔ̰́ɔ́   bɛ̀ɛ sà̰   ŋé
   person.SBJV pig buy.IRR NEG
   'Let's not buy a pig.' [sos150317e]

e. ì   á   ɲá   pìɔn fíɛ   ně í   səgɔ̌ ŋé
   COMP 2SG be.NEG flute blow.REAL.NOM LOC LOG good NEG
   '[He said] you are not playing the flute well.' [sos150626t4:50]

f. óo   nìgì jîo   ŋé òo
   2SG.EMPH cow see.REAL.PFV NEG EXCL
   'You didn't get any cows!' [sos161009t1:231]

As the example in (70e) shows, the clause-final negative particle is still used even with the negative auxiliary ɲá̰.

14 Non-verbal predicates

This chapter turns to predicates without the regularly inflected verbs described in the last chapter. These include constructions using one of two 'be' verbs, the copula *ké* (§14.1) or the auxiliary verb *sǐ* seen in the last chapter in the progressive (§13.3.1.1) and stative (§13.3.3); this latter, *sǐ*, forms the basis of a wide range of predicate types. I will address the copula first, then turn to the use of *sǐ* in existential (§14.2), adjectival (§14.3), possessive (§14.4), and volitional (§14.5) constructions.

14.1 Copula *ké*

The copula is an equative linker, the equals sign in X = Y. It has an almost invariant shape in Seenku, though there is some variation in the vowel depending on speaker. In the speech of SCT (and most likely in the speech of GET, though measurements are inconclusive), the form of the copula is *ké*, but in the speech of some other speakers who have a four-way front vowel distinction (/i, ɪ, e, ɛ/), the copula is pronounced *ké*. The transcription in the examples below will reflect that speaker's pronunciation.

The only variants we find of the copula are a past tense formed by tone raising (*ké̋*, discussed in §14.1.2) and a portmanteau discourse definite copula (*kóʊ*, discussed §14.1.3).

The Seenku copula is interesting from a Mande-internal standpoint in that the order differs from the Mande languages in Schreiber's (2008) typology. When both an argument and a predicate NP are present, the order is the same as in all of the other Mande languages (N_{arg} COP N_{pred}), but when just the predicate is present, the copula still precedes it (COP N_{pred}); see below.

For the use of the copula in focus marking, see §21.1.3.

14.1.1 Basic function

As defined in the introduction to this section, the copula has an equative function. While it can be used exactly like an equals sign between two nouns or pronouns (X *ké* Y), the subject X is most often omitted. This is somewhat surprising, since the language typically does not tolerate null arguments and instead resorts to dummy 3sg pronouns (e.g. when citing an inalienable noun, §8.6.1, or in headless NPs with adjectives, §8.3.4).

Examples of these null subject copulative constructions are shown in (1):

(1) a. ké kótê məŋě
 COP calabash small
 '[It] is a little calabash.' [sos170711t1:106]

 b. ké gɔ́ɔ sɔ́ɛn, bɛ́nɛ́-gɔ́ɔ
 COP wood one tree.sp-wood
 '[It] is a single [kind of] wood, *Pterocarpus erinaceus*.' [sos170711t1:71]

 c. mɛ̏ í bɛ̋ ɩ̀ ôőɩ̀ ké kəré-bɔ́ɔ lé təgǒ
 3SG.SUBORD LOG do.IRR COMP no COMP COP man-old REL sit.PTCP
 bɛ́ lɛ̏ ké kʊ́
 be.REL PRES COP D.DEF
 'He said, no, [it] is the old man who is sitting there, it's him.' [sos170711t1:23]

The subject 'it' in these examples is implied; there is no need to fill the subject slot with a pronoun.

If the subject is other than a basic 'it', then it is overt and precedes the copula, as shown in (2):

(2) a. mó təgɔ̀n ké Màmǎdû
 1SG.EMPH name COP Mamadou
 'My name is Mamadou.' [sos171009t1:10]

 b. bá̰a̰-brɛ̋ ké kɛ̋
 balafon-play.NOM.PL COP griot.PL
 'Balafon players are griots.' [sos171009t1:18]

 c. óo ké kərṳ̀
 2SG.EMPH COP hyena
 'You are a glutton (=hyena).' [sos150626t4:17]

As we can see, there is no other special marking or inflection on the copula when an overt subject is present. The copula simply equates the subject with the noun that follows.

We likewise see no changes in form when the copula construction is negated; the copula retains its same form, and the clause is simply followed by the clause-final negation particle ŋé:

(3) a. ké á wóò nìgì ŋé dò̰, ké Fàatűu nı̋gı̋
 COP 2SG EMPH.DAT cow NEG EMPH COP Fatou.DAT cow
 '[It] is not your cow, it's Fatou's cow!' [sos161009t1:62]

b. ké kɔ́ jèn-jèn bé yɛ̏rɛ̏ ŋé
COP D.DEF RED-story DEM self NEG
'[It] is not that same story.' [sos161009t1:87]

c. méɛ lɛ̏ kà bâa gɔ̀ sô dzʋ̈ kǎa
REL.PRO SUBORD go.REAL.PFV balafon learn.IRR road edge next.to
tsɛ̋-ké mǐ nɔ̋ ké sɔ́en ŋé
and 1PL that.for COP one NEG
'Those who went and learned the balafon on the side of the road and what we do, [it] is not the same.' [sos170711t1:75]

This is in contrast to the existential auxiliary 'be', which has a suppletive negative form; see §14.2 below.

14.1.2 Past tense

The one case in which the copula sees its form altered is in the past tense. Instead of regular past tense marking, either with the segmental TAMP marker lɛ̋ or with its tone and length (§13.4), the copula has a portmanteau form kɛ̋. The effect of this tonal change is shown in the following pair of forms from elicitation:

(4) a. ké tɔ́ɔsǐ
COP flashlight
'[It] is a flashlight.' [sos170802e]

b. kɛ̋ tɔ́ɔsǐ
COP.PST flashlight
'[It] was a flashlight.' [sos170802e]

This past tense form is far less common in the text corpus, but we find a few examples:

(5) a. mǐ jərá-ŋɛ̋ kərúǐ kɛ̋ kɛ̋ ŋé
1PL family-HUM.PL all.PL COP.PST griot.PL NEG
'My whole family were not griots.' [sos171009t1:34]

b. mǐ nɔ̋ kɛ̋ kûɛ tsɛ̋-ké sì
1PL for COP.PST calabash and jars
'For us, it was the calabash and the clay water jar.' [sos170702t1:74]

c. kűɛ kɛ̋ gbɛ̀nɛ̋-sɛ̋
others COP.PST before-thing.PL
'Those were things of the past.' [sos170702t1:75]

d. mais *kʊ́ bíaa-cɪ́ bɛ́ kɛ̋ sâŋgə̰́nsɔ̋*
but.FR D.DEF mud-house DEM COP.PST two.story.house
'But those mudbrick houses were two-story houses.' [sos170702t1:58]

Note that the speaker in (5a) pronounces the copula with the vowel /e/, which forms a minimal pair with the plural form *kɛ̋* 'griots' that follows it.

14.1.3 Discourse definite copula

If the subject of a copula construction is the discourse definite, then the copula is absorbed into this discourse definite pronoun, resulting in vowel lengthening. This is generally less common than the plain copula with a null subject, but it appears to be the construction of choice in responding to riddles, where the discourse definite refers back to the clue given by the riddle teller:

(6) a. *kʊ̋ʊ mɔ̰̏ ɲənȁ-ɲənȁ*
D.DEF.COP person RED-shadow
'It's a shadow.' [sos161009t1:16]

b. *kʊ̋ʊ jəgȅ*
D.DEF.COP dog
'It's a dog.' [sos161009t1:69]

c. *kʊ̋ʊ ɲəgɔ̋-jʊ̋*
D.DEF.COP potash-water
'It's potash water.' [sos150626t1:4]

However, we do find this construction outside of the context of riddles as well, as the following examples show:

(7) a. *kʊ̋ʊ nȉgȉ tsɛ̰̋ mó tȅ*
D.DEF.COP cow how 1SG.EMPH GEN
'How many cows is that for me?' [sos161009t1:26]

b. *á wôo ȁ kárə̰́ lɛ́ lɛ̏ jɪ́o nɛ̋ kʊ̋ʊ*
2SG EMPH.SUBORD DEF school REL PRES say.REAL.NOM LOC D.DEF.COP
sɔ̏kó-kû
Jula-thing
'That "school" that you are saying, that's Jula.' [sos170702t1:32]

c. *ȉ kʊ̋ʊ fɛ́n tsɔ́ lɛ́ wɛ́ ȁ kȁ*
COMP D.DEF.COP thing type which FOC 3SG in.hand
'[They asked] what is that thing that he was holding.' [sos170711t1:34]

In each case, there is a discourse salient referent indicated by the use of *kóʋ*.

14.2 Existential predicates

While the equative 'be' is indicated in Seenku through the copula *ké*, other translations of 'be' such as existentials or locatives use the form *sǐ*. I will first address affirmative examples before turning to the suppletive negative form *ɲá* in §14.2.1.

We first saw *sǐ* as an auxiliary verb in the progressive (§13.3.1.1), which I noted to be identical in form to locative expressions. In this section, I will focus exclusively on these existential and locative predicates, which form the foundation of possessive and volitional predicates discussed in §14.4-14.5.

Unlike the copula *ké*, *sǐ* always requires a subject. We can see that with the following examples with the 3sg:

(8) a. *ǎ   sǐ sɔ̀kɔ́-kû   nɛ̀   lìbúúrú nɛ̀*
       3SG be Jula-thing LOC book   LOC
       'It's in Jula in a book.' [sos161009t1:196]

   b. *ké ǎ   sǐ mɔ̰̀mɑ̰́*
       COP 3SG be a.lot
       'There are a lot [of generations].' [sos171009t1:77]

   c. *ké ǎ   sǐ kʋ́   tɔ̋*
       COP 3SG be D.DEF like
       'It's like that.' [sos170714t3:93]

Even though the 3sg *ǎ* in these cases doesn't contribute anything that is not already evident from the discourse, it still must be used. For the use of *ké* in focus constructions like these, see §21.1.3.

At its core, the auxiliary *sǐ* is an existential; it implies the existence (or non-existence, in the case of the negative) of the subject. Location can be left unspecified, in which case the clause simply means existence:

(9) a. *á   wó tɛ̋-mənǐ   sǐ, mənǐ-dərő̃n tsɛ̋ sǐ á   wó jǔnǐ*
       2SG EMPH dear-woman be woman-child INDF be 2SG EMPH eye.PL
       bǔɔ   sǐ kʋ́   tɛ̀
       go.out.PTCP be D.DEF GEN
       'There is your girlfriend, there is a girl who you like...' [sos170714t2:83]

b. *kʊ́ kʊ́ kὲ   bɛ̋   fáná sɪ̌*
   D.DEF D.DEF griot.PL DEM.PL also be
   'There are also those [kinds of] griots.' [sos171009t1:92]

c. *bṵ̀ɛ̀-dɪ̀   təgɔ̋ɛ   sɪ̌ wétənɛ̌, ĩi   ɲṵ́ɪ̰-cɪ́   ɲɛ̋*
   djinn-child.PL certain.PL be now   3PL.PST honey-house build.IRR
   wɛ̋
   HAB
   'There were some djinns who were in the process of building an apiary.'
   [sos130828t2:1]

In (9a), there are two existential clauses in a row, both denoting the existence of a young woman and implying that she is there when the young men are farming, but this latter part is left unsaid. The third clause also contains the auxiliary verb *sɪ̌*, but in a participial predicate; see §13.3.3 below. The example in (9b) summarizes the discussion of another kind of griot, and the speaker reiterates their existence with this sentence. Finally, the example in (9c) is the clearest existential, since it is the first line of a folktale and simply sets up the existence of some key players in the story.

Locative predicates take these existential predicates as their base and simply add a locative PP or adverb after *sɪ̌*. For instance:

(10) a. *mɔ̀ɛ   bɔ̋ɛɛ   sɪ̌ ɲì   ì   à   fó-nȅn   trù*
       person.PL old.PL be there 3PL 3SG fonio-grain sweep.IRR
       'Old people are there sweeping up fonio grains.' [sos170714t3:145]

   b. *mó   ɲəgɔ́n-kɔ̀sɪ́   sɪ̌ kʊ́   dəgɔɔ bé   nɛ̏*
       1SG.EMPH same-friend.PL be D.DEF place DEM LOC
       'My agemates are there in that place.' [sos170711t1:267]

   c. *kɛ́ á wó kɛ̏ɛ sɪ̌ ằ nɛ̏*
       COP 2SG EMPH taboo be 3SG LOC
       'Your taboo is in it.' [sos170711t1:282]

   d. *ì-ǎ-lɔ́   kɛ́ kɔ̀ɛɛ   tsɛ̋ sɪ̌ ằ   nɛ̏, kɛ́ kɔ̀ɛɛ   nɔ̀ dərɔ̂*
       you.know.JU COP hole.PL how be 3SG LOC COP hole.PL five only
       'You know there are some holes in it, only five holes.' [sos170711t1:343]

The first example, (10a), employs an adverb *ɲì* 'there' to indicate location. The other three examples use PPs with the general locative postposition *né*, either with a more specified locative phrase as in (10b) or simply with the 3sg pronoun, which makes reference to something else in the discourse (the balafon in (10c) and a flute in (10d)).

For more examples of locative predicates, see Chapter 10 on postpositions and adverbials.

14.2 Existential predicates

While these existential or locative uses are the most common for sį̌, we find occasional examples where it is used in a copula-like manner:

(11) a. móő   sį̌ dəró-mɔ̌
    1SG.EMPH.PST be child-HUM.SG
    'I was a child.' [sos170711t1:158]

b. jằnkʊ́ ằá   sį̌ kâ
    even.if 3SG.SBJV be griot
    'Even if it is a griot.' [sos170711t1:246]

Example (11a) shows that past tense marking with the auxiliary sį̌ is regular, using the TAMP marker lɛ̌ (here elided with the subject pronoun). Interestingly, in (11b), we see that the 3sg subject is still required with sį̌, even though it has an equative usage here. When asked whether the copula ké could be used in place of sį̌ in these examples, a consultant agreed that the two are interchangeable for (11a) but not for (11b). More data are required to determine when sį̌ may be used in place of the regular copula.

14.2.1 Negative existential ɲá

Unlike the copula, the existential auxiliary sį̌ has a suppletive negative form ɲá, which must co-occur with regular clause-final negation (that is, negation is marked twice in these sentences). The examples below include a mix of existential and locative predicates in the negative:

(12) a. mais kʊ́ ɲá sɛ́ɛ-kû   nɛ̌ ŋé
    but.FR D.DEF be.NEG Sambla-thing LOC NEG
    'But that is not in Seenku.' [sos171009t1:45]

b. bɑ́ɑ-brɛ̌   ɲá Gbéné-gʊ̀   ŋé
    balafon-play.NOM.PL be.NEG Bouende-under NEG
    'There are no balafonists in Bouende.' [sos170711t1:443]

c. kʊ́ǔ ɲá ằ nɛ̌ ŋé
    D.DEF.PST be.NEG 3SG LOC NEG
    'That wasn't part of it.' [sos170714t3:117]

d. mənǐ nɔ̰́ ké fó-nèn ɲì, parce-que gbə̀nə̋
woman that.for COP fonio-grain pick.up.NOM because.FR before
wótərő ɲá ŋé, fú-fú ɲá ŋé, ké ḭ̀ fó-nèn
cart be.NEG NEG RED-nothing be.NEG NEG COP 3PL fonio-grain
ɲì
pick.up.NOM
'For women, it was carrying fonio, because before, there were no carts, there was nothing, it was them carrying fonio.' [sos170714t3:156]

The examples in (12a-b) show simple negative locative predicates, (12a) with a locative PP and (12b) with a place name used adverbially. The example in (12b) shows a past negative locative, with past tense marking on the subject and negation marked through the suppletive verb ɲá and clause-final negation. The example in (12d) is more complex, but there are two consecutive negative existential clauses, first saying that no carts existed, and then that nothing existed.

For the suppletive negative ɲá in progressives, see §13.5.

14.3 Adjectival predicates

Section 8.3 introduced adjectives and their use as modifiers in the NP. Here we turn to adjectival predicates, which use the existential auxiliary sɪ̰̌. Curiously, adjectives in adjectival predicates are always preceded by the logophoric pronoun í. This construction is schematized in (13):

(13)   *Schematization of adjectival predicates*
        Subject sɪ̰̌ í Adjective

The copula ké is never used with adjectives. The logophoric pronoun is co-indexed with the subject and surfaces as í in every person/number combination except the 1sg, in which case ń is used instead; for more on the logophoric pronoun, see §6.7.

Adjectival predicates are only rarely attested in the text corpus, and the attested examples are largely in the plural. Thus for simplicity of presentation, I provide elicited examples of singular adjectival predicates here first. The distinction between the 1sg logophoric pronoun ń and the regular logophoric pronoun can be seen in the following examples:

(14) a. mó   sɪ̰̌ ń sɪ̰̀ɛ
          1SG.EMPH be 1SG red
          'I am red.' [sos130821e]

b. ằ sḭ́ í sḭ̀ɛ
3SG be LOG red
'He is red.' [sos130821e]

c. mǽ sḭ́ í sí-sḭ̀ɛ
1PL be LOG RED-red
'We are red.' [sos130821e]

The example in (14c) shows that not all first person subjects take *ń*; it is just the combination 1sg that is exceptional in which pronoun is used before the adjective.

This last example also illustrates how plural is marked on the adjective in plural adjectival predicates, via initial CV reduplication; for schematizations and examples, see §8.3.3.2. In this case, we find three examples of plural adjectival predicates with parallel structure in a text:

(15) a. təgɔ́́ɛ sḭ́ í bú-bəlě təgɔ́́ɛ sḭ́ í mú-məɲě
some.PL be LOG RED-big.PL some.PL be LOG RED-small.PL
'Some are big, some are small.' [sos170711t1:86]

b. təgɔ́́ɛ sḭ́ í jú-jṵ̀i
some.PL be LOG RED-long.PL
'Some are long.' [sos170711t1:88]

In addition to initial CV reduplication (with semi-fixed vocalism), the adjectival stem itself is marked for plural via regular nominal plural inflection (§5.3.1), including vowel fronting and tone raising. In (15a), both are vacuously applied to *bəlě* (which already ends with a front vowel and S tone), and *məɲě* is an irregular plural form of singular *mŏén* 'small'. The vowel fronting effect can be seen in (15b), where singular *jṵ̆* becomes the back-front diphthong *jṵ̀i*.

Negative adjectival predicates are formed as expected, by replacing *sḭ́* with its suppletive negative form *ɲá* in conjunction with the clause-final negative particle:

(16) jʊ̀ŋmǎ ɲá í kǎ̰ ŋé
cat be.NEG LOG white NEG
'The cat is not white.' [sos160825e]

Note that in some cases, it is difficult to discern whether a qualifier is an adjective, participle, or ideophone. As a modifier, all three share largely the same construction (see §8.3.3), but in predicates, they diverge. Participial predicates will be discussed in §13.3.3. Before leaving this section, I will briefly illustrate what appears to be the predicate structure for ideophonic qualifiers:

(17) a. bǎ ɲá   pètè ŋé
       table be.NEG flat NEG
       'The table is not flat.' [sos160825e]

   b. ǎ sɪ̌ kɔ́kɔ́
      3SG be short
      'He is short.' [sos170728e]

Like regular adjectival predicates, the qualifier 'flat' or 'short' follows the auxiliary verb *sɪ̌* 'be'. But unlike these adjectives, no logophoric pronoun is present (and it is in fact ungrammatical to include one). It is only a very small class of qualifiers that work this way, and as the examples in (17) show, their stem shape sets them apart from regular Seenku vocabulary; thus I treat these as ideophonic in nature and as such outside of regular adjectival predicates. Note that the one case in the text corpus in which a predicate with 'short' is attested, the speaker uses a copular construction:

(18) í wó à jərà í wó ké m̰̀ kɔ́kɔ́
     LOG EMPH 3SG think LOG EMPH COP person short
     'I thought I was short [lit. a short person].' [sos161009t1:154]

We thus cannot tell if this X *sɪ̌* Ideo construction would be naturally used in speech or not.

14.4 Possessive predicates

Possessive predicates in Seenku are essentially existential in nature. There is no explicit verb 'have'—instead, the semantically possessed noun is the subject of an existential predicate (with *sɪ̌* 'be'), and the possessor is encoded in a postpositional phrase, most commonly with the genitive postposition *tě* but occasionally with the dative postposition *lě* or the postposition *ká* 'in hand'.

I first illustrate possessive predicates with simple examples from elicitation:

(19) a. bî sɪ̌ mó   tḛ̀
       goat be 1SG.EMPH GEN
       'I have a goat' [sos170705e]

   b. bî ɲá ǎ tê ŋé
      goat be.NEG 3SG GEN NEG
      'He doesn't have a goat.' [sos170705e]

An affirmative clause is shown in (19a), with the auxiliary verb *sɪ̌*; this is replaced by *ɲá* in the negative in (19b), coupled with the clause-final negative particle.

From texts, we find the following examples of possession with the genitive *tě*:

(20) a. gɔ̋ɛɛ sɪ̰ mó tɛ̀ dó
wood.PL be 1SG.EMPH GEN EMPH
'I have wood at my house.' [sos170822t1:48]

b. jén-jɛ̋en sɪ̰ mó tɛ̀ mɔ̀mɑ̋ mɛ̀ fɑ̰
RED-story.PST be 1SG.EMPH GEN a.lot 3SG.SUBORD pass
'I used to have so many stories.' [sos150626t2:27]

c. mənɪ̋-dərṍn kɔ̋nɑ̋ ɲá ɪ̀ tê ŋɛ́
woman-child elder be.NEG 3PL GEN NEG
'They don't have an elder daughter.' [sos170714t3:113]

d. ɪ̀ kɔ́ bɑ̰̀ɑ̰ ɲá ɪ̀ tê ŋɛ́
COMP D.DEF balafon be.NEG 3PL GEN NEG
'[They said that] they don't have a balafon.' [sos171009t1:93]

Examples (20a-b) are affirmative, but (20b) is also additionally inflected for past tense (via the elision of the past tense clitic lɛ̋ into the subject/possessed noun). The examples in (20c-d) are negative. As these examples suggest, the genitive postposition tɛ̋ is most common in possession because it indicates a kind of general possession, where the possessed noun may not be on the person at the time but they do own it. In (20a) especially, we see an overlap between the use of tɛ̋ in a possessive predicate vs. its use to indicate one's abode, like French *chez*. Thus, *mó tɛ̀* in this example could also be understood as 'at my house' or *chez moi*.

If the possessed noun is understood to be currently on the person, then the postposition ká 'in hand' is used in place of tɛ̋:

(21) a. kɛ́ nìgɪ̀ tsìi sɪ̰ mó kɑ̀ lɛ̋
COP cow six be 1SG.EMPH in.hand EMPH
'I have six cows!' [sos161009t1:76]

b. á jɛ̀nflɛ́n dəgɛ̋ ɲəgɔ́ɔ́ sɪ̰ nɛ̋ á kɑ̀ á ɲəgɔ́
2SG soap make.IRR potash.SBJV be if 2SG in.hand 2SG potash
bɛ̋
do.IRR
'You make soap, if you have potash, you make potash.' [sos170822t1:75]

In these two examples, the possessed noun has more immediate relevance and the person is expected to either literally or metaphorically (in the case of "cow" rewards for answering riddles, (21a)) have the possessed noun on them.

Other postpositions are also attesed with less frequency, including locative nɛ́ (specifically pertaining to illnesses), the associative wɛ̀, and the dative lɛ̋:

(22) a. ɛ̂ɛ́   dəgɛ̀ təgɔ́ kʊ́   nɔ̀gɔ̀ bɛ́ sĭ mó   nɛ̀
 3SG.LOG make like D.DEF illness DEM be 1SG.EMPH LOC
 'It's as if I had that illness.' [sos170822t2:39]

  b. fűi   ɲá   mɔ̀ɔ̀   ŋɛ́
   nothing be.NEG person.with NEG
   'We have nothing [wrong].' [sos170822t1:20]

  c. dzɔ̋   sĭ mɔ̀ɛ   dəgě   lɛ̋
   hunger be person.PL remainder.PL DAT
   'The other people were hungry.' [sos170714t3:85]

Thus, as I see it, while the least marked form of possessive predicates may contain the genitive postposition *tɛ̋*, there is nothing obligatory about this form for possession. In fact, we may go so far as to say that there is no explicit possessive predicate construction in Seenku, but rather that they form a subset of locative predicates.

For a discussion of possession in the NP, see §8.6.

14.5 Volitional predicates

The last predicate type to discuss in this chapter is the volitional predicate, the Seenku equivalent of "want". In Seenku, there are no verbs meaning specifically 'want' or 'desire'. Rather, periphrastic constructions are used instead. There are two different constructions used to express this meaning, one that resembles possession and can be used for both NP and clausal arguments ('want X' vs. 'want to X'), and one that can only be used with NP arguments. I refer to these as "want predicates" and "desire predicates", respectively, and address them in turn below.

14.5.1 'Want' predicates

The 'want' predicate is a non-verbal predicate since there is no explicit verb meaning 'want' in Seenku. Once again we find the existential *sĭ* in these expressions in what looks like a reverse of the possessive predicate, with the one experiencing the wanting as the subject and the thing that is desired in a PP with the genitive *tɛ̋* after *sĭ*. This predicate construction is schematized in (23):

(23) *Schematic of 'want' predicates*
   Subject *sĭ* Object *tɛ̋*

For instance:

(24) a. ń sį̀ kǜ tḛ̀
       1SG be toh GEN
       'I want toh.' [sos120108e]

   b. ń sį̀ bǎ̰ pètérté tḛ̀
       1SG be table flat GEN
       'I want a flat table.' [sos160825e]

If the order of the arguments were reversed, then these examples would mean 'I have toh' and 'I have a flat table', respectively.

Examples from the text corpus include:

(25) a. ń sį̀ sáa té̋ tsé̋-ké jḛ̀nflé̋n
       1SG be tobacco GEN and soap
       'I want tobacco and soap.' [sos170822t3:124]

   b. Dípè ɲá kṍ tḛ̀ ŋé, Dípè sį̀ ä̀ sṳ̀kǎrǎ nǒ̰n té̋
       Dipe be.NEG D.DEF GEN NEG Dipe be DEF sugar that.for GEN
       'Dipe doesn't want that, Dipe wants what is sweet.' [sos170822t3:44]

   c. íwí̋ ɲá bö̀ ä̀ tê ŋé
       1PL.EXCL be.NEG anymore 3SG GEN NEG
       '[They said that] they don't want her anymore.' [sos171009t1:67]

The example in (25a) shows that when two arguments are conjoined, only the first is followed by the genitive postposition. The example in (25b) illustrates an affirmative and negative volitional predicate back-to-back, with the negative formed as expected with the suppletive form ɲá and the clause-final negative particle. The negative form is shown again in (25c).

This particular volitional construction is far more commonly used to introduce a subordinated clause, as in:

(26) mó sį̀ ń tḛ̀ móo cȅrȅ
       1SG.EMPH be 1SG GEN 1SG.EMPH.SBJV sleep.IRR
       'I want to sleep.' [sos170811e]

For more on subordination with 'want', see §19.3.1.1.

14.5.2 'Desire' predicates

If the volitional predicate is expressing a desire for something, another construction can be used. In this 'desire' construction, a noun which I gloss as 'desire' is added after the desired noun. Two forms are attested: kű and kɔ̋rɔ̋. The first is invariant, always S-toned, whereas the second undergoes sandhi with the desired noun. This noun-noun sequence is followed by *sį̀*, which is in turn followed by a postpositional phrase containing the NP experiencing the desire. This construction is schematized in (27) with "desiree" and "desirer" rather than "subject" and "object":

(27) *Schematic of 'desire' predicates*
    Desiree *kű/kɔ̀rɔ̀ sį̀* Desirer P

As in possessive predicate constructions, P can be a range of postpositions, including *wɛ̀* 'with' (28a), *kɔ̃n* 'on' (28b), or the locative postposition *né* (28c). The following examples all employ the noun *kű*:

(28) a. *ɲų̋į̋ kű sį̀ à wɛ̀*
        honey desire be 3SG with
        'He want[ed] honey.' [sos130828t2:36]

   b. *jɛ̰̀nflɛ́n kű sį̀ ń kɔ̃n*
        soap desire be 1SG on
        'I want/need soap.' [sos170822t1:62]

   c. *sǻa kű sį̀ ń nɛ̰̀*
        tobacco desire be 1SG LOC
        'I want tobacco.' [sos170717e]

More data are required to tell whether the different postpositions lend different meanings to these expressions, such as degree of urgency.

With *kɔ̀rɔ̀*, we find the following examples:

(29) a. *bɛ̀ɛ tòo kɔ̀rɔ̀ sį̀ mó wɛ̋*
        pig ear desire be 1SG.EMPH with
        'I want a pig ear.' [sos150707e]

   b. *dɔ̀ɔ kɔ̀rɔ̀ sį̀ ń nɛ̰̀*
        beer desire be 1SG LOC
        'I want beer.' [sos170717e]

This form is less common than *kű*. In discussions with consultants, the strength or urgency of *kɔ̀rɔ̀* appears to be less than that of *kű*, which can also be translated as 'need'.

15 Comparatives

In this chapter, I will be following the terminology laid out in Dixon (2008). The subject of a comparative clause will be referred to as the **comparee**; the person or thing to which the subject is compared will be referred to as the **standard of comparison**; finally, the quality being compared (typically expressed as an adjectival or verbal predicate) will be referred to as the **parameter of comparison**.

15.1 Asymmetrical comparison

There is no comparative morphology on adjectives or adverbs in Seenku. Instead, asymmetrical comparison (e.g. 'better than', 'bigger than', etc.) involves some combination of the following elements: a comparative adverb or predicate *fő̃n*, a standard of comparison carrying the associative postposition *wɛ̀* or the postpositional noun *jɛ̃̀n* 'in front of', or the verbal predicate *fà̰* '(sur)pass'.

15.1.1 *fő̃n* 'better, more'

The most common way of marking asymmetrical comparison is with the comparative *fő̃n*. Typically, this immediately follows the verbal or adjectival predicate and precedes the standard of comparison, which appears in a postpositional phrase. It is not immediately apparent how this comparative *fő̃n* should be analyzed syntactically: a verb? An adverb? In many Mande languages, the equivalent of *fő̃n* in comparatives is either synchronically or diachronically a verb stem meaning '(sur)pass' or 'exceed'. For example, in Gban (Fedotov 2013), the verb *zà(lè)* 'exceed, fly over' is the comparative index which either acts as the second predicate in a bi-clausal comparative or precedes an infinitive indicating the parameter in a monoclausal comparative. In Jalkunan (Heath 2017), an "adjoined verb" *blé* '(sur)pass' follows the verbal predicate expressing the parameter. However, Jalkunan also uses what appears to be a cognate of Seenku *fő̃n*, *fɔ̃ ~ fɔ̰́*, which is itself a predicate meaning 'be better'; this is optionally followed by the '(sur)pass' verb. The Seenku equivalent can be used in both ways: as a stand-alone predicate or following another predicate.

In Seenku, *fő̃n* is invariable; it carries no identifiable morphology that would point to it being a regular verb or an adjectival verb. It closely resembles the verb *fà̰* '(sur)pass', discussed in §15.1.4, which could indicate a common origin, but this may also be coincidence. It is also used in non-comparative constructions as a clause-initial modal meaning 'should' (sometimes pronounced [fɔ̰́]), a construction that is also attested in Jula and Dzùùngoo (Solomiac 2007), which could indicate that a core meaning of 'best' (i.e. the modal interpretation is 'it is best that...'; see §19.3.1.2).

In other words, given the difficulty in categorizing *főn*, it is unclear whether Seenku comparatives should be treated as Type A where *főn* is a special index or Type B, where it is an exceed-type serial verb.

While qualificational predicates in Seenku are normally expressed with a copular auxiliary and an adjective, in comparatives, the adjectival stem is used verbally. It is this stem that is followed by *főn*:

(1) a. *jŭŋmǎ sɔ̀ főn jəgè wè*
       cat   pretty better dog with
       'The cat is prettier than the dog.' [sos130821e]

   b. *kű̃ɛ   kɔ́-kɔ́   főn   à   wò   wè*
      other.PL RED-short more 3SG EMPH with
      'They are shorter than him.' [sos161009t1:155]

   c. *kʊ́   nɛ̀ wé dò̃, ń   tɛ̃́ sân   kú-tsío   főn   ń   tɛ̃́*
      D.DEF LOC FOC EMPH 1SG dear rabbit thing-know.PFV better 1SG dear
      kərù   wè   âa
      hyena with NEG.Q
      'At that moment, Mr. Rabbit was cleverer than Mr. Hyena, wasn't he.' [sos150626t2:22]

   d. *ń   təgŏ   gɔ̀ɔ   bɔ́ɔ főn   ń   təgĭ   ń   tsɪ̰̀ɛ   mè*
      1SG sit.PTCP ground.with tall better 1SG stand.PTCP 1SG foot.PL with
      wè
      with
      'If I am sitting on the ground, I am taller than when I stand on my feet.' [sos161009t1:58]

In the simple elicited example in (1a), the adjective 'pretty' uses its verbal stem *sɔ̀*, rather than its typical adjectival stem *sagɔ́*; for examples of the predicate structure of the latter, see §14.3. This is followed by *főn*, which is in turn followed by the standard of comparison, *jəgè* 'dog', marked with the associative postposition *wè* (the two raise to *jəgè wè* by argument-head tone sandhi; §4.4.2). In (1c), the predicate is the compound verbal expression *kú-tó* (here *kú-tsío* in the perfective), which is again followed by *főn* and an associative-marked comparandum. Finally, (1d) (a riddle) displays nominalized clauses as both the subject and comparandum; this explains the stacking of two assocative postpositions at the end, where the first forms a constituent with 'my feet', and the second forms a constituent with the nominalized clause of the standard of comparison.

There is no special construction for negative comparisons; the comparative clause is simply followed by the clause-final negative marker:

(2) jəgə̀ bələ̀ főn   jʊ̀ŋmǎ wɛ̋   ɲé
    dog big better cat   with NEG
    'The dog is not bigger than the cat.' [sos120109e]

The preceding examples are the most explicit and complete form of asymmetrical comparatives. Elements besides *főn* are, however, optional, depending on the meaning of the clause. First, the standard of comparison can be omitted. A few utterances after (2d) in the text, the meaning of the riddle is explained, and the utterance ends with the comparative *főn*:

(3) jəgə̏ə́   təgǒ   sĭ nɛ̋ tő-tərő   í   tɔ̀ɔn kɔ̀n, ằ   təgĭ   sĭ tő-tərő
    dog.SBJV sit.PTCP be if RED-like LOG butt on   3SG stand.PTCP be RED-like
    ằ   təgǒ   lé lȅ   kʊ̋   bɔ́ɔ főn
    3SG sit.PTCP REL PRES D.DEF tall better
    'If a dog is sitting like that on its butt, it stands up like that, [when] it sits down, that is taller.' [sos161009t1:71]

Here, the standard of comparison is implied or understood by context; it is omitted from the utterance, leaving the comparative *főn* in final position. Other examples of omitted standards of comparison include:

(4) a. mó   ɲằa   kʊ̏ lɛ́ tằa   kʊ̋ dzɛ̋
       1SG.EMPH mother.SUBORD toh REL cook.IRR.HAB D.DEF delicious
       főn   môe
       better 1SG.EMPH.DAT
       'I prefer the toh that my mother makes [Lit. the toh that my mother makes is more delicious to me].' [sos170729e]

   b. ì-ǎ-lɔ́   mɔ̀ɔ́   dȅn flằ   nɛ̋ ằ
      you.know.JU person.SBJV bean thrash.REAL.PFV if 3SG
      kóò   főn
      produce.fruit.IRR.HAB better
      'You know if beans are thrashed, they produce more fruit.' [sos150626t2:7]

The PP after the comparative in (4a) is not a standard of comparison, but rather a dative pronoun expressing the opinion of the speaker ('to me').

In addition to omitting the standard of comparison, it is also possible to omit the adjectival/verbal predicate (the parameter of comparison) and simply use the comparative *főn* to mean 'better', with (5a) or without (5b) a copular auxiliary:

(5) a. mó yɛ̀rɛ̀ fő̋n Fátűmátáà wè
1SG.EMPH self.JU better Fatoumata with
'I myself am [still] better than Fatoumata.' [sos161009t1:177]

b. dő̋nké, səsɛ̋ nǰ né bɛ́ wé kú̋ sǐ fő̋n ǎ sä̀fɛ̋ jɛ̋n
SO.FR spider that.for REL be.REL FOC D.DEF be better DEF bag front
'So, the spider's stuff, that's better than the bag.' [sos170711t1:127]

Note in (5b) that the standard of comparison takes the postpositional noun *jɛ̋n* 'front' instead of the associative postposition *wɛ̀*.

Finally, in one case, the location of the comparative *fő̋n* is moved from after the predicate to the end of the clause:

(6) mí̋ fəgậ jö̀ màa Təmî-ŋɛ̀ wè fő̋n
1PL power see.IRR gain Karangasso-HUM.PL with better
'We get more power than [balafon players from] Karangasso.' [sos170711t1:416]

Consultants report that it could occur in its regular position after the verb.

15.1.2 Comparative APs

The comparative *fő̋n* is also used in AP comparison. In this construction, the AP does not take its usual place after the noun it modifies but rather it is placed at the end of the clause. There, it is preceded by the logophoric pronoun *í*, just as we see in adjectival predicates (§14.3). For example:

(7) a. ń jəgɛ̀ tsɛ̋ jîo í bəlĕ fő̋n cî̀ wè
1SG dog INDF see.REAL.PFV LOG big better house with
'I saw a dog bigger than a house.' [sos190803e]

b. ń tsïo tsɛ̋ kəɾɛ́` wè í bő̋ɔ fő̋n gɔ́ɔ̀-kù wè
1SG meet.REAL.PRF INDF man with LOG tall better wood-thing with
'I met a man taller than a tree.' [sos190803e]

As usual, the standard of comparison follows the adjective.

I have seen no examples of this construction in the text corpus.

15.1.3 Bare predicates

In both elicitation and texts, comparative expressions of age never use the comparative *fő̋n*. The predicate 'be old' can appear in two forms: either as a pure verbal expression, with intransitive stem *bɔ̌ɔ* marked with the habitual *wɛ̀*, or as an adjectival predicate with the stem form *bő̋ɔ*:

(8) a. mɛ́ɛ lɛ̀ bɔ́ɔ̂ wè mó wɛ́̋
REL.PRO SUBORD be.old.IRR HAB 1SG.EMPH with
'someone older than me' [sos171009t1:124]

b. dənṳ̀ ké bḭ́ɛ-säa bɔ́ɔ̂ wè
talking.drum COP play.REAL.NOM-thing.SUBORD be.old.IRR HAB
bá̰à̰ wè
balafon with
'The talking drum is an older instrument than the balafon.' [sos170711t1:312]

c. ké dənṳ̀ yéré ké kɔ́nâ, kʊ́ bɔ́ɔ bá̰à̰ wè
COP talking.drum self.JU COP older.sibling D.DEF old balafon with
'It's the talking drum itself, that's the older sibling, it is older than the balafon.' [sos170711t1:311]

The verbal stem 'be old' is attested in (8a-b) and the adjectival stem in (8c).

It is unclear why 'old' resists the comparative marker while other qualificational predicates do not. In elicitation, speakers accept *fő́n* with age predicates, as in:

(9) mó bɔ́ɔ̂ fő́n á wɛ́̋
1SG.EMPH be.old.IRR.HAB best 2SG with
'I am older than you.' [sos180716e]

15.1.4 *fa̰* '(sur)pass'

There is another form of bare comparative predicate, which I treat separately here as it uses a specific verb *fa̰*, which can mean 'enter' or 'pass' but in the context of comparatives takes on the meaning 'surpass' or 'be better'. It is used in exactly the same way as *fő́n* when used alone, raising the question of whether the similarity in phonological form is an indication of common roots.

Examples of *fa̰* comparatives include:

(10) a. í wó fà̰ á wɛ́̋, kʊ́ mʉ̰̀ fǎ̰ mʉ̰̀ɔ ŋé
LOG EMPH pass 2SG with D.DEF person pass.NOM person.with NEG
'[Saying] I'm better than you, that's not being better.' [sos170714t1:37]

b. ké kʊ́ nɛ̀ à Tími-ŋɛ́   jűnɨ́ cɛ̰́ ïi
   COP D.DEF LOC DEF Karangasso-HUM.PL eye.PL open 3PL.SUBORD
   fà̰   mí́ wɛ́ dəgɔ̌ɛɛ lé   nɛ̀ ké à   lê
   pass 1PL with place   REL LOC COP 3SG PRES
   'That's how people from Karangasso have gotten more enlightened than us in this regard.' [sos170702t1:102]

c. sân ɲɨ̀   í   cɛ̰́n fà̰   mɛ̀ à   mɔ̀nəgɔ̀ wè âa
   rabbit run.REAL.PFV LOG leg.PL pass.IRR HAB DEF toad   with NEG.Q
   'The rabbit ran, his legs are better than those of the toad, aren't they.' [sos170805t15:61]

This construction is rarer than *fő́n* comparatives, and more examples are necessary to fully understand its intricacies, such as the inflectional properties of *fà̰*.

15.1.5 Superlatives

There is no construction specific to superlatives. Rather, the typical asymmetrical comparison construction is used, but the standard of comparison includes a universal quantifier (typically *kúrúú* 'all') rather than a specific individual or group of individuals.

(11) a. səgɔ̂   kù-tɔ̀   fő́n jəmɨ̰̀-kɛ̀kɛ́   kúrúíi wɛ́
      partridge thing-know.IRR best bush-meat.PL all.PL with
      'The partridge is the most clever of all the animals.' [sos180716e]

  b. mó   sɔ́ɔ̀   fő́n kɔ̀ee   lɛ̀ ì kúrúíi wɛ́
     1SG.EMPH be.able.IRR.HAB best sing.ANTIP.NOM DAT 3PL all.PL with
     'I sing the best [out of anybody].' [sos180716e]

Both of these examples could be read as standard comparatives, meaning 'the partridge is more clever than all of the animals' and 'I sing better than everyone', respectively.

15.2 Symmetrical comparison

In symmetrical comparison, the comparee and the standard are stated to be the same or equal in some quality or ability. The current data do not contain many examples of symmetrical comparison, but those examples that are attested are varied in form. I divide symmetrical comparison into three categories of form: simile comparisons, identity comparisons, and quantitative comparisons with 'one'.

15.2.1 Simile comparisons

As the name suggests, simile comparisons involve expressions where the subject has a quality compared to and equated with some standard of comparison, but with a simile-like figurativeness. An example is given in (12):

(12) a. sì-tán-jô sĩ í bɔ́ɔ təgɔ́ gɔ́ɔ̀ tɔ̀
Sy-Tan-Jo be LOG tall or tree like
'Sy-Tan-Jo is as tall as a tree.' [sos170719e]

b. ằ ɲììn nɛ̰̋ màa fìɔ təgɔ́ sò tɔ̀
3SG run.IRR.HAB CMPV again fast or horse like
'He runs as fast as a horse.' [sos180716e]

The standard appears after a conjunction təgɔ́, also found in disjunction (see §11.2). It takes the postpositional noun tɔ̀, which undergoes argument-head tone sandhi. This relational noun appears to have a more general meaning of likeness rather than physical resemblance (in which case sərḭ́ is used instead); tɔ̀ is frequent in texts in the expression kʊ́ tɔ̋ 'like that'. In example (12b), a particle lɛ̋ (here nasalized to nɛ̰̋) appears after the verbal predicate; it is not clear what the identity of this particle is. Since it appears after the verb, it cannot be the S-toned past tense TAMP marker. It is also found in simile predicates without təgɔ́, such as the following:

(13) ằ sĩ í səgɔ̋ lɛ̋ màa í ɲà tɔ̀
3SG be LOG pretty CMPV again LOG mother like
'She is as pretty as her mother.' [sos180716e]

As this example shows, it often (but not obligatorily) co-occurs with the adverb màa. This example shows it appearing after an adjectival predicate, where it is clearer that we are not dealing with a nominalized verb. Pending further data, I simply gloss it as CMPV for a particle involved in the comparative.

Finally, we find examples of simile comparatives where neither the particle lɛ̋ nor təgɔ́ appear:

(14) a. mó dʊ̀n nǎ ằ bɔ́ɔ-bɛ́ nʊ̀ ń tɔ̋
1SG.EMPH child PROSP 3SG tall-NOM eat.IRR 1SG like
'My child will be as tall as me.' [sos180716e]

b. ằ sĩ í səgɔ̋ í ɲà tɔ̀
3SG be LOG pretty LOG mother like
'She is as pretty as her mother.' [sos180716e]

In (14a), we see once again the idiomatic expression combining a deadjectival noun and the verb 'eat'; see §5.2.1 for further discussion.

15.2.2 Identity comparisons with *ɲəgɔ̃n*

I use the term "identity comparison" to describe a class of symmetrical comparisons using the root *ɲəgɔ̃n*, meaning roughly 'same'. The stem can be used in at least two ways: as a relational noun "possessed" by the parameter (expressed nominally), or as a participial predicate (in which case the tone is exceptionally S rather than the usual LS we might expect from an X-toned stem; see §13.3.1). The former is illustrated in (15a) and the latter in (15b):

(15) a. mó dòn nǎ móò bɔ̀ɔ-bɛ̀ ɲəgɔ̀n jò
1SG.EMPH child PROSP 1SG.EMPH.DAT tall-NOM same see.IRR
'My child will reach my height [lit. will find my same tallness].' [sos170719e]

b. á wó tɛ̀ cəbɛ́ɛ ɲəgɔ̃n sı̌ mó tɛ̀
2SG EMPH GEN shoe.PL same be 1SG.EMPH GEN
'Your shoes are the same as mine.' [sos170719e]

The same stem is used to mean 'agemate', as in the expression *ɲəgɔ̃n kɔ̀sî* meaning a friend of the same generation.

15.2.3 Comparisons with *sɔ́ɛn* 'one'

The last form of symmetrical comparison involves the numeral *sɔ́ɛn* 'one' to indicate that two or more things are the same. The noun *tsɔ̂* 'type, kind' is optional.

(16) a. á wó tɛ̀ cəbɛ́ɛ tsɛ́-kɛ́ mó tɛ̀ cəbɛ́ɛ sı̌ (tsɔ̂) sɔ́ɛn
2SG EMPH GEN shoe.PL and 1SG.EMPH GEN shoe.PL be type one
'Your shoes and my shoes are the same.' [sos170719e]

b. ké jén-jɛ̌n tsɔ̂ sɔ́ɛn ɲɛ́
COP RED-story type one NEG
'They are not the same story.' [sos161009t1:55]

c. bon, kərɔ̀ ä-né dɔ̀n ɩ̀ ɲá sɔ́ɛn ɲɛ́ kú lɛ́ tɔ̋
well.FR yesterday and today 3PL be.NEG one NEG thing which like
'Well, just like how yesterday and today are not the same...' [sos170702t1:53]

As these examples show, symmetrical comparisons with 'one' do not involve any compared quality but rather full identity.

16 Interrogation

This chapter covers interrogative strategies in Seenku. I begin with polar interrogatives (§16.1), which display lax question prosody, then wh-expressions in main clauses (§16.2). For the interrogative *tsɛ́* 'how' in relative clauses, see §17.6. For other embedded interrogatives, see §19.2.2.

16.1 Polar interrogatives

Polar interrogatives in Seenku take two forms, depending on whether the question is affirmative (§16.1.1) or negative (§16.1.2). The two are similar in that they share a long low or falling contour at the end of the sentence, an example of "lax question prosody" (Rialland 2007, 2009) that is common to many African languages, including other Mande languages such as Guro and Wan (Grégoire 1990). As Rialland (2009) notes, lax question prosody is more commonly documented among Southeastern Mande languages, presumably due to contact with Kru and Kwa languages where such prosody is the norm. She notes that in many other Mande languages, the question marker is high-pitched. Lax question prosody is also common to Gur languages, and thus the situation for Seenku is likely similar to that of Southeastern Mande, with lax question prosody spreading through extended contact.

16.1.1 Affirmative polar interrogatives

Affirmative polar interrogatives involve no special morphology or syntax. The only aspect distinguishing them from declaratives is the intonational elongation of the final vowel of the last word, accompanied by a long falling pitch. In the following transcriptions, this prosodic pattern will be indicated with a downward-pointing right arrow (↘) at the end of the clause.

If the final tone of the word is X, then lengthening of the vowel becomes the primary means of expressing interrogation; the vowel in these cases is much more lengthened than a vowel where intonation can also carry some of the weight. Consider the spectrogram and pitch track in Figure 16.1 for the phrase *á sḭ̀ cěrë̀ nɛ̋*↘ 'are you sleeping?'. The vowel of the X-toned postposition *nɛ̋* is significantly lengthened, allowing a slight pitch drop to be audible.

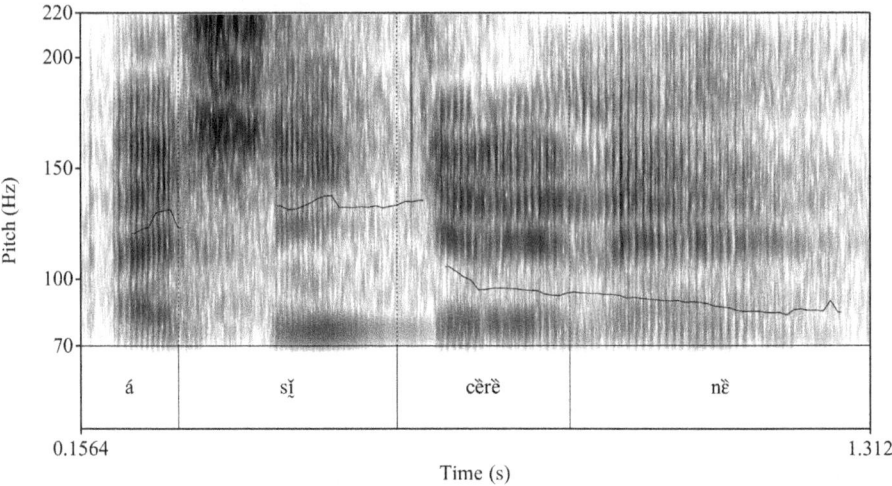

Fig. 16.1: Wave-form, spectogram, and pitch tracing for polar interrogative 'are you sleeping?'

We can compare this to the pitch drop and lesser lengthening in a phrase like *á cërë̈ í səgɔ́*↘ 'did you sleep well?', shown in Figure 16.2, where the falling tone of the final syllable signals interrogation.

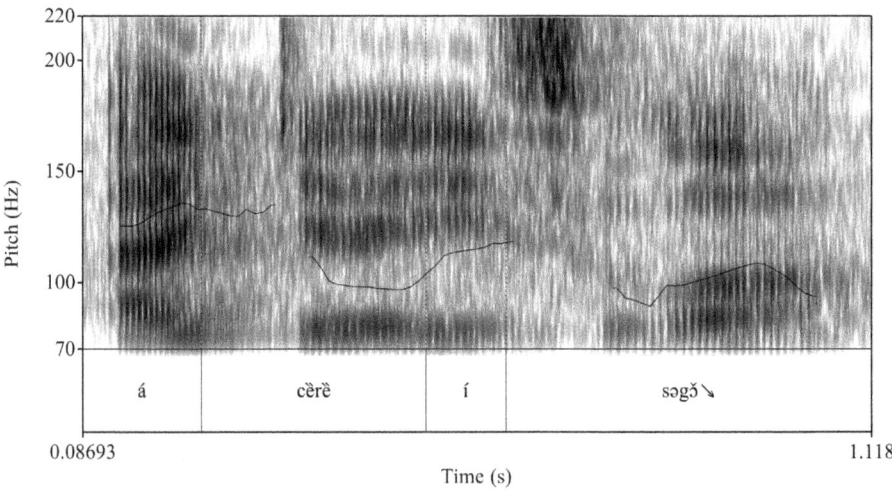

Fig. 16.2: Wave-form, spectogram, and pitch tracing for polar interrogative 'did you sleep well?'

This same strategy is used in all tenses and aspects. Examples from the text corpus include:

(1) a. ế! í wó nă màa jîoo kʊ́ tsío↘
INTERJ 2PL EMPH PROSP again fail.IRR D.DEF know.REAL.Q
'Eh! Would you fail to know it?' [sos161009t1:15]

b. á mḭ̀ɛ↘
2SG hear.REAL.PFV.Q
'Do you understand? [Lit. did you hear?]' [sos150626t4:72]

c. Fàatū́ óo sḭ̀ ằ tê áa fắ mó wɛ́↘
Fatou 2SG.EMPH be 3SG GEN 2SG.SBJV fight 1SG.EMPH with.Q
'Fatou, do you want to fight me?' [sos161009t1:96]

d. ằ sḭ̀ sɔ̀kɔ́-kû nɛ̈↘
3SG be Jula-thing LOC
'It's in Jula?' [sos161009t1:197]

e. áa yɛ̀rɛ̈ tsḭ́ nɛ̋ á kʊ́ dzḭ̀ wè ằ lɛ́↘
2SG.SBJV self.JU cut.REAL.PFV if 2SG D.DEF put.IRR HAB 3SG DAT
'If you cut yourself, then you put that on it?' [sos170714t2:13]

These examples show lax question prosody in a variety of contexts, including on verbs (1a-b) and on postpositions (1c-e).

This lax question prosody can even be used to confirm a single word, as in:

(2) mó↘
1SG.EMPH.Q
'Me?' [sos161009t1:227]

As we will see in the next subsection, however, negative polar question marking is far more common in the current corpus, even if the expected answer is affirmative.

16.1.2 Negative polar interrogatives

Negative polar interrogatives follow more or less the same prosodic pattern as affirmative interrogatives, but the usual negative particle *ŋé* from declaratives is replaced with *âa*, which carries the prosodic interrogative fall. This vowel has an extragrammatical feel to it, since it doesn't trigger hiatus resolution in the same way other vowel-initial elements like pronouns do (see §3.5.4).

In (3), I show the negative question equivalent of Figure 16.1, and to compare, the negative indicative:

(3) a. á ɲá cě̀rě̀ nè̤ âa↘
2SG be.NEG sleep.REAL.NOM LOC NEG.Q
'Aren't you sleeping?' [sos150622e]

b. á ɲá cě̀rě̀ nè̤ ŋɛ́
2SG be.NEG sleep.REAL.NOM LOC NEG
'You are not sleeping.' [sos130821e]

Comparing the two examples in (3), we can see that in both cases, any irregular negative forms will be used earlier in the clause, but that the clause-final negative particle ŋɛ́ is replaced by âa in the polar question.

What we find in texts is that âa tends to be used almost like negative tag questions in English ("isn't it?", "aren't you?"). In other words, the expected answer is affirmative. This is particular common with copular predicates (§14.1):

(4) a. ì̤ kɛ́ sìɛbè̤ âa
COMP COP truth NEG.Q
'[They said], it's true, isn't it?' [sos170711t1:47]

b. e! ì̤ kɛ́ à cî kɛ́ á wó tè̤ âa
INTERJ COMP COP DEF house COP 2SG EMPH GEN NEG.Q
'[He said] Eh! That's your house, isn't it?' [150626t4:22]

c. kɛ́ à̤ bón âa kɛ́ mɔ̰̂ bɔ̂ɔ âa
COP 3SG back NEG.Q COP person old NEG.Q
'It's his back, isn't it, he's an old person, isn't he?' [sos170714t2:71]

d. kűɛɛ nìgì nàa âa
other.PL.COP cow.PL four NEG.Q
'That's four cows, no?' [sos161009t1:25]

In each case, the speaker is seeking validation through the use of the negative question.

Negative question marking in other constructions is shown in (5):

(5) a. í dɔ̀ɔ á jɛ́n âa
LOG finish.REAL.PFV 2SG front NEG.Q
'Have I not finished before you?' [sos170714t1:35]

b. á à̤ jîo âa
2SG 3SG see.REAL.PFV NEG.Q
'You see, no?' [sos170714t3:49]

c. est-ce que m̰ɔ̰̈ sɔ́ɔ̀ m̰ɔ̰̈ɔ́ tsîɛɛ təg͏̈ɛ
Q.FR person be.able.IRR.HAB person.SBJV word certain.PL
jǔ bâ̰a̰ nɛ̀ mais m̰ɔ̰̈ sɔ́ɔ̀ m̰ɔ̰̈ɔ́ ï̀
say.IRR balafon LOC but.FR person be.able.IRR.HAB person.SBJV 3PL
jú í dzʊ̈ âa
say.IRR LOG mouth NEG.Q
'Are there words you can say with your mouth that you can't say on the balafon?' [sos170711t1:229]

The first two examples also act like tag questions or validation seeking, but (5c) shows a use where the question really is negative. The tag question in (5b) is very common in texts as a way of making sure the listener is keeping up with the narrative.

16.2 Wh-interrogatives

Unlike polar interrogatives, wh-interrogatives have no special prosodic marking. The fact that they are questions is clear from the use of wh-words alone. These words are left in situ (i.e. there is no wh-movement), though adverbial wh-words like 'where', 'when' and 'how' are flexible in their linear order, as most adverbs are.

16.2.1 Which/what

There is no single morpheme meaning 'what' in Seenku. Instead, 'what' is formed by combining the wh-word *lé* 'which', typically with one of two light nouns for 'thing' though also in other expressions like 'which kind'. Note that this form *lé* is the same morpheme used as a relativizer, which will be discussed in Chapter 17.

Let us begin with the core 'what' expressions, in which *lé* combines with light nouns meaning 'thing'. For abstract referents, *kú* is used, yielding the complex wh-form *kú lé* ('which [abstract] thing?'); for concrete referents, *fên* is used, yielding the complex wh-form *fên né* ('which [concrete] thing?'); note that the latter has an unusual tone pattern, with L on 'thing' rather than expected H. Both of these terms can be used as I have just shown, as a clear bimorphemic phrase, but they also both show contracted monomorphemic forms; in this case, what would have been the light noun becomes the half syllable of a sesquisyllabic form, yielding *kəré* and *fəlé*, respectively; note that in the second case, the latent nasal coda is lost (but the irregular tone pattern remains). In fluent speech, these contractions are more common than the phrasal forms.

First, the following examples illustrate questions with abstract *kú lé/kəré*:

(6) a. kú lé lẽ̀ ì bɔ́ í sí nɛ̈̀
thing which SUBORD 3PL take.out.IRR LOG RECP LOC
'What differentiates them?' [sos170711t1:404]

b. kʊ́ kɔ́rɔ́ ké wé kəré
D.DEF meaning COP FOC what
'What does it mean?' [sos170822t2:368]

c. í wôo bǎrǎ ké kəré wétənɛ̌ ì̀ tê
2PL EMPH.DAT work COP what now 3PL GEN
'What is your work with them?' [sos170822t12:36]

In these examples, the noun corresponding to the wh-expression kəré/kú lé is not a physical object, but rather an abstract concept like a meaning or an action.

If the noun is concrete, then fəlé/fèn né is used instead:

(7) a. fôn-bá̰-trḭ́ ké fəlé
fonio-beat.NOM-medicine COP what
'What is fonio beating medicine?' [sos170714t3:33]

b. kʊ́ʊ fèn né
D.DEF thing which
'What is it?' [sos161009t1:43]

c. ì ä̀ trẽ̀ wé ì̀ wò̀ nä̀ fèn né
3PL 3SG ask.REAL.PFV FOC 3PL EMPH come.REAL.PFV thing which
sòo lɔ́
search.IRR here
'They asked him what they came to look for here.' [sos170711t1:16]

d. óo fóo bé ɲḝ̰ɛ fəlé tsẽ́-ké fəlé wẽ́
2SG.EMPH basket DEM weave.IRR.HAB what and what with
'You weave that basket with what and what?' [sos170822t10:131]

In each case, the response to the question will be a concrete noun: a kind of medicine (7a), a person or thing that embodies the answer to the riddle (7b), the thing that the hunter came to look for (7c), or the tools for weaving (7d).

In a few cases, təré is used in place of either kəré or fəlé. As I will discuss in §17.7, all three of these can be used as relative pronouns, or as "embedded what" in phrases like "I know what he ate". In terms of comparative distribution between relative clauses vs. use as a wh-interrogative, təré is found more commonly in relative clauses, but in a couple of instances, we see it used as a wh-pronoun:

(8) a. mais təré ŋərɔ̀n dzɔ̀ bəgǔ főn
but.FR which oil amount plentiful better
'But which [one] gives more oil?' [sos170822t1:186]

b. ou bien tərêɛ nɛ̀-dəgǎ főn
or.FR well.FR which.SUBORD TRANS-be.fast.PTCP better
'Or which [one] is faster?' [sos170822t1:187]

c. donc ìi təré cèrè wè ằ sûinỉ dó
SO.FR 3PL.SUBORD which call.IRR HAB DEF small.basket EMPH
'So, which one is it that they call *suini*?' [sos170822t10:273]

d. mais á wó sɪ̌ ɲɛ̀ɛ nɛ̀ ằ dzìa ké təré
but.FR 2SG EMPH be weave.REAL.NOM LOC 3SG fatigue COP which
'But you're weaving, which [part] is tiring?' [sos170822t10:482]

In some instances, these can be understood as relative clauses that stand in as questions: "[And] the one that gives you more oil?", "[And how about] the one that they call *suini*?" However, this cannot be said for (8d). It is interesting, though, that *təré* is consistently used in these cases where the speaker is asking someone to distinguish between two or more options, i.e. it expresses a meaning "which one" as opposed to a more open-ended "what".

Of course, as a modifier 'which', *lɛ́* can be used with any noun and not just these light nouns that lend the meaning of 'what'. A common expression is *tsɔ́ lɛ́*, 'which kind', as shown in (9):

(9) a. ì̀ kóʊ fèn tsɔ́ lɛ́ ằ kằ
COMP D.DEF.COP thing kind which 3SG in.hand
'[They asked] what kind of thing he had with him.' [sos170711t1:34]

b. mɔ̀-bɛ́ɛ́-kǔ tsɔ́ lɛ́
person-do.NOM-thing kind which
'What kinds of things?' [sos170702t1:37]

But we find examples in the text corpus with other nouns modified by *lɛ́*:

(10) a. cəběe tə̀nɔ̌n né fɑ̋n mɛ̋ í wó kằ
shea.nut benefit which put.in.IRR HAB 2PL EMPH in.hand
'What benefit do shea nuts give you?' [sos170822t1:69]

b. í kằ wé ằ jəgí mằasɪ́n né nɛ̀ wé
2PL go.REAL.PFV FOC 3SG grind.IRR machine which LOC FOC
'Which machine did you go grind it in?' [sos170822t2:468]

c. *mǎmù lɛ́*
   Mamou which
   'Which Mamou?' [sos170822t10:457]

In both (10a) and (10b), a latent nasal coda on the noun (*tə̀nɔ̰̀n* 'benefit' and *mǎasĩ́n* 'machine', respectively) nasalizes *lɛ́* to *nɛ́*. It is also important to note that 'which', like the homophonous relative marker and demonstratives, allows H-final nouns to surface with final H rather than having to epenthesize a final X-tone; see §4.3.2.1 for more.

Though rare in texts, *lɛ́* can also be inflected for plural through regular plural formation (§5.3.1), resulting in the raised form *lɛ̋*. In (11), I give one textual example and one elicited example:

(11) a. *í bîɛ kú lɛ̋ nɛ̋*
       2PL play.IRR thing which.PL LOC
       'Which things do you play for?' [sos170711t1:384]

   b. *ɑ̀ nǎ bɛ̀ɛ lɛ̋ kɔ̰̋n-tsɨ̰́*
      3SG PROSP pig.PL which.PL head-cut.IRR
      'Which pigs will he slaughter?' [sos150622e]

As is the usual pattern for plural marking in NPs, the noun preceding the plural-marked modifier only optionally inflects for plural.

For the use of *lɛ́* in locative interrogation, see §16.2.3; in temporal interrogation, see §16.2.4; and in the wh-expression 'why', see §16.2.6. For the use of the wh-word in relative clauses, see Chapter 17.

16.2.2 Who

The pronoun 'who' in Seenku is expressed by *té*, which can be pluralized to *tɛ̋* when the expected answer is multiple people. Of the two, the singular is by far more common. Examples from the text corpus include:

(12) a. *ì té nǎ kʊ́ tò ɑ̀ wò kà*
       COMP who PROSP D.DEF take.IRR 3SG EMPH in.hand
       '[They asked] who would take it from her?' [sos170805t9:49]

   b. *ì kɛ́ té lɛ̀ ɑ̀ nɨ̈ɨ fɑ̀ wé á nɛ̈*
      COMP COP who SUBORD 3SG pregnancy put.in.REAL.PFV FOC 2SG LOC
      '[They asked] who was it who got you pregnant?' [sos171009t1:61]

c. kòee-sərà   ké té
   sing.ANTIP-master COP who
   'Who is a singer?' [sos170822t12:459]

d. mais dɔ̀ɔ sĭ wé té tè̀
   but.FR beer be FOC who GEN
   'But who has beer?' [sos170822t12:109]

In these examples, we see *té* 'who' in subject position (12a-b), in a copular predicate (12c), and as the complement to a postposition (12d).

I have not seen any examples of plural 'who' in the text corpus. Elicited examples are provided in (13):

(13) a. ké tɛ̋   lɛ̋ nằ   lɔ̋
       COP who.PL PST come.REAL.PFV here
       'Who all came here?' [sos150619e]

   b. á á tê jằnɛ̋ bằ   tɛ̋ kǎ́
      2SG 2SG GEN corn put.REAL.PFV who.PL in.hand
      'Who all did you give your corn to?' [sos190803e]

The S tone on *tɛ̋* marks plurality.

16.2.3 Where

I have seen three expressions translating to 'where' in Seenku. The first appears to be a loanword from Jula, *mḭ̋*:

(14) a. mais á cènèn-sǎ́n   kǎ́ fɔ̋ mḭ̋
       but.FR 2SG palm.frond-buy.NOM go until where
       'But where do you go to buy palm fronds?' [sos170822t10:157]

   b. mais gbɛ̆nɛ̋ ăa   súù   mḭ̋
      but.FR before 3SG.PST get.up.IRR.HAB where
      'But where did it come from before?' [sos170822t10:493]

   c. mɛ̀̀   í bɛ̋ ì̀ à wò̀ à ɲṵ̋ḭ nɛ̋
      3SG.SUBORD LOG do.IRR COMP 3SG EMPH DEF honey DEM
      jîo   mḭ̋
      see.REAL.PFV where
      '…[and] he asked where he found this honey.' [sos130828t2:24]

This is a very general term for 'where', typically offered first in elicited questions like 'where are you going?' (á sị̈ kằ nɛ̀ mị́ [sos150619e]). Like the adverb ɲì 'there' with its variant ɲì-nà 'towards there', mị́ can also have the variant mị́-nǎ:

(15) a. m᷉ɔ̀ nǎ wɛ́ ɲəgɔ̋-jő jő wɛ́ mị́-nǎ
person PROSP FOC potash-water find.IRR FOC where-towards
'Where will we [be able to] find potash water?' [sos170822t2:48]

b. ń nǎ ằ cɛ̏nɛ̏n-jŏon səgɔ̆ jő mị́-nǎ
1SG PROSP DEF palm-leaf good find.IRR where-towards
'Where will I find a good palm leaf?' [sos170822t10:328]

I have glossed -nǎ as 'towards', since consultants will sometimes translate it in this way. Combined with 'where', it may give a flavor like 'whereabouts'; in other words, there is not a large semantic difference, and when asked, consultants will typically accept mị́ anywhere that mị́-nǎ has been used. For more on nà, see §10.1.8.2 and §10.2.1.2.

Native Seenku expressions of 'where' combine the interrogative lɛ́ 'which' from §16.2.1 above with nouns meaning 'place'. The most common of these is dəgɔ̆ɔ (with its central Bouendé variant dəgɔ̆ɛɛ, used uniformly in the plural) which yields the expression dəgɔ̆ɔ lɛ́ nɛ̏ or dəgɔ̆ɛɛ lɛ́ nɛ̏ 'in which place?'. This complex interrogative expression can be used in the same contexts as mị́. In elicitation, for instance, we find that the two are interchangeable:

(16) a. á sı̈o mị́
2SG get.up.PTCP where
'Where are you from?' [sos150619e]

b. á sı̈o dəgɔ̆ɛɛ lɛ́ nɛ̏
2SG get.up.PTCP place.PL which LOC
'Where are you from?' [sos150619e]

I have seen no textual examples of this expression used as an interrogative.
Finally, a reportedly less common expression dǎn né nɛ̏ is attested in texts, which my consultant also translates as 'where', but using French *lieu* instead of *endroit*. It is unclear what exactly the difference is between dǎn and dəgɔ̆ɛɛ. Examples include:

(17) ń tɛ̋ kərù sı̈o mɛ̏ kɛ̋ ń tɛ̋ sân
1SG dear hyena get.up.REAL.PFV 3SG.SUBORD go.IRR 1SG dear rabbit
tərɛ̏ ɩ̀ óő kằ búè̩-dɩ̀ bɛ̋ jő
ask.IRR COMP 2SG.EMPH.PST go.REAL.PFV djinn-child.PL DEM.PL see.IRR
dǎn né nɛ̏
place which LOC
'Mr. Hyena got up and went to ask Mr. Rabbit, where did you go to find those djinns?' [sos130828t2:29]

When asking for this expression in elicitation, my consultants reported it is not as common, and they preferred to offer either *mɹ̰́* or *dəgɔɛɛ lɛ́ nɛ̀*. It may be a more archaic term, reserved for traditional contexts like storytelling. More data are required to decide this question.

16.2.4 When

The text corpus lacks any naturally occurring 'when' interrogatives. From elicitation, we can identify a general expression *cı̀cı̋*, found in examples like the following:

(18) a. *á wó kôo   cı̀cı̋*
2SG FOC be.born.REAL.PFV when
'When were you born?' [sos150619e]

b. *á wó kɔ̀sî nǎ nɛ̀   cı̀cı̋*
2SG EMPH friend PROSP come.IRR when
'When is your friend going to come?' [sos150619e]

This wh-expression is quite general, and can be used in contexts expecting responses of years, months, hours, etc. Like other wh-expressions, it is commonly found in relative and subordinated clauses, as in the following proverb:

(19) *óo   búɔ   nɛ̋ áa bî sà̰   nɛ̋*
2SG.EMPH.SBJV go.out.REAL.PFV if 2SG.SBJV goat buy.REAL.PFV if
fɛ̰̋ ŋɛ́ âa   təgê sà̰   nɛ̋ cı̀cı̋ á bà̰
already NEG 2SG.SUBORD chicken buy.REAL.NOM LOC when 2SG rope
dzɨ̰̀   ä̀ gù lɛ̀
put.IRREAL 3SG neck DAT
'If when you are born you have not already bought a goat, then when you buy a chicken, you will put a rope on its neck (Proverb meaning 'Don't content yourself with what little you already have').' [sos150710e]

More specific temporal interrogatives can be formed by combining *lɛ́* 'which' with time referents like *jṵ̀* 'year' or *cèrɛ̀* 'day', as shown in the following elicited examples:

(20) a. *á wó kôo   jṵ̀ lêɛ*
2SG EMPH be.born.REAL.PFV year which.LOC
'What year were you born?' [sos150619e]

b. *á wóő   nà̰   cèrɛ̀ lɛ́ wɛ̋*
2SG EMPH.PST come.REAL.PFV day which with
'What day did you come?' [sos150619e]

In (20a), the contraction *lêɛ* is supposedly composed of *lé nè*, which is unusual in that the locative *né* typically does not undergo clitic elision (§4.4.3). The combination *lé wé* in (20b) can likewise be contracted to *léé*. This difference in postposition use between 'year' and 'day' is systematic; 'year' always uses *né*, 'day' always uses *wè*, and the two cannot be switched. See Chapter 10 for more on postpositions.

16.2.5 How (many)

The Seenku wh-word *tsɛ́* covers the semantic ground of both 'how' and 'how many'. Its pronunciation is closer to [tsɜ́] or [tsə́], due to vowel centralization after the alveolar affricate (§3.5.5). I begin with examples illustrating the 'how' reading:

(21) a. í   dəgè   tsɛ́   íi   tsîɛ   à   nè̀
         2PL make.IRR how 2PL.SUBJ speak.IRR 3SG LOC
         'What do you do to speak on it [the balafon]?' [sos170711t1:205]

   b. í   sĭ   kʊ́ tằ bé mɛ́̃ɛ   nɛ̋ tsɛ́ ì   à
         LOG be D.DEF fire DEM ignite.REAL.NOM LOC how COMP 3SG
         kpîi   wè kʊ́ tɔ́
         extinguish.IRR HAB D.DEF like
         'How are you lighting the fire such that it keeps going out like that?' [sos130828t2:20]

   c. ì   kʊ́ cèrè wè tsɛ́
         3PL D.DEF call.IRR HAB how
         'What do they call that?' [sos170822t10:100]

   d. í   kʊ́ bɔ̀   wè tsɛ́
         2PL D.DEF take.out.IRR HAB how
         'How do you remove that?' [sos170822t10:280]

In every case, the wh-word *tsɛ́* immediately follows the verbal complex (consisting of the verb and any verbal particles). Though translated as 'what' in (21a) and (21c), these examples fit the same pattern of 'how' in Seenku ('how do you do it that....', 'how do they call it...'), i.e. an interrogative manner adverb.

However, the same form *tsɛ́* can also be used as an interrogative quantifier meaning 'how many'. If one went to the market, for instance, one could ask the price simply by saying (22a) for one item or (22b) if the quantifier is distributive:

(22) a. ké tsɛ́
         COP how
         'How much is it?' [sos150619e]

b. ké tsɛ̋-tsɛ̋
COP RED-how
'How much are they each?' [sos150619e]

As we can see here, *tsɛ̋* can be used on its own as an interrogative adverb; however, it can also be used as an interrogative modifier on a noun, with no change in form:

(23) a. ằ sóen są́ ké wɛ́n tsɛ̋ tɔ́-trɔ̋
3SG one buy.NOM COP money how RED-like
'How much money is it to buy one like that?' [sos170822t10:160]

b. í bą́ą̀ gɔ̀ɔ jǜ tsɛ̋ tɛ̋
2PL balafon learn.IRR.HAB year how GEN
'At what age do you learn the balafon?' [sos170711t1:146]

c. mais á wó bű̋ɔ ằ fòlò ɲɛ̰̀ɛ tê á
but.FR 2SG EMPH go.out.PTCP DEF basket weave.ANTIP.NOM GEN 2SG
wó mɔ̀ɛ tsɛ̋ gü̋ɔ fòlò ɲɛ̰̀ɛ lɛ̀
EMPH person.PL how learn.REAL.PRF basket weave.ANTIP.NOM DAT
'But since you've started weaving baskets, how many people have you taught to weave baskets?' [sos170822t10:255]

When used as a nominal modifier, *tsɛ̋* immediately follows the noun, and this NP can then appear anywhere non-interrogative NPs can appear: in a copular predicate (23a), as the complement to a postposition (23b), or even as an object NP in (23c).

16.2.6 Why

The last wh-expression to be considered here is 'why', which is not its own root in Seenku but rather a postpositional phrase employing the already complex wh-expression 'what' (§16.2.1). The postposition involved is the genitive *tɛ̋* (see §10.1.8), leaving the full expression to translate to something like 'for what thing/reason'?

This can be a simple interjection, without being embedded in a larger clause:

(24) ɛ̋! kəré tɛ̀ wɛ́
INTERJ what GEN FOC
'Eh! Why?' [sos170822t2:325]

It can also be used to question a longer proposition; in this usage, it most commonly comes at the end of the clause (25a), but it is also attested at the beginning of the clause (25b):

(25) a. á wó sɪ̌ ằ mɪ̈ɛ nɛ́ kəré tɛ̀
2SG EMPH be 3SG listen.REAL.NOM LOC what GEN
'Why are you listening to it?' [sos170828t1:42]

b. kəré tɛ̀ á wó í bɛ́̋ ɪ̀ mɔ̰̀ɔ̰́ à mɪ̰ í
what GEN 2SG EMPH LOG do.IRR COMP person.SBJV 3SG drink.IRR LOG
sí tɛ̀
RECP GEN
'Why do you say we should drink together?' [sos170828t1:44]

In elicitation as well, we find this variable order:

(26) a. á wóő nằ kú lέ tɛ̀
2SG EMPH.PST come.REAL.PFV thing which GEN
'Why did you come?' [sos150619e]

b. kú lέ tɛ̀ dôn sɪ̌ sâ nɛ̀̋
thing which GEN child be cry.REAL.NOM LOC
'Why is the child crying?' [sos150619e]

In (26a), 'why' is clause-final, while in (26b), it is clause-initial.

17 Relative clauses

Relative clauses in Seenku, as in most Mande languages, are head-internal. This means that the head of the relative clause is not extracted and pre-posed (as in English or French) or post-posed (as in Japanese); it remains in situ. The head is identifiable despite the lack of change in word order as it is marked with the relative marker lé, which is the same morpheme used as a wh-word for 'which' (see §16.2.1). For ease of comprehension, I gloss it in relative clauses as REL but in interrogatives as 'which'.

The following examples show the relative marking when the head of the relative clause (in boldface) is the subject (1a), object (1b), or complement of a postposition (1c); the whole relative clause is placed in square brackets:

(1) a. [**bí** lé lɛ̀ bû ŋmǎ nɛ́] mó nǎ kʊ́
goat REL SUBORD grass eat.REAL.NOM LOC 1SG.EMPH PROSP D.DEF
sǎ
buy.IRR
'I will buy the goat that is eating grass.' [sos170718e]

b. [mənǐ lɛ̀ à lɛ̀ **jǎn-dɛ́n** né sərě nɛ́]
woman SUBORD 3SG SUBORD corn-grain REL pound.REAL.NOM LOC
mó nǎ kʊ́ sərǎ
1SG.EMPH PROSP D.DEF gather.IRR
'I will gather the corn that the woman is pounding.' [sos170718e]

c. [mó lɛ̀ ɲəgâan jîo **sì** lé gʉ̀] mó
1SG.EMPH SUBORD scorpion see.REAL.PFV jar REL under 1SG.EMPH
nǎ kʊ́ nɛ̀-kɔ̀
PROSP D.DEF TRANS-break.IRR
'I will break the water jar that I saw the scorpion under.' [sos170718e]

The relative clause in each case precedes the main clause. Both clauses show the same word order: S Aux O V X. As we can see in the examples above, the head of the relative clause remains in its regular position of subject (1a), object (1b), or adjunct (1c). The head is identifiable by the relative particle lé that immediately follows it. A phonologically similar subordinating particle lɛ̀ marks the subject of the relative clause (following the relative particle lé when the head is the subject); if the non-head subject of a relative clause is a noun, it is often resumed by a pronoun.

Relative clauses cannot appear inside of the main clause, and so they are generally pre- or post-posed, with a coreferential pronoun (often the discourse definite kʊ́) occurring in the argument position of the main clause; alternatively, the overt copy of the noun occurs in the main clause, with a coreferential relative pronoun in the relative clause. The latter strategy is more common when the relative clause is post-posed.

In (1a), we see that the head of the relative clause is the H-toned noun *bí* 'goat'; it is only when followed by the relative marker *lé* or the demonstrative *bé* (§8.2.3) that this level H tone is allowed to surface. In other environments (isolation, followed by an adjective, etc.), underlyingly H-toned nouns surface as HX (e.g. *bî*) via the process of X epenthesis; for further discussion, see §4.3.2.1. This is the only phonological difference that we find between nouns acting as the head of the relative clause vs. in any other position.

Another common relativization strategy in Seenku is to use relative pronouns ('the one which') in a post-posed relative clause (i.e. the noun that is co-referential with the relative pronoun occurs before it in the main clause, which itself precedes the relative clause). The relative pronoun equivalents of each of the phrases in (1) are given in (2):

(2) a. mó nǎ bî̀ sà̰ [tənɛ́ lɛ̀ bṵ ŋmǎ
 1SG.EMPH PROSP goat buy.IRR REL.PRO SUBORD grass eat.REAL.NOM
 nɛ́̃]
 LOC
 'I will buy the goat that is eating grass.' [sos170718e]

 b. mó nǎ jǎn-dɛ́n sərǎ [mənǐ lɛ̀ tré
 1SG.EMPH PROSP corn-grain gather.IRR woman SUBORD REL.PRO
 sərĕ nɛ́̃]
 pound.REAL.NOM LOC
 'I will gather the corn that the woman is pounding.' [sos170718e]

 c. mó nǎ sḭ̀ nɛ̰̈-kɔ́ [môo ɲəgâan
 1SG.EMPH PROSP jar TRANS-break.IRR 1SG.SUBORD scorpion
 jîo tré gṵ̀]
 see.REAL.PFV REL.PRO under
 'I will break the water jar that I saw the scorpion under.' [sos170718e]

There is free variation in the form of the relative pronoun, between *tənɛ́* (2a) and *tré* ~ *tərɛ́* (2b-c). This is the same form that we saw in §16.2.1 as a wh-word, meaning roughly 'which one'. We can still classify these post-posed relative clauses as head-internal, since the relative pronoun remains in its usual sentential position.

The structure of the chapter is as follows: First, in §17.1 I discuss verb inflection in the relative clause, including placement of the subordinating particle with respect to other TAM markers. I then turn to subject relatives (§17.2), object relative (§17.3), and PP relatives (§17.4); in each case, the head remains in situ and is marked with the relative marker *lé*. Section §17.7 is dedicated to the use of relative pronouns.

17.1 Verb inflection and subject marking in the relative clause

The conjugation of verbs in relative clauses differs very little from main clauses. On the lexical verb itself (i.e. not the auxiliary), there is no difference; it takes its regular realis or irrealis forms, depending upon TAM categories. However, the subject must be obligatorily subordinated, and this subordinating TAMP marker interacts in sometimes interesting ways with other predicative markers and auxiliaries. Given the close interaction between TAMP marking and subordination, I discuss them together in this section.

17.1.1 Prospective

When the verb of the relative clause is prospective (§13.2.1), the regular prospective auxiliary *nǎ* is used; the subordinating particle *lɛ̋* follows the prospective auxiliary. This is unusual, since the TAMP marker slot typically precedes auxiliary verbs (see e.g. the past prospective; §13.4.1). Simple examples from elicitation are provided in (3) to illustrate the construction:

(3) a. *mɔnǐ lɛ̋ ǎ nǎ lɛ̋ jǎn-dɛ́n né sɔrɛ̋*
woman SUBORD 3SG PROSP SUBORD corn-grain REL pound.IRR
mó nǎ kʊ́ sɔrǎ
1SG.EMPH PROSP D.DEF gather.IRR
'I will gather the corn that the woman will pound.' [sos170718e]

b. *kɔré lé nǎ lɛ̋ sɔmâ mó à tò*
man REL PROSP SUBORD dance.IRR 1SG.EMPH 3SG know.IRR
'I know the man who is going to dance.' [sos170718e]

As with many other TAMP markers, such as the segmentally identical past tense marker *lɛ̋*, the subordinating marker can simply lend length and tone to the preceding element; in other words, in (3b), *nǎ lɛ̋* can be replaced by *nǎǎ*. Interestingly, the relative marker *lé*, though equally identical in its segments, never elides in this way. As (3a) shows, if the subject of the relative clause is a noun and is not the head, it is typically followed by a resumptive pronoun; both the original noun and the resumptive pronoun are followed by the subordinating particle. These two examples show that the subordinating particle appears after the prospective auxiliary, regardless of whether the subject or the object is the head of the relative clause.

Prospective aspect in relative clauses is rare in the text corpus. The example in (4) is a headless relative clause, where the null head indicates a location. What is important here is that the subordinating TAMP marker *lɛ̋* appears after the prospective auxiliary verb:

(4) ì nǎ lɛ̀ tő mű í sűː...
3PL PROSP SUBORD meet.IRR where LOG RECIP.with
'[The place that] they are going to meet each other....' [sos170714t1:15]

See §17.6 below for further discussion of headless relative clauses.

17.1.2 Habitual

The habitual does not use an auxiliary verb, and so its inflection in relative clauses is simpler; the subordinate marker simply follows the subject, and the verb retains its regular form (discussed in §13.2.2). The text corpus contains many examples of habitual aspect in relative clauses, a selection of which are presented here:

(5) a. kṵ̀i̤ lɛ́ fánâa   səsɛ́ bɛ̋ wɛ̋ kű̃ɛ ɲá bɔ̀
       bug REL also.JU.SUBORD spider do.IRR HAB other.PL be.NEG anymore
       kɔ́ tő ŋɛ́
       D.DEF NEG
       'The bug that makes the spider egg sacs, it doesn't exist that much anymore.' [sos170711t1:140-141]

   b. ì̤ kərúú lɛ̀   à bǎrǎ̰ lɛ́ bɛ̋ɛ   bá̰à̰   kɔ̀n íi
      3PL all   SUBORD DEF work REL do.IRR.HAB balafon on 2PL.SBJV
      sɔ́ nɛ̋ íi kɔ́ sɔ̰̋   dɔ̀ɔnì
      be.able if 2PL.SBJV D.DEF present.IRR a.little
      'The work that all of them do on the balafon, if you could talk about that a little bit.' [sos170711t1:194]

   c. ì̤   sűɛ   lɛ̋   brɛ̰̋   wɛ̋ est-ce que ì̤ tsɛ̋-kɛ́ dɔ̀n
      3PL.SUBORD song.PL REL.PL play.IRR HAB Q.FR   3PL and   today
      ì̤   təné   lɛ́ brɛ̰̀ wɛ̀, est-ce que ì̤ kɛ́ sóen
      3PL.SUBORD REL.PRO REL play.IRR HAB Q.FR   3PL COP one
      'The songs they [used to] play, those and what they play today, are they the same?' [sos170711t1:254]

   d. mɔ̰̀ lɛ̀   à kótɛ̋   lɛ́ fã́n   mɛ̋ à bá̰à̰
      person SUBORD DEF calabash.PL REL.PL put.in.IRR HAB DEF balafon
      gù
      under
      'The calabashes we put under the balafon....' [sos170711t1:284]

The example in (5a) is a subject relative clause, and so the head noun kṵ̀i̤ 'bug' is first marked by the relative marker lɛ́; it is modified by 'also', which is followed by the subordinate marker, here elided into fáná to create fánâa. The other three examples are object relative clauses, and so the subject is followed directly by the subordinate marker, which is elided in (5b-c) and overt in (5d). The examples in (5c-d) show that the relative marker *lé* is raised to *lɛ́* in the plural, following regular rules of plural formation (§5.3.1).

17.1.3 Progressive

Section 13.3.1.1 details the form of the progressive in main clauses; importantly, in main clauses, the existential auxiliary verb *sĭ* (*ná* in the negative) intervenes between the subject and the nominalized VP. In relative clauses, the affirmative auxiliary is almost always absent; in its place, the subordinating particle is found. The following examples are a mix of elicited and naturally occuring:

(6) a. mənǐ   lɛ̀   à   lɛ̀   jăn-děn   né sərĕ   nɛ̋
         woman SUBORD 3SG SUBORD corn-grain REL pound.REAL.NOM LOC
         mó   nǎ   kʊ́   sərɑ̋
         1SG.EMPH PROSP D.DEF gather.IRR
         'I will gather the corn that the woman is pounding.' [sos170718e]

   b. kəré lé lɛ̀   səmâ   nɛ̀ mó   à   tò
         man REL SUBORD dance.REAL.NOM LOC 1SG.EMPH 3SG know.IRR
         'I know the man who is dancing.' [sos170718e]

   c. kűɛ   lɛ̀   à   sʊ́   lɛ́   kŏo   nɛ̋ à kűɛ
         other.PL SUBORD DEF song REL.PL sing.REAL.NOM LOC 3SG other.PL
         brɛ̰̋ɛ̰   lé
         play.IRR.HAB PART
         'The songs that they were singing, he played those.' [sos170711t1:40]

   d. á   wó   lɛ̀   mɛ́ɛ   cɛ̋rɛ̋   nɛ̋....
         2SG EMPH SUBORD REL.PRO call.REAL.NOM LOC
         'The one you are calling...' [sos170711t1:247]

In all of these cases, the subordinating particle *lɛ̀* appears where we would expect to see *sĭ*. It is unclear what the H-toned particle *lé* is doing in (6c), so I have simply glossed it as PART for 'particle'.

Nevertheless, in natural speech, I have seen one instance in which the auxiliary verb *sĭ* is used, in this case after the subordinate TAMP marker:

(7) ì   á   wôo   sį̀ ã̀   məgŏn-cəbèe lé   kǎa   nḗ
     COMP 2SG EMPH.SUBORD be DEF   monitor-lizard REL chase.REAL.NOM   LOC
     ì   á   wó   à   tò   wé   lɔ́
     COMP 2SG EMPH 3SG know.IRR   FOC here
     'The monitor lizard you were chasing, do you see him here?' [sos170711t1:22]

It is unclear why this example deviates from the usual construction.

In the negative, on the other hand, the suppletive negative auxiliary consistently appears; this time, it is the subordinating particle after the resumptive pronoun that is absent, though it remains on the subject noun itself.

(8) mənĩ́   lɛ̀̃   à̰   ɲá   jăn-dḗn   né   sərĕ   nḗ ŋé
     woman SUBORD 3SG be.NEG   corn-grain   REL pound.REAL.NOM   LOC NEG
     mó   nă   kṹ   sərǎ
     1SG.EMPH   PROSP D.DEF   gather.IRR
     'I will gather the corn that the woman isn't pounding.' [sos170729e]

As usual, the negative marker ŋé is clause-final, even when the clause is relative. Currently, just this single example is attested of the negative progressive in relative clauses; more examples will be required to confirm this construction.

17.1.4 Perfective

In the perfective, the verb takes its usual realis form with its tone lowering to [-raised] (see §13.3.2.1). If the verb is inflected for the present perfective, then the subordinate marker simply follows the subject:

(9) a. méɛ   lɛ̀̃   kà   bâ̰a̰   gɔ̃̀   sô-dzʊ̀   kǎa
         REL.PRO SUBORD   go.REAL.PFV   balafon learn.IRR road-edge   next.to
         tsɛ̋-ké mĩ́ nɔ̃̋   ké   sɔ́ɛn ŋé
         and   1PL   that.for COP   one NEG
         'Someone who went and learned the balafon on the side of the road and what we do, it's not the same.' [sos170711t1:75]

     b. ỹ̀   dzɔ́ lé   kṵ́   í   lé   dɔ̃̀ɔ
         3PL.SUBORD   row REL catch.REAL.PFV LOG   SBJV finish.IRR
         'The row that they took to finish...' [sos170714t2:43]

c. fén né lȅ búɔ bi̠ɛ-sắn nêɛ
   thing REL SUBORD go.out.REAL.PFV play-thing REL.SUBORD
   búɔ
   go.out.REAL.PFV
   'The thing that came out, the instrument that came out....' [sos170711t1:308]

The example in (9a) is a subject relative clause, where a relative pronoun mɛ́ɛ is used in subject position; it is followed by lȅ which is in turn followed by a perfective-marked intransitive verb. The object relative clause in (9b) shows the subordinate marker subsumed into the subject and the object with overt relative marking; once again, the verb takes its regular H-toned perfective form. In (9c), we see two parallel subject relative clauses, the first with a generic noun 'thing' as the subject, which is then replaced by the more specific 'instrument' in the second repetition; the relative marker is followed immediately by the subordinate TAMP marker, and the verb surfaces in the perfective.

In the past perfective, we see competition for the TAMP marker slot: Past tense means that the TAMP marker lɛ̋ should be used, while the relative clause mandates the use of a subordinate TAMP marker after the subject. In this case, past tense blocks the subordinate marker, regardless of whether the subject is the head or not (i.e. regardless of where the relative marker itself appears). I have not seen any past tense relative clauses in the text corpus, so elicited examples are provided below:

(10) a. kərɛ́ lɛ́ lɛ̋ səmâ jĭee mó à tò
        man REL PST dance.REAL.PFV last.year 1SG.EMPH 3SG know.IRR
        'I know the man who danced last year.' [sos170718e]

   b. dón nɛ́ɛ̋ səgû ŋmá ăa cǜɛ
      child REL.PST caterpillar eat.REAL.PFV 3SG.PST vomit.REAL.PFV
      'The child who ate caterpillars vomited.' [sos170729e]

In other words, these relative clauses give us evidence that only a single TAMP marker can be present, and that the one contributing tense marking takes precedence over the one encoding subordination.

17.1.5 Existential and participial predicates

Existential and participial predicates employ the existential auxiliary sĭ in place of a main verb. Just as we saw in §17.1.3, the subordinate TAMP marker takes the place of sĭ, even when it is the only verbal element:

(11) a. bǐ lɛ̋ lȅ lű-ŋǎa ì sá wè gərû
        goat.PL REL.PL SUBORD courtyard-inside 3PL cry.IRR HAB too.much
        'The goats in the courtyard cry too much.' [sos150622e]

b. ké ằ dìnǚ sǐ lêɛ   Sì-Flâ   kằ
   COP DEF drum female REL.SUBORD first.son-Fula in.hand
   'It's a type of drum that Sy-Fla has on him.' [sos170714t1:55]

In main clauses, *sĩ* would appear where the subordinate marker is occuring. In §17.1.4, we saw that the past tense marker and the subordinate marker do not co-occur. (11a) shows that this is not a phonological restriction, i.e. *lɛ́ lɛ̀* is an acceptable sequence when *lɛ́* is the plural relative marker; rather, this restriction is a case of morphosyntactic slot blocking.

We also commonly find a form *bé* in this environment, which appears to be a suppletive form of *sĩ* in subordinate clauses. For example:

(12) a. ì   ké kəré-bɔ́ɔ lɛ́ təgŏ   bé   lɛ̀   ké kʊ́
        COMP COP man-old REL sit.PTCP be.SUBORD SUBORD COP D.DEF
        '[They said that] it's the old man that is sitting there.' [sos170711t1:23]

   b. ằ wò   təgŏ   béɛ   tsɛ̃́, ké Jɛ̀   âa
      3SG EMPH.SUBORD sit.PTCP be.SUBORD how COP first.girl NEG.Q
      'How she is sitting, it's Jɛ, right?" [sos170711t1:207]

   c. ằ   béɛ   tsɛ̃́
      3SG.SUBORD be.SUBORD how
      'The way that it is...' [sos170714t3:63]

In (12b-c), the subordinate marker *lɛ̀* does not appear, but instead, the suppletive form *bé* is lengthened. Both of these are headless relative clauses, with an implied manner head; see §17.6 for further discussion. The expression in (12c) is very common in discourse to introduce another statement.

Like progressives, in the negative, the suppletive negative form *ɲá* reappears:

(13) a. tré   kùä   ɲá   ằ nɛ̀ fɛ̃́ ɲé fôn sɛ́ɛ
        REL.PRO farm.PTCP.SUBORD be.NEG 3SG LOC yet NEG fonio throw.PTCP
        ɲá   kʊ́   nɛ̀ ɲé
        be.NEG D.DEF LOC NEG
        'Where it has not been farmed yet, fonio has not been thrown there.' [sos170714t1:29]

   b. ń nǎ   kə̀kâ ŋmằ   təré   cəmǜ   ɲá   ɲé
      1SG PROSP meat eat.IRR REL.PRO grill.PTCP.SUBORD be.NEG NEG
      'I will eat the meat that isn't grilled.' [sos190803e]

In both of these examples, the subordinate marker *lɛ̀* is elided, leaving its X tone on the preceding participle.

17.2 Subject relatives

When the head of the relative clause is the subject, it is marked by an immediately following relativizer *lé*, then by the subordinate marker *lȅ*, if present (i.e. if not blocked by the past tense marker). This marking is the same whether the subject is of a transitive verb or an intransitive verb, as the examples below illustrate.

Subject relative clauses look like head-initial relative clauses, but this is purely due to the SOV word order of the language; object relative clauses or PP relative clauses, discussed below, show that the head is left in situ.

From elicitation, we find examples like the following:

(14) a. bí   lé   lȅ   bṷ   ŋmǎ   nɛ̋ mó   nǎ   kʊ́
          goat REL SUBORD   grass eat.REAL.NOM   LOC 1SG.EMPH   PROSP D.DEF
          sǎ̰
          buy.IRR
          'I will buy the goat that is eating grass.' [sos170718e]

   b. mǐ   lɛ̋   sío   lȅ   bɛ̀ɛ   sɔ́ɔ   nɛ̋
       1PL REL.PL REC.PST   SUBORD   pig.PL   sell.REAL.NOM   LOC
       'We who have just sold pigs' [sos150201e]

   c. kəré lé lɛ̋   səmâ   jiee   mó   à   tò
       man   REL PST dance.REAL.PFV   last.year 1SG.EMPH   3SG   know.IRR
       'I know the man who danced last year.' [sos170718e]

   d. mʋ̈   lé   lȅ   nǎ   á   wó   lɛ̋ ǟ   jîo↘
       person REL SUBORD come.REAL.PFV   2SG EMPH   PST 3SG see.REAL.PFV.Q
       'Did you see the person who came?' [sos150620e]

Examples (14a-b) show transitive relative clauses whose head is the subject. In (14a), both the relative marker and the subordinate marker are present, but the subordinate marker replaces the auxiliary verb *sɪ̰* in the progressive (§17.1.3). In (14b), we find an example of the immediate past used in a relative clause, and here, the subordinate marker follows the immediate past auxiliary *sío*, as it does for the prospective auxiliary; for more on the immediate past, see §13.3.1.2. Examples (14c-d) illustrate intransitive verbs. In (14c), the past tense marker *lɛ̋* replaces the subordinate marker, which can be seen in (14d). In both cases, these TAMP markers follow the relativizer.

In (15), I provide a couple of examples from the text corpus showing subject relative clauses:

(15) a. fén né lɛ̏ búɔ,   bíɛ-sǎn nêɛ
     thing REL SUBORD go.out.REAL.PFV play-thing REL.SUBORD
     búɔ
     go.out.REAL.PFV
     'The thing that came out, the instrument that came out...' [sos170711t1:308]

 b. kṳi lé fánâa   səsɛ̋ bɛ̋ wɛ̋ kű́ɛ ɲá bò
    bug REL also.SUBORD spider do.IRR HAB other.PL be.NEG anymore
    kʊ́ tʊ̋ ŋé
    D.DEF like NEG
    'The bug that makes the spider egg sacs, it doesn't exist that much anymore.' [sos170711t1:140-141]

Both of these examples have nominal heads (fên 'thing', bíɛ-sǎn 'instrument', kṳi 'bug'); for relative pronouns in subject position, see §17.7 below.

17.3 Object relatives

The head-internal nature of relative clauses becomes clear when we look at object relative clauses, where the head remains in its position between the subordinated subject and the verb. It is likewise marked with the relative marker lé, but it is now preceded by the subordinate TAMP marker, which consistently marks the subject of the relative clause.

The text corpus is replete with examples of object relative clauses, a selection of which I provide here:

(16) a. ɩ̀   á   wôo   sɪ̏ ä̀ məgŏn-cəbȅe lé kǎa
       COMP 2SG EMPH.SUBORD be DEF monitor-lizard REL chase.REAL.NOM
       nɛ̋ ɩ̀ á wó à tò   wé lʊ̋
       LOC COMP 2SG EMPH 3SG know.IRR FOC here
       'The monitor lizard you were chasing, do you see him here?' [sos170711t1:22]

 b. ɩ̏i   dzɔ́ lé kṵ́   í   lé dɔ̋ɔ
    3PL.SUBORD row REL catch.REAL.PFV LOG SBJV finish.IRR
    'The row that they took to finish...' [sos170714t2:43]

c. kűɛ   lȅ   à̰   sʊ́   lɛ̋   kŏo   nɛ̋ à̰ kűɛ
    other.PL SUBORD DEF song REL.PL sing.REAL.NOM LOC 3SG other.PL
    brɛ̰̋ɛ̰   lɛ́
    play.IRR.HAB PART
    'The songs that they were singing, [he took those] and played them.'
    [sos170711t1:40]

d. á   wôo   à̰   kárán lé   jĭo   nɛ̋ kʊ́ʊ
    2SG EMPH.SUBORD   DEF school REL say.REAL.NOM   LOC D.DEF.COP
    sò̰kó-kû
    Jula-thing
    'The *kalan* (school) that you are saying, that is Jula.' [sos170702t1:38]

As these examples show, the relative clause tends to be topicalized and front-dislocated, with the head noun resumed by a pronoun. In other words, instead of putting the relative clause into the object position of the main clause by saying "do you see the monitor lizard that you were chasing here?" it stands alone at the front, with a resumptive pronoun (typically 3sg *à̰* or discourse definite *kʊ́* for singular nouns) in the main clause.

17.4 PP relatives

PP relative clauses relativize the complement of the postposition. Following the general pattern of Seenku relativization, this head is left in situ before the postposition, but the relative marker *lé* intervenes between the two. Examples from elicitation illustrate this construction more clearly:

(17) a. mó   lȅ   ɲəgâan   jĭo   sḭ̀   lé   gʊ̰̀   mó
         1SG.EMPH SUBORD scorpion see.REAL.PFV jar   REL under   1SG.EMPH
         nǎ   kʊ́   nȅ-kɔ̀
         PROSP   D.DEF TRANS-break.IRR
         'I will break the water jar that I saw the scorpion under.' [sos170718e]

     b. ôo   nà̰   kəré lé   wɛ̋   kɛ̋   té
         2SG.EMPH.SUBORD come.REAL.PFV man   REL with COP who
         'Who is the man that you came with?' [sos170718e]

     c. dɔ̋ɔ   lȅ   kún   né   nȅ kʊ́   bɛ̋   à̰   kà̰
         beer SUBORD calabash REL LOC D.DEF do.IRR 3SG in.hand
         'Give him the calabash with the millet beer in it!' [sos170718e]

The head of the relative clause remains in its PP, and the PP remains in its usual location after the verb. As before, the relative clause is topicalized, and the main clause following it contains a resumptive pronoun (the discourse definite *kʊ́* in (17a) and (17c) and a null pronoun in the copular predicate in (17b)).

PP relatives are infrequent in the text corpus. Both examples I have seen come from songs (the first on the balafon and the second as part of a folktale); both involve existential constructions:

(18) a. *á wó lɛ̀   ɲá   nɛ́ wé cí   lɛ́ nɛ̀ ŋɛ́*
        2SG EMPH SUBORD be.NEG if   FOC house REL LOC NEG
        'The house in which you do not live....' [sos161003e]

    b. *ɩ̀   jəgɛ̀ lɛ̀   sɪ̌ nɛ́ gṹɔ lɛ́ nɛ̀ ɩ̀   kʊ́ gṹɔ bé*
        COMP dog SUBORD be if   country REL LOC COMP D.DEF country DEM
        kɛ́ gṹɔ   səgɔ̌ kɛ́ɛ ŋɛ́
        COP country good at.all NEG
        'A land with a dog, that is not a good land at all.' [sos150626t6:59]

We also commonly find a codified PP relative as an expression of time: *sɔ́ń tɛ̀*. The head noun *sɔ́ń*, homophonous with 'sky', in this case means 'time' or 'moment'; while we would expect the relative PP to sound like *sɔ́ né tɛ̀*, the expression is common enough to have undergone reduction to *sɔ́ń tɛ̀*. The following examples illustrate its placement and use, which follow the general rules for PP relatives:

(19) a. *mó   à   bə̂ə   gṹɔ   mó   lɛ̀   sɔ́ń*
        1SG.EMPH DEF balafon learn.REAL.PFV 1SG.EMPH SUBORD time.REL
        tɛ̀ jù nɔ̌
        GEN year five
        'I learned the balafon when I was five years old...' [sos171009t1:21]

    b. *bə̂ə   lɛ̀   nằ   wé sɔ́ń   tɛ̀ mɪ́ jərá-ŋɛ́*
        balafon SUBORD come.REAL.PFV FOC time.REL GEN 1PL family-HUM.PL
        kərúĩ kɛ́   kɛ́   ŋɛ́
        all.PL COP.PST griot.PL NEG
        'When the balafon arrived, none of our family were griots.' [sos171009t1:33-34]

The use of 'time' as the head of the PP relative subordinates the clause, setting the scene for the main clause that follows without the need for a resumptive pronoun, since the head of the relative clause is not an argument in the main clause.

17.5 Possessor relatives

Possessor relatives are constructions where the head of the relative clause is the possessor DP (e.g. 'the woman whose child...') rather than the whole possessed DP ('the woman's child who...'). Elicited examples include:

(20) a. à tɘgò kɘrê lɛ̀ mɘlé nì̀ cìe jĩee
3SG sit.REAL.PFV man DAT REL.PRO father cie.REAL.PFV last.year
'She married the man whose father died last year.' [sos190803e]

b. mɘnĩ́ lɛ́ɛ̀ nìgì kóo à̀ fócêɛn mɔ̰̀mɑ̰́
woman REL.DAT cow give.birth.REAL.PFV 3SG milk a.lot
jĩo
see.REAL.PFV
'The woman whose cow gave birth got a lot of milk.' [sos190803e]

In (20a), the main clause precedes the relative clause; a relative pronoun mɘlé resumes the indirect object of the main clause 'man', and this relative pronoun acts as the possessor of nì̀ 'father'. In (20b), the relative clause is first; the possessor 'woman' is head of the relative clause and thus is marked with the relativizer lé, which combines with the elided dative postposition used in alienable possession (§8.6.2.2).

In the corpus, possessor relatives generally look more like (20a), involving a relative pronoun instead of an overt noun (though the speaker switches back to the original noun in (21b)).

(21) a. tɘné gɘrɛ̋ jɘgă lɛ̀ kṹ gṳ̀,
REL.PRO voice descend.PTCP SUBORD D.DEF under
jĩo-bǎ̰a-dɛ̌n, mɔ̰̀ kṹ kòtɛ̀ bé fɑ̋ né
fetish-balafon-grain person D.DEF calabash DEM put.in.IRR FOC
kṹ gṳ̀
D.DEF under
'The one whose voice follows that, the fetish balafon key, we put that calabash underneath it.' [sos170711t1:96]

b. téné kóté lé gɘrɛ̋ sɨ́ɔ à ɲá nɛ̋ ŋé mɔ̰̀
REL.PRO calabash REL voice arrive.PTCP 3SG be.NEG if LOC person
à dzʊ̀ ɲɛ̀ɛ
3SG mouth build.IRR.HAB
'The one, the calabash whose voice doesn't come out, we build up its mouth.' [sos170711t1:97-98]

In (21a), the head of the relative clause is the pronoun tɘné, which possesses the noun gɘrɛ̋ 'voice'. In (21b), the speaker starts out with the relative pronoun téné but then decides to use the noun kóté 'calabash' instead. Once again, this is a possessor, possessing the noun *garɛ̋* voice. When the relative pronoun is used as head, as in (21a), the overt noun is used in the following main clause; if the noun itself is used in the relative clause, as in (21b), a pronoun (here the 3sg *ằ*) is used in the following main clause.

17.6 Headless relatives

In all of the relative clauses presented thus far, the head of the relative clause is overt and fills one of the core arguments of the relative clause. In texts, we find cases of headless relative clauses, that is, subordinate clauses that follow the same structure as the relative clauses we have seen thus far but without a head noun (or a relativizer *lɛ́*). Typically, the null head indicates something like manner, and the whole relative clause is followed by the wh-word *tsɛ̋* 'how'. Consider the following examples:

(22) a. ì dənɨ̋ lɛ̀ ì lɛ̀ ằ jío tsɛ̋ ì ké
   3PL child.PL SUBORD 3PL SUBORD 3SG say.REAL.PFV how COMP COP
   kʊ́ tő
   D.DEF like
   'The way the children said it, it's like that.' [150626t4:15]

b. ǐi béɛ tsɛ̋ í wó kằ tsɛ̋ gùɔ
   3PL.SUBORD be.SUBORD how LOG EMPH go.REAL.PFV INDF country
   nɛ̀
   LOC
   'The way that it is [=as they say], I went to a country.' [161009t1:147]

c. bâ̰a̰ nằ tsɛ̋ sɛ́ɛ-ŋɛ̀ tè íaa, mɨ̋
   balafon.SUBORD come.REAL.PFV how Sambla-HUM.PL GEN TOP 1PL
   nɨ̋ bú-blɛ̆ kű̋ɛ lɛ̀ ằ jú tsɛ̋ mɨ̋ tsɛ̋-ké
   father.PL RED-big.PL other.PL SUBORD 3SG say.IRR how 1PL.DAT and
   mɨ̋ nɨ̋ lɛ̀ ằ jú tsɛ̋, ké kərê sı̋o
   1PL father SUBORD 3SG say.IRR how COP man get.up.REAL.PFV
   jṵ-jɔ́ɔ wɛ̋, mɛ̀ ké jṵ-jɔ̀ɔ jəmṵ
   mountain-stroll.NOM with 3SG.SUBORD go.IRR mount-stroll.IRR bush
   'Well, as for how the balafon came to Sambla country, as our grandfathers told us and how our fathers told us, there was a man who started hunting, he went out hunting in the bush.' [sos170711t1:5-7]

In each of these examples, there is no overt head; rather the relative clause as a whole, marked with *tsɛ̋* 'how', refers to the manner in which the subject of the relative clause said or did something, and this then serves as a topic or context relating to the main clause that follows.

In one instance, this same construction is used with a temporal meaning similar to 'since':

(23) í wó lɛ̏ kəná tsɛ̃́ gṹɔ-dəgɛ̀ɛ tsɛ̃́ mɔ̀ bậa
LOG EMPH SUBORD wake.REAL.PFV how morning.LOC INDF person balafon
dzǔ-tsí̧ fɛ̃́ í wó tè fɔ̃́ɛ̃́-fɔ̃́ɛ̃́ ŋɛ́
mouth-cut.REAL.PFV yet LOG EMPH GEN RED-at.all NEG
'Since I woke up this morning, no one has opened up the balafon [=given money to the balafon] at all.' [sos161005e]

Regular temporal subordination, on the other hand, tends to be achieved through a reduplicated verb construction or the use of the conditional; see §20.3.3 and §20.3.4, respectively.

17.7 Relative pronoun

Instead of using a noun followed by the relativizer *lɛ́* as the head of the relative clause, Seenku also uses relative pronouns, evolved from a combination of light nouns ('thing', 'person') and the relative marker. There are four forms: *fəlɛ́/fɛ̀ nɛ́*, *kərɛ́/kú lɛ́*, *tərɛ́/tənɛ́/tɛ́ nɛ́*, and *məlɛ́/mɛ́ɛ* (possibly from *mɔ̀ lɛ́*). Of these, the first three are used also as wh-expressions; see §16.2.1. As the slashes indicate, there is free variation in how compressed or integrated the relative marker is into the relative pronoun, from still being two identifiable words (*kú lɛ́*) to being completely subsumed (*mɛ́ɛ*); this elision pattern is otherwise unseen with the relative marker.

I will discuss each relative pronoun in turn, as they have distinct but overlapping contexts in which they can be used.

17.7.1 *fəlɛ́/fənɛ́/fɛ̀n nɛ́*

The relative pronoun *fəlɛ́/fənɛ́* (with two-word variant *fɛ̀n nɛ́*) can be used as a wh-word meaning 'what' (for concrete things) or it can be used as the head of a relative clause. For example:

(24) a. mó nəgǐ büɔ kǎtő fəlɛ́ɛ̃́
1SG.EMPH mind go.out.REAL.PRF even.though REL.PRO.PST
dzɛ̃́ môee kɛ́ ằ fəlêɛ
be.good.PTCP 1SG.EMPH.with COP DEF REL.PRO.PRES
'I have forgotten even though what I liked was that.' [sos161009t1:57]

b. á lɛ̏ fə̀lé kərűii ɲɛ́ɛ yè tsɨ̰̀n-bűɔ
   2SG SUBORD REL.PRO all.PL weave.IRR.HAB PART beginning
   gɔ̏ɔ   fɔ̰́ wɛ́
   be.difficult more FOC
   'Everything that you are weaving, it's the beginning that is the hardest part.' [sos170822t10:205]

The relative pronoun appears twice in (24a), first as the subject head of the relative clause, marked with the past tense TAMP marker and second as the argument of a copular predicate, marked with the presentative (likely related to relative marking; see §8.2.3.2). In (24b), the relative pronoun is the object head of the relative clause.

See §16.2.1 for further discussion of this form as an interrogative.

17.7.2 kəré/kú lɛ́

Like fə̀né/fɛ̀n né, the expression kəré/kú lɛ́ can be used as a relative pronoun or as a wh-word meaning 'what' (abstract concepts). Both expressions mean something like 'the thing that', with the difference between the two being whether this thing is concrete or abstract.

(25) a. gbɛ̏nɛ̋ mɔ̰̋ɔ   kú lɛ̋ bɛ̋ wɛ̋ tsɛ̋-ké dɔ̀n ɨ̀
        before person.PST thing REL.PL do.IRR HAB and today 3PL
        bɛ́ɛ-cé
        do.NOM-manner
        '...what people did before and how they are done now.' [sos170702t1:41]

   b. fôn-bɛ̰́ɛ̰̋   màa fəná dəró-ŋɛ́ɛ   sőn   mɛ̋
      fonio-beat.ANTIP.NOM again also child-HUM.PL.PST play.IRR HAB
      kəré wɛ̋ à   bɛ́ɛ   tsɛ̰̋ ɨ̀ í bɛ̋ ɨ̀
      REL.PRO with 3SG.SUBORD be.SUBORD how 3PL LOG do.IRR COMP
      fón-bṵ̀   sɨ̰̏ kɔ́ kâa quoi
      fonio-grass be D.DEF fight what.FR
      'For fonio beating also, what the children used to play with, how it was, there was fonio grass, it was a war.' [sos170714t3:63]

In (25a), the two word expression is used, with the S-toned relative marker lɛ̋ marking the plural ('things that people did'); in (25b), the relative pronoun is the complement to a postpositition in a PP relative.

For kəré/kú lɛ́ as an interrogative wh-expression, see §16.2.1.

17.7.3 tərɛ́/tənɛ́/tɛ́nɛ́

The most common relative pronoun is *tərɛ́/tənɛ́/tɛ́nɛ́*. Recall from §16.2.1 that this form could be used as a wh-word meaning 'which one', but this interrogative use is far less common than its role in relative clauses, where it can translate to something like 'the one that'. While *kərɛ́* and *fə̀lɛ́* are built off of identifiable light nouns (*kû* and *fên*, respectively, both meaning 'thing'), there is no light noun in modern Seenku that shows us the diachronic path of *tərɛ́*; the likeliest suspect is *tɛ́*, the wh-word 'who' (§16.2.2), but *tərɛ́* is exclusively used for non-human referents while 'who' is a wh-word exclusively for humans.

This relative pronoun can be used in any position in a relative clause (subject (26a), object (26b), in a PP (26c), as a possessor (26d), etc.), but in every case, it indicates a non-human argument.

(26) a. tɛ́nɛ́ lɛ̏ jṳ̀ tsi̋ì bàä á kằ, mí̋ kʊ́
REL.PRO SUBORD year six do.REAL.PRF 2SG in.hand 1PL D.DEF
bɔ̀ wɛ̀
take.out.IRR HAB
'What has done six years with you, we take that out.' [sos170711t1:64]

b. mó lɛ̏ tɛ́nɛ́ tő bậạ nɛ̋
1SG.EMPH SUBORD REL.PRO know.IRR balafon LOC
'That which I know about the balafon.' [sos171009t1:24]

c. mó nǎ sì̋ nɛ̋-kɔ̀ môo ɲəgâan
1SG.EMPH PROSP jar TRANS-break.IRR 1SG.EMPH.SUBORD scorpion
jîo tərɛ́ gṳ̀
see.REAL.PFV REL.PRO under
'I will break the water jar that I saw the scorpion under.' [sos170718e]

d. tənɛ́ gərɛ̋ jəgǎ lɛ̏ kʊ́ gṳ̀,
REL.PRO voice descend.PTCP SUBORD D.DEF under
jîo-bậạ-dɛ̋n, mɔ̋ kʊ́ kòtɛ̀ bɛ́ fɑ̋ nɛ́
fetish-balafon-grain person D.DEF calabash DEM put.in.IRR FOC
kʊ́ gṳ̀
D.DEF under
'The one whose voice follows that, the fetish balafon key, we put that calabash underneath it.' [sos170711t1:96]

All of the examples in (26) are naturally occurring except for (26c), from elicitation; note that this example is the equivalent of (17a) above; there, the noun 'water jar' appeared in the relative clause, marked by the relative marker *lɛ́* and followed by the resumptive pronoun *kɔ́*; here, 'water jar' appears in the main clause, with a relative clause following that elaborates on the head indicated with the relative pronoun *tərɛ̀*.

17.7.4 *məlɛ́/mɛ́ɛ*

The last relative pronoun *məlɛ́/mɛ́ɛ* is reserved for human referents. Given this, it is likely that it evolved from *mɔ̰̌ lɛ́* 'person who', though any trace of the original vowel of *mɔ̰̌* 'person' or its nasalization has been lost. It is also the only case in which I have seen the relative marker *lɛ́* fully elided; otherwise, *lɛ́* is impervious to clitic elision (§4.4.3). The plural form of *mɛ́ɛ* is *mɛ́ɛ́*, as shown in (27d) below.

Examples of this relative pronoun include:

(27) a. mɛ́ɛ   lɛ̀   kà   bâa   gɔ̀   sô   dzʊ̌   kǎa
      REL.PRO SUBORD go.REAL.PFV balafon learn.IRR road edge next.to
      tsɛ̋-kɛ́ mǐ nɔ̰̌   kɛ́ sɔ́ɛn ŋɛ́
      and   1PL that.for COP one NEG
      'Someone who went and learned balafon on the side of the road and what we do, it's not the same.' [sos170711t1:75]

   b. mɛ́ɛ   lɛ̀   bɔ́ɔ̀   wè   mó   wɛ̋   kɛ́ mó   nǎ
      REL.PRO SUBORD be.old.IRR HAB 1SG.EMPH with COP 1SG.EMPH PROSP
      kɛ̋   fɛ̰̋ kɔ́   sərà̰   tərɛ̰̀
      go.IRR yet D.DEF master ask.IRR
      'Someone older than me, I will ask him first.' [sos171009t1:124-125]

   c. mɔ̰̌   sɔ́ɔ̀   mɔ̰̌ɔ́   à̰   kərúú jù   bâa   nɛ̰̀
      person be.able.IRR.HAB person.SBJV 3SG all   say.IRR balafon LOC
      et   puis   mlɛ́   lɛ̀   à̰   mḭ̀ɛ   nɛ̋ est-ce que
      and.FR then.FR REL.PRO SUBORD 3SG hear.REAL.NOM LOC q.FR
      ḭ̀   kərúú bá̰à̰   dàn-kù   mɛ̰̀   wè
      3PL all   balafon mouth-thing hear.IRR HAB
      'Can one say anything on the balafon, and then the one who is listening, can everyone understand balafon speech?' [sos170711t1:218]

   d. ḭ̀   lɛ̀   mɛ́ɛ́   cɛ̋rɛ̋   wɛ̋   kɛ̋
      3PL SUBORD REL.PRO.PL call.IRR HAB griot.PL
      'Those who are called griots...' [sos171009t1:30]

The examples in (27a-c) show *mɛ́ɛ* (or *mlɛ́* in the case of (27d)) in subject position (i.e. they are subject relative clauses), while it appears in object position in (27d).

In one example, I have seen the relative pronoun *mɛ́ɛ* used in the distributive reduplication pattern X-òo-X (§10.2.2.4), here with a L tone on the reduplicating linker rather than the H found in adverbial constructions:

(28) ì   lɛ̀   mɛ́ɛ-òo-mɛ́ɛ   cèrè   wè kâ
      3PL SUBORD REL.PRO-LINK-REL.PRO call.IRR HAB griot
      'Whoever is called a griot...' [sos171009t1:99]

As the gloss indicates, this reduplication pattern gives the reading 'whoever'. It is unclear whether the other relative pronouns can undergo this reduplication.

Unlike the other relative pronouns, I have never seen *məlɛ́/mɛ́ɛ* used as an interrogative, presumably because the human-specific interrogative *tɛ́* 'who' is used instead.

18 Conditional constructions

This chapter focuses on all manner of conditional phrases, including hypotheticals and counterfactuals, which share the same basic form. Conditionals are very common in texts, used both for true hypotheticals as well as for more temporal subordination in discussing a sequence of events ("when X happens, then Y", or "if X happens, then Y"). For the latter, see §20.3.4. For other types of subordination, see Chapter 19 on complement clauses and modal expressions, and Chapter 20 on clause chaining.

18.1 Basic form

All hypotheticals share the same basic structure: The subject is followed by a subjunctive particle *lé* (not to be confused with the relative subject subordinating particle *lɛ̀*). More often than not, this particle undergoes clitic elision (§4.4.3), leaving only a H-toned mora that lengthens the subject. The verb takes its perfective form (see §13.3.2.1) but is followed immediately by the conditional marker *nɛ́*. This particle is homophonous with the locative particle used with transitive verbs, but can be distinguished with intransitive verbs, which would otherwise take an X-toned version *nɛ̀* via argument-head tone sandhi (§4.4.2); in other words, the conditional particle does not form a sandhi domain with the preceding verb. The hypothetical clause (the antecedent) typically precedes the subsequent clause, though the order can be reversed.

In the interest of clarity, I provide elicited examples in (1) illustrating these basic principles:

(1) a. áa bî sɔ́ɔ nɛ́ á à jú ń nɛ̀
2SG.SBJV goat sell.REAL.PFV if 2SG 3SG say.IRR 1SG DAT
'If you sell a goat, tell me.' [sos170803e]

b. móo kʉ̀ níɔ nɛ́ ŋɛ́ ì nəgǐ nǎ dəbɛ̀ ŋɛ́
1SG.SBJV toh eat.REAL.PFV if NEG 3PL mind PROSP be.good.IRR NEG
'If I don't eat toh, they won't be happy.' [sos170803e]

c. mɔ̰̂ɔ̰́ tsîo nɛ́ cícǐ í síǐ mɔ̰̀ nǎ í
person.SBJV meet.REAL.PFV if when LOG RECP.with person PROSP LOG
sí bà̰
RECP hit.IRR
'When we meet each other [again], we will fight.' [sos161007e]

For more on hypotheticals, see §18.2.

Counterfactuals share this basic form but use a fixed clause in the antecedent ǎá jərá nɛ̋ 'if it happens that', which itself subordinates the semantic content of the counterfactual:

(2) ǎá jərá nɛ̋ á bî sa̰ mɔ̰̋ɔ̰ nǎ ǎ
    3SG.SBJV become.REAL.PFV if 2SG goat sell.IRR person.PST PROSP 3SG
    nɔ́ í səgɔ́
    eat.IRR LOG good
    'If you had bought a goat, we would have eaten well.' [sos170803e]

In the clause subordinated by the conditional clause, there is no subordinating particle after the subject and the verb is irrealis. For more counterfactuals, see §18.3.

18.2 Hypotheticals

Hypotheticals are the most basic form of conditionals. The verb is uniformly perfective, and hence realis. From a mood perspective, this is surprising, since the antecedent verb in a conditional construction has by definition not yet taken place, and hence we may expect an irrealis verb form. However, as Bybee (1992) and Givón (1994) have shown, the use of the perfective in conditionals may have diachronic origins in a past subjunctive in counterfactuals, and from this position, they expand out and "colonize" other conditional forms. If we look to related languages in the Samogo group, we see possible evidence for this hypothesis. For example, in Jowulu, counterfactual conditionals put the antecedent verb in the perfective, but normal conditionals use the more semantically felicitous irrealis verb form (Kim 2002). Dzùùngoo (Solomiac 2014) lies somewhere in between; though the verb in a conditional construction is typically in its uninflected form, which corresponds to the Seenku irrealis, the verb can also be inflected for either imperfective or perfective, depending upon the relation of the conditional clause to the point of reference. In Seenku, it appears, the perfective marking has become semantically bleached and is now simply part of conditional constructions.

In (3), I present a selection of simple hypotheticals from the text corpus:

(3) a. íi sɔ́ɔ̰ nɛ̋ íi expliquer dəgɔ̃ɛɛ lɛ́ lɛ̏
       2PL.SBJV be.able.IRR.HAB if 2PL.SBJV explain.FR place.PL REL SUBORD
       ȉ bɔ́ í sí nɛ̏
       3PL take.out.IRR LOG RECP LOC
       'If you could explain where they differ from each other.' [sos170702t1:42]

b. í wóo sío nɛ́ ì ằ sú, í
   LOG EMPH.SBJV get.up.REAL.PFV if COMP 3SG get.up.IRR LOG
   wóo təgɔ̀ nɛ́ ì ằ təgɔ̀ íi sənáŋ
   EMPH.SBJV sit.REAL.PFV if COMP 3SG sit.IRR LOG.SBJV lie.down.REAL
   nɛ́ ì ằ sənáŋ
   if COMP 3SG lie.down.IRR
   '[They say that] if I get up, he gets up, if I sit down, he sits down, if I lie down, he lies down.' [sos161009t1:34]

c. ǐi í bǎ nɛ́ wɛ́ kɛ́ jén-jɛ́n fín wɛ́
   3PL.SBJV LOG say.REAL.PFV if FOC COP RED-story two FOC
   'If they say that, then they are two different riddles.' [sos161009t1:52]

d. móo kǎ nɛ́ cɔ̀ mó nǎ tsɛ́ɛ
   1SG.EMPH.SBJV go.REAL.PFV if village 1SG.EMPH PROSP ask.IRR
   'If I go to the village, I will ask.' [sos161009t1:162]

In all of these examples, the hypothetical clause precedes the subsequent clause; the verb is inflected for perfective, even though by virtue of being a hypothetical, the action has not necessarily taken place. In (3c), we see a common pattern where the conditional particle is followed by a broad focus marker *wɛ́*; for further discussion, see §21.1.2.1.

18.2.1 Conditionals with non-perfective verb forms

While the perfective is the typical unmarked form that a verb will take in a hypothetical conditional, we also find conditional constructions where the verb is in an inflectional category with an auxiliary (either the progressive or the prospective). In this case, the conditional particle *nɛ́* follows the auxiliary verb.

First, the following examples illustrate the conditional with progressive verbs:

(4) a. ou bien mɔ̀ɔ́ sɪ̌ nɛ́ ằ bǎ nɛ́ ɲì-nà
   or.FR well.FR person.SBJV be if 3SG put.REAL.NOM LOC there-towards
   jəmɪ̀, wótrɔ́ lɛ́ à ɲì wɛ ǐi ằ kɛ̀ɛ tásîa
   bush cart PST 3SG pick.up.IRR HAB 3PL.SBJV 3SG gather.IRR plate
   nɛ̀ tsɪ̀ɔ nɛ̀
   LOC stalk LOC
   'Or if we were putting [things] down in the bush, the cart would pick it up and gather it into containers in the stalks...' [sos170702t1:52]

b. áa sĭ ně wé nân nǐɔ ně á á tsɛ̀ fɛ̀ɛ
2SG.SBJV be if FOC sauce eat.REAL.NOM LOC 2SG 2SG hand lick.IRR
tɔ́-tɔ́ɔ
RED-like
'If you are eating sauce, you lick your hand like that.' [sos170711t1:27]

c. ä́á ɲá ně ä̀ mĭɛ ně ŋé, mɔ̀̃ kʊ́ cɛ̏rɛ̏
3SG.SBJV be.NEG if 3SG hear.REAL.NOM LOC NEG person D.DEF call.IRR
mɔ̀̃ ä̀ jú küɛ ï̈ ä̀ jú ä̀ lɛ́
person 3SG say.IRR other.PL.DAT 3PL.SBJV 3SG say.IRR 3SG DAT
'If he doesn't understand, we call them and tell them to tell it to him.'
[sos170711t1:241]

The examples in (4a-b) show affirmative progressives, where the conditional particle *ně* follows the auxiliary verb *sĭ*; in (4b), we once again see the focus particle *wé* after the conditional. In (4c), a negative progressive is shown, which follows the same pattern but uses the suppletive negative verb *ɲá* instead. It should be noted that the locative postposition in the progressive is homophonous with the conditional, since these verbs are transitive, but speakers know to interpret these as the locative, given the presence of the auxiliary and conditional particle earlier in the clause.

For the non-verbal conditional predicates with existential *sĭ*, see §18.2.2.

In the prospective, we find one of two auxiliaries in the conditional: either the regular prospective auxiliary *nǎ* or the auxiliary verb *lò*, derived from another verb for 'come'. In both of these cases, the conditional particle follows the auxiliary verb, and the content verb is left in the irrealis.

(5) a. m̋-m̋ mó nəgì̀ lò ně bɔ́ ń nṳ̀ dəgɔ̆ɛ tsɛ̋
INTERJ 1SG.EMPH mind come if go.out.IRR 1SG that.for place INDF
lɛ̋ á wó nǎ kʊ́ jṳ̀ âa
DAT 2SG EMPH PROSP D.DEF say.IRR NEG.Q
'If I forget something that I'm supposed to say, you would say it, right?'
[sos150626t6:5]

b. ä̀á nǎ ně sɔ́ á kpénén-kó wɛ̋, kʊ́ nǎ
3SG.SBJV PROSP if arrive.IRR 2SG finger-thumb with D.DEF PROSP
fä̀ í bòn mè
enter.IRR LOG back with
'If you get to your thumb, it enters [your mouth] backwards.' [sos170711t1:27]

c. bon, mí tě lɔ̋ à́ jáné̋ ké kərê-dərǒn ǎa ná
well.FR 1PL GEN here 3SG become.if COP boy-child 3SG.SBJV PROSP
né̋- mɔ̰̋ɔ̰́ ná né̋ à́ gɔ́ bậa lḛ̀ ké jṳ̀ ɲḛ̀ɛ
if person.SBJV PROSP if 3SG learn.IRR balafon DAT COP year seven
'Well, for us here, if it's a boy, if he will–, if we will teach him balafon, it
[will be when he is] seven years old.' [sos170711t1:147]

For more on lɔ̀ as an auxiliary, see §19.5.3.

18.2.2 Hypotheticals with non-verbal predicates

Non-verbal predicates, including copular predicates, existential predicates, or volitional predicates, can also be put into the conditional. If the copula *ké* or the existential *sɪ̰* is present, as in (6a-b) and (6c-d), respectively, the conditional particle follows it:

(6) a. ì́ áa ké né̋ kərê ì́ á nḛ̀
COMP 2SG.SBJV COP if man COMP 2SG come.IRR
'[They said] if you are a man, then follow [me].' [sos170714t1:38]

b. óo ké né̋ kəré-tsî, məní́ ɲá á tḛ̀ ŋé...
2SG.EMPH.SBJV COP if man-unmarried woman be.NEG 2SG GEN NEG
'If you are a bachelor, you don't have a wife...' [sos170714t3:101]

c. jəgḛ̀ təgǒ sɪ̰ né̋ tɔ́-tərɔ́ ì́ tɔ̀ɔn kɔ̀n à́ nǎ– à́ təgɪ̌ sɪ̰
dog sit.PTCP be if RED-like LOG butt on 3SG PROSP 3SG stand.PTCP be
tɔ́-tərɔ́ à́ təgǒ lɛ́ lḛ̀ kʊ́ bɔ́ɔ fő̰n
RED-like 3SG sit.PTCP REL PRES D.DEF be.tall.IRR.HAB more
'If a dog is sitting like that on his butt, he will stand up like that, his sitting
down is taller.' [sos161009t1:71]

d. ì́ ằa sɪ̰ né̋ à́ tê gṳ̀ɔ nḛ̀ kɛ̰́ɛ bő̰n né̋
COMP 3SG.SBJV be if 3SG GEN country LOC tomorrow back LOC
lê
REL.PRES
'[That] if he wanted, in the village the day after next...' [sos170805t9:15]

Copular predicates with *ké* are shown in (6a-b); a participial predicate with the existential auxiliary *sɪ̰* is shown in (6c), while (6d) provides an example of a volitional predicate, also with the auxiliary *sɪ̰*. It should be noted that another speaker of Seenku found the use of the copula followed by the conditional to be non-ideal; he says the best way to form these sentences would be to use *jáné̋* (discussed below in this section), and that this construction with the copula sounds like "city Seenku". Indeed,

(6a-b) were produced by a young man who has grown up largely in Bobo-Dioulasso, and it is clear that there are differences between the Seenku spoken in town and that spoken in the more traditional Sambla villages.

The copular predicates in (6a-b) have an overt 2sg subject, which is lengthened by the subjunctive. Recall from §14.1 that the subject is null if it would be a 3rd person pronoun. To form the conditional in this case, the copula itself can be omitted and the conditional marker *ně* directly follows the predicate noun. For example:

(7) puisque mɔ̂ɛ̌ɛ ně kó nɛ̀ mɔ̀ mɔ̀ɛ̀ɛ tsi̋i ɲì-nà
  since.FR millet.SBJV if D.DEF LOC person millet cut.IRR.HAB there-towards
  kpéɛ̀ wɛ̀, í à ɲì tásîa nɛ̀ í né à bè wótrő
  knife with LOG 3SG pick.up.IRR plate LOC LOG come.IRR 3SG put.IRR cart
  ně
  LOC
  'If it was millet, we would harvest millet with a knife and pick it up in containers and come put it in a donkey cart...' [sos170702t1:51]

This form is rare, however, compared to a construction in which a conditional predicate *jáně*, derived from *jərâ ně* 'become (conditional)', is used instead to introduce a noun:

(8) a. ằá jáně kó tɔ̋ ń jəbǎ ɲá ằ wò nɛ̀ ŋé
    3SG.SBJV become.if D.DEF like 1SG care be.NEG 3SG EMPH LOC NEG
    'If it's like that, I don't care.' [sos171009t2:21]

  b. ằá jáně səsằanɛ̀ mɔ̀ɛ tsi̋i ɲəgɔ̀ɛ
    3SG.SBJV become.if right.now person.PL six equal.PL
    'If there were six people now....' [sos170714t3:19]

  c. ằá jáně gʉ̀ɔ-dəgɛ̀ tsɛ̋-ké sɔ̋n-tsìe-nɛ̀
    3SG.SBJV become.if morning and sky-black-LOC
    'If it's the morning and the evening...' [sos170711t1:436]

In each of these cases, the conditional predicate takes a generic 3sg as the subject; the predicate is followed by the noun in (8b-c) or by an adverbial phrase as in (8a).

Further evidence that *à jáně* is the conditional equivalent of the copula *ké* comes from the fact that it can also be used to introduce clauses, in the same way that the copula does (with a likely tie to focus; §21.1.3). For example:

(9) a. bon àá jáné fəná bą́ą-brɛ̃́ sĭ kúɛ
well.FR 3SG.SBJV become.if also balafon-play.NOM.PL be other.PL
nǎ í nè-sɔ̀ɔ à bą́ą̀ wɛ̀
PROSP LOG TRANS-approach.IRR DEF balafon with
'If balafon players are there as well, they will approach the balafon...'
[sos170714t3:51]

b. ì̀ nǎ í bɛ̃́ ì̀ àá jáné ì̀ J̀àakáa kúɛ
3PL PROSP LOG do.IRR COMP 3SG.SBJV become.if 3PL Jaakaa other.PL
ɲəgɛ̃́ sĭ à bą́ą bɛ́ brɛ̃́ nɛ̃́ kɛ́ ì̀-á-lɔ́ kɛ́
?? be DEF balafon DEM play.REAL.NOM LOC COP you.know.JU COP
sóen ŋɛ́
one NEG
'They will say, if Jaakaa and the others are playing the balafon, you know
that it's not the same.' [sos170711t1:259]

Just as we saw with main clauses introduced by the copula *ké* in §21.1.3, the clause following *à jáné* does not display any unusual inflectional properties, nor does *à jáné* contribute much meaning that could not be encoded by simply making the clause that follows it conditional.

This conditional predicate can also surface in its full form *jərâ nɛ̃́*, in which case it means 'if X becomes', as shown in the following example:

(10) kɛ́ á wó dzʊ̀ kɔ̀n àá jərâ nɛ̃́ cén-fəgâ fɔ́ kɛ́ à
COP 2SG EMPH mouth on 3SG.SBJV become if breast-full must COP 3SG
nǎ nɛ̀ lɛ́ màa á wó tɛ̀
PROSP come.IRR FOC again 2SG EMPH GEN
'She is for you, if she becomes a young woman, she has to come [live with] you.'
[sos170714t3:114]

For more on non-verbal predicates in main clauses, see Chapter 14.

18.2.3 Conditionals as temporal subordination

The same construction used for hypothetical conditionals can also be used as a kind of temporal subordination; in this case, the subordinate clause takes on a meaning of 'when' rather than 'if'. This construction is extremely common in narratives as a way of setting up an order of events. For example:

(11) a. ǎ jánɛ̀ɛ́ síɔ nɛ́ wɛ́ lɔ́ trɔ́ ǎ
DEF evening.SBJV arrive.REAL.PFV if FOC here like.that DEF
dəró-ŋɛ́ ì sú wè küɛ kɛ́ són
child-HUM.PL 3PL get.up.IRR HAB other.PL.SUBORD go.IRR play.IRR
ǎ tərǔkű nɛ́
DEF trash LOC
'When evening comes here like that, the children go out and play behind the house.' [sos170711t1:38-39]

b. ì kɛ́ í wóo sǐ jɯ̰̀-jɔ́ɔ nɛ́,
COMP COP LOG EMPH.SBJV be mountain-stroll.REAL.PFV if
məgɔ̌n-cəbɛ̀ɛ́ fɑ̰̀ nɛ́ í gɯ̀ kɔ̌ɔ lɛ̀ í wó
monitor.lizard.SBJV enter.REAL.PFV if LOG under hole DAT LOG EMPH
lɛ́ ǎ sḭ̀ɛ nɛ́ lɛ́...
SBJV 3SG dig.REAL.PFV if FOC
'[He said] when he was hunting, when a monitor went into a hole underneath him, and when he was digging...' [sos170711t1:17-18]

c. ǎ bö̀-kɔ̌ɔ lɛ́ tsîɛɛ nɛ́ ɛ̀ɛ́ bí ǎ!
DEF billygoat PST talk.REAL.PFV if 3SG.LOG do.IRR.COMP INTERJ
ì fèn nêɛ kɛ́ bö̀-kɔ̌ɔ ŋɛ́
COMP thing REL.PRES COP billygoat NEG
'When Billygoat spoke, he said, ah! it's not a billygoat.' [sos161009t1:209]

d. nɛ́ dəgɔ̀̃ nɛ́ kɔ́ tɔ́ í lɛ̀ mó nǎ màa
1SG.SBJV greet.REAL.PFV if D.DEF like 2PL DAT 1SG.EMPH PROSP again
jiaa mó ń təgɔ̀n nɛ̀-jɯ̀ í wó lɛ̀
return.IRR 1SG.EMPH 1SG name TRANS-say.IRR 2PL EMPH DAT
'Now that I have greeted you, I'll come back now and tell you my name.' [sos171009t1:8-9]

In each of these examples, the clause marked with the conditional particle actually takes place in the narrative, so it is not a hypothetical statement. Instead, the use of the conditional here signals to the listener that that clause takes place and is completed before the action described in the subsequent main clause. In (11b), multiple subordinated clauses are strung together to create a series of actions occurring one after the next.

The conditional subordination is similar in meaning to reduplicative subordination, described in §20.3.3. For more on clause chaining beyond temporal subordination, see Chapter 20.

18.3 Counterfactual conditionals

Counterfactual conditionals describe an alternative reality in the conditional clause; the action did not, in fact, take place, but **if it had**, then we would see the result stated in the main clause that follows. In Seenku, these do not look much different from regular conditionals, with the exception that we see the conditional predicate ǎá jáně̋ more often introducing the clause. In this case, the focus reading of this construction (and the non-conditional ké) could be co-opted to indicate a counterfactual reading. In the main clause, we find past tense marking, since it indicates an option that was available in the past (but no longer, because the alternate reality in the conditional clause did not play out). I first show elicited examples in (12), which represent translations offered by consultants in response to a counterfactual prompt:

(12) a. ǎá   jərá   ně̋ á   bî   sà̰   mɔ̰̌ɔ̰   nǎ   à
        3SG.SBJV become if 2SG goat buy.REAL.PFV person.PST PROSP 3SG
        nɔ́   í   səgɔ̌
        eat.IRR LOG good
        'If you had bought a goat, we would have eaten well.' [sos170803e]

   b. móo   bî   sɔ́ɔ   ně̋ móő   nǎ   wě́n
      1SG.EMPH.SBJV goat sell.REAL.PFV if 1SG.EMPH.PST PROSP money
      jő
      find.IRR
      'If I had sold a goat, I would have gotten money.' [sos170811e]

As these two examples show, the conditional predicate ǎá jáně̋ (here with its full form ǎá jərá ně̋) is not necessary to encode a counterfactual. From texts, we find:

(13) a. móő   à   tò   ně̋ né á wó nǎ
        1SG.EMPH.PST 3SG know.REAL.PFV if 1SG.COMP 2SG EMPH PROSP
        mó   cè̋rḛ̀   kó̰ tè móő   nǎ nḛ̀   ŋé
        1SG.EMPH call.IRR D.DEF GEN 1SG.EMPH.PST PROSP come.IRR NEG
        'If I had known that you would come call me for this, I would not have come.' [sos150626t6:10]

   b. ḭ̀   ǎá   jərâ   ně̋ ḭ̀   tsě̋ mɔ̰̌   bě̋
      COMP 3SG.SBJV become if COMP INDF person stranger
      búɔ   kərɔ̀   lő̰n á wó kő̰n ḭ̀ nǎ   lé   à
      go.out.REAL.PFV yesterday here 2SG EMPH on 3PL PROSP FOC 3SG
      bá̰   ḭ̀   à   bó
      hit.IRR 3PL 3SG kill.IRR
      '[They said that] if someone had seen him here yesterday, they would have beat him and killed him.' [sos170730t1:77]

c. íì   ằ̀ bá̰   nɛ́́ í   cèɛ́́   nǎ   fà̰   ằ
    LOG.SBJV 3SG hit.REAL.PFV if LOG hand.PL.PST PROSP enter.IRR 3SG
    lɛ́
    DAT
    '[He said that] if I had hit him, it would have been worse.' [sos170730t1:83]

d. ằ́á   jánɛ́́   áǎ́   nǎ   sɔ́   áa   à   tò
    3SG.SBJV become.if 2SG.PST PROSP arrive.IRR 2SG.SBJV 3SG know.IRR
    íaa, mó   yɛ̀rɛ̀ɛ́́   nǎ   à   bè   á   kằ   áa   ằ
    TOP 1SG.EMPH self.PST PROSP 3SG put.IRR 2SG in.hand 2SG.SBJV 3SG
    tsésɛ̀̀
    try.IRR
    'If you were going to learn it, I would have given some to you for you to try.' [sos170822t10:89]

The examples in (13b) and (13d) both contain *ằ́á jánɛ́́*, but (13a) and (13c) do not.

18.4 'Even if'

I now turn to ways of expressing more extreme conditionals in Seenku, roughly equivalent to English "even if" or French *même si*. There are three constructions I have seen in the text corpus to express this meaning: with *gbằ*, with Jula loanword *áǎ́lí* (or variants thereof), or with a simple conditional with the adverb *màa*. I address each in turn.

First, the native Seenku way of expressing 'even if' conditionals is to use a form *gbằ*. It immediately follows the subject, before the subjunctive TAMP marker, which often elides leaving *gbằá̰*:

(14) a. ằ   gbằá̰   jánɛ́́   ké   də̀nǐ-brɛ̰̂   ŋɛ́   òo
          3SG even.SBJV become.if COP drum-play.NOM NEG EXCL
          'Even if there wasn't a drum player...' [sos170711t1:245]

    b. ằ   gbằá̰   á   wó   nḭɛ   nɛ́́, est-ce que á   wó
        3SG even.SBJV 2SG EMPH insult.REAL.PFV if Q.FR   2SG EMPH
        gbằá̰   ằ   tsîo   nɛ́́ ḭ̀   à   sǐ   á   wó
        even.SBJV 3SG know.REAL.PFV if COMP 3SG be 2SG EMPH
        nḭɛ   nɛ́́ nəgɔ̀   nɛ̀̀
        insult.REAL.NOM LOC initiate LOC
        'Even if he is insulting you, even if you knew he was insulting you in his initiated speech....' [sos170823t8:405]

In (14a), the conditional is in a copular clause which uses *jánɛ́́*. In (14b), there are two conditional clauses back-to-back; the first conditional clause contains a full verb *nḭɛ* 'insult' and the second the verb *tsîo* 'know', both in the perfective.

However, I have also commonly seen it used without any conditional marking, i.e. the conditional reading is imparted by *gbǎ* itself:

(15) a. á gbǎ lɛ́ à bà ɲì mɛ̀ kɛ̋ jṳ̀ jərá òo
       2SG even SBJV 3SG put.REAL.PFV there 3SG.SUBORD go.IRR year next EXCL
       'Even if you put it there until next year...' [sos170822t3:194]

b. mɔ̰̀ɛ gbǎá̰ kà̰ òo né débrouiller lɛ̏ cí-dzʊ̀ʊ
   person.PL even.SBJV go.REAL.PFV EXCL 1SG.SBJV make.do.FR DAT house-inside
   'Even if people go, I make do at home.' [sos170822t10:19]

c. ḭ̀ gbǎá̰ nà̰ cɔ̰̏ ì cè kṵ́ṵ̀ bɔ̏ à̰ lɛ́ ŋɛ́
   3PL even.SBJV come.REAL.PFV village 3PL hand grasp.IRR.HAB anymore 3SG NEG
   'Even if they come to the village, they no longer touch it.' [sos170822t10:265]

We could perhaps view these forms without the conditional as the equivalent of English subjunctive clauses like "Were people to go....", which implies a conditional without explicitly using "if".

In many people's speech, especially younger people's speech (all of the examples above were by speakers over the age of 50), *gbǎ* is being replaced by the Jula loan *áǎlí* (originally from Arabic). Not only has the word been borrowed, but its clause-initial structure as well. For example:

(16) a. Emma *drée*, non, kʊ́ dəgɔ̰̏ nɛ̏ fáná áǎlí móo dzïa kɛ̰̏
       Emma in.love no.FR D.DEF place LOC also even.JU 1SG.EMPH.SBJV be.tired.REAL.PRF EMPH
       'I love Emma, no, in that case, even if I'm tired....' [sos170714t3:136]

b. áǎlí ǎá sį̌ gɔ̀ɲǎ   òo á ằ tsį́-bɔ̀ lɛ́
   even 3SG.SBJV be big.basket EXCL 2SG 3SG cut-take.out.IRR FOC
   tɔ̋-trɔ̋ ǎá kɛ̋ lɛ́ blɛ̀-bɛ́ nɔ̋
   RED-like 3SG.SBJV go.IRR FOC big-NOM eat.IRR
   'Even if it's a big basket, you start like this until it reaches its size.'
   [sos170822t10:207]

c. áǎlí á wóo dzía   sį̌ nɛ́ gərû áa
   even 2SG EMPH.SBJV be.tired.REAL.PTCP be if too.much 2SG.SBJV
   tɛ́rɛ́kɛ́ lɔ̋ à wɛ̀ gʉ̀ɔ-cɛ̋rɛ̋ nɛ́ á bɔ́ lɔ̋ fəgáa nɔ̋
   scrub.JU here 3SG with next.day LOC 2SG go.out.IRR here relaxed here
   'Even if you are too tired, you scrub it [shea butter] on your body and the next day you come out feeling fine.' [sos170822t3:280]

In (16a-b), we see that expressions with áǎlí also do not require a conditional marker; áǎlí appears at the beginning of the clause, whose subject is marked with the subjunctive. The example in (16b) also shows the clause final exclamative particle òo, which plays an important role in 'whether or not' conditionals; see §18.6 below. In (16c), we see that áǎlí and the conditional particle can combine, just as we saw with gbǎ above.

Finally, two other strategies appear in the text corpus, each translated into French in the same way by a consultant (*même si* 'even if'):

(17) a. gɔ̋n nɛ́ sį̌ nɛ̋ màa á nɛ̀ á à fà̰   á brʉ̀ nɛ̀
       cold SBJV be if again 2SG LOC 2SG 3SG put.in.IRR 2SG nose LOC
       áa sɔ́ áa ɲűa
       2SG.SBJV be.able. 2SG.SBJV breathe
       'Even if you have a cold, you put it in your nose so you can breathe.'
       [sos170822t3:281]

   b. áa kằ   lɛ̋ jəmì òo mïi   à̰   mʉ̀ɛ
      2SG.SBJV go.REAL.PFV PART bush EXCL 1PL.SUBORD 3SG hear.REAL.PFV
      tsɛ̋ ḭ̀ í jòo   ɛ̏ɛ́ cìɛ səgùa lɔ̋ tɔ̋-trɔ̋
      how 3PL LOG say.IRR.HAB 3SG.LOG hand.PL stack.IRR here RED-LIKE
      í sí nɛ̀
      LOG RECP LOC
      'Even if you go to the bush, from what we've heard, they say you cross your arms like this....' [sos170823t8:32]

In (17a), the only thing that could contribute the meaning of 'even' to the conditional clause is the adverb *màa* 'again, also' after the conditional particle. In (17b), the conditional particle is not even present, but instead we see a particle *lɛ̋* and then the clause-final exclamative *òo*, as in 'whether or not' conditionals. It is not entirely clear what this particle *lɛ̋* (glossed simply as PART for 'particle') is; it is not the same as the conditional particle, which consultants report could also be used in conjunction with it (i.e. ǎá kà̰ nɛ̋ lɛ̋).

Clearly Seenku speakers have a wide range of options at their disposal to intensify the meaning of a conditional.

18.5 'If not'

I include in this chapter a discussion of strategies to encode the expression 'if not' (cf. French *sinon*), which in some of its translations draws on elements from conditional marking. Regardless of their form, all of these expressions appear before the main clause.

First, we find an expression *tà̰a kʋ́ nɛ̋ ŋé*, which includes the conditional marker *nɛ̋*. In (18a-b), I show two expressions translated from balafon speech (see §22.2.1), both of which show the full version of this expression, and in (18c), I show an abridged version from natural speech:

(18) a. ì tà̰a kʋ́ nɛ̋ ŋé í wó lɛ̏ kəná
COMP otherwise D.DEF if NEG LOG EMPH SUBORD wake.REAL.PFV
tsɛ̋ gṵ̀ɔ-dəgɛ̏ɛ tsɛ̋ mɔ̰̀ bâ̰a̰ dzʋ̏-tsḭ́ fɛ̋ í
how morning.LOC INDF person balafon mouth-cut.REAL.PFV yet LOG
wó tɛ̏ fɔ́ɛ̋-fɔ́ɛ̋ ŋé
EMPH GEN RED-nothing NEG
'If not, since I woke up this morning, no one has opened the balafon [given me anything] at all.' [sos161005e]

b. ì tà̰a kʋ́ nɛ̋ ŋé gɛ̰̀nfəlén-sâ̰n ɲá í wó tɛ̏
COMP otherwise D.DEF if NEG soap-buy.NOM be.NEG LOG EMPH GEN
fɔ́ɛ̋-fɔ́ɛ̋ ŋé
RED-nothing NEG
'If not, I don't even have [enough money] to buy soap.' [sos161005e]

c. táanɛ̋ ké mí yɛ̏rɛ̏ à̰ kóté bé tsʋ̋ wɛ̋
if.not COP 1PL self.JU DEF calabash DEM pierce.IRR HAB
'If not, we attach those calabashes ourselves.' [sos170711t1:111]

In (18c), *tà̰a kʋ́ nɛ̋ ŋé* is abbreviated to *táanɛ̋*; otherwise, the constructions remain the same, with regularly inflected main clauses following.

More commonly, we find an expression *nɔ́ɔ́ntɛ̋*. Though it does not contain any trace of the conditional marker *nɛ̋*, it is translated by consultants in the same way as *sinon*. I find that the better English translation in these instances is 'otherwise' rather than 'if not'. For instance:

(19) a. à dəŋ̌ fáná kʊ́ ɲá bʊ̀ tê né à səsɛ̌
DEF child.PL also D.DEF be.NEG anymore GEN COMP 3SG spider
sőo nɛ̋ ŋɛ̂, nɔ̋ɔ́ntɛ̋ ké mɔ̰̀ à sòo wɛ̀ kʊ̀ɔ nɛ̰̀
search.IRR LOC NEG if.not COP person 3SG search.IRR HAB bush LOC
'The children don't want to look for spiders anymore, otherwise, we used
to look for them in the bush.' [sos170711t1:138]

b. nɔ̋ɔ́ntɛ̋ mǎn-ŋərɔ̌n-bǎrǎ bəlɛ̀ lɛ̋
if.not shea-butter-work be.big EMPH
'Otherwise, shea butter takes a lot of work!' [sos170822t3:275]

c. nɔ̋ɔ́ntɛ̋ kʊ́ dǒo blɛ̀-bé nía dɔ́ɔní
if.not D.DEF though.PST big-NOM eat.REAL.PFV a.little
'Otherwise, it was big though.' [sos170822t10:403]

It sometimes seems like speakers use this expression *nɔ̋ɔ́ntɛ̋* less so as a way of expressing conditions for the following clause (as we see in (19a)), but rather as a way to bring attention back to what they are about to say. In this sense, *nɔ̋ɔ́ntɛ̋* takes on a meaning closer to "but anyway" or "in any case" in English.

18.6 Whether or not conditionals

The last kind of conditional to be addressed in this chapter is the 'whether or not' conditional, where two options are set up in the conditional phrase, both of which are stated to have little influence on the following main clause ("irrelevance conditionals", like 'even if' above; §18.4). In the conditional phrase, both clauses are followed by the particle *òo* (see also §21.3.2); no conditional marking is used, but like the conditional clauses discussed in §18.2, the verb is in the perfective (despite the fact that it is a hypothetical and has not actually taken place). First, the following simple examples from elicitation demonstrate the form of this construction:

(20) a. ằá bi̯ɛ òo ằá bi̯ɛ ŋé òo mí̋
3SG.SBJV rain.REAL.PFV EXCL 3SG.SBJV rain.REAL.PFV NEG EXCL 1PL
nǎ kɛ̋ jəmɯ̰̀
PROSP go.IRR bush
'Whether it rains or not, we're going to the bush.' [sos150702e]

b. ǎá bî kɔ̰̀-tsḭ́ òo ǎá səgà
3SG.SBJV goat head-cut.REAL.PFV EXCL 3SG.SBJV sheep
kɔ̰̀-tsḭ́ òo mɔ̰̀ nǎ nɔ́nɛ́sǎn nő í səgɔ̌
head-cut.REAL.PFV EXCL person PROSP food eat.IRR LOG good
dɔ̌n jánɛ̏
today evening
'Whether he slaughters a goat or a sheep, we are going to eat well tonight.'
[sos150702e]

The subjects of the conditional clauses are marked with the subjunctive TAMP marker (here elided), but the clause-final particle *òo* takes the place of the conditional marker *nɛ̋*.

From texts, we find the following:

(21) a. áa cɛ̏n fəŋɛ̏ lɛ̋ òo áa mɔ̰̂ɛɛ
2SG.SBJV peanut plant.REAL.PFV PART EXCL 2SG.SBJV millet
fəŋɛ̏ lɛ̋ òo áa jǎnɛ̋ fəŋɛ̏ lɛ̋ òo
plant.REAL.PFV PART EXCL 2SG.SBJV corn plant.REAL.PFV PART EXCL
ǎá səbɛ̏
3SG succeed
'Whether you plant peanuts, millet or corn, it works.' [sos170822t3:348]

b. íi kú-tòo bǎ í tɛ̏ gṵ̀ɔ-sərǎ òo, íi
2PL.SBJV thing-bad do.REAL.PFV 2PL GEN village-chief EXCL 2PL.SBJV
tsɛ̋ mɔ̰̀ fɛ́ɛ sḭ̌ òo, kòkő lɛ̂, ǎ
INDF person attach.REAL.PTCP be EXCL koko REL.PRES 3SG
jǎn təgɔ̰̌ lɛ̏ ǎ lɛ̏ ǎ jío tsɛ̋ ké ǎ
become.PTCP like DAT 3SG SUBORD 3SG say.REAL.PFV how COP 3SG
nǎ lɛ́ né á wó kǎ í mɔ̰̀
PROSP FOC come.IRR 2SG EMPH in.hand LOG all
'Whether you did something bad to your chief, or you tied someone up, the koko, it will be like as they said, he will come for you.' [sos170823t8:195]

It is by virtue of stacking up clauses marked by *òo* that we get the reading of 'whether or not' conditionals. As we say above, in §18.4 for instance, it is also possible to use a single conditional clause with *òo*. As we can see in (21a), conditionals sometimes contain an S-toned particle *lɛ̋* after the verb whose meaning is unclear; it can also be seen in (17b) above. Further work is needed to elucidate the meaning of this particle.

19 Complement and purposive clauses

This chapter addresses complement and purposive clauses in Seenku, as the two are syntactically very similar. Note that I will be using the term "complement clause" here, though according to Dixon's (2006) typology, Seenku generally displays "complementation strategies" rather than true complement clauses, since in many cases the clause itself does not fill an argument position of the main clause verb. For instance, with 'want' (itself a periphrastic predicate; §14.5.1), the argument position for what is desired is filled with the default 3sg pronoun à; what functions as the complement clause is simply a subordinate clause that follows the main clause. In other cases, the complement clause is nominalized, i.e. no longer a true clause. For the ease of presentation, I will take a functional approach and refer to all of these cases as complement clauses. The syntactically similar subordinate clauses indicating purpose will be referred to as purposive clauses.

We find three kinds of complement clauses: 1. Complement clauses with an overt complementizer; 2. Subjunctive and/or subordinated complement clauses; 3. Nominalized complement clauses. Purposive clauses take the same form as the subordinated complement clauses. Generally speaking, complement clauses with an overt complementizer are inflected in the same way as main clauses, while those constructions that cannot take a complementizer take subordinating TAMP markers, much as we saw in the conditional (Chapter 18) or relative clauses (Chapter 17).

This chapter first addresses the morphological form of complementizers, which show limited subject agreement, in §19.1. Complement clauses that use this overt complementizer are then addressed in §19.2 (including quotative complements §19.2.1, complements of 'know' §19.2.2, and complements of 'think' verbs §19.2.3). I then turn to subjunctive/subordinate complement clauses, which include complements of 'want' (§19.3.1.1), 'be able' (§19.3.2.1), 'must' (§19.3.1.2), 'try' (§19.3.2.2), 'help' (§19.3.2.3), 'ask' (§19.3.1.3), and periphrastic causative constructions with 'make' (§19.3.2.4). Nominalized complements (whether used as an NP or in a PP) are addressed in §19.4. Finally, I turn to purposive clauses in §19.5.

19.1 Complementizers

Before turning to different complement clause constructions, I will first address the different complementizers that we find in Seenku. This is an interesting area, since the language shows limited subject agreement with the complementizer. Complementizer agreement has been demonstrated in a few other Mande languages, including the Samogo language Jowulu (Idiatov 2010). Seenku follows the pattern found in Jula of Samatiguila (Braconnier 1987-1988) and some dialects of Mandinka, where the 1sg shows a distinct form from all other person-number combinations. The two attested complementizers are shown below:

(1)   1sg   né
       non-1sg   ì̀

To illustrate, consider the following examples with the matrix verb 'know':

(2)   a.   mó   à   tò   né   á   wó   sɔ́ɔ̀
           1SG.EMPH 3SG know.IRR 1SG.COMP 2SG EMPH be.able.IRR.HAB
           səmâ   lɛ̈
           dance.REAL.NOM DAT
           'I know you can dance.' [sos181016e]

      b.   ì   à   tò   ì̀   á   wó   sɔ́ɔ̀   səmâ
           3PL 3SG know.IRR COMP 2SG EMPH be.able.IRR.HAB dance.REAL.NOM
           lɛ̈
           DAT
           'They know you can dance.' [sos181016e]

      c.   mí̈ à   tò   ì̀   á   wó   sɔ́ɔ̀   səmâ
           1PL 3SG know.IRR COMP 2SG EMPH be.able.IRR.HAB dance.REAL.NOM
           lɛ̈
           DAT
           'We know that you can dance.' [sos181016e]

The examples in (2) are identical save for the subject of the matrix clause: 1sg in (2a), 3pl in (2b), and 1pl in (2c). The quotative complementizer in (2a) takes the form *né*, but in all other cases, including the 1pl, the quotative complementizer is *ì̀*; *né* is rejected with all other subjects, though *ì̀* is marginally accepted with the 1sg subject (as can be seen in §19.2.2, for instance).

The constructions in which these complementizers are used will be discussed in §19.2. In all other complement clauses, the complementizer is null, regardless of person-number; these constructions are discussed in §19.3.

19.2 Complement clauses with an overt complementizer

Verbs that take a complement clause with an overt complementizer tend to be verbs of saying, knowing, thinking, or perceiving. These different expressions will be discussed in turn in the subsections below.

19.2.1 Quotatives

Quotative constructions are used to express reported speech. There is one general template for quotatives in Seenku, which can take two different verbs:

(3)   *Schematic of quotative construction*

    a.   Subject Log *bɛ̀* ì {Clause}

    b.   Subject Log *jű* ì {Clause}

The verbs *bɛ̀* and *jű* are addressed in §19.2.1.1 and §19.2.1.2, respectively. Rarer expressions with other verbs of speech are discussed in §19.2.1.3.

The complementizer, ì or *né* depending on person and number, introduces the complement clause, which is inflected in exactly the same way as a main clause. Canonically, the complementizer immediately follows the verb of saying (as shown in §19.2.1.1 and §19.2.1.2), but it can also be used on its own to indicate hearsay.

(4) a. *ɔ̀hɔ̰́!* ì   à   *kɔ́εε-cíɛ*   ì   *ké bö̀-kɔ̃ɔ,* ì à
       INTERJ COMP 3SG walk.ANTIP-MANNER COMP COP billygoat COMP 3SG
       bɔ́ɔ-bé, ì   *ké bö̀-kɔ̃ɔ*
       tall-NOM COMP COP billygoat
       '[They say] that from his way of walking, that it was a billygoat, that from his height, that it was a billygoat.' [sos161009t1:201-202]

  b. *tsɛ̋ sḭ̀ wé* ì   *dəgɔ̃́ kúrúú jḭ̀*   *füi*   ì   *Pátárá*
      INDF be FOC COMP place all   burn.REAL.PFV nothing COMP Patara
      mɔ̰̀   *sóen kɛ̋* *təgö̀ ɲì*
      person one go.IRR sit.IRR there
      'There is another one that goes, "The whole place is burned, but Patara is the one person remaining."' [sos161009t1:38]

The example in (4a) stacks up multiple clauses, and each is introduced by the complementizer. In (4b) as well, ì introduces a riddle and appears to be repeated after *füi*, though it is difficult to say definitively, since it would be preceded by another high front vowel.

The complementizer can also be used initially without a verb of speech if it is mimicking or quoting back something that someone just said. Consider the following exchange, with Speaker 1 in (5a) and Speaker 2 in (5b):

(5) a. *kètè-kètè-gbímì   kóʊ   tâ*
UNTRANSLATABLE D.DEF.COP fire
'*Kete-kete-gbimi* [phrase used before saying the answer to a riddle] it's fire.'
[sos161009t1:103-104]

b. *ì̀   kètè-kètè-brṳ̀   ì̀   kóʊ tâ*
COMP UNTRANSLATABLE COMP D.DEF fire
'[She says] *kètè-kètè-brṳ̀*, it's fire.' [sos161009t1:108]

Speaker 2 repeats back what Speaker 1 said after much laughter, using just the complementizer as a quotative particle. Once again, it is placed before each clause.

Most typically, as we will see, complementizers follow a verb of speech, marking the following clause as its complement. Multiple complement clauses can be stacked up, sometimes extending three or four clauses of a narrative, thus putting a good deal of space between the complementizer and the verb that introduced it.

19.2.1.1 Quotative clauses with *bɛ̋* 'do'

The most common verb indicating 'say' is *bɛ̋*, which is a highly versatile verb that can mean 'do', 'put', or 'give' in other configurations. The form *bɛ̋* is irrealis (what we see most commonly in narratives), with the irregular realis form *bä̀*. In its use as 'say', the verb takes a reflexive/logophoric pronoun as its object, which is *ń* for the 1sg and otherwise *í* (§6.7).

In fluent speech, vowel hiatus resolution typically takes place between *bɛ̋* and the complementizer *ì̀*; we would expect this to yield *bï*, with a SX contour accounting for both tones, but it appears that this combination is so common that it may have led to a reanalysis in which the irrealis form of 'say' is itself *bí̌* for some speakers. This is audible when a pause is introduced between 'say' and the complementizer (which phrases with the following clause). Generally, though, we cannot tell whether speakers have reinterpreted *bɛ̋* as *bí̌* or not, since vowel hiatus resolution with a following *ì̀* will neutralize the distinction.

Examples of quotative constructions from the text corpus include:

(6) a. *ì̀   í   bɛ̋̋   ì̀   kərṳ̀ sío,   ì̀   ä̀   sǐ*
3PL LOG do.IRR COMP hyena get.up.REAL.PFV COMP 3SG be
kä̀   nɛ̀̋ jəmṳ̀, ì̀   ä̀   sǐ jɔ́ɔ   nɛ̀̋ nɔ́nésã́n
go.REAL.NOM LOC bush COMP 3SG be look.for.REAL.NOM LOC food
nɛ̋̋
DAT
'They say that the hyena got up, that he is going to the bush and that he is looking for food.' [sos161009t1:181-182]

b. ǎ lɛ̀ í bɛ́ ì̀ kóʊ fəlé, ì̀ kóʊ
   3SG SUBORD LOG do.IRR COMP D.DEF.COP what COMP D.DEF.COP
   bö̀-kɔ̌ɔ
   billygoat
   'He asked, "What is that, is that a billygoat?"' [sos150626t1:7]

c. mɛ̌ í bɛ́ ì̀ mɔ̀̃ sɔ́ wɛ̀ mɔ̀̃ɔ́
   3SG.SUBORD LOG do.IRR COMP person be.able.IRR HAB person.SBJV
   kűnı̰́ í wó lɛ̀↘
   help.IRR 2PL EMPH DAT.Q
   '[and] he asked, "would it be possible to help you?"' [sos130828t2:62]

These examples show that any TAM marking can occur in the complement clause: perfective or progressive as in (6a), habitual as in (6c), or just an uninflected copular predicate as in (6b).

This quotative construction can also be used with just an NP complement, i.e. without a full clause as the complement. We see this construction used if someone is defining terminology. For example:

(7) a. ì̀ í bɛ́ ì̀ fóǹ-sɛ̀
       3PL LOG do.IRR COMP fonio-fly.NOM
       'They call it "making the fonio fly".' [sos170714t3:37]

   b. ì̀ í bɛ́ ì̀ fôn-bɛ̰́ɛ̰́-tǎa
       3PL LOG do.IRR COMP fonio-beat.ANTIP-open.space
       'They call it "the open space for beating fonio".' [sos170714t3:1]

   c. mɔ̀̃ɔ́ í bɛ́ ì̀ mı̋́ jərá-ŋɛ̋
       person.SBJV LOG do.IRR COMP 1PL family-HUM.PL
       'So let's say, "our family".' [sos171009t1:108]

Unsurprisingly, this construction is found most commonly with a semantically empty 3pl subject (7a-b), though other configurations are possible, as the hortative expression in (7c) shows.

19.2.1.2 Quotative clauses with *jű* 'say'

Seenku does have a verb 'say': irrealis *jű*, with corresponding realis *jío*. This verb is far more commonly used with an NP representing what is being said (the word, the speech act, etc.) as the direct object without a complementizer, as in (8):

(8) a. á wó á nɔ̀ⁿn jǜ
2SG EMPH 2SG that.for say.IRR
'Say yours [your riddle]!' [sos161009t1:50]

b. ì ǎ jú tsɛ̰́
3PL 3SG say.IRR how
'How do they say it?' [sos161009t1:78]

The verb bà̰/bɛ̀ is completely impossible in this context.

However, the reverse is not true: We do find a small number of cases of jǘ/jío used to introduce a quotative complement clause. In this usage, the construction is the same as we saw in §19.2.1.1, usually with the logophoric pronoun filling the object slot of the verb and the complement clause introduced with ì. For example:

(9) a. kʊ́ jáa kʊ́ nɛ̀ ǎ jú ì ɛ́ɛ bʉ̀bá ì ké
D.DEF return.IRR D.DEF LOC 3SG say.IRR COMP INTERJ dad COMP COP
kʊ́ tɔ́
D.DEF like
'She returned and said, "Eh! Dad, it's like that."' [sos150626t4:14]

b. ɛ́ɛ jío ì ǎ sǐ sòkó-kû nɛ̰̀↘
2SG.LOG say.REAL.PFV COMP 3SG be Jula-thing LOC.Q
'You said that it's in Jula?' [sos161009t1:215]

This use of jǘ/jío is rare compared to both the use of bà̰/bɛ̀ in the same construction or compared to the use of jǘ/jío with a direct object NP complement. Note that the example in (9a) does not use the logophoric pronoun.

19.2.1.3 Quotative clauses with other verbs of saying

In the text corpus, there are a few examples of verbs other than bɛ̀/bà̰ or jǘ/jío being used with quotative complements. Specifically, we find two verbs of asking tərɛ́ and jɔ́ɔ and one instance of the verb cɛ́rɛ́ 'call'. Unlike the constructions above, where the direct object slot of the main verb was filled with a logophoric pronoun, in these cases, if there is a direct object slot, it is filled with a more contentful noun or pronoun:

(10) a. mɛ̀ ì tərɛ̀ ì mɔ̰̀ sɔ́ɔ̀ mɔ̰̀ɔ́
3SG.SUBORD 3PL ask.IRR COMP person be.able.IRR.HAB person.SBJV
kǔnǐ í wêe↘
help.IRR 2PL EMPH.DAT.Q
'He asked, "Would one be able to help you?"' [sos130828t2:3]

b. ń tɛ́ kərǜ sú   mɛ̀   kɛ̃́   ń tɛ́ sân
    1SG dear hyena get.up.IRR 3SG.SUBORD go.IRR 1SG dear rabbit
    tərɛ̋ ì   á wóó   kà   bṹɛ̰̀-dɩ̰̀   bɛ̃́
    ask.IRR COMP 2SG EMPH.PST go.REAL.PFV djinn-child.PL DEM.PL
    jő   dǎn né   nɛ̀
    find.IRR place which LOC
    'Mr. Hyena got up and went to ask Mr. Rabbit, "Where did you find those djinns?"' [sos130828t2:29]

c. ì̀ wɛ̀   jɔ́ɔ   wétənɛ̃̀ ì̀   kɛ́ tɛ́ lɛ̀   ǎ   n̋ìi
    3PL SUBORD ask.IRR now   COMP COP who SUBORD DEF pregnancy
    fǎ   wɛ́ á nɛ̀
    put.in.REAL.PFV FOC 2SG LOC
    'They asked now, "Who was it who got you pregnant?"' [sos171009t1:61]

d. ǎ dö̀   kʊ́ bá̰à̰   brɛ̰̀   wè ŋɛ́ mais ì̀ wɛ̀ ǎ
    3SG though D.DEF balafon play.IRR HAB NEG but.FR 3PL NARR 3SG
    cɛ̋rɛ̀   ì̀ kɛ́ kâ
    call.IRR COMP COP griot
    'Him, though, he doesn't play the balafon, but they say that he is a griot.' [sos171009t1:90]

In (10a-b), the main clause verb introducing the quotative clause is tərɛ́ 'ask'; in (10c), we see jɔ́ɔ, also translating to 'ask'. Finally, in (10d), we find cɛ́rɛ́ 'call'.

19.2.2 Complements of 'know'

The verb 'know' is tò, which is almost invariably used in the irrealis. Its object position in the main clause is filled with the dummy 3sg pronoun ǎ, yielding the expression Subject ǎ tò, which is in turn followed by the complementizer ì̀ or né introducing the complement clause. Simple elicited examples include the following:

(11) a. ǎ   kɔ̈́sî là   tò   ì̀   Rene sɔ́ɔ̀   ǎ́á   ǎ
         3SG friend L-3SG know.IRR COMP Rene be.able.IRR.HAB 3SG.SBJV DEF
         kənún nê ǎ ɲ̋ì
         stone DEM 3SG pick.up.IRR
         'His friend knows that Rene can pick up the stone.' [sos170807e]

b. mó   à   tò   né   á   wó   ɲá   cĕrȅ
    1SG.EMPH 3SG know.IRR 1SG.COMP 2SG EMPH be.NEG sleep.REAL.NOM
    nȅ̀ ŋé
    LOC NEG
    'I know that you aren't sleeping.' [sos181015e]

c. móő   à   tò   né   á   wóő   ɲá
    1SG.EMPH.PST 3SG know.IRR 1SG.COMP 2SG EMPH.PST be.NEG
    cĕrȅ   nȅ̀ ŋé
    sleep.REAL.NOM LOC NEG
    'I knew that you weren't sleeping.' [sos181015e]

The example in (11a) has a non-1sg subject, and so the complementizer is ì̀. The examples in (11b-c) are identical except for tense. Both have a 1sg subject, and so the complementizer is *né*; (11b) is in the present, while (11c) is in the past. The form is identical, except that the past marker *lĕ́* (surfacing here as tone and lengthening due to clitic elision) appears on the subject of both the main and embedded clause. The verb 'know' remains in the irrealis.

From texts, we find:

(12) a. á   à   tò   ì̀   ì̀   ǎ   jén-jĕ́n   bɛ́
         2SG 3SG know.IRR COMP 3PL DEF RED-story DEM
         nȅ̀-jərán-jərân   sȍkó-kû   nȅ̀↘
         TRANS-RED-change.REAL.PFV Jula-thing LOC.Q
         'You know they translated that story into Jula?' [sos161009t1:199]

b. ǎ́lí   bîɛ   bâa   nȅ̀ ì̀ à   tò   gbǎ ì̀   óo
    even.JU play.IRR balafon LOC 3PL 3SG know.IRR even COMP 2SG.EMPH
    tĕ́-mənî́   təgĭ   sǐ
    dear-woman stand.PTCP be
    'Even while playing, they know even that your girlfriend is standing there.'
    [sos170714t3:134]

In the vast majority of cases of texts in the corpus, the subject is non-1sg, and so the complementizer ì̀ is used.

In negative constructions, when the origin of negation is the main clause (i.e. 'know' is negated), the negative particle doesn't appear until the end of the **complement** clause. Interestingly, as the elicited example in (13c) shows, the negation of the main clause scopes over the complement cause, triggering the suppletive negative of the auxiliary verb, even though the complement clause is itself affirmative:

(13) a. Bon,   mó   kʊ́   à   tò   ì̀   ì̀   brḭ́-brḭ́
        well.FR 1SG.EMPH D.DEF 3SG know.IRR COMP 3PL RED-go.around.IRR
        cḭ̀ɛ   dzɔ́ lé   ŋé   sá̰
        time amount which NEG PART
        'Well, I don't know how many times they go around.' [sos170714t3:13]

   b. mó   à   tò   yèrè   "hɔ́rɔ́n"   né   ké fèn
      1SG.EMPH 3SG know.IRR self.JU farming.caste.JU 1SG.COMP COP thing
      né   ŋé
      which NEG
      'I don't even know what a *horon* is.' [sos171009t2:40]

   c. mó   à   tò   né   á   wó   ɲá   cḛ̌rḛ̌
      1SG.EMPH 3SG know.IRR 1SG.COMP 2SG EMPH be.NEG sleep.REAL.NOM
      nḛ̀   ŋé
      LOC NEG
      'I know that you aren't sleeping.' [sos181015e]

In each of these examples, *ŋé* appears at the end of the complement clause, despite the fact that the negation is introduced by the main clause. In (13a), we see an example where the generic complementizer *ì̀* is used with a 1sg subject. The main clause contains negative focus marking in the form of the discourse definite *kʊ́* that appears before the object of the transitive verb; such marking is incompatible with an affirmative clause, lending yet further evidence that negation originates in the main clause. In both other examples, the 1sg complementizer *né* appears. In (13c), the negation of the main clause triggers the use of *ɲá* as the auxiliary of the complement clause.

19.2.3 Complements of 'think' verbs

There are several expressions in Seenku to indicate thought (and related translations like belief); all of them can take complement clauses with overt complementizers, but in each case, they also surface with null complementizers. Whether the complementizer is overt or null, the complement clause retains regular inflection (i.e. it is not inflected for subjunctive, as the clauses in §19.3 are).

19.2.3.1 *jərǎ* 'think'

The most common expression of thought in Seenku seems to be the verb *jərǎ*. Like *tò* 'know', this verb is used invariably in the irrealis with a dummy 3sg object *ǎ*, meaning both will raise to L by argument-head tone sandhi (§4.4.2); this yields *à jərà*. In some examples, the explicit habitual particle *wě* (*wè* by sandhi) appears after the verb, and in others, the habitual is marked by lengthening. In still others, I hear only an unmarked irrealis verb with no lengthening. The examples below represent what I hear in the speaker's pronunciation.

Complements of 'think' are typically marked with the overt complementizers *né* and *ì̵*. For instance:

(14) a. *ä̰ wò lɛ́ í cɛ̰̀ fɛ̀ɛ,   ä̰ wò là jə̀rà*
         3SG EMPH PST LOG hand lick.REAL.PFV 3SG EMPH L-3SG think.IRR
         ì̵ ì̵ í wó jîo   ŋé
         COMP 3PL LOG EMPH see.REAL.PFV NEG
         'He licked his hand, he thought that they didn't see him.' [sos130828t2:66]

    b. *í wó à jə̀rà ì̵ í wó ké mɔ̰̀ kɔ́-kɔ́*
         LOG EMPH 3SG think.IRR COMP LOG EMPH COP person RED-short
         '[The riddle goes like:] I thought I was a short person.' [sos161009t1:154]

    c. *Roukiatou à jə̀rà ì̵ sɔ́n nă sɪ̰̌ bɛ̰̂ɛ̰ nɛ̰̈*
         Roukiatou 3SG think.IRR COMP rain PROSP be rain.REAL.NOM LOC
         'Roukiatou thinks that it must be raining.' [sos170802e]

    d. *mó à jə̀rà né ä̰ nà̰ fɛ̰́ ŋé*
         1SG.EMPH 3SG think.IRR 1SG.COMP 3SG come.REAL.PFV yet NEG
         'I think that he hasn't come yet.' [sos170811e]

The examples in (14a-b) come from texts, where in both cases the complementizer *ì̵* is followed by another high front vowel, making it difficult to say with certainty that it is there. In (14c-d), the examples are elicited, and in (14d), the complementizer agrees with the 1sg subject.

If the verb 'think' has more than one complement, both are introduced with the complementizer:

(15) *Gilles là jə̀rà wɛ̀ ì̵ jə̀gɛ̰̈ nă jó cîe ŋé ì̵*
      Gilles L-3SG think.IRR HAB COMP dog PROSP see.IRR house.LOC NEG COMP
      ä̰ nă jó sə̀rɛ̰́
      3SG PROSP see.IRR outside
      'Gilles thinks that the dog might not be in the house, it might be outside.' [sos181206e]

The complementizer, however, is not obligatory. In many cases, when the complement clause begins with the copula (see §21.1.3 for clause-initial copulas), the complementizer is omitted. For instance:

(16) a. mḛ̀   cəbâa-dənǒn kə̀nä,   ằ   à   jə̀rà   ké
     3SG.SUBORD orphan-child wake.up.REAL.PRF 3SG 3SG think.IRR COP
     ȉ   dǒn   âa
     LOG.DAT child NEG.Q
     'She woke up the orphan thinking it was her child.' [sos130828t1:23]

   b. mó   yèrḛ̀ à jə̀rà   ké á   nǎ   jô̰   dzı̰̀ nṍ
      1SG.EMPH self.JU 3SG think.IRR COP 2SG PROSP water put.IRR here
      wé mʋ̰̀ʋ́   à fèn-bɛ́   mʋ̰̀ʋ́   à tsə́sɛ̰̀
      FOC person.SBJV 3SG thing-do.IRR person.SBJV 3SG look.IRR
      'I thought we were going to put water here and mix it and see [how it turns out].' [sos170822t3:126]

   c. móő   à   jə̀rà   ké mó   nǎ   né
      1SG.EMPH.PST 3SG think.IRR COP 1SG.EMPH PROSP come.IRR
      'I thought that I would come.' [sos170720e]

If the complementizer would be *né*, as in (16c), consultants report that it would be possible to stack *né* before *ké* but it is preferable to use one or the other. If the complementizer would be *ȉ*, as in (16a-b), consultants appear to feel it there even though it is "swallowed" by the copula. We do find cases, however, with an overt sequence *ȉ ké*, showing that it is possible:

(17) ằ̰   à jə̀ràa   ȉ   ké mó   kʋ̈   nío
     3SG 3SG think.IRR.HAB COMP COP 1SG.EMPH toh eat.REAL.PFV
     'He thought that I ate toh.' [sos170724e]

19.2.3.2 *mīrī́* 'think'

Another verb for 'think', *mīrī́* (variant: *məri̋*), is attested in elicitation (though not in texts). It is a loanword from Jula which is used in the progressive in the main clause. Like expressions with *jə̀rà̰*, the complementizer is optional. For example:

(18) a. mó   sı̰̀ ằ mīrī́   nɛ̋ né   à sı̰̀
        1SG.EMPH be 3SG think.JU.REAL.NOM LOC 1SG.COMP 3SG be
        cɛ̈rɛ̰̀   nɛ̰̀
        sleep.REAL.NOM LOC
        'I think that he is sleeping.' [sos170811e]

b. ǎ sį̌ ǎ mərǐ́   nɛ́̈ ì̀ mó   sį̌
   3SG be 3SG think.JU.REAL.NOM LOC COMP 1SG.EMPH be
   cə̀rə̈   nɛ̀̈
   sleep.REAL.NOM LOC
   'He thinks that I am sleeping.' [sos181206e]

c. ǎ sį̌ ǎ mį́rį́   nɛ́̈ í wóo   kà̀   nɛ́̈
   3SG be 3SG think.JU.REAL.NOM LOC LOG EMPH.SBJV go.REAL.PFV if
   Sį́a
   Bobo
   'He is thinking about whether he will go to Bobo-Dioulasso.' [sos170724e]

d. móő̋   sį̌ ǎ mį́rį́   nɛ́̈ nɛ́   ké
   1SG.EMPH.PST be 3SG think.JU.REAL.NOM LOC 1SG.COMP COP
   mó   nǎ   nɛ́
   1SG.EMPH PROSP come.IRR
   'I thought that I would come.' [sos170720e]

Each of these examples except (18c) contain an overt complementizer.

19.2.3.3 səmį́ 'think/be afraid that'

A third 'think' verb is found, səmį́, though it is rarer than the other two expressions seen thus far in the data corpus, despite one consultant telling me that it is the best and most common verb 'think'. However, she also notes that unlike the other expressions seen thus far, səmį́ has a negative connotation to it, translating better to 'be afraid that' or 'fear' than a neutral meaning of 'think'. It can appear either in the irrealis (with habitual lengthening, yielding səmį̃) or in the progressive, a realis form. In all attested examples, the complementizer is present.

(19) a. mó   ǎ səmį̃   nɛ́   jʊ̈ŋmǎ̋ sį̌ í bɔ́̈ɔ
        1SG.EMPH 3SG fear.IRR.HAB 1SG.COMP cat be LOG tall
        'I think that the cat is tall.' [sos160825e]

    b. mó   sį̌ ǎ səmį́   nɛ́̈ nɛ́   ǎ nǎ   nɛ́
       1SG.EMPH be 3SG fear.REAL.NOM LOC 1SG.COMP 3SG PROSP come.IRR
       dɔ̈́n
       today
       'I fear that he will come today.'

This is the same verb root found in the expression á ŋǎa səmį́ 'excuse me', or literally, 'think about your inside'. In that context, it does not carry any negative connotations of fear.

19.2.3.4 lǎ sɪ̰̌ 'believe/be certain'

Finally, the last expression for 'think' is also a loan from Jula, a participial predicate *lǎ sɪ̰̌* 'be certain' or 'believe'. Like the other 'think' expressions, the complementizer is optional. Whereas the verbal 'think' expressions we saw before had a dummy 3sg direct object, *lǎ sɪ̰̌* takes a dummy 3sg in a PP, which is then followed by the complement clause:

(20) a. mó   lǎ   sɪ̰̌ ằ nɛ̀ né   á nǎ mó   nəgɪ̀
      1SG.EMPH certain be 3SG LOC 1SG.COMP 2SG PROSP 1SG.EMPH mind
      bằa
      destroy.IRR
      'I am sure that you will disappoint me.' [sos170724e]

   b. mó   lǎ   ɲá   ằ nɛ̀ ằ nǎ nɛ̀   ɲɛ́
      1SG.EMPH certain be.NEG 3SG LOC 3SG PROSP come.IRR NEG
      'I don't believe that he will come.' [sos170811e]

   c. ằ lǎ   sɪ̰̌ ằ nɛ̀ ɪ̀   gɔ̂ɔ-kù   lê ằ sɔ́ɔ
      3SG certain be 3SG LOC COMP wood-plant PRES 3SG be.able.IRR.HAB
      ằá   fɔ́   lɪ̌
      3SG.SBJV grow.IRR here
      'She believes that that tree should be able to grow here.' [sos170807e]

   d. mó   lǎa   sɪ̰̌ ằ nɛ̀ né   á nǎ
      1SG.EMPH certain.PST be 3SG NEG 1SG.COMP 2SG PROSP
      kùaa   môe
      farm.ANTIP.IRR 1SG.EMPH.DAT
      'I was confident that you would farm for me.' [sos170724e]

Examples (20a-b) contrast an affirmative and negative expression in the present. The complementizer is absent in the negative, but this is not due to the negative, as there are cases in the corpus where affirmatives lack the complementizer or vice versa. The example in (20c) shows a 3sg subject that uses the ɪ̀ complementizer, while (20d) shows that the expression is placed into the past by S-toned lengthening of the participle, characteristic of participial predicates (§13.3.3).

19.3 Subjunctive complement clauses

In this section, I cover complement constructions where a complementizer is ungrammatical (and not just optionally absent, as in many of the constructions we saw above). In this class of constructions, the complement clause is subordinated, either with the subjunctive TAMP marker *lé* or with the subordinate TAMP marker *lě*. In both cases, the verb of the complement clause is in its bare irrealis form.

While complement clauses with an overt complementizer were selected by verbs of saying or perception, subjunctive complement clauses are selected by modal verbs like 'must' or 'be able', in addition to verbs like 'want', 'help', or 'try', which Dixon (2006) classifies as "secondary concepts".

Amongst these verbs, however, we find an interesting split: some verbs select complement clauses that are invariably subjunctive, while others select complement clauses that are subjunctive when the verb is non-completive aspect and subordinate when it is completive (i.e. perfective or perfect). I suspect that this difference emerges from whether the complement clause was logically achieved if the main clause verb was completed or not.

I first address invariably subjunctive complement clauses in §19.3.1, then turn to subjunctive/subordinate complement clauses in §19.3.2.

19.3.1 Invariably subjunctive complement clauses

Three verbs take invariably subjunctive complement clauses: 'want' (§19.3.1.1), 'must' (§19.3.1.2), and 'ask' (§19.3.1.3).

19.3.1.1 'want' (*sɪ̰ ǎ tê*)

The meaning 'want' is expressed with a non-verbal predicate involving the existential auxiliary *sɪ̰* and the genitive particle *tě*, as laid out in §14.5. When the complement of 'want' is an NP, as in a phrase like 'I want coffee', 'coffee' fills the X slot in <Subject *sɪ̰* X *tě*>. If, on the other hand, the complement is a clause, then this position is filled with a 3sg pronoun *ǎ*. The complement clause then follows without any overt complementizer. The subject is marked with a subjunctive TAMP marker *lé*, which I first described in §18.1 in the context of conditionals, and the verb is inflected in the irrealis.

Examples of complement clauses with 'want' from the text corpus are provided in (21):

(21) a. Fàatú kűɛ   sɪ̰ ǎ tê   îi   fǎ   mó   wɛ̋↘
       Fatou other.PL be 3SG GEN 2PL.SBJV fight 1SG.EMPH with.Q
       'Fatou and all, you want to fight me?' [sos161009t1:96]

   b. ǎ̰ sɪ̰ ǎ tê ǎá   ǎ̰ ŋmǎ̰
      3SG be 3SG GEN 3SG.SBJV 3SG eat.IRR
      'He wanted to eat him.' [sos161009t1:211]

c. á wó sị̌ ằ tê mɔ̀ɔ́ à ɲɛ̀ ằ súìnì wè
   2SG EMPH be 3SG GEN person.SBJV 3SG weave.IRR DEF rachis with
   'You want us to weave with the rachis [hard middle part of the frond].'
   [sos170822t10:277]

d. mɛ̀ í bɛ̌ ì ké í wó sị̌ ằ tê í wó
   3SG.SUBORD LOG do.IRR COMP COP LOG EMPH be 3SG GEN 2PL EMPH
   kűéɛ ɲűi bɛ̌ í wó kằ
   other.PL.SBJV honey put.IRR LOG EMPH in.hand
   'She said she wanted them to give her some honey.' [sos130828t2:22]

As each of these shows, the genitive postposition that forms part of the volitional predicate is immediately followed by the subject of the complement clause; in all of the examples in (21), subjunctive is marked by lengthening the final vowel of the subject and adding a H tone (in other words, the TAMP marker lέ has undergone clitic elision; §4.4.3). The subject of the main and complement clauses can be either the same (21a-b) or different (21c-d), with no difference in overall structure. In (21d), the volitional predicate introducing the complement clause is itself a quotative complement; note that the logophoric pronoun subject í wó of the volitional predicate is homophonous with the 2pl subject of the complement clause.

In the negative, the existential auxiliary sị̌ in the main clause is replaced with the suppletive negative ɲá; as we saw in §19.2.2 above, the clause-final negative marker follows the complement clause, not the negative volitional predicate in the main clause. This is characteristic of negation in complex utterances; the negative particle always appears at the end. For example:

(22) a. mó ɲá ằ tê móo dâmbù ŋé
    1SG.EMPH be.NEG 3SG GEN 1SG.EMPH.SBJV lie.IRR NEG
    'I don't want to lie.' [sos171009t1:121]

b. məlêɛ ɲá ằ tê íi bără bɛ̌ ŋé
   REL.PRO.SUBORD be.NEG 3SG GEN LOG.SBJV work do.IRR NEG
   'He who does not want to work...' [sos170823t8:31]

Example (22a) shows the volitional predicate in a main clause, taking the irrealis-marked complement. In (22b), the whole expression is a relative clause, indicated by the use of the relative pronoun for the subject followed by the subordinate TAMP marker.

When the main clause is in the past tense, the complement clause retains subjunctive marking rather than being marked with the subordinate. For instance:

(23) a. móő   sǐ ă tê né   bî sà̰   mais móő
       1SG.EMPH.PST be 3SG GEN 1SG.SBJV goat buy.IRR but.FR 1SG.EMPH.PST
       ă̰ tsíɔ   ɲì
       3SG leave.REAL.PFV there
       'I wanted to buy a goat but I left it.' [sos181210e]

   b. ăa   sǐ ă̰ tê ă̰á   cȅrȅ
      3SG.PST be 3SG GEN 3SG.SBJV sleep.IRR
      'He wanted to sleep.' [sos181210e]

In each case, the embedded subject shows the H tone of the subjunctive rather than the X of the subordinate.

Note that the subject of the embedded clause can differ from that of the main clause. In this case, it gives the reading *Subject₁ wants Subject₂ to...*:

(24) a. mó   sǐ ă̰ tê á wóo   cȅrȅ
       1SG.EMPH be 1SG GEN 2SG EMPH.SBJV sleep.IRR
       'I want you to sleep.' [sos170811e]

   b. mó   ɲá   ă̰ tê ă̰á   mó   jȍ
      1SG.EMPH be.NEG 3SG GEN 3SG.SBJV 1SG.EMPH see.IRR
      cȅrȅ   nḛ̏ ŋé
      sleep.REAL.NOM LOC NEG
      'I don't want him to see me sleeping.' [sos170816e]

In (24a), the main clause subject is the 1sg, but the embedded subject is the 2sg. In (24b), the embedded subject is the 3sg. There are no other formal differences between same-subject and different-subject complements.

19.3.1.2 'should' or 'must'

The modal 'must' or 'should' is typically expressed in Seenku with one of two loan expressions from Jula: *ká-ɲì* or *ká-kạ̃n*. In Jula, the first comes from *ká ɲì*, which consists of an attributive TAMP marker *ká* and the stem for 'good' *ɲì*. The other expression, *ká kạ̃n*, on the other hand, comes from the homophonous Jula expression meaning 'be normal'. In both cases in Seenku, under negation, *ká* is replaced by *mạ́*, the Jula suppletive negative of *ká*. Of the two, the form *ká-ɲì* is most likely to be offered in translation of 'must' (or French *doit*) while *ká-kạ̃n* is more common as a translation of 'should' (or French *devrait*).

These expressions of modality introduce a subjunctive-marked clause. First, I illustrate examples of *ká-ɲì* from elicitation:

(25) a. *Brahima ká-ɲɨ̀   ǎá   ɲɨ̀   màa-màa*
Brahima AFF-good.JU 3SG.SBJV run.IRR slow-slow
'Brahima should drive slowly.' [sos170807e]

b. *Rene ká-ɲɨ̀   ǎá   kɛ̋   sɔ̋n-kɔ̌-nɛ̋-səgɨ̋   nɛ̋*
Rene AFF-good.JU 3SG.SBJV go.IRR sun-cool-LOC-market LOC
'Rene should go to the eastern market.' [sos170809e]

The modal *ká-ɲɨ̀* appears first in the main clause, treated as an intransitive verb; in the complement clause that follows, a pronoun marked with the subjunctive resumes the main clause subject.

I have only seen one example of *ká-ɲɨ̀* in a text:

(26) *mɔ̀   ká-ɲɨ̀   mɔ̀ɔ́   í   bɛ̋   ì   ɔ̀ɔ̋ɔ̀*
person AFF-good.JU person.SBJV LOG say COMP INTERJ
'We should say "ɔ̀ɔ̋ɔ̀"' [sos170802t1:29]

Elicitation has revealed other inflected forms of this construction, including the past and the negative:

(27) a. *móő   ká-ɲɨ̀   né   kɛ̋*
1SG.EMPH.PST AFF-good.JU 1SG.SBJV go.IRR
'I had to go.' [sos181210e]

b. *móő   mạ́-ɲɨ̀   né   kɛ̋   ŋé*
1SG.EMPH.PST NEG-good.JU 1SG.SBJV go.IRR NEG
'I didn't have to go.' [sos181210e]

The expression in (27a) demonstrates that 'must' takes an invariably subjunctive complement clause. In (27b), we see the Jula affirmative marker *ká* replaced by *mạ́*.

More common in the corpus of texts (though curiously not in elicitation) is the expression *ká-kạ́n*. The form of the complement clause is the same. Looking first at the affirmative, there is nothing different about this expression:

(28) a. *ǎ   dôn mɔ̀   ká-kạ́n   mɔ̀ɔ́   à   bɛ̀   í*
DEF child person AFF-normal.JU person.SBJV 3SG do.IRR LOG
síí
RECP.with
'Kid, we should work [do it] together.' [sos170822t3:203]

b. donc *mó   ɲá   à   tê   móo   dâmbṳ̈ ŋé*
SO.FR 1SG.EMPH be.NEG 3SG GEN 1SG.EMPH.SBJV lie.IRR NEG
mó   lḛ̀   dəgɔ̌ɔ lé tsɨ́ɛ̰́ɛ tő   à   nɛ̰̀ mó
1SG.EMPH SUBORD place REL very know.IRR 3SG LOC 1SG.EMPH
ká-kạ̣n   móo   à   jú   í   səgɔ̌
AFF-normal.JU 1SG.EMPH.SBJV 3SG say.IRR LOG good
'So I don't want to lie, the places that I really know, I should say those well.' [sos171009t1:121]

As these examples show, the form of the complement clause is identical; the only difference is the use of *ká-kạ̣n* instead of *ká-ɲḭ̀*.

As with *ká-ɲḭ̀*, Seenku has borrowed the Jula negation pattern for *ká-kạ̣n*, replacing the affirmative TAMP marker *ká* with the negative *mạ̣n*, yielding the expression *mạ̣n-kạ̣n*:

(29) a. *mó   mạ̣n-kạ̣n   né   kɛ̰̋   ŋɛ́*
       1SG.EMPH NEG-normal.JU 1SG.SBJV go.IRR NEG
       'I don't have to go.' [sos181210e]

   b. *kʊ́ tɛ̰̀ mənì̋ mạ̣n-kạ̣n   ằá   à   fɛ̰̀   ŋɛ́*
      D.DEF GEN woman NEG-normal.JU 3SG.SBJV 3SG blow.IRR NEG
      'That's why a woman must not play [the flute].' [sos170823t8:79]

The phrase in (29b) or a variation on it is repeated multiple times in the text by all participants, including GET, the younger interviewer. The construction is also attested once, not with a modal reading, but as an expression meaning that something is not good or normal:

(30) *á   wóo   tsɛ̋   kú-tòo   bằ   nɛ̰̋ mɛ̰̀   í   dəgɛ̰̀*
     2SG EMPH.SBJV INDF thing-bad do.REAL.PFV if 3SG.SUBORD LOG make.IRR
     təgɔ̌ áa   mɔ̰̌ büo   lé   òo, á   wôo
     like 2SG.SBJV person kill.REAL.PRF FOC INTERJ 2SG EMPH.SUBORD
     kú-tòo   lé bằ   à   mạ̣n-kạ̣n   Sɛ̰́ɛ-gûa   ŋɛ́,
     thing-bad REL do.REAL.PFV 3SG NEG-normal.JU Sambla-country NEG
     ằá   blɛ̰̀-bé   nìɔ   nɛ̰̋ főn kòkő nǎ   bɔ́
     3SG.SBJV big-NOM eat.REAL.PFV if until Koko PROSP go.out.IRR
     'If you do something bad like killing someone, bad thing you have done that shouldn't be done in Sambla country, if it's a big thing, the Koko [a bad monster/spirit] could come out.' [sos170823t8:178]

The expression *mạ̣n-kạ̣n* here is found as part of a relative clause, and it qualifies that the bad thing that is the subject of most of the utterance is not normal or good in Sambla country.

For comparison of meaning, I provide the elicited examples that resulted in *ká-ką́n* in (31):

(31) a. *Fàtű ká-kąn̄   ằá   jó   bìrő   ně̋*
Fatou AFF-normal.JU 3SG.SBJV see.IRR office LOC
'Fatou should be in the office.' [sos170807e]

b. *mó   ká-kąn̄   móo   ké̋   parce-que   mó kǎ   ső̋n sïɔ*
1SG.EMPH AFF-normal.JU 1SG.EMPH.SBJV go.IRR because.FR 1SG.EMPH
go.REAL.NOM time arrive.REAL.PRF
'I have to go because my time to go has arrived.' [sos170728e]

The first example differs in meaning from those using *ká-ɲì̋*; while the use of *ká-ɲì̋* here would express that Fatou should for moral purposes (or other value judgments) be at the office, the example in (31a) indicates more the idea that all things being equal, given what the speaker knows about Fatou's patterns, she should be at the office at this time of day. The example in (31b), on the other hand, could be said with either *ká-kąn̄* or *ká-ɲì̋*.

I end this section with two other 'must' constructions, even though they are not constructions with complementation. First, many examples similar in translation to (31a) resulted not in the *ká-kąn̄* construction but rather in a Seenku expression, the prospective auxiliary *nǎ*:

(32) a. *ằ   nǎ   jó   C ŋàa*
3SG PROSP find.IRR C inside
'It must be in C.' [sos170802e]

b. *Robert nǎ   sɪ̌ dɔ̋ɔ-cîe*
Robert PROSP be beer-house.LOC
'Robert must be at the maquis.' [sos170802e]

Like the example with Fatou at the office, these examples also indicate deduction on the part of the speaker: given what he or she knows about the state of the world and available evidence, it must be the case that it is in location C or that Robert is at the maquis (bar). It is unclear whether there are any subtle semantic differences between expressions with *ká-kąn̄* and those with the prospective. For more on regular prospective inflection, see §13.2.1.

Finally, we find a clause-initial modal strategy with *fő̋*. This looks almost identical to *főn* found in comparative (§15.1.1), which can be translated as 'better' or 'more', suggesting that there could be a common origin to the two expressions (i.e. 'must' = 'it is best that'). The clause introduced by *fő̋* is inflected normally.

Examples include:

(33) a. fő á   wó   tíi   môee
        must 2SG EMPH accept.IRR 1SG.EMPH.DAT
        'You need to trust me!' [sos181015e]

   b. fő mó   á   wó   nɔ̰̀   kɔ́rɔ́   tő
      must 1SG.EMPH 2SG EMPH that.for meaning.JU know.IRR
      'I have to know the answer to what you're talking about.' [sos161009t1:47]

   c. Măadù, vraiment, fő   mɔ̰̌ɔ   nà   wé jén-jěn
      Madou really.FR   must person.PST come.REAL.PFV FOC RED-story
      təmɛ̋   dɔ̀n nő
      tell.IRR today here
      'Madou, really, we had to tell this riddle here today.' [sos161009t1:12]

More data are needed to disentangle semantic differences between the various 'must' expressions in Seenku.

19.3.1.3 'ask'

The verb 'ask' (also used for 'beg') is *səmê*. The person being asked (the addressee) to do something is the direct object of the verb (i.e. it fills the verb's internal argument position), and then the pronoun is repeated again as the subject of the complement clause, marked by the subjunctive. For example:

(34) a. mó   ằ   səmê   ǎá   kəní   mó   lɛ̏
        1SG.EMPH 3SG ask.REAL.PFV 3SG.SBJV help.IRREAL 1SG.EMPH DAT
        mó   ń   tɛ̏ cî̂   ɲɛ̀
        1SG.EMPH 1SG GEN house build.IRR
        'I asked him to help me build my house.' [sos170816e]

   b. ằ   nǎ   mó   səmɛ̏   ǎá   sɔ́   nɛ̋ ǎá
      3SG PROSP 1SG.EMPH ask.IRR 3SG.SBJV be.able.IRR if 3SG.SBJV
      nɛ̀   mí̋ tɛ̋
      come.IRR 1PL GEN
      'He will ask me if he can come with us.' [sos170816e]

As (34a) shows, the verb 'ask' always takes the subjunctive in the complement clause, presumably since its action is never necessarily realized (i.e. even if one asks someone to do something, he may not necessarily do it). The example in (34b) is a complex clause, with a conditional of the verb 'be able' in the complement clause which itself takes another complement clause; see §19.3.2.1 below for more on 'be able'.

There are not many examples of this 'ask' complement construction in the corpus.

19.3.2 Subjunctive/subordinate complement clauses

The verbs for which the subjunctive TAMP marker is replaced by the subordinate in completive contexts are 'be able' (§19.3.2.1), 'try' (§19.3.2.2), 'help' (§19.3.2.3), and 'make' (§19.3.2.4).

19.3.2.1 'be able' (sɔ́ wè)

There are two ways of expressing ability in Seenku. In the main clause, both use the verb sɔ́ 'arrive' (cf. French *arriver à faire*). Most commonly, it is inflected in the irrealis with the habitual particle wè; these can both be pronounced independently as sɔ́ wè or the habitual can undergo clitic elision (§4.4.3), leaving sɔ́ɔ̀.

The complement can be a PP with a nominalized verb (discussed in §19.4.1) or a subordinated clause. In non-completive aspects, this clause takes the subjunctive TAMP marker lé after the subject, as we saw in the preceding sections. Examples from the text corpus include:

(35) a. mó   sɔ́ɔ̀   móo   ǎ   jú   í   wêe...
          1SG.EMPH be.able.IRR.HAB 1SG.EMPH.SBJV 3SG say.IRR 2PL EMPH.DAT
          mí̋ tȅ sɛ́ɛ-gûa...
          1PL GEN Sambla-country
          'I can tell you... in our Sambla country...' [sos171009t1:28-29]

    b. mɔ̰̀   fáná sɔ́ɔ̀   ǎá   mənı̋ jő   ǎ   tê
          person also be.able.IRR.HAB 3SG.SBJV woman find.IRR 3SG GEN
          'One could also find a wife that way.' [sos170714t3:100]

    c. tsȅ sɔ́ɔ̀   yèrè ǎá   màan dəgȅ
          INDF be.able.IRR.HAB self.JU 3SG.SBJV rice cook.IRR
          'Someone could even make rice.' [sos170714t3:75]

    d. ı̀   sɔ́ɔ̀   ı̏i   fôn   bä̋   tsı̰̋-kű
          3PL be.able.IRR.HAB 3PL.SBJV fonio beat.IRR cut-take.IRR
          gùɔ-dəgèɛ
          morning.ADV
          'They can start cutting fonio in the morning.' [sos170714t3:53]

For other examples of complements of 'start', see §19.4.7.

The subjunctive TAMP marker is also found when the main clause is negated:

(36) a. î̀   dòn-mənì-dənòn   sɔ́   wè   ǎá   təgò̀   à̀
        LOG.DAT child-woman-child be.able.IRR HAB 3SG.SBJV sit.IRR 3SG
        bá̰a̰-brɛ̰́   lɛ̰́ à̀ lé ŋɛ́
        balafon-play.NOM DEM 3SG DAT NEG
        '[Everyone said that] their daughter cannot get married to that balafon player.' [sos171009t1:42]

   b. ì̀   kʊ́ sɔ́   wè   ǐí   fên kùa   bè   ŋɛ́
      3PL D.DEF be.able.IRR HAB 3PL.SBJV thing other do.IRR NEG
      'They could not do anything else.' [sos171009t1:94]

The example in (36b) shows negative focus marking with the discourse definite before sɔ́ (§21.1.4).

All of the examples in the text corpus are inflected in the present habitual (whether affirmative or negative). In elicitation, I was able to get 'be able' in the prospective and the past:

(37) a. mó   nǎ   sɔ́   móo   kɛ̰́   cɔ̀̃ ŋɛ́
        1SG.EMPH PROSP be.able.IRR 1SG.EMPH.SBJV go.IRR village NEG
        'I will not be able to go to the village.' [sos150618e]

   b. móő   sɔ̌ɔ̀   móo   bǎrǎ bɛ̰́
      1SG.EMPH.PST be.able.IRR.HAB 1SG.SBJV work do.IRR
      'I used to be able to work.' [sos190803e]

Both of these tense/aspect combinations trigger subjunctive in the complement clause; (37b) in particular shows that the subjunctive/subordinate distribution is not tied to tense but rather to aspect.

In completive aspects like the perfective or the perfect, however, we see the subjunctive predicate marker replaced with subordinate wḛ̀ or lɛ̰̀:

(38) a. nɛ̰́   síɔ   ń   mḛ̀   kɛ̰́   cɔ̀̃   ŋɛ́
        1SG.PST be.able.PFV 1SG SUBORD go.IRR village NEG
        'I was not able to go to the village.' [sos150618e]

   b. Carole sìɔ   mḛ̀   bɔ́   kərḛ́̀-dəròn mè
      Carole arrive.REAL.PRF 3SG.SUBORD go.out.IRR man-child with
      'Carole can [now] go out with the boy.' [sos170807e]

In (38a), the form mḛ̀ is due to the nasal of the first singular; in (38b), mḛ̀ is the 3sg same subject allomorph of the subordinate; while à̀ wḛ̀ (using the 3sg pronoun explicitly) is possible here, it is more common for different subject configurations. See §20.2 for further discussion.

For PP complements of 'be able', see §19.4.1.

19.3.2.2 'try'

The expression 'try' employs the verb *tsə̌sə̋* 'look at' (realis: *tsə̌sí̋ɛ*); some younger speakers pronounce the verb with an initial [s] rather than the affricate [ts], leading to forms *sə̌sə̋* and *sí̋sí̋ɛ*, respectively. Like many of the other verbs we have seen thus far that take complement clauses, the direct object slot of the main clause is filled with the dummy 3sg pronoun *ǎ*. However, the verb does not take a complementizer, and the complement clause that follows is inflected in the subjunctive.

I have found no textual examples of the 'try' construction. From elicitation, we find forms like the following:

(39) a. *mó   nǎ   ǎ   tsə́sɛ̀   móo   səmâ*
          1SG.EMPH PROSP 3SG look.at.IRR 1SG.EMPH.SBJV dance.IRR
          'I will try to dance.' [sos181107e]

  b. *ǎ   nǎ   ǎ   tsə́sɛ̀   ǎá   səmâ*
      3SG PROSP 3SG look.at.IRR 3SG.SBJV dance.IRR
      'She will try to dance.' [sos181107e]

  c. *mó   nǎ   ǎ   sə́sɛ̀   móo   kʊ̀ tà*
      1SG.EMPH PROSP 3SG look.at.IRR 1SG.EMPH.SBJV toh cook.IRR
      'I will try to cook toh.' [sos170816e]

In each of the cases, the subject of the complement clause is followed by the subjunctive *lé*, which typically undergoes clitic elision (§4.4.3), as seen in (39).

Like 'be able to', if the main clause with 'try' is inflected for the perfective, the subject of the complement clause is followed by the subordinator *wɛ̀* or *lɛ̀* rather than the subjunctive *lé*:

(40) *móő   ǎ   tsə̂síɛ   môo   səmâ*
      1SG.EMPH.PST 3SG look.at.REAL.PFV 1SG.EMPH.SUBORD dance
      'I tried to dance.' [sos181107e]

In (40a), the embedded subject can also be realized as *ń mɛ̀* or *ń*.

In elicitation, I have also seen the French loanword *sáyə̋* (from *essayer*) used to express 'try'. It uses the same construction as the native Seenku verb *tsə̌sə̋*:

(41) a. *mó   nǎ   ǎ   sáyé   móo   kʊ̀ tà*
          1SG.EMPH PROSP 3SG try.FR 1SG.SBJV toh cook.IRR
          'I will try to cook toh.' [sos170816e]

  b. *ǎ   ǎ   sáyé mɛ̀   mó   bɔ̋*
      3SG 3SG try.FR 3SG.SUBORD 1SG.EMPH kill.IRR
      'He tried to kill me.' [sos170816e]

The example in (41b) is also attested with *à lɛ̌* as the subject of the embedded clause, rather than *mɛ̌*, though because it is the same subject, *mɛ̌* appears to be preferable.

For NP complements of 'try', see §19.4.5.

19.3.2.3 'help'

The verb 'help' in Seenku takes the form *kəní* (sounds like [kúní]) in the irrealis and *kənî* in the realis (at least the perfective). It is an intransitive verb, with the benefactor of helping expressed in a PP after the verb. Since helping implies an action undertaken by both the helper and the benefactor, the subject of the complement clause is always plural (the generic 1pl *mɔ̰̌* with a first person participant and the 3pl *ï* for non-first person; I suspect a second person participant would trigger the 2pl embedded subject *í*, but I have no examples in the corpus). Like 'try', the form of the complement clause changes depending on whether the main clause is perfective or non-perfective. Examples of prospective main clauses include:

(42) a. mó   nǎ   kəní   à   lɛ́   mɔ̰̌ɔ̰̌   kʊ̀ tà
       1SG.EMPH PROSP help.IRR 3SG DAT person.SBJV toh cook.IRR
       'I will help her make toh.' [sos181210e]

   b. ǎ   nǎ   kəní   môe   mɔ̰̌ɔ̰̌   jô   jɔ̃̌
      3SG PROSP help.IRR 1SG.EMPH.DAT person.SBJV water draw.IRR
      'She will help me draw water.' [sos181210e]

In both of these examples, the subject of the embedded clause is *mɔ̰̌*, regardless of whether the 1sg is the subject or oblique object of the main clause. It is marked with the subjunctive TAMP marker *lɛ́* (realized here as lengthening).

When the main clause is in the perfective, the subordinate marker takes the place of the subjunctive:

(43) a. móő   kənî   à   lɛ́   mɔ̰̌ɔ̰̀   kʊ̀ tà
       1SG.EMPH.PST help.REAL.PFV 3SG DAT person.SUBORD toh cook.IRR
       'I helped her make toh.' [sos181210e]

   b. ǎ   ɲǎ   kənî   à   lɛ́   ïi   jô   jɔ̃̌
      3SG mother help.REAL.PFV 3SG DAT 3PL.SUBORD water draw.IRR
      'Her mother helped her draw water.' [sos181210e]

In (43b), both participants in the main clause are third person, and so the embedded subject is *ï*. The subordinate marker *wɛ̀* has taken the place of *lɛ́* in the embedded clause, triggering X-toned lengthening.

19.3.2.4 Periphrastic causative expressions with 'make'

There is no morphological causative in Seenku as is found in some Mande languages like Mandinka or Soninke (see e.g. Creissels 2012). Instead, Seenku shows a periphrastic causative construction with the verb bɛ̀ 'make/do' (realis bä̀) in the main clause. The complement clause follows the same patterns as we saw with 'try' in §19.3.2.2 above, namely that if the main clause is non-perfective, then the complement clause is inflected in the subjunctive, but if it is perfective, the subject of the complement clause takes instead an X-toned subordinate marker.

(44) a. mó   á   bä̀   âa   səmâ
       1SG.EMPH 2SG do.REAL.PFV 2SG.SUBORD dance.IRR
       'I made you dance.' [sos181204e]

   b. á   nǎ   mó   bɛ́   né   səmâ
      2SG PROSP 1SG.EMPH do.IRR 1SG.SBJV dance.IRR
      'You will make me dance.' [sos181204e]

   c. mó   nǎ   dóǹ bɛ̀   ǎ́á   təgö̀
      1SG.EMPH PROSP child do.IRR 3SG.SBJV sit.IRR
      'I will make the child sit.' [sos150622e]

   d. sǒn-tǎ   lɛ̀   bɔ́   gərû   mɛ̀   à   bɛ̀
      sky-fire SUBORD go.out.IRR too.much 3SG.SUBORD 3SG do.IRR
      gǜɔ-né-kâ   lɛ́   î   màantɔ̀n bɔ́   í
      country-LOC-go.REAL.NOM SBJV LOG.DAT coat   take.off.IRR LOG
      wɛ̋
      with
      'The sun came out [=shone] too much and made the traveler take off his coat.' [sos170807t1]

In (44a), the main clause is perfective, and so the embedded subject surfaces as âa with subordinate marking. In (44b-d), the main clause contains an irrealis verb, either in the prospective or in subordinate chaining form in (44d), and so the embedded clause subject is marked with the subjunctive.

19.4 Nominalized complements

Some complement clauses appear as nominalized, often in a PP construction. In some cases, like 'be able', the same verb can take both a clausal complement (§19.3.2.1) and a PP complement (§19.4.1), whereas in others like 'fail' (§19.4.4), the verb uniformly takes a PP complement. For other verbs, the nominalized complement clause appears in direct object position.

As discussed in §13.3.1, nominalized verbs typically take the realis form as base. Most commonly, the PP complement uses the dative postposition lɛ̋, though in one case ('forbid'), the genitive postposition tɛ̋ can be used.

For PP complements in temporally subordinated clauses, see §20.3.1.

19.4.1 'be able' with a PP complement

In §19.3.2.1, we saw that the verb sɔ́ 'be able/arrive' takes as its complement a full clause inflected in the subjunctive. However, we also find cases where the complement is a PP with a nominalized verb instead. The postposition used in this case is always the dative lɛ̋ (modulo tone changes resulting from argument-head tone sandhi, §4.4.2). From elicitation, we can identify the construction:

(45)   a.   mó   sɔ́   wɛ̀ səmâ   lɛ̏ í   səgɔ́
            1SG.EMPH be.able.IRR HAB dance.REAL.NOM DAT LOG good
            'I can dance well.' [sos150703e]

       b.   mó   sɔ́ɔ̀   nân tǎ   lɛ̋
            1SG.EMPH be.able.IRR.HAB sauce cook.REAL.NOM DAT
            'I can cook sauce.' [sos181016e]

The ability predicate is followed immediately by the nominalized VP, itself the complement of the postposition lɛ̋. In some cases like (45a), there are no overt tonal or segmental changes showing that the verb has been nominalized, though in (45b), the LS rising tone on the X-toned verb tǎ clearly demonstrates nominalization.

Consultants explain to me that there is a subtle difference in meaning between the PP complement of sɔ́ and the clausal complement. Namely, the PP complement indicates general ability or know-how, whereas the clausal complement suggests that the person may be able to do the action at that moment if necessary.

A few instances of this construction are found in the text corpus, including:

(46)   a.   ì̀   á   wó   à   jío   ì̀   í   sɔ́ɔ̀
            COMP 2SG EMPH 3SG say.REAL.PFV COMP LOG be.able.IRR.HAB
            kùaa   lɛ̏
            farm.NOM DAT
            '[He would say] you said that you could farm!' [sos170714t1:33]

b. *fôn-bą́-trí̃*   *ké fəlé kú kərúú áa   æ̀*
    fonio-beat-medicine COP what thing all   2SG.SBJV 3SG
    gûɔ   ně́ á sɔ́ɔ̀   æ̀ lě
    learn.REAL.PFV if 2SG be.able.IRR.HAB 3SG DAT
    'What is fonio beating medicine, everything if you learn it, you can do it.'
    [sos170714t3:33]

In (46a), the nominalized verb *kùaa* 'farm' is used in the PP complement. The form in (46b) is exactly the same construction, except a pronoun is used instead of a nominalized verb.

19.4.2 'accept' with a PP complement

The verb stem for 'accept' is *tîi*, unusual for the fact that the /t/ does not undergo affrication before the /i/ (a regular phonological process in the language, §3.5.1.2). When it takes a nominalized complement, it appears in a PP after the verb. Attested postpositions include the dative *lě* and the genitive *tě*. For example:

(47) a. *tsě́ mɔ̌ tîi   í blǎ   tě́ ŋé*
        INDF person accept.IRR LOG fell.REAL.NOM GEN NEG
        'No one accepts being knocked down.' [sos170714t3:70]

   b. *ì̀ á kʊ́ tîi jɔ́ɔ̀   lě̀ ŋé*
        COMP 2SG D.DEF accept stroll.REAL.NOM DAT NEG
        '[She said] you never agree to go out walking.' [sos130828t2:27]

   c. *dəró-mɔ̌   cìamą́ tîi kǎ*
        child-HUM.SG a.lot.JU accept GO.REAL.NOM
        fón-bę́ę̌   ŋé
        fonio-beat.ANTIP.REAL.NOM.DAT NEG
        'A lot of kids don't accept going to beat fonio.' [sos170714t3:64]

   d. *í wó dəró-ŋě́   kʊ́ tîi wé à cěně̀*
        2PL EMPH child-HUM.PL D.DEF accept FOC DEF palm.frond
        są̌   ně́ mɔ̌ cìe ŋé
        buy.REAL.NOM DAT person give NEG
        'You kids won't agree to buy us palm fronds.' [sos170822t10:153]

In (47a), the genitive postposition *tě* is used in the complement. In all other cases, it is the dative, even in (47d) where *ně́* is the result of nasalizing the initial /l/.

19.4.3 'forbid' with a PP complement

The expression 'forbid' takes as its main verb *káa* (literally 'chase'). Like the PP complement of 'accept', 'forbid' can take either the dative *lɛ́* or the genitive *tɛ́*. Attested examples, shown in (48), come from elicitation:

(48) a. ä́ ní l-ä̀ káa təgɔ̀ tɛ̆̀ ä̀ kərɛ́ lê ä̀
3SG father L-3SG chase.REAL.PFV sit.REAL.NOM GEN DEF man PRES 3SG
lɛ́
DAT
'Her father forbade her to marry that man.' [sos181204e]

b. ä̀ mó káa nä̀ tê
3SG 1SG.EMPH chase.REAL.PFV come.REAL.NOM GEN
'He forbade me to come.' [sos181204e]

c. ä̀ mó káa kʊ̈ nɪ́ɔ lɛ́̆
3SG 1SG.EMPH chase.REAL.PFV toh eat.REAL.NOM DAT
'He forbade me to eat toh.' [sos181204e]

In each case, either the dative or the genitive could be used.

19.4.4 'fail' with a PP complement

The verb *jôo/jíoo* means something like 'fail' or 'be unable to'. It has an inherently negative meaning to it which is cancelled under negation, leading to an interpretation like 'manage to (despite thinking one would not be able to)'.

First, examples in the affirmative (thus meaning 'fail' or 'be unable to') are given in (49):

(49) a. í wó nǎ màa jôo kʊ̌ tsíoo↘
2PL EMPH PROSP again fail.IRR D.DEF know.REAL.NOM.DAT.Q
'Would you fail to know it?' [sos161009t1:15]

b. mó jóò kùaa lɛ̈̀
1SG.EMPH fail.IRR.HAB farm.REAL.NOM DAT
'I can't farm.' [sos181210e]

c. ä̀ jíoo nä̀a
3SG fail.REAL.PFV come.REAL.NOM.DAT
'He failed to come.' [sos181210e]

In each case, the construction is grammatically affirmative, but the reading is negative, thanks to the inherent negative meaning of the main verb. The complement clause is nominalized and embedded in a postpositional phrase with the dative postposition *lɛ̌* (other postpositions are ungrammatical).

If clauses like these are negated, the construction takes on a reading of 'manage to do' (lit. 'did not fail to')—that despite thinking it would not be possible, in the end, the action was able to take place. For instance:

(50) a. mó   jíoo   kṳ̀aa   lɛ̌   ŋɛ́
          1SG.EMPH fail.REAL.PFV farm.REAL.NOM DAT NEG
          'I managed to farm.' [sos181210e]

      b. ằ   jíoo   nằa   ŋɛ́
          3SG fail.REAL.PFV come.REAL.NOM.DAT NEG
          'He managed to come.' [sos181210e]

      c. ĭi   jíoo   sô   kǒo   ŋɛ́
          3PL.PST fail.REAL.PFV song sing.REAL.NOM.DAT NEG
          'They managed to sing the song.' [sos181210e]

Examples (50a-b) are negations of previous affirmative examples; (50c) provides another illustration of the construction.

It appears that more commonly, the modal *sɔ́* 'be able' is simply negated to express the idea of inability, rather than this specific verb.

19.4.5 'try' with an NP complement

While all of the other nominalized complements in this section have appeared post-verbally in a PP, the verb *tsɛ̋sɛ̋* 'try' takes its nominalized complement as a direct object. I have just a single instance of this construction, shown in (51):

(51) mó   jằnɛ̋ kǔa   tsɛ̋síɛ   nɛ́   nǎ   nɛ̋
      1SG.EMPH corn farm.REAL.NOM try.REAL.PFV 1SG.SBJV PROSP if
      sɔ́
      be.able.IRR
      'I tried farming corn to see if I could.' [sos181107e]

Here, the nominalized phrase *jằnɛ̋ kǔa* 'corn farming' is the direct object of *tsɛ̋sɛ̋*.

19.4.6 'finish' with an NP or PP complement

The verb ɲà (realis: ɲìa) 'finish' can be used either transitively or intransitively, both with a nominalized complement. If the verb is used transitively, the NP complement appears in direct object position, as in the following examples:

(52) a. ì   fôn   bǎ   ɲìäa   lɔ́
3PL fonio beat.REAL.NOM finish.REAL.PRF here
'They have finished thrashing fonio here.' [sos170714t3:62]

b. ì   ǎ   kǔa   ɲìäa   lɔ́
3PL 3SG farm.REAL.NOM finish.REAL.PRF here
'They have finished farming it here.' [sos170714t1:57]

c. ì   lɛ̀   ǎ   kɔ̀ɔ   sɨ́ɔ   ɲìa-ɲìa   wétǝnɛ̌...
3PL SUBORD DEF hole bury.REAL.NOM RED-finish.REAL.PRF now
'When they were done burying him now....' [sos170711t1:42]

It is also possible to use the verb 'finish' intransitively, in which case the complement appears as a PP after the verb. The postposition used is the locative *né*, which means that the construction is indistinguishable from realis forms with auxiliaries, such as the progressive (§13.3.1.1) or the immediate past (§13.3.1.2):

(53) a. mó   ɲìäa   cěrɛ̀   nɛ̀
1SG.EMPH finish.REAL.PRF sleep.REAL.NOM LOC
'I finished sleeping.' [sos170811e]

b. ǎ   ɲìäa   nɔ́nɛ̌sǎn nɨ́ɔ   nɛ̋
3SG finish.REAL.PRF food   eat.REAL.NOM LOC
'He finished eating.' [sos181204e]

These examples show that the PP complement can be either transitive or intransitive.

19.4.7 'start' with an NP complement

The expression for 'start' can only be used transitively with an NP complement; intransitive uses with a PP complement are unattested. The verb 'begin' is a compound verb *tsɨ́-kű*, though whether it is a verb-verb compound ('cut-catch') or a noun-verb compound ('part-catch') is not clear; I will gloss it as 'cut-catch'. For more on verbal compounds, see §12.5.

Natural examples from the text corpus are shown in (54):

(54) a. ì nǎ   fôn   tsį̋   tsį̋-kų̋
        3PL PROSP fonio cut.REAL.NOM cut-catch.IRR
        'They will start cutting fonio.' [sos170714t2:5]

   b. ì sɔ́ɔ̀   ǐi   fôn   bǎ̰   tsį̋-kų̋
        3PL be.able.IRR.HAB 3PL.SBJV fonio beat.REAL.NOM cut-take.IRR
        gùɔ-dəgèɛ
        morning.ADV
        'They can start cutting fonio in the morning.' [sos170714t3:53]

   c. óő   ɲɛ̰̀ɛ̰   tsḭ̀-kṵ́   á   jű   tsɛ̰̋
        2SG.PST weave.ANTIP.REAL.NOM cut-catch.REAL.PFV 2SG year how
        'How old were you when you started to weave?' [sos170822t10:68]

The example in (54b) is a complex construction in which the 'start' clause is itself the subjunctive complement of the modal sɔ́ 'be able to'.

19.5 Purposive clauses

I finish this chapter with purposive clauses due to their syntactic similarity to subjunctive complement clauses. Indeed, both constructions show the juxtaposition of a main clause and a subjunctive-marked subordinate clause. The only difference is the verbal semantics of the main clause. In the case of complement clauses, the semantics of the main clause differ without the complement clause. For instance, while 'want' could stand alone in a predicate without the complement clause, this would mean something like 'I want it' rather than wanting to do something; 'be able to' without its complement clause would simply mean 'arrive'.

With purposive constructions, on the other hand, the absence of the purposive clause doesn't change the meaning of the main clause. The purposive clause simply adds information about why the main clause action is undertaken.

Some cases blur the boundary between complement and purposive clauses. The verb 'help', for instance, could be seen as a complement clause, as shown above in §19.3.2.3; or it could be read as a purposive clause (e.g. 'I helped him so that we could build his house'). It is not clear how it is interpreted by speakers.

I discuss two related purposive constructions below—the first with an overt conjunction 'in order to' (§19.5.1) and the second with a bare subjunctive clause (§19.5.2). I end with a subsection on motion verbs in particular, which can be used as auxiliaries in a purposive-like construction.

19.5.1 Explicit conjunction *sân-kɄ́/jân-kɄ́*

I first address purposive clauses that are introduced with an explicit conjunction functioning like 'in order to'. This conjunction takes two forms, which are seemingly interchangeable: *sân-kɄ́* and *jân-kɄ́*. The purposive clause following the conjunction is always in the subjunctive.

For example:

(55) a. mɔ̰̀   dərḭ́   à   dzʊ̀   kɔ̀n jân-kɄ́ à   gùrè lé
person put.ANTIP.IRR 3SG mouth on so.that 3SG voice SBJV
sɔ́   ằ   bậg̰-dɛ̀n   bé   tề
arrive.IRR DEF balafon-child DEM GEN
'We add [more] to its mouth so that its voice comes out the same as that balafon key.' [sos170711t1:99]

b. kɄ́   kɄ́   tề   mó   ằ   tsíɛ   lê   kɄ́   búɔ
D.DEF D.DEF GEN 1SG.EMPH DEF word PRES D.DEF take.out.REAL.PFV
sân-kɄ́ móo   í   nəgí nề-təgò̰   ằ   nề   kú   lé
so.that 1SG.EMPH.SBJV 2PL mind TRANS-sit.IRR 3SG LOC thing REL
lḛ̂̀   fạ̰ạ̰
REL.SUBJ go.past.REAL.PERF
'That's why I have said the things I did, in order to remind you all of things that have passed.' [sos171009t1:117-118]

c. ḭ̀   jân-kɄ́ íwḯ   sɔ́   íwḯ   səré-bɔ̋
COMP so.that 1PL.EXCL.SBJV be.able.IRR 1PL.EXCL.SBJV see-go.out.IRR
í   tsḭ́   mɛ̋
LOG bottom with
'[They said] so that we can pass the time here on our butts.' [sos170711t1:46]

The examples in (55a-b) include both the main clause and the conjoined purposive clause, introduced by *jân-kɄ́* in (55a) and *sân-kɄ́* in (55b). In (55c), the main clause was in a separate intonational phrase, resumed by a quotative complementizer and the purposive clause as presented above. There appears to be no difference between the two conjunctions, but rather it is a matter of taste; SAD, the speaker in (55a) and (55c), consistently uses *jân-kɄ́*, while MD, the speaker in (55b), consistently uses *sân-kɄ́*.

19.5.2 Purposive clauses with no conjunction

We also find cases of purposive clauses where there is no explicit conjunction; rather, the main clause is simply followed by a subjunctive clause. Examples include:

(56) a. ń nɛ̀   ǎ tâ dəgɛ̃́   nɛ̃́ wé ǎ gʉ̀ ǎ tâ lɛ́
       1SG SUBORD DEF fire make.REAL.NOM LOC FOC 3SG under DEF fire SBJV
       kɛ̀ɛ
       light.IRR
       'Here I am arranging the coals [lit. the fire] underneath it so the fire will light.' [sos170822t4:165]

   b. donc í ǎ nɛ̀-kəkɛ̀ɛ   ǎ jʊ̈ʊ́   jəgǎ
      SO.FR 2PL 3SG TRANS-spread.IRR 3SG water.SBJV go.down.IRR
      'So you spread it out so that its water comes out.' [sos170822t1:107]

In elicitation, I have seen examples such as the one in (57) where consultants explicitly point out the optionality of the conjunction, suggesting that there is no change in meaning whether or not the conjunction is present:

(57) mó   bî sǎ̰   (sân-kʊ́) mó   nḭ̀ lɛ́ à jɔ̰̀
     1SG.EMPH goat buy.REAL.PFV (so.that) 1SG.EMPH father SBJV 3SG grill.IRR
     'I bought a goat so that my father will grill it.' [sos150618e]

Bare purposive clauses like these most closely resemble the complement clauses discussed in §19.3 above.

19.5.3 Verbs of motion as auxiliary verbs

Seenku does not have verb chaining or serial verbs, which is otherwise a common phenomenon in many West African languages (e.g. Stahlke 1970, Lord 1973, Aikhenvald 2006, etc.). Generally speaking, if the speaker wishes to put together multiple verbs, it is necessary to use multiple clauses or to nominalize one or more of the verbs.

The exception is verbs of motion. Verbs of motion can combine with other verbs in a single clause by taking the place of the auxiliary verb. The following verb is inflected in the irrealis and the meaning is akin to a purposive construction. The three verbs that participate in this construction are kà̰/kɛ̃́ 'go' (realis/irrealis), nà̰/né 'come' (realis/irrealis), and lö 'come'.

Examples with 'go' are shown first in (58):

(58) a. óo   yérɛ́ ǎ tsíɛɛ   á kɛ̃́   tùbábú-kû
       2SG.EMPH self.JU 3SG speak.IRR 2SG go.IRR white.person-thing
       dzɪ̰̈   ǎ nɛ̀
       put.IRR 3SG LOC
       'You yourself speak, you go and add French into it.' [sos170702t1:24]

b. óo   ké̋   ằ   nɔ́nɛ̋sǎn nɔ̋   màa á wó nɛ́   ằ
   2SG.EMPH go.IRR DEF food   eat.IRR again 2SG EMPH come.IRR DEF
   fôn   bá̰   tsḭ́-kṵ́
   fonio beat.REAL.NOM cut-catch.IRR
   'You go eat and come back to start beating fonio.' [sos170714t3:87]

c. mɛ̏   ké̋   ằ   ɲṵ́i   jő   mɔ̰̋má̰ ń   té̋   sân   kű́ɛ
   3SG.SUBORD go.IRR DEF honey see.IRR a.lot 1SG dear rabbit other.PL
   té̋   mɔ̰̋má̰
   GEN a.lot
   'She went and saw a lot of honey, a lot at Mr. Rabbit's family house.'
   [sos130828t2:12]

In (58b-c), the meaning of the motion verb is literal: movement away from the fonio beating or from the character's house takes place before the following verb (eating or seeing honey). In (58a), it is more figurative: the speaker means that as you speak (as you go through speaking), you add in French words. There is no literal motion involved.

The example in (58b) put together two clauses, the first with 'go' as the auxiliary and the second with 'come' as the auxiliary. In both cases, the following VP is inflected in the irrealis; note that in the second clause, *tsḭ́-kṵ́* 'begin' is the main verb, which takes a nominalized VP complement headed by *bá̰* 'beat'. Other examples include:

(59) a. ɛ̏ɛ́   bé̋   ì   í   nằ   tâ   sù̀
        3SG.LOG do.IRR COMP LOG come.REAL.PFV fire take.IRR
        'She said that she came to get fire.' [sos130828t2:13]

   b. ì̀   ằ   tərɛ̏   wé ì̀   ŏo   nằ   fènɛ́
      3PL 3SG ask.REAL.PFV FOC COMP 3SG.EMPH come.REAL.PFV what
      sò̰o   lɔ̋
      search.IRR here
      'They asked him what he came to look for here.' [sos170711t1:16]

   c. ằ   jɔ̋ɔ-jɔ́ɔ   tóò wè ằ   lɛ̏   nɛ́   ằ   gɔ̂ɔ
      3SG RED-search.REAL.PFV axe with 3SG SUBORD come.IRR DEF wood
      tsḭ̀
      cut.IRR
      'Having looked for the axe, she came to cut down the tree.' [sos130828t1:42]

The examples in (59a-b) show that even when the auxiliary is inflected in the perfective, the verb in the main VP is always in the irrealis. These examples also give a clear indication of the origins of the prospective, which differs only tonally; see §13.2.1 for further discussion of the prospective.

19.5 Purposive clauses

In elicitation, we find also cases using the auxiliary *lò*. This is also translated as 'come', but one consultant drew a distinction between *lò* and *nà*, where the former indicates cases where the subject in question is still en route or heading towards the speaker, while *nà* (a perfective form) indicates that the person has already arrived.

(60) a. á lò kəré jù
2SG come what say.IRR
'What have you come to say?' [sos150806e]

b. à̰ lò bɛ̀ɛ sà̰
3SG come pig buy.IRR
'He is coming to buy a pig.' [sos150804e]

c. ń nò̰ cî brḭ́-brḭ́
1SG come house RED-go.around.IRR
'I came to go around the house.' [sos150804e]

Given the translations of some of these examples, it is difficult to see how the subject could not have arrived yet. More data are needed to fully understand the *lò* construction.

In texts, however, *lò* is more commonly found in cases with a figurative future or desiderative reading for 'come' rather than a physical one. For example:

(61) á kɛ̰́ à̰ kúwɛ́ɛ bɛ̰́ à̰ gṵ̀ təgɔ́ á lò à̰ tsḭ̀
2SG go.IRR 3SG sickle put.IRR 3SG under like 2SG come.IRR 3SG cut.IRR
'You go put the sickle underneath him as if you were going to cut him.'
[sos170714t2:18]

As the main verb, *lò* is attested with a ventive motion reading in texts, as in:

(62) ḭ̀ í bɛ̰́ wétənɛ̆ ḭ̀ sì-brɔ́ lò ḭ̀ Bəbâ lò
3PL LOG do.IRR now COMP first.son-brɔ come COMP Bouba come
'They say now, "Si-Brɔ is coming, Bouba is coming."' [sos170823t8:351]

Here, we clearly see the reading of *lò* where the subject is still en route.

20 Clause coordination and event sequencing

This chapter covers remaining ways of combining clauses, especially as it relates to constructing larger discourse. In terms of clause coordination strategies, Seenku displays two major patterns. The first is the use of explicit coordinating conjunctions (§20.1), specifically 'because' (§20.1.1), 'but' (§20.1.2), and 'as though' (§20.1.3), but crucially absent is a clause-level conjunction 'and'. Instead, Seenku makes wide use in narratives of a second strategy, namely clause chaining, which combines aspects of coordination and subordination. This latter strategy is discussed in §20.2.

Clause chaining implies a sequence of events; the action of the first clause takes place, then the second, then the third, and so on. If a speaker wishes to be more explicit about event sequencing, temporal subordination strategies are used. These strategies are discussed in §20.3.

It should be noted that Seenku does not have serial verb constructions. The closest construction we find to serialization is the use of motion verbs as auxiliaries; see §19.5.3.

20.1 Coordination with explicit conjunctions

This section addresses clause-level coordination in Seenku using explicit conjunctions; for conjunction and disjunction at the word- or phrase-level, see Chapter 11.

We find a small handful of common conjunction strategies depending on the intended meaning. Specifically, we find the conjunctions 'because' (§20.1.1), 'but' (§20.1.2), and 'as though' (§20.1.3).

20.1.1 Because

Conjunctions of causality, like 'because' or 'since', are almost entirely French loanwords in Seenku: either *páskɛ̋* ~ *pásíkí̋* (< French *parce que* 'because') or *kɔ́mì* (< French *comme* 'like, since'). These loanwords are common in younger people's speech and even older males' speech; it is only elderly females who appear not to use these words, though the corpus of texts is smaller in this demographic and no sentences are attested in which 'because' is offered as a translation.

First, sentences with *páskɛ̋* are illustrated in (1):

(1) a. ké ằ pìɔn kʊ́   kʊ́   ằ   bíɛ-sắn   prɔ́mîe yèrè
       COP DEF flute D.DEF D.DEF DEF play.REAL.NOM-thing first.FR self.JU
       páskɛ̋   kʊ́ kʊ́ sìɔ   jəmʋ̀ bʋ́ɛ̰ɛ-dʋ̀ì kà
       because.FR D.DEF D.DEF arrive.REAL.PRF bush jinn-child.PL in.hand
       'The flute is the very first instrument because it arrived in the bush in the hands of jinns.' [sos170711t1:339]

   b. ằ   cě kɑ̰̀   lɛ́ nằ   nɛ̋ɲì ké ằ nằ í
       3SG hand empty SBJV come.REAL.PFV if there COP 3SG PROSP LOG
       kpɛ̀nɛ̀ tsɹ̀   súu, páskɛ̋   ằ fôn jô   bɔ̀   ŋɛ́
       finger cut.IRR directly because.FR DEF fonio see.IRR anymore NEG
       'When his empty hands comes up there, he will cut his finger directly, because there isn't any fonio there anymore.' [sos170714t2:19]

These examples show a usage of *páskɛ̋* that exactly mirrors how it would be used in French, i.e. to link two clauses together. However, some speakers use *páskɛ̋* to introduce clauses in ways that differ from canonical French usage. Consider the following exchange between a question in (2a) and the response in (2b):

(2) a. í   bʋ́ɛ̰ɛ   kú lɛ̋   nɛ̋?
       2PL play.IRR.HAB thing which.PL LOC
       'What kinds of things do you play for?' [sos170711t1:384]

   b. páskɛ̋   mǐ té lɔ̋ ì̀ bʋ̂ɛ   kú   lɛ́ nɛ̀̀
       because.FR 1PL GEN here 3PL play.IRR thing which LOC
       'Because where we are here, we play for what.' [sos170711t1:385]

The speaker in (2b) then goes on to indicate the kinds of situations in which the balafons would play (e.g. if an old person dies). It is not clear what role *páskɛ̋* is playing in the mind of the speaker at the beginning of this utterance; this distribution is not uncommon, particularly with older speakers, suggesting that there may have been a native conjunction with a similar distribution, one that overlaps with the French *parce que* distribution but extends beyond it.

We find only one hint for what such a native conjunction might be, in a single utterance shown in (3):

(3) ằ̀ ɲəgé-səgû   jîo,   ằ̀ ằ̀ jərà ì̀   ké cəbâa-dərɔ̋n
    3SG salt-rub.NOM see.REAL.PFV 3SG 3SG think COMP COP orphan-child
    jáǎá   ɲəgê səgǔ   sɹ̀ ằ dòn mè
    because salt rub.PTCP be 3SG child with
    'She saw the one with salt and she thought it was the orphan, since her child had salt rubbed on him.' [sos130828t1:20]

Here, the speaker uses a conjunction *jáǎá* where we would otherwise see the use of the French conjunction. However, this is the only time I have seen this conjunction used. More data are required to determine its range of uses and its frequency in current Seenku (though the example in (3) was spoken by a young man, SCT).

A related expression meaning 'since' is *kɔ́mì*, borrowed from French *comme* 'like/since'. In French, the clause introduced by *comme* tends to come utterance-initially, followed by the consequence of the 'since' clause; the structure is the same borrowed into Seenku:

(4) a. *kɔ́mì   ǎ   Dɛ́ɛ   là   bǎsǐ-krűn   bà   lɔ̌   mǐ*
       since.FR DEF Madeline DEF couscous-ball put.REAL.PFV here 1PL
       ká̌   âa   mǐ kűɛ   jəgɔ̌
       in.hand NEG.Q 1PL other.PL munch.IRR
       'Since Madeline gave us couscous balls here, we ate those.' [sos170822t7:16]

   b. *kɔ́mì   brȩ̀m-bą̂   sɔ́-səgɔ̀ɛ   sǐ Bùrùkìnǎ té   Màlǐ nǎ*
       since.FR ball-hit.REAL.NOM RED-good.PL be Burkina GEN Mali PROSP
       sɔ́   ǎá   ǎ   bàatí   ɲɛ́
       be.able.IRR 3SG.SBJV 3SG beat.FR.IRR NEG
       'Since Burkina has a better team, Mali will not be able to beat them.'
       [sos170809e]

Even older speakers who do not speak French use *kɔ́mì*; the utterance in (4a) was spoken by a woman in her late middle ages.

20.1.2 But

Another French conjunction that has been borrowed into Seenku is *mais* 'but', realized as *mɛ̀* in Seenku (though typically throughout the grammar, I have indicated it in unitalicized French orthography). This conjunction is even more widespread than *páskɛ́* or *kɔ́mì*, used by virtually all speakers, regardless of age or gender. For instance:

(5) a. *mɛ̀   kʊ́   ɲá   bɔ̀   ɲɛ́*
       but.FR D.DEF be.NEG anymore NEG
       'But that doesn't exist anymore.' [sos170822t10:165]

   b. *ǎ   dɔ̀   kʊ́   bą́ą̀   brȩ̀   wɛ̀   ɲɛ́ mɛ̀   ì̀   wɛ̀ ǎ*
       3SG though D.DEF balafon play.IRR HAB NEG but.FR 3PL SUBORD 3SG
       cȩ̀rȩ̀   ì̀ kɛ́ kâ
       call.IRREAL COMP COP griot
       'Him, though, he doesn't play the balafon but he is [still] called a griot.'
       [sos171009t1:90]

c. ì̀   kərúú sɔ́   ǐi   à   bá̰a̰   dàn-kù
    3PL all be.able.IRR 3PL.SBJV 3SG balafon mouth-thing
    mɛ̰̀   ŋé, mɛ̰̀   təgɔ̆ɛ   lê   à   mɛ̰̀   wè
    understand.IRR NEG but.FR certain.PL PRES 3SG understand.IRR HAB
    'Not everyone understands the balafon speech, but there are some who understand it.' [sos170711t1:219]

Unlike the homophonous 3sg subordinate TAMP marker mɛ̰̀ (§20.2), the French conjunction is not subject to vowel hiatus resolution, so the sequence mɛ̰̀ ì in (5b) is pronounced with both vowels.

We do find native Seenku equivalents, though. What I have most commonly heard suggested is ŋ́gáa, as in:

(6) ŋ́gáa ké ằ   sŭ́məŋằ lê   í   bὲɛ   kʊ́ tɔ̆ ŋɛ́ ké
    but   COP DEF god   REL.SUBORD LOG do.IRR.HAB D.DEF like NEG COP
    sὺɛ dərón-ŋɛ̆   lé lɛ̀
    three child-HUM.PL REL SUBORD
    'But since God decided otherwise, I have just three children left [lit. they are three, those children there].' [sos170822t12:78]

I have been told by consultants that this is the Seenku equivalent of 'but', but it is nearly non-existent in my data corpus.

In one other case, jăa is used like 'but'. It is unclear whether this is a version of jáǎá 'because' that has been mistranslated or has a broader range of uses, or whether it simply resembles this other conjunction. The example is provided in (7):

(7) dɔ́ŋ́ké mɛ̰̀   jəgă-jəgằ   wétənĕ ɲì-nà
    so.FR 3SG.SUBORD RED-go.down.REAL.PFV now there-towards
    mɛ̰̀   ằ   táasɔ̆   ằ   bɛ̆   wé mɔ̰̀ɛ   dəgŭaa jăa ké
    3SG.SUBORD 3SG surprise 3SG take.place FOC person.PL between but COP
    bûɛ̰-dɔ̀n
    djinn-child
    'So, when he had descended there, to his surprise, he was surrounded by people but they were djinns.' [sos170711t1:14]

More examples will be needed to clarify the usage of jăa and determine its distinctiveness from jáǎá.

20.1.3 As though

The last clause conjunction strategy discussed in this chapter is təgɔ́ 'as though'. We first saw this form in §11.2 in its use as an NP disjunction 'or'. It can be used on its own to join two clauses; the clause following təgɔ́ is inflected normally, i.e. it is not subjunctive or otherwise explicitly subordinated. I have only seen one example of this construction in the text corpus, shown in (8):

(8) óo   sɔ́ɔ̀   áa   á   fírá   dǎa   á   kḗ   à̰
     2SG.EMPH be.able.HAB 2SG.SBJV 2SG colleague trick.IRR 2SG go.IRR DEF
     kúwéɛ́ bḗ   à   gù   təgɔ́   á   lò̰   ä̀   tsị́
     sickle put.IRR 3SG under as.though 2SG come 3SG cut.IRR
     'You can trick your adversary and put your sickle underneath him as though you were going to cut him.' [sos170714t2:18]

More commonly, we find *təgɔ́* or a variant *tɔ́ɔ* in a fixed expression *ɛ̌ɛ dəgɛ̀ tɔ́ɔ* 'it is as though', which is then followed by a regularly inflected clause:

(9) a. ɛ̌ɛ   dəgɛ̀   təgɔ́   jʊ́   béɛ   bəgû nḗ ä̀   nɛ̌ ä̀
        3SG.LOG make.IRR as.though water DEM.SBJV a.lot if 3SG LOC 3SG
        nǎ   mụ̈ɔ   fìɔ   ŋɛ́
        PROSP cook.IRR fast NEG
        'It is as though if the water becomes too much, it doesn't cook quickly.' [sos170822t4:80]

   b.   kɛ́   jì-kû   dərɔ̀n tɛ̰̀   ŋɛ́,   âa   ä̀   jío   tsɛ̰́
        COP fetish-thing only GEN NEG 2SG.SUBORD 3SG say.REAL.PFV how
        lɔ̰́n   ɛ̌ɛ   dəgɛ̀   tɔ́ɔ   kʊ́ʊ   ä̀   nə̀fóo-nəgé-sä́n
        here 3SG.LOG make.IRR as.though D.DEF.COP DEF animal-herd-thing
        'It's not just a thing for the fetishes, as you've said here, it's also something for animal herders.' [sos170823t8:87]

We also find cases where *ɛ̌ɛ dəgɛ̀ tɔ́ɔ* is instead realized without the logophoric pronoun as *ä̀ dəgé tɔ̀ɔ* in (10a), or even with other subjects, such as the example in (10b) with the 2sg:

(10) a. ä̀   dəgé   tɔ̀ɔ   tré   bä́rä́ bǎa   dzíɛ   nḗ
         3SG make.IRR as.though REL.PRO work do.REAL.NOM.SBJV be.good if
         fɔ́n   á   nǎ   lɛ́   bä́rä́ bḗ   kʊ́   wḗ
         more 2SG PROSP FOC work do.IRR D.DEF with
         'It's as though whichever is easier to work with, that is the one that you will use.' [sos170822t10:115]

   b.   á   ä̀   dəgɛ̀   tɔ́ɔ   á   sị̌ ä̀ təgǐ   nḗ í
        2SG 3SG make.IRR as.though 2SG be 3SG stand.REAL.NOM LOC LOG
        tsị̀ɛ   kɔ̀n
        foot.PL on
        'It's as though you are standing it up on its feet.' [sos170822t10:190]

It may be that *dəgɛ́* 'make' in this expression acts as a raising verb, like English 'seem', allowing the subject of the conjoined clause to be repeated as the subject of the 'as though' expression.

20.2 Clause chaining

Clause chaining refers specifically to a syntactic strategy that combines aspects of coordination and subordination, and which can be quite common in narratives. Formally, clause chaining involves (sometimes long) sequences of dependent clauses (Dooley 2010), which show morphosyntactic subordination, and one main clause situating these dependent clauses in space and time. In many languages, the main clause comes at the end of the chain (e.g. Kumyk, Haspelmath 1995; Kanite, Longacre 2007), but in Seenku, the main clause comes first. This main clause shows the full range of TAM marking, whereas subsequent clauses use the subordinate TAMP marker (*wɛ̀*) after the subject with the verb in its bare irrealis form.

Though Seenku and Mande languages more generally are not known for having switch reference systems, Seenku clause chaining shows a small pocket of emergent same subject marking. When the subject of the main clause is 3sg, a same subject referent in subsequent clauses is indicated by the portmanteau TAMP marker *mɛ̀*, which subsumes the subject; if the subject will change to a different 3sg subject, then the transparent sequence *ä̀ wɛ̀* is used instead.

Clause chaining and same subject marking are both clearly illustrated in the following examples, consisting of the first six lines of a narrative. As is typical, the narrative begins with a few regular main clauses inflected for TAM. After the timeframe has been set by these phrases, clauses can then be chained together. Whenever the subject is the same as the preceding clause, *mɛ̀* is used; if the subject changes, *ä̀ wɛ̀* is used instead (11d). Consider the beginning lines of a billygoat and hyena folktale [sos150626t4]:

(11) a. Donc, *kʊ́ nɛ̀ wétənɛ̆ kərʊ̀ íaa tsɛ́ké sà-bö̀-kɔ̌ɔ sɔ́n*
    SO.FR D.DEF LOC now hyena TOP and second.son-billygoat rain
    bəlɛ̆ bǎa tsɛ́ bḭ̀ɛ
    big INTENS INDF rain.REAL.PFV
    'So, now, the hyena and the billygoat, a really big rain fell.' [sos150626t4:1]

   b. *sà-bö̀-kɔ̌ɔ ì-ǎ-lɔ́ sà-bö̀-kɔ̌ɔ kʊ́*
    second.son-billygoat you.know.JU second.son-billygoat D.DEF
    təgì wɛ̀ ä̀ sɔ́n-nɛ́n-jʊ̆ jɛ́n ŋɛ́
    stand.IRR HAB DEF rain-grain-water front NEG
    'Billygoat, you know, billygoat won't stand in the rain.' [sos150626t4:2]

c. sɔ́n   nà̰   wé bɛ̰́   wétənɛ̆ mɛ̰̀   né   à̰
    rain come.REAL.PFV FOC rain.IRR now   3SG.SUBORD   come.IRR DEF
    bò̰-kɔ̆ɔ   jő
    billygoat find.IRR
    'The rain came and found the billygoat.' [sos150626t4:3]

d. à̰   wɛ̰̀   í   təbɛ̰̀   wétənɛ̆ lő   à̰   kərṵ̀   kűɛ
    3SG SUBORD LOG stand.next.to.IRR now   here DEF hyena other.PL
    tɛ̋   dân   tɛ̰̀
    GEN wall GEN
    'He huddled next to the wall of hyena's family's house.' [sos150626t4:4]

e. à̰   dôn mɛ̰̀   bɔ́   mɛ̰̀   kɛ̋   à̰   cɛ̰̋n-kɛ̋
    3SG child SUBORD go.out.IRR 3SG.SUBORD go.IRR DEF peanut-shell.PL
    sɛ̰̋ɛ   ɲḭ̀
    throw.IRR.NE there
    'His [=hyena's] child went outside to throw out some peanut shells.'
    [sos150626t4:5]

f. mɛ̰̀   kɛ̋   mɛ̰̀   í   bɛ̋   ɛ̰̋!   ḭ̀   bṵ̀bǎ tsɛ̋
    3SG.SUBORD go.IRR 3SG.SUBORD LOG do.IRR INTERJ COMP dad INDF
    fên   sı̰̆   nɔ̆-ŋɛ̋   à̰   dân gṵ̀
    thing be here-NEG DEF wall under
    'and he went out and said "Eh! Dad, there is something over there next to the wall!"' [sos150626t4:6]

The first two lines consist of entirely inflected clauses, first in (11a) a perfective clause setting the scene for the story, then in (11b) a habitual clause reminding the listener that billygoats do not like to stand in the rain. In (11c), the clause begins with a perfective, whose subject is the noun sɔ́n 'rain', but it is chained with a subordinate clause about coming to find the billygoat. It is a subsequent clause, indicating a series of events: first, the rain came to fall, then it came and found the billygoat. The subject of the subordinate clause is indicated with mɛ̰̀, since the same subject (the rain) is found in both clauses. In (11d), the subject changes, now to the billygoat who is huddled against the wall. Since the subject has changed, à̰ wɛ̰̀ must be used instead. The subject changes once again in (11e) to the hyena's child. The child is introduced as an NP in the first clause, followed by the subordinator wɛ̰̀ (nasalized to mɛ̰̀ due to the latent nasal coda of dôn 'child'); this clause is chained with another in the same intonation group, and here the subject remains the same, so mɛ̰̀ is used. This same subject then carries over into two more clauses in (11f).

In cases like those in (11) where all participants are 3sg, mɛ̰̀ functions as a same subject marker. However, it is not a canonical same subject marker in that it can also be used to refer to another argument in a preceding clause if it is the only 3sg argument. For example:

(12) a. ì̀ fəgǎ sḭ plə̌ngṵ̀ nɛ̀ bŏ-kɔ́ɔ tɛ́ mɛ̀
3PL be.full.PTCP be traditional.bag LOC billygoat GEN 3SG.SUBORD
sú mɛ̀ né təgò̀ tâ lɛ̀
get.up.IRR 3SG.SUBORD come.IRR sit.IRR fire DAT
'They [birds] were full in the billygoat's bag, and then he came and sat by the fire.' [sos150626t4:28]

b. móő ǎ tsə̂síɛ mɛ̀ féɛ
1SG.EMPH.PST 3SG look.at.REAL.PFV 3SG.SUBORD before
səmâa
dance.REAL.NOM.DAT
'I looked at her before she danced.' [sos181107e]

The example in (12a) is drawn from a narrative; the subject of the first clause is the 3pl ì̀; 'billygoat' is the complement of the postposition tɛ́. Nevertheless, mɛ̀ in the subsequent picks out 'billygoat' because it is the only 3sg argument available. The situation is similar in (12b), an elicited phrase. The subject of the main clause is the 1sg, and the direct object is 3sg. The subordinator mɛ̀ in the subsequent clause is co-referent with the object and not the subject. However, speakers report that if ǎ wɛ̀ were used instead, it would still be understood in the same way, i.e. with coindexation of the object of the main clause and the subject of the subsequent clause.

Further, mɛ̀ can only be used for 3sg subjects, not for any same subject. The following examples show cases where the subject of the dependent clause is the same as a preceding clause but is not the 3sg:

(13) a. ì̀ í tsə̂síɛ ì̀ wɛ̀ səmâa
3PL LOG look.at.REAL.PFV 3PL SUBORD dance.REAL.NOM.DAT
'They looked at each other and then danced.' [sos181107e]

b. ǎ̀ jánɛ̀ɛ́ síɔ nɛ́ wé lɔ́ trɔ́ ǎ̀
DEF evening.SBJV arrive.REAL.PFV if FOC here like.that DEF
dəró-ŋɛ́ ì̀ sú wɛ̀ küɛɛ kɛ́ sőn ǎ̀
child-HUM.PL 3PL get.up.IRR HAB all.SUBORD go.IRR play.IRR DEF
tərṵ̀kű nɛ́
trash LOC
'When evening comes here like that, the children, they get up and go out and play behind the house.' [sos170711t1:38-39]

In both of these cases, the co-referent pronoun—ì̀ in (13a) and küɛ in (13b)—must be repeated in the dependent clause, followed by the subordinate TAMP marker, which

20.3 Temporal subordination

The clause chains with *mɛ̈* indicate a general pattern of sequence: First clause1, then clause2, then clause3, etc., but there is no clear sense of hierarchy or explicit temporal subordination in the construction. This section turns to different temporal subordination strategies, including *fɛɛ* 'before' (§20.3.1), *fɔ̃* 'until' (§20.3.2), a verbal reduplication strategy indicating precedence or completion (§20.3.3), and a brief discussion and cross-reference to conditional clauses as a form of temporal subordination (§20.3.4).

20.3.1 Subordination with 'before'

Clauses subordinated with 'before' in Seenku always appear after the main clause. They use a fixed verbal expression *fɛɛ*, the subject of which appears in the subjunctive or the subordinated form, depending on the TAMP marking of the main clause (see §19.3 for further discussion of TAMP marking in subordinate clauses). The complement of *fɛɛ* 'before' is nominalized and embedded in a PP with the postposition *lɛ̋* or *wɛ̀*, as we saw with other complement clause types in §19.4.

First, the following elicited examples illustrate the construction with irrealis (14a-b) and realis (14c-d) inflection in the main clause:

(14) a. á cè fəgɔ̀ áa fɛɛ nɔ́nɛ̋sán nǐɔɔ
 2SG hand.PL wash.IRR 2SG.SBJV before food eat.REAL.NOM.DAT
 'Wash your hands before eating!' [sos170728e]

 b. ä̀ nǎ kṳ̈ nɔ̈ fɛ̋ ä̀á fɛɛ səmá` wɛ̀
 3SG PROSP toh eat.IRR yet 3SG.SBJV before dance.REAL.NOM with
 'He will eat toh before dancing.' [sos181204e]

 c. ä̀ mó tsə̀síɛ mɛ̈ fɛɛ
 3SG 1SG.EMPH look.at.REAL.PFV 3SG.SUBORD before
 səmâa
 dance.REAL.NOM.DAT
 'She looked at me before dancing.' [sos181107e]

d. ì̀   dɔ̈ɔ̈   wétənĕ ̀ìi   fɛ́ɛ   í
   3PL finish.REAL.PRF now   3PL.SUBORD before LOG
   gù-ɲïi
   neck-lift.REAL.NOM.DAT
   'They finished now before getting up.' [sos170728e]

In (14a-b), the subjunctive TAMP marker is used with the subject of the 'before' clause, while we find the subordinate in (14c-d). In most cases, the nominalized complement of 'before' appears with the dative postposition, but in (14b), the associative wɛ̀ is used instead. It is likely that fɛ́ɛ 'before' is verbal in nature, since it is the only candidate for an inflected verb in the subordinate clause; it appears after the subject and TAMP marker and before the nominalized PP complement.

It is not necessary that the subject of the main clause and the subject of the temporally subordinated clause be the same, as illustrated in (15):

(15) ä̀   mó   tsə̀síɛ   môo   fɛ́ɛ   səmâa
     3SG 1SG.EMPH look.at.REAL.PFV 1SG.SUBORD before dance.REAL.NOM.DAT
     'She looked at me before I danced.' [sos181107e]

From the text corpus, we find the following examples:

(16) a. á   ä̀   kú   bɛ́   mïŕï̈́   á   ŋáa   áa   fɛ́ɛ   ä̀   kú
        2SG 3SG thing DEM think.IRR 2SG inside 2SG.SBJV before 3SG thing
        bɛ́   jïoo
        DEM say.REAL.NOM.DAT
        'You have to think about that thing [=the words] before you can say it.'
        [sos170711t1:213]

     b. mɔ̰̌   nă   à   wè-fəgɔ̀   âa   ä̀á   wɛ́-gɛ̀ii
        person PROSP 3SG TRANS-wash.IRR NEG.Q 3SG.SBJV TRANS-clean.IRR
        wɛ́ íi   fɛ́ɛ   wɛ́ ä̀   dzïï̈   ä̀ tâ
        FOC LOG.SBJV before FOC 3SG put.REAL.NOM.DAT DEF fire
        'You have to wash it, right, so that it is clean before putting it on the fire.'
        [sos170822t3:308]

Both cases involve irrealis in the main clause, and thus subjunctive marking in the complement clause. In (16b), there is an unusual change from the generic mɔ̰̌ 'person' in the main clause to what appears to be the logophoric subject (or 2pl) subject in the 'before' clause; this may represent different ways of expressing general statements without an explicit subject in mind.

Finally, another example shown in (17) trades off between two speakers, with one speaker (GMT) speaking the main clause in (17a) and another (GKT) following up with the temporally subordinated clause in (17b):

(17) a. à kǎá   kəmɛ̀   nɛ̋ á à   jəgà   wétənɛ̆
       3SG side.SBJV bleach.REAL.PFV if 2SG 3SG go.down now
       'If it becomes white now, you take it down.' [sos170822t3:57]

   b. áa   fɛ́ɛ   à   jʊ́ bɛ́ cḭ́ɔ̰ɔ̰   wétənɛ̆
      2SG.SBJV before DEF water DEM scoop.REAL.NOM.DAT now
      'Before you scoop out the water.' [sos170822t3:58]

Once again, the main clause in (17a) has an irrealis verb, and so the temporally subordinated clause in (17b) uses the subjunctive TAMP marker.

20.3.2 Subordination with 'until'

Another temporal subordinator is *fɔ̋* 'until', this one much more canonically conjunction-like in its distribution than semi-verbal *fɛ́ɛ* 'before' in the last subsection. We see *fɔ̋* at the beginning of the subordinated clause, which usually shows subordinate marking after the subject and an irrealis verb. This can be seen clearly in the following elicited examples:

(18) a. mɔ̰̀   səmâ   fɔ̋   sɔ̋n-tâa   kɛ̋   bɔ́
       person dance.REAL.PFV until sun-fire.SUBORD go.IRR go.out.IRR
       'We danced until the sun came up.' [sos170728e]

   b. mó   ɲù̀   fɔ̋   kʊ́ tɔ̋ môo   kɛ̋
      1SG.EMPH run.REAL.PFV until D.DEF like 1SG.EMPH.SUBORD go.IRR
      dzìa
      tire.IRR
      'I ran until I got tired.' [sos150617e]

As the example in (18b) shows, *fɔ̋* can also be followed by *kʊ́ tɔ̋* 'like that'. The subject in both cases is subordinated and the verb (a motion verb *kɛ̋* 'go' chained with a following verb; §19.5.3) is in the irrealis.

Examples from the text collection complicate the subordinate clause a little:

(19) a. kʊ́   í   məgòo   wè kʊ́   sənáà   à   kǎ à tê fɔ̋
       D.DEF LOG hide.IRR HAB D.DEF lie.down.IRR.HAB 3SG go 3SG GEN until
       kûʊ   kɛ̋   à   nîi   bɛ̀
       D.DEF.SUBORD go.IRR 3SG pregnancy do.IRR
       'He would go and sleep with her in secret until he got her pregnant.'
       [sos171009t1: 57-58]

b. á wó bǎrǎ bɛ́ɛ   fɔ̰́   kʊ́ʊ   á wó jîo
   2SG EMPH work do.IRR.HAB until D.DEF.SBJV 2SG EMPH see.REAL.PFV
   nɛ́̃ kʊ́   nəgɩ̀   dəbë
   if D.DEF mind be.good.REAL.PRF
   'You would work until if she saw you, she would be happy.' [sos170714t2:83]

c. fɔ̰́   fôn   bǎ̰   ɲɩ̀a   íi   fôn
   until fonio beat.REAL.NOM finish.REAL.PFV 2PL.SBJV fonio
   bǎ̰á̰   ɲɩ̀a   nɛ́̃ í   fɛ́ɛ   kʊ́   dəgɔ̰̀
   beat.REAL.NOM.SBJV finish.REAL.PFV if 2SG before D.DEF moment
   nɛ̰̀   nɔ́nɛ́ sǎ̰n nî ɔɔ
   LOC food   eat.REAL.NOM.DAT
   'Until the fonio beating is done, if you finished beating the fonio, then you could go eat.' [sos170714t3:92]

In (19a), we see the same subordinate construction in the temporally subordinated clause 'until he got her pregnant'. In (19b), though, the temporal conjunction *fɔ̰́* is followed by a conditional clause, with regular conditional marking, and that conditional clause is then followed as normal by a regularly inflected clause. Finally, in (19c), the clause following *fɔ̰́* appears to be regularly inflected. There is no trace of a subordinate marker after the deverbal subject, though the verb *ɲɩ̀a* sounds more like *ɲía* here, an unexpected tonal form for this class of verb; I assume this has to do with non-final intonation. After the 'until', we see another conditional clause, followed by what looks to be a clause with the 'before' construction from §20.3.1, but here better translated as 'then'.

Rather than introducing a full clause, *fɔ̰́* can also be used with a temporal adverb or noun, as the following examples show:

(20) a. mɔ̰̀   nǎ   səmâ   fɔ̰́   kɛ̰́ɛ̰
        person PROSP dance.IRR until tomorrow
        'We will dance until tomorrow.' [sos170717e]

   b. fɔ̰́   ɲəmà-cíɛ   gó-gó-gó nɛ̰̀   áa   sɔ́   nɛ́̃ áa   kɛ̃́
      until hot.season RED-IDEO LOC 2SG.SBJV be.able if 2SG.SBJV go.IRR
      təgɔ̰̀   dɔ̀ɔ-cîe   ɲəgɔ̰̀ nɛ̰̀ à   mɔ̰̀ɛ   ɲənágbɛ́`   wè
      sit.IRR beer-house.LOC like LOC DEF person.PL entertain.IRR HAB
      ì   á   cíɛ dɔ̀ɔ wè áa   à   mì
      3PL 2SG give beer with 2SG.SBJV 3SG drink.IRR
      'Until the hot dry season, if you can go sit in somewhere like a cabaret and entertain people, they will give you beer to drink.' [sos170711t1:365]

In (20a), from elicitation, the temporal expression follows the main clause, while in (20b), from a text, it precedes it.

20.3.3 Subordination with verbal reduplication

In narratives, we find a kind of verbal reduplication that serves to temporally subordinate the clause. While in §20.3.1-§20.3.2, the subordinated clause usually followed the main clause, clauses with this verbal reduplication precede the main clause, and the temporally subordinated clause has the meaning of 'once' or 'after', i.e. its action is completed before the action of the main clause.

Because it it is full reduplication, it is difficult to say which copy is the base and which the reduplicant. Segmentally, the verb takes its realis stem form, and the second copy carries the perfective tone (X for X-toned verbs and H for H- and S-toned verbs). The first copy surfaces as LS for X-toned verbs, and as S with H- and S-toned verbs, as in verb nominalization (§13.3.1). Table 20.1 illustrates these tone patterns.

Tab. 20.1: Temporally subordinated reduplication

Base form	Reduplicated form	Gloss
fà̰	fă̰-fà̰	'enter'
kà	kă-kà	'go'
ŋmá	ŋmă-ŋmá	'eat (meat)'
sú	sío-sío	'get up'
bá̰	bá̰-bá̰	'hit'
nɔ̋	nɔ́-nɔ́	'eat'

The first copy of H- and S-toned verbs sounds a little bit like a SH contour tone, but I suspect this is an anticipatory effect of the following H tone.

Since the meaning of the reduplicated verb is perfective and the second copy is identical to regular perfective verbs, I will gloss the first copy as the reduplicant and the second copy as perfective.

The following elicited examples illustrate the basic use of this reduplicated verb form:

(21) a. *móő cěrě-cěrë̀ jəgěe fà̰ mó*
 1SG.EMPH.PST RED-sleep.REAL.PFV dog.PST enter.REAL.PFV 1SG.EMPH
 tḛ̀ cîe
 GEN house.LOC
 'When I had fallen asleep, the dog entered my house.' [sos150806e]

 b. *móő fă̰-fà̰ móő səŋâ*
 1SG.EMPH.PST RED-enter.REAL.PFV 1SG.EMPH.PST lie.down.REAL.PFV
 'When I got home, I went to bed.' [sos150620e]

As these examples show, the clause with the reduplicated verb comes first, and it indicates that the action has already taken place and has set the stage for the next clause. Consultants translate it into French either with *quand* or *lorsque* ('when' or 'once').

This form is very common in narratives, serving to subordinate a clause and set its action as the background to the subsequent main clause. For example:

(22) a. ǎ jɔ́ɔ-jɔ́ɔ tóò wè, ǎ lɛ̀ né ǎ gôɔ
3SG RED-search.REAL.PFV axe with 3SG SUBORD come.IRR DEF wood
tsɪ̀
cut.IRR
'Once she had looked around for the axe, she came to cut down the tree.'
[sos130828t1:42]

b. ǎ kǎ-kà wé tsɛ́ fên sɪ̌
3SG RED-go.REAL.PFV FOC INDF thing be
'When he went, there was something [there].' [sos170711t1:9]

c. ǎ ɲǐa-ɲìa ɪ̀ ɲɯ́ɪ bä̀ ǎ kä̀ mɔ̀mä́
3SG RED-finish.REAL.PFV 3PL honey do.REAL.PFV 3SG in.hand a.lot
mɛ̀ kɛ́ à wè í jərâ
3SG.SUBORD go.IRR 3SG with LOG home
'When it was finished, they gave him a lot of honey and he took it home.'
[sos130828t2:10]

d. ǎ dənɪ́ bɛ́ fəgɔ̌-fəgɔ̀, mɛ̀ ŋənɔ̂ səgù,
DEF child.PL DEM.PL RED-wash.REAL.PFV 3SG.SUBORD oil apply.IRR
mɛ̀ sú ìi kɛ́ ìi lő ŋənɔ̂
3SG.SUBORD get.up.IRR LOG.SBJV go.IRR LOG.SBJV come.IRR oil
səgù í dòn mɛ̀
apply.IRR LOG child with
'Once she had washed those children, she applied oil, she got up to put oil on her child.' [sos130828t1:8]

These examples show that the subsequent clauses to the reduplicated clause can either be regularly inflected main clauses (22a-c) or chained clauses (22d) as discussed in §20.2.

20.3.4 Conditionals as temporal subordination

A common form of temporal subordination similar in meaning to the reduplicated forms in §20.3.3 is the use of the conditional. This construction is discussed in greater depth in §18.2.3. Illustrative examples are given in (23):

(23) a. mɛ̏   í   bɛ̋   ì̀   wɛ́ ä!   ì̀   ké í   wóo
3SG.SUBORD LOG do.IRR COMP FOC INTERJ COMP COP LOG EMPH.SBJV
sǐ   jṳ̀-jɔ́ɔ   nɛ̋ məgǒn-cəbɛ̏ɛ̏   fə̀
be mountain-stroll.REAL.PFV if monitor.lizard.SBJV enter.REAL.PFV
nɛ̋ í   gṳ̀   kɔ́ɔ lɛ̏ í   wó   lé   ə̏   sḭ̀ɛ   nɛ̋ lé í
if LOG under hole DAT LOG EMPH SBJV 3SG dig.REAL.NOM if FOC LOG
wóo…   í   ə̀   tò   wɛ́ ŋɛ́
EMPH.SBJV LOG 3SG know.IRR FOC NEG
'He said, "Ah! I was hunting, when a monitor went into a hole underneath me and when I was digging I…. I don't know."' [sos170711t1:17-19]

b. né   dəgɔ̏   nɛ̋ kʊ́   tɔ̋ í   lɛ̏ mó   nə̌   màa
1SG.SBJV greet.REAL.PFV if D.DEF like 2PL DAT 1SG.EMPH PROSP again
jíaa   móo   ń̀   təgɔ̋n nɛ̏-jṳ̀   í   wó lɛ̏
return.IRR 1SG.EMPH.SBJV 1SG name TRANS-say.IRR 2PL EMPH DAT
'Now that I have greeted you, I will come back and introduce myself.'
[sos171009t1:8-9]

In both of these examples, the clause with the conditional is not hypothetical; the action has already taken place, and it, like the reduplicated verb form in §20.3.3, sets the stage for the main clause that follows.

For further discussion of conditionals more broadly, see Chapter 18.

21 Information structure and discourse

This chapter addresses aspects of information structure and discourse in Seenku. I begin with a discussion of possible focus strategies in §21.1, though as we will see, none of these constructions are unequivocally related to focus as opposed to emphasis or topicalization. I turn to explicitly topicalizing constructions in §21.2, which tends to be clause-level topicalization in Seenku. The chapter concludes with sections related specifically to discourse, including discourse particles (§21.3), interjections (§21.4), greetings and benedictions (§21.5), and finally some brief remarks on discourse structure in narratives (§21.6), including observations about turn-taking and back-channeling.

21.1 Focus and information structure

Focus is linguistic encoding of new or contrastive information, seemingly a task that every language should be equipped to carry out. However, focus strategies familiar in European languages like English are not used in Seenku—we do not see clefting or fronting of focused elements, nor do we find prosodic cues for focus like higher pitch (given the high functional load of tone) or even expanded pitch range. Indeed, my early attempts at focus elicitation appeared to yield no results whatsoever for focus marking. Unlike other West African languages like Fulfulde or the Dogon languages (e.g. Heath 2008, McPherson 2013, etc.), there is no effect of focus on verb inflection. And even focus strategies from other Mande languages like Toura (Bearth 1992), with a mobile focus marker *le*, or Wan (Nikitina 2018), with a subject focus marking *laa*, find no parallels in Seenku.

Of course, Seenku speakers are just as capable of expressing subtleties of information structure, but exact parallels between Seenku strategies and more familiar focus strategies are not forthcoming. Some of the constructions I will discuss here do not even encode focus so much as other aspects of information structure, like emphasis.

The constructions covered in this section include the following: First, like many Mande languages, Seenku has a range of emphatic pronouns (analyzed as focalized in some Mande languages), formed by the addition of the particle *wó*. These were first discussed in the context of the pronominal system in §6.2, but I will treat them in §21.1.1 below as they pertain to information structure. Second, there are a couple of particles (§21.1.2) which appear to indicate broad focus. Third, clauses introduced by the copula (§21.1.3) may also be involved in broad focus marking. Finally, in negative clauses, the appearance of the discourse definite *kʋ́*, typically before the auxiliary, indicates focus on the negation (§21.1.4). As stated above, all of these strategies are only tentatively related to focus, but all of them pertain to information structure. Deeper and more systematic investigation will be required to clarify the uses and meanings of each. I provide ample examples in each subsection below to illustrate the distribution and usage so that the reader can evaluate for him- or herself these hypotheses.

Before turning to these subsections, I will first illustrate the lack of explicit focus marking turned up by some common focus elicitation strategies. Focus marking commonly occurs cross-linguistically in response to wh-questions, focalizing the new information added by the response. In Seenku, there is no overt marking in this environment:

(1) a. á ná kǘɔ mḭ́
    2SG PROSP go.IRR where
    'Where are you going?' [sos150630e]

 b. mó ná kɛ́̃ Sía
    1SG.EMPH PROSP go.IRR Bobo
    'I am going to Bobo-Dioulasso.' [sos150630e]

 c. á sḭ̀ fə̀lé tǎ   nɛ́̃
    2SG be what cook.REAL.NOM LOC
    'What are you cooking?' [sos120109e]

 d. ń sḭ̀ kʊ̀ tǎ   nɛ́̃
    1SG be toh cook.REAL.NOM LOC
    'I'm cooking toh.' [sos120109e]

In the question-answer pair in (1a-b), the wh-word mḭ́ 'where' is replaced by Sía 'Bobo-Dioulasso'. This location is not marked with any focus particles or with any pitch changes, nor is it fronted or otherwise displaced. The difference in the form of the verb in the question likewise does not play any role—consultants reported that kɛ́̃ could be used in (1a) with no difference in meaning. Similarly, in (1c-d), fə̀lé 'what' in the question is replaced with the answer kʊ̀ 'toh' with no overt focus marking. Notice also that the form of the pronoun does not appear to be correlated with any focus on the response to the question; the emphatic 1sg mó is used in (1b) but the regular 1sg ń is used in (1d).

I also tried to find contrastive focus in elicitation, but here too, no clear focus strategies were revealed:

(2) a. á wó lɛ́̃ kʊ̀ níɔ↘
    1SG EMPH PST toh eat.REAL.PFV.Q
    'Did you eat toh?' [sos150630e]

b. őȍő	mó	lɛ̋	kɜ̀kâ	ŋmá
   INTERJ 1SG.EMPH PST meat eat.REAL.PFV
   'No, I ate meat.' [sos150630e]

c. mó	nǎ	kòee	ŋɛ́ mó	nǎ	səmâ
   1SG.EMPH PROSP sing.ANTIP.IRR NEG 1SG.EMPH PROSP dance.IRR
   'I'm not going to sing, I'm going to dance.' [sos150630e]

First, I tried a question-answer pair shown in (2a-b), where the response corrects false information in the polar question. There was no focus marking; instead, kʊ̀ 'toh' was simply replaced by kɜ̀kâ 'meat' without any prosodic or morphosyntactic marking. Even the verb, which had to change from níɔ for the eating of soft foods to ŋmá for the eating of meat and other foods requiring chewing, showed no special marking that would draw attention to this difference. In (2c), where the speaker contrasts something that did not occur with what actually occurred, no special marking was used in either clause. The structure is exactly parallel.

In the subsections below, I lay out some elements and constructions that appear to relate to focus, again with the caveat that these would benefit from further research.

21.1.1 Emphatic pronouns

Like many Mande languages, Seenku has a range of emphatic pronouns (also referred to as focalized pronouns in some languages, see e.g. Babaev 2010). These are formed by adding the emphatic particle wó after the pronoun. In combination with 1sg ń, it systematically merges to form the emphatic pronoun mó, and 2sg and 3sg combinations á wó and ǎ wǒ can optionally merge to create óo and ǒo, respectively.

I refer to these pronouns as emphatic rather than focalized or focused, since they do not obligatorily encode a focus reading on the argument represented by the pronoun. Nikitina (2018) likewise writes that for Wan, emphatic pronouns are used when the subject is in focus or the pronoun is topicalized but that they typically do not co-occur with explicit focus marking. In Seenku, we find these emphatic pronouns even when another argument is focused in the clause, such as in the wh-question/response pair in (3):

(3) a. á	wó	sı̋o	bî	sǎ	nɛ̋	té	c̀ɪɛ
       2SG EMPH REC.PST goat buy.REAL.NOM LOC who give.IRR
       'Who did you just buy a goat for?' [sos150619e]

   b. mó	sı̋o	ǎ	sǎ	nɛ̋	ń	ní	c̀ɪɛ
      1SG.EMPH REC.PST 3SG buy.REAL.NOM LOC 1SG father give.IRR
      'I just bought it for my father.' [sos150619e]

Here, the indirect object is the focused element in the clause, but the subjects in both the question and the response still use the emphatic pronouns. Note also in (3b) the omission or backgrounding of given information (the direct object *bî* 'goat' replaced with the 3sg pronoun *ǎ*), which contributes to the overall focus placed on other arguments in the clause.

We find a hierarchy in terms of how frequently the emphatic particle is used with different person/number combinations:

(4)   1sg > 2sg,pl > 3sg

In the corpus of glossed texts, the emphatic 1sg *mó* outnumbers the plain pronoun 5-to-1 (132 to 26); in other words, it appears to be the default form of the 1sg. For the 2sg, we find an even split: 187 instances of both the emphatic and the non-emphatic pronouns. The emphatic 3sg is extremely rare, attested only 13 times compared to the non-emphatic *ǎ*, which shows up an impressive 974 times. This latter figure is perhaps unsurprising if we consider that most of the time, if focus will be placed on a noun, then it will not be replaced by a pronoun; for the 1st and 2nd person, on the other hand, the only option is to use a pronoun, but still, we see a difference between the the 1sg and 2sg in terms of distribution. As laid out in §6.2, the 1pl has no emphatic form (*mǐ wő).

In the following conversational exchange, we find nothing but emphatic pronouns used for both the 1sg and the 2pl:

(5)   a.   mó   nəgì sĭ ǎ   jén-jén   təmé-cę̧   nὲ̀ mais mó
           1SG.EMPH mind be DEF RED-story tell-manner LOC but.FR 1SG.EMPH
           nəgì́ ɲá   ǎ   kɔ́rɔ́   nὲ̀ ɲέ
           mind be.NEG 3SG meaning.JU LOC NEG
           'I remember how that riddle is told, but I don't remember its answer.'
           [sos161009t1:10]

      b.   donc, mó   nǎ   wé   nìgì   mɔ̀mɛ̧̆   tő   dɔ̀n   í   wó
           SO.FR 1SG.EMPH PROSP FOC COW.PL a.lot.PL take.IRR today 2PL EMPH
           kὰ̀
           in.hand
           'So, it's me who will get a lot of cows with you all today.' [sos161009t1:11]

The 1sg in both subject NPs in (5a) takes the emphatic form *mó*, even though there is nothing in the context that would indicate that the subject should be focused. In the response, on the other hand, the subject could be understood with focus ("so I'm the one who's going to be getting a lot of cows", the figurative prize for stumping others with riddles), or it could be broad focus on the whole statement. Either way, the focus here appears to be indicated not with the emphatic pronoun *mó* (since the 2pl in the

PP is also emphatic), but rather with the focus particle *wé* following the prospective auxiliary; I will address this focus particle in §21.1.2.1 below.

21.1.2 Focus particles

In natural speech (but only rarely in elicitation), we see two particles *wé* and *ŋǎ*, which share a similar distribution: after an auxiliary, if present, otherwise after a wh-word or after the VP and any other particles associated with it (including the conditional particle *nɛ̋* 'if'); however, we cannot say that they are clause-final, since they can be followed by other adverbs or PPs or the negative. The two particles differ in that *ŋǎ* is more narrow, used only in interrogatives, whereas *wé* can be used in both interrogatives and indicatives; in interrogatives, it has a more polite reading than *ŋǎ*, which has an element of abruptness, exasperation, or directness to it. However, consultants report that the two can be used together (in the order *wé ŋǎ*) in interrogatives, which means they do not occupy the same position or fulfill the same function.

My best interpretation is that these particles encode broad focus, and as such, I will gloss them as FOC; this is, however, only a tentative analysis, and they may be involved in information structure in another way. Further analysis will have to await future work.

I will discuss each particle in turn.

21.1.2.1 *wé*

The particle *wé* almost never appears in elicited speech, but is quite frequent in naturally occurring speech. Since it can appear after irrealis verbs, it can sometimes look like the habitual marker, but the habitual never surfaces with H tone (instead surfacing as *wè* or *wɛ̋*, depending upon the sandhi trigger). The focus particle *wé*, on the other hand, is invariably H-toned.

Consultants cannot articulate what this particle does—sentences are just as grammatical without it, often even in the same contexts. The distribution, however, is consistent with broad focus, bringing attention to the whole clause in which it appears.

The placement of the particle in the clause is predictable: If there is an auxiliary verb, it appears after the auxiliary, even if the auxiliary is in the conditional (6c):

(6) a. donc, *mó   nǎ   wé nìgì   mɔ̀mɛ̋ tő   dɔ̀n í   wó*
       SO.FR 1SG.EMPH PROSP FOC COW.PL a.lot.PL take.IRR today 2PL EMPH
       kä̀
       in.hand
       'So, it's me who will get a lot of cows with you all today.' [sos161009t1:11]

b. ŋ́gǎa mó   nǎ   wé ǎ   jú   í   lɛ̀   né   í
but 1SG.EMPH PROSP FOC 3SG say.IRR 2PL DAT 1SG.COMP 2PL
pó-pǒe   kúnâ   wé
RED-all.PL good.morning FOC
'But I will say to all of you, "good morning".' [sos171009t1:7]

c. áa   sɪ̌ ně wé nân   nı́ɔ   ně á   á   cè
2SG.SBJV be if FOC sauce eat.REAL.NOM LOC 2SG 2SG hand
fɛ̀ɛ   tɔ́-tɔ́
lick.IRR.HAB RED-like
'If you are eating sauce, you lick your hand like that.' [sos161009t1:27]

In (6a-b), the focus particle comes after the prospective auxiliary. The example in (6a) was translated to me with this cleft construction, suggesting that the focus could be on the subject, but the whole clause, with its statement of finding a lot of cows, is relatively new in the discourse and could have broad focus. In (6b), the subject is an emphatic 1sg, as it is in (6a), but there is no subject focus reading. The example in (6c) shows that it is not necessary to have an emphatic pronoun in these constructions. It also shows the focus particle following the conditional; focus is commonly placed on conditional clauses in Seenku.

If there is no auxiliary, then the particle appears after the predicate (be that verbal or non-verbal):

(7) a. á   kʊ́   jù̀   wé   ŋé
2SG D.DEF say.IRR FOC NEG
'Don't even say that!' [sos161009t1:17]

b. ı̌ı   í   bà   ně wé kɛ́   jén-jén   fı́n wé
3PL.SBJV LOG do.REAL.PFV if FOC COP RED-story two FOC
'If that's what they say, then they are two different riddles.' [sos161009t1:52]

c. ı̀   wɛ̀   ǎ   tɛ̀ɛ   wé ɲì-nà   mɛ̀   təgʊ̀ wé
3PL SUBORD 3SG leave.IRR FOC there-towards 3SG.SUBORD sit FOC
ǎ   kɔ̀ɔ lɛ̀   kʊ́rʊ́ʊʊ
DEF hole DAT long.time
'They left him there and he sat in that hole for a long time.' [sos170711t1:27]

In (7a), the focus particle follows the irrealis verb of an imperative, where no auxiliary is present. In (7b), there are two instances of the focus particle: first, after the conditional verb in the first clause (showing again the predilection of the conditional for focus), then again after the non-verbal predicate *jén-jén fı́n* 'two stories'. In (7c), it likewise appears twice, once after each irrealis verb.

Interestingly, we also see an example where the focus particle occurs after a wh-word, despite there being an auxiliary present earlier in the clause:

(8) m̰ǎ ná kʊ́ jù tsɛ̰́ wé sɛ́ɛ̰-kû nɛ̰̀
person PROSP D.DEF say.IRR how FOC Sambla-thing LOC
'How do you say it in Seenku?' [sos161009t1:114]

When asked, consultants note that the particle could also have been said after the auxiliary.

We find *wé* in questions, both polar questions and wh-questions. For instance:

(9) a. m̰ǎ ná wé ɲəgɔ̰́-jʊ̋ jʊ̋ wé mḭ́-nǎ
person PROSP FOC potash-water find.IRR FOC where-towards
'Where will we [be able to] find potash water?' [sos170822t2:48]

b. mais dɔ̀ɔ sḭ̌ wé té tɛ̀
but.FR beer be FOC who GEN
'But who has beer?' [sos170822t12:109]

c. ḭ̀ kɛ́ té lɛ̰̀ à̰ nɨ̈i fà̰ wé á nɛ̰̀
COMP COP who SUBORD 3SG pregnancy put.in.REAL.PFV FOC 2SG LOC
'[They asked] who was it who got you pregnant?' [sos171009t1:61]

d. í kà̰ wé ǎ̰ jəgí mǎasín né nɛ̰̀ wé
2PL go.REAL.PFV FOC 3SG grind.IRR machine which LOC FOC
'Which machine did you go grind it in?' [sos170822t2:468]

In (9a) and (9d), we see two occurrences each of the focus particle.

21.1.2.2 ŋǎ̰

Another focus particle, *ŋǎ̰*, follows the same placement rules as *wé*, but it is only attested in questions.

(10) a. á sḭ̌ ŋǎ̰ kʊ́ tʊ́̋ kú lɛ́ bǎ nɛ́̋
2SG be FOC D.DEF like thing which do.REAL.NOM LOC
'What are you doing like that?' [Mamadou Diabate, p.c.]

b. kɛ́ fɛ̀n né ŋǎ̰
COP thing which
'What is it?!' [Mamadou Diabate, p.c.]

I have been told that both of these questions would have an insisting or aggressive feeling to them (unless they are played on the balafon, in which case that aggressiveness is not felt; see §22.2.1). For instance, for (10b), it could be said in a case where someone looks at something, looks away, looks back at it again, looks away, and repeats this several times until the person with them becomes exasperated and asks the question in that way with *ŋǎ̰*.

Examples from texts include:

(11) a. mó   sĩ ằ tê fɔ̋   ằ   mɔ̰̀   kɔ́-kɔ̋ɛ   lê   ké fə̀né
       1SG.EMPH be 3SG GEN must 3SG person RED-short.PL PRES COP what
       ŋằ
       FOC
       'I want to know those short people there, what are they?' [sos161009t1:172]

   b. ì̋   fên   kű ɔ-ɲènènènè lê   ằ   sï ɔ   ŋằ   mí̋
      COMP thing fresh-IDEO   PRES 3SG arrive.REAL.PRF FOC where
      mɔ̰̀   gṵ̀
      person under
      '[They asked] that wet thing there, where did it come from here underneath us?' [sos170805t15:86]

The emphasis or focus encoded with ŋằ in (11a) is because the speaker is bringing attention back to this question after the conversation got derailed. In (11b), the emphatic use of ŋằ encodes disgust at the presence of a toad.

When asked whether both wé and ŋằ could be used together in (11b), consultants answered in the affirmative (i.e. ằ sïɔ wé ŋằ mí̋ mɔ̰̀ gṵ̀, sos190803e).

For emphatic discourse particles, not tied to focus but instead encoding speaker attitude, see §21.3.

21.1.3 Clauses introduced by the copula as a focus strategy

In §14.1, I introduced the equative copula ké (or variant kê), which precedes the predicate NP. In natural speech, it is not uncommon to find full regularly inflected clauses introduced by the copula. According to speakers, there is no great difference in meaning whether or not the copula is used. The contexts in which it is found, however, are consistent with the interpretation that this copula marks broad focus. Consider the example in (12b), with its context provided in (12a):

(12) a. mí̋ nḯi   bú-bəlĕ   kűɛ   lɛ̋   ằ   jú   tsɛ̋̃   mí̋i
       1PL father.PL RED-big.PL other.PL SUBORD 3SG say.IRR how 1PL.DAT
       tsɛ̋̃-ké mí̋ nḯi   lɛ̋   ằ   jú   tsɛ̋̃
       and   1PL father.PL SUBORD 3SG say.IRR how
       'How our grandfathers tell us, and how our fathers tell it...' [sos170711t1:6]

   b. ké   kərê sío   jṵ̀-jɔ́ɔ   wɛ́
      COP man get.up.REAL.PFV bush-stroll.NOM with
      'A man got up to go hunting.' [sos170711t1:7]

As (12b) shows, the copula occurs at the beginning of the sentence and is followed by a regular indicative clause; there is no difference in verb inflection, TAMP markers, or anything else between this expression and one without the copula. Here, we could say that the copula is equating what it was that the fathers and grandfathers said (12a) with the beginning of the story of the arrival of the balafon ("[What they said] is that a man got up to go hunting."). However, this is all new information for the listener, and the use of the copula *ké* may be placing broad focus on it.

In other cases, there is no clear way to tie the copula to an equative reading like this to something else that was explicitly mentioned in the discourse. For instance, preceding the example in (13), another speaker was talking about how putting a spider egg sac over a hole in the calabash resonator augments the sound of the balafon. His interlocutor chimes in:

(13) ké kʊ́ à gərè dəbè wè
 COP D.DEF 3SG voice make.good.IRR HAB
 '[It is the case that] it makes its voice nice.' [sos170711t1:123]

Once again, this is consistent with broad focus marking, bringing attention to the purpose of putting these spider egg sacs onto the instrument.

These focused clauses can occur in any aspect; above, we have seen a perfective and a habitual; the examples in (14) illustrate a prospective, a progressive, and even two non-verbal predicates:

(14) a. ké mó cè nǎ wétənɛ̌ ǎ kú bé jǜ
 COP 1SG.EMPH hand PROSP now DEF thing DEM say.IRR
 'My hand will now say the thing [on the balafon].' [sos170711t1:210]

 b. kʊ́ʊ í sı̌ bʋ̰̀ɛ kǎa nɛ̋
 D.DEF.COP 2PL be djinn chase.REAL.NOM LOC
 'That there is you chasing the djinn.' [sos170714t3:11]

 c. ké kű́ɛ fáná ké kɛ̋
 COP other.PL also COP griot.PL
 '[It is the case that] they are also griots.' [sos171009t1:96]

 d. ké ǎ sı̌ mɔ̰̀mɑ̋
 COP 3SG be a.lot
 'There are a lot [of generations].' [sos171009t1:77]

In (14b), we see that the discourse definite copula (§14.1.3) can also be used to introduce clauses. Here, the discourse definite is referring to the action the speakers are watching in the video, which this speaker has just been describing. He states that that action is what is known as "chasing the djinn" (a fonio farming technique). In this case, the discourse definite copula does appear to be adding more information, not only drawing attention to the whole clause but also linking it to a salient entity in the discourse (the action in the video).

To check whether *ké* and the focus particle *wé* can co-occur, I asked a consultant about the grammaticality of including both in (14a). Once again, the two are able to occur together, as follows (though the consultant preferred it without the discourse adverb *wétənĕ* 'now'):

(15) ké mó cè̌ nǎ wé à̌ kú bé jǜ
 COP 1SG.EMPH hand PROSP FOC DEF thing DEM say.IRR
 'My hand will now say the thing [on the balafon].' [sos190803e]

The focus particle takes its usual place after the prospective auxiliary.

I refer readers to the archive to see these examples in their natural contexts, which set them up for a broad focus interpretation.

21.1.4 Focused negation with discourse definite *kʊ́*

The last focus strategy I will discuss is specifically tied to focus of negation. When speakers wish to emphasize negation (or perhaps a whole negative clause—the scope of focus is not entirely clear), they may use a discourse definite pronoun *kʊ́* that precedes the predicate. Linearly, this means that *kʊ́* will either appear before the auxiliary, if present, before the object of a transitive verb if no auxiliary is present, or directly before an intransitive verb in the absence of an auxiliary.

I first present examples from elicitation, though in the case of (15c), the phrase was elicited during the translation of a folktale (sos150626t2).

(16) a. mó kʊ́ nǎ sɔ́ móo kɛ́ cɔ̌ ɲɛ́
 1SG.EMPH D.DEF PROSP arrive.IRR 1SG.SBJV go.IRR village NEG
 'I would not be able to go to the village.' [sos150618e]

 b. à̌ ɲá A nè̌ ɲɛ́, à̌ kʊ́ ɲá B nè̌ ɲɛ́
 3SG be.NEG A LOC NEG 3SG D.DEF be.NEG B LOC NEG
 'It's not in A, it's not in B.' [sos170802e]

 c. dên kʊ́ ɲá kərù̌ tè̌ bò̌ ɲɛ́
 black.bean D.DEF be.NEG hyena GEN anymore NEG
 'The hyena no longer has any black beans.' [sos150704e]

The discourse definite cannot be interpreted as an object in any of these examples, since the slot between the subject and an auxiliary is not an argument position.

In texts, we find examples like the following:

(17) a. kərṳ̀ dzía-dzía sɔ́ŋ́ nɛ̰̀, dzɔ́ sḭ̌ ằ lé, ằ
hyena RED-tire.REAL.PFV moment.REL LOC hunger be 3SG DAT 3SG
kʊ́ ɲá füi jǐo nɛ́̋ ŋɛ́
D.DEF be.NEG nothing see.REAL.NOM NEG
'When hyena got tired out, he was hungry, he wasn't finding anything.'
[sos161009t1:186]

b. dɔ́ɔní âa tsíɛɛ á kɛ̋ dɔ̋ɔ tsɛ̋ dəgɔ̌ɛɛ nɛ̋
a.little 2SG.SUBORD speak.IRR 2SG go.IRR finish.IRR INDF place LOC
ằ kʊ́ nǎ ɲá sɛ́ɛ̰-kû ŋɛ́
3SG D.DEF PROSP be.NEG Sambla-thing LOC
'You speak a little and you go end up somewhere that is not Seenku.'
[sos170702t1:26]

c. ằ dö̀ kʊ́ bá̰à̰ brɛ̰̀ wè ŋɛ́ mais ḭ̀ wɛ̀ ằ
3SG though D.DEF balafon play.IRR HAB NEG but.FR 3PL SUBORD 3SG
cɛ̀rɛ̰̋ ḭ̀ kɛ́ kâ
call.IRR COMP COP griot
'Him, though, he does not play the balafon, but they [still] call him a griot.'
[sos171009t1:90]

d. mó kʊ́ ɲà̰ fɛ̰̋ ằ nɛ̰̀ ŋɛ́
1SG.EMPH D.DEF finish.REAL.PFV yet 3SG LOC NEG
'I haven't finished with that yet.' [sos171009t1:115]

Deeper study will be required to definitively say that *kʊ́* in these cases contributes focus, and if so, what the scope of that focus is.

As with *kɛ́* above, the particle *wé* can co-occur with *kʊ́* negatives. A consultant accepted the following rendition of (17d) as grammatical:

(18) mó kʊ́ ɲà̰ fɛ̰̋ wé ằ nɛ̰̀ ŋɛ́
1SG.EMPH D.DEF finish.REAL.PFV yet FOC 3SG LOC NEG
'I haven't finished with that yet.' [sos190803e]

The focus particle *wé* occurs after the adverb *fɛ̰̋* but before the PP. It is not entirely clear what the difference in meaning is with and without the focus particle.

21.2 Topicalization

We find a couple of discourse markers with an explicitly topicalizing function. The first is phrase-final *íaa*, which can topicalize an NP or a clause (§21.2.1). The second is a loanword from Jula *kɔ̀nì*, with more nativized variants like *kʊ́ nɛ̰̀* (§21.2.2).

21.2.1 Phrase-final *íaa*

The phrase-final discourse particle *íaa* (IPA [jaː]) introduces a new topic of discussion. It can follow a full clause, as in (19a-b), or more commonly, it follows a noun phrase, as in (19c-d):

(19) a. í   wó   kɔ̀sî   sagɔ̌ bɔ̀ɔ tsɛ́   sı̌   wé   íaa
         LOG EMPH friend good old INDF be FOC TOP
         'They say, there is a good old friend from a long time back.' [sos161009t1:33]

     b. dɔ̃nké kʊ́   nɛ̀   wétanɛ̌ dɔ̀,   ń   tɛ́   bɔ̃̀-kɔ̃ɔ   à
         SO.FR D.DEF LOC now   EMPH 1SG dear billygoat 3SG
         síɔ   ì   wɔ̀   lɛ̀   kʊ́   dagɔ̌εε bé   nɛ̃̀   íaa
         be.able.REAL.PFV 3PL EMPH DAT D.DEF place   DEM LOC TOP
         'So, as for that now, Mr. Billygoat showed them up there.' [sos150626t4:69]

     c. à   kǎa-kà   wé   tsɛ́ fên   sı̌   ɲì,   magɔ̌n-cabèè   íaa, á
         3SG RED-go.REAL.PFV FOC INDF thing be there monitor-lizard TOP 2SG
         magɔ̌n-cabèè   tó   kɛ̃̀
         monitor-lizard know.IRR EMPH
         'When he had gone, there was something there, a monitor lizard, you know the monitor lizard!' [sos170711t1:9]

     d. bậạ   nằ   tsɛ̃́ sɛ́ɛ-ŋè   tè   íaa
         balafon.SUBORD come.REAL.PFV how Sambla-HUM.PL GEN TOP
         'The way the balafon came to Sambla country....' [sos170711t1:5]

In (19a), the discourse particle *íaa* follows the first line of a riddle that the speaker is introducing. In (19b), the use of *íaa* after this clause highlights the situation that the billygoat was triumphant in defeating the hyena and his family, and the speaker returns to this point in the next sentence. More canonically, though, *íaa* follows NPs, whether they are simple nouns, as in (19c), or nominalized clauses, as in (19d). The particle identifies the NP as being the topic of discussion in the coming discourse.

In both configurations (following a clause or following an NP), *íaa* marks the end of a phonological phrase. That is, we do not find *íaa* after an NP in situ, such as a subject or object. The NP must stand alone as its own phrase.

21.2.2 *kɔ̀nì* 'as for'

Another topicalizing strategy uses the phrase *kɔ̀nì*. This expression is found in other languages of the region, including Jula and Jalkunan (Heath 2017). Because of its Jula origins, I will gloss it as TOP.JU.

(20) a. tsɛ́ sḭ̌ kɔ̀nì mɔ̌ɔ̰ kʊ́ tə̀mè wè kʊ́ kɔ̀nì ké
INDF be TOP.JU person.PST D.DEF tell.IRR HAB D.DEF TOP.JU COP
sɛ́ɛ̰-kû ŋé, mais mɔ̌ɔ̰ à tə̀mè wè
Sambla-thing NEG but.FR person.PST 3SG tell.IRR HAB
'There was one that people used to tell, it wasn't in Seenku, but people used to tell it.' [sos161009t1:111]

b. puisque mɔ̂ɛ́ɛ nɛ́ kɔ̀nì mɔ̰̌ mɔ́ɛ̰̀ɛ̰ tsḭ̀ḭ
since.FR millet.SBJV if TOP.JU person millet cut.IRR.HAB
ɲì-nà kpéè wè
there-towards knife with
'Since if it was millet, we would harvest millet with a knife.' [sos170702t1:44]

In (20a), we see it immediately after a subject, whereas in (20b), it comes at the end of the conditional clause.

There is some variation in this form. Some speakers appear to have reinterpreted it as kʊ́ nɛ̀, or the discourse definite pronoun followed by the locative; others use kɔ̀nɛ̀, a sort of intermediate form between kɔ̀nì and kʊ́ nɛ̀. For instance:

(21) a. ȉi à jío tsɛ́ ǎ kɔ̀nɛ̀ lɛ́ sḭ̌ təgɔ́ɛɛ tɛ́
3PL.SUBORD 3SG say.REAL.PFV how 3SG FOC.JU PST be certain.PL GEN
jȉ nɛ̀
fetish LOC
'As they said, it [the flute] was at some other people's houses for their fetishes.' [sos170823t8:99]

b. donc kʊ́ nɛ̀ wétə̀nɛ̌ kə̀rṳ íaa (tsɛ́ké) sà-bɔ̀-kɔ̌ɔ sɔ́n
SO.FR D.DEF LOC now hyena TOP and second.son-billygoat rain
bə̀lɛ̌ bǎa tsɛ́ bḭ̀ɛ̰
big IDEO INDF rain.REAL.PFV
'So, now, there was once a hyena and a billygoat, and there was a really big rain.' [sos150626t4:1]

The reinterpretation as kʊ́ nɛ̀ is especially common as shown in (21b), where it forms a phrase of its own, often followed by wétə̀nɛ̌ 'now' (§21.3.4). This example is the slow beginning of a folk tale as the speaker tries to recall its various elements. The phrase kʊ́ nɛ̀ wétə̀nɛ̌ attracts the listener's attention and alerts him that a new topic is coming, while íaa after 'hyena' flags this actor as a key participant in the following tale. For more on íaa, see §21.2.1 above.

21.3 Discourse markers

Seenku displays a range of discourse markers; discourse particles tend to be clause-final, while discourse adverbials may appear in multiple places. Many of the particles find cognates or correlates in Jula or other Mande languages of the region. I first address two emphatic particles, *lɛ́* and *kɛ̀* in §21.3.1. I then turn to the clause-final particle *òo* in §21.3.2, which has uses as both a disjunctive particle as well as an exclamatory particle. The impatience particle *sá̰* is addressed in §21.3.3, and finally the discourse adverbial *wétə̀nɛ̌* 'now' is covered in §21.3.4.

21.3.1 Emphatic particles

21.3.1.1 *lɛ́*

The Seenku cognate of the Jula emphatic *dé* is S-toned *lɛ́*. Its addition to the end of a clause adds a sense of insistence or emphasis:

(22) a. *Fátù, á jǐjǎ lɛ́*
 Fatou 2SG try.hard.JU EMPH
 'Fatou, think hard! Try hard!' [sos161009t1:49]

 b. *dɔ̌nké ké kəré-bé lɛ̀ lɔ́ lɛ́*
 SO.FR COP man-NOM PRES here EMPH
 'So that there is manliness!' [sos170714t2:21]

 c. *ǎ ɲəmǎkórɔ̀ sìɔ lɛ́*
 EXCL Nyumakoro arrive.REAL.PRF EMPH
 'Ah, Nyumakoro has arrived!' [sos170714t2:86]

This particle is comparatively less common in the corpus of texts than *kɛ̀*, addressed in the next subsection.

21.3.1.2 *kɛ̀*

By far the most common emphatic particle in Seenku is *kɛ̀*, which has no discernible difference in meaning from *lɛ́*. This particle is also attested in related Dzùùngoo (Solomiac 2007:257), though not in local Jula, to the best of my knowledge. Examples of *kɛ̀* include:

(23) a. ké ǎ nìgì nǒo ɲì í wó lɛ̏, í wó kʊ́ jṳ̀
COP DEF COW.PL come.NE there 2PL EMPH DAT 2PL EMPH D.DEF say.IRR
kɛ̏
EMPH
'There are the cows coming towards you, say the answer!' [sos161009t1:46]

b. né né mɔ̈ɔ́ ǎ ŋmǎ̀ kɛ̏
come.IRR come.IRR person.SBJV 3SG eat.IRR EMPH
'Come, come, let's eat!' [sos161009t1:224]

c. mais kűɛ nəgí́ dəbɛ̋ sɪ̰ kɛ̏
but.FR other.PL mind be.good.PTCP be EMPH
'But they are happy!' [sos170714t1:47]

d. mɔ̈ ǎ jú sɛ́ɛ-kû nɛ̈ kɛ̏
person 3SG say.IRR Sambla-thing LOC EMPH
'It is said in Seenku too!' [sos161009t1:113]

Examples (23a-b) show the use of *kɛ̏* with imperatives and hortatives, while the examples in (23c-d) show that it can be equally used on indicative clauses.

21.3.2 Exclamative *òo*

Another common clause-final particle, not only in Seenku but in many other languages of the region, is the particle *òo*, which I will describe as 'exclamative'. We first saw this particle in §18.6, where it formed part of the 'whether or not' conditional construction. Like the particles in §21.3.1, *òo* also gives a flavor of emphasis, but more in a way that feels as though the speaker is making sure that the listener is keeping track of the points being made.

The following examples illustrate the kinds of environments in which we find this exclamative particle:

(24) a. óo nɛ̋ óo nəgì jîo ŋɛ́ òo
2SG.EMPH if 2SG.EMPH COW see.REAL.PFV NEG EXCL
'As for you, you didn't get any cows.' [sos161009t1:231]

b. mó   ń   bɛ̌   né   à   sɪ̌ mó   tőrɔ́
    1SG.EMPH 1SG do.IRR 1SG.COMP 3SG be 1SG.EMPH mistreat.REAL.NOM
    nɛ̋, mais   dɔ̀n wɛ́ dɔ̀n kʊ́ kʊ́ ɲá   dɔ̀n ŋɛ́ mais
    LOC but.FR today FOC today D.DEF D.DEF be.NEG today NEG but.FR
    mó   yɛ́rɛ́ sɪ̌ dɔ̀n ń yɛ́rɛ́ tɛ̀ wɛ́ òo
    1SG.EMPH self.JU be today 1SG self.JU GEN FOC EXCL
    'I used to say that he was mistreating me, but today, that isn't there today, today I am my own master.' [sos170711t1:161]

c. páskɛ̋   ì-ǎ-lɔ́   mǐ nɔ̌   tsɛ̋-kɛ́ ì   wò   nṳ̀   kɛ́
    because.FR you.know.JU 1PL that.for and   3PL EMPH that.for COP
    sɔ́ɛn ɲì-nà   ŋɛ́ òo kʊ́ tɔ̋ ŋɛ́
    one there-towards NEG EXCL D.DEF like NEG
    'Because you know that ours and theirs, it's not the same thing, not like that!' [sos170711t1:435]

d. kʊ́   kùi   bé   fáná ɲìäa   òo
    D.DEF thing.PL DEM also finish.REAL.PRF EXCL
    'Those things don't exist anymore!' [sos170711t1:139]

In each of these examples, we can imagine the particle *òo* as meaning something like an insisting 'you see' or 'you know', emphasizing the point and making sure that the listener is following.

In related Dzùùngoo, Solomiac (2007:258) describes the meaning of *ò* as marking various elements in a complex utterance that lead to a particular conclusion. I suspect that this is similar if not the same as we see in Seenku. Nevertheless, defining clause-final particles like *òo* is a challenge, since they are not obligatory and do not significantly alter the meaning of the clause, but rather reflect some combination of the speaker's attitude, the relationship between the clause and the larger discourse, and the intended effect on the listener.

21.3.3 Impatience particle *sá̰*

The particle *sá̰* indicates insistence or impatience; I will gloss it as IMP for 'impatience' (alternatively, this gloss could also be understood as 'imperative', which is also consistent with the distribution of the particle). According to Solomiac (2007:259), both Dzùùngoo and Jula have the same particle, though in these languages, it contains an oral vowel (*sá*, H-toned in the two- or three-toned languages).

(25) a. á kòo   sā́
          2SG sing.IRR IMP
          'Sing please!' [sos150626t5:36]

      b. á kṵ̄n fā́   á gṵ̀ ŋé sā́
          2SG head enter.IRR 2SG under NEG IMP
          'Please don't lower your head!' [sos150626t5:2]

I have included 'please' in the glosses of these examples, not to indicate politeness, but rather to indicate impatience with the person being addressed.

21.3.4 wétənɛ̌ 'now'

The adverb *wétənɛ̌* is very common in folk tales. Consultants have translated it as 'now', though it appears to play a larger discourse role than a temporal one; if a speaker wishes to express '(right) now' as a temporal statement, they will typically use a different adverb, *sǎsàa nɛ̀* (§10.2.2.11).
  Examples of *wétənɛ̌* include:

(26) a. ằ jərā́-jərá   wétənɛ̌ səmɛ̂ɛ-sərằ
          3SG RED-become.REAL.PFV now   beg.ANTIP-master
          'Once he had become a beggar now...' [sos171009t1:38]

      b. mɔ̰̂mâa   sɩɔ   à kərù wɛ̀, ḭ̀ í bɛ̋   wétənɛ̌
          association arrive.REAL.PRF DEF hyena with 3PL LOG do.IRR now
          ḭ̀   íwí̋   kɛ̋
          COMP 1PL.EXCL go.IRR
          'Hyena's turn arrived, they told him now, "Let's go".' [sos150626t2:5]

      c. də̀ŋ̋ nɔ̰̋ wétənɛ̌ kʊ́ kʊ́ à dá̰ wè í sí̋
          drum that.for now D.DEF D.DEF 3SG add.IRR HAB LOG RECP.with
          'As for the drums now, that is added in.' [sos170711t1:317]

      d. dɔ́ŋ́ké mɛ̀   jəgǎ-jəgằ   wétənɛ̌ ɲì-nà
          SO.FR 3SG.SUBORD RED-go.down.REAL.PFV now there-towards
          mɛ̀   ằ   táaső ằ bɛ̋   wé mɔ̰̀ɛ   dəgǔaa jǎa
          3SG.SUBORD 3SG surprise 3SG take.place FOC person.PL between but
          kɛ̋ bṵ̂ɛ-dʊ̀n
          COP djinn-child
          'So, when he had descended there, to his surprise, he was surrounded by people but they were djinns.' [sos170711t1:14]

As these examples show, the use of *wétənɛ̌* 'now' is akin to a topicalizer, shifting the attention of the discourse to the clause in which it is used; if it carries any literal temporal meaning, it is very weak.

In terms of distribution, *wétənɛ̌* typically appears post-verbally, though as (26c) shows, it can also be used after a simple NP placed clause-initially as a topic. Similar to the distribution of the focus particle *wé* (§21.1.2.1), it can also come immediately after the auxiliary verb:

(27) ké mó cȅ nǎ wétənɛ̌ ȁ kú bɛ́ jȕ
      COP 1SG.EMPH hand PROSP now DEF thing DEM say.IRR
      'It is my hand that will say it now.' [sos170711t1:210]

Here, it follows the prospective auxiliary *nǎ*.

21.4 Interjections

This section covers common interjections, with the exception of back-channeling interjections, which will be addressed in §21.6.2.

21.4.1 Yes and no

The affirmative interjection 'yes' in Seenku is ɔ̌ɔ. Tonally, I have seen two variants, a level H-toned ɔ́ɔ and a bell-shaped tone ɔ̌ɔ̂ (seen in (31) below). Examples include:

(28) a. ɔ́ɔ ȁ ɲá í gɔ̌ɔ ŋɛ́
        yes 3SG be.NEG LOG hard NEG
        'Yes, it's not hard.' [sos170822t10:520]

   b. ɔ́ɔ mɔ̏ ȁ cȅɛ tɔ́-tɔ́ sɔ́n-sóen sɔ́n-sóen sɔ́n-sóen
        yes person 3SG sort.IRR RED-like RED-one RED-one RED-one
        'Yes, we sort through them one by one by one.' [sos170822t1:73]

I have also heard *ɛ̌ɛ* used as an affirmative, as in:

(29) a. ɛ̌ɛ á wó ȁ kòo kɛ̋
        yes 2SG EMPH 3SG sing.IRR EMPH
        'Yes, you should sing it!' [sos170823t8:148]

   b. ɛ̌ɛ á sùinì jərà áa ɲɛ̏ɛ kʊ́ wɛ́
        yes 2SG leaf.spine take.IRR 2SG.SUBJ weave.ANTIP.IRR D.DEF with
        'Yes, you take the palm leaf spine and weave with it.' [sos170822t10:357]

To express 'no', we find variations on a form with a trough-shaped (HXH) tone. In its strongest form, it is realized as óòó:

(30) a. óòó ké kǔ nɔ̌n ké nìgì tsǐi mó nɔ̌n ké nìgì
no COP D.DEF that.for COP COW.PL six 1SG.EMPH that.for COP COW.PL
nàa
four
'No, for him, it's six cows, for me, it's four cows.' [sos161009t1:230]

b. ì wɛ̃́ í bǐ́ wé ǎ lé ǎ! ì ǎ
3PL SUBORD LOG do.IRR.COMP FOC 3SG DAT INTERJ COMP 3SG
wǒo sǐ ǎ məgɔ̌n-cəbèe lé kǎa nɛ̃́ ì
EMPH.SUBORD be DEF monitor REL chase.REAL.NOM LOC COMP
ǎ wǒ ǎ tò wé lɔ́? mɛ̀ í bɛ̃́ ì óòó
3SG EMPH 3SG know FOC here 3SG.SUBORD LOG do.IRR COMP no
'They said to him, ah! the monitor that you were chasing, do you recognize him here? He said no.' [sos170711t1:22]

It can also be realized with a nasal vowel ɔ̌ɔ̀ɔ́ or even simply as a nasal ńǹń. What remains characteristic is the trough-shaped tone pattern.

However, it is now common to use French *oui* and *non* in place of native Seenku equivalents, to the extent that speakers are noticing and commenting on it:

(31) ah ouais nɛ̃́ ké tùbábú-kû âa, mɔ̌ ká-ɲì
ah.FR yes.FR if COP white.person-thing NEG.Q person AFF-good.JU
mɔ̌ɔ́ í bɛ̃́ ì ɔ̌ɔ̂
person.SBJV LOG do.IRR COMP yes
"'Ah ouais' is French, isn't it, we should say 'ɔ̌ɔ̂'" [sos170702t1:28-29]

I have heard similar sentiments when using Jula 'yes' and 'no' equivalents.

21.4.2 ì-ǎ-lɔ́ 'you know'

A common interjection heard in narrative is ì-ǎ-lɔ́, meaning 'you know'. This is a borrowed expression from Jula, where lɔ́ has a nasal vowel lɔ́; this nasalization is typically missing in Seenku. Examples of its usage include:

(32) a. ì-ǎ-lɔ́ bǒ-kɔ́ɔ kərǎ təgǐ́ sǐ ǎ sǎn mɛ̃́
you.know.JU billygoat tail stand.PTCP be DEF above with
'You know how the billygoat holds his tail in the air.' [sos161009t1:189]

b. ì-ǎ-lɔ́   sà-bö̀-kɔ̌ɔ   kʊ́   təgì   wè ằ
    you.know.JU second.son-billygoat D.DEF stand.IRR HAB DEF
    sɔ́n-nɛ́n-jʊ̈   jɛ̌n   ŋɛ́
    rain-child-water under NEG
    'You know, the billygoat won't stand under the rain.' [sos150626t4:2]

Though the phrase translates to a complementizer clause, it does not function like one in Seenku grammar; unlike regular Seenku 'know' (§19.2.2), it does not trigger the use of a complementizer or of a subjunctive in the following clause.

21.5 Greetings and benedictions

21.5.1 Greetings

This section summarizes the basic greetings of Seenku. Like most West African societies, greetings are very important in Sambla culture. There is a fairly rigid structure to greeting sequences, which depend on factors like time of day, gender, and whether one of the participants has just arrived in the village.

I begin this section with different time of day greetings, then move on to circumstantial greetings, then finally turn to the questions that follow any of these specific starts to a greeting sequence.

21.5.1.1 Time of day greetings
Morning
When first seeing someone in the morning, the greeting sequence begins with *á kű-nằ wê* to a single person or *í kűnằ wê* to a group of people. After acknowledging the greeting with either *ḿmâa/ḿbâa* (spoken by a man) or *fő́omɛ̋* (spoken by a woman), the respondent will typically pose the question *ằ gǜdəgɛ̀-kù kṵ̂ə âa* 'has your morning been good?'. This exchange is illustrated in (33):

(33) A (male): *á kűnằ wê*.
      (Good morning.)

      B (female): *ɛ̀ɛ, fő́omɛ̋. Ằ gǜdəgɛ̀-kù kṵ̂ə âa*.
      (Indeed. Has your morning been good?)

      A (male): *Ằ kṵ̂ə sǐ*.
      (It is good.)

Other morning-specific questions and greetings include the following:

(34) a. á kənä   í mŭi↘
       2SG wake.up.REAL.PRF LOG in.shape.Q
       'Have you woken up well?' [sos150624e]

   b. á cěrȅ   í səgɔ̌↘
       2SG sleep.REAL.PFV LOG good.Q
       'Did you sleep well?' [sos150624e]

   c. ȁ kȉekű wέ òo
       DEF sleep FOC EXCL
       'How was your sleep?' [sos170822t1:9]

After these morning-specific questions, the rest of the greeting sequence asking about various people in each participant's entourage can begin (§21.5.1.3).

For a textual example of a morning greeting sequence, see the first few lines of sos170822t1.

Middle of the day

In the middle of the day (between roughly 10 and 3), a more generic greeting is used to begin a greeting exchange:

(35) ń dəgɔ̀ wὲ á lὲ̏
     1SG greet.IRR HAB 2SG DAT
     'I greet you.' [sos150624e]

If more than one person is being addressed, 2sg *á* would be replaced with 2pl *í*.

Instead of then asking about the morning, the person being greeted might ask instead:

(36) sɔ̌n-tǎ-něˊ wέ òo
     sun-fire-LOC FOC EXCL
     'How about the afternoon?' [sos150624e]

I have also heard this question posed as *sɔ̌n-tǎ-něˊ-kűˊ kŷ̰ɔ âa*, following the same format as we saw for the morning, but my impression is that the simple *wέ òo* greeting is the most common.

For an example of middle of the day greetings, see the beginning of sos170822t10.

After 3pm
Starting at approximately 3pm, the greeting changes to *á jánɛ̀* for one person and *í jánɛ̀* to a group, both based on the term *jánɛ̀* meaning 'evening'. In response, after acknowledging the greeting, the person being greeted will respond with *jánɛ̀ wɛ́ òo* 'How about the evening?'. This greeting can be used through night time.

21.5.1.2 Arrival greetings
In certain circumstances, special greetings are used rather than time of day greetings. One common occasion of this sort is when someone arrives in a village. In this case, it is the responsibility of the person who lives in that village or who was there first to greet the newly arrived with the following:

(37) á nàä   wɛ́
      2G come.REAL.PRF FOC
      'You have come [i.e. welcome]!'

This greeting can be acknowledged in the same way as time of day greetings (i.e. with *ḿmâa* for men and *fő́omɛ̋* for women). The follow-up looks a lot like time of day greetings, with the person able to ask about the morning, the afternoon, or the evening. In the core of the greeting sequence, it is customary in this case to ask about the well-being of people where the person has come from; see §21.5.1.3 for further discussion.

21.5.1.3 Core greeting sequence
Once the appropriate greeting sequence has been initiated, greetings become a series of questions about the well-being of various people in the interlocutor's family and entourage. There are at least four different formats for asking about well-being, which I illustrate in (38) with the noun *dənį̋* 'children':

(38) a. ä̀ dənį̋   wɛ́ òo
          DEF child.PL FOC EXCL
          'How about the children?'

      b. ä̀ dənį̋   ɲá   í   wɛ̋-kų̌ɔ   âa
          DEF child.PL be.NEG LOG TRANS-cool.REAL.PFV   NEG.Q
          'The children are well, aren't they?' [sos170822t1:8]

      c. ä̀ dənį̋   kų̌ɔ   âa
          DEF child.PL cool.REAL.PFV NEG.Q
          'Are the children well?' [sos170822t1:9]

d. *ằ dənǐ kŭɔ lɛ̌ ɲì*
   DEF child.PL cool.PTCP PST there
   'Were the children good there?' [sos170822t10:6]

I am told that especially (38b) and (38d) are used when the people whose well-being is being asked about are not present where the conversation is taking place.

The responses are fairly uniform, typically one of the following:

(39) a. *ằ kŭɔ sǐ*
      3SG cool.PTCP.(PST) be
      'It is/was good.'

   b. *ì kŭɔ sǐ ɲì-nà*
      3PL cool.PTCP.PST be there-towards
      'They were good there [i.e. when I last saw them].'

   c. *ì sǐ ɲì-nà*
      3PL be there-towards
      'They are there.'

Answers with *ɲì-nà* 'there' can be offered even if it is not present in the question. I have put PST in parantheses since it results in no audible difference: the vowel is already lengthened, by virtue of being a rising tone, and it already ends in S. It was not until a consultant actively broke down the meaning of (39b) and offered an equivalent with overt *lɛ̌* (*ì kŭɔ lɛ̌ sǐ ɲì-nà*) that I became aware of the past tense interpretation.

Another possible answer is as follows:

(40) *füi ɲá (mɔ̀ɔ) ŋɛ́*
     nothing be.NEG (person.with) NEG
     'We have nothing wrong.' [sos170822t1:11]

This response can be used both when questioning a person's well-being as well as in response to questions about the time of day, waking up, etc.

Whose well-being is questioned depends on who is being greeted. Children are always amongst the first to be asked after, regardless of whether the person being greeted is male or female. If the person is female, then the husband is asked about (41a), and if the person is male, then the wives are asked about (41b):

(41) a. *á səná wɛ́ òo*
      2SG husband FOC EXCL
      'How about your husband?'

   b. *ằ mənǐ kûɔ âa*
      DEF woman(.PL) cool.REAL.PFV NEG.Q
      'Are the women well?'

A common generic question in the greeting sequence is the following, in either this or another question format discussed above:

(42) cí-dɔ̀ɔ wɛ́ òo
house-inside FOC EXCL
'How is the household?'

Other people whom I have seen asked about in regular greeting sequences include friends kɔ̀sí and old people mɔ̀ bɔ̌ɛɛ.

If the greeting sequence is taking place with someone who has just arrived (as in §21.5.1.2), then people at the traveler's point of origin are also asked about. To do so, the human plural suffix -ŋɛ̌ is added to the place name, as shown in (43):

(43) ằ Sĭa-ŋɛ̌ wɛ́ òo
DEF Bobo-HUM.PL FOC EXCL
'How are the people in Bobo?' [sos150624e]

In response, the traveler (arriver) can ask about the people where he or she has arrived:

(44) a. lɔ̌-ŋɛ̌ wɛ́ òo
here-HUM.PL FOC EXCL
'How are the people here?' [sos150624e]

b. ń jɛ̌n-ŋɛ̌ wɛ́ òo
1SG front-HUM.PL FOC EXCL
'How are the people in front of me?' [sos150624e]

For examples of greeting sequences, see the beginnings of the texts sos170822t1 and 170822t10.

21.5.2 Benedictions

Benedictions are exchanged at the end of nearly every greeting sequence. These uniformly begin as follows:

(45) (ằ) sŭməŋǎ/sǎn lɛ́...
DEF God SBJV
'May God...'

There are two variants of the word for 'god' in Seenku, a simplex sǎn and a (diachronically) complex form sŭməŋǎ, which looks like a compound combining sɔ̆n 'sky' and məŋằ 'rain chief'. Either variant may be optionally preceded by the definite determiner ằ.

In greeting sequences, it is common to exchange benedictions regarding the day, that it may end well. Commonly, we find benedictions like the following:

(46) a. sŭməŋǎá sɔ́n-tǎ nɔ̌gɔ̌yá
      god.SBJV sky-fire calm.JU
      'May God bless this day.' [sos120107e]

   b. sŭməŋǎ lɛ́ ǎ dɔ́n dəbɛ̋ á wɛ́
      god   SBJV DEF today make.good.IRR 2SG with
      'May God give you a good day.' [sos150624e]

   c. sŭməŋǎ lɛ́ ǎ sɔ́n-tǎ wɛ̋-kɔ̋
      god   SBJV DEF sky-fire TRANS-cool.IRR
      'May God let this day end well.'

The benediction in (46a) can have sɔ́n-tǎ replaced with gṵɔ-fɛ̰́ 'night' to wish someone a good night in the evening. The expression nɔ̌gɔ̌yá seems to be a loanword from Jula, meaning 'calm' or 'simplify'.

Other common benedictions include:

(47) a. ǎ sŭməŋǎ lɛ́ í kɔ̋ nɛ̋-dəbɛ̋
      DEF god   SBJV 2PL head TRANS-make.good.IRR
      'May God give you good luck/intelligence.' [sos150624e]

   b. sŭməŋǎ lɛ́ á tɔ̌ mó kərɛ̀
      god   SBJV 2SG leave.IRR 1SG.EMPH near
      'May God leave you near me.'

   c. sŭməŋǎá wɛ̋-kɔ̋ bɛ̋ í kǎ
      god.SBJV TRANS-cool.NOM do.IRR 2PL in.hand
      'May God give you health.' [sos170822t12:81]

In a long string of benedictions, rather than repeating sŭməŋǎ or sǎn each time, subsequent benedictions can simply begin with ɛ̆ɛ́ '3SG.SBJV', or 'May he...'.

The most common response to benedictions is a loanword from Jula (originally from Arabic), ǎmḭ́ or ǎmḭ́nǎ̀. This has come to replace the native Seenku response wéěyó.

21.6 Discourse structure

I end this chapter with some brief observations on discourse structure in Seenku, including patterns of turn-taking and back-channeling strategies.

21.6.1 Turn-taking

Seenku speakers tend not to leave any space between turns when speaking. Silence in conversation is minimalized. Either the turn passes to the next person who will speak, or gaps between a single speaker's utterances are filled with back-channeling strategies discussed in §21.6.2. This tendency is especially noticeable in women's speech, especially in conversations whose participants are entirely female. Good examples of this kind of discourse style are the texts sos170822t1-10.

In a narrative speech style, men tend to do less back-channeling and leave more space around each utterance. See, for instance, sos170702t1 or sos170823t8.

21.6.2 Back-channeling

Back-channeling refers to the feedback a listener gives to let a speaker know that he or she is listening and following what is being said. My observations suggest that back-channeling is most commonly done by lower status people, especially younger people (when an older person is talking) or women. Women will commonly back-channel even when speaking amongst themselves. Older men are the least likely to back-channel.

We find a few common back-channeling strategies and interjections, summarized in the subsections below.

21.6.2.1 ɛ̌ɛ́ kɛ̌

The interjection ɛ̌ɛ́ kɛ̌ is commonly found as a backchannel. It appears to be made up of ɛ̌ɛ́, a portmanteau of the 3sg and the logophoric pronoun (à + í) and the emphatic particle kɛ̌ (§21.3.1). Its use suggests a meaning like 'that's right' or 'indeed', as shown in the following exchange:

(48) a. ké kʊ́ ì təmá ká̰↘
        COP D.DEF 3PL praise.IRR go.Q
        'She's praising them as she goes?' [sos170714t2:75]

      b. ɛ̌ɛ́   kɛ̌
        3SG.LOG EMPH
        'Indeed.' [sos170714t2:76]

In other words, it affirms what the speaker has just said. A more casual variant ň́ń kɛ̌ is also attested.

21.6.2.2 kɛ́ kʊ́ tɔ́

A more explicitly affirmative backchannel is the expression kɛ́ kʊ́ tɔ́ 'it is like that'. The following exchange illustrates the use of this backchannel:

(49) a. jəgèé   təgǒ   sɪ̰̌ nɛ̋ tɔ́-tərɔ̋   í   tɔ̀ɔn kɔ̀n ȁ   nǎ   ȁ
        dog.SBJV sit.PTCP be if RED-like   LOG butt on 3SG PROSP 3SG
        təgĭ   sɪ̰̌ tɔ́-tərɔ̋ ȁ   təgǒ   lé   lɛ̏   kʊ́   bɔ́ɔ fő́n
        stand.PTCP be RED-like 3SG sit.PTCP REL PRES D.DEF tall more
        'If a dog is sitting like that on its butt, when it stands up, [the way that] it sits down is taller.' [sos161009t1:71]

   b. kɛ́   kʊ́   tɔ́
       COP D.DEF like
       'It's true [lit. it is like that].' [sos161009t1:72]

21.6.2.3 ɛ̀ɛ

Often, non-lexical backchannels like ɛ̀ɛ (possibly interpreted as 'yes'; §21.4.1) or ǹn are used simply to engage with the speaker and show that the listener is listening.

(50) a. ɛ̋!   áa   kà   nɛ̋ mŏén lé jŏ   kʊ́   fő́n kɛ̀
        INTERJ 2SG.SBJV go.REAL.PFV if small RED find.IRR D.DEF more EMPH
        'Eh! If you go, the little bit that you will get is better [than nothing].'
        [sos170822t1:22]

   b. ɛ̀ɛ...
       yes
       'Yeah...' [sos170822t1:22]

The listener acknowledges the first statement in (50a) with a simple ɛ̀ɛ, showing that she is listening and (at least nominally) agrees.

21.6.2.4 Shadowing

A final form of back-channeling to be discussed here is shadowing, where the listener repeats back what the speaker has just said, either right after the utterance has finished or even nearly simultaneously if the listener has determined what the speaker is about to say. For instance, in folk tales, where the listener may know how the story goes and know what comes next, he or she may speak the same line a word or two behind the main storyteller.

This back-channeling strategy is difficult to illustrate in print; I refer the reader to the folktales in sos170805t15, where this back-channeling strategy is particularly apparent with the listener NKT.

22 Artistic adaptation of language

Though not a canonical topic in reference grammars, I include here a chapter on the artistic adaptation of Seenku in song and music. This topic is of considerable interest for Seenku especially thanks to the presence of a complex musical **surrogate language** played on the balafon, a kind of resonator xylophone common to this area of West Africa.

I begin with a brief discussion of the linguistic considerations of sung music in Seenku, then turn to surrogate speech, both on the balafon and in its more limited role on a traditional horn known as the *gbên*.

22.1 Sung music

Vocal music is likely one of the oldest musical traditions in Sambla society, though in the last couple hundred years (Strand 2009) seemingly instrumental balafon music has come to take on the most prestige; this has triggered some attrition in knowledge of the sung music repertoire, especially traditional *griot* praise songs, which are now more likely to be played on the balafon. Sung music falls into a number of genres, including:
1. Women's work songs
2. Play songs
3. Praise songs
4. Ritual songs

The study of Seenku vocal music is still in its infancy, compared to the study of its balafon tradition (Strand 2009, McPherson 2018), so any observations about differences between genres are preliminary. One noticeable difference between (women's) play songs and the other genres is that the play songs involve a high frequency call-and-response format, where a soloist sings one line and a chorus repeats a consistent phrase in between. For example, consider the following excerpt from a woman's play song [sos170823t3]:

(1)   a.   *jəbě báa   wé*
              cloth ruin.REAL.PFV FOC
              'The cloth is ruined.'

        b.   *kərê nă   tsě sǎ*
              man PROSP INDF buy.IRR
              'The man will buy something.'

c. mɔ̰̂tɛ̂ɛ   báa   wɛ́
   clothing ruin.REAL.PFV FOC
   'The clothing is ruined.'

d. kərê nă   tsɛ̋ sɑ̰̋
   man PROSP INDF buy.IRR
   'The man will buy something.'

(1a) and (1c) are the soloist's lines, while the whole chorus chimes in for lines (1b) and (1d); the song goes on like this, alternating between specific things that are ruined, ripped, broken, etc., and the chorus replying that the man will buy something.

No other genre that I have heard has this sort of call-and-response format.

22.1.1 Linguistic features of vocal lyrics

Here, I briefly lay out some of the linguistic features of song lyrics. Like poetry in most languages, Seenku lyrics contain some elements that differ either in their form or their frequency from regular speech, and in terms of content, they can be tricky to interpret even for native speakers due to their highly proverbial and abstract nature.

22.1.1.1 Vocables

The term **vocable** refers to syllables that are used in song without any specific meaning (e.g. English *oh*, *oo*, or *la*). These are commonly held for a long duration, either at the beginning or the end of a line. In praise music, for instance, sung by female griots, I have seen two phrase-initial vocables, *biɔɔ* and *eŋaa*, both of which are held for a couple of seconds before launching into the lyrics of the line. See sos170822t12:121 for the former and sos1985m1 for the latter.

At the ends of lines, we also find vocables, typically *(y)oo*, which could simply be a lengthened version of the discourse particle *òo*, but sometimes also *aa* or *waa*.

22.1.1.2 Bouncing ball intonation

The bouncing ball intonation pattern discussed in §9.1.2.2 appears to be especially common in Seenku music, both sung and instrumental. It appears on ideophones at the ends of lines. While in regular speech, these ideophones may be repeated 3-4 times, it is not uncommon in song to find up to six repetitions of the stem. See, for instance, sos181217t1 around 7m20s for a prime example of this intonation pattern. As in spoken language, where this intonation pattern is found only on ideophones with a single (flat) tone, the sung melodies for the intonation pattern are likewise level.

This rhythmic pattern is also clearly audible in instrumental flute and balafon music, whose main melodies are simply instrumental renditions of vocal music; see §22.3 for further discussion and references to the data corpus.

22.1.1.3 Proverbs

Turning to the content of vocal music, song lyrics in most genres (with the exception, maybe, of play songs) are highly proverbial. Consultants, especially younger consultants, admit not fully understanding what the lyrics are supposed to mean. The following excerpt of lyrics from the song *kókő tế sô* 'Song of the Koko' is a prime example of this proverbiality:

(2) a. ằ   kṹ   blẽ̀   ŋέ   òo
        DEF   D.DEF be.big   NEG   VOC
        'That's not big, oo...'

   b. í   wằ   tɔ̀   sɯ̋mənắ   kắ
        2PL 3SG   leave.IRR   god   in.hand
        'Leave him in the hands of God.'

   c. nɛ́   cɔ́ɔ-bɛ̋ɛ́   ŋənɔ̂   dəgɛ́   nɛ̋ ằ
        1SG.COMP sorcery-do.NOM.PL.SBJV oil   make.REAL.PFV if   DEF
        gɯ̏ɔtəgằ-nɛ̏
        late.night-LOC
        'I said, if the sorcerers make oil late at night.'

   d. ɩ̀   jǎa   ɩ̀   kɛ́   Gò-bằsɯ̋   bɛ́   kɔ̀kɛ̋   nɔ̋n   tɛ̋
        COMP because COMP COP third.son-Basu DEM meat.PL that.for GEN
        'They say it's because it's for Go-Basu's meat.' [sos170823t8:159]

The song *kókő tế sô* is about a mythical creature, the Koko, that will come at night and catch any wrong-doers and make them pay a fine for their sins. Given this context, there is no literal connection to oil making late at night; and as is characteristic of many of these old Seenku songs, the song contains references to people and places, like Go-Basu here. The song goes on to talk about how sorcerers will tire themselves out trying to get at Go-Basu, who is in the hands of God, perhaps a proverb meaning that if one has done good and sided oneself with the forces of good, then one has nothing to fear from the Koko (here referred to proverbially as sorcerers).

Seenku song lyrics would provide a wealth of interesting material for those interested in oral tradition or Mande poetic structure.

22.1.2 Tone-tune association

A key question in studying vocal music in a tone language is the degree to which the linguistic tones are respected or represented musically. Rates of **tone-tune association** have been surveyed in a number of tonal languages from all around the world; see, for instance, the survey in Schellenberg (2012) or the references in McPherson

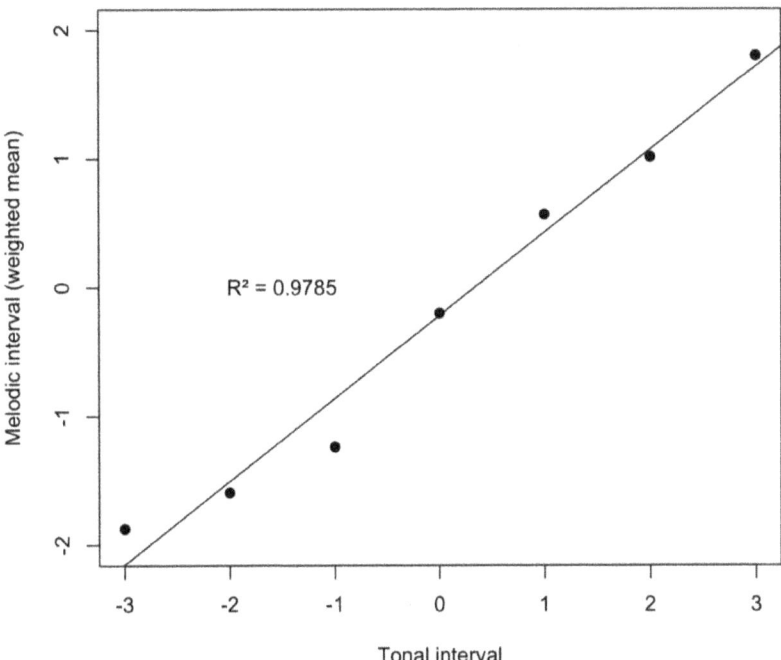

Fig. 22.1: Correlation between tonal and melodic interval size

and Ryan (2018). It turns out that there is no one way that languages will behave. For instance, Mandarin popular music pays little heed to tones, while typologically similar and geographically close Cantonese is very strict in its tonal text-setting (Ho 2006, Schellenberg 2013). Most languages, however, seem to fall somewhere in the middle; for example, in the Dogon language Tommo So (McPherson and Ryan 2018), both parallel mappings of tone to melody (i.e. up with up, level with level, down with down) and oblique mappings (i.e. level to either up or down) are equally tolerated, allowing the singer a good deal of freedom in how the lyrics are set to music.

The study of tonal text-setting in Seenku is still preliminary, but results suggest a high degree of correspondence between tone and melody. In a study of four songs (including Song of the Koko), only 3% of note-to-note transitions are contrary mappings, where tonal direction and melodic direction contradict one another. This means that 97% of the transitions are non-opposing. Breaking that figure down further, we find that a solid 74% of tonal transitions are parallel—if the tone goes up, the melody goes up; if the tone is level, the melody stays level. Finally, 23% of transitions are oblique.

What is more, the size of the tonal interval appears to be closely correlated with the size of the melodic interval. The graph in Figure 22.1 plots the tonal interval size (from -3 for an S to X interval, to 3 for an X to S) against the weighted mean for melodic interval size in scale degrees.

In some ways, the strictness of text-setting is audible in Seenku sung music. Given the tonal complexity of the language with its four tones, level sequences of tones are rare, and tone sequences are just as likely to go up as they are to go down in the spoken language. As a result, the sung melodies likewise involve frequent changes in note, both up and down, resulting in lines with little sense of the overarching melodic contour common to Western music.

More data are required to bolster these findings and investigate possible differences between genres.

22.2 Surrogate speech

The most fascinating aspect of the artistic adaptation of Seenku is the presence of an elaborate speech surrogate system on the balafon, a resonator xylophone with many variants throughout the region. A more limited speech surrogate system is also found on a horn known as the *gbên*. I will address each in turn here.

22.2.1 Balafon surrogate language

Though the balafon (*bə̰ə̰* in Seenku) is relatively recent in Sambla country, having been borrowed from the neighboring Toussian just 200 years ago (Strand 2009), it has become perhaps the most importantly musical tradition in Sambla culture. The instrument is played by specific families of *griots* (Jula *jeli*), a musician caste. Balafon musicians never sing, lending the impression that this is a purely instrumental tradition. This is, however, an illusion—almost everything played by the soloist is linguistically-grounded, either a balafon rendition of sung lyrics (§22.3) or a speech surrogate, communicating via notes on the balafon with the spectators, the other musicians, or even the spirits.

The Sambla balafon is a resonator xylophone, typically with 23 keys. It is tuned to a pentatonic scale, corresponding roughly to Western 1, minor 3, 3, 5, and 6 (the same scale found in vocal music). A single instrument is played simultaneously by three players. Seated on one side and playing the simplest middle part of the music is *bə̰ə̰-lé-kpə̂*, "the one who closes the balafon". This is the youngest of the three players. The next oldest player sits opposite the *bə̰ə̰-lé-kpə̂* and plays the *bə̰ə̰-ɲǎ*, "the balafon mother", or the bass notes. Finally, the oldest and most skilled player is the soloist on the treble notes; he is seated on the same side as the one playing the *bə̰ə̰-ɲǎ*, and it is he who is in charge of "singing" lyrics and communicating with the audience without ever opening his mouth.

I will not go into detail here on the musical or cultural aspects of the Sambla balafon; I refer interested readers to Strand (2009) or McPherson (2018). In this chapter, I will briefly sketch out the basics of the surrogate language. It is largely an "abridging" speech surrogate (Stern 1957), meaning that it musically encodes phonemic aspects of the language. In particular, the balafon represents tonal and rhythmic aspects of Seenku, while foregoing the representation of segmental contrasts.

22.2.1.1 Tonal encoding

The notes of the balafon scale are used to represent the four tones of Seenku. There is no one-to-one correspondence, e.g. the 5th is L, the 6th is H, etc. The precise encoding of tone depends on the mode of the song being played—whatever note forms the tonal center of the mode typically encodes S tone; the other three tones cascade down the scale from there, usually skipping the minor third. This key is known as the *jĩo-bə̀ə̀-dĕn* 'fetish balafon key' and is generally reserved for more spiritual uses.

The table in (3) summarizes the correspondences between notes of the scale and tonal encoding in a corpus of 823 words "spoken" on the balafon:

(3) *Tone-note correspondence in the balafon surrogate corpus*

	1	b3	3	5	6	8
S	0	1	8	22	38	**158**
H	4	0	72	85	**154**	28
L	2	1	9	**73**	15	7
X	**101**	2	93	57	14	15

The most frequent note for each tone is in boldface; while this corpus contains songs played in multiple modes, the most common mode is the *bə̀ə̀-ɲǎ* mode, the name for note 1, which at higher octaves (noted here with 8) is known as *sərǎkùa*. In this mode, S is played most often on the octave of the tonic (8), H on the 6th, L on the 5th, and X evenly distributed between the 3rd and the 1st. As this table shows, the minor 3rd (b3) is almost always avoided.

To illustrate the speech surrogate, I use a grid system, showing the notes down the lefthand side and the syllables along the bottom, with shaded-in squares of the grid indicating a note strike. The following example shows the difference between the subject pronouns *mǐ* (1pl, S-toned), *mó* (1sg, H-toned), and *mʲ̀* (generic 'person', X-toned):

(4) *Pronominal tone contrast on the balafon, in the phrase '___ will dance'*

	8			
	6			
	5			
	3			
	b3			
➤	1			
Words	mí̋ mó m̰̋	nă		səmâ

The pronouns are arranged vertically on the word tier, with the order corresponding to the notes above. In other words, *mí̋* is represented on the octave of the tonic (shaded with horizontal lines), *mó* on the 6th (shaded with a trellis), and *m̰̋* on the 3rd (shaded with vertical lines). The arrow on the left points out the tonal center that defines the mode.

This example also illustrates the encoding of contour tones: the note corresponding to each component tones is played, the first as a grace note (i.e. with a shorter duration). Thus, *nă* sees both its L- and S-tones played, while *səmâ* 'dance' sees both its H- and X-tones played on their corresponding notes.

The balafon surrogate language has been a surprising and valuable source of data on the tone system, especially since many of the postlexical tone processes like downstep (§4.5.2) and tonal absorption (§4.5.3) are not encoded, thus providing a glimpse at the underlying representation of contour tones.

22.2.1.2 Rhythmic encoding

While segmental identity (e.g. the difference between /b/ and /k/ or between /i/ and /ɛ/) is not encoded, aspects of syllable structure that influence the rhythm of the language are. In particular, the difference between short and long vowels and between mono- and sesquisyllabic words are encoded on the balafon.

Interestingly, both long vowels and sesquisyllabic words are encoded in the same way: by striking the same note twice (for level-toned words), with the first strike as a grace note. This creates a good deal of ambiguity. For instance, the following sequence of notes could be interpreted in at least the two ways listed beneath the notes:

(5)   *Balafon encoding of 'boar' or 'ram'*

8			
6		▓	
5			
3	▓		▓
b3			
⋗ 1			
Words	səgä̀ bě̀ɛ	bâ	kərê

The double-strike on 3 can either represent the sesquisyllabic form *səgä̀* 'sheep' or the long-voweled *bě̀ɛ* 'pig'. As this example also shows, words with contour tones are even more ambiguous, since the technique of striking the balafon twice for the syllable has already been used to encode the two tones of the contour. Thus, the 6-3 sequence could be either a simple, short-voweled monosyllabic *bâ* or a sesquisyllabic form *kərê* (or a long-voweled contour tone like *bâ̰a*, balafon, in another context).

22.2.1.3 Usage and comprehension of the surrogate

The balafon surrogate language is used mainly to request money and goods from the audience—the griot's livelihood. It can also be used, however, to criticize people, to joke and flirt, to direct other musicians, or to communicate with the spirits. The system is entirely productive—anything that can be said in Seenku can be said on the balafon.

Conversely, not everyone understands the surrogate language, and thus comprehension is a limiting factor. Given enough context to disambiguate the message, the balafonists themselves can understand what is being said almost perfectly, as can drum-playing griots who frequently accompany the balafon. Regular Seenku speakers will understand their names and common requests, but will otherwise need the speech translated to them. It is taboo for the balafonist himself to translate what has been said (otherwise the request sounds like it comes from him, rather than being made by the balafon and hence deflecting any negative feelings that might be had). If there are any younger members of the balafon family present, they can translate it to the person being addressed, otherwise a drum player will often fill this role.

For further information about the balafon surrogate language, see McPherson (2018).

22.2.2 Horn surrogate language

The balafon is not the only instrument in Sambla culture to speak. In fact, any instrument capable of producing different pitches could be used for speech (and I have seen rare examples of drum-playing griots communicating with their tension drums); but the only other instrument whose express purpose it is to communicate is a traditional horn known as the *gbên*. This is a horn constructed out of two different species of animal horn fused together. It is played to the side, with the pitch manipulated by the amount of air blown through it.

Like the balafon surrogate language, the horn surrogate language likewise encodes notes and rhythms. However, since the mechanics of the instrument are such that pitch glides are possible, we do not find the fixed two-note sequences to encode contour tones. Because of this, the pitch contours on the horn are considerably more speech-like.

It appears that the horn plays only a ritual function to call people together for certain ceremonies. Every time the *gbên* has been demonstrated in the text corpus, it only plays one thing, translated to me as:

(6)   a.   ằ   báà   kó   tɔ̋   kɛ̀
              3SG do.ANTIP.IRR.HAB D.DEF like EMPH
              'It was done like that.'

         b.   ì   sɛ́ɛ-gûa   tsìɛɛ
              COMP Sambla-country word
              '[They said] in the words of Sambla country.' [sos170806m1]

Another speaker instead translated the first line as *ằ báà ằ kɛ̋ kɛ̀*, which supposedly means roughly the same thing but looks instead to contain the irrealis form of 'go' *kɛ̋*.

It is unclear whether there was a time when the horn was used to communicate more productively and that this is simply the last remaining vestige of the tradition, or whether it has always been a highly specialized instrument.

22.3 Instrumental versions of vocal music

A lot of instrumental Sambla music, whether played on the balafon or on a traditional wooden traverse flute known as the *pîɔn*, can also be sung; in other words, what appear to be instrumental melodies do in fact have linguistic underpinnings. While this may at first glance appear to be another use of the speech surrogate system, we find that it is in fact one step removed. For instance, when looking at the balafon, the correspondence between tones and notes in these musical passages is not nearly as strict as what we find in speech mode.

In fact, what the balafon is encoding is not the basic linguistic structure of the lyrics but rather the melodies on which the lyrics would be sung in vocal music. As described in §22.1.2, these melodies are shaped by the linguistic tones of the lyrics, but only in the sense that the movement of the tone must match the movement of the melody; there are no fixed correspondences between tones and notes.

Thus, the "singing" of the balafon is filtered through a stage of tone-tune association for vocalic melodies, but it is still linguistically grounded. The musical repertoire on the *pîɔn* works in the same way. All of the *pîɔn* songs have sung equivalents (and typically also balafon equivalents), using the same melodies across the two modalities. See sos181217m1 for examples of songs on the *pîɔn* and their sung forms.

To date, I have seen no examples of purely instrumental music. There may be short passages in balafon songs that do not have corresponding words, but these are always embedded in larger compositions that are based around lyrics and speech. In other words, music cannot be divorced from speech in Sambla culture.

23 Texts

I give two examples of interlinear glossed texts here to illustrate the grammatical structures laid out in this grammar. Both of these and many others are accessible from the Seenku collection at the Endangered Languages Archive (ELAR). Transcriptions in the archive are in time-aligned ELAN format and are downloadable together with video and audio:

https://elar.soas.ac.uk/Collection/MPI1080582

23.1 Explanation of traditional fonio farming, part 1

This text is a discussion between two young adult speakers, Sy Clément Traoré and Gni Emma Traoré. They are narrating a video of a traditional fonio farming demonstration that we recorded a few days prior in the village of Bouendé. Fonio is a high-labor low-yield crop that is only rarely cultivated in Sambla country today. Planting, harvesting, and thrashing the grains involve synchronized dance-like motions carried out by men and accompanied by traditional musicians. In the following text, the two speakers narrate the video demonstrating how fonio is planted.

I recorded this text on July 14, 2017 in Bobo-Dioulasso using a Zoom Q8 video recorder and two Shure SM-93 lavalier microphones. This text is archived under the ID sos170714t1; the video that they are narrating is also available in the archive under the ID sos170711m1.

(1) Sy Clément:

   Voila   ké   mɔ̀̃   n-í   bě   ì̀   ké   ằ   sɛ́ɛ-məgɔ́-bê
   you.see.FR COP person L-LOG do.IRR COMP COP DEF Sambla-person-NOM
   lê
   PRES

   'You see, we could say that that's what it means to be Sambla.'

(2) Gni Emma:

   ǹ́ńkɛ̀̃
   INTERJ

   'That's right.'

(3) Sy Clément:

ké mə̰̀ kʊ́ cèrɛ̀ɛ ằ sɛ́ɛ̣-məgɔ́-bê
COP person D.DEF call.IRR.HAB DEF Sambla-person-NOM

'That's what is called being Sambla.'

(4) (Cont.)

ɛ̀ɛɛ ké lɔ̰́ ké ḭ̀ kàä ằ gɔ̀ɔ nɛ̰̀
HES COP here COP 3PL go.REAL.PRF DEF field LOC

'Ehh, here, they have already gone to the field.'

(5) (Cont.)

ı̰̈ kằ nɛ̰́ ằ gɔ̀ɔ nɛ̰̀ ı̰̈ ké mə̰̀ɛ nəgì dəbɛ̀
2PL.SBJV go.REAL.PFV if DEF field LOC 2PL.SUBORD go.IRR person.PL mind be.good.IRR

'If you go to the field, you go entertain people.'

(6) (Cont.)

ı̰̈ sɔ́ ı̰̈ bằrằ bɛ̋
3PL.SUBORD be.able.IRR 3PL.SUBORD work do.IRR

'So that they can work.'

(7) (Cont.)

ằ bı́ɛ̣-sɛ̋ lë ḭ̀ kằ, ké ḭ̀ kűɛ cɛ́rɛ̋ dìnı̰̋
DEF play-thing.PL PRES.PL 3PL in.hand COP 3PL D.DEF.PL call.IRR dinin

'The instruments that they are holding, they're called *dinin* (barrel drums).'

(8) (Cont.)

dìnı̰̋
dinin

'Dinin.'

(9) (Cont.)

dìnɨ̋ lê lő ké dìnɨ̋ tsɛ̋ sǜɛ sɨ̌ nɔ̋ ì kǎ̀ tsɛ̋-ké dìnɨ̋
dinin PRES here COP dinin INDF three be here 3PL in.hand and dinin
sɨ̋ tsɛ̋-ké sèn-sèn tsɛ̋-ké kɔ̰̀-kɔ̰̀ ǎ̀-né ǎ̀ dənɨ̰̀
female and sen-sen and kon-kon then DEF talking.drum

'The *dinin* here that they have, there are three kinds: the female *dinin*, the *sen-sen*, the *kon-kon*, and then the talking drum (tension drum).'

(10) Gni Emma:

ǎ̀-né dùnɨ̰̀
then talking.drum.PL

'And then the talking drums.'

(11) Sy Clément:

ké lő ì lɛ̂ ǎ̀ gɔ̀ɔ-jèn gɑ̋a nɛ̋
COP here 3PL SUBORD 3SG field-border pull.REAL.NOM LOC

'It's here they put a border around a field.'

(12) (Cont.)

mɔ̰̋ɔ̋ lò̰ nɛ̋ kùaa ǐi gɔ̋ɔ-jɛ̋n gɑ̋a
person.SBJV come if farm.ANTIP.IRR 3PL.PST field-border.PL pull.IRR
jǎnkʊ́ ǐi sɔ́ ǐi fôn sɛ̀ɛ kʊ́ nɛ̀ í
so.that LOG.SBJV be.able.IRR LOG.SBJV fonio dump.IRR D.DEF LOC 2PL
nǎ sɔ́ dəgɔ̀ɛɛ lɛ́ kùaa kʊ́ kù ǎ̀a
PROSP be.able.IRR place.PL REL farm.ANTIP.HAB D.DEF thing 3SG.SBJV
ɲǎ̀ nɛ̋ ǐi ké màa tsɛ̋ jɛ̋n gɑ̋a ǐì
finish.REAL.PFV if 3PL.PST go.IRR again INDF border pull.IRR 3PL.SUBORD
ǎ̀ fôn sɛ̀ɛ kʊ́ nɛ̀ ǐi ǎ̀ kùa
DEF fonio dump.IRR D.DEF LOC 3PL.SUBORD 3SG farm.IRR

'If one wanted to farm, they drew out borders of where they would dump the fonio where you could farm, if we finished farming that part, they would go draw out another area and dump fonio there to farm it.'

(13)　(Cont.)

ä jén gǎa lé kùa kùa fɛ̋ ŋé ä dəgé tɔ̋
DEF border pull.IRR PART farming farming already NEG 3SG make.IRR like
ké ä dán-bű̋ɔ ì̀ dəgɔ̀ɛɛ dán-bű̋ɔ ì̀ fôn
COP 3SG mouth-go.out.PTCP 3PL place.PL mouth-go.out.PTCP 3PL fonio
sɛ̀ɛ kʋ́ nɛ̀
dump.IRR D.DEF LOC

'With the border drawn out, there's not farming right away, it's like the borders have been made, a border is designated and the fonio is dumped.'

(14)　(Cont.)

Voila ké ì̀ l-ä̀ kŭa tsí̠-kú̠ wétənĕ lɔ̋, ì̀
you.see.FR COP 3PL L-3SG farm.NOM cut-catch.REAL.PFV now here 3PL
fôn sɛ̈ɛ, ké ä̀ Báa-blĕ ä̀ fôn sɛ̈ɛ lɔ̋
fonio dump.REAL.PRF COP DEF Baa-Ble DEF fonio dump.REAL.PRF here
ä̀ nɛ̀ ì̀ lɛ̀ wétənĕ ä̀ kŭa tsí̠-kú̠ nɛ̋
3SG LOC 3PL SUBORD now 3SG farm.NOM cut-catch.REAL.NOM LOC

'You see, they started farming here, they have dumped the fonio, it's Baa-ble that has dumped the fonio here now, and now they are starting to farm.'

(15)　(Cont.)

Páakáa tsɛ̋-ké Fìɛ-fɔ́, voila ké ì̀ kʋ́ cɛ̀rɛ̀ gùrên-blă
Pascal and Fiɛ-Fɔ you.see.FR COP 3PL D.DEF call.IRR hoe-drop.NOM

'Pascal and Fiɛ-Fɔ, you see, that's what we call dropping the hoe.'

(16)　Gni Emma:

gùrên-blă
hoe-drop.NOM

'Dropping the hoe.'

(17) Sy Clément:

Voila   ì̀   lé   gùrên blằ   né̋ wétənê̌ ïi   ằ
you.see.FR 3PL SBJV hoe drop.REAL.PFV if now   3PL.PST 3SG
búɔ   i   sí   gṳ̀   ì̀   nǎ   lë̋   tő   mé̋ í
take.out.REAL.PFV LOG RECIP under 3PL PROSP SUBORD meet.IRR HAB LOG
síí̋   ì̀   í   bé̋   ì̀   kʊ́   ằ   búɔ   í   sí
RECIP.WITH 3PL LOG do.IRR COMP D.DEF 3SG take.out.NOM LOG RECIP
gṳ̀
under

'There, now that they are dropping hoes, they took it out underneath them, where they are going to run into each other, that's what we call taking out under them.'[1]

(18) (Cont.)

ïi   i   cề   fǎ   né búɔ   ká̋ ì̀   í
3PL.SUBORD LOG hand put.in.REAL.NOM REL go.out.PFV go 3PL LOG
bé̋   ì̀   á   cề   nề-jərán-jərán   á   á   cề
do.IRR 3PL 2SG hand TRANS-RED-change.REAL.NOM 2SG 2SG hand
nề-jərǎn-jərǎn   á   ằ   kằ   jîo   âa
TRANS-RED-change.IRR 2SG 3SG go.REAL.PFV see.REAL.PFV NEG.Q

'From how they put their hands in, we call that changing your hand, you change your hand, you see him go?'[2]

(19) (Cont.)

Voila   i   né   wétənê̌ ằ   bɔ́   i   sí   gṳ̀   i
you.see.FR 2PL come.IRR now   3SG take.out.IRR LOG RECIP under 2PL
ké̋   blǎ   i   sɔ́n-sɔ́ɛn í   jáa   i   ké̋   nề   tő
go.IRR fall.IRR LOG RED-one 2PL return.IRR 2PL go.IRR come.IRR meet.IRR
í   síí̋   brɔ̰́-nề
LOG RECP.with middle-LOC

'You see, you come now and take out beneath each other, you go and fall into place one by one [side-by-side to farm], you come back and come meet in the middle.'

---

[1] Two men alternate bending over and digging with handheld hoes towards the outside, then turning in towards each other and digging between each other.
[2] The correct gloss of *né búɔ ká̋* in the first clause is not entirely clear.

(20) (Cont.)

ké mɔ̰̀ kʊ́ cɛ̀rɛɛ à gùrên-blǎ
COP person D.DEF call.IRR.HAB DEF hoe-drop.REAL.NOM

'That's what we call dropping the hoe.'

(21) (Cont.)

ké à kəré-bé tsḭ́ɛ tò wè kʊ́ nɛ̀, kằfɔ ì sḭ̀ ằ
COP DEF man-NOM IDEO know.IRR HAB D.DEF LOC dont.say.JU 3PL be 3SG
kṹ nɛ̋ dzʊ́ tɛ̀, í wó kằ à dɔ̀ɔ à
take.REAL.NOM LOC line GEN LOG EMPH go.REAL.PFV 3SG finish.IRR 3SG
jɛ̀n, kʊ́ ɲá ằ nɛ̀ ŋɛ́ ɛ̋ɛ́ dəgɛ̀ ì̀ mɔ̰̀
in.front D.DEF be.NEG 3SG LOC NEG, 3SG.LOG make.IRR 3PL person
cɛ̀rɛɛ ằ bón kpǎ́ ằa béɛ-cɛ̋ á wó
call.IRR.HAB 3SG back close.PTCP 3SG.SUBORD be.REL-manner 2SG EMPH
fṹrǎ́á gù̀-ɲǐ ɲá nɛ̋ ŋɛ́ á wó nǎ á
partner.SBJV neck-pick.up.PTCP be.NEG if NEG 2SG EMPH PROSP 2SG
gù̀-ɲǐ tsɛ̋
neck-pick.up.IRR how

'It was there we could tell who was a true man; one wouldn't say, I'll take a line and go finish first, there wasn't that, they were called closed backs, from the way of doing it, if your partner doesn't get up, how would you get up?'[3]

(22) Gni Emma:

kʊ́ kɔ̀nì á sɔ́ áa gù̀-ɲǐ ŋɛ́
D.DEF TOP.JU 2SG be.able 2SG.SBJV neck-pick.up.IRR NEG

'That's right, you can't get up.'

(23) Sy Clément:

á wó sɔ́ áa gù̀-ɲǐ ŋɛ́ ì́ á wó bȍn
2SG EMPH be.able 2SG.SBJV neck-pick.up.IRR NEG 3PL 2SG EMPH back
kpǎ̰
close.REAL.PRF

'You can't get up, they have closed your back!'

---

[3] "Closed backs" because the farmer is bent over at the waist to dig with the handheld hoe.

(24) (Cont.)

í bón kpǎ kǎ fʃ̰ í kḗ lɛ̏ á ä̀ jô fʃ̰ í jáa í nɛ̏-tő í síí
2PL back close.PTCP go must 2PL go.IRR EMPH 2SG 3SG see.IRR must 2PL go.back.IRR LOG TRANS-meet LOG RECIP.with

'Your backs are closed to the extent that you have to go, you see, you have to come back and cross paths with each other.'

(25) (Cont.)

fʃ̰ ì̀ kǎ blä̀ ì̀ dɔ̌ɔ nɛ̋
must 3PL go fall.IRR 3PL finish.REAL.NOM LOC

'They must finish them [the lines].'

(26) Gni Emma:

ì̀ dɔ̌ɔ nɛ̋
3PL finish.REAL.NOM LOC

'[They] finish them.'

(27) Sy Clément:

Voila ì̀-ǎ-lɔ́ ì̀ dɔ̌ɔ̋ wétənɛ̌ ìi féɛ í gǜ-ɲìi, bíɛ̰-sán-brɛ̰́ sḭ̌ wétənɛ̌ ɲì
you.see.FR you.know.JU 3PL finish.REAL.PRF now 3PL.SUBORD before LOG neck-lift.REAL.NOM.DAT play-thing-play.ANTIP.NOM.PL be now there

'There, you know that they have finished now before getting up, the musicians are there now.'[4]

---

[4] This is one of the primary roles of *griots* in Sambla society, to entertain and provoke the men farming to encourage them to work hard.

(28) Gni Emma:

küɛ bɛ́ɛ lő lɛ̏ ì tənì̧
other.PL.SUBORD put.IRR.HAB come PART 3PL behind

'They follow them.'

(29) Sy Clément:

küɛ bɛ́ɛ lő lɛ̏ ì tənì̧
other.PL.SUBORD put.IRR.HAB come PART 3PL behind

'They follow them.'

(30) (Cont.)

ằ fôn ǐi dəgɔ̌ɛɛ lɛ́ kùäa ằ dəgɛ́ tɔ̋ fôn
DEF fonio 3PL.SUBORD place.PL REL farm.REAL.PRF 3SG make like fonio
sɛ́̋ɛ sɪ̌ kʊ́ nɛ̏, təɾɛ́ kŭa ɲá ằ nɛ̏ fɛ̋́ ŋɛ́
dump.PTCP be D.DEF LOC REL.PRO farm.PTCP be.NEG 3SG LOC yet NEG
fôn sɛ́̋ɛ ɲá kʊ́ nɛ̏ ŋɛ́
fonio dump.PTCP be.NEG D.DEF LOC NEG

'Where they have farmed, it's like they have thrown fonio there, where it hasn't been farmed, they haven't thrown fonio.'

(31) Gni Emma:

fôn sɛ́̋ɛ ɲá kʊ́ nɛ̏ ŋɛ́
fonio dump.PTCP be.NEG D.DEF LOC NEG

'Fonio hasn't been thrown there.'

(32) Sy Clément:

Voila
you.see.FR

'You see.'

(33) (Cont.)

kɛ́ kʊ́ dəgɔ̌ɛɛ bɛ́ lɛ̏ kɛ́ kʊ́ ȁ kùaa gbɛ̏nɛ̋
COP D.DEF place.PL DEM PRES COP D.DEF DEF farm.REAL.ANTIP.NOM before

'It's like that there, that was farming before.'

(34) (Cont.)

mais mí̋ sə̋sȁa nɛ̏ dənı̀ mí̋ í bɛ̋ ı̏ í wó ı̏
but.FR 1PL right.now LOC child.PL 1PL LOG do.IRR COMP LOG EMPH 3PL
dzɔ̂ kų̀ í kȁ ı̏ dɔ̀ɔ á jɛ̋n ı̏ á
line take.IRR LOG go.REAL.PFV 3PL finish.REAL.PRF 2SG in.front COMP 2SG
wó jío ı̏ í sɔ́ɔ kùa lɛ̏
EMPH say.REAL.PFV COMP LOG be.able.IRR.HAB farm.NOM DAT

'But us kids today, we say we take a line, that we've finished it before you, that you said you could farm.'

(35) Gni Emma:

ɛ̏ɛ í dɔ̋ɔ á jɛ̋n âa
yes LOG finish.REAL.PFV 2SG in.front NEG.Q

'Yes, that I finished before you, didn't I.'

(36) Sy Clément:

í dɔ̋ɔ á jɛ̋n âa
LOG finish.REAL.PFV 2SG in.front NEG.Q

'That I finished before you, didn't I.'

(37) Gni Emma:

í wó fų̏ á wɛ̋ òo
LOG EMPH surpass.IRR 2SG with EXCL

'That I'm better than you!'

(38) Sy Clément:

í wó fã̰   á wɛ́̃ kʊ́ʊ   mɔ̰̀   fã̰
LOG EMPH surpass.IRR 2SG with D.DEF.COP person surpass.REAL.NOM
mɔ̰̀ɔ   ŋɛ́
person.with NEG

'That I am better than you, [but] that's not being better than someone.'

(39) Gni Emma:

ḭ̀   áa   kɛ́ nɛ́̃ kərê ḭ̀   á   nɛ̀̃
COMP 2SG.SBJV COP if man COMP 2SG come.IRR

'[We say] if you are a man, then come here.'

(40) Sy Clément:

kɛ́ ä̰ tərê   í wóo   bä̰   nɛ́̃ mɔ̰̀   wè fɔ̰̃́
COP 2SG REL.PRO.PRES 2PL EMPH.SBJV do.REAL.PFV if person with must
ä̰ sərä̰ kɛ́̃   nɛ́   í bɛ́̃   ḭ̀   kərê í tîi   á
DEF master go.IRR 1SG.COMP LOG do.IRR COMP man LOG accept 2SG
nɔ̰́   nɛ̀̃
that.for LOC

'That's what.... that's what will make it so that that person has to come and say, "Man, I accept you" [=your challenge]'

(41) (Cont.)

í tîi á nɔ̰́   nɛ̀̃, parce que *á dő   kʊ́ dəgɔ̰́ nɛ́̃,*
LOG accept 2SG that.for LOC because.FR 2SG though D.DEF place LOC
óo   nă á gṵ̀-ɲḭ̀   óo   kɛ̃́ mɪ̰́̃
2SG.EMPH PROSP 2SG neck-pick.up.IRR 2SG.EMPH.SBJV go.IRR where

'I accept, because you are there like that, where would you get up to go?'

(42) Gni Emma:

á kä̰   mɪ̰́̃
2SG go.REAL.PFV where

'You'll go where?'

(43) Sy Clément:

kóʊ kằ nɛ́ sɔ́ń tɛ̀ jôo lɛ̀, á wó ằ
D.DEF.SBVJ go.REAL.PFV if time.REL GEN fail.NOM DAT 2SG EMPH 3SG
jú á fírá́-kərê lɛ̀, ắ, mó ằ tsíɔ
say.IRR 2SG colleague-man DAT INTERJ 1SG.EMPH 3SG abandon.REAL.PFV
á nų́ nɛ̈
2SG that.for LOC

'If you can't take it anymore, you tell your adversary, "Ah, you beat me."'

(44) (Cont.)

mó ằ tsíɔ á nų́ nɛ̈
1SG.EMPH 3SG abandon.REAL.PFV 2SG that.for LOC

'You beat me.'

(45) (Cont.)

kʊ́ jərá óo tɛ̀ kənâ. Voila.
D.DEF become.REAL.PFV 2SG.EMPH GEN older.brother you.see.FR

'He became your big brother [stronger than you]. You see.'

(46) Gni Emma:

bíɛ-sán-brɛ̌ nəgǐ dəbɛ̌ sǐ wétənɛ̌ kʊ́ sɔ̀n
play-thing-play.ANTIP.NOM.PL mind be.good.PTCP be now D.DEF time
nɛ̈
LOC

'The drummers are happy now.'

(47) Sy Clément:

Mais *kűɛ nəgǐ dəbɛ̌ sǐ kɛ̀, ké kűɛ í dăa*
but.FR other.PL mind be.good.PTCP be EMPH COP other.PL 2PL flatter
mɛ̈ í dzį́ í sí tɛ̀ âa
SUBORD 2PL put.IRR LOG RECIP GEN NEG.Q

'But they are happy, they flatter you and pit you against one another, don't they.'

(48) (Cont.)

ké bíɛ-sán-brɛ̃́   í dǎa i dzí   i sí tɛ̀
COP play-thing-play.ANTIP.NOM.PL 2PL flatter 2PL put.IRR LOG RECIP GEN
âa
NEG.Q

'The musicians flatter you and pit you against one another, right.'

(49) Gni Emma:

ńjʋ́wɛ́ n-í cé-tǎa nɛ̃́-bǎ̰a̰   ì́ lɛ́
Njʋwɛ N-LOG hand-palm TRANS-beat.IRR.HAB 3PL DAT

'Njʋwɛ claps her hands for them.'

(50) Sy Clément:

Voila   kʋ́ kòee   kʋ́ ì̀ təmàa-sʋ́ à̰ lɛ́ jouer ì̀
you.see.FR D.DEF sing.IRR.HAB D.DEF 3PL praise-song 3SG DAT play.FR 3PL
lɛ́
DAT

'You see, she sings their praise songs, plays for them.'[5]

(51) (Cont.)

Voila   ké à̰ ńjʋ́wɛ́ nɛ̀̃   lɔ̃́... kʋ́ nɛ̀̃
you.see.FR COP DEF Njʋwɛ SUBORD here D.DEF LOC

'You see, that's what Njʋwɛ does there.'

(52) Gni Emma:

kʋ́ʋ kû səgɔ̃
D.DEF thing good

'That's a good thing.'

---

[5] There appears to be a verb missing in the clause containing 'praise song'; it is unclear what this should be, especially with the verb in the following clause being a French loanword.

(53) Sy Clément:

    á   ǎ   jĩo   âa
    2SG 3SG see.REAL.PFV NEG.Q

    'You see.'

(54) (Cont.)

    Voila   *sì-flâ*
    you.see.FR Sy-Fla

    'There, Sy-Fla.'[6]

(55) (Cont.)

    Voila   *ké   ǎ   dìn̄   sí́   lɛ̀*   *sì-flâ   kǎ*
    you.see.FR COP DEF drum female SUBORD Sy-Fla in.hand

    'There, that's the "female barrel drum" that Sy-Fla has.'

(56) (Cont.)

    Voila   René *lò̌   ǎ   fôn-   ké   ǎ   məni-sán   nê*
    you.see.FR René come DEF fonio COP DEF woman-thing PRES

    'There, René [is bringing] the fonio– that's a plate.'

(57) (Cont.)

    ké gbə̌nə̋ ké fónô,   ĩi   ǎ   bɛ̀ɛ   ì̀   kǎ   fónô,
    COP before COP basket 3PL.PST 3SG do.IRR.HAB 3PL in.hand basket
    voila   *dɔ̋nké* maintenant *ké ì̀   ɲìäa   lɔ̋,   ì̀   ǎ*
    you.see.FR so   now   COP 3PL finish.REAL.PRF here 3PL DEF
    kŭa   ɲìäa   lɔ̋
    farm.NOM finish.REAL.PRF here

    'Before, it was a small basket, they would be given small baskets, okay, so now it's done here, they are done farming here.'

---

[6] The name 'Sy-Fla' means 'first son-Fulani', i.e. this man is the firstborn son of his mother and his birth had some relation to the Fulani people.

23.2 The toad and the rabbit

The following text is a folktale told by three middle-aged women, Ga-Kənɔn Traoré (mother of Gni Emma), Ga-Masa Traoré (mother of Sy Clément), and Nyuma-Koro Traoré. It is the story of the toad and the rabbit. The rabbit is usually the trickster in Sambla stories, the animal that outsmarts all the others, but in this case, the toad gets the upper hand. This folktale has many examples of shadowing, a discourse strategy where interlocutors repeat what the primary speaker has just said; see §21.6.2.4. I have transcribed some but not all of these instances.

The story was recorded on August 5, 2017 in Bouendé, Burkina Faso. It was recorded by Sy Clément Traoré and Gni Emma Traoré using a Zoom Q8 video recorder. It can be found in the archive under the ID sos170805t15.

(1) Ga-Kənɔn:

Bon   mó   sĭ à   tê   móo   jón-jŏn   tsɛ́   təmɛ́
well.FR 1SG.EMPH be 3SG GEN 1SG.SBJV RED-story INDF tell.IRR

'Well, I want to tell a story.'

(2) (Cont.)

à   sân   dzʊ̀   kʊ́   tsɔ́ǹ   mè   à   kűi   nɛ́   ŋɛ́   yèe,
DEF rabbit mouth D.DEF miss.out.IRR HAB DEF thing.PL LOC NEG EXCL
kʊ́   ké à   wò   ké à   kû   tsḭ́-kə̄rḭ́ǐ   âa,   kû
D.DEF COP 3SG EMPH COP 3SG thing cut-take.ANTIP NEG.Q thing
tsḭ́-kúnḭ́
cut-take.ANTIP.NOM

'The rabbit doesn't miss out on anything, is it not him who starts things, that he is the start of things?'

(3) (Cont.)

sân   kűɛɛ   sío   à   mɔ̀nəgɔ̀ wè,   íwǐ   kɛ́   à
rabbit other.PL.PST get.up.REAL.PFV DEF toad with LOG.PL go.IRR DEF
gɔ̀nfɑ́   cənḭ́   jəgɛ̀ nɛ̀
couscous trade.IRR dog LOC

'The rabbit and the toad got up to go trade couscous[7] for a dog.'

---

[7] I am glossing gɔ̀nfɑ́ here as couscous, but it is a snack made from ground millet mixed with powdered peanuts and rolled into little balls.

(4) (Cont.)

ì lɛ̈ à gɔ̀nfǎ dəgɛ̋ ì wɔ̀ yέrέ tê, ì-ǎ-lɔ́ à
3PL SUBORD DEF couscous make.IRR 3PL EMPH self.JU GEN you.know.JU DEF
mɔ̋nəgɔ̋ sɪ̌ dɔ́n-dɔ́ní ɛ̈ɛ́ bɛ̋ ì ləgɔ̀-ləgɔ̀-ləgɔ̀
toad be RED-a.little 3SG.LOG do.IRR COMP IDEO

'They made the couscous themselves, and you know, the toad is there little by little, like ləgɔ-ləgɔ-ləgɔ [sound of throat moving].'

(5) (Cont.)

sân nɛ̈ í bɛ̋ ì ɛ̋! í tɛ̋ mɔ̋nəgɔ̋, ì kέ
rabbit SUBORD LOG do.IRR COMP INTERJ LOG dear toad COMP COP
óo sɪ̋ ì fəlɛ̂ɛ̂ ì jəgɔ́ɛ̋ɛ nɛ̋↘
2SG.EMPH be 3PL thing.PRES 3PL munch.ANTIP.REAL.NOM LOC.Q

'The rabbit said, Eh! My dear toad. Are you there munching on your things?'[8]

(6) (Cont.)

ɛ̈ɛ́ bɛ̋ ì í nǎ fên tɔ̀ í kɔ̋n ìi
3SG.LOG do.IRR COMP LOG PROSP thing leave.IRR LOG head LOG.SBJV
cì̀ ŋέ
die.IRR NEG

'He [the toad] said he wasn't going to leave it [the food] there on his head to die [of hunger].'

(7) Nyuma-Koro:

ìi fέn bέ í kɔ̋n ìi cì̀ ŋέ
LOG.DAT thing DEM LOG head LOG.SBVJ die.IRR NEG

'That thing on his head to die of hunger.'

---

8 This is an example of an antipassive-marked verb being used with a direct object; this gives the meaning that the toad is accused of eating some but not all of his couscous. See §12.3 for further discussion.

(8) Ga-Kənɔn:

sân í nȷ̈ɛ cɛ̋ɛ kʊ́ʊ kűɛ jəgő
rabbit LOG that.for.PL take.out.IRR D.DEF.SBJV other.PL munch.IRR

'The rabbit also took out some of his to munch on it.'

(9) Ga-Masa:

sân í nȷ̈ɛ cɛ̋ɛ kʊ́ʊ kűɛ jəgő
rabbit LOG that.for.PL take.out.IRR D.DEF.SBJV other.PL munch.IRR

'The rabbit also took out some of his to munch on it.'

(10) Ga-Kənɔn:

kʊ́ tő lɛ́ kərʊ́ʊʊ
D.DEF like PART long.time

'[It was] like that for a long time.'

(11) Ga-Masa:

ïanɛ́ ì kɛ̋ sɔ́ ä cṵ̂-dəgɔ̀ɛɛ
moment.JU 3PL go.IRR arrive.IRR DEF trade-place.PL

'As soon as they arrived at the trading ground…'

(12) Ga-Kənɔn:

sân nɛ̋ îi gɔ̀nfä́ kərúú jəgɔ̆ ɲìäa
rabbit PST LOG.DAT couscous all munch.NOM finish.REAL.PRF

'The rabbit had eaten up all of his couscous.'

(13) Ga-Masa:

ȍo nȷ̈ jóo wétənɛ̆ ä̀ jəgɛ̈ səgɔ̆ tɛ̋
3SG.EMPH that.for fail.REAL.PFV now DEF dog good GEN

'His wasn't enough to get a good dog.'

(14) Ga-Kənɔn:

ăa cənį́-cənį́ kʊ́ tɔ́ ŏo nɔ̰̀
3SG.SUBORD RED-trade.REAL.PFV D.DEF like 3SG.EMPH that.for
jóo wétənɛ̌ ǎ jəgɛ̰̀ kùkù tɛ̰̀
fail.REAL.PFV now DEF dog entire GEN

'When he had traded now, his wasn't enough to get a whole dog.'

(15) (Cont.)

sân nɔ̰̀n jərâ jəgɛ̰̀-kų̂n
rabbit that.for become.REAL.PFV dog-head

'The rabbit's [was only enough for] a dog head.'

(16) (Cont.)

mɔ̰̌nəgɔ̰̌ nɔ̰̀n mɛ̰̀ jərâ wétənɛ̌ ǎ jəgɛ̰̀ səgɔ̌, ì
toad that.for SUBORD become.REAL.PFV now DEF dog good 3PL
kʊ́ cɛ̀rɛ̀ɛ ì Sɔ̰́n-fɔ̋n
D.DEF call.IRR.HAB COMP Sɔnfon

'For the toad, it was enough for a good dog, he was called "Sɔnfon" [=character-better].'

(17) Ga-Masa:

sân nɔ̰̀n kɛ̋ Tɔ̌fɔ́dzìa
rabbit that.for COP.PST Tɔfɔdzia

'For the rabbit, it was "Tɔfɔdzia" [=Jula for 'we don't say the rest'].'

(18) Ga-Kənɔn:

sân nɔ̰̀n kɛ̋ Tɔ̌fɔ́dzìa, ǎ wò nɔ̰̀ síɔ
rabbit that.for COP.PST Tɔfɔdzia 3SG EMPH that.for arrive.REAL.PFV
jəgɛ̰̀-kɔ̰̂n tɛ̰̀
dog-head GEN

'For the rabbit, it was Tɔfɔdzia, all he got for his was a dog head.'

(19) (Cont.)

kʊ́ʊ Tɔ̂fɔ́dzìa
D.DEF Tɔfɔdzia

'That was Tɔfɔdzia.'

(20) (Cont.)

ì   wɛ̀   cèrè,   ɔ̰̂hɔ̰̂,   ằa   təgŏ-təgò   kʊ́ tɔ̋, ì
3PL SUBORD sleep.IRR INTERJ 3SG.SUBORD RED-sit.REAL.PFV D.DEF like 3PL
kǎ   sɔ́   kʊ́ gʊ̋ɔ bɛ́ nɛ̀
go.REAL.PTCP arrive.IRR D.DEF country DEM LOC

'They slept, uh-huh, since it had turned out like that, they were going to arrive in this country.'

(21) (Cont.)

sân   mɛ̀   í   bɛ̋   ŋɛ́ ǐi   kằ   nɛ̋ sɔ́   ằ
rabbit SUBORD LOG do.IRR NEG 3PL.SBJV go.REAL.PFV if arrive.IRR DEF
gʊ̀ɔ   bɛ́ nɛ̀
country DEM LOC

'The rabbit said if they were going to arrive in that country'

(22) (Cont.)

ǐi   í   bằ   nɛ̋ì   í   màa kʊ̀ tò
3PL.SBJV LOG do.REAL.PFV if COMP LOG again toh take.IRR

'if they said to take toh'

(23) (Cont.)

ǐi   à   bɛ̀   mɔ̰̋   tʊ̋ḭ   kɑ̋
3PL.SBJV 3SG do.IRR person pot.PL in.hand

'to give it to strangers'

(24) Ga-Masa:

ì̀ kóʊ məŋä̀ tûn kűɛ nɔ̋
COMP ANAPH.COP rain.chief pot other.PL that.for

'That that's for the new rain chief.'

(25) Nyuma-Koro:

ì̀ kóʊ məŋä̀ tûn kűɛ nɔ̋
COMP ANAPH.COP rain.chief pot other.PL that.for

'That that's for the new rain chief.'[9]

(26) Ga-Kənɔn:

ä̀ wɔ̀ nɔ̀̃n bɛ́ síɔ wɛ́ ä̀ jəgěé
3SG EMPH that.for DEM arrive.REAL.PFV FOC DEF dog.SBJV
jərǎ-jərǎ ä̀ Tɔ̋fɔ̋dzìa ä̀ tê
RED-become.REAL.PFV DEF Tɔfɔdzia 3SG GEN

'For him, he got Tɔfɔdzia.'

(27) (Cont.)

ì̀ wɛ̀ jáa wétənɛ̌ í tsín mɛ̋
3PL SUBORD return.IRR now LOG back with

'They returned now.'

(28) (Cont.)

ì̀ nà-tɔ́ lë̀ bɛ́ wɛ̀ dərɔ̰́ ìi nɛ́ tàaső
3PL come-while.JU PRES be.REL HAB only 3PL.SUBORD come.IRR surprise
kòe lë̀ ká̰
hyrax.PL SUBORD go

'When coming back, to their surprise, they came across some hyraxes.'[10]

---

9 At this point, there was low unintelligible conversation between the women. It appears that they had started down the wrong path in the story, hence the abrupt change of subject in the next line.
10 A hyrax is a small mammal; though rodent-like, its closest relative is the elephant.

(29) (Cont.)

    kòe lɛ̀ kā́-kā́ dərɔ́ ằ sɔ̃̀n-fɔ́n l-í yìrè wétənĕ
    hyrax.PL SUBORD RED-go.REAL.PFV only DEF Sɔnfon L-LOG ?? now
    mɛ̀ ằ kòe kàa
    3SG.SUBORD DEF hyrax.PL chase

    'When the hyraxes were leaving, the dog Sɔnfon chased them.'[11]

(30) Ga-Masa:

    ằ mɔ̃nəgɔ̃ kʊ́ sɔ́ɔ̀ ằá ɲì̀ nɛ̀̃ ɲé, ằ
    DEF toad D.DEF be.able.IRR.HAB 3SG.SBJV run.REAL.NOM LOC NEG DEF
    sɔ̃̀n-fɔ́n lɛ̀ sɔ́ ằá ɲì̀ nɛ̀̃
    Sɔnfon SUBORD be.able.IRR 3SG.SBJV run.REAL.NOM LOC

    'The toad couldn't run, but Sɔnfon could run.'

(31) Ga-Kənɔn:

    mɔ̃nəgɔ̃ fɛ̀n-jɔ̀ fɛ̀n-jɔ̀ fɛ̀n-jɔ̀
    toad IDEO IDEO IDEO

    'The toad limped along like fɛn-jɔ, fɛn-jɔ, fɛn-jɔ.'

(32) ằ sân kʊ́ sɔ́ɔ̀ ằá ɲì̀ nɛ̀̃ ằá
    DEF rabbit D.DEF be.able.IRR.HAB 3SG.SBJV run.REAL.NOM LOC 3SG.SBJV
    krɛ̀̃n-krɛ́̃n ằá kɛ̃́ lɔ̃́
    IDEO 3SG.SBJV go.IRR here
    'The rabbit could run, he would run with short fast steps here.'

(33) Nyuma-Koro:

    ằá krɛ̀̃n-krɛ́̃n ằá kɛ̃́ lɔ̃́ ằá krɛ̀̃n-krɛ́̃n ằá
    3SG.SBJV IDEO 3SG.SBJV go.IRR here 3SG.SBJV IDEO 3SG.SBJV
    jáa lɔ̃́
    return.IRR here

    'He ran here and then he ran there.'

---

[11] It is not clear what yìrè means here. It could be a pronunciation of the Jula loan yéré 'self', but that would leave the clause without a verb.

(34) Ga-Masa:

à wò bɛ́ wétənĕ nɛ́...
3SG EMPH put.IRR now LOC

'He [followed] them now....'

(35) Ga-Kənɔn:

à sɔ̀n-főn kà̰ wétənĕ nɛ́ kôʊ kɛ́ à kò
DEF Sɔnfon go.REAL.PFV now LOC D.DEF.SUBORD go.IRR DEF hyrax
kṵ̀
catch.IRR

'Sɔnfon went now and caught the hyrax.'

(36) (Cont.)

sân ɲĭ-cɛ̰́ fà̰n mè mɔ̀nəgɔ̀ wè âa
rabbit run.NOM-leg.PL surpass.IRR HAB toad with NEG.Q

'The rabbit's running legs pass up the toad's, don't they.'

(37) (Cont.)

ɔ̀o kɛ́ wétənĕ sɔ́ mɛ̀ à sɔ̀n-főn
3SG.EMPH.SUBORD go.IRR now arrive.IRR 3SG.SUBORD DEF Sɔnfon
kǎa âa
chase.IRR NEG.Q

'He [the toad] caught up and chased away Sɔnfon.'

(38) Ga-Masa:

mɛ̀ à Tɔ̀fɔ́dzìa jəgĕ-kɔ̂ bɔ̀ í tê
3SG.SUBORD DEF Tɔfɔdzia dog-head take.out.IRR LOG GEN

'Then he took out Tɔfɔdzia the dog head.'

(39) Ga-Kənɔn:

mɛ̈   à   Tɔ̈fɔ̈dzìa jəgɛ̈-kɔ̂   bɔ̈   í   tê
3SG.SUBORD DEF Tɔfɔdzia dog-head take.out.IRR LOG GEN

'Then he took out Tɔfɔdzia the dog head.'

(40) Ga-Masa:

mɛ̈   kɛ̋   à   dɛ̀   ä̀   kö   lɛ̀
3SG.SUBORD go.IRR 3SG stick.IRR DEF hyrax DAT

'And he stuck it to the hyrax.'

(41) Ga-Kənɔn:

mɛ̈   kɛ̋   à   dɛ̀   ä̀   kö   lɛ̀
3SG.SUBORD go.IRR 3SG stick.IRR DEF hyrax DAT

'And he stuck it to the hyrax.'

(42) (Cont.)

mɛ̈   í   bɛ̋   ŋé...
3SG.SUBORD LOG do.IRR ???

'He said... '[12]

(43) Ga-Masa:

ä̀   mɔ̈nəgɔ̈ nä̀   lɛ̋   sɔ́...
DEF toad   come.REAL.PFV PST arrive.IRR

'When the toad arrived...'

---

[12] Ga-Kənɔn has a tendency to use the particle ŋé in quotative constructions, among other places. It does not mean the negative here. When I asked other consultants about it, they report that it is optional.

(44) Ga-Kənɔn:

ì ɛ́! ɛ́! ń tɛ́ sân! ì ké jəgḛ̀ lé lɛ̀ à
COMP INTERJ INTERJ 1SG dear rabbit COMP COP dog which SUBORD 3SG
kṵ́
catch.REAL.PFV

'[He said] Eh eh! Mr. Rabbit! Which dog caught it?'

(45) (Cont.)

à Tɔ̀fɔ́dzìa dzʊ̀ dzìɛ jó wè à lé âa
DEF Tɔfɔdzia mouth stick.REAL.PFV see.IRR HAB 3SG DAT NEG.Q

'You don't see that it's Tɔfɔdzia's mouth that's stuck to it?'

(46) Ga-Masa:

ì ké ǎ tɔ̀fɔ́ɔ́ nɛ̃́ ŋɛ́ yèe, ì ké à tɔ̀fɔ́ lɛ̀ à
COMP COP DEF Tɔfɔ.SBJV if ??? EXCL COMP COP DEF Tɔfɔ SUBORD 3SG
kṵ́, ì sɔ̀n-fɔ́n nǎ ŋà̰ à jó mḭ́-nǎ,
catch.REAL.PFV COMP Sɔnfon PROSP FOC 3SG see.IRR where-towards
ì ké à tɔ̀fɔ̀ɔ âa
COMP COP DEF Tɔfɔ.SUBORD NEG.Q

'If it's not Tɔfɔ, who is it? Tɔfɔ caught it, where would Sɔn-Fon find it, it was Tɔfɔ!'

(47) Ga-Kənɔn:

ì ké à tɔ̀fɔ́ lɛ̀ à kṵ́
COMP COP DEF Tɔfɔ SUBORD 3SG catch.REAL.PFV

'It was Tɔfɔ who caught it.'

(48) (Cont.)

ì ké à tɔ̀fɔ́ lɛ̀ à kṵ́
COMP COP DEF Tɔfɔ SUBORD 3SG catch.REAL.PFV

'It was Tɔfɔ who caught it.'

(49) Ga-Masa:

ì   ä̀   wò̰ yéré lɛ̀   ä̀   dzʊ̀ dzǐɛ   jő   wɛ́ ä̀
COMP 3SG EMPH self.JU SUBORD 3SG mouth stick.PTCP see.IRR HAB 3SG
lɛ́   âa
DAT NEG.Q

'[He said] that couldn't he see for himself that his mouth was stuck to it?'

(50) Ga-Kənɔn:

ä̀   dzʊ̀   dzǐɛ   ä̀   lɛ́, ä̀   sɔ̀n-fő̰n käa   kʊ́   sɔ̀n nɛ̰̀
3SG mouth stick.PTCP 3SG DAT 3SG Sonfon chase.REAL.PRF D.DEF time LOC
mɛ̰̀   kʊ́   dzʊ̀   bɔ̰̀   kò̰ lɛ̰̀
3SG.SUBORD D.DEF mouth take.off.IRR hyrax DAT

'The mouth was stuck to it, at that time he had already chased away Sonfon to get his mouth off of the hyrax.'

(51) Nyuma-Koro:

ì   ä̀   dzʊ̀   dzǐɛ   lɛ̰̀   bɛ́ɛ   ä̀   lɛ́
COMP 3SG mouth stick.PTCP SUBORD be.REL 3SG DAT

'That here his mouth is stuck to it.'

(52) Ga-Masa:

ä̀   mɔ̀nəgɔ̀ mɔ̰̀mä̰̀   wɛ́
DEF toad   be.quiet.REAL.PFV FOC

'The toad was quiet.'

(53) Ga-Kənɔn:

mɛ̰̀nəgɔ̀ mɔ̰̀mä̰̀
toad   be.quiet.REAL.PFV

'The toad was quiet.'

(54) (Cont.)

ǐi kɛ́ à bɛ̀ í kǔlɛ̌, ǐ wɛ̀ ǎ gɔ́́εε
3PL.SUBORD go.IRR 3SG put.IRR LOG close 3PL SUBORD DEF wood.PL
ŋɛ́́εn
gather.IRR

'They put it next to them and they gathered wood.'

(55) Ga-Masa:

ǐ wɛ̀ ǎ gɔ́́εε ŋɛ́́εn wétənɛ̌
3PL SUBORD DEF wood.PL gather.IRR now

'They gathered wood now.'

(56) Ga-Kənɔn:

mɛ̀nəgɔ̀ í bɛ́ ǐ wétənɛ̌ ǎ! í wó kʊ́ sɔ́ɔ̀
toad LOG do.IRR COMP now INTERJ LOG EMPH D.DEF be.able.IRR.HAB
kɔ́́ɔ lɛ́́ ŋé yèe
walk.NOM DAT NEG EXCL

'The toad said, ah! I can't go out walking!'

(57) Ga-Masa:

í wó yɛ̀rɛ̀ ǎ kǔ bé kʊ́ dzɛ́́ ǎ mənǐ lɛ́́
LOG EMPH self.JU 3SG thing DEM D.DEF be.good.PTCP DEF woman.PL DAT
ŋé yèe
NEG EXCL

'[The toad said] that women don't like him.'

(58) Ga-Kənɔn:

í wó... ǎ mɔ̀̃ε lɛ̀ ŋé
LOG EMPH DEF person.PL DAT NEG

'That people.... [didn't like] him.'

(59) (Cont.)

ì   wóo   tsí-tsí   nḗ lé   í   wóo   kḗ
LOG EMPH.SBJV RED-jump.REAL.PFV if PART LOG EMPH.SBJV go.IRR
sɔ́   sə́sə̀a   nɛ̀ ŋɛ́ dərɔ̰́ ì   nǎ   í   bḗ   ḭ̀   fên
arrive.IRR right.now LOC NEG only 3PL PROSP LOG do.IRR COMP thing
kű͂ɔ-ɲènènènè lê
IDEO   PRES

'[He said that] if he comes jumping up now, they will say that thing, that is too fresh [=slimy].'

(60) Ga-Masa:

ḭ̀   fên   kű͂ɔ-ɲènènènè lê   ằ   sìɔ   ŋằ mű͂   mɔ̀͂
COMP thing IDEO   PRES 3SG arrive.REAL.PRF FOC where person
gṵ̀,   ḭ̀   ằ   mənű͂   nǎ   lɛ̰̀   í   sű   ṵ̋   í
under COMP DEF woman.PL PROSP FOC LOG pick.up.IRR 3PL.SBJV LOG
fí   ɲì   sə́sə̀a   nɛ̀
throw.IRR there right.now LOC

'[They will say,] where did that fresh thing come from underneath us? And then they will pick him up and throw him away.'

(61) Ga-Kɔnɔn:

ḭ̀   ɛ̰̋ɛ́   fí   ɲì   sə́sə̀a   nɛ̀, ḭ̀   ằ   wɔ̀   lɛ̰̀
COMP 3SG.LOG throw.IRR there right.now LOC COMP 3SG EMPH SUBORD
sɔ́ɔ̀   ɲì   nɛ̀
be.able.IRR run.REAL.NOM LOC

'[He said that] she will pick me up and throw me, [but] that he [the rabbit] is there who knows how to run.'

(62) Nyuma-Koro:

ḭ̀   ằ   kḗ   í   bḗ   ḭ̀   kű͂ɔ   [sɪ̰̌]
COMP 3SG go.IRR LOG do.IRR COMP cool.PTCP [be]

'[They will] say that [it's] fresh.'

(63) Ga-Kənɔn:

ì ǎ wò lɛ́ nǎ ǎ krèn-krɛ́n ì ǎ wòó kɛ́ ŋɛ̋
COMP 3SG EMPH SBJV PROSP 3SG IDEO   COMP 3SG EMPH.SBJV go.IRR Nɛ

'[The toad said] that he [the rabbit] should go and run away from here!'

(64) Nyuma-Koro:

ì ǎá kɛ́ ǎ tâ sʉ̀
COMP 3SG.SBJV go.IRR DEF fire get.IRR

'To go get fire.'

(65) Ga-Kənɔn:

ì ǎá kɛ́ ǎ tâ sʉ̀ ì ǎá nɛ̏
COMP 3SG.SBJV go.IRR DEF fire get.IRR COMP 2SG.SBJV come.IRR

'That he should go get fire and bring it.'

(66) Ga-Masa:

sân n-í bɛ̋ ì wétənɛ̌ í wó lɛ̏ í wó təgɔ̀n
rabbit L-LOG do.IRR COMP now LOG EMPH SUBORD LOG EMPH name
kʉ́ dzɛ̋ ŋé, í wóo kǎ nɛ̋ ŋɛ̋...
D.DEF be.good.PTCP NEG LOG EMPH.SBJV go.REAL.PFV if Nɛ

'The rabbit said now that he doesn't have a good name, if he goes...'

(67) Ga-Kənɔn:

ì nǎ í bɛ̋ ì sân sïɛ
3PL PROSP LOG do.IRR COMP rabbit fly.REAL.PRF

'They will say the rabbit has darted out.'[13]

---

[13] This seems to imply that people will try to hunt him.

(68) Ga-Masa:

ȉ nǎ í bɛ́ ȉ sân sïɛ ȉ ǟ sïɛ-
3PL PROSP LOG do.IRR COMP rabbit fly.REAL.PRF COMP 3SG fly.REAL.PRF
ȉ ǟ sïo ŋǟ mḭ́
COMP 3SG get.up.REAL.PRF FOC where

'They will say the rabbit has darted out, he has darted out–, where did he come from?'

(69) Nyuma-Koro:

sân sïɛ ɲì
rabbit fly.REAL.PRF there

'The rabbit has darted out there!'

(70) Ga-Kənɔn:

sân sïɛ sân sïɛ!
rabbit fly.REAL.PRF rabbit fly.REAL.PRF

'The rabbit has darted out, the rabbit has darted out!'

(71) (Cont.)

kʊ́ tɔ́ kʊ́rʊ́ʊʊ ǟ mɔ̀nəgɔ̀ gùrè nɛ̀-fä ǎ
D.DEF like long.time DEF toad   voice TRANS-convince.REAL.PRF 3SG
wɔ̀ wɛ̀
EMPH with

'After a long time like that, the toad convinced him.'

(72) (Cont.)

ȉ ǟ wɔ̀ nɔ̰̀ fɔ̰́ fɔ́n í wó nɔ̰̀ wɛ̀
COMP 3SG EMPH that.for better more LOG EMPH that.for with

'That his [skills] were better.'

(73) Ga-Masa:

ì   ǎ̀   wɔ̀   sɔ́ɔ̀   ɲï̀   nɛ̈
COMP 3SG EMPH be.able.IRR.HAB run.REAL.NOM LOC

'That he could run.'

(74) Ga-Kənɔn:

ǎ̀   wɔ̀   kɛ̋   ǎ̀   tâ   sṳ̀
3SG EMPH go.IRR DEF fire get.IRR

'He went to get fire.'

(75) (Cont.)

ǎ̤á   fa̤-fa̤   í   jɛ̋n mɛ̋   mɔ̈nəgɔ̈ lɛ̈   sú
3SG.SBJV RED-pass.REAL.PFV LOG front with toad   SUBORD get.up.IRR
mɛ̈   ǎ̀   brɛ̀nɛ̀n kɛ̀ɛ
3SG.SUBORD DEF switch break.IRR

'When he had gone ahead, the toad got up and broke off a switch.'

(76) (Cont.)

mɛ̈   ǎ̀   brìnì̤   səŋà   lɔ̋   ǎ̀   wɔ̀   cɛ̰̈ɛ
3SG.SUBORD DEF switch.PL lay.IRR here 3SG EMPH aside

'He laid the switches to the side to wait.'

(77) (Cont.)

mɛ̈   təgɔ̋ɛ   kɛ́ɛ   mɛ̈   kűe   frǎ̰   kə̀nú`
3SG.SUBORD certain.PL break.IRR 3SG.SUBORD other.PL thrash.IRR stone
jɛ̀n
front

'He broke some them and thrashed them against a stone.'

(78) (Cont.)

mɛ̀	frá̰	wétənĕ
3SG.SUBORD	fray.IRR	now

'It frayed now...'

(79) Ga-Masa:

mɛ̀	kűɛ	lé	dɔ́ɔ	í	mà̰-məlĕ	pó-pó-pó-pó
3SG.SUBORD	other.PL	SBJV	fray.IRR	LOG	RED-all	RED-IDEO

'Until all of them were frayed.'

(80) Ga-Kənɔn:

mɛ̀	fà̰	mɛ̀	í	məgŏ	wétənĕ	ǎ	kò	ŋəmà
3SG.SUBORD	pass.IRR	3SG.SUBORD	LOG	hide.IRR	now		DEF	hyrax blood

nɛ̀
LOC

'Then he went and hid himself in hyrax blood.'

(81) (Cont.)

ǎ	búɔ	wétənĕ	mɛ̀	í	fɔ̰́	mɛ̀
DEF	go.out.REAL.PFV	now	3SG.SUBORD	LOG	inflate.IRR	3SG.SUBORD

təgḭ̀	lɔ́
stand.IRR	here

'He came out now and inflated himself and stood there.'

(82) Ga-Masa:

mɛ̀	í	bá̰	wétənĕ	ǎ	kòo-məŋà	nɛ̀	kűrűʊ	ǎ
3SG.SUBORD	LOG	beat.IRR	now	DEF	burrow	LOC	long.time	3SG

kà̰	təgò	wétənĕ	nɛ̋	sá̰ɠə	sɔ̋ń	tɛ̋	mɛ̀
go.REAL.PFV	sit.IRR	now	LOC	IDEO	time.REL	GEN	3SG.SUBORD

bɔ́	wétənĕ	í	təgò	lɔ́
go.out.IRR	now	LOG	sit.IRR	here

'He rubbed himself against [the walls of] the burrow until his skin turned bright red, then he went out and sat down.'

(83) Ga-Kənɔn:

ằa kằ wétəně ì ɓɔ̋ ɓɔ̋ ɓɔ̋ ɓɔ̋
3SG.SUBORD go now COMP IDEO IDEO IDEO IDEO

'He went, "ɓɔ, ɓɔ, ɓɔ, ɓɔ" [=sound of croaking].'

(84) Ga-Masa:

ɓɔ̋
IDEO

'ɓɔ.'

(85) Ga-Kənɔn:

ɓɔ̋
IDEO

'ɓɔ.'

(86) Ga-Masa:

ɓɔ̋
IDEO

'ɓɔ.'

(87) Ga-Kənɔn:

ằ wò sú wétəně...
3SG EMPH get.up.IRR now

'He got up now...'

(88) Ga-Masa:

sân sïo lěɛ ɲì-nà mɛ̋ nɛ̋
rabbit get.up.REAL.PRF SUBORD.NE there-towards 3SG.SUBORD come.IRR
tàaső ằ mɔ̋nəgɔ̋ lɛ̋ kő tő
surprise DEF toad SUBORD D.DEF like

'The rabbit left where he was and came back to find to his surprise the toad like that.'

(89) (Cont.)

sə́ə̣ə̣ ì   ə̋!
IDEO COMP INTERJ

'Bright red, [he said] eh!'

(90) (Cont.)

í	tə̋	mɔ̀nəgɔ̀ ì	kú	lɛ́	ä̀	wò̰	jîo?
LOG	dear	toad COMP	thing	which	3SG	EMPH	find.REAL.PFV

'[He said] my dear toad, what happened to you?'

(91) (Cont.)

ḭ̀   ké   á   wó   l̰ȅ   lɛ̆   ḭ̀   kú   lɛ́   l-í   wó   jîo   âa
COMP COP 2SG EMPH SUBORD there COMP thing which L-LOG EMPH find.REAL.PFV NEG.Q

'[He replied] that you are there asking what happened to me, no?'

(92) (Cont.)

ḭ̀	á	wó	ä̀	brìnḭ̀	sənə̋	jő	wɛ́	âa
COMP	2SG	EMPH	DEF	switch.PL	lie.PTCP	see.IRR	FOC	NEG.Q

'You don't see the switches lying here?'

(93) Ga-Kənɔn:

ḭ̀   sə̋mənə̋ l-í   jío   íwí̋   sí̋o   í   wôo   bì-sənḛ̀   kṵ̋   nə̋
COMP god L-LOG say.REAL.PFV 1PL.EXCL REC.PST LOG EMPH.DAT goat-castrated catch.REAL.NOM LOC

'[He said] that god said that we had just caught his castrated goat.'

(94) (Cont.)

íwɨ́   lɛ́   à̰   bó,   ɨ̀   kɛ́   à̰   wɔ̀   lɛ́   í   wó   frá̰
1PL.EXCL SBJV 3SG kill.IRR COMP COP 3SG EMPH SBJV LOG EMPH thrash.IRR

'To kill it, that he would beat me.'[14]

(95) (Cont.)

í   wó   ŋəmɑ̋   lɛ̏   bɛ́ɛ̀   wɛ̀
LOG EMPH blood SUBORD be.SUBORD HAB

'Here's my blood.'

(96) Ga-Masa:

ɨ̀   à̰   təré   kűɛ   bä̰   wé   ɲì-nà   à̰   wɔ̀
COMP 3SG REL.PRO other.PL put.REAL.PFV FOC there-towards 3SG EMPH
cɛ̰̋ɛ̀
aside

'[He said] that he put these [switches] aside for him.'

(97) Ga-Kənɔn:

ɨ̀   à̰   təré   kűɛ   bä̰   wé   ɲì-nà   à̰   wɔ̀
COMP 3SG REL.PRO other.PL put.REAL.PFV FOC there-towards 3SG EMPH
cɛ̰̋ɛ ɨ̀   ȍo   məlɛ́   lɛ̏   jəgɛ̏-sərä̰
for COMP 3SG.EMPH REL.PRO SUBORD dog-owner

'[He said] that he put these aside for him, he who is the owner of the dog.'

(98) (Cont.)

ɨ̀   à̰   kɛ́   à̰   təré   kűɛ   bä̰   wé   ɲì-nà
COMP 3SG COP 3SG REL.PRO other.PL put.REAL.PFV FOC there-towards
ȍo   cɛ̰̋ɛ
3SG.EMPH for

'[He said] that he put these aside for him.'

---

[14] Proverbial statement that he was being punished for catching the hyrax.

(99)   (Cont.)

   sân   mɛ̀   îi   jəgɛ̈-kɔ̂   sù   ì   ö!   ì
   rabbit SUBORD LOG.DAT dog-head pick.up.IRR COMP INTERJ COMP
   jəgɛ̈-kɔ̂   kʊ́   kə̀ká`kừụ   tsɛ̋
   dog-head D.DEF meat catch.IRR.HAB how

   'The rabbit picked up his dog head and said, how could a dog head catch meat?'

(100)   Ga-Masa:

   ì   kú-bɛ́n   sɪ̌   ǎ   wò   kằ   lɛ̋,   ì   jəgɛ̈-kɔ̂
   COMP thing-miracle be 3SG EMPH in.hand EMPH COMP dog-head
   kʊ́ʊ̋   kə̀kâ kụ́↘
   D.DEF.PST meat catch.REAL.PFV.Q

   '[He said] you have a miraculous thing there! A dog head could catch meat?'

(101)   (Cont.)

   ì   ké   sɔ̀n-főn lɛ̀   ǎ   kụ́   nɛ̋,   ì   ké
   COMP COP Sɔnfon SUBORD 3SG catch.REAL.PFV EMPH COMP COP
   Tɔ̀fɔ̀   ŋɛ́
   Tɔfɔ.SUBORD NEG

   'It was Sɔnfon who caught it, not Tɔfɔ.'

(102)   Ga-Kənɔn:

   ɔ̂ɔ,   ì   ké   sɔ̀n-főn lɛ̀   ǎ   kụ́
   INTERJ COMP COP Sɔnfon SUBORD 3SG catch.REAL.PFV

   'Yeah, it was Sɔnfon who caught it.'

(103)   Ga-Masa:

   ì   ké   ǎ   sɔ̀n-főn lɛ̀   ǎ   kụ́
   COMP COP DEF Sɔnfon SUBORD 3SG catch.REAL.PFV

   'Yeah, it was Sɔnfon who caught it.'

(104) Ga-Kənɔn:

í wó Tɔ̃fɔ̃dzìa lê ì̀ jəgə̈-kɔ̂ kʊ́ nă kə̀kâ kǜ
2PL EMPH Tɔfɔdzia PRES COMP dog-head D.DEF PROSP meat catch.IRR
tsɛ̋
how

'Your Tɔfɔdzia there, how will a dog head go catch meat?'

(105) (Cont.)

mɛ̈ ı̂ı fɛ̀n-kɔ̂ sʊ̀ mɛ̈ ä̀ dzį́ í
3SG.SUBORD LOG.DAT thing-head take.IRR 3SG.SUBORD 3SG put.IRR LOG
tê
GEN

'He picked up the thing's head and held it.'

(106) Ga-Masa:

mɛ̈ ı̂ı jəgə̈-kɔ̂ sʊ̀ mɛ̈ ä̀ dzį́ í
3SG.SUBORD LOG.DAT dog-head take.IRR 3SG.SUBORD 3SG put.IRR LOG
tê
GEN

'He picked up his dog head and held it.'

(107) Ga-Kənɔn:

mɛ̈ ɲì̀ mɛ̈ fə̀ í jɛ́n mɛ̋
3SG.SUBORD run.IRR 3SG.SUBORD pass.IRR LOG front with

'He ran away [into the distance].'

(108) Ga-Masa:

mɔ̃nəgɔ̃ mɛ̈ í kő găa
toad SUBORD LOG hyrax pull.IRR

'The toad grabbed his hyrax.'

(109) (Cont.)

 mɛ̏   à   gɔ̀rɔ̀   mɛ̏   í   kő   kə̀ká`ɲì
 3SG.SUBORD 3SG skin.IRR 3SG.SUBORD LOG hyrax meat take.IRR
 mɛ̏   kɛ̋   à   wɛ̀
 3SG.SUBORD go.IRR 3SG with

'He skinned it and picked up the meat of his hyrax and took it with him.'

(110) (Cont.)

 í   tɛ̏   sân   fǎa̰   sɪ̰̌   gərû
 LOG dear rabbit pass.PTCP be too.much

'The rabbit had gone too far [and missed out].'

(111) Nyuma-Koro:

 í   kəré   lɛ̋ɛ̋   ɲì-nà   ǎá   klɛ̏n-klén kʊ́   nɛ̏
 LOG thing REL.NE there-towards 3SG.SBJV IDEO   D.DEF LOC

'All those things there, he hops in them.'

(112) Ga-Masa:

 ɪ̏   ǎá   klɛ̏n-klén kʊ́   nɛ̏
 COMP 3SG.SBJV IDEO   D.DEF LOC

'[They say] he hops in them.'

(113) (Cont.)

 kʊ́   tő   màa....
 D.DEF like again

'Like that...'

(114) Ga-Kənɔn:

kṹ-tɔ́n-kṹ-tɔ́n-mərɔ̃ kṹ   kɛ̃́   kɔ́nán-bɔ̃́ɛɛ tɛ̃́ súǹ   mɛ̀
UNTRANSLATABLE   D.DEF go.IRR elder-old.PL GEN weaving.basket with

'Little by little, it went into the old people's weaving basket (little by little, we save the words like this).'[15]

(115) (Cont.)

kɛ̃́ kṹ   dɛ̀ɛ-dəgɔ̃ɛɛ   lê
COP D.DEF end.ANTIP-place.PL PRES

'That's the end.'

---

[15] The phrase *kṹ-tɔ́n-kṹ-tɔ́n-mərɔ̃* is a phrase used to end folk tales, the ending equivalent of "once upon a time". The proverbial phrase 'it went into old people's weaving basket' is a way of simply saying, "This is the story as we heard it".

Bibliography

Aikhenvald, Alexandra. 2004. *Evidentiality*. Oxford: Oxford University Press.

Aikhenvald, Alexandra. 2006. *Serial verb constructions: a cross-linguistic typology*. Oxford University Press.

Albright, Adam. 2009. Feature-based generalization as a source of gradient acceptability. *Phonology* 26:9–41.

Ameka, Felix. 2001. Ideophones and the nature of the adjective word class in Ewe. In *Typological studies in language*, ed. F.K. Erhard Voeltz and Christa Kilian-Hatz, 25–48. Benjamins.

Babaev, Kirill. 2010. *Zialo: the newly-discovered Mande language of Guinea*. Lincom Europa.

Babaev, Kirill. 2011. On the reconstruction of some tense/aspect markers in Proto-Mande. *Journal of Language Relationship* 6:1–23.

Bailey, Todd, and Ulrike Hahn. 2001. Determinants of wordlikeness: phonotactics or lexical neighborhoods. *Journal of Memory and Language* 44:568–591.

Bearth, Thomas. 1992. Constituent structure, natural focus hierarchy and focus types in Toura. *Folia Linguistica* 26:75–94.

Bearth, Thomas. 1995. Nominal periphrasis and the origin of the predicative marker in Mande languages – an alternative view. *Afrikanistische Arbeitspapiere* 41:89–117.

Berlin, Brent. 1992. *Ethnobiological classification: Principles of categorization of plants and animals in traditional societies*. Princeton, NJ: Princeton University Press.

Bird, Charles. 1968. Relative clauses in Bambara. *Journal of West African Languages* 5:35–47.

Blench, Roger. 2010. The sensory world: ideophones in Africa and elsewhere. In *Perception of the invisible: religion, historical semantics, and the role of perceptive verbs*, ed. Anne Storch, 275–296. Cologne: Köppe.

Boone, C.J.L. 2016. Tone in the Bobo Madare North noun system. Master's thesis, Leiden University.

Braconnier, Cassian. 1987-1988. Kò/nkò à Samatiguila. *Mandenkan* 14-15:47–58.

Bybee, Joan. 1992. The semantic development of past tense modals in English. Symposium on Mood and Modality, UNM, Albuquerque, May 1992.

Cahill, Michael. 2007. More universals of tone. *SIL Electronic Working Papers*.

Chen, Matthew Y. 2000. *Tone sandhi: Patterns across Chinese dialects*. Cambridge Studies in Linguistics vol. 92. Cambridge: Cambridge University Press.

Clements, George N., Alexis Michaud, and Cédric Patin. 2010. Do we need tone features? In *Tones and features: Phonetic and phonological perspectives*, ed. John A. Goldsmith, Elizabeth Hume, and Leo Wetzels, Studies in Generative Grammar vol. 107, 3–24. De Gruyter Mouton.

Congo, Rasmane. 2013. L'esquisse d'analyse phonologique du sembla (parler de Bouendé). Master's thesis, Université de Ouagadougou.

Connell, Bruce. 2001. Downdrift, downstep, and declination. Bielefeld University: Typology of African Prosodic Systems Workshop.

Connell, Bruce, and D. Robert Ladd. 1990. Aspects of pitch realization in Yoruba. *Phonology* 7:1–29.

Coulibaly, Samadou. 1989. Interrogation in sambla and english. Master's thesis, University of Ouagadougou.

Courtenay, Karen. 1974. On the nature of the Bambara tone system. *Studies in African Linguistics* 5:303–323.

Creissels, Denis. 1978. A propos de la tonologie du bambara: realisations tonales, système tonal et la modalité nominal 'défini'. *Afrique et langage* 9:5–70.

Creissels, Denis. 2012. The origin of antipassive markers in West Mande languages. In *Proceedings of the 45th Meeting of the Societas Linguistica Europaea*. Stockholm, Sweden.

deZeeuw, Peter Howard. 1979. Western Mande compound tone rules. Master's thesis, Michigan State University.

Dingemanse, Mark. 2012. Advances in the cross-linguistic study of ideophones. *Language and Linguistics Compass* 6:654–672.

Dixon, R.M.W. 2006. Complement clauses and complementation strategies in typological perspective. In *Complementation*, ed. R.M.W. Dixon and Alexandra Aikhenvald, 1–48. Oxford University Press.

Dixon, R.M.W. 2008. Comparative constructions: a cross-linguistic typology. *Studies in Language* 32:787–817.

Djilla, Mama, Bart Eenkhoorn, and Jacqueline Eenkhoorn-Pilon. 2004. *Phonologie du jôwulu ("samogho")*. Mande Languages and Linguistics. Cologne: Rüdiger Köppe Verlag Köln.

Dooley, Robert A. 2010. Exploring clause chaining. SIL Electronic Working Papers 2010-001, February 2010.

Dryer, Matthew. 2009. Verb-object-negative order in Central Africa. In *Negation patterns in West African languages and beyond*, ed. Norbert Cyffer, Erwin Ebermann, and Georg Ziegelmeyer, 307–362. Amsterdam: John Benjamins.

Dwyer, David. 1973. The comparative tonology of Southwestern Mande nominals. Doctoral Dissertation, Michigan State University.

Fedotov, Maxim. 2013. Comparative constructions in Gban (South Mande).

Garber, Anne. 1988. A double-tiered analysis of Sicite tone. *Journal of West African Languages* 18:21–33.

Givón, Talmy. 1994. Irrealis and the subjunctive. *Studies in Language* 18:265–337.

Goldsmith, John A. 1976. Autosegmental phonology. Doctoral Dissertation, MIT.

Green, Christopher. 2015. The foot domain in Bambara. *Language* 91:e1–e26.

Green, Christopher. 2018. A survey of word-level replacive tonal patterns in Western Mande. *Mandenkan* 59:1–35.

Green, Christopher, Stuart Davis, Boubacar Diakite, and Karen Baertsch. 2014. On the role of margin phonotactics in Collquial Bamana complex syllables. *Natural Language and Linguistic Theory* 32:499–536.

Grégoire, Claire. 1990. Tonétique et tonologie d'un groupe de langues Mande Sud. etude théorique et expérimentale. Doctoral Dissertation, Université de la Sorbonne-Nouvelle, Paris.

Haspelmath, Martin. 1995. The converb as a cross-linguistically valid category. In *Converbs in cross-linguistic perspective*, ed. Martin Haspelmath and Ekkehard König, 1–55. Berlin: Mouton de Gruyter.

Haynie, Hannah, Claire Bowern, Patience Epps, Jane Hill, and Patrick McConvell. 2014. Wanderwörter in languages of the Americas and Australia. *Ampersand* 1:1–18.

Heath, Jeffrey. 2008. *Grammar of Jamsay*. Mouton de Gruyter.

Heath, Jeffrey. 2017. *A grammar of Jalkunan*. Language Description Heritage Library.

Ho, Wing See Vincie. 2006. The tone-melody interface of popular songs written in tone languages. Paper presented at the 9th international conference on music perception and cognition, Bologna, August 22-26, 2006.

Hombert, J.M. 1974. Universals of downdrift: their phonetic basis and significance for a theory of tone. *Studies in African Linguistics* 5:169–183.

Hyman, Larry. 2010a. Amazonia and the typology of tone systems. *UC Berkeley Phonology Lab Annual Report* 376–394.

Hyman, Larry. 2010b. Do tones have features? In *Tones and features: Phonetic and phonological perspectives*, ed. John A. Goldsmith, Elizabeth Hume, and Leo Wetzels, Studies in Generative Grammar vol. 107, 50–80. Berlin: De Gruyter Mouton.

Hyman, Larry, and Russell Schuh. 1974. Universals of tone rules: Evidence from West Africa. *Linguistic Inquiry* 5:81–115.
Hyman, Larry M. 2001. The limits of phonetic determinism in phonology. In *The role of speech perception in phonology*, ed. Elizabeth Hume and Keith Johnson, 141–185. Academic Press, San Diego.
Idiatov, Dmitry. 2010. Person-number agreement on clause linking markers in Mande. *Studies in Language* 34:832–868.
Idiatov, Dmitry. 2015. Clause-final negative markers in Bobo and Samogo: Parallel evolution and contact. *Journal of Historical Linguistics* 5:235–266.
Idiatov, Dmitry. 2016. Development of TAM and polarity marking conditioned by transitivity status in Western Mande. Ms. LLACAN.
Jauro, Luka Barnabas, John Ngamsa, and John Peter Wappa. 2013. A morphosemantic analysis of the Kamue personal names. *International Journal of English and Linguistics Research* 1:1–12.
Jones, Ross. 2000. Co-reference marking in Boko - logophoricity or not? *Journal of African Languages and Linguistics* 21:135–159.
Kastenholz, Raimund. 1997. *Sprachegeschichte im west-mande*. Köln: Rüdiger Köppe Verlag Köln.
Kastenholz, Raimund. 2003. Auxiliaries, grammaticalization, and word order in Mande. *Journal of African Languages and Linguistics* 24:31–53.
Keïta, Boniface. 1989. Les préverbes du dialonké. *Mandenkan* 17:69–80.
Khachaturyan, Maria. 2015. Grammaire du mano. *Mandenkan* 54:1–254.
Khachaturyan, Maria. 2017. Bound noun plus verb combinations in Mano. *Mandenkan* 57.
Kim, Hae-Kyung. 2002. Aspect, temps et modes en jowulu. Bamako: SIL Mali.
Labov, William. 1990. The intersection of sex and social class in the course of linguistic change. *Language Variation and Change* 2:205–254.
Le Saout, Joseph. 1979. *Notes sur la phonologie du Gouro (zone de Zuénoula)*. Nice: C.E.P.L.A.N.
Longacre, Robert E. 2007. Sentences as combinations of clauses. In *Language typology and syntactic description*, ed. Timothy Shopen, volume 2, 372–420. Cambridge University Press.
Lord, Carol. 1973. Serial verbs in transition. *Studies in African Linguistics* 4:269–296.
M. Paul Lewis, Charles D. Fennig, Gary F. Simons, ed. 2016. *Ethnologue: Languages of the world, eighteenth edition.*. Dallas: SIL International. URL http://www.ethnologue.com.
Makeeva, Nadezda. 2009. Les préverbes en kla-dan. *Mandenkan* 50:85–102.
Matisoff, James A. 1990. Bulging monosyllables: Areal tendencies in Southeast Asian diachrony. In *Proceedings of the 16th Annual Meeting of the Berkeley Linguistics Society*, 543–559.
Matisoff, James A. 2008. *The Tibeto-Burman reproductive system: toward an etymological thesaurus*. University of California Press.
McPherson, Laura. 2013. *A Grammar of Tommo So*. MGL 62. Berlin: De Gruyter Mouton.
McPherson, Laura. 2016. Culminativity and ganging in the tonology of awa suffixes. *Language: Phonological Analysis* 92:e38–e66.
McPherson, Laura. 2017a. The morphosyntax of adjectives in Seenku. *Mandenkan* 57.
McPherson, Laura. 2017b. Multiple feature affixation in Seenku plural formation. *Morphology* 27:217–252.
McPherson, Laura. 2017c. On (ir)realis in Seenku (Mande, Burkina Faso). In *Africa's endangered languages*, ed. Jason Kandybowicz and Harold Torrence, 297–320. Oxford: Oxford University Press.
McPherson, Laura. 2017d. Tone features revisited: Evidence from Seenku (Mande, Burkina Faso). In *Selected Proceedings of the 46th Annual Conference on African Linguistics*, ed. Doris Payne, Sara Pacchiarotti, and Mokaya Bosire, 5–21. Berlin: Language Science Press.
McPherson, Laura. 2018. The talking balafon of the Sambla: grammatical principles and documentary implications. *Anthropological Linguistics* 60:255–294.

McPherson, Laura. 2019. Seenku argument-head tone sandhi: allomorph selection in a cyclic grammar. *Glossa* 4:22.

McPherson, Laura, and Kevin Ryan. 2018. Tone-tune association in Tommo So (Dogon) folk songs. *Language* 94:119–156.

Mithun, Marianne. 1999. *The languages of Native North America*. Cambridge: Cambridge University Press.

Nikitina, Tatiana. 2011. Categorial reanalysis and the origin of the s-o-v-x word order in Mande. *Journal of African Languages and Linguistics* 32:251–273.

Odden, David. In press. Tone in African languages. In *Handbook of African languages*, ed. Rainer Vossen. Oxford University Press.

Peterson, David A. 2007. *Applicative constructions*. Oxford University Press.

Pittayaporn, Pittayawat. 2015. Typologizing sesquisyllabicity. In *Languages of mainland Southeast Asia: The state of the art*, ed. Nick Enfield and Bernard Comrie, 500–528. Berlin/Boston: De Gruyter Mouton.

Prince, Alan, and Paul Smolensky. 1993. Optimality theory: constraint interaction in generative grammar. Rutgers University and the University of Boulder, Colorado.

Prost, André. 1971. *Eléments de sembla: Phonologie - grammaire - lexique*. Lyon: Afrique et Langage.

Pulleyblank, Douglas. 1986. *Tone in lexical phonology*. Studies in Natural Language and Linguistic Theory vol. 4. Springer.

Rialland, Annie. 2007. Question prosody: an African perspective. In *Tones and tunes: Studies in word and sentence prosody*, ed. Carlos Gussenhoven and Tomas Riad, 35–56. Mouton.

Rialland, Annie. 2009. The African lax question prosody: Its realization and geographic distribution. *Lingua* 119:928–949.

Richtsmeier, Peter. 2011. Word-types, not word-tokens, facilitate extraction of phonotactic sequences by adults. *Laboratory Phonology* 2:157–183.

Roberts-Kohno, Rosalind Ruth. 2000. Kikamba phonology and morphology. Doctoral Dissertation, Ohio State University.

Royer, Patrick Yves. 1996. In pursuit of tradition: Local cults and religious conversion amongst the Sambla of Burkina Faso. Doctoral Dissertation, University of Illinois.

Samarin, William J. 1965. Perspective on African ideophones. *African Studies* 24:117–121.

Schellenberg, Murray. 2012. Does language determine music in tone languages? *Ethnomusicology* 56:266–278.

Schellenberg, Murray. 2013. The realization of tone in singing in Cantonese and Mandarin. Doctoral Dissertation, University of British Colombia.

Schreiber, Henning. 2008. Copula constructions in Mande - an overview. *Mandenkan* 44:63–77.

Segerer, Guillaume. 2008. Closed adjective classes and primary adjectives in African languages. Halshs-00255943.

Shluinsky, Andrey. 2014. Verbal prefixes mà- and rà- in Susu and lexical features of verbal stems. *Mandenkan* 52:73–110.

Smith, Jennifer L. 2001. Lexical category and phonological contrast. In *PETL 6: Proceedings of the workshop on the lexicon in phonetics and phonology*, ed. Robert Kirchner, Joe Pater, and Wolf Wikely, 61–72. Edmonton: University of Alberta.

Solomiac, Paul. 2007. Phonologie et morphosyntaxe du Dzùùngoo de Samogohiri. Doctoral Dissertation, Université Lumière Lyon, Lyon.

Solomiac, Paul. 2014. *Phonologie et morphosyntaxe du Dzùùngoo de Samogohiri*. Cologne: Rüdiger Köppe Verlag Köln.

Sproat, Richard, and Chilin Shih. 1991. The cross-linguistic distribution of adjective ordering restrictions. *Interdisciplinary approaches to language* 565–593.

Stahlke, Herbert. 1970. Serial verbs. *Studies in African Linguistics* 1:60–99.

Stern, Theodore. 1957. Drum and whistle "languages": an analysis of speech surrogates. *American Anthropologist* 59:487–506.

Stewart, John. 1965. The typology of the Twi tone system. *Bulletin of the Institute of African Studies, Legon* 1:1–27.

Strand, Julie. 2009. The Sambla xylophone: tradition and identity in Burkina Faso. Doctoral Dissertation, Wesleyan.

Traoré, Ali, Fabé Traoré, and Paul Solomiac. 1998. *Lexique orthographique dzùùngoo - francais*. Ouagadougou, Burkina Faso: SIL.

Tröbs, Holger. 2008. Duun. In *La qualification dans les langues africaines*, ed. Holger Tröbs, Eva Rothmaler, and Kerstin Winkelmann, 71–86. Köln: Köppe.

van der Hulst, Harry, and Keith Snider, ed. 1993. *The phonology of tone: The representation of tonal register*, volume 17. Berlin: Mouton de Gruyter.

Vydrine, Valentin. 2004. Areal and genetic features in West Mande and South Mande phonology: In what sense did Mande languages evolve? *Journal of West African Languages* 30:113–125.

Vydrine, Valentin. 2006. Emergence of morphological cases in South Mande: From the amorphous type to inflectional? In *Case, valency, and transitivity*, ed. Leonid Kulikov, Andrej Malchukov, and Peter de Swart, 49–64. Benjamins.

Vydrine, Valentin. 2009a. On the problem of the Proto-Mande homeland. *Journal of Language Relationship* 1:107–142.

Vydrine, Valentin. 2009b. Prjevjerby v jazykje dan-gueta [preverbs in dan-gweetaa]. *Voprosy Jazykoznanija* 2:75–84.

Vydrine, Valentin. 2011. Déclinaison nominale en dan-gwèètaa (groupe mandé-sud, Côte-d'Ivoire). *Faits de Langues: Les Cahiers* 3:233–258.

Vydrine, Valentin. 2016a. Tonal inflection in Mande languages: The cases of Bamana and Dan-Gwèètaa. In *Tone and inflection: new facts and new perspectives*, ed. Enrique L. Palancar and Jean Léo Léonard, 83–105. Berlin: De Gruyter Mouton.

Vydrine, Valentin. 2016b. Toward a Proto-Mande reconstruction and an etymological dictionary. *Faits de Langues* 47:109–123.

Welmers, William, and Beatrice Welmers. 1969. Noun modifiers in Igbo. *International Journal of American Linguistics* 35:315–322.

Wiesmann, Hannes. 2001. Les classes nominales en win (toussian du sud). SIL.

Winans, Lauren. 2016. Inferences of "will". Doctoral Dissertation, UCLA.

Wood, Esther. 2007. The semantic typology of pluractionality. Doctoral Dissertation, University of California Berkeley.

Yip, Moira. 1980. The tonal phonology of Chinese. Doctoral Dissertation, MIT, Boston, MA.

Yip, Moira. 2002. *Tone*. Cambridge: Cambridge University Press.

Zaugg-Coretti, Siliva. 2005. Le syntagme nominal en toussian du nord (langue voltaïque du Burkina Faso). Master's thesis, University of Zürich.

Zhang, Jie. 2004. Contour tone licensing and contour tone representation. *Language and Linguistics* 5:925–968.

Index

'all', 207–212
Adjective, 188, 300, 302
Adverb, 274
Affrication, 67
Anaphor, 146–147, see Discourse definite
Antipassive, 315–322
Aspect, 335

Benedictions, 514

Causative, 465
Classifier, 203
Clause chaining, 481
Comitative, 257, 264
Comparative, 259, 385
– asymmetrical, 385
– superlative, 390
– symmetrical, 390
Complement clause, 441
Complementizer, 441
Compound
– noun, 159
– tonology, 161–164
– verb, 327–332
Conditional, 426, 489
– counterfactual, 434
Conjunction, 295
– clause-level, 476–481
Consonants, 40–50
Copula, 371–374, 498

Dative, 223, 267
Declination, 122
Definite, 179–180
Demonstrative, 182–184
Discourse definite, 180–182, 374, 500
Disjunction, 301
Dissimilation, 71

Emphatic, 147, 493, 504

Focus, 491–493, 495–501
Future, see Prospective

Genitive, 261
Greetings, 510–514

Habitual, 343, 410
Hortative, 349

Ideophone, 231
Immediate past, 356
Imperative, 345
Indefinite, 186
Instrumental, 256
Insubordination, 351
Interrogative, 497
– polar, 393
– wh-, 397
Intonation, 124–126, 235, 393

Lenition, 69–71
Locative, 253
Logophor, 153

Modal, 456
Modifier, 188, 192
Mood, 336
– irrealis, 336
– realis, 336

Negation, 369
Noun
– deadjectival, 132
– deverbal, 134–137, 173–176, 353
Noun phrase, 177–178
NPI, 212
Numeral, 197
– cardinal, 201
– distributive, 204
– ordinal, 205
– partitive, 203

Onomastics, 129
Onomatopoeia, 244

Palatalization, 65–67
Participial, 188, 362
Perfect, 360
Perfective, 358, 412
Plural, 137–143, 193
Possession, 151, 219, 419
– alienable, 222–227, 270
– inalienable, 219–222
Postposition, 249
Pre-verb, 322
Predicate
– adjectival, 155, 190, 300, 303, 378
– existential, 375
– participial, 413
– possessive, 380
– volitional, 382, 454
Predicate marker, *see* TAMP marker
Presentative, 185
Progressive, 355, 411
Pronoun, 144–146
Prospective, 341, 409
Purposive, 471

Quotative, 154, 443–447

Reciprocal, 157
Reduplication, 130, 234, 284, 332, 488
Reflexive, 155
Relative clause, 407
– headless, 420
Relative pronoun, 421–425
Resultative, 362

Song, 518
Stative, 362
Surrogate speech, 522–526

Syllable structure, 51
– coda nasal, 54–61
– monosyllable, 51
– sesquisyllable, 25, 52, 61

TAMP marker, 149
– past, *see* Past
– subjunctive, 426, 454
– subordinate, 409, 461
Temporal subordination, 432, 484
Tense, 365
– past, 365
– present, 365
Tone
– contours, 83–87
– downstep, 114
– features, 80, 139, 358
– grammatical, 97–101
– levels, 78–80
– register, 113
– sandhi, 102–110, 336
Tone bearing unit, 89
Topic, 501

Variation
– dialect, 4
– interspeaker, 69
Verb
– intransitive, 310–313
– labile, 313
– transitive, 307–310
Vocable, 519
Volitional, 265, 382
Vowels, 20
– ATR, 20
– diphthongs, 23
– hiatus, 72–75
– length, 21

www.ingramcontent.com/pod-product-compliance
Lightning Source LLC
Chambersburg PA
CBHW060451300426
44113CB00016B/2559